Advanced Business

Level 3

For Alun and Stuart

Advanced Business

LEVEL 3

Jon Sutherland
and
Diane Canwell

Hodder & Stoughton
A MEMBER OF THE HODDER HEADLINE GROUP

© 1994 Jon Sutherland and Diane Canwell

First Published in Great Britain 1994

British Library Cataloguing in Publication Data

A Catalogue for this title is available from the British Library

ISBN 0-340-61075-1

Typeset by GreenGate Publishing Services, Tonbridge, Kent
Printed and bound in Great Britain for Hodder and Stoughton Educational, a division of Hodder Headline plc, 338 Euston Road, London NW1 3BH, by Butler and Tanner Ltd., Frome, Somerset

Contents

Introduction

Anyone who actually runs a business will tell you how easy it all seemed before they started. On the face of it, you have to make something and sell it for more than you paid for the materials and any other costs. The trouble is that it is really not that simple. If things are as simple as all that, why do so many businesses fail? Why is the economy not booming with thousands of people running businesses and making millions? As we will see, the economy itself has a lot to do with business failure. Perhaps the main reason for business failures is mismanagement.

An individual may have a great idea when he or she starts a business, but lacks many of the skills needed to run it successfully. It may be all very well to know how to be an employee, but what about being an employer?

This book will give you valuable information as a potential employee, but will also give you useful insights into the operations and problems that employers face.

Our book contains practical and above all, relevant, activities and tasks which are designed to meet all of the criteria required to complete a GNVQ Level 3 award in Business, now known as Advanced Business.

We have attempted to follow all of the Performance Criteria, Ranges and Evidence Indicators, element by element, across the eight Units of the learning programme. At all times, we have endeavoured to use the most up-to-date documentation from GNVQ in the preparation of the materials.

Successful completion of all Student Activities and Element Assignments will provide candidates with sufficient evidence for their Portfolios. Throughout these assignments and activities, we have attempted to use the three Core Skills as often as is practicable. We are sure that those responsible for the delivery of this programme at various institutions will find their own ways of organising candidates' portfolios. Some guidance on this matter is given in the section headed 'Portfolio Building'.

The 10 multiple choice questions at the end of each Unit should form the basis of a useful summative test in the style of those proposed by GNVQ.

A few last words, directed towards the candidates themselves. We are sure that your institution will have created its own way of undertaking this programme of study. Whichever method has been have chosen, the key to success is to be systematic and to take each Element independently. You will be required to show that you understand the coverage of the range of subject-matter before you are considered to have successfully completed the Element.

We hope that you will find the text interesting and informative and the Student Activities useful and practical.

Jon Sutherland and Diane Canwell
September 1994

Acknowledgements

The authors would like to acknowledge the help and support of the following organisations in the preparation and illustration of this book:

Alliance & Leicester Building Society
Allied Lyons plc
Anglia Television Group plc
Avon Cosmetics Ltd
Barclays Bank plc
British Airports Authority plc
British Nuclear Fuels plc
British Petroleum plc
British Union for the Abolition of Vivisection
Cunard Line Ltd
Department of Trade & Industry
Fisons plc
Geest plc
Inland Revenue Department
Ipswich & Norwich Co-operative Society Ltd
Kingfisher plc
Kwik-Fit Holdings plc
Ladbroke Group plc
Marks & Spencer plc
Mercury Communications Ltd
Mobil Oil Company Ltd
Peugeot Talbot Motor Company Ltd
Rank Organisation
Rentokil Ltd
Sharp Electronics (UK) Ltd
Smith & Nephew plc
Storehouse plc
Tesco Stores Ltd
Yorkshire-Tyne Tees Television Holdings plc

We would also like to thank the following for their assistance in producing this book:

Christine Shorten
Alan Hopley
Maurice Cowley

Portfolio building and core skills
– a note for lecturers

PORTFOLIO BUILDING

GATHERING EVIDENCE FOR THE PORTFOLIO

Throughout the book we have designed a series of **Student Activities** and **Unit Assignments** which are both formative and summative in nature. **Formative** means that the students will be learning while they are doing, **summative** means that the students will be tested after a specific block of information to ensure understanding. In addition, at the commencement of each Element, we have listed the Performance Criteria and Range as specified by GNVQ.

The **Student Activities** and **Unit Assignments** cover not only the **GNVQ Performance Criteria** and **Range**, but also the **Core Skills** - i.e. students apply technology, are asked to communicate in a variety of ways and show application of number.

Because these **Activities** and **Assignments** cover all the necessary criteria and **Core Skills**, it is therefore possible to use these to help build up the **Student Portfolio of Evidence.**

WHAT THE PORTFOLIO SHOULD CONTAIN

The **Student Portfolio** should contain evidence either that the student has achieved outcomes or proved competence in the past, that he or she has carried out tasks which test both knowledge and competence during the GNVQ programme. In effect, this means that the Portfolio can contain evidence obtained within the institution of study, as well as that derived from any external activities.

Examples of evidence which a student could use to claim **Accreditation for Prior Learning or Experience** might be:

- *Certificates* of qualifications already gained, proving that learning has taken place
- A *reference* from an accredited assessor stating that the student has carried out a certain task competently on a number of occasions
- A *log of visitors* with whom a student may have dealt regularly over a period of time
- Evidence based on a student's part-time *work experience*

This is not an exhaustive list. Other evidence may be negotiated with the Assessor, an Internal Verifier and an External Verifier.

The **Portfolio** *must* contain evidence of assessment of all the **GNVQ Elements.** The **Range** and **Evidence Indicators** assist in suggesting how this could be carried out.

The **Portfolio** *must* contain evidence of achievement of the **three Core Skills** It is not essential that **Additional Core Skills** be contained in the **Portfolio**, as they will not be required to prove competence at Level 3. If, however, these Additional Core Skills have been assessed, then obviously the evidence should be included in the **Portfolio.**

The **Student Activities** and **Unit Assignments** in this book are designed to assist in the preparation of the **Evidence Portfolio**, although naturally, additional evidence will also be required or preferred. When students have to prove competence on a number of different occasions, then obviously the institutions responsible for delivering the programme of study will need to provide additional means of assessment.

GNVQ CORE SKILLS

We designed the learning and assessment activities bearing in mind the **unit specifications** demanded within the programme. You should think of the **Core Skills**, as an integral part of the course. It is a good idea to map the **Core Skills** coverage on a **Programme Assessment Sheet**. The Core Skills require continuous assessment throughout the programme of study. Sufficient evidence should be generated from the **Student Activities** and **Unit Assignments** to confirm the candidates' ability to fulfil the specific elements of each core skill. In practice, not only will you assess the same core skills on more than one occasion, but also you will find that the particular elements that make up each core skill are similarly tested repeatedly. This process is perfectly acceptable, since it reaffirms the candidate's ability to reproduce a particular achievement on a number of occasions. In this respect, the candidate has shown a **consistent performance**.

I. COMMUNICATION LEVEL 3

Element 3.1 – Take part in discussions with a range of people on routine matters.
Element 3.2 – Prepare written material on a range of matters.

Element 3.3 – Use images to illustrate points made in writing and in discussions with a range of people on a range of matters.
Element 3.4 – Read and respond to written materials and images on a range of matters.

2. INFORMATION TECHNOLOGY LEVEL 3

Element 3.1 – Set system options and set up, use, and input data into storage systems.
Element 3.2 – Edit, organise and integrate information from different sources.
Element 3.3 – Select and use formats for presenting complex information from different sources.
Element 3.4 – Select and use applications when they are an effective way of working with information.

3. APPLICATION OF NUMBER LEVEL 3

Element 3.1 – Gather and process data using group 1, 2 and 3 mathematical techniques.
Element 3.2 – Represent and tackle problems using group 1, 2 and 3 mathematical techniques.
Element 3.3 – Interpret and present mathematical data using group 1, 2 and 3 mathematical techniques.

ELEMENT I.I

Explain the purposes and products of business

I DEMAND
needs, wants, effective demand, consumption and income, demand and price,
elastic and inelastic

2 INDUSTRIAL SECTORS
primary, secondary and tertiary

3 PRODUCT
goods, services

4 PURPOSES
profit making, public service, charitable

DEMAND

NEEDS AND WANTS

No matter whether you are a customer or an organisation, young or old, we all have various wants and needs. The difference between these two desires has a great effect upon how we try to get them and what we will do in the process. You could say that I want a new car, but what I need is a reliable form of transport. It doesn't have to be a new car.

We all make a series of regular purchases every day, newspapers, cigarettes, canned drinks, chocolates and other food items. The reasoning behind our purchases can be related to our tastes or our opinion of a particular product. Organisations will seek to influence our decision-making when we make a purchase, but we will be looking at this later.

Also, every now and then, we make special purchases. These are things that we really have to think about before we buy them. Perhaps they are expensive, perhaps they are a luxury. Organisations which make these products, like cars, TVs, stereo systems and furniture, have to try to predict what the demand will be for these products and make sure that they have produced enough of them to satisfy demand. These producers of products will have to be ready to react to sudden changes in demand, and be prepared to gear up their production should demand increase in a short space of time. Above all, the product that they make should aim to satisfy the demands of the buyer. If it doesn't then the buyer will not be satisfied and is unlikely to buy from that organisation again. To be successful, the organisation has to have sufficient products available, at the right price and in the right place. These are the basic business skills required to succeed and survive in a very competitive area of activity. In business jargon, we can use the words **production**, **pricing** and **distribution**.

EFFECTIVE DEMAND

The demand for a particular product or service is sometimes reliant on the price the consumer is willing to pay, but this is not the whole story. We need to consider something called 'market demand'. This is the amount of a product or service that will be demanded during a particular period of time. Here are some of the factors that will influence that consumption rate:

1 *Price* – in most cases the higher the price charged for a particular product or service, the lower the demand for it. As the price falls, there should be a correspondingly higher demand for that product or service. One thing to note here is that despite the cost, even if it is very low, there is only a comparatively limited demand. Eventually, all those who need it will have it.

2 *Income* – this refers to the income of consumers. They may well want the product or service, but may be unable to afford to consume it at the rate they would really like. A basic assumption is that when income increases, consumers can consume more (as they have more income that they can spend), however, this is not exactly the case. If we split the range of goods and services into two different categories, calling them inferior and superior, then we can begin to see the choices consumers have. The inferior goods and services are comparatively cheap. The superior goods and services are expensive. When consumers have more income, they can spend it on more inferior goods and services, which in effect means that, the consumers are consuming more. Consumers could switch over to superior goods and services, which are more expensive so they would use up the additional income, but not actually **consuming** more. The alternative way of looking at this is to say that they do actually consume more just by buying more superior goods and services.

CONSUMPTION, INCOME, DEMAND AND PRICE

Income elasticity of demand describes how responsive demand is to changes in income. Simply, a rise in income should signal a rise in demand. This effect is more likely at the luxury end of the market, and is unlikely to affect products and services at the lower end of the market. In fact, in some cases, a rise in income can signal a negative demand. In this case, products or services which are considered inferior or substandard are shunned by consumers as they can afford more expensive alternatives. The formula for calculating income elasticity of demand is:

$$\text{Income elasticity of demand} = \frac{\text{Percentage change in quantity demanded}}{\text{Percentage change in income}}$$

To complicate matters, there is another formula which describes the effect on demand for one product when the price changes on another. This is called the Cross elasticity of demand:

$$\text{Cross elasticity of demand} = \frac{\text{Percentage change in demand for product } x}{\text{Percentage change in price of product } y}$$

This formula is only useful when the two products are substitutes for one another.

Supply obviously refers to the quantity of products or services available. As you may have already realised, demand is not necessarily the quantity actually bought. Equally, supply is not the quantity actually sold. Generally speaking, the higher the price a product or service can command in the market, the greater the quantity there is available. High prices will give many new producers the ability to enter the market, as well as encouraging existing producers to make more. The relationship between price and quantity is reflected in the way the supply curve slopes upwards. This is similar to the demand curve, but assumes that all other factors remain the same. When there is a rise in the costs of producing something, this automatically reduces the profitability of that product or service. Price elasticity describes the responsiveness of supply to changes in price. This is known as PES (Price elasticity of supply).

$$\text{PES} = \frac{\text{Percentage change in quantity supplied}}{\text{Percentage change in price}}$$

Supply tends to be elastic for only short periods of time. Rises in price will tempt organisations to supply more, but this is only possible if they are immediately able to use existing labour, materials and machinery.

If we combine supply and demand curves on to the same graph, we can attempt to calculate something known as the **equilibrium price**. Equilibrium price is when the quantity actually bought equals the quantity offered on the market. At all other prices there is what is known as **disequilibrium**. Competition between purchasers of the products or services will force the price up to the equilibrium (this is when demand exceeds

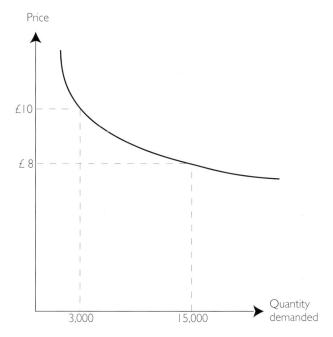

FIG 1.1.1 *Demand curve.*

supply). Competition between sellers will force the equilibrium down when supply exceeds demand. Equilibrium price is often referred to as the natural market price as market forces will always have an effect on the equilibrium.

ELASTIC AND INELASTIC

Elasticity of demand is a term used to describe the quantity of a product or service demanded and how that demand is affected by price changes. Merely for the consumer to want a product or service is not sufficient; there are several other factors to be taken into consideration. These are:

● the consumer's ability to pay
● the other demands on the consumer's income
● the desire the consumer has to acquire the product or service
● the benefits and advantages that may be received by acquiring the product or service
● other sacrifices that may have to be made in order to acquire the product or service

Some products or services will be purchased regardless of the price. There has only been a gradual decline in the sales of cigarettes, for example, despite enormous price rises. When we consider the simple relationship between supply and demand, we are not taking sufficient note of price sensitivity. This means that certain products or services may be price sensitive, in other words, the demand may be directly affected by price.

Demand tends to be elastic if the product or service has some of the following features:

● if it is a luxury
● if there are cheaper alternatives
● if it is very expensive in relation to total income

Alternatively, some products or services are inelastic, which means that regardless of the price, we will still be

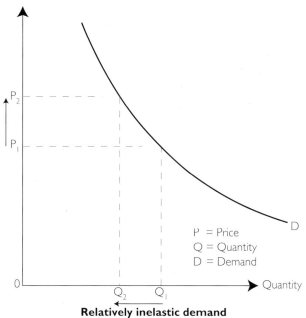

Relatively inelastic demand

FIG 1.1.2 *Inelastic demand graph.*

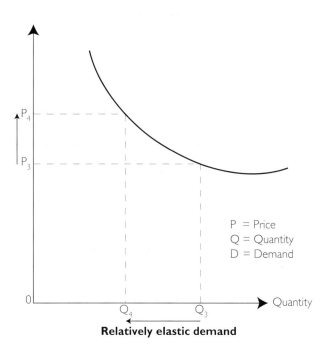

Relatively elastic demand

FIG 1.1.3 *Elastic demand graph.*

3

prepared to pay. A good example of this would be the services of a professional such as a photographer or a solicitor. There is a simple formula which describes the elasticity of demand:

Price elasticity of demand

$$= \frac{\text{Percentage change in quantity demanded}}{\text{Percentage change in price}}$$

Calculating elasticity is quite difficult, but all organisations will consider this when thinking about price changing. In some circumstances, reducing the price will have little effect on the demand, particularly if the demand is insensitive to price. When demand is sensitive to price, the organisation will have to risk losing some of their market share.

student activity

Individually, calculate the elasticity of demand for an organisation which produces products at £20 each and sells 10,000 units. Then it increases its price to £24 and finds that sales fall to 5,000 units.

TYPES OF INDUSTRY AND INDUSTRIAL SECTORS

All types of organisations that actually produce something are also known as industry.

Industry comprises organisations that make things or produce raw materials, but it also includes Banking, Insurance and Retailing.

The government actually splits the different sorts of organisation into 111 different types, but really it all boils down to three different headings:

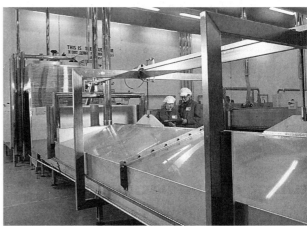

FIG 1.1.5 *Geest's pasta and bread factory in South Humberside was constructed at a cost of £6 million. The illustration shows machines which pasteurise fresh pasta. This food-processing operation is a good example of secondary sector business activity.*

The first is known as primary. These are industries that are concerned with producing raw materials. They include agriculture, fishery, forestry and mining.

student activity

In groups of two, identify at least five other major extractors of raw materials.

FIG 1.1.4 *Offshore oil and gas production such as the extensive operations carried out by BP in the North Sea. This is a good example of primary sector business activity.*

The second major group is secondary. These are industries concerned with the manufacturing of different products or the processing of them. These include car making, food processing and iron and steel working.

FIG 1.1.6 *Kwik-Fit has some 610 fitting centres throughout the UK, Holland and Belgium and services some four million customers per year. This operation is a prime example of tertiary sector business activity.*

The third group is known as the tertiary group. These include all the industries that do not actually produce the goods, but sell them. These are called services.

The tertiary sector, for this reason, is commonly known as the service sector. In this category are included banking, all of the retailing and distribution businesses and tourism.

Many organisations operate in one of these sectors, but sell in another. In other words, a coal-mine belongs to the primary sector but sells its product in the secondary sector. Some organisations will operate a cross-sector range of businesses, for example, a poultry farmer may grow the foodstuffs required to feed his stock (primary sector), he may slaughter and process the poultry (secondary sector) and he may distribute and retail the finished products (tertiary sector).

Businesses like this are known as **vertically integrated organisations**. They have built their business in a logical and progressive manner, to reap the benefits of business activity from the differing sectors in which they operate. They will be able to benefit from all the profits generated at each stage of the business process.

PRODUCTS - GOODS AND SERVICES

If, for the moment, we ignore raw materials and concentrate on manufactured goods and services, we can investigate how relatively few organisations share international markets and the ease to which a product manufactured in one country may be suitable for use in another.

Companies are always looking to move into markets that are expanding. This has been somewhat difficult in recent years due to a global recession. However, if we look into the recent past, we can find a number of organisations, which have seized upon a good idea, and manufactured a product or service to cater for potential demand. It becomes obvious that such organisations have grown enormously as demand for their products has increased.

There is an obvious link between the number of products an organisation sells, and its potential to grow. When a company needs to grow more quickly, it may choose to buy or merge with another company. However, most early growth is made by identifying and exploiting a gap in the market. If traditional markets for products are in decline, a company which is well-positioned to sell its excess production elsewhere is less likely to be seriously affected. An alternative way of dealing with this problem is to look for another way customers can use the product that is made. In the case of whisky distilleries, which have seen a gradual decline in demand, they have found it impossible to discover an alternative use for their product. They had, to some extent, coped with earlier declines in demand by exporting the majority of their whisky to the Far East. In Japan, which had been a huge market for Scotch whisky, the tables were turned as enterprising Japanese businessmen started producing their own version of whisky.

As we mentioned earlier, a good way of expanding your business is to increase the number of products you produce. As the number of products manufactured gradually increases, so do the profits, as the individual cost for each product falls. This fact is known as an **economy of scale**. It basically means that companies can buy in greater bulk, they can use their premises and employees more efficiently and all their overheads are spread more thinly. Overheads refer to such things as heating, lighting, insurance, rent, rates and loans. In addition, with this increased profitability, they are able to keep pace with technological changes and invest money in research and development and always be in a position to raise additional money for emergencies or the purchase of another company.

When an organisation becomes a large-scale manufacturer, it is able to mass-produce goods at relatively low prices, will always be catering for comparatively stable markets (in other words, the future demands for its products are fairly safe), but it will have had to invest very heavily in machinery.

student activity

In groups of three investigate one of the following areas of business activity:

- car production
- frozen foods
- soft drinks manufacturers
- brewers
- sport and leisure wear manufacturers
- confectionery manufacturers

Try to identify the top 10 organisations engaged in one of these business activities. Organise your top 10 in ranking order in terms of market share.

Present your findings in report format, written for an organisation which wishes to establish itself in the UK.

The ideal situation for a large-scale producer of manufactured goods is to create a global market for its products. It would be even more ideal if this product did not have to be substantially changed before it could be sold in various countries. The fewer the changes, the lower the cost to the manufacturer.

On the other hand, being a large-scale manufacturer, involved in various different countries, an organisation is likely to suffer quite badly if there is a recession across the world. Some of the largest organisations have had to contend with losses running into billions of pounds as a result of over-extending themselves. The growth process needs to be carefully considered and must not outstrip the real demand for the product.

These companies which have suffered massive losses have blamed various features of their organisation, including:

- The more widespread the company is, the harder it is to manage efficiently.
- Organisations tend to have what is known as an 'optimum' size. In other words, it would have been better to have created another company to handle the production and not to have produced the goods themselves.

- Large organisations with huge numbers of staff tend to suffer from poor communications.
- There is a tendency for considerable numbers of employees to feel that they have no real power in the organisation and therefore they are not well motivated.

These reasons, taken together, are known as **'diseconomies of scale'**.

Increasingly, the service sector is dominated by large companies. We have already pointed out that the service sector is, indeed, a large one. Many of the same problems that face a large-scale manufacturing organisation will be faced by service organisations. The major difference is that they do not necessarily produce products, but provide services. In effect, if they suffer problems, they will have to shed staff and dispose of premises.

The ultimate success of any company is related to providing for the needs and wants of the customer. Indeed, to be really successful, an organisation must stay ahead of all its competitors. Having a large market share is one thing, but being a market leader is just as important.

Let us return to the question of customers' needs

CHIEF EXECUTIVE'S REVIEW

CARLSBERG-TETLEY

FIG 1.1.7 *Carlsberg Tetley, a division of Allied Lyons, shows that large organisations have the ability to not only produce the product but retail it too.*

and wants. Just what is the difference between the two? A need is to require something essential. This, of course, includes the need to eat, drink and keep warm. On the other hand, a want is a specific desire for something you may not necessarily need. If you are hungry, this is a need, but you may want a MacDonalds.

Organisations spend huge amounts of money on trying to assess and manipulate the wants of customers. If it were not for our wants, then there would be no choice in products at all. Marketing experts know this and attempt, by various means, to influence what customers want.

As we have already seen, the nature of the goods that make up the consumer market are limited to just three different types of goods or services. Within each of these three categories, there is a vast array of alternatives, all of which would satisfy our needs. The simple fact that one product or another has slightly different features, colours, taste or smell means that our essential need is transformed into a want.

The same can be said, to some extent, in the industrial sector of the market. Organisations here will also purchase consumer durables (in their case capital goods like machines), consumables (in industry these will be oil, raw materials and office stationery) and services

(perhaps the services of an advertising agency or an accountant). Perhaps the choice is not so great as in the consumer market, but there are definite differences between similar products and services offered by a range of companies.

Technology, design, research and development are continually introducing new products and services on to the market. In many cases, new products or services simply replace older ones, making them obsolete. Occasionally, a new product or service may enter the market that offers possibilities that could not have been even been dreamt of a few years ago. No-one would have believed that there could one day be a machine which would replace the need to hand-write additional copies of a book, but it happened when the first printing press was designed. No-one would have believed that the huge pools of copy-typists which most large organisations employed would be replaced by a machine called a photocopier.

These products, whether they are replacing an existing one or not, have to cater for either a need or a want. In the case of replacement, there is an existing need. In the case of a want, this may have to be generated by an expensive advertising campaign which tries to convince the consumers that they really do want one!

PURPOSES AND FUNCTIONS OF ORGANISATIONS

As we will discover, there are a wide variety of different forms of business organisations. This also means that they all have a wide variety of different goals. Perhaps a good start is to have a look at how different many organisations are at their very core.

student activity

Before you read any more of this section, in pairs discuss the following statement:
  The purpose of business is to make a profit, pure and simple.
How far do you think this is true? Do all organisations have this goal? Can you identify some organisations which do not have this goal?

FORMAL AND INFORMAL ORGANISATIONS

Formal organisations can be defined as those that have established the express purpose of achieving a particular goal or aims or objectives. These sorts of

organisations have clearly defined rules and instructions as well as quite highly developed communication between different parts of the organisation. Good examples of these sort of operations include most businesses, governments and international institutions.

The opposite to formal is an **informal organisation**, also known as a social organisation. These organisations do not tend to have clearly defined goals and examples of these organisations include families or communities.

Productive and non-productive organisations

Because there are so many different forms of formal organisation, we need to classify this large group a little more carefully. One of the easiest ways is to separate them into productive and non-productive categories.

Productive organisations are all of those that are concerned in some way with producing something, or production. These can be privately or public owned. Also they do not necessarily have to make a product, they could provide a service.

All the industries that we have mentioned so far tend to sell something or offer their services to the community. There are a number of publicly owned services such as Health and Education. These are still considered to be productive organisations, but they do not trade. Therefore we can also subdivide this large category into **trading** and **non-trading**.

There are many organisations which do not make any goods or offer any services at all, and these are the ones that we can call **non-productive**, but they are not unimportant. Good examples of these are the courts, unions or the churches. They all play an important role in our lives.

PURPOSES OF ORGANISATIONS

In most ways, the **purpose** of any organisation is to be successful. This success is, however, measured in many different ways, which are dependent upon the type of organisation concerned. A good starting point for any organisation is to set down guidelines for activity that act as a standard from which it can measure itself.

There is always likely to be a major difference between the organisation itself, and how it operates, and the ideal type of organisation to achieve success. It is only when the organisation has clearly set out its goals and objectives that it can identify shortcomings or problems and seek solutions to them.

BUSINESS PLANS

Many businesses begin with setting out their aims, purposes and objectives in a **business plan**. This is a formal statement of their goals. However, in reality, the day-to-day achieving of these goals may differ from the business plan. Organisations do not exist in isolation. The environment in which they operate is constantly changing. Therefore the organisation must be flexible. Any change may require organisational change when old ways of operating are no longer efficient or advisable in the new circumstances.

student activity

What would you expect to find in a business plan? How would a business plan be organised? Who would be responsible for putting the business plan together? Who would want to see a business plan? How closely do businesses stick to their business plans?

MISSION STATEMENTS

A **mission statement** differs from a business plan as it looks at what the organisation actually stands for. Generally, this is an agreement between both managers and employees. These agreed goals are often more valuable as they have the common consent of all those involved in the organisation. The individuals involved have a shared point of view and perhaps some common ideas of how to achieve them.

student activity

The institution in which you are studying this programme will probably have a mission statement. Try to discover what it is and put it into your own words.

GOALS TO ACTION

Once an organisation has established its goals, it must then find methods of achieving them. These are known as the **strategy** and **tactics**.

Strategies are the major ways to achieve the objectives and tend to be fairly long-term in their approach, e.g. increase turnover by 50 per cent in 10 years.

Tactics, on the other hand, are more short-term and flexible. These are the individual parts of the main strategy, e.g. in order to increase turnover by 50 per cent in 10 years we need to increase our product range and find cheaper suppliers.

So, strategy answers the question of how the organisation intends to get where it wants to go, and tactics are the means by which it achieves the strategy.

As we have said, businesses exist for many different reasons, and perhaps the most common is profit, but it is certainly not the only one. Being happy and satisfied is as strong a reason for running an organisation, and this is why many people like to work for themselves. The freedom to make your own choices is good compensation for having to work for an organisation that is only interested in profit.

The following are some of the main objectives of organisations:

Maximising profits

This is when there is the largest possible difference between how much something has cost to produce, and how much you can sell it for. In order to achieve this the organisation needs to know as much about the customer and the market as possible. It needs to know where to get its supplies at the cheapest possible rate, the most economical way of getting the product to the customer and the maximum price the customer would be prepared to pay for the product.

Being the market leader

A **market leader** is an organisation that tries to sell more products than all of its rivals, or perhaps all of its rivals combined. There are considerable advantages to being a market leader, since every other organisation's products are compared to yours. Once this status has been achieved profit maximisation may also follow as you can produce products more cheaply than your rivals because you are producing so many more than they are.

A part-way stage of achieving market leadership is to set an achievable level of market share. In other words, the organisation may not directly seek to be the market leader straight away, but will move towards this in stages by gradually increasing its market share.

This year's results

	1992 £M	1991 £M
Turnover	1,082	1,042
Operating profit	328	339
Profit on ordinary activities before taxation	161	156
Profit for the financial year	143	136
Dividends	52	50
Profit retained	91	86
Capital expenditure	590	605
Assets employed	4,347	4,109
Shareholders' interest (average for year)	601	513
Profit before taxation related to average shareholders' interest	27%	30%
Number of employees	15,783	15,327

FIG I.I.8 *This is a summary of Mobile Oil's Annual Results which include profits before and after taxation and payment to shareholders.*

Maximising sales

On the face of it, this would appear to be similar to maximising profits, but this is not the case. It does not necessarily follow that by achieving high sales you are achieving high profits. There may be only a small profit to be made from each product. It is only when you sell many thousands of a product that you make a reasonable profit. This particular objective is most common in the retail trade, when different branches of the same organisation compete with one another to achieve high sales figures. After all, the employees of the branches may be given considerable cash bonuses to encourage them to sell more.

Organisational growth

The larger an organisation is, the more likely it is to attract investors and to be able to produce products on a vast scale. Being big brings its own particular problems. Keeping track of business activity such as sales, stock and profit requires many extra employees. Should a company grow too quickly and overtake its ability to keep track of things, it runs the risk of overtrading. It is, therefore, very important for an organisation to be able to monitor all activities when it is growing fast.

Providing a steady income

In some ways, this is the opposite to sales and profit maximisation. An organisation which states that providing a steady income is its principal objective is saying that it would rather attain realistic goals than overstretch itself. This is perhaps a cautious approach to business, but it is one that is often the most workable. Being able easily to meet sales targets, deliver goods on time and maintain high standards of quality may mean the difference between survival and failure in an uncertain business world. Many of the organisations which grew very quickly in the 1980s over extended themselves in pursuit of short-term profits. We can now see that companies which plodded along throughout the 1980s are still trading successfully, having provided themselves with a steady income in good times and bad.

Expanding the range of products or services

The more products or services an organisation offers, the more likely that organisation is to survive and succeed. Organisations which only offer a single product or service can often find themselves in great difficulty if demand for what they offer reduces or disappears.

There are, however, dangers of offering too wide a range of products or services as an organisation may not be considered to be expert or a market leader in any of them. In addition, the organisation is also exposing itself to the risks of several markets failing.

Freedom

As we have already mentioned, many people set up a business in order to work for themselves. They prefer the opportunity to make their own decisions and be their own boss, and, of course, take all the profits and risk all the losses.

Provide a return for shareholders and owners

This objective aims to provide a steady and acceptable level of profit to the owners of the organisation. In this sense, we have made a distinction between owners and shareholders. This will be covered in greater detail later.

Shareholders are owners of the business, but may only have a small stake in it and look for profits in the form of dividends from the shares they own.

The term **owners**, on the other hand, may refer to sole traders, partners or major shareholders, who again are looking for income from the organisation related to how much of that organisation they own.

Beating the competition

This objective in a sense is similar to being a market leader, however, beating the competition may just relate to achieving higher sales. Measuring this objective in terms of success is difficult, but can usually be assessed by the level of profit or reputation.

Survival

When times are bad and the economy is in recession, a company may simply seek survival. This may be measured by the company's ability to maintain existing staff levels, keeping customers and not having to close branches or retail outlets.

Breaking even

This objective can often be used to describe the attitude of a charity or non-profit-making organisation (e.g. a local authority or a Government Department). Any profits that are made are simply ploughed back into the organisation to cover running costs and purchase more products in order to continue the cycle. This can be termed 'ticking over' and is another objective often adopted by organisations in times of recession.

student activity

We have tried to identify the ten major objectives of most organisations. Which do you think are the most important? Put the 10 objectives into ranking order of importance. Once you have done this, look at your top five and try to come up with reasons why you have chosen these as being the most important.

Compare your decisions with those of the rest of the group.

Explain government influences on business

I ECONOMIC MANAGEMENT
free market, command economy, mixed/social market

2 INTERVENTION IN NATIONAL MARKETS
government policy, EC policy

3 INTERVENTION IN INTERNATIONAL MARKETS
protectionism, trade agreements (GATT etc.)

4 REASONS FOR GOVERNMENT INTERVENTION
competition, eliminate trade barriers, eliminate inequalities of opportunity, subsidise essential needs, support favoured businesses, employment

5 GOVERNMENT AND EC POLICY
interest rates, competition, employment, regional, transport, environmental protection, common standards, taxation (company and VAT)

ECONOMIC MANAGEMENT

One of the ways of looking at the different economies is to measure the amount of influence the Government has on decision making.

FREE MARKET

In a free market the government is not involved in controlling the resources. All decisions are made by buyers or sellers. Buyers will only buy goods when they believe they are getting value for money. If buyers, or consumers, think they would get better value from buying something else, then they will buy that. Those that make the goods, known as producers, have to constantly ad-

just their output of goods to match consumer demands. In the real world there is not a single country that can claim to be a truly free market. To a greater or lesser extent, all governments meddle with the economy.

Advantages

1 Consumers will buy what they think will give them the most satisfaction and value for money.
2 The most popular goods are likely to be produced in huge quantities and at low prices.
3 Most resources will be channelled into goods which are popular. It is unlikely that unpopular goods will be widely available. Scarce resources are not wasted on goods which will not sell.

4 The free market can respond to change very quickly when buying trends make the producing of old-fashioned goods unprofitable.

Disadvantages

1 Large and powerful companies have much more influence than smaller companies.

2 Although all production is linked to the consumers' willingness to buy, those consumers with more money have more influence.

3 The free market does not guarantee that the poorest consumers will have their basic needs provided for.

4 In a free market it is common for some large companies to be the only producers of particular goods (these are known as monopolies).
The free market only really works when consumers know exactly where and at what price they can buy goods, in other words, when they know where the best bargain is.

5 Advertising in a free market is very powerful. The information given to consumers is often misleading. It is difficult for consumers to know when they are being told the truth.

PLANNED/COMMAND ECONOMY

This is a system at the other end of the scale from a free market system. The government, through central planning, needs to know how much each region of the country is able to produce and exactly what their needs will be. From this information the government can then give out the available resources. This system has not worked very well in the long run and only China and Cuba still operate this system.

Advantages

1 The whole effort of the country can be used to achieve targets of production.

2 All parts of the country are dependent upon one another and this is a powerful way of ensuring all areas of the country remain united in their efforts.

3 Basic needs of the people can be fulfilled. If there is high unemployment, then these basic needs can be reduced in price so that people can afford them.

4 Long-term planning can be made for all resources and all industries.

5 There is no wasteful duplication of production. All goods and services can be distributed fairly.

Disadvantages

1 Since there is no competition, the quality of the products suffers. This also removes the rewards that individuals would normally get for their own effort and enterprise.

2 Factory managers and regional planners will always overestimate what they need to complete a project so that they can obtain more than their fair share of the resources. This means that resources are wasted because all the regions of the country like to think that they are more important than others

3 Because everything is centrally planned, a lot of paperwork needs to be completed. This is known as bureaucracy, and means that the cost of running a planned system is high.

4 Because all decisions must go through the bureaucracy, decision making is slowed down.

5 When the planned economy fails to produce enough of particular goods, individuals who can obtain these goods will sell them at high prices themselves. This is known as a 'black market'.

MIXED/SOCIAL ECONOMY

Mixed economies have features of both the free market and planned systems. The mixed economy is also the most common. There is a level of government involvement, but also a large element of private enterprise. Most Western European countries use this system in which three main groups are of equal importance, the producer, the government and the consumer.

The **producers** are private owners who are free to decide how their own resources are used. They decide what to produce, how many to produce (quantity), and the quality of the product.

The **government** has control over some resources and runs most of the services the country needs, e.g. health, welfare and defence. It has the power to influence producers and consumers. This is usually done by imposing laws or high rates of tax to discourage the over-buying of certain goods, e.g. alcohol and tobacco products.

Consumers are a very powerful but disorganised group. Each individual has his or her own needs and wants. They have the choice to buy from a range of goods that are on offer. Their decisions are heavily influenced by price, availability and advertising.

Advantages

1 The mixed economy combines the best elements of planned and free markets.

2 The government should be able to influence how resources are used.

3 The government also provides a 'safety net' for the weaker members of society who are unable to provide for themselves, e.g. the unemployed, the elderly, the sick.

4 The government with the help of the producers is able to make sure that the market runs smoothly, and ensure that there is effective competition within the market to keep prices low.

Disadvantages

1 The mixed economy also combines the worst elements of the free market and planned economies.
2 The government interferes with initiative and enterprise by imposing restrictive laws.
3 Competition will always favour the strong at the expense of the weak. Larger businesses will always be able to offer what appears to be a better deal as they are in a position to buy the resources they need at lower cost.

INTERVENTION IN NATIONAL MARKETS

GOVERNMENT POLICY

One would assume that in a free or mixed market, the individual consumer has the maximum freedom to consume and spend as he or she sees fit. Consumption patterns will determine the supply of all products and services and ensure that any scarce resources are not wasted. Unfortunately, there are several problems with this system and successive governments have intervened to control or manipulate the market. Above all, governments do not want the market to fail. Market failures unfortunately are all too common and may have resulted from the following circumstances:

- the economy is not sufficiently developed to accommodate changes in demand
- products or services are not available in sufficient quantities to match demand, or there has been over-production which has resulted in a glut in the market
- demand in a particular market may have collapsed suddenly
- Small or new organisations may be unable to compete due to the dominance of a market by a particular organisation

The market system is usually more than able to provide a wide range of products and services as demanded by the consumer. These are more often than not produced by the private sector and consumed by private consumers. Private goods on their own, however, cannot meet all the demands or requirements of the economy or country. The country needs additional products or services which are not usually supplied by the private sector. These are known as public goods or merit goods.

Public goods

The term **public goods** or **services** refers to provisions provided for the country as a whole. These include the police force, the prison service and the fire service. It is not feasible for each individual in society to pay directly for these services. Although some individuals may be able to afford expensive personal or property protection, the majority of the population require a society-wide protection. Increasingly, some of these public goods or services are being privatised, but this does not mean privatisation in the accepted sense of the word. The privatisation of prisons, for example, merely refers to private organisations subcontracting from the government the responsibility of running the service. There are two further important considerations to look at when we are considering public goods or services. These are:

- *Non-rival in consumption* - this refers to the point that if a particular individual benefits from a public good or service this does not prevent other individuals from consuming or benefiting at the same time. The level of service should be sufficient for a number of simultaneous demands on the service to be met fairly easily. The state, in providing the service, will try to ensure that the costs of providing that service do not exceed the overall benefit that society gains.

- *Non-exclusive* - if individuals refuse to pay their share towards the service provided, it is very difficult to exclude them from the benefits that all individuals receive. If someone has not paid his or her council tax, this does not mean that the police force (which receives some of its funding from this source) will not respond to an emergency call. Individuals who do not pay their contribution towards services are effectively enjoying a free ride at the expense of those who are willing to pay. In the final analysis, this means that all willing payers will end up paying more to subsidise the free-riders.

student activity

Present government policy seems to be moving towards reducing the number of publicly owned providers of goods and services. What is your opinion of this privatisation process? Should certain vital goods and services be controlled by the government and not by private enterprise?

Merit goods

Products or services which fall into this category are described as merit goods as they could be provided by the private sector. Examples of merit goods include the National Health Service, museums and education. There are two main reasons why the government chooses to provide these merit goods. These are:

- *Equity* - in a society which recognises equality of opportunity, it is important to give all individuals a fair chance. In this respect, the provision of free education to all tries to address the fact that the poorer sections of the community could not afford a good education for their offspring. Those with high incomes can always choose to use private education, but the majority of the population have no other choice but to use state education.
- *Externalities* - by providing a particular service from which all members of the population can benefit, this has positive benefits to society as a whole. If the majority of the population is literate and well educated, then the assumption is that the economy will be more successful. These are also known as the **social benefits**, but they are hard to quantify. In some respects the government may choose to ignore the social benefits and concentrate on the social costs of providing the service. This is a rather negative view to adopt, but an increasingly more popular one. The philosophy behind looking at social costs and ignoring social benefits is linked to the desire of many

individuals to allow everyone to choose exactly where and how to spend their income. Following on from this, we must assume that if key services are not provided by the state, then we can expect lower taxation – which in turn releases more income to be expended as and where the individual sees fit.

student activity

Since merit goods and services include hospitals and given that they are gradually becoming fund holders in their own right (in other words they are required to manage their own budgets), carry out research on your local hospital and try to discover the impact this process may have had. You may also find useful information on this subject in your local press.

FISCAL POLICY

Fiscal policy refers to the government's policy on the following:

- public spending
- various taxes
- public borrowing

The government tries to influence the level of demand within the economy by changing the amount it spends in relation to the amount of money received from tax.

At nearly every point in recent history, the government has been operating a deficit budget. This is when they are spending more than they receive in taxes. In order to make up the shortfall, they must acquire money from other sources. This is known as the **public sector borrowing requirement** (PSBR). A balanced budget occurs when government spending is matched by tax income. Recent governments have attempted to reach this balance by spending as little as possible and relying on private individuals to provide for themselves. Rarely does a government have a surplus budget, as this would mean that the government had taken in more taxes than it was spending.

There are additional advantages and disadvantages of these various forms of 'balancing the books'. If the government is operating a deficit budget, there is a danger of inflation growing, as it becomes increasingly more expensive to borrow money. A surplus budget, on the other hand, can help reduce inflation by cutting down the amount of disposable income each individual has, in other words, reducing demand.

The main sources of tax income are:

- income tax taken from each individual from money earned
- corporation tax paid by businesses on their profits

- value added tax paid on the value of products or services at each stage of their production (this VAT proportion increases as products move from raw materials to finished goods)
- national insurance paid by both employees and employers to provide benefits
- inheritance tax paid on property and money left in wills
- stamp duty paid on financial transactions which involve large sums of money

student activity

Find out the latest figures on government expenditure plans. Try to compare how these figures differ from those of last year. What have been the most significant changes in the expenditure? Have some particular departments gained or suffered as a result of expenditure realignment?

MONETARY POLICY

Monetary policy is concerned with the control of the quantity and price of money in the economy. As long as individuals are spending money at a rate faster than the supply of products or services, then prices will inevitably rise. There is a strong link between the quantity of money available and the level of inflation.

FIG 1.2.1 *Interest rates naturally affect all bank borrowing and influence deposits in banks, loans and overdrafts.*

Money cannot simply be described as coins and notes. There are many other forms of money. These include credit cards, cheques and credit payments. In order to control the amount of money available, the government will set the interest rate at a level to deter people from borrowing, or encouraging them to do so. As well as attempting to control the quantity of money the government will also try to set the price of money. Such

activity relates also to the interest rate. In addition, the government will keep a close eye on the **retail price index** which serves as an indicator of inflation. By keeping pay settlements below the increase in the RPI, the government will be effectively reducing the amount of money available in the economy. On the other hand, if the government allows pay settlements to exceed the change in the RPI then it will be allowing the injection of more money into the economy. In the first instance, the RPI will drop, in the latter it will increase. Both of these circumstances may give the government cause for concern.

Student banking

Starting student life means all sorts of changes. As well as studying hard and having a good time, you'll need to pay for all types of living expenses such as rent, food, household bills, books and so on. You may find your grant just won't stretch to cover all of this. Barclays have produced a package to help you manage your money more effectively.

THE BARCLAYS STUDENT BANK ACCOUNT PACKAGE

WHAT DOES IT GIVE ME?

The choice is yours. You may just want a cheque book and a Barclaybank card, which is a cash dispenser card only. Or maybe you'd prefer the versatility of the Barclays Connect card – a debit card, cash dispenser and cheque guarantee card all in one – so you have less to carry around. You may also need a credit card – Barclaycard Visa. You can apply for whatever card best suits your needs.

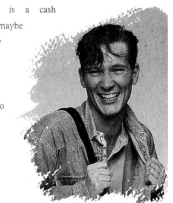

FIG 1.2.2 *Banks have recognised the importance of providing services for individuals even before they actually reach the job market.*

PRIVATISATION

Ever since 1979 the process of **privatisation** has been taking place. There are two reasons for this privatisation process:

- Many people argue that state-run businesses are not very efficient, perhaps because they have no competition, and they never have a threat of going bankrupt because the government will always bail them out.

- It is believed that as many people as possible should have shares in businesses. The idea is that everyone, no matter how rich or poor they may be, should be encouraged to buy a few hundred pounds' worth of shares in major enterprises like British Telecom. And indeed they have done so.

As privatisation rolls into areas which have not previously been affected, such as the National Health Service, where Trust status is almost another word for privatisation, there have been considerable worries. Competition in areas such as health can often lead to costcutting policies which will only mean the deterioration of standards.

One of the major arguments against privatisation is the question of whether it is right to sell peoples' shares in industries which are in fact already owned by them. The theory behind this is that if the government is representative of the people of the country and runs services for the people then those services are owned by the people, since they are state-owned.

student activity

Investigate the privatisation process of an industry of your choice and consider the following questions:
- What were the processes of privatisation?
- How has the ownership of the industry changed since privatisation?
- What problems were encountered during and after privatisation?
- Is it possible to measure the comparative success of the privatised industry?

Compile your findings in a short report format which should be word processed.

THE GOVERNMENT AND PUBLIC-SECTOR ORGANISATIONS

When we look at the relationship of the government and the managers of these public sector organisations we find that there is always conflict. The government has one set of objectives and the organisation is likely to have another one. The government usually states its objectives in relation to public organisations in terms of providing a good service. The government may see its job as cutting costs. It also may have other reasons for demanding that the service be run in a particular way. For example, there may be an election soon.

Public-sector organisations, just like any other organisation, are interested in survival, expansion and efficiency. It may not always be possible to reach these three main targets. The bottom line often is that the service should give value for money. When public sector organisations have been starved of investment, as so many claim nowadays, then the managers of these organisations find it very difficult to offer an efficient service which provides value for money.

EC POLICY

FIG 1.2.3 *It is likely that the EC will be enlarged with the inclusion of 12 further nations. This process may be slowed down by the creation of the European Economic Area and Association Agreements with East European Countries. This intermediate step is intended to give the current member states time to complete the programmes of economic and monetary union.*

The European Community (EC) Commission, based in Brussels, prepares and proposes a range of laws based on the agreed treaties signed by member states. Once these are passed, the implementation of the policies is monitored by the Commission.

The Council of Ministers decides whether policies should become law. These Ministers (one from each member state) consider the proposals and must all agree before a policy can become law. Increasingly, the European Parliament is becoming involved in decision making. The impact of EC law has had wide-ranging effects at all levels and activities of businesses.

The Maastricht Treaty

Many people will have heard of this treaty, but despite a considerable amount of press coverage, there is still confusion as to the point and nature of the legislation. Its main points are that:

- individuals whose country is part of the EC have the right to live or work anywhere within the community
- there is some level of co-operation and agreement with regard to transport networks, energy policies and communications throughout the EC
- the EC fund a variety of research and development projects
- the EC monitors environmental issues
- throughout the EC there is some common recognition of academic and vocational qualifications

- the EC strictly monitors and controls the entry of new countries into the EC
- member states co-operate on educational issues
- member states co-operate on public health issues
- member states develop a range of consumer laws
- particular attention is paid to the protection of regional culture and language
- the EC states move towards a single market (which allows the free movement of goods and services throughout the EC)

student activity

Try to assess the reasons why the UK is refusing to adopt the Social Chapter of the Maastrich Treaty. Discuss the probable reasons as a group.

Another aspect of the Maastricht Treaty is the Social Chapter. Although this has not been adopted by the UK, it has been accepted by all other EC members (1989). The Social Chapter contains some of the following proposals:

- a maximum 48-hour working week
- the improvement of working conditions of employees
- an EC-wide attempt to reduce high levels of unemployment
- the formalisation of the negotiation process between employees and employers
- the goal of preventing "social dumping" whereby organisations move to EC member states which have lower pay rates and less protection for employees

student activity

Can you find any evidence of social dumping in the UK? Use newspapers as your main source of information.

The **exchange rate mechanism** was created to control the rate of exchange of currencies between members of the EC. The purpose of the exercise is to give organisations and individuals the opportunity to purchase products and services in any EC currency and be well aware of the exact exchange rate (within some limits). Many EC members consider that the adoption of a standard currency throughout Europe is essential to ensure that Europe operates effectively as a single, strong market. To this end, they have created the ECU (European Currency Unit) which, although it has been minted in many countries, has not been generally accepted as a viable exchange currency.

The UK, in particular, sees the Maastricht Treaty as being the first stage in a process leading to the eventual loss of **sovereignty** power and ability to make it's own decisions. By giving up its Sovereignty, a country is passing on decision making to the European Commission, the European Parliament, the European Central Bank, and this could lead to joint decision making by Europe as a whole. If countries were to accept a single currency, many people feel that the government would lose its ability to use monetary policy to control the supply of money and the level of interest rates.

INTERVENTION IN INTERNATIONAL MARKETS

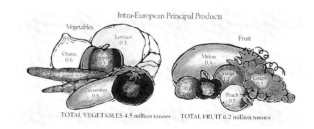

FIG 1.2.4 *This illustration shows the internal trade within Europe of fruit and vegetables as calculated by Geest.*

Trade throughout the world creates employment and income for all countries involved. Different countries have a range of attitudes to the potential advantages and disadvantages of international trade. Some may adopt a protectionist attitude, while others freely accept the costs and benefits of international trade.

To a greater or lesser extent, all countries are dependent upon one another for a variety of different products and services. It is rare to find a country which can produce everything its economy requires. Many factors influence what a country produces:

- the climate may not allow the growth of certain produce
- the geography of the country may be such that there is a disproportionate area of mountains, deserts or swampland
- the country may lack vital raw materials
- the country may not be able to afford the machinery needed to produce certain items

- the country may not have the labour expertise to run certain plant and machinery
- the country may be poor and may lack the ability to invest in industry

There are two different ways of looking at the advantages particular countries will have over one another. They are known as absolute or comparative advantages.

1 *Absolute advantages.* Countries which enjoy an absolute advantage in one particular area of business activity are able to produce something which other countries cannot. The West Indies, for example, have an absolute advantage in the production of tropical fruits, whereas they do not benefit from the ability to produce the farming machinery that is necessary for their industries. The UK, on the other hand, has an absolute advantage in the production of a variety of goods and services. The UK is renowned for its production of whisky, steel and farming equipment. It is therefore the case that countries will concentrate on areas of business activity in which they have an advantage. It is unlikely that West Indian countries, for example, would invest vast sums of money to build up industry in areas at present dominated by other countries.

FIG 1.2.5 *Despite Europe's wide differences in climate it is still unable to produce certain types of fruit and vegetables and indeed cannot fully supply demand for products normally grown within Europe. These figures have also been calculated by Geest.*

2 *Comparative advantages.* Having a comparative advantage may only be a temporary state of affairs. When using its comparative advantage to the best effect, a country would concentrate on the production of products and services which are relatively low in cost. More goods can be produced using fewer of the countries economic resources.

All countries benefit from trade for the following reasons:

- individuals within the country may enjoy a higher standard of living since they are producing products and services for the international market rather than relying purely on the domestic market
- international trade greatly widens the choice of products and services available to all
- each country, in concentrating on what it is good at producing may benefit from economies of scale (this is the theory that recognises that mass production means lower individual costs per product)
- international co-operation is developed through international trade by the establishment of a wide variety of economic and political agreements

PROTECTIONISM

Despite the fact that trade offers many advantages some countries attempt to restrict it by the imposition of protectionist legislation. This can take the form of:

- *tariffs* – also known as import duties, which make imported goods more expensive
- *quotas* – these are used to limit the quantity of imports allowed
- *embargoes* – these are the banning of all trade with a particular country
- *exchange controls* – which attempt to restrict the supply of foreign currency in order to reduce the quantity imported
- *patents and trade marks* – to legally protect the ideas and products of a home-producer

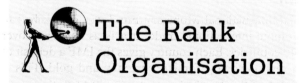

FIG 1.2.6 *The Rank symbol and name can officially appear in a variety of different formats. However, the use of the company 'signature' is closely guarded.*

- *licensing* – permitting imports only when there is a shortage of products in the country
- *subsidies* – government-provided finance to enable products and services produced in the domestic market to be sold at lower prices, thus reducing the demand for imports

Countries choose to impose these various barriers to trade for the following reasons:

● to reduce balance of payments problems
● to reduce unemployment (which will be caused by high import levels)
● to protect new industries at home
● to encourage the country to become self-sufficient
● to prevent 'dumping' when surplus goods are sold abroad at a lower price

TRADE AGREEMENTS

Most countries readily accept the need to involve themselves in international trade. To this end, a variety of trading agreements have been agreed and signed to facilitate this:

GATT

GATT (General Agreement on Tariffs and Trade) is a landmark agreement involving over 100 countries and accounting for nearly 90 per cent of all world trade. GATT attempts to combat protectionist policies by:

● establishing a set of rules regarding international trade
● by acting as a negotiation medium to attempt to liberalise trade and eliminate trade barriers
● operating as an arbiter and court to which governments can appeal when faced with trading disputes

student activity

Try to identify at least three countries which are not GATT signatories.

IMF

The International Monetary Fund was established to promote international trade. It acts as banker to over 140 countries. Each country gives the IMF a deposit of its own currency, foreign currency and gold. This is known as the country's quota. Member countries may then draw on these deposits, or borrow in excess of their deposit to help balance their payments. Any loans are repaid once the present balance of payments problem is solved. The IMF will impose certain conditions upon borrowers which must be met or the loan will not be agreed. All policies are controlled by a Board of Governors. Although the IMF is primarily concerned with short term loans, it has in recent years, been issuing loans to developing countries on a long-term basis.

G7

The Group of 7 are the seven most advanced industrial countries. These are:

● Canada
● France
● Germany
● Italy
● Japan
● UK
● USA

Between them they produce almost 70 per cent of the world's output of products and services. They meet annually and their goal is to create a solid foundation for international trade.

In addition to the strictly economic considerations, G7 is also interested in the following:

● supporting GATT
● assisting developing nations in their debt management
● encouraging the growth of international trade and the world economy
● monitoring and controlling environmental policies
● organising aid for the former Soviet Union and other eastern European countries
● international co-operation in combating drug trafficking

student activity

Can you identify at least one other country which could claim membership of G7 on the grounds that its economy has developed significantly in recent years?

REASONS FOR GOVERNMENT INTERVENTION

Prior to this century, the government played only a minor part in the running of the economy. However, various circumstances have determined that the government should play a greater role and involve itself in almost every aspect of business activity. It is important to realise that the government must take a macro view (wide view) of the operations of businesses and how they impact upon the economy. It is for this reason that the government is involved in all of the areas detailed below. You should not consider this to be a comprehensive list as we are sure you can think of other areas of the economy in which the government is involved.

TO ENCOURAGE COMPETITION

Since 1948, successive governments have produced a range of legislation in order to stimulate competition within the economy. Generally known as competition policy, these Acts try to ensure free and fair competition in the market place.

The 1948 Monopolies and Restrictive Practices (Inquiry and Control) Act

We say there is a **monopoly** when a single organisation substantially controls a particular market. This is not an acceptable state of affairs, as the organisation may be able to control both price and supply within that market. As far as the government is concerned, a monopoly situation is not in the public interest. In recent years those responsible for monitoring monopolies have been re-named the Monopolies and Mergers Commission (MMC). They investigate organisations which dominate particular markets and are empowered to refer serious cases to the Secretary of State, who can then make an order to counterbalance the state of affairs.

student activity

Using national newspapers as your major research tool, try to identify a monopolies and mergers case in the last year. Try to prepare your findings in chronological order and present your research to the rest of your group in the form of an oral presentation.

The 1956 Restrictive Trade Practices Act

Under this Act, a Restrictive Practices Court was established to investigate and rule upon organisations working together to fix market prices. Such an agreement between organisations is known as a **Cartel**.

Interestingly, in variance with the basic premise of English law, under which a suspect is presumed innocent until proven guilty, in restrictive practices cases, the organisations must prove that it is not against the public interest in order to avoid action being taken against them.

The 1965 Monopolies and Mergers Act

With this Act the government provided itself with the means to automatically refer merger proposals to a Mergers Panel. This panel would report back within six months and simply state whether or not the proposed merger was against the public interest. The actions of the Mergers Panel came under serious criticism from a number of different directions.

The 1973 Fair Trading Act

This key Act attempts to tackle the problem of competition. Defining a monopoly as an organisation controlling more than 25 per cent of a market, this gave the Director General of Fair Trading considerable powers. Of particular interest to the Director was any organisation attempting to distort the operation of a market by using anti-competitive pricing practices. Should the Director rule that the organisation's activities are unacceptable, the organisation is automatically referred to the MMC. Again, the Secretary of State may rule that the organisation must immediately cease this unacceptable behaviour.

student activity

If you were concerned as to the price charged for a particular product or service, how would you go about complaining? Which agencies would offer you help and advice? You can begin your research by visiting your local Citizens' Advice Bureau.

The 1980 Competition Act

This Act effectively broadened the scope of activities that could be undertaken by the Director General of Fair Trading and the MMC. They could now investigate public sector organisations, which were brought into the range of the legislation. Each case is still investigated as regards its particular benefits and costs to the free running of the market, but it is no longer the view that mergers in themselves are undesirable. Indeed, a monopoly may be acceptable under certain circumstances.

TO ELIMINATE TRADE BARRIERS

As we mentioned in the previous section on governments' intervention in international markets, successive agreements have been made internationally to ease the flow of world-wide trade.

Over the centuries, many countries have been involved in trade wars with one another. In some cases these have occurred when particular countries have developed new areas of business activity to replace imported foreign goods. Increasingly, as developing countries find themselves in a position to replace imported goods, their old suppliers are faced with serious and long-term problems. To some extent these old suppliers may be able to find alternative markets for their products, but in many cases they have found their products unwanted and obsolete. Further barriers to trade are gradually being eliminated by such agreements as GATT and this can only be to the advantage of all signatories. There are some countries which refuse to involve themselves in any trade agreements. In the short term this may not affect them, but in the long term they may find themselves isolated and without trading partners. By imposing trade barriers, a country signals to others that their goods and services are unwanted. In turn, potential trading partners may choose to create their own barriers in response.

The UK, finding its old trading partners in the Commonwealth looking to find alternative trading partners within their own regional areas, has realised that it must look to Europe for the future. With this in mind, the UK has, albeit begrudgingly, begun to accept the concept of a free market within Europe. This process began with the entry of the UK into Europe in the 1970s. There is a feeling that the UK has relied upon its old trading advantages for too long and that its reluctance to involve itself in Europe has left it lagging behind. The UK now accepts that its principal trading partners find trade barriers unacceptable and, as a result, has eliminated most trade barriers with European countries. Barriers are only found among trading partners from further afield. These, too, are gradually disappearing.

The government has now recognised that in order for UK industry to be truly competitive throughout the world, it must not discriminate against any foreign imports. If it does, it can only expect the same treatment for its own products and services abroad. This realisation has had a drastic impact upon the UK economy, since many foreign countries have an absolute or comparative advantage in the production of certain products. Many traditional UK industries have been forced out of business as they cannot compete with the lower wage and production costs abroad. At the same time, the UK strengths have begun to be exploited abroad, particularly in the high technology field.

TO ELIMINATE INEQUALITIES OF OPPORTUNITY

In a free market it is very difficult for a government to establish conditions under which organisations can compete on an equal basis. Since the key feature of a free market is that market forces determine the success or failure of an organisation, it should not be forgotten that smaller and less efficient organisations tend to fail. As far as government intervention in the operation of organisations is concerned, it is able to keep a close eye on fair trading, monopoly situations and potential mergers. It is at the individual level that the government finds it difficult to provide the ideal circumstances for equality of opportunity. True equality of opportunity may only be established when all individuals in society begin with the same base chance of success or failure. We know that inequalities exist even before an individual is born. His or her parents may be comparatively rich and therefore able to offer their offspring a better start in life. However, the establishment of universal, compulsory education, at least to the age of 16, has gone some way towards levelling the chances and opportunities. In the present political climate it is believed that with intelligence, good ideas and some assistance from government agencies, any individual may be successful. To this end, the government has established a range of advice and information centres, together with incentive programmes to assist new entrepreneurs and enterprises. The Enterprise Allowance Scheme (which has now reached the end of its life) provided new business people with a safety net of £40 per week during their first year of operation. Despite this, there was still upwards of a 90 per cent failure rate. New businesses in particular suffer from lack of funding, knowledge and opportunity to succeed.

TO SUBSIDISE ESSENTIAL NEEDS

In nearly all countries, governments have involved themselves in providing for essential needs. These include health, education, law enforcement, transport and housing. Governments provide these services, funded by taxation, to ensure that the basic infrastructure of the economy is maintained. Without the maintenance of these services, individuals and businesses alike would find it impossible to operate. Although some individuals and businesses may be able to provide for themselves in almost all of these areas, the vast majority of the population find themselves reliant upon the government subsidised services. There has been a gradual move towards the privatisation of many of these services, but privatisation does not necessarily mean the elimination of the provision of these services by the government itself. In many cases, the privatisation process merely means that the provider of the service is no longer a government department or agent, but effectively is a subcontractor who provides the service on the government's behalf.

TO SUPPORT FAVOURED BUSINESSES

The government has established a variety of departments whose function is to deal with specific forms of business activity. Each government department liaises with and assists these industries. Key government departments involved in this area are:

Agriculture, Fisheries and Food

This government department deals with the agricultural industry and is involved in the inspection and development of business activity in this area.

Trade and Industry

The main function of this department is to support all forms of industry and commerce and it is a key player in the formation of government policy. In addition, it will provide resources and assistance to organisations involved in exporting.

Energy

The main function of this department is to co-ordinate all energy policies and assist the development of the energy industry in general.

Employment

This department is specifically involved in the development of the country's human resources and will take particular notice of industry's human resource requirements.

Transport

This department is responsible for the co-ordination of transportation policy and the implementation of EC directives relating to transportation.

Other government departments, are involved either directly or indirectly, in supporting UK business. These include:

- **The Treasury**, which analyses economic affairs
- **The Bank of England**, which not only issues the

currency, but acts as the government's banker and monitors all other banking providers
- **The Central Office of Information**, which produces detailed reports, surveys, statistics and forecasts useful to industry
- **The Office of Fair Trading**, which monitors trading practices and the legality of business activities
- **The Health and Safety Commission**, which monitors and controls the health and safety of both employees and customers
- **The Monopolies and Mergers Commission**, which rules on monopolies and mergers and decides whether these are in the public interest
- **The Advertising Standards Authority**, which monitors advertising and investigates complaints
- **The Independent Television Commission**, which fulfils a similar role to the ASA within television
- **The Factories and Public Health Inspectorates**, which regularly inspect business premises to make sure that health and safety legislation is being adhered to fully
- **Industrial Tribunals**, which were set up to arbitrate and adjudicate in employment matters
- **The Registrar of Companies**, who not only maintains a national registry of private limited companies and shareholdings, but also is responsible for the monitoring of the use of trade marks and trade names
- **County and District Councils**, which are responsible for the implementation of government policy and legislation which relates to businesses. Specific areas of interest include:
  – collecting business rates
  – collecting taxes on premises
  – giving planning consents
  – monitoring trading standards
  – public health

In conjunction with specific regional policies, which are aimed at developing areas suffering from high levels of unemployment, the government will seek to improve the general environment in which UK businesses operate. It will identify key exporters and assist them in every way in order to aid the balance of payments, since high levels of exporting mean that additional funds will flow into the country. This is obviously beneficial to the economy in general, and generally enhances the wealth of the nation.

TO CREATE EMPLOYMENT

To be classified as being unemployed, an individual must be **actively seeking work**. The way in which this figure is calculated has come under severe criticism from a variety of sources. The Department of Employment uses a fairly broad measure to calculate unemployment, this being those who are registered as unemployed and eligible for benefit payments. However, the official figures are said to grossly underestimate the true levels of unemployment. The figures do not include the following:

- those who have not registered as being unemployed, as they are too proud to admit to being unemployed
- students and housewives
- those who are on YT or other employment training programmes
- those who are working part time or in seasonal or temporary occupations

The reasons for unemployment are three-fold:

- there has been a growth in the number of people seeking work over the last 20 years, in fact it has risen by nearly three million
- with the elimination of many trade barriers, the UK in particular has suffered from high levels of market penetration from foreign competition
- the UK unfairly has a poor industrial relations reputation. It is widely believed that the British worker is not as reliable or stable as some of his/her European counterparts

Unemployment itself may take many forms. Some of the main types of unemployment are as follows:

1 *Structural unemployment.* This is where there is a mis-match of available labour skills to industrial needs. It may be the case that skilled workers are available in different parts of the country, but they are not necessarily available where they are required.

2 *Cyclical unemployment.* This form of unemployment is caused by periods of down-turn in business activity. Typically these cycles are known as 'booms' and 'slumps'. A slump is best defined as a recession, and is a time in which there are higher levels of unemployment.

3 *Frictional unemployment.* This type of unemployment, although temporary, refers to individuals moving from one job to another. The time spent unemployed between these jobs is a permanent feature of the economy. A small percentage of individuals can always be found in this classification.

4 *Seasonal unemployment.* This should not be confused with cyclical unemployment, although the two have many of the same features. Typically, seasonal unemployment refers to the tourist and leisure industry.

student activity

Identify five major types of seasonal employment in your own area.

5 *Regional unemployment.* Certain areas within the UK suffer from lower wage levels as they are comparatively at a disadvantage in terms of their location. In such areas, the loss of any industries have a more serious effect as it is less likely that alternative employment may be found.

student activity

Can you think of any particular regions which are currently suffering from severe regional unemployment? Why do you think this has occurred?

6 *Technological unemployment.* As industries become automated, information technology equipment in its various forms will replace workers.

7 *Real wage unemployment.* This is caused by wages being too high for all members of the workforce to be in employment. Employers simply cannot afford to take on new staff. These periods are marked by the activities of powerful trade unions and possibly weak government.

8 *Residual Unemployment.* There is always a small percentage of the population who, for various reasons, are unable to work. While strictly they may not be classed as being unemployed (as technically they are not seeking work), this category will include the physically and mentally disadvantaged.

Unemployment can have severe effects on the economy. These include:

- *Loss of income to the country.* The unemployed not only pay little or no taxation, but they actually cost the Exchequer funds. It is calculated that the average unemployed person costs the country upwards of £10,000 per year.
- *Inequality.* Unemployed people are, naturally, worse off than their employed peers. The levels of benefit do not adequately compensate them for being unemployed.
- *Resource wastage.* The mere fact that a number of individuals are unemployed means that the economy is not performing to its maximum potential. If we

consider working individuals as a resource, the economy is not using its resource potential to full effect.

In addition to these economic considerations, there are also social effects arising from unemployment. These include:

- **increased crime** as a result of boredom and frustration
- **poorer health** arising from the inability of unemployed individuals to provide for themselves nutritionally and medically
- **loss of status** as a net result of being unemployed, particularly in the long term
- **loss of the work ethic** as unemployed people become depressed and demoralised and eventually lose the will to work

Unemployment itself can have serious implications for businesses. These include:

- a reduction in demand for products and services, which, in turn, will affect sales and profits
- reduced wage rates, although beneficial to the employer, mean that some jobs would be considered marginal by employees, as they may pay only slightly more than the available benefits
- reduction in trade union power. Again, this may be welcomed by employers, but, as trade unions lose power and members through unemployment, they become easier prey for unscrupulous employers who wish to take advantage of the situation

We shall be looking at how governments attempt to control unemployment in the next section of the book.

student activity

Using local and national newspapers as your research tools, identify any social problems in your own area which have been associated with unemployment.

GOVERNMENT AND EC POLICY

In this section we will be looking at the relationship between the implementation of policy and the influence that the EC has had on government legislation. Again, we have provided a list of key issues, although there may be more areas which impact upon business activity in general.

INTEREST RATES

The simplest way to think about interest rates is to assume that these control the price of borrowing money. The Bank of England, in consultation with the government, sets the general level of interest rates, in particular economic situations. By changing the interest rate government policy has the following impact on businesses:

1. High interest rates will reduce the money tied up in stock and release capital as organisations seek to avoid overdrafts. The net effect of this is that organisations produce less and employ fewer people.
2. Higher interest rates will also affect suppliers who face similar problems and may be required to increase prices to the consumer. This, in turn, may have a detrimental effect on an organisation's ability to compete in the international market.
3. As interest rates increase, demand will fall, since consumers will have to pay more for their credit facilities. Some goods, as we have already seen, are

price-sensitive and this increase in credit costs may deter consumers from purchasing products.

4. Rises in interest rates will, however, strengthen the pound, thus encouraging foreign investors to put money into the UK economy. In order to invest in the UK foreign, organisations must buy sterling and their buying activities will increase the demand on that currency. As we know, greater demand may increase price. This is also true for currencies.
5. A rise in interest rates does, as we have already said, make UK firms less competitive, but on the other side of the coin, it does mean that the prices of imports into the UK will also fall. This may lead to a further problem as imports outpace exports.

student activity

How will interest rates affect an organisation's ability to manage its debts?

The effects of changes in the interest rate depend on the size of the change. If higher interest rates are coupled with a high inflation rate then organisations and consumers alike are not overly concerned. But when inflation is low and interest rates are high we are less likely to borrow.

Increasingly, the UK Government has been interested in the comparative interest rates of other European countries. This new level of inter-dependence has been promoted by the EC, which is keen to see interest rates in harmony throughout Europe. Nevertheless, certain EC member states are suffering from more serious economic problems than others and are forced to increase their interest rates correspondingly. The effects of these increases may be seen as either advantages or disadvantages, depending upon whether one is importing from or exporting to those countries.

student activity

Find out the interest rates of the following countries:

- UK
- Germany
- USA
- Japan

As a group discuss the reasons for the differences in interest rates in these countries.

COMPETITION

As we have already stated when considering such trade agreements as GATT, the EC and the UK are concerned with assisting businesses to compete on an equal and fair basis. With the reduction in restrictive trading practices throughout Europe it is now possible to compete on a Europe-wide basis. However, certain countries are still keen to protect key elements of their economies. This may be because they are comparatively unsuccessful or inefficient within the European context. If a country has a core business which provides for the majority of employment and wealth of that nation, it is understandable that such a country would be rather reluctant to expose this business to the full effect of market forces.

FIG 1.2.7 *Mercury Communications, a division of Cable and Wireless, was granted a telecommunications operator licence in 1984. Cable and Wireless was formerly a publicly owned industry.*

When we consider world-wide competition, we find that, despite numerous trade agreements, there are still barriers to trade in various countries.

EMPLOYMENT

At various times, governments have employed both fiscal and monetary policy to control unemployment. **Fiscal** policies used by governments include:

- increasing public spending which, in turn, generates economic activity and helps to expand employment
- reduction in taxation, which gives individuals more disposable income and helps to generate additional demand
- general support for businesses by offering incentives to investment and assisting and reducing the complexities of exporting

Since 1979 the government has been preoccupied with the use of **monetary** policy to manage the economy. The manipulation of interest rates has been used to control the money supply. Lower interest rates are more attractive to borrowers than savers, thus encouraging people to take on credit or loans in order to spend. With the availability of cheaper money, businesses are likewise more inclined to invest. It is believed that this policy will help reduce unemployment. In reality, it is only just beginning to have an effect after nearly 15 years.

Specific policies, or direct measures, taken by the government to tackle unemployment include:

1 *Investment in education and training.* Funded through the Technical Enterprise Councils, a number of schemes, such as YT and Training for Work, are run which are specifically aimed at the long-term unemployed and at employers.
2 *Enterprise schemes,* which offer various financial and tax incentives to help, in particularly, small or new businesses.
3 *Reducing the value of social security* to act as a disincentive to individuals and force them back into work. Present government philosophy is moving towards the introduction of a 'Workfare' along American lines, where individuals who receive benefits are required to involve themselves either in training or in community programmes. If they do not, then the benefit will be suspended.
4 *Reduction in trade union power.* As we will see in Unit 4, the government has introduced a wide range of legislation aimed at reducing trade union power. The policy has been targeted at removing the 'closed shop', and reducing the power of picketing and the effectiveness of strikes. In addition, as we have already mentioned, weaker Trade Unions mean lower pay settlements.

5 *Advice and information.* The government has sought to create a comprehensive range of advice centres throughout the country to aid the unemployed. These include Job Clubs, Restart and enhanced Job Centres.

6 *Regional assistance programmes.* Depressed areas may benefit from a variety of grants and tax relief schemes to businesses. These policies are specifically aimed at areas with high unemployment in the hope that they will alleviate pressure on local businesses.

REGIONAL POLICY

Regional policy seeks to address the inequalities between particular regions. Some economists feel that regions should be left to their own devices and that market forces should determine whether a region succeeds or fails. If a region is suffering from high unemployment, then it is inevitable that organisations which establish themselves there can demand lower pay rates from their workers. The theory is that this comparative advantage which results from high unemployment will mean that the region will benefit in the medium to long term. Unfortunately, the market is not as discriminating as these economists feel it should be. The UK, in particular, has a national wage bargaining system, which means that in certain occupations, the wage rates are exactly the same despite regional variations in employment. There are many other factors that may determine the location of an industry in a particular region, such as the availability of raw materials or communication links. It is too simplistic to cite labour skills as being the sole reason for location of industry in a particular region. The theory of market forces also presupposes that labour is comparatively mobile and is able to move from region to region in search of employment. The fact of the matter is that the majority of individuals are immobile. This is for two main reasons:

1 *Occupational immobility.* This form of immobility is related to the fact that many people have only some skills and are untrained in other skills. They are thus unsuitable for employment in alternative occupational areas. The government provides a range of retraining programmes to help ease this form of immobility.

2 *Geographical immobility.* Individuals are reluctant to move to new areas of the country, or to Europe for that matter, for a variety of reasons. These include:

- family ties
- social ties
- housing difficulties
- children
- comparative additional expenses of moving into dearer areas

The young are more likely to be willing and able to move, but it is they who contribute significantly to local economies. If we assume that most younger people are in employment, then it is the case that they are contributing a large proportion of their income to local businesses and this, in turn, generates more employment. Emigration of these people from an area has a multiplier effect on that area, since demand for local goods and services will be reduced, thus increasing unemployment. Gradually, the area will suffer a decline as organisations close or move from that area.

Government policy on regional development can take a number of different forms. These include:

1 The **siting of central government departments** in regional areas. The government operates a policy of positive discrimination in choosing a depressed area to site its services. The Vehicle Licensing Agency, which is responsible for the monitoring and licensing of all motor vehicles within the UK, has been sited in Swansea. This area had been suffering from high levels of unemployment and the move has resulted in many positive effects on the local economy.

2 The government offers a range of **incentives to industry** to help reduce costs in moving to or setting up in a depressed area. The government has built a number of purpose-made factories and lowered the cost of rent and rates to encourage organisations to resettle in depressed areas.

3 Labour costs can also be reduced by offering a **subsidy to industries** to attract them to select a depressed area when considering a move.

4 Certain regions can be designated as **special areas** which will, in turn, receive additional help and assistance from the Government. Development areas can be split into three distinct types:
- special development areas - those in need of the maximum help
- intermediate areas - those with particularly high levels of unemployment
- development areas

The EC assists these regions through its regional development fund and encourages its money to be spent on building up the infrastructure as well as encouraging organisations to establish their businesses there.

student activity

Try to identify the nearest area which benefits from some form of assistance from the government. Assess the impact of this enhanced status. How has it affected the unemployment figures?

FIG 1.2.8 *Geest's distributive wholesale division offers the food service industry the widest range of fruit, vegetables and prepared foods via chilled distribution from nine depots situated throughout the UK. The organisation has a fleet of 140 temperature controlled vehicles of various sizes to provide a flexible response to customer needs.*

TRANSPORT

The business community benefits greatly from government spending on the infrastructure of the UK. Infrastructure includes the following:

- roads
- rail
- water and sewers
- communication
- power

Although the private sector has become involved in many of these areas of activity it is still the government that provides the majority of funding for transportation projects, especially transportation links. Having said this, such projects as the Channel Tunnel have been almost solely funded by private enterprise.

The EC is particularly interested in the development of trans-European links between member states. To this end, the EC is beginning to become involved in policy formulation relating to the building and maintenance of transportation networks. In addition to this, the EC is keen to harmonise the rules relating to transportation in general, one example being the increase of the legal weight limit on trucks operating throughout Europe.

Transportation costs are particularly crucial if raw materials, or finished goods for that matter, are bulky or heavy. In order to ensure that all parts of the EC are accessible to various modes of transport, the EC has begun to formulate general policies on the establishment of improved transportation systems.

The UK government is presently considering the introduction of toll motorways throughout the country in the hope of encouraging private contractors to build new road systems. This is a common feature in Europe and has greatly improved transportation networks on the Continent. It is hoped that it will have a similar effect in the UK.

ENVIRONMENTAL PROTECTION

Organisations are becoming increasingly aware of the environmental concerns of the public. Whether they have adopted this interest in environmental issues as a marketing ploy, as the sceptics would say, or whether they truly believe that they should take a greater interest in this area is open to debate.

Despite the age of the planet, it has only been in the past few decades that man has managed to destroy and pollute extensively. Environmental awareness has been forced to the top of the agenda by a variety of pressure groups, political organisations and the media.

As far as government is concerned, the only way to ensure that businesses adhere to environmental considerations is by regulation. In the UK the 1990 Environmental Protection Act has begun to regulate industrial pollution. The integrated pollution control (IPC) relates to some 5,000 industrial processes and aims to regulate all pollution whether it be on land, air or water. This Act is enforced by the Inspectorate of Pollution. In addition to this comprehensive coverage, local authorities are required by central government to monitor another 27,000 more complex processes. Organisations are required to render all potential pollutants harmless before releasing them.

In 1986 the American Government formed the Environmental Protection Agency which publishes a toxics release inventory which obliges organisations to submit an annual list of pollutants released. Meanwhile, in the UK the Environmental Protection Act established the notion of environmental auditing. These 'green' audits are intended to show any weaknesses in environmental management systems and any breaches of standards.

The European Commission in 1990 produced a draft of their own environmental audit which proposed to require companies to submit similar lists, although, at present, this is only a voluntary scheme.

THE ENVIRONMENT: A CHALLENGE FOR BUSINESS

The DTI launched its Environmental Programme in May 1989. It did so because the protection and improvement of the environment is a major issue at home and abroad – and not least an issue for business.

Since then the pressures for environmental improvement have grown apace and have a significant impact on business. There have been strengthened controls on substances which deplete the ozone layer; negotiations have started on an international Framework Convention on Climate Change; and consumers have continued to demonstrate a desire for goods which have minimal impact on the environment.

The *White Paper on the Environment, This Common Inheritance*, set out the Government's environmental policies and objectives for the 1990s and stressed the important role business needs to play in achieving a better environment.

All these developments, and others, continue to present both threats and opportunities for your business. It is now more than ever the case that, to remain competitive, and indeed to survive, firms need to develop environmental strategies incorporating better environmental performance and products.

In keeping with this gathering momentum DTI has continued to develop and expand its own activities in the environmental field. DTI's Environment Unit brings together all of the Department's widespread interests in environmental issues.

This brochure sets out what the Environment Unit does and what business can do to meet the environmental challenge. It gives guidance too on the practical ways DTI can help business by offering advice, encouraging best practice and supporting research and development.

Environmental issues impact on all businesses. If you are not already planning your firm's response, the time to do so is now.

FIG 1.2.9 *The DTI's environmental programme was launched in May 1989 as a result of the government's white paper on the environment called 'This Common Inheritance'.*

COMMON STANDARDS (HARMONISATION)

The concept of common standards, either in the UK or Europe-wide, is a tricky and complex issue to tackle. We must assume that all countries have a wide variety of different standards which they apply to employment, business activity and social concerns. The blanket imposition of common standards may prove to be difficult where cultural and language differences prevail. In certain countries behaviour regarded as acceptable in business operations may be difficult to overturn despite the fact that it may be unacceptable to the majority of other member states. There is a wide variance of attitudes and the EC will be fighting an uphill battle to establish common standards.

TAXATION

Taxation can be best described as the government or other public authority's levying a compulsory contribution to finance their expenditure. The main functions of taxation are:

- to raise funds to **finance government activity**
- to assist the **regulation of the economy**
- to **correct market failures**

We can further identify taxation as being in two distinct areas. These are:

- direct taxation
- indirect taxation

There are a number of advantages and disadvantages relating to direct and indirect taxation.

Direct taxation

1 Advantages

- this is usually progressive in the sense that, taken with benefits, it is effectively redistributing income in favour of low income groups
- the amount raised by direct taxation increases as income rises
- it is anti-inflationary
- the exact cost to each individual in society is easily measured and calculated

2 Disadvantages

- there is a dis-incentive effect, in that the more you earn, the more you pay
- it is said that direct taxation stifles initiative and enterprise by over-taxing
- it is comparatively easy to evade or avoid payment of taxation
- direct taxation may act as a disincentive to foreign investors as well as those at home
- it is comparatively expensive to collect
- by taxing savings, the value of these savings is substantially reduced

Indirect taxation

1 Advantages

- payment is often convenient as indirect taxation may be paid in instalments or at source
- to some extent indirect taxation can be considered to be voluntary since its payment is linked to consumption

- unlike direct taxation, it does not adversely affect incentive or enterprise
- since it is often paid at source, it is harder to evade payment
- indirect taxation is considered to be a fairly flexible form of taxation
- the funds received from indirect taxation can be used to fund specific purposes

2 Disadvantages

- indirect taxation can be considered to be a regressive form of taxation in that, although it takes a lower percentage of an individual's income, it may not necessarily take a lower amount as income rises
- indirect taxation tends to penalise certain types of consumption. If the taxation policy is not sufficiently thought through, then it may adversely affect the ability of a particular industry to operate
- unlike direct taxation, the burden of indirect taxation is hard to calculate since it is only when specific purchases are made that the indirect taxation comes into operation

student activity

Find out the total, and the sources of taxation income that contributed to the Government's income last year. How much difference is there between this income and the expenditure of the Government?

Investigate the supply of goods and services by business

1 BUSINESS SECTORS
public, private

2 RELATIONSHIPS
costs, supply and prices, wealth and welfare

3 EVALUATION
trends in the UK and Europe, quantitatively in financial terms, qualitatively

4 INFORMATION SOURCES
UK government, EC, business press, reference texts, media, sources within business

BUSINESS SECTORS

THE PUBLIC SECTOR

A variety of goods and services are provided by the public sector. We have already mentioned the major reasons for governments involving themselves in national markets. The principal aim of the public sector is to provide 'free' goods and services to the general public. The public sector businesses have been targeted by the government in recent years and many have been sold to shareholders. In this respect these public sector organisations have become part of the private sector. Existing public sector organisations include British Coal, the National Health Service, British Rail, local amenities (e.g. libraries and swimming pools).

Essentially, public sector organisations fall into two main categories, these are central government enterprises and local government enterprises. We shall look at these in a little more detail:

student activity

How financially accountable are public sector corporations and to whom must they report? Identify three further public sector corporations and assess their relative accountability.

Central government enterprises

Central government enterprises are run as one of the following three types:

1 *A government department.* This organisation has a minister in overall control and is supported by civil servants. The Department of Trade and Industry is an ideal example of this.

FIG 1.3.1 *The DTI is a large and extremely valuable central government department which provides considerable support to all sectors of the UK economy.*

2 *A partly-owned government company.* This sort of organisation is partly owned by the government in that it holds some of the shares. This is also a form of support to particular key businesses such as Rolls Royce. A further reason for government involvement in companies like this is to avoid unnecessarily high levels of unemployment within a particular region. In recent years the Government has been disposing of its shareholding in these companies.

student activity

Identify another partly owned government company and find out why this is partly owned by the Government.

3 *A Public Corporation.* Public corporations are set up by an Act of Parliament and are owned by the Government itself. They are run by a Chairperson and Managers appointed by the Government. They aim to act as a public service as well as having general commercial goals. The Government sets yearly targets for the particular industry to meet and requires the corporation to provide an acceptable service of the highest quality as well as being efficient. Formerly, these public sector organisations were given financial subsidies by the Government, but, this is much less likely to happen now. The main reasons for the subsidies were:

- protection of jobs in declining industries
- to provide non-profitable services
- to provide services of social benefit to particular communities

In recent years public corporations have been encouraged to concentrate on meeting stringent financial targets. At the same time they need to produce higher profit levels and be more consumer-oriented.

Local government enterprises

Most people routinely use a variety of local government enterprises. These include:

- bus services (those which are not already privatised)
- parks
- nurseries
- leisure centres
- swimming pools

Increasingly, many of these services have been offered to private organisations to run on behalf of the local authorities. All services are financed by local taxation, the current forms of which are council taxes and business rates.

student activity

Assess your local government's expenditure on local government enterprises and consider their impact on both employment and the local economy in general.

Recent implications for public-sector organisations

The duties and responsibilities of the organisation will directly affect the way in which it is structured. The more diverse and complex its operations, the more complicated the structure will be. It may also be required by law to provide certain additional services (e.g. an information office) and monitoring services to keep a constant check on spending and budget control.

The geographical extent of the organisation's responsibility will affect not only the size of the organisation, but also its structure. From the smallest parish to the organisation responsible nationally for delivering a range of services, we can see some basic similarities, but obviously the former is far less complex than the latter. Other types of organisation which can be identified by their size are borough, district, town, city, county and regional.

The ever-changing Government policies which impact upon the running of public-sector organisations may well influence the structure of the organisation. In recent years Rate Departments were transformed into Community Charge Departments, then into Council Tax Departments, meaning rapid reorganisation, retraining and redeployment of staff.

The amount of income an organisation has and the source of this income – whether it comes directly from central government or from payments made by the public, – will determine the complexity of the structure. In cases when much of the finance is collected by the organisation itself, large departments may be solely responsible for collection of money. In addition, the organisation must have other departments to oversee the services provided to the public.

Technological change has had a general impact on all types of organisation. Many have developed complex and sophisticated computer systems in order to handle as many of the routine tasks as possible. The availability of computers and their relative fall in price has made them accessible to even the smallest types of public-sector organisation.

The public make many more demands on public-sector organisations now than in the past. One of the most significant is their interest in how and why decisions are made on their behalf. Public-sector organisations must therefore be ready, willing and able to provide a wide variety of information instantly and on demand. Public Relations Departments and Liaison Officers have become common in nearly all public-sector organisations. Meetings are nearly always open to the public and information packs are available on request.

student activity

Why does the public make more demands on public-sector organisations than in the past? Is this a symptom of individuals' inability to handle their own affairs?

As in the private-sector, public sector organisations are finding it increasingly difficult to operate in isolation. Many factors which influence decision making in a private organisation also apply to them. Important decisions may have been made nationally or internationally that public sector organisations cannot ignore, therefore the structure needs to be flexible enough to cope.

Some public-sector organisations may have direct contact with the public. Those which provide goods, services or advisory assistance will need to devote part of their activity to this area. Those which do provide these types of services are similar in many ways to either private-sector manufacturing or retailing organisations.

A great many public-sector organisations, however, only have minimal direct contact with the public.

THE PRIVATE SECTOR

You will find a full listing of the different forms of private-sector organisation in Unit 4 of the book. However, the main difference between the private and the public sector is that the former is controlled by private individuals or groups.

The diversity of different goods and services provided by the private sector is enormous. Equally, the private-sector is involved in all sectors of the economy, from primary to tertiary. The size of private-sector organisations can range from single person businesses to enormous organisations which employ thousands of people.

FIG 1.3.2 *Sir Derek Palmar is the Chairman of Yorkshire-Tyne Tees Television Holdings PLC, a major private-sector employer. Yorkshire Television produces such television programmes as 'Emmerdale', 'Heartbeat', 'The Darling Buds of May', 'Jimmy's' and 'Countdown'.*

RELATIONSHIPS

The price an organisation chooses to charge for its products and services may be dependent upon the total costs incurred in producing it, plus a particular level of profit. In addition to this consideration, the organisation must be aware of how much a customer would be willing to pay. The costs of production can be determined in a number of different ways, as we shall see. These costs will inevitably affect both supply and prices. Another consideration worthy of note at this point is the relationship between wealth and welfare. We shall look at all these points in turn:

COSTS, SUPPLY AND PRICES

The production costs that an organisation must meet are largely dependent upon the type of business activity in which it is involved. Costs include the following:

- premises
- machinery
- other capital equipment
- workforce
- development costs
- storage costs

- training costs
- cleaning costs
- administration costs

student activity

Considering a typical manufacturing organisation, identify which of the above costs would account for the majority of its budget. Try to put all of the others into ranking order of cost.

Costs are either short term or long term.

Short-term costs

These tend to be fairly fixed in the sense that it is difficult to change the level of expenditure in a short period of time. If an organisation needs to respond financially to sudden changes in the market, then it may be unable to find the additional funding required.

Long-term costs

These tend to be, by their very nature, rather more variable. The further we look into the future, the more variable an organisation's costs may be. The organisation is able to identify, through forecasts, potential changes in output and amend its expenditure to match. It is at this point that we should look at the nature of fixed and variable costs.

1 *Fixed Costs.* Fixed costs consist of the following:

- rent
- rates
- mortgages
- loans
- administration

These costs will be incurred whether the organisation is producing anything or not. Therefore, the eventual pricing policy will have to incorporate these fixed costs. Fixed costs rise as the organisation increases its scale of operations, as new fixed costs are taken on.

2 *Variable Costs.* Certain production costs come into operation only when they are required. In other words, these costs may be increased or decreased in line with the level of production itself. These costs will include:

- raw materials
- energy costs
- distribution costs

Variable costs will always increase in relation to the output of the organisation.

3 *Semi-variable costs.* A semi-variable cost can be best described as any expenditure which is incurred in the process of the organisation stepping up output. If we take the case of payment to the workforce, then we will see that elements of this expenditure fall into fixed, variable and semi-variable categories:

- the basic wage is fixed
- the overtime is variable
- the frequency with which overtime is paid may be semi-variable

We will look at how these additional costs are calculated when we consider the formula relating to average and marginal costs.

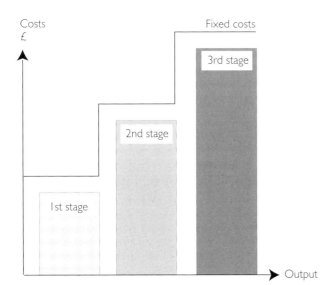

FIG 1.3.3 *Fixed costs increase as output increases.*

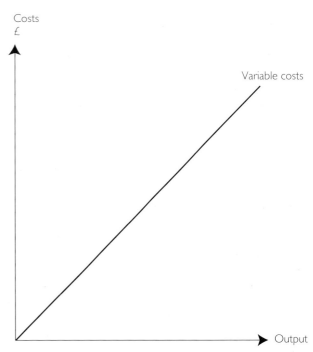

FIG 1.3.4 *Variable costs increase proportionately with output.*

student activity

A small business which produces hand-knitted jumpers sells each unit at an average of £25.00. The organisation has identified that fixed costs are some £18,000 and the variable costs are £13.00 per unit. It is the intention of the organisation to try to generate a profit of £18,000 per year. Calculate the following:

- the **number of units** that will need to be sold to achieve the £18,000 profit.
- the **total sales value** that will have to be achieved to reach the £18,000 profit.
- the break-even point in terms of **units**.
- The break-even point in terms of **sales value**.

Break-even

The concept of break-even is used to discover the amount of profit or loss an organisation will have at particular levels of output. Break-even itself is when output covers all costs of production. There is a simple formula which is used to calculate the break-even point. This is:

Break-even point

$$= \frac{\text{Fixed cost}}{(\text{Selling price per unit} - \text{variable cost per unit})}$$

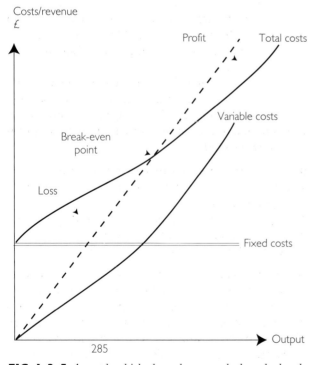

FIG 1.3.5 *A graph which shows how to calculate the break-even point.*

Once this break-even point has been reached, the organisation will be operating in profit. However, if the variable costs rise then profits will fall. The use of a graph to calculate the break-even point is common and as you can see in Figure 1.3.5 the graph shows the following:

- fixed costs
- variable costs
- total costs
- total revenue

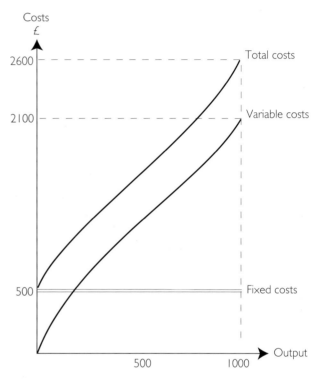

FIG 1.3.6 *A graph showing an organisation's total costs, fixed costs and variable costs.*

Where the total revenue line crosses the total costs line, we find the break-even point. At all points below the break-even point, the organisation is operating at a loss. At all points above the break-even point, the organisation is operating at a profit.

Average and marginal costs

It is valuable to calculate both the average cost per unit and the marginal cost per unit. Each has its own formula. We shall look at each formula and describe the implications:

$$\text{Average cost per unit} = \frac{\text{Total cost}}{\text{Quantity}}$$

$$\text{Marginal cost} = \frac{\text{Extra cost}}{\text{Extra output}}$$

Both types of cost produce a U-shaped curve on a graph, *see* Figure 1.3.7. In the case of average cost, this is because the fixed costs determine average costs up to a certain point. Within the limitations of the range of fixed costs, there are sufficient flexibility and economies of scale to show that increased production reduces the average cost per unit. Once variable costs are included in the equation, thus adding additional expenditure, average costs per unit begin to rise slightly. Marginal costs, however, are more prone to the additional costs incurred at higher levels of productivity and as such, show a steeper rise.

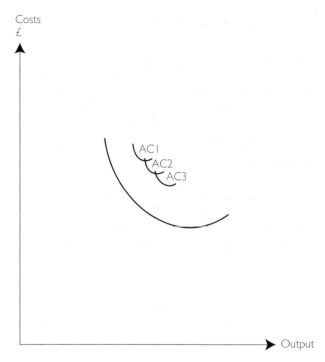

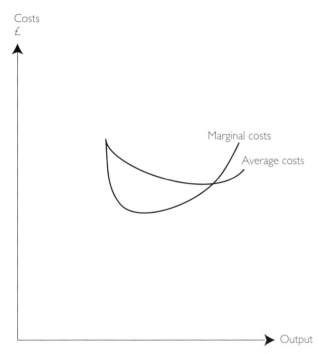

FIG 1.3.7 *A graph showing an organisation's marginal and average costs in the short term.*

FIG 1.3.8 *A graph showing an organisation's average costs in the long term.*

student activity

How would you use marginal costs techniques to work out whether a business would be viable?

Long-term costs

We return now to long-term costs. The concept of 'long term' is difficult to grasp since we are dealing with a number of different organisations involved in various forms of business activity. The individual organisations' costs will be dependent upon the type of production involved. Organisations must try to assess the potential demand in the future for their products and services and try to ensure that their level of production meets this potential demand. They must also be aware of the problems of maintaining an optimum level of production in order to avoid unnecessary variable costs. Even if an organisation steps up its production for a short period of time it will incur additional variable costs, thus pushing up the average costs per unit. Organisations do, however, gain economies of scale as they move from one production level to another and although short-term costs may be high, (in the case of buying new machinery or transportation) the longer-term benefits may outweigh these.

If an organisation fails to maintain an adequate and stable level of production and finds itself in a position of having to step up then drastically reduce production over a period of time, it may suffer a number of problems. These include:

- inability to source raw materials at short notice
- having to pay premium prices for raw materials required at short notice
- employees with the correct skills are difficult to find
- these employees (if found) are expensive
- industrial unrest from existing employees

If the organisation fails to meet immediate demand for its products or services, then it is giving its competitors a distinct advantage. This situation, where an organisation does not provide adequate supply into the market place, is known as 'imperfect competition'. In extreme cases, this may cause an 'oligopoly' to be formed as the organisation relinquishes control of its market share to its competitors.

WEALTH AND WELFARE

There is a direct relationship between the wealth of individuals and their general happiness, which is known as welfare. Whilst economic growth tends to make individuals more wealthy, it does not necessarily affect their welfare.

Although economic growth may enable individuals to consume more products and services, little attention is paid to the individual's ability to enjoy a worthwhile life. What actually constitutes a worthwhile existence will obviously differ from person to person, but, generally speaking, welfare may relate to the following:

- the comparative amount of a person's income that can be considered to be disposable

- the amount of time, comparatively, the person has to pursue leisure activities
- the security the individual enjoys at work
- the comparative health and physical well-being of the individual
- the stability of the individual's domestic situation
- the distribution of income throughout society and its relationship to an individual's output and value

student activity

Calculate in percentage terms what you think to be the actual disposable income of an average worker who receives some £250 per week.

EVALUATION OF THE SUPPLY OF GOODS AND SERVICES BY BUSINESS

In order to evaluate the supply of goods and services by business, you will have to look at the various data sets available from a variety of agencies and government departments. In the remaining part of this Element we shall be looking at the data sets and trying to evaluate their worth.

student activity

How would you identify the trends in demand and supply of a particular product or service?

UK AND EUROPE

Measuring the exact output or performance of a particular area of business activity can be very difficult. It is almost impossible to quantify some of the business activity at all. Indeed, how can gatherers of information ensure that they know the exact output in any industry? Are they sure that all of the businesses involved are giving any, or the correct information to them?

The supply of goods and services by businesses will ultimately depend upon the actual demand for these products and services. Seasonal fluctuations may also have a role to play. Equally, it is sometimes the case that a product or service falls out of favour with the consumer for other reasons. These reasons may include health scares, unfortunate associations with particularly unpleasant production processes or temporary anger towards a particular country for reasons out of the control of the industry.

In other words, the trends in the UK and Europe are continually moving. An organisation should always base its forecasts and plans on the latest available data and not operate from information that is no longer relevant.

QUANTITATIVE EVALUATION

As we have mentioned already, and will be covering in the last part of this section, the data sets available make up the quantitative element of the evaluation. The data are available from a variety of sources and care should be taken in agreeing the comparative importance of the data. Data must be collected in a totally scientific manner and must not have been collected for reasons other than that for which the organisation wishes to use it.

student activity

What sources of information would you use in order to make a quantitative evaluation?

QUALITATIVE EVALUATION

This type of evaluation is based on conjecture and opinion. Organisations often employ a consultancy company to offer their opinion on the state of the market. As with any individual or group of individuals with opinions, it is prudent to ensure that they are basing their assumptions on the latest available data. The opinions they express should be considered to be only that and not actual fact.

Equally, if an organisation takes too much notice of opinions expressed by the media, it may suffer the same consequences. Media speculation is always dangerous and must be regarded as suspect.

Information provided by the industry itself will always be tainted by enthusiasm, so it should also be treated with a great deal of scepticism.

With regard to opinions expressed by those within the organisation, certain individuals will have a jaundiced view of the situation, while others have an altogether more optimistic one. If you refer to the matter of forecasting (covered in Units 3, 7 and 8) you will see that this type of opinion also needs to be handled carefully.

student activity

How valuable are qualitative assessments? Can they be relied upon? Can you make a qualitative assessment of the potential demand for the following?

- DAT tapes
- hair gel
- cruelty-free products

INFORMATION SOURCES ON THE SUPPLY OF GOODS AND SERVICES

Obviously, depending upon the type of information you are looking for in relation to the supply of goods and services, you will be able to use a variety of different sources. We have categorised them into several different areas. While the list cannot be exhaustive, it shows the main sources available to the business researcher.

student activity

Using the list, find out the location of the reports and other information. Indicate where in your local area you are likely to find these.

THE UK GOVERNMENT

The UK Government offers a comprehensive range of information sources including:

- *Annual Abstract of Statistics*
- *Economic Trends*
- *Family Expenditure Survey*
- Financial statistics
- *The Blue Book – National Income and Expenditure*
- Central Statistical Office Reports
- *Social Trends*
- *Overseas Trade Statistics of the UK*
- *Guide to Official Statistics*
- The enormous range of DTI publications
- The Department of Employment's *Euro Action*
- *Economic Intelligence Unit Quarterly Reviews*
- The *OECD Reports*

THE EC

Similarly, the EC provides a range of material and information which take a Europe-wide look at the supply of goods and services. Some information is specific to particular industries or areas of business activity, while others take a wider view. The best place to begin your search for information provided by the EC is the *Guide to EC Publications* available at all European Information Centres.

student activity

Discover the location of your local European Information Centre and find out whether they have any useful materials for students.

THE BUSINESS PRESS

This category covers an enormous range of different publications. The following list can be only a partial attempt to cover the available materials. This category will also include non-written sources of information (e.g. data bases etc.):

- The Market Research Society's *Reports*
- *Directory of Information Sources in the UK*
- *Key British Enterprises* (Dunn and Bradstreet)
- *UK and EC Company Information, Products and Services* (Kompass)
- *Handbook of Market Leaders* (Extel)
- *Statistical Yearbook* (Eurostat)
- British Statistical Office *Reports*
- *The A-Z of UK Brand Leaders* (Euromonitor Ltd)
- *The A-Z of UK Marketing Data* (Euromonitor Ltd)
- *Jordan's Business Reviews and Surveys*
- Phillips & Drew *Monthly Economic Forecasts*
- Mintel Information Services
- ICC Database Dialog
- ICC Eurocompany Information Service
- Extat Online Database
- Datastream Online Database
- Dataline Online Database
- Datacards Online Database

student activity

Does your institution's library or any local library stock any of the above in their reference section? Having discovered this, research one of the above and orally feedback to the remainder of your group the usefulness of this source of information.

REFERENCE IN TEXTS

The major danger with this type of information is that it will date quickly, due to the long period of production time involved in getting the text ready for publication.

Many business analysts have written very worthwhile material on a variety of business issues, but these should be read with consideration to the economic situations prevailing at the time of writing.

THE MEDIA

The media, on the other hand, provide pertinent and up-to-date information on a variety of issues relating to the supply of goods and services. Good media sources will include:

- *The Financial Times* (and its *Business Information Service*)
- *The Times*
- *The Daily Telegraph*
- *The Guardian*
- *The Independent*
- *The New York Herald Tribune*

student activity

As business studies students you should naturally be reading the quality press. How accessible is the information and the language included in this branch of the media? Which of the above is most user-friendly and why?

SOURCES WITHIN BUSINESS

We have taken this category to mean the information provided by specific industries on themselves. In this category we will find detailed information that is, perhaps, only accessible to those very interested in the specific area of the business activity concerned. Examples include:

- *Management Today*
- *Marketing Weekly*
- *Banking World*
- *The Grocer*
- *PC User*

UNIT I

a s s i g n m e n t

'A PRODUCT AND THE ECONOMY'

In order to fulfil the various criteria of this Unit, it is essential for you to carry out the following tasks:

1 Identify a particular product in which you may be interested.
2 Identify the type of business which produces this product or service.
3 Identify the sector to which this business belongs.
4 Identify whether this business is in the private or public sector of the economy.
5 Identify any economic factors which may influence the supply of this product or service.

6 Identify any UK legislation which may relate to this product or service.
7 Identify any EC Directives which may relate to this product or service.

In order to assist you in your research, you should begin by identifying the appropriate sources of information listed in this Unit and refer to them. In these sources of information you will find the basic necessary information required.

You should present your report on this product or service and the businesses involved and any economic considerations in a word processed format.

UNIT I

t e s t q u e s t i o n s

1 The advantages of a planned economy would not include:

(a) elimination of wasteful competition
(b) lack of competition
(c) use of resources for the benefit of the community
(d) equal distribution of income

2 The Body Shop supplies products to a number of retail outlets. The conditions of this supply is known as a:

(a) co-operative
(b) retail chain
(c) franchise
(c) independent company network

3 Which of the following organisations operate in the public sector of the economy?

(a) J. Sainsbury Ltd
(b) Ladbrokes
(c) Yorkshire Television
(d) British Coal

4 If the pound has depreciated against other currencies, what does this mean?

(a) It is worth less
(b) It is worth more

(c) It is worth proportionately less
(d) It is worth the same

5 Which of the following organisations are interested in stabilising exchange rates?

(a) GATT
(b) EC
(c) IMF
(d) ECGD

6 Countries will tend to produce goods and engage in international trade under which of the following circumstances?

(a) Because they cannot get them from abroad
(b) Because they can produce them cheaply
(c) Because they cannot obtain them easily because of tariffs
(d) Because they have a comparative advantage

7 Which of the following statements concerning the UK is correct?

(a) We have an increasingly younger population
(b) Death rates are falling
(c) People live for shorter periods of time
(d) Birth rates are falling

8 Which of the following social factors will not have an affect on an organisation?

(a) The level of competition
(b) Education
(c) Pressure groups
(d) Culture

9 Under the Trade Descriptions Act which of the following is required of retailers?

(a) To sell merchantable quality goods
(b) To accept responsibility for faulty products
(c) To give accurate information about the products or services
(d) To display readily accessible notices about products or services

10 Unemployment caused by automation may be classed as which of the following types of unemployment?

(a) Cyclical
(b) Technological
(c) Frictional
(d) Structural

Investigate administrative systems

1 PURPOSES
routine functions, non-routine functions, supporting human, financial, physical resources, recording and monitoring business performance

2 LEGAL AND STATUTORY REQUIREMENTS
health and safety, Companies Act, employment law, fiscal VAT, PAYE, pensions

3 ADMINISTRATION SYSTEMS
accounting, sales, distribution, personnel, services (maintenance/catering etc.)

4 EVALUATION CRITERIA
efficiency of operation, effective control of business functions

In order for organisations to meet their business objectives, it is essential for them to manage their resources. The efficiency with which the resources are managed will determine the success of the business itself. As we will see in Unit 4, organisations adopt a variety of different structures to meet their individual needs.

However, whichever organisational structure they choose, they must be able to handle three key areas of business activity. These are:

- administration systems
- communication systems
- information processing systems

PURPOSES OF ADMINISTRATION SYSTEMS

The term administration systems needs to be defined before we can accurately determine its purposes. These are the generally accepted descriptions of administration systems:

- Activities carried out by managers to determine the aims and policies of the organisation
- Controlling the day-to-day running of the business. The latter definition of administration is the one that we will be using within this Unit.

As we have said, the running of an organisation requires an organised approach to all administration, and administrative tasks will be undertaken at every level of the organisation. In a large organisation, administration will be carried out by the Administration Department (see Unit 4 for a full description of their activities), but in smaller businesses the administration may be carried out by a single individual who will be responsible for all forms of administration.

Whoever is responsible for carrying out these administrative tasks, the basic purposes remain the same. These are:

1 providing **support systems** for all resources used by the organisation

2 the keeping of **records** relating to the activities of the organisation

3 **monitoring** the performance of the business' activities

ROUTINE AND NON-ROUTINE FUNCTIONS

The activities of an organisation may be classified as routine or non-routine.

1 *Routine.* Routine activities mean those carried out on a regular basis. Some individuals will be responsible for administration functions which will not differ regardless of any other activities carried out by the organisation. Examples of such functions may include:

- the processing of invoices
- the filing of business documents and information

2 *Non-routine.* Other individuals will carry out a series of non-routine activities. They will have to be more adaptable as the demands of each day will differ greatly. These individuals will not be able to predict the demands upon them with any great accuracy. On a single day they may have a series of meetings or tasks to perform without prior notice or instruction.

Routine functions of an office can be easily organised through the establishment of systems to handle them. An office organised in this way will base its organisation upon previous experience and will know with considerable accuracy the demands that will be placed upon it. In situations when an individual or department must carry out a non-routine function, they must be able to rely upon a separate series of systems to support them. It may be the case that a support system has to be created for that specific purpose.

SUPPORTING HUMAN, FINANCIAL AND PHYSICAL RESOURCES

Many organisations have recognised that their **human resources** are the most important resource they have. The deployment of these human resources, as much as any other factor, will determine the successfulness of the organisation.

The **financial resources** are the capital (or money) that the organisation has received from its trading activities.

The **physical resources** are slightly more complex and may include the following:

- land
- premises
- equipment

FIG 2.1.1 *This is a major engineering works carried out by Fisons in Jurong, Singapore and shows the complexity of industrial equipment..*

- plant and machinery
- copyrights
- patents
- trade marks

In managing any of these resources, it is a priority of the organisation to establish a series of systems, which often take the form of a departmentalised structure to assist the efficient running of the administration function.

RECORDING AND MONITORING BUSINESS PERFORMANCE

Maintaining an efficient and accurate recording system of business activity is essential to all forms of businesses. Records are kept for the following four main reasons:

1 *To fulfil statutory obligations.* Various legislation requires organisations to keep detailed records of business activity. In the main, these tend to focus on financial and staff considerations. A record of business activity should be kept for VAT and tax inspections and with regard to staff, both tax and National Insurance deductions and contributions should be recorded. Company legislation requires organisations to provide information for investors, customers and company employees.

IR 53

THINKING OF TAKING SOMEONE ON?

PAYE for Employers

FIG 2.1.2 *The Inland Revenue provides comprehensive guidance to employers on such matters as the calculation of PAYE for their employees. This booklet, IR53, is particularly useful and extremely informative.*

2 *To assist future planning.* Comprehensive data on the following may be vital to assist managers in future decision making:

- costs
- product details
- market research
- customer complaints
- profit margins
- supplier details

These records are maintained in order to allow managers to make decisions on the basis of past experience.

3 *Evidence of transactions carried out.* These records keep a track of all income and expenditure relating to the organisation's business activities. These will include the following:

- purchases made
- sales made
- organisations and individuals with whom transactions have been made
- dates of transactions
- payments received and pending
- personnel records
- stock levels
- staff training and development
- accurate minutes of meetings

4 *Monitoring performance.* An organisation must attempt to identify any problems arising from its business activities and have in place a system that can highlight these quickly.

Finance is the key area to monitor. Financial information may be sourced from various parts of the organisation. Each individual manager is responsible for controlling and monitoring the expenditure of his or her department and will need to analyse the department's expenditure to assist in future planning.

Comparing expenditure from year to year may be undertaken from two different viewpoints. These are:

- intra-firm comparisons, where expenditure is compared with that of last year
- inter-firm comparisons, where comparisons are made in relation to the expenditure of competitors.

Many organisations have adopted management information systems provided by computer software packages to organise, store and monitor their financial data. The information stored is accessible to all interested parties within the organisation and can be used to provide necessary information on an immediate basis. We will be looking at this aspect of business systems later in this unit.

student activity

For what reasons would an organisation make intra-firm comparisons and inter-firm comparisons? What would be the outcome of these comparisons?

LEGAL AND STATUTORY REQUIREMENTS

Organisations are required by law (both civil and criminal) to comply with various obligations. If they do not adhere to various laws they may be subject to fines, confiscation or compensation. In the main, the legislation refers to two of the resources of the organisation, the **human** and the **financial**.

student activity

Identify the main pieces of legislation which relate to the human and financial features of an organisation.

HEALTH AND SAFETY

Although we will be looking at health and safety in some detail in Unit 5, we must consider the basic aims of the Act here. The key act is the Health and Safety at Work Act 1974. This Act aims to minimise the potential risks to employees. This Act is backed up by a range of health and safety regulations and a number of EC directives. In order to provide an efficient system which addresses the requirements of the health and safety legislation, an organisation must:

1 have a clear understanding of the scope of the legislation and know what it must do to stay within the law
2 identify an individual within the organisation to take responsibility for all health and safety matters. This person should be trained and be in a position to apply the legal obligations to the functions of the organisation. In short, this individual must create systems, policies, procedures and structures to handle the health and safety legislation.

A well-organised health and safety system should include the provision of the following:

- create a company policy on health and safety
- organise the training of staff in health and safety matters
- create a safety committee
- appoint various safety representatives throughout the organisation
- provide comprehensive first aid and training
- ensure that legally required display notices are positioned in key locations within the organisation's premises
- establish a system by which all injuries and accidents are recorded

HEALTH AND SAFETY

Divisional Policy

We give the highest priority to developing, promoting and maintaining safe and healthy working conditions, in line with the Health & Safety at Work Act and good practice.

Managers have a duty to do everything possible to prevent injury or damage to health, and this aspect of their work is given the highest priority. This responsibility extends to all areas of the Division's operations.

Your Manager and the Personnel Office hold a copy of the detailed Health and Safety Procedures. You are welcome to consult these documents on request.

The Director/General Manager has the ultimate responsibility for effective Health and Safety.

FIG 2.1.3 *An extract from the Divisional Policy on Health and Safety from Smith and Nephew's Personal Hygiene and Toiletries Division.*

COMPANIES ACTS

The Companies Acts (especially the Act of 1985) define the legal liabilities of company directors. Specifically the Act relates to directors of private and public limited companies. These liabilities include the following:

1 the calling of annual shareholders' meetings
2 responsibility for the presentation of tax and VAT returns
3 adherence to various other Acts, such as:

- Health and Safety at Work Act 1974
- Factories Act 1961
- Employers' Liability (Compulsory Insurance) Act 1969
- Offices, Shops and Railway Premises Act 1963
- Data Protection Act 1984

It is within the Companies Act of 1985 that we find the organisation's responsibility to ensure that accounting records are kept. These should show the following:

- all transactions made
- explanation of transactions made
- full accuracy
- sufficient details to create a balance sheet
- sufficient details to create a profit and loss account

student activity

Why is it important to keep records of all of the accounting transactions? Is it just because the legislation requires it? To what uses can the organisation put this information?

Although we will be dealing with the exact nature of balance sheets and profit and loss accounts in Units 6 and 7, it is important to understand the basics of them here, since they are a key and integral part of administration systems.

Accounting records should contain a daily breakdown of all incoming and outgoing payments. They should also give details of the transactions and act as a tally of all assets and liabilities. Assets are on the positive side of the business' balance sheet and include all monies received and owed to it. Liabilities are the negative and are all payments owed to external organisations. The accounting records should also keep an accurate record of stock held by the business and any other stock currently being held by customers, but not yet paid for.

The auditors will need access to the balance sheet, profit and loss account and other financial information, together with any accompanying relevant Directors' reports. It is a legal requirement that registered companies present all these financial statements at their Annual General Meeting. The format in which these financial statements must be presented is laid down by the 1985 Act, which, in turn, meets the requirements of the EC's Fourth Directive on Company Law.

In order to produce these financial statements, the organisation must install a number of systems of bookkeeping to keep track of its financial affairs. These are known as the double entry system, the main features of which are:

1 *Ledgers* – which are used to keep a record of financial transactions and include the personal accounts of customers (known as Sales or Debtors Ledgers) and suppliers (known as Purchase or Credit Ledgers). In addition, the organisation must maintain a system which records any payments of wages or monies spent on machinery or property.
2 *Cash Books* – in cash books we would find each transaction entered twice, once on the debit side of the account and once on the credit side. This aspect of the maintenance of financial transactions is handled in Units 6 and 7.

student activity

Identify the main headings you would expect to find in a ledger and in a cash book and rough out a typical page.

EMPLOYMENT LAW

As we will be looking at human resources in more detail in Unit 4, it is sufficient to note here that organisations, via their personnel managers or departments, are responsible for adhering to a number of pieces of key employment legislation. As a routine function, they handle the full range of activities that relate to employees, from recruitment to termination of employment. They must be able to identify accurately any possible breaches of employment law and advise the relevant manager(s) of action required to be taken. This function is particularly important in cases of dismissal where, if the legislation is not followed to the letter, the organisation may be laying itself open to claims of unfair dismissal and considerable compensation claims.

FISCAL - VAT, PAYE AND PENSIONS

Organisations must keep accurate financial records to meet their obligations regarding their tax liability. All organisations have direct taxes to pay which are related to their profits (known as Corporation Tax), and they may also be responsible as a tax collector with regard to the PAYE (Pay As You Earn) of their employees.

The employer also has the additional responsibility of the calculation and collection of National Insurance and will have an individual responsible for the monitoring of this function. The calculations need to be correct and paid on time.

An individual may receive a pension from two different sources, both of which involve the employing organisation in some respect. These are:

1 *State Pension.* The organisation has an administrative responsibility for the collection of contributions from the individual until he or she retires. From then the state takes over responsibility for the payment and administration of the pension. In addition, an individual may choose to pay SERPS (State Earnings Related Pension Scheme) contributions in order to 'top up' his or her pension.

2 *Occupational pension schemes.* The other form of pension is known as an Occupational Pension Scheme, by which the individual pays the employer separate contributions which may be topped up by the employer. Although the employing organisation is responsible for carrying out all the administrative tasks related to this pension scheme, it does receive the benefit of all its contributions being tax-deductible.

A BRIEF WORD ON SALARIES

When are salaries paid?

- salaries for monthly paid staff are generally paid on the 14th of each month. Paid two weeks in advance and two weeks in arrears, they can be paid into a bank account or a Society account.

How do I change the details of where my salary is paid?

- simply notify the Payroll Department in writing, preferably giving a month's notice.

How is my National Insurance contribution worked out?

National Insurance contributions are paid to finance State benefits such as unemployment pay, State sickness benefits and State pensions and are calculated as a percentage of gross earnings.

- Your N.I. letter as shown on your payslip will most probably be a 'D' or an 'A'.

- if you pay 'D' rate National Insurance it means you are a member of the Society's pension scheme.

- if you pay 'A' rate National Insurance it signifies that you are not.

- you contribute less on 'D' rate than on 'A' rate because in return for lower N.I. contributions, the Pension Scheme gives the D.H.S.S. certain guarantees about the benefits payable at retirement.

What about my income tax?

Income tax is paid on taxable income and is determined by your tax code and the rate of income tax currently in force. It is a complex area where a variety of factors govern the amount you will pay.

- if, for example, your code is 260L this will mean you are able to earn up to £2,600 p.a. before paying tax. Any money earned after that will be subject to Income Tax.

- for more information about **calculating your Income Tax,** contact the Payroll Department.

- if you have a query about your **code,** contact: H M Inspector of Taxes, 44 Abbey Street, Leicester. Tel: Leicester (0533) 510041. Tax reference number: L6273. Always quote your personal tax reference number.

FIG 2.1.4 *The Alliance and Leicester Building Society provides all employees with a very user-friendly booklet called 'Your Pay'. The section on salaries explains very clearly an employee's obligations in terms of PAYE and national insurance.*

Pensions

We have two first class contracted-out Company pension schemes which will help you to protect your dependants and provide for your retirement.

If you are aged 20 or over you can apply to join the relevant scheme immediately. If you are 25 or over with 1 year's service you are automatically included in the appropriate scheme, unless you have completed the form available from the Pensions Department to say you do not wish to join. (Our pension schemes are for permanent employees only).

+ You can obtain a pensions guide and question and answer booklet along with further details from your Staff Manager.

Additional Voluntary Contributions (AVCs)

Members of both pension schemes have the opportunity to improve their pension benefits by making Additional Voluntary Contributions (AVCs). AVCs are worth considering if you think your pension may be too small when you retire.

However, AVCs should only be considered as a long term investment because you cannot gain access to the funds until you retire. Whether AVCs are for you depends on various factors such as age, length of service, etc.

+ Pension arrangements are very important. Your Staff Manager will be able to give you more details before you make a decision.

FIG 2.1.5 *Tesco PLC, the national food retailing giant, offers an attractive company pension to its employees who are given additional opportunities to make voluntary contributions to enhance their pension benefits.*

ADMINISTRATION SYSTEMS

The operation of administration systems is vital since the activities of an organisation must be co-ordinated and planned. If inadequate administration systems are in operation, then the organisation may suffer from a lack of efficiency and effectiveness since it does not have access to all relevant information. Administration systems inevitably involve some form of filing, whether it be a paper-based filing system or one housed within a computer system. We must look at the various areas of business activity and identify the main types of system and the reasoning behind the adoption of these systems.

ACCOUNTING

The main function of accounting systems, as we have already mentioned, is to provide managers with the means to exercise **financial control** over their departments. They are interested in budgetary control. A budget relies on a plan which is made on the basis of estimates of future spending and income. The budget will also try to allocate any expenses in relation to particular objectives set by the organisation. Depending upon the size of the organisation, this may be across the whole of the organisation, or on a departmental basis. Budgetary control is established by careful consideration of the following:

1 the organisation will define its **objectives** and try to allocate the expenditure related to each of them

2 the organisation will establish standard operating **procedure** which relates to specific strategies and tactics in meeting the objectives

3 the organisation will establish systems to monitor the **actual spending** on each objective as opposed to the estimated expenditure

4 the above monitoring of the objectives in relation to the standards set will be made at various times and may take the form of **Interim Reports**

Profit & Loss Account
FOR THE 26 WEEKS ENDED 3RD JULY 1993

53 weeks ended 2nd January 1993 £000		Notes	26 weeks ended 3rd July 1993 £000	26 weeks ended 27th June 1992 £000
	Turnover			
605,826	Continuing	2	332,687	325,478
53,101	Discontinued	2	-	33,284
658,927			332,687	358,762
(586,278)	Cost of sales	2	(302,243)	(318,983)
72,649	**Gross profit**		30,444	39,779
(55,943)	Administrative expenses	2	(26,369)	(27,371)
2,412	Less 1991 provision	2	-	1,584
(1,839)	Operating exceptional items	3	(734)	-
17,279	**Operating profit**	2	3,341	13,992
174	Income from investments in associated undertakings		(35)	143
(1,176)	Provision for loss on operations to be discontinued			-
(20,860)	Loss on disposal of discontinued operations			-
4,788	Less 1991 provision			-
205	**Profit on ordinary activities before interest**		3,306	14,135
2,922	Interest receivable		255	1,288
3,127	**Profit on ordinary activities before taxation**	1	3,561	15,423
(5,966)	Taxation on profit on ordinary activities		(1,139)	(4,473)
(2,839)	**Profit on ordinary activities after taxation**		2,422	10,950
117	Minority interest		124	(42)
(2,722)	**Profit/(loss) for the financial period**		2,546	10,908
(5,793)	Dividends		(2,655)	(2,645)
(8,515)	**Retained (loss)/profit**		(109)	8,263
(3.8p)	**Earnings per ordinary share**	4	3.6p	15.3p
8.1p	**Dividend per ordinary share**		3.7p	3.7p

FIG 2.1.6 *The Profit and Loss Account from Geest PLC, covering the first half of 1993. Also contained in the Interim Report are the balance sheet, cash flow statement and interim financial statements.*

Geest PLC Interim Report 1993

5 The organisation must have in place a series of procedures in order to react to any **differences in the estimated and actual spending**. This is particularly important if there is an overspend and may result in the re-examination of the organisation's operating systems. Most organisations expect to have to constantly redefine their operating standards and monitoring systems in order to maintain efficiency

The accurate monitoring of budgets is essential to all businesses for the following reasons:

1 it allows the organisation to clearly define its **aims and policies**

2 it allows the organisation to develop an **overall corporate strategy**

3 it allows the key decision-makers of the organisation to keep a careful eye on all **budgets**

4 it allows the organisation to **monitor** actual performance against estimated activity

5 it should improve the organisation's **efficiency** and the deployment of resources towards the meeting of specific objectives

SALES

The key functions of sales staff are to control and organise the selling and distribution of the organisation's products and services. The sales function may often be found within the Marketing Department of an organisation, but the sales operation will always be supported by administrative personnel and various sales representatives. As with any other managerial function, the Sales Manager will be responsible for the establishment and revision of systems which will ensure the smooth-running of the sales operations. In addition, he/she may have specific targets to meet and must maintain budgetary control over these. Communication is a key feature of a good Sales Department, as the staff must be able to handle all communications with customers. They will also be responsible for the maintenance of any relevant records and exercise some control (via a Credit Controller) over the availability of credit to customers.

Dealing with customers requires the establishment of systems to handle enquiries and problems efficiently. These systems will also require the Sales Department to keep records of any enquiries made, orders received and other documentation which maintains an up-to-date record of customer transactions.

YOUR PERSONAL COMMITMENT

It cannot be stressed enough that the considerable benefits available to your staff and your company from the Customer Awareness Training programme will depend more upon you and your manager's commitment and involvement than upon any other factor.

This detailed guide outlines the scope of the programme and has been produced to help with the task ahead.

However, should you have any queries regarding aspects of the C.A.T. Programme, please contact the Sales and Marketing Institute on 0203 884400.

FIG 2.1.7 *Peugeot Talbot's Pride programme for its dealers which concentrates on customer awareness training.*

When sales staff have contact with customers, whether this is by telephone or personal visit, administration systems must be in place to ensure that the details of any conversation, negotiation or problems have been recorded accurately. This information will be held by the Sales Department and will include many of the following:

- name and phone number of customer's Chief Buyer
- discounts agreed
- credit worthiness
- specific customer requirements
- delivery arrangements
- size of customer orders
- frequency of customer orders

In relation to the creditworthiness of a customer, most organisations will have set a particular policy at high management level. In large organisations, there may be an individual with specific responsibility for credit control and the setting of customers' credit levels. In smaller organisations, as we have mentioned, an individual may have to take on this responsibility in addition to other tasks. Regardless of the particular situation in the organisation, an efficient credit system should include the following features:

- *Credit checks* - which include the taking up of bank and trade references and reference to credit agencies
- establishment of *credit levels* and what terms apply to these limits
- action to be taken in the case of *credit breaches* - this will involve a system being created to determine at what stage particular action will be taken. It will include a series of letters requesting payment. The style and tone of these letters is important in order to avoid unnecessary complications, both legally and personally, with the customer.

Credit ratings are often based on sales experience with a particular customer. Credit ratings given to customers should reflect their ability to pay at some point in the future.

student activity

Design and write a series of letters aimed at obtaining an outstanding debt from a customer. Bear in mind that you should always be clear and courteous.

DISTRIBUTION

Since distribution deals with the transferring of products from the supplier to the customer, there needs to be an accurate and efficient system in place to monitor the location and status of all dealings. The distribution function may fall under the control of the Marketing Department, just like sales. It is the aim of the Distribution Department to seek to fulfil the following requirements:

- keep distribution costs competitive
- evaluate alternative distribution methods
- decide whether to deal directly with retailers
- decide whether to rely on wholesalers
- reduce administrative costs by dealing directly only with larger customers
- analyse and evaluate seasonal fluctuations in distribution

- accurately identify the location of all products at all stages of the distribution process (from a centrally located warehouse within the organisation, through transportation, to arrival and storage at the customer's premises)

FIG 2.1.8 *As part of their service to customers, Geest Wholesale Services have a network of nine distribution points throughout the UK, making it the only national operator in its market sector.*

Specifically, administration systems must be in place to handle the following functions:

- checking goods **into** the warehouse
- checking goods **out of** the warehouse
- a selection system for **choosing** products to be distributed. This is particularly important in the case of perishable goods where a stock rotation system is essential in order to ensure that products do not deteriorate as a result of being stored when they should have been earmarked for distribution. There are two versions of this system known as:

  - FiFo – the first in first out system. This bases distribution on the premise that goods stored for the longest period of time should be distributed first
  - LiFo – this system is particularly important for organisations which distribute seasonal or fashionable products which require immediate distribution as opposed to their standard items, which are held in bulk storage.

- **moving** products around within the warehouse, whether this be done by a manual or automated system.
- establishing a system which identifies specific **locations** within the warehouse for particular products
- keeping **stock control** levels in order to assist the reordering function of the organisation

student activity

How would you identify the differences between the distribution and warehousing facilities of an organisation?

PERSONNEL

The main features of the Personnel Department will be looked at in Units 4 and 5, but the key considerations are the management of the human resources of the organisation. In addition, they are responsible for the well-being of the workforce so that they can contribute fully to the organisation itself. Specifically, a Personnel Department will deal with the following areas related to employees:

- hiring and firing
- education and training
- staff welfare
- industrial relations

In order to carry out these functions, the staff must deal with a range of administration work, which mainly relates to the maintenance of personnel records. The Personnel Department will maintain records on all members of the workforce, both full and part time. The organisation will require the Personnel Department to store information regarding the following:

- name, address and date of birth of employee
- sex, marital status, number of dependants and next of kin of employee
- nationality and place of birth of employee
- National Insurance number and tax details of employee
- education and qualifications of employee
- past and present employment record of employee
- present job, role(s) and responsibilities of employee
- salary details of employee
- appraisal interview(s) and outcome(s)
- any disciplinary action taken against the employee
- an assessment of the potential of the employee
- any staff development undertaken or required by the employee

The system by which this information is collected and

stored must be flexible enough to be updated on a regular basis. The information relating to particular employees should be available to relevant members of staff upon request (but only those with authority to access such records).

student activity

Design a personnel record which would allow for the successful storing of all of the above details of an employee. This record would need to be flexible in its use. You may use computer software to produce this record.

SERVICES (MAINTENANCE/CATERING ETC.)

It is essential for an organisation to establish administration systems to cope with the various service functions. A maintenance system will be required to fulfil the following requirements:

FIG 2.1.9 *The Office Machine Maintenance Division of Rentokil PLC provides a service for leasing, rental, sales and maintenance of photocopiers and fax machines. Rentokil brings its experience and reputation for high quality service to an industry sector in which service is vital. Major brands are sold with service and maintenance provided under contract with the aim of reducing down-time from breakdowns and maximising the reliability and performance of equipment.*

- regularly **inspect** all plant and machinery
- record any **actions** taken as a result of inspections
- instruct maintenance staff to deal with any **problems** identified by the inspection
- maintain **records** of action taken by maintenance staff
- create a full **inventory** of all plant and machinery
- identify particular plant and machinery which may be **prone to deterioration or breakdown**
- establish an additional maintenance schedule for **vulnerable** plant and machinery

The catering functions of an organisation need a system to handle the following:

- identify the level of **catering needs** within the organisation
- install an efficient **stock control system** to ensure there are sufficient catering materials
- ensure that the catering function conforms with all **statutory obligations**

- establish the catering function as a **separate cost centre** (which may mean that it has to make a profit in its own right)
- in relation to the above point, there needs to be a system which identifies **other cost centres** which should be billed for the use of catering facilities
- in the case of organisations which provide a **subsidised catering service** to their employees, there needs to be some assessment of the general impact and appreciation of the service
- the establishment of specified **catering areas and personnel** to fulfil catering functions

THE EVALUATION OF CRITERIA

The systems which an organisation has in place should aim to establish a means by which the efficiency and effectiveness of all operations are assessed. All systems rely on the way in which the organisation is structured and the comparative importance with which individuals within the organisation view the systems.

Any system is only a series of sub-systems which themselves may be split into additional sub-systems. It is, therefore, important that the organisation monitors all parts of the system. The systems should be designed in such a way that they can be amended or can evolve to meet the requirements of the organisation. In order to understand the ways in which organisations work, we need to understand how they can assess the efficiency and effectiveness of all their operations.

EFFICIENCY OF OPERATION

The simple way of describing the **efficiency of** operations is to consider how the organisation uses its available resources to produce specific outputs. Efficiency requires the organisation to make this process as smooth as possible.

EFFECTIVE CONTROL OF BUSINESS FUNCTIONS

Effectiveness is concerned with how the organisation achieves its objectives and goals. At its simplest, if an organisation meets its declared objectives and goals, then it is being effective. However, the amount of resources deployed to achieve these objectives or goals should also be measured in order to assess effectiveness.

In other words, we cannot assess how successful an organisation is simply by considering efficiency or effectiveness separately. We need to consider both, since an organisation needs to operate efficiently and effectively and its operations need to be co-ordinated. Even if only one part of the organisation fails in its task then we cannot state that the organisation is truly efficient or effective. One or more feature in the organisation's systems must be deficient if one part of the organisation is under-achieving.

Systems obviously play a vital role here. They are the means by which the organisation is able to operate as a whole entity. Any organisation can have good ideas and well-motivated personnel, but without systems to ensure that vital functions are carried out, then these may be doomed to failure. Organisations need not necessarily rely on their own personnel to provide the design and running of systems. They may employ outside specialists or consultants who are conversant with Organisation and Methods (O&M) Analysis. In recent years many organisations have employed this vital tool to improve efficiency and effectiveness. They have often done this by engaging outside agencies to study and analyse their existing systems.

Whether the systems of an organisation evolve from existing systems, or are radically redesigned, O & M base their assessment on scientific analysis of the organisation's systems. As we have seen, systems are vital to measure the performance of an organisation and to assess whether it is reaching its declared objectives. However the systems have originated, they will always be open to criticism and to the charge that it is the systems themselves that are responsible for inefficiencies or their lack of effectiveness.

Investigate communication systems

1 PURPOSES
internal, external, handling information, taking decisions, informing actions

2 COMMUNICATION SYSTEMS
internal, external, face-to-face, correspondence, telecommunications, computer-aided

3 ELECTRONIC TECHNOLOGY
network computer systems, electronic mail, enhanced telephone systems

4 EVALUATION CRITERIA
accuracy, efficiency, cost-effectiveness, security

PURPOSES

Central to the efficient running of any organisation is the clear and effective channelling of all communications. It is a fundamental requirement of all those in a position of authority, and some who are not, to be able to communicate in a clear and effective manner. To be a good manager or administrator, an individual will need to spend a great deal of time communicating with others. Communication is, of course, a two-way process, since ideas and information may come from any source.

It is important to identify the main sorts of communication and look at their purposes within the organisation.

INTERNAL

The way in which an organisation is structured will determine the channels through which communication is made. There is a definite relationship to be identified in terms of an individual's position, authority and status within an organisation. Depending on these factors, an individual will be more receptive and accessible by the establishment of an effective communications system. Information needs to flow freely around the organisation. In a small business, it is easy for everyone to know exactly what is going on, but, in larger organisations, the flow of information may be awkward and disrupted at various points. Indeed, certain individuals within the organisation will put in place barriers to communication to avoid information overload. They will not be interested in or able to handle the sheer volume of information and will have nominated other individuals to perform monitoring tasks on their behalf.

In order to determine how effective the channels of communication are within an organisation, we must look at whether the right information has reached the right person at the right time. If there are any barriers that prevent this from happening, then they must be overcome in order to increase the effectiveness of that individual. The way in which an organisation is structured will often determine how hard or easy it is to get the information through to the right person. Organisations may consider fundamental changes in their structure if these barriers appear to be insurmountable.

Once the information has reached the correct person, it must be in such a format as to allow that individual immediate understanding. If the information is unclear, misleading or ambiguous in any way, then the channels of communication, however good they are, have been wasted.

EXTERNAL

Organisations are often more concerned with the way in which external organisations view them. The view of external organisations is often affected by the way in which they receive information from that organisation. While the organisation will try to respond in an appropriate manner, it must take care to ensure that its reputation is maintained at a high level in all the communication methods it uses.

HANDLING INFORMATION

To handle information efficiently and effectively, the organisation needs to establish and maintain an information system. The key purposes of information will be to:

- give instructions
- ask for advice
- allocate tasks
- praise or criticise
- evaluate

This information may be transferred in a variety of different ways, which we will look at in more detail later, but the essential forms of information are:

- oral
- written
- non-verbal
- electronic
- telecommunication

Information is a vital part of any organisation since it is essential to inform the correct person. Without an efficient information system, individuals may not be

FIG 2.2.1 *Fison's unique cohort computer system is used by sales representatives to give customers up-to-the minute product and ordering information.*

able to utilise existing data to help them make decisions. The nature of handling information will later require us to look at all the various forms of communications.

TAKING DECISIONS

In order to make the correct decision an individual needs to obtain and interpret all available information. Without the correct information all the individual can do is guess. It is important for the manager to have the most accurate and relevant information, as well as the most up-to-date data. It would be a courageous manager who chooses to make a decision without reference to existing information.

Many organisations have systems in place in order to assist decision making. These systems will attempt to ensure the following:

- what kind of information is required
- by whom the information is required
- what decision the individual may make
- what implications the decision may have

In a fully formed system which facilitates decision making, the following process may be in operation:

1 The manager who is required to make the decision writes a report detailing all the implications the decision will have.

2 This report is submitted to his/her immediate superior who produces an additional short report and recommends actions.

3 A copy of the original report is sent to any appropriate directors who will, in turn, produce a briefing paper and any cost implications.

4 The original report and any other additional documentation is entered on to the agenda of the next full meeting of the board of directors meeting. It is an essential part of this system that all members of the board should receive copies of all relevant documents prior to the meeting.

5 The board will discuss the proposal and attached documents. On the basis of information received they will decide to accept or reject the proposal. If there is some dispute, then the proposal is put to the vote and the decision of the board is then transmitted to the appropriate manager(s).

student activity

What other information-gathering systems could be used to keep the board of directors informed as to the nature and problems that the business currently faces?

INFORMING ACTIONS

It can often be the case that individuals will receive information which they do not understand. Generally, information is given to an individual for a particular purpose. The information may require the individual to act upon it. However, this is not necessarily always the case. It may just be information that must be filed for future reference. Much information is channelled to various individuals so that they may use it as a basis

for decisions. Other information may be passed on to individuals purely to process it. This is often true of the information handled by people whose jobs entail routine clerical duties. Information can provide the trigger for a manager to take some action, perhaps by informing others as a result of receiving this information.

There are, essentially, two forms of information system which operate within most organisations, these are:

Formal system

This usually takes the form of a **management information system** (MIS) which provides a broad view of the business and assists managers in making decisions regarding budgets and other key management issues.

FIG 2.2.2 *Bernard Cassley, Director of Information Services for Kwik-Fit Holdings PLC provides a network of information systems to aid decision making, management and customer service.*

Informal system

This system, as you may have realised, does not rely on structured information systems, but relies on personal communication between individuals within the organisation. Informal information systems operate when managers have a good working relationship with their employees.

FIG 2.2.3 *Marks and Spencer PLC have recently developed a franchise operation overseas. Here we see Sue Knight advising Portuguese franchisees on stock selection.*

COMMUNICATIONS SYSTEMS

Communication systems cover the five main types of communication skills. These are:

- listening
- speaking
- reading
- writing
- information technology

In addition, we must also consider communication that is carried out using none of the above. This is known as **non-verbal communication** or **body language**.

Let us look at these skills in a little more detail:

1 *Listening.* During the course of a day, we may listen to a number of different people. It is a rare person who will remember everything that has been said to him or her. This is particularly the case if the way in which conversation is listened to is unstructured and confused.

In order to use listening as effectively as possible, the individual must:

- actually hear the message itself
- interpret the message
- evaluate the message
- act upon the message and make use of the information it contains

It is often a good idea to take notes during a conversation. Some people find it very useful to use a tape recorder.

2 *Speaking.* Speaking need not necessarily take place face to face. It may also take the form of a telephone conversation. The use of questioning techniques is important in clarifying the exact nature of the message.

To be an effective communicator the individual should have the following qualities:

- Clearly know his/her own role in the conversation
- Be aware of the receptiveness and interest of those listening
- Have an accurate knowledge of the listener's own knowledge of the subject of the conversation

Being an effective communicator means making sure that the listener is always attentive and that any points raised within the conversation are not ambiguous.

3 *Reading and writing.* We have chosen to take these two skills together since the writer of a message must be acutely aware of how the message will be received by the reader.

To be an effective writer an individual must take the following facts into account when presenting the information:

- that the information will be read by a variety of people in different situations
- that complex information needs to have sufficient background description in order to make it clear
- that the information should be capable of having a long life, in the sense that it may be referred to many times in the future

As with many other forms of communication, the written word may suffer from being ambiguous. Even the most informal of messages needs to be clear. Organisations use standard formats for a variety of written communication. These systems have been designed to avoid ambiguity. Certain forms of written communication can be easier to understand than others, but the writer should ensure that the reader always has sufficient information in order to form an opinion if required. The presentation of data, for example, should be carefully considered since financial information, in particular, can often be misleading or unclear.

4 *Information technology.* Information technology has transformed the way in which much information is processed, handled and distributed. The availability of computer facilities throughout organisations has meant that information can be relayed quickly and effectively. This is, of course, vital to the success of a business, but does require that individuals within the organisation be sufficiently trained on many different computer software systems.

5 *Non-verbal communication/body language.* As we will see, not all messages rely on the spoken or written word. We can 'read' a great deal into the way in which someone uses his or her body to convey information. Each gesture or facial expression has its own particular meaning. Being able to read these gestures and expressions is a skill in itself, not to mention being able to use these gestures and expressions yourself. An individual will use non-verbal communication in order to support the message he or she is giving or receiving. This form of communication is intended to make the message clearer.

It was rightly judged strong enough to help see off the challenge posed by the BBC's lavishly funded new soap opera 'Eldorado.'

And above all *Emmerdale*, under its new producer, Morag Bain, was continually freshened with new and strong story lines, attractive characters and appealing visions of the Yorkshire Countryside.

It remains among the most appreciated of all the television serials and twice a week provides a strong foundation for the night's ITV schedules.

Yorkshire Programmes enters the new ITV era with an exceptionally strong hand. David Jason, who has given us such phenomenal successes as *A Bit Of A Do* and *The Darling Buds of May*, overwhelmed the schedules before Christmas with his new series *A Touch Of Frost* attracting three quarters of the whole British television audience. This series will be back next year. Similarly Nick Berry, after his great success with *Heartbeat*, will be returning in two more series in 1993.

We are excellently placed with a new current affairs series *3D*, the continuing presence of *Jimmy's* as one of the most appreciated programmes in the whole schedule, Dennis Waterman in a new role as well as the familiar one of Thomas in *Stay Lucky*, and a very large number of children's and educational programmes for both ITV and Channel 4.

We confidently expect 1993 and 1994 to see as many, if not more, Yorkshire programmes on ITV and elsewhere as we have in these last few years, which themselves have reached new records.

FIG 2.2.4 *This is an extract form Yorkshire-Tyne Tees Television Holdings PLC'S Annual Report and Accounts, which illustrates how a great deal of information can be relayed to the reader in a concise and accessible format.*

student activity

Read the text in Figure 2.2.4 and further summarise the information, in no more than 100 words.

INTERNAL AND EXTERNAL

Many basic forms of communication are applicable to both internal and external situations. The skills of communication are similar whether one is dealing with colleagues or customers. The different needs these two groups have may determine the exact style of the communication. External situations may require a more formal approach, whereas internal communications can be dealt with in an informal manner. We shall look at the various forms of internal and external communication in turn.

Verbal communication (internal and external)

To be a good communicator takes practice and experience. Here are some of the key things to remember when you are communicating. It does not matter who you communicate with – it could be friends, parents, teachers or potential employers – they will all gain an insight into you, and how you conduct yourself, by what you say and how you say it.

1   You should always speak clearly.
2   You should not speak too quickly or too slowly.
3   You should use the right words for the situation; do not be too complicated or simplistic.
4   You should be able to listen to what the other person is saying so that you can respond properly.
5   You should show confidence, both in yourself and in what you say.
6   You should try to put the other person at ease.
7   You should think about what you say and try to make your responses logical and easy to follow.
8   You should try to use the right tone for the situation; do not be too aggressive or passive or allow your feelings to confuse what it is you have to say.
9   If you have a regional accent, while this is fine in most situations, if it is too strong or broad, you should talk slightly more slowly than normal.
10 If you think that your voice is not pleasant to listen to, perhaps too high, try to lower the pitch of your voice a little. You can help counter this problem by controlling your excitement or speed of talking.
11 You should never interrupt someone who is speaking, wait until he or she is finished.
12 Take care to use the right tone of voice, as this can affect how the other person receives what you say. The same statement may be either acceptable or unacceptable, depending on your tone.

EFFECTIVE COMMUNICATION

2. We can see from this the importance of **communication - not only with customers and prospective customers, but within** our dealership itself.

In big organisations you may have heard it said that: "The right hand doesn't know what the left hand is doing". (This is true of some branches of government too!)

When communication breaks down, there can be high costs sustained - both in financial and human terms.

There are several forms of communication breakdown that we need to be aware of. Can you think what these are? Please make a list of them.

■ ....

■ ....

■ ....

■ ....

■ ....

■ ....

■ ....

 STOP

3. Organisations do not have to be all that large for communication to fail.

It can happen between two or more people!

It can happen between husband and wife, boss and employee, between colleagues, or between staff and customers. Big and small, it can happen in our dealership.

So the key to the successful "One Dealership" idea is effective communications.

3

FIG 2.2.5 An extract from Peugeot Talbot's 'One Dealership Workbook' on customer awareness training which stresses the importance of effective communication with customers and within the organisation.

Non-verbal communication (internal and external)

Although you may not have ever heard of the term, we all use non-verbal communication (NVC). It is important to know how to use it, what it means and how you can read other people's NVC.

Let's start with the face and what that can give away about what you are really saying!

- raising the eyebrows could show surprise or disbelief
- if your pupils dilate, this could mean either anger or love
- opening your eyes wide might show hostility
- grinning would show that you accept what is being said or are simply friendly

We are sure that you can think of many more of these facial expressions.

Gestures, on the other hand (no pun intended), can also give interesting clues as to what the speaker really means.

- pointing, to identify someone or something directly when referring to it
- giving a thumbs-up sign, to signify agreement or acceptance
- shaking your head, to show disagreement
- fiddling with something, such as jewellery, a tie or the strap of a bag may infer nervousness
- pacing up and down may show impatience or boredom
- looking at your hands, or fiddling with something may show disinterest

Posture shows some interesting things too:

- standing upright shows alertness
- sitting in a hunched position shows nervousness
- lounging in a chair, on the other hand, shows ease
- standing with your shoulders hunched, shows that you are miserable or depressed

Where you are standing or sitting, in relation to the person you are talking to, can show some important things:

- you are likely to stand closer to a person whom you know well
- where you stand, and how close to a person, may depend upon your nationality or upbringing
- the nature of the circumstances in which you met people will have an effect on how close you stand to someone

student activity

In pairs, discuss a topic of your choice, preferably one which interests you. While communicating note the different NVCs used by your partner. What do they indicate to you? After five minutes compare your lists with one another.

Reports (mainly internal)

Although **reports** issued or received by an organisation can be either informal or very formal, both types contain certain common elements, although not necessarily the same format.

A report may contain research which has been carried out for a specific purpose. It may be the findings and recommendations of work that has been carried out for a specific purpose. Or it may be an account of something which has taken place and been reported on.

A report will contain the following headings:

1 *Terms of Reference.* This will state what you have been asked to do. It may be that you have been asked to conduct research on a particular aspect or topic.
2 *Procedure.* This will say how you have gone about gathering the information you are stating.
3 *Findings.* In this section you would state what facts you have found out. You would not make statements about your recommendations at this stage, but simply state facts.
4 *Conclusion.* This would be a general statement about your findings. Again this is not the place you would make recommendations, but is when you would conclude and sum up your findings.
5 *Recommendations.* On the basis of your findings and conclusions you would make recommendations for future research or projects.

It is usual to sign and date a report.

Using numbers within a report

Sometimes it is helpful to break down the headings used in a report. This could be done by using a series of numbers. For example:

1. Establishment of company catering facilities
(a)   Lunch period arrangements
  (i) Arrangement of seating

Or alternatively:

1. Establishment of company catering facilities
   1.1 Lunch period arrangements
     1.1.1   Arrangement of seating

student activity

Compile a report on the effectiveness of different forms of communication. In this report you should include all the advantages and disadvantages as well as the features of each communication type. You should use the correct report format, which should be word processed.

Forms (internal and external)

In everyday life, as well as life in the business world, there are a large variety of forms to complete. When carrying out this task, there are some useful guidelines you should follow to ensure that you make a neat and accurate job of completing forms:

1 If possible take a photocopy of the form so that you can practise first. If this is not possible, complete in pencil first to avoid messy crossings out.
2 Read the form thoroughly before you even consider starting to complete it.

Form initiation

The initiation and design of forms is a specialised activity and the following guidelines are, of necessity, technical in nature. Basically, one can distinguish between forms that are wholly, or in part, subject to data processing constraints and those free from such constraints.

Form design

There are two important aspects of form design. Firstly, there is the efficiency of the form which, because of its appearance and layout, aids use. Secondly, there is the Rank corporate style which by its consistent application creates a positive impression.

The visual arrangement and appearance of any form should aid clarity of information content as well as legibility and ease of use, both by the person entering information on the form and by the person who needs to retrieve selected information from the form.

Where there is a hierarchy of importance, a distinction must be made between hierarchy in terms of form content and structure, and hierarchy in terms of actual reading. When forms are regularly used by staff, most wording is no longer actually read and the typography must aid recognition and location; but considerations of familiarity do not as a rule apply to forms or those portions of forms used by members of the public, and the typography must aid legibility.

It should be borne in mind that type size is not an indicator of importance and that simultaneous emphasis on many items is counter productive.

Design guidelines for forms

Plan the basic layout giving consideration to the contents, order and general position of the information to be included. Take any constraints into account at the planning stage. Position the name of the company, title of the form and symbol. Divide the form into horizontal positions and vertical columns, based on the likely amount of information each entry will require. Use the entire printable area of the paper and try to achieve a balanced appearance.

Plan and lay out the form roughly first, using the grid printed at the end of this section.

When the basic layout has been finalised, fine detailing can begin. Each caption should be positioned exactly on a grid co-ordinate, therefore conforming to 12pt vertical divisions and 5 or 6 character horizontal divisions. This will enable the typist to position all entries automatically without constant re-alignment and adjustment.

Align all information horizontally and vertically into columns wherever possible.

When all wording required has been positioned use vertical and/or horizontal rules to create boxes and separate the areas of information. Distances between words and rules should be consistent both vertically and horizontally. One weight of rule is generally sufficient, but a thicker weight can be used for emphasis or the division of information into areas.

Check that the layout is appropriate, clear and the positioning of all information is correct before involving a printer.

FIG 2.2.6 *Within Rank Organisation's corporate identity manual, they clearly detail exactly how forms should be created and designed. This attention to detail ensures that the corporate image is consistent throughout the organisation.*

3 Make sure you know how to complete the form before you start, and that you have all the information required readily to hand.

4 Check to see if there is any instruction regarding the colour of pen to use. Some forms stipulate 'use black pen'.

5 Check to see if there is any instruction regarding the style in which you have to complete the form. Some forms stipulate 'use block capitals only'.

6 Use your neatest handwriting.

7 Try to complete all parts of the form. If there is some information you do not have readily to hand, then do not send the form off until it is fully completed.

8 Check thoroughly everything you have completed before you send it off. If possible ask someone else to look at it – sometimes you cannot find your own mistakes!

Preparing a summary (mainly internal)

It may be that during the course of your work you will be asked to use the written form of communication called **summarising**. This means that you are given a long article or report and have to read it and present the information more briefly. The original document may be long and complicated to start with, so it is necessary that you understand the information you read before you start. You would then take out the unnecessary facts and write a shorter information pack. The following are guidelines for carrying out this task:

1 Read through the whole document first, rather than trying to understand everything as you go through.
2 Re-read the document more thoroughly. You could highlight the areas of importance at this stage, or cross out the unnecessary information.
3 Make a list of the items you have to use and that it is important to include.
4 Compare your list with the main document to make sure you haven't forgotten anything important.
5 Write a draft summary. It may be that a superior could check this for you at this stage. Once you are happy with this draft, you may want to write a final draft.
6 Once the final draft has been agreed, you can write the final Summary.

Writing a project (mainly internal)

Just as you write projects for your College work, so you may be asked by your employer to write a project for him/her. If this task is new to you, it may be useful to look at some guidelines for completing projects:

1 *Preparation.* The first thing you need to find out is the date for completion of the project. Allow yourself plenty of time to research and write up the information. Don't leave things until the last minute – you will not feel good about it and your work will not be of the highest possible standard.
2 Secondly, find out exactly what is required of you. How long does the project have to be? How many pages of typing or writing is expected? Is there a limit to the number of words you submit?
3 Next, do you have to submit the project in a certain format? Are there set headings you are expected to use?
4 Lastly, where will you find out the information you need? Make a list of the sources of information you will need to use:

(a) Your local library – the library staff will be very pleased to help you in your research. Facilities the library may offer are:

- photocopying
- books and magazines for reference
- an indexing system that you can refer to in order to find the literature you require
- ordering of specific books, or reserving them for you when they are returned to the library
- quiet areas where you can carry out research without being disturbed

(b) local and national newspapers
(c) local and national radio and television
(d) banks
(e) building societies
(f) post offices
(g) citizens' advice bureaux
(h) chambers of commerce

Many other organisations offer assistance in project work. It will obviously depend on the type of research you are carrying out.

Different methods of displaying information (internal and external)

Whether you are writing a project or preparing for a presentation to a group of people, there are many different ways you could display this information in order to vary the methods already used. It is often said that something is easier to understand if you can see it rather than be told about it. With that in mind, we are going to mention a few alternative methods of displaying information, maybe for use as visual aids:

1 *Charts, photographs, sketches, pictograms and diagrams.* When you are talking about a complicated piece of machinery or the layout of a new extension, it is obviously easier for you and for your audience to see a diagram of the proposed topic. Charts and diagrams not only make something easier to visualise, but are also more pleasant to look at than page after page of script. You know yourself that very often when you pick up a newspaper or magazine, what you tend to do is look at the pictures first.
2 *Bar charts, line graphs and pie charts.* This method of producing and displaying information is increasingly prepared using computer software. You might use this method to show percentages, to prove an increase or decrease in current trends, or to make comparisons.

Agendas (internal and external)

The success of a meeting will be largely determined by the way in which it has been organised in advance. The document that is used to inform those who are to attend a meeting about the nature of that meeting is known as an **Agenda**.

Essentially, an agenda has the following format:

1 Apologies for absence
2 Minutes of the last meeting

3 Matters arising
4 Reports
5 Motions
6 Any other business
7 Date of the next meeting

Minutes (internal and external)

Minutes are the record of meetings and include the following:

1 An account of those present at the meeting
2 Decisions made
3 Discussions which have taken place
4 Tasks allocated to individuals
5 Reports received from individuals
6 Actions to be taken in the future
7 Details of individuals to whom decisions made at the meeting refer

It is the responsibility of an appointed individual (usually a secretary capable of taking shorthand) to record and prepare formal minutes. These are then typed and distributed to members present at the meeting together

```
                    A G E N D A

for the Annual General Meeting of the Gt Yarmouth Camera Club

1    Apologies for absence

2    Minutes of the last meeting

3    Matters arising

          3.1  Subscription fees

          4.2  Planned exhibition

4    Final plan for next exhibition

5    Purchase of new equipment

6    Any other business

7    Date of next meeting
```

FIG 2.2.8 *This shows the normal layout of a typical agenda. the format is standard for most organisations.*

OPERATING CAPITAL EMPLOYED – STERLING

Operating capital employed (i)					£ million
	1987	1988	1989	1990	1991
By business					
Exploration and Production	7,996	11,032	11,705	10,019	10,074
Refining and Marketing	4,512	4,608	5,695	5,717	5,926
Chemicals	1,479	1,630	1,941	2,081	2,436
Nutrition	730	851	1,027	949	970
Other Businesses and Corporate	2,524	2,068	298(ii)	380	509
Total	17,241	20,189	20,666	19,146	19,915
By geographical area					
UK (iii)	2,625	5,374	5,829	6,135	6,415
Rest of Europe	2,526	2,327	2,932	3,137	3,533
USA	9,432	9,210	8,552	7,029	6,847
Rest of World	2,658	3,278	3,353	2,845	3,120
Total	17,241	20,189	20,666	19,146	19,915

(i) Operating capital employed is defined as fixed assets plus working capital less long-term liabilities and provisions, excluding liabilities for current and deferred taxation.
(ii) During 1989, the group sold the majority of its Australian and South African coal interests, and most of its minerals interests.
(iii) UK area includes the UK-based international activities of BP Oil.

FIG 2.2.7 *This chart of figures shows one particular way of displaying information. The chart shows the operating capital employed in sterling by the British Petroleum Company PLC in the years 1987–1991.*

student activity

To complete this task you will need to refer to Figure 2.2.7. Although BP illustrated this information in various graphical forms in their Financial and Operating Information Brochure, we are not as kind as that! Your task is to create appropriate graphs which would better illustrate this information.

with the agenda of the next meeting. This is to ensure that a correct and true account has been made of the previous meeting and that it may be agreed in the next meeting that these are an accurate reflection of what happened.

MINUTES OF THE ANNUAL GENERAL MEETING

OF THE GT YARMOUTH CAMERA CLUB

Held at the Bendix Hotel, at 7.30 on Friday 7th January 199-.

Present: Mr J Clyde (in the Chair)
              Mr B Butler
              Miss S Smith
              Mr J Thompson
              Mrs B Brett
              Mr A Sharman
              Mrs P Hunt

1   Apologies for absence

     Apologies for absence were received from Mrs Bryant and Miss Leech.

2   Minutes of the last meeting

     The Minutes were read and signed as being a true and accurate record.

3   Matters arising

     3.1 Subscription fees

          It was agreed that the fees would be increased to £15 with effect from 6 April.

     4.2 Planned exhibition

          A sub-committee was formed in order that plans for next year's exhibition could begin to be under way. Mr Sharman would chair the sub-committee and volunteers would be sought to assist in some fund-raising activities.

4   Final plan for next exhibition

     As the exhibition is only now 3 weeks away, it was decided to hold an Extraordinary Meeting to discuss the final arrangements in more detail. It was felt that more could be achieved by doing this than trying to cover all items on this Agenda.

5   Purchase of new equipment

     The Treasurer reported that funds are very low at the moment, and although members had been requesting some new dark-room equipment, he felt it would be unwise to spend any money until after the exhibition had been held.

6   Any other business

     There being no further business, the meeting closed at 9.15.

7   Date of next meeting

     The date of the Extraordinary Meeting was arranged for Friday 14th January at 7.30.

     The date for next year's Annual General Meeting would be arranged at a later date.

....
     Chairman

FIG 2.2.9 *The minutes shown here relate to the agenda in Figure 2.2.8. You will see that all items appearing on the agenda have been covered in the minutes, showing the outcomes of discussions.*

The taking of minutes and the subsequent distribution of the minutes further assists members present by reminding them of decisions made and any actions which they personally have to take. Although minutes should be concise and precise, they should not lose any accuracy in this process. The writing style required may seem short and abrupt and often a form of numerical recording is used against each minuted item.

Certain organisations, in particular local authorities, must have their minutes available for public inspection. The details of any motions voted upon or amendments made to these motions must be clearly detailed in the minutes for public perusal.

Papers and briefs (mainly internal)

These documents take the form of additional information provided by individuals to assist decision-makers. In other words, their key function is to enable others to make the right decision. These documents will include essential background information on a particular subject, usually written by an individual with a particular interest or experience in this area. A discussion document also gives essential background material, but in addition offers advice as to the decision which should be made. It is usually the case that these documents will include a series of arguments for and against a particular course of action in the process of arriving at a preferred conclusion.

Notes (mainly internal)

These short, often informal, forms of communication take the form of handwritten pieces of information. Under this heading, we may include telephone messages, informal arrangements and details of informal short meetings.

Invitations (mainly external)

Informal and formal invitations may be sent or received by organisations. When these are being issued in bulk, it is normal that they will be printed by a specialist company and simply prepared for postage within the organisation. An invitation will usually contain the following information:

1 the address of the person sending out the invitation
2 the date the invitation is sent out
3 the names of the people acting as host/hostess at the event
4 the date of the event
5 the venue of the event
6 the time of the event
7 the reason for the event (e.g. 18th birthday party)
8 RSVP – this is a request for a reply and is taken from the French *respondez s'il vous plait*. Sometimes a deadline for replies is also given.

Notices (internal and external)

If an organisation wishes to pass a message on to a number of employees, it may place information on its staff noticeboards. These messages may be formal or informal. Perhaps there is a change to normal organisational procedures, or maybe a social event is being planned by the organisation's Personnel Department.

Notices allow the quick and easy sending of information to a large number of people. Noticeboards can also be used by individuals wishing to inform colleagues of items for sale or events planned.

FACE-TO-FACE

When you are actually communicating directly with someone, you will use a mixture of verbal and non-verbal communication. You will also be able to see what he or she is feeling by taking careful note of his or her non-verbal communication.

When talking to a customer, whether they are a new customer or an established one, you should always remember the following rules:

1 Always be polite
2 Always try to be helpful
3 Try not to distract the customer with an irritating habit (such as chewing gum or sniffing)
4 To help make the customer feel valued, use his or her name in the conversation
5 Always close the conversation by saying 'goodbye', otherwise you may give the impression that the business is unfinished.

Regular customers are vitally important to any organisation. A great deal of hard work, not to mention advertising and other costs, have been incurred in making a buyer a regular customer. It is, therefore, essential to build and maintain customer relations. Poor customer relations can ruin the work of years or months. The following rules are important:

1 Always use the customer's name when greeting him or her
2 Give the customer favourable treatment, such as refreshments, offering them a seat or additional information regarding business
3 Try to remember something about the customer or his or her family. Failing that, try to remember something about the customer's business
4 Always try to tell regular customers the truth, inform them of special offers pending, or changes in stock **before** they actually happen

Even when you are dealing with new customers, you should always observe some conventions:

1 Greet the customers
2 Be friendly
3 Be helpful and tell them you are there for their benefit
4 Do not harass customers, let them have time to look before pouncing on them
5 Be available if they look as if they need help

Many of these points are applicable to face-to-face interactions with colleagues. One major advantage with face-to-face communication is that feedback is instant. It should, therefore, be relatively easy to sort out any disagreements. Face-to-face communications can be disadvantageous in the sense that they are rather time consuming and often suffer from the fact that those involved have not taken any permanent record of the inter change of views. It is also the case that discussion may not be focused and may lead to misunderstandings.

If we consider internal communications specifically, we should take into account the following:

- What is it that I need to say?
- What do I hope to achieve by saying it?
- To whom am I communicating?
- How will they react?
- What is my relationship with the person I am talking to?
- Will this affect the way in which he or she reacts to my message?
- What do I need to tell this person in addition to my message?
- Which particular techniques shall I use to help get my message across?

student activity

In the role of a manager who has to deal with a senior member of staff who has failed to complete a task and seems unconcerned, advise as to the communication techniques that should be employed.

As we have mentioned, most verbal communications give the advantage of an instant feedback. However, the nature of the feedback may be determined by the type of organisation in which the individual is operating. As we will see in a later Unit, there are essentially two different types of structure that may determine the way in which information is accepted and reacted to. These are:

- *Democratic* – in organisations which employ a democratic structure, managers will be keen to encourage individuals and will always give positive feedback. In addition they will try to ensure that misunderstandings are cleared up as quickly as possible.
- *Authoritarian* – in organisations which prefer an authoritarian structure, managers will be more used to giving orders and instructions to their employees. They will not necessarily expect their instructions to be questioned in any way and, as a result, misunderstandings are common.

student activity

Compare these two types of organisation and assess the comparative problems in effective communication.

CORRESPONDENCE

Most business organisations spend a considerable amount of their time communicating with their customers. Some of this communication, as we have seen, will take the form of face-to-face or verbal communication. However, it is essential that some of these communications are supported by written evidence of agreements made.

In our day-to-day life, we use **written communication**, and it is just as important when writing a personal letter to a friend or a note to one of the family as in business correspondence, that we ensure our spelling and grammar are correct.

In all organisations neat, accurate and reliable written communication is vitally important. Written communication in the business world takes several forms:

Passing on messages

It may be that someone has taken a telephone message for a colleague who is unavailable at the time. It is essential that the information contained in this message is correct and legible.

Memoranda

Internal memoranda are used for communication between different departments within the same organisation. These are often called **Memos**. An example of a Memo is given in Figure 2.2.10. You will see that it is normally shorter than a business letter and usually deals with one particular subject. When more than one point is being made it is normal to number them.

Memos are not signed in the same way as a business letter, but the person issuing the Memo would normally initial it at the end.

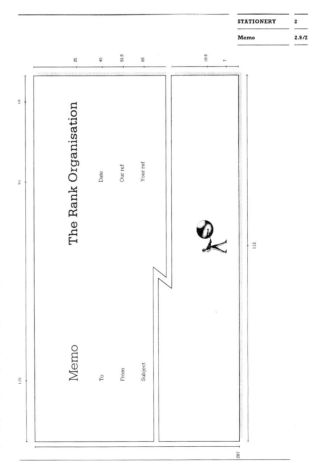

FIG 2.2.10 *This illustration shows another example of Rank's standard stationery requirements. Note the structure of the memorandum document.*

Business letters

A **business letter**, unlike a memorandum, is one that would be sent outside the organisation. It is important then that they are neat, accurate and well presented.

The headed paper used by the organisation for its business letters would form part of its **corporate image**. The example shown gives the information an organisation would wish each of its customers or clients to see regularly:

1 The name and address of the organisation.
2 The telephone number, fax number and/or telex number of the organisation.
3 The registered address of the organisation, as this may be different from the postal address.
4 The company registration number.
5 The names of the directors of the organisation.
6 Any other companies the organisation may represent or be affiliated to.

The layout or format of the business letter will usually also be part of the organisation's corporate image, and different organisations have their own rules about the way in which a letter should be displayed. It is common nowadays to use the fully blocked method of display,

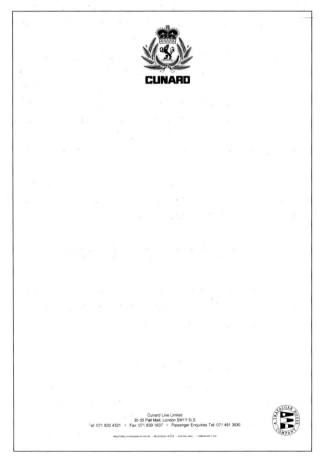

FIG 2.2.11 *Cunard Line Ltd's rather impressive letterhead.*

Peugeot Talbot Motor Company PLC
Registered Office: Aldermoor House, P.O. Box 227, Aldermoor Lane, Coventry CV3 1LT
Telephone: 0203 884000 Fax: 0203 884001 Telex: 311914
Registered in England No. 148545

FIG 2.2.12 *Peugeot Talbot's Company Training Division's letterhead. Note the inclusion of the crest following the gaining of the Queen's Award for Export Achievement 1992.*

which means that each part of the letter commences at the left-hand margin.

The following format can be used as a guideline:

1 *Our Reference* – this can be initials and/or numbers which the organisation sending the letter will use for filing purposes.
2 *Your Reference* – this again is usually initials and/or numbers which the organisation receiving the letter has used in previous correspondence.
3 The *date* – all letters must be dated.
4 The *name and address* of the recipient (the person or organisation to which the letter is being sent) – when using the fully blocked style of business letter, it is normal to use 'open punctuation' in this section. That means that no punctuation is required in the name and address.
The name of the town should be in capital letters, and the postcode should be on a line of its own.
5 The *salutation* – this is the 'Dear Sir/Madam/Mr/Ms/Mrs/Miss' etc.

6 The *heading* – very often, after the salutation, an organisation will give the letter a title. This is normally either typed in capitals, with initial capital letters only, and may be underlined or emboldened.

7 The *body of the letter* is then typed. Each line of the paragraph would commence at the left-hand margin, and a line space would be left between paragraphs.

If you are replying to previous correspondence, it is usual to start your letter with 'Thank you for your letter', or 'I refer to your letter dated ...'. The first paragraph would also state what the letter is about. The subsequent paragraphs would contain the purpose of the letter – what you are writing about and what information you are passing on or requiring. The final paragraph would conclude the letter. In this section you may mention any enclosures you have included. It may also be that you say things like 'I look forward to hearing from you soon' or 'Should you require any further information, please do not hesitate to contact me'.

8 The *complimentary close* – this is the 'Yours faithfully' or 'Yours sincerely'. The complimentary close will match the salutation. When you are using 'Dear Sir/Madam', you will use 'Yours faithfully'. When using 'Dear Mr/Ms/Mrs/Miss' at the beginning, you should use 'Yours sincerely' at the end.

After allowing space for a signature, you type the name of the person signing the letter, as well as his or her title.

9 *Enclosure(s)* – if you have mentioned in the body of the letter that you are enclosing additional information with the letter, then it is usual to indicate this at the foot of the letter. This is done by typing 'Enc(s)' after the complimentary close.

By indicating the number of enclosures, you ensure that the recipient knows that everything needed has actually been received.

student activity

In your own student role, write a letter in correct business format requesting information from an organisation of your choice. You should ask specifically for their company report.

Letters of complaint

Organisations will, in the course of their business activities receive a number of complaints from their customers, or indeed suppliers. Many will express strong emotions, particularly if money is involved. It is important for the organisation to respond in a helpful and constructive manner. A good letter of complaint from the complainant's point of view should follow these guidelines:

- set out the facts clearly
- be relevant
- be polite
- state that the complainant requires a favourable response

student activity

In the role of an irate customer, write a letter of complaint concerning the poor service you have received when requesting information from a sales assistant in a retail outlet.

It may be that the organisation in response to the letter of complaint may have to write a letter of apology. This may involve the following, in addition to the apology:

- financial compensation
- an offer to replace the goods
- an undertaking that the situation will not arise again
- an undertaking that an individual within the organisation has been disciplined

If the organisation discovers that the complaint is without justification, then in order to maintain customer goodwill, a token offer may be made.

Whatever the circumstance, justified or unjustified, letters relating to customer complaints should be carefully put together. They should always use restrained language, such as 'Please be assured that this situation will not arise again'. With the best will in the world an organisation is prone to errors and cannot really guarantee that something similar will not happen at some point in the future.

All letters of complaint should be dealt with promptly but some may need enquiries to be undertaken before the complaint can be addressed.

student activity

In the role of the management of the retail outlet concerned in the previous activity, write a letter of apology in response to the complaint.

Circulars, standard letters and direct mail

These forms of letters are often used for advertising purposes. Standard letters, in the main, can also be used for inviting individuals to attend job interviews.

These sorts of letters take the form of a word-processed basic letter which is merged using computer software with a datafile containing names and addresses.

Such letters are not always personally addressed and they may simply refer to 'the occupier'. This is particularly the case for circulars as many thousands are distributed in a particular mail shot. Circulars have three main goals. These are:

- to **create an impact** by using a striking headline or picture
- to **encourage the reading of the letter** by using the appropriate language or stating boldly that the individual will receive a free gift for example
- **be memorable** by using appropriate slogans in large type

References and testimonials

Many organisations are required at various times to provide references or testimonials for individuals. References are much more common and testimonials need not necessarily relate to an employee of the organisation.

1 *References.* Often references are written on a standard form provided by a potential employer. In other cases, a letter can be written in relation to a number of guidelines laid down by the potential employer. These references are always written by an individual who has some knowledge of the applicant and will contain statements regarding that individual's abilities, character, quality and performance.

student activity

In the role of a manager write a reference for one of the members of your group.

2 *Testimonials.* A testimonial is essentially a letter of commendation. It has not been written with a particular job in mind, but contains general information regarding the individual. Organisations may be asked to write testimonials for other individuals who are not necessarily employees.

The writing of references and testimonials provides the organisation with some moral problems. A reference should be truthful as far as the organisation is aware. The organisation must be careful not to make defamatory statements which could harm the reputation of an individual. The writer needs to strike a balance between the truth and tact. In other words, when reading a reference, one should often look for what is not said. There is no legal obligation to provide a reference or a testimonial and much can be inferred from an employer choosing not to give a reference on an individual. It should be noted that employers must give permission before their name and address be given to a potential employer. In some cases, a potential employer will contact a previous employer by telephone if a quick decision is needed.

TELECOMMUNICATIONS

Telecommunications have had a drastic impact on the communications systems of organisations. At a stroke, many of them have replaced traditional forms of communication. We shall begin by looking at the three main forms of telecommunication.

Telephone

The basic problem with communication via the telephone is that you do not have non-verbal communication to fall back on.

To make the most effective use of the telephone, it is wise to remember some of the following points:

1 Always pick up the telephone as quickly as possible
2 Always have a pen and paper handy to take a message
3 Always be helpful and polite
4 If the caller needs information that is not readily to hand, then phone him or her back
5 If you have promised to ring back, then you should not forget
6 Always remember that, unless you put the caller on HOLD, then he or she will be able to hear what you say
7 Make sure that you do not give out confidential information without checking with your superior first
8 If the call is interrupted and you are cut off, then the person who made the call should always ring back
9 In order to make sure that you have the facts correct, figures right or a complicated name spelt correctly, it is acceptable to ask the caller to repeat. If you are still unsure, then you can repeat the message back to the caller
10 If you have been asked for details or information and are ringing back with this, make sure that you have all the necessary information to hand
11 Always quote figures in pairs as they are easier to understand and remember
12 Always complete the call by saying 'thank you'.

If a caller wants someone who is not available you should follow the procedure below:

1 Having established that the person the caller wants to speak to is not available, you should then ask if there is someone else who can help them
2 Offer to help yourself
3 If this is not acceptable then either ask the caller to ring back, or promise to get the person the caller wanted to call back

4 If necessary, take a message and ensure that it gets to the right person

If you are in the position of taking a call for someone who is available, you should follow this procedure:

I After the caller has asked for someone in particular, ask the caller who he or she is
2 Ask the caller to hold the line, while you find or contact the person requested
3 Contact the person required and say who is calling, and if relevant, what the call is about

Facsimile machines

Another way an organisation may choose to communicate with its customers or clients is by the use of the facsimile machine colloquially known as the 'fax' machine. The word 'facsimile' means an exact and faithful reproduction of and this applies to text, photographs or graphic images. This means that an added benefit of a fax is that an organisation is not limited to what it can send. It is also useful for organisations which may need to contact companies overseas. A fax machine is left on for 24 hours a day, and it does not have to be continually monitored through the night. This means that the time differences between countries are not a problem. The procedure for sending a facsimile message via the telephone line is as follows:

I Prepare the original document (this may be typed, handwritten, contain graphs, charts, diagrams etc.).
2 Look up the fax number of the recipient. Often an organisation will keep such numbers readily to hand. If, however, the company is being contacted for the first time, then a Fax Directory is available. This works in the same way as a Telephone Directory.
3 Prepare a covering sheet which will contain a short message, show the name of the recipient of the document, the name of the sender, the fax numbers involved and the number of pages being sent.
4 Place the document face-down on the machine.
5 Key in the number of the recipient. Machines vary slightly, but the machine will give you instructions as to the correct procedure to follow.
6 Provided a connection has been made, the original document will pass through the machine and you will be informed that transmission is taking place. Should the recipient's line be engaged, the machine will automatically redial the number for you at intervals.

7 Once transmission has taken place, the machine will issue you with a Transmission Report. This will state the date, time and length of the call, the recipient's number, the sender's number, the number of pages sent and that transmission was acceptable. Should there have been a problem in transmission, the report will indicate this and re-transmission may be necessary.

Telex machines

The telex is an older form of transmission which uses much the same principle as the facsimile machine. The telex is more limited in its use. It is not possible to transmit charts and diagrams via the telex. However, the same advantages apply regarding the transmission of messages to countries overseas and confirmation of transmission. Telex messages can also be prepared and saved on electronic file and transmitted at a later time when they are despatched automatically. The procedure for sending a telex message is as follows:

I Find the telex number of the recipient. This will be done in the same way as for the fax machine, but using the Telex Directory.
2 Prepare the text of the telex – this is typed on the telex machine.
3 Make contact with the recipient by keying in the telex number.
4 Obtain confirmatory answerback code from the recipient.
5 Provide identification in the form of the answerback code of the sender.
6 Despatch the telex.

COMPUTER AIDED COMMUNICATION

It is our intention to look at the main forms of electronic and computer-aided technology in the next section of this book.

More than anything else, computer-aided communication has revolutionised business activity over the last few years. There is virtually no part of business activity that has not been affected by the development of computer systems. These systems include:

- Networked computers
- Electronic mail
- Enhanced telephone systems

ELECTRONIC TECHNOLOGY

The installation of information technology was initially met with a great deal of scepticism. Many organisations adopted information technology without any serious regard to the uses to which it would be put. However, in recent years, organisations have recognised the need to use information technology and to develop employee skills to handle its functions.

The skills required fall into two main categories – general and specialist skills. We shall look at these in detail first before considering the nature of the electronic technology itself.

1 *General skills.* Nearly all jobs have been affected in some way by the adoption of electronic technology. As a result, most employees must know in general terms how this technology works. Increasingly, technological systems have been integrated via a networking system and are no longer the relatively simple 'stand alone' desktop PC.
2 *Specialist skills.* Approaching one per cent of the working population can now be considered to have specialist technology skills in relation to the use of computers. Specialists will have particular skills in one or more computer functions, and these may include the following:

- word processing
- desk top publishing
- databases
- spreadsheets
- graphics

student activity

As a group, audit the specialist technology skills available between you. How were these skills acquired and are there areas concerning information technology that all of you lack?

As we have said, technology has transformed businesses and as a result many benefits have been enjoyed. These benefits include the following:

- cost reductions
- simplified and efficient workflows
- increased responsiveness to customer needs
- additional job satisfaction
- ability for employees to learn new skills

While the adoption of technology can be seen as a positive step, it is essential that all computers be 'user friendly'. The recent introduction of the Graphical User Interface has allowed technology to be more easily understood by the use of icons. All an operator need do is to use a 'mouse' to 'click' on an icon which, in turn, redraws the screen and offers a new set of options.

The 'windows' system allows the operator to undertake a series of simultaneous tasks by over-writing new screens on to the existing screen. In this way, other files may be perused and referred to and the user may then return to the original document. This system is fast becoming the industry standard.

As we have already mentioned, computer systems enable an individual to carry out the following main tasks. These include:

- the recording of information
- the checking of information
- the sorting and classification of information
- the summarising of data
- the calculation of financial data
- the storage and retrieval of information
- the reproduction of information
- the communication of information to remote terminals

Specifically, these processes are covered by the following:

1 *Word Processing.* The main function of a word processing package is the manipulation, storage and retrieval of text. In addition, a modern word processing system will allow graphics to be inserted into the text and via a database will provide names and addresses for mail shots.
2 *Desktop publishing.* Desktop publishing (DTP) systems have been developed by merging the functions of word processing and graphics packages. On a DTP system the operator has the facility to use a variety of different typefaces, fonts and styles in conjunction with various illustrations. It is possible to produce a very professional document using a DTP package.
3 *Databases.* The storage of information is important to most business organisations. The construction of a database that will provide the information you require needs careful consideration. When constructing a database the designer must know what information will be required from the database and what information needs to be input into the database in order to fulfil these demands.

    The database is capable of producing information in various forms such as bar charts or line graphs. To get the full benefit from a database it is essential to ensure that the information recorded is constantly updated.
4 *Spreadsheets.* The task of a spreadsheet package is to manipulate and organise numbers. Spreadsheets are

used when making calculations and making forecasts. Provided the correct information has been entered into the spreadsheet package, then the computer can calculate a number of useful totals

Through networking and the creation of integrated software packages, an operator is able to access all of these key technological functions simultaneously and gain access to information from the individual terminal and the mainframe computer system.

NETWORKED COMPUTER SYSTEMS

Many organisations will have a number of computers connected to one another so that data may be transferred between terminals. These will take the form of either a LAN system or a WAN system. We shall look at these in some detail.

LAN system (local area network)

A LAN system consists of a number of terminals connected together so that information and functions may be shared. In this respect each terminal can be considered to be a workstation.

Information should be considered a resource and the sharing of this information will provide benefits to all those involved. Users do not have to rely on disk-based updates of information, as the simple inputting of information at one terminal instantly fulfils the task.

LAN systems are protected from external tampering by the use of security mechanisms to ensure that only authorised users can gain access to particular files and functions.

WAN system (wide area network)

This slightly more sophisticated variety of networking enables terminals to be linked in various remote locations in much the same way as a LAN system. In the UK British Telecom provides the majority of land lines connecting terminals in a WAN system. The use of satellites extends WAN systems world-wide. This enables individuals to engage in tele-working as well as providing offices abroad with instant access to the information stored by the parent company.

Major corporations will employ a LAN and a WAN system working together in order to provide a full range of network facilities. Each office will have its own LAN system but be connected with all other offices by a WAN system. They will all have access to the head office's mainframe via the WAN system.

SOFTWARE USED WITHIN PEUGEOT

WINDOWS - Word :- A word processing package used primarily for typed documents.

- Lotus :- A package used for spreadsheets.

- Freelance :- Used primarily to produce OHP's and slides.

The Company is moving steadily towards a total windows environment. Windows and the packages that go with it require modern hardware. Those people who have slightly older machinery use some of the older packages, primarily Displaywrite which is a word processing package and DOS Lotus which is a spreadsheet package. These are increasingly being phased out as the company continues to expand its modern hardware.

Another form of software used by the company are databases. These are used to set up large databanks of information. An example is the Assisted Development Programme (ADP) in which a record is kept of all employees partaking on some sort of course within the scheme. The records holds their names, address, course, cost, date of course and tax paid.

FIG 2.2.13 *A brief summary of software employed by Peugeot Talbot from their detailed information package on information technology.*

Other than the software used above the company is linked up through a mainframe network. A couple of examples of the uses of this are included, these being MEMO an electronic Mail System and Cyborg a Computerised Personnel Information System.

ELECTRONIC MAIL

Electronic mail offers all of the facilities provided by fax and telex, but is paperless. Electronic mail offers the additional advantage of being able to store messages when the destination terminal is busy. Electronic mail systems offer a variety of common features. These include:

- terminals to prepare and store messages
- a communications link with other work stations within the network
- a central controlling computer
- a directory of addresses
- a central mailbox
- a system which dates the message
- a function that notes that the message has been received by the addressee
- a facility to multiple-address so that all members of a particular working group are sent the message simultaneously

It's easy to pick up a Mercury Compatible phone from your local high street retailer.

To help you choose the one which best meets your needs, start by consulting this leaflet.

All the phones featured in this leaflet are Mercury Compatible, which means they have a dedicated Mercury button and display the "Mercury Compatible" symbol.

Mercury Compatible phones enable you to make fast, trouble-free connection to Mercury's network at the convenient touch of a button.

There is a wide range of styles of Mercury Compatible phones available with up-to-the-minute features to choose from at affordable prices. You can buy them from high street retailers – stockists for each phone are listed in this leaflet. Alternatively, you can buy any of them from the Mercury Customer Centre at 67 Theobalds Road, London WC1 (near Holborn Tube). Telephone 071 971 8500 for details of their mail order service.

So... the choice is yours.

FIG 2.2.14 *A page from Mercury Communications''Mercury Compatible Phones' booklet which lists some 30 different enhanced telephone systems.*

- a prioritising system so that messages can be identified as important or routine
- a storage facility in order to keep in the memory those messages that have not yet been received
- compatibility with existing equipment and computer systems

Electronic mail offers a number of advantages in relation to other forms of communication. These include:

- savings on stationery and paper costs
- savings on telephone costs
- rapid transmission
- integration with other systems
- recording of all transmissions so that accurate costings may be obtained
- allowing employees to tele-work
- allowing the addressees to peruse their electronic mail at their leisure

Another version of the electronic mail system may be found in the **electronic data interchange** which enables individuals to exchange business documents using the same communication system.

Electronic diaries and **calendars** are becoming increasingly common and allow individuals to make diary entries and searches on particular days or events, thus avoiding the need manually to enter information in a personal handwritten business diary.

Electronic noticeboards and **Viewdata** now allow a mass of information to be accessed via workstation screens. This is provided in the UK by Prestel and is essentially an interactive system which allows not only the viewing of information but the transmission as well.

student activity

In the role of office services manager, what positive steps could you take to ensure that information within the organisation reached its destination quickly and efficiently?

ENHANCED TELEPHONE SYSTEMS

In recent years modern telephone systems have been developed to provide many new features, including:

- visual display of number dialled
- a redial button
- a secrecy button
- a timer so that the call cost may be estimated
- a memory facility for all regularly dialled numbers
- the day, date and time
- conferencing

Switchboards, too, are much more sophisticated and allow the telephone operator to assess the status of each individual line on the system. It can also identify which extension should be dialled in response to a particular call. Switchboards also have the facility to log calls and record them. This assists in the monitoring of unauthorised personal calls made by employees. The logging itself enables the cost of the call to be attributed to a particular department and its budget.

Cellular phones enable individuals to be contacted in remote locations and important information to be transmitted wherever that individual may be. With regard to car phones in particular, a hand-free system has been developed in order to avoid the perils of telephone use and driving.

An alternative to cellular phones, and in many respects cheaper, is the radio-pager. These enable the individual carrying the radio-pager to be contacted and given a short message or telephone number. Additional facilities available on a radio-pager are:

- using the PABX system (private automatic branch exchange) an individual may be 'bleeped' to inform him or her that there is a message
- multiple radio-pagers may be 'bleeped' simultaneously
- there is a short visual display consisting of either the telephone number to be contacted or brief details of the message

Answering machines have become a vital part of business communication, despite the fact that people are not keen on talking to machines. When the individual called is not available, or when there is no-one to take the message on an extension, then the answering machine can receive the message.

student activity

In the role of a sole trader operating a washing machine repair service, devise a suitable message which could be left on the answering machine.

EVALUATING COMMUNICATION SYSTEMS

In order to evaluate the impact that communication systems have on specific businesses, it is essential that we consider a number of common business measures:

- accuracy of the system
- whether the system creates efficiency
- whether in relation to alternative methods of communication, the system used is cost-effective
- whether the system is secure against unauthorised access

We shall look at each of these in a little more detail:

ACCURACY

We shall be dealing with the subject of **accuracy** in relation to business documents in more detail in Unit 6. However, suffice it to say that it is imperative for all business documentation to be error-free. Communication systems specialists take the view that the reduction in human involvement with the processing of information and communication takes many of the errors out of the processes. If a business can rely on a fool-proof communications system, then the accuracy factor is taken for granted. Others may take a more sceptical view and state that reliance on electronic technology means that humans are less aware of the process, therefore they find it more difficult to identify errors and inaccuracies. The sophistication of systems should mean that to a large extent the systems are totally reliable.

EFFICIENCY

A sophisticated communications system should offer a business greater flexibility and the ability to respond to change and market requirements. With improved communications between remote parts of an organisation a greater interchange of information should occur. The sharing of ideas can be problematic at a more traditional level based on paper. Paper-based filing systems, for example, lack the immediacy of access that can be enjoyed from on-screen systems. A good communications system should also help efficiency in terms of workflow and operations by ensuring that congestion and delays in the interchange of information can be identified and information re-routed by an alternative channel.

With increased efficiency the organisation will receive a useful additional benefit in that it will appear to external organisations to be more responsive and professional.

If the communications system is sufficiently user-friendly then employees will enjoy a more stimulating and satisfying work experience. If employees can be freed from boring and routine tasks then there is more opportunity for them to stretch their talents to the benefit of the organisation. This will, in itself, increase efficiency since fewer employees are involved in mundane duties.

student activity

In the role of the business administration manager of an organisation, list the criteria that you would use in order to assess the accuracy and efficiency of communications systems.

COST-EFFECTIVENESS

Since communications systems have inevitably replaced humans in a variety of job tasks, there is a need to measure the comparative cost-effectiveness of the new and traditional forms of operations. Indeed, in addition to this there is also a need to measure the comparative cost-effectiveness of different systems themselves. Where new systems have been introduced, an organisation may have to defer its measurement of the benefits until employees have been able to learn the new systems thoroughly. In regard to choosing between systems, it is often trial and error that eventually identifies the right system for an organisation. Often it is only after large sums of money have been expended on unsuitable, unusable or near-obsolete systems that an organisation finally reaches the point when it has the correct system for its needs. When we are considering cost-effectiveness we should also refer to the enhanced efficiency of the organisation and consider whether this increase in efficiency has made the system inherently more cost-effective. Obviously, the initial outlay on a new communications system will be large, but organisations tend to take a longer view and look to the future cost-effectiveness that the system will bring. If the communications system can ensure that the right information reaches the right person at the right time, then unnecessary wastage can be avoided, thus contributing to the cost-effectiveness of the business.

SECURITY

Regardless of the nature of the organisation's business activities, there is always a need for certain security measures to be in place. This may simply mean that the organisation does not wish its competitors to know some of the following:

- the names and addresses of its customers
- the discount rates offered
- the credit terms and credit limits of its customers
- the production costs of the organisation
- the distribution arrangements of the organisation
- the current financial status of the organisation

Other organisations may have more sensitive data which need to be transferred throughout the organisation. This is particularly true of organisations involved in financial and credit activities. Perhaps even more sensitive in terms of security are organisations involved in the production of military equipment, for example. In recent years there have been a number of court cases relating to computer 'hackers'. These individuals, extremely adept at breaking their way into organisations' computer systems, have gained access to extremely sensitive information. While in many cases the act of hacking has been simply an intellectual challenge to the individual, in other cases, this has been done for industrial espionage purposes. The communications systems of an organisation are particularly vulnerable to unauthorised access, since they rely upon shared channels which connect computer systems. The widespread use of security codes has gone some way to address this problematic area. Other organisations have installed additional security devices. Of particular note is a system which only allows certain levels of access into the system. Depending upon the individual's security code number, he/she will only be able to gain access to a limited number of levels of the system. This serves a dual purpose in the sense that it disbars junior employees (who may not be security cleared) from accessing information other than that relating to their immediate job role. Additionally, it serves as a back-up security system which means that a potential hacker needs to know about the way in which an individual can gain access to the more sensitive material.

student activity

In the role of the owner of a small business, who stores information regarding customers on a database, list the measures you would take to ensure that only those who need to have access to this information are able to do so.

Investigate information processing systems

I PURPOSES
storing information, distributing information, using information, communicating information

2 INFORMATION PROCESSING SYSTEMS
manual, electronic

3 EVALUATION CRITERIA
security, efficiency, cost-effectiveness

4 DATA PROTECTION ACT
individual rights, access to information, security, usership

5 EFFECTS OF TECHNOLOGY
speed, accuracy, costs, health, skills, access to information

PURPOSES

Information processing systems may be either manual or electronic. They both handle data, processing them in some specific way in order to produce an end goal.

With regard to electronic systems, the processing systems comprise of both hard and software. The information processing system itself is carried out by a program. It is useful to define these three key terms at this point:

I *Hardware*. This describes the physical, mechanical components of the computer system, such as the keyboard, monitor, disk drive(s) and printer(s).

2 *Software*. Software is a predesigned computer package which provides the information and processes by which the hardware can handle particular forms of information. These are also known as programs.

3 *Programs*. As you may have realised, programs are software, but are written in a complex computer language aimed at providing a flexible and fool-proof system by which information may be processed.

Let us now have a look at the particular forms of hardware and how each part of that hardware interrelates with the whole system:

I *Memory*. Often known as RAM (random access memory) it has five specific purposes:

- to store programs being utilised in the processing of data
- to temporarily store the data itself

- to store information awaiting processing
- to store information being processed
- to store information generated as a result of the processing function

2 *The CPU.* The CPU (central processing unit) can be considered to be the real brain of the computer. It performs the following functions:

- monitors current operations
- ensures that all components within the system meet the requirements of the software in use
- carries out arithmetic processing of data
- carries out logical processing of data

3 *Input and Output.* In order for the machine to process data it must be in a form which the machine understands. Computers cannot understand the same language that we speak or write. The computer has to convert all information into a binary language. This information, once it has been translated into the binary language, is known as **input**.

Output essentially translates binary language back into a format which is understandable to us. The computer converts the binary language and displays it, either on the screen or on to paper via a printer.

4 *Backing store.* In order to fulfil many of the functions that are required, the computer must be able to file information. This information may be found in two places:

- *Memory.* It is not practical or desirable to store much information here since it may be destroyed or over-written. Certain computers do not have an inbuilt resident memory and all files stored in memory are destroyed if the computer is turned off.

- *Magnetic disks.* An alternative location for the storage of information is on either magnetic tape or disk. Datafiles can be stored in these locations for retrieval in the future.

We will return to other features of computer systems shortly.

Before we begin to look at the different sorts of computer and features of computer technology, we should begin by looking at the basic uses of information processing systems. We shall also compare the manual against the electronic in each case. The main considerations are:

- the storing of information
- the distribution of information
- the use of information
- the communication of information

Let us look at these individually:

STORING INFORMATION

A useful comparison to make here is the difference between a filing cabinet and a computer storage system. Both have the following features:

- information is stored in a logical manner
- the information is readily retrievable, provided the user is aware of where that information is stored
- a system has been created in order to ensure that the right information goes to the correct place 'in the files'
- it is possible to update and amend information as required
- there is the opportunity to access and duplicate the information when required
- there should be a system by which irrelevant or out-of-date information is 'weeded out' periodically to ensure that the system is not overloaded with irrelevant details

Obviously, the manual version of information storage will require greater physical space. There is also the danger that important documents may be mis-filed or lost. This is also true of computer systems. At a key stroke, a file may be accidentally erased or routed to a location not intended.

FIG 2.3.1 *The Alliance and Leicester's use of advanced information technology has helped the company to offer a high quality service and competitive rates.*

student activity

In groups of three, consider all the ways in which a computer could be beneficial in the storage of information. How would an organisation ensure that there is easy access to this information at all times?

DISTRIBUTING INFORMATION

The common method for distributing information manually is:

- circulation of the relevant files to interested parties
- the duplication of specific documents to individuals
- the attachment of a circulation list which requires the listed individuals to read the document, indicate that they have done so, then pass it on to the next person on the list. This method is called 'routing'
- the physical distribution of material via internal or external mailing

The common method for distributing information electronically is:

- if the organisation is using a network system, then the distribution of information may be carried out using electronic mail
- if the organisation is using a less sophisticated form of computer system, then the information may be distributed using magnetic tape or disks
- if the organisation prefers a mixture of both electronic and manual distribution, then the information may be printed on to paper then distributed in the conventional manner

USING INFORMATION

A manual system can suffer from the restrictions of there being only one file in existence. This means that only one individual may have access to this file at a time. A way around this problem is to duplicate the file so that all interested parties may gain access to a copy simultaneously. However, this simply adds to the paper mountain and adds considerably to the overall storage problems. Certain computer systems can suffer from the same problems. Unsophisticated computer systems may only allow a single user access to a file at a particular time. Equally, if the system is disk-based, then access to the relevant files relies on a number of disk copies being made. With this system, there is always the danger of a file being updated by a particular user, while all other users are dealing with out-of-date information.

COMMUNICATING INFORMATION

As we mentioned earlier in this Unit, there is a wide variety of communication systems. Some of the manual systems do have their advantages in as much as they are, to a large extent, *personal* communication processes. Computer communication systems can suffer from being impersonal and give a sense of isolation to the user. Whether the information being communicated to a particular individual is routed via a manual or electronic system, there is still no guarantee that the individual will read or take note of the information. To date, there has been no system designed to ensure that the recipient does respond to information given. Certain computer systems will, however, require the recipient to acknowledge receipt of the information, but this is really no more sophisticated than ticking a circulation list.

INFORMATION PROCESSING SYSTEMS

Many organisations have skilfully avoided the computer revolution and are still grounded in conventional manual methods of information processing. Many other organisations actually prefer the 'personal touch' which manual systems offer both internally and to their customers. The benefits which may accrue from the implementation of computer systems is undeniable, but is largely dependent upon the nature of the business activity. Precisely what the business needs to do determines whether it decides to install electronic systems.

Many of the manual systems are better described in Unit 6, so we shall be concentrating on the electronic information processing systems in this section of the Unit.

We shall begin by looking at some specific information processing equipment and methods:

DISPLAYS

Commonly, a display is the viewing screen. Normally, the viewing screen or VDU (visual display unit) will show a combination of text and graphics. Depending on the screen resolution (in other words, the sharpness or clarity of the monitor), the viewer will be able to see various images made up of pixels (picture elements). The more pixels there are on the screen, the better the quality of picture.

KEYBOARDS AND ALTERNATIVES

The keyboard is perhaps the most common, but not necessarily the most convenient, method of inputting

FIG 2.3.2 *Barclays Computer Operations was formed to provide services to the commercial market and boasts some of the most sophisticated computer technology in the UK. Its operations are extremely highly thought of by customers and its customer service teams have recently gained BS 5750.*

information into the system. A keyboard will be touch-sensitive and arranged in a standard QWERTY format. There are a number of alternatives to the keyboard however. These include:

- *Mouse* – a hand-held device which is used to move the cursor around the screen. Clicks on the mouse allow the user to perform various functions from on-screen icons or text.
- *Joystick* – commonly used in computer games, these operate in a similar manner to a mouse. However, they are slightly more sophisticated in the sense that they allow greater flexibility in terms of angles of movement.
- *Light pen* – this is a photo-electric or light-sensitive device which interacts with the screen once touched. A light pen is particularly useful in computer aided design (CAD).
- *Touch screen* – this is a logical extension of the light pen but allows the user to interact with the screen by the use of his/her finger.

PRINTERS

There is a wide diversity of printer types available. They are usually identified by use of the following criteria:

- speed
- quality of print
- impact
- non-impact

Specifically, printers may be identified as being one of the following:

- impact dot-matrix printers
- line printers
- thermal printers
- electro-sensitive printers
- laser printers
- ink-jet printers

DATA CAPTURE EQUIPMENT

As we have already mentioned, most information is normally originally formatted in a manner in which humans can read it. Computers need to be able to 'read' this information and to transform it into their own binary language. The principal devices that have been designed to capture information, in other words to allow the computer access to this information, include the following:

- *optical character readers* – which are able to read stylised characters also readable by humans
- *optical mark readers* – which enable the computer to read marks in pre-set positions, such as multiple choice or market research questionnaires
- *bar code readers* – commonly found in many shops, which enable the computer to read via a light pen or laser scanner
- *magnetic ink character readers* – commonly used for sorting and processing cheques. These are very stylised characters, printed in ink containing iron
- *digitisers* – which automatically transform graphics in particular into a binary format on the screen
- *voice recognition devices* – this relatively new system allows the computer to understand simple words and phrases and interpret them as commands.

SOFTWARE

The processes by which computer systems handle information can be categorised under the following headings:

- word processing
- spreadsheets
- databases
- graphics packages
- accounts packages
- sales packages
- invoicing packages
- stock control packages
- desktop publishing
- computer aided design and manufacture
- management information systems

We shall now look at each of these in a little more detail:

Word processing

Essentially, a **word processor** is a computer with a keyboard used for entering text. Word processors may thus be used for all forms of business documentation. They have a number of advantages over the manual system (typewriters):

- it is comparatively easy to identify and correct typing errors (there is usually a spell-checking facility available)
- page numbering may be available automatically
- an instant word count may be available
- the document may be edited and re-edited, particularly useful when sending a similar letter to various addressees
- multiple copies may be made
- all printed copies are of the same quality
- documents may be saved for future reference or use
- a line-draw facility may be available to aid the ruling of tabulated work
- a wide variety of print styles and character fonts is available

Spreadsheets

Spreadsheets are designed to manipulate numerical data. Spreadsheet programs consist of the following:

- a number of cells – each of these cells may be labelled to perform a particular function
- the cell may be a number or text or a formula
- calculations may be made, provided the spreadsheet has been pre-designed to perform a particular function

Spreadsheets are particularly useful in the displaying of numerical data. A good example of the use of a spreadsheet would be in the updating of a football league table, when the spreadsheet has been organised in such a manner that:

- results of football matches are inputted
- the spreadsheet updates the league table by allocating the appropriate number of points to each team
- the spreadsheet then re-sorts the league after each football result has been entered

Spreadsheets offer a number of advantages over their manual counterparts. These are:

- they are designed to be easy to learn and use
- they have a wide variety of uses
- they are comparatively cheap
- they can be personalised for each organisation
- they have been 'debugged' and tested

However, spreadsheets need to be carefully designed prior to use and may suffer from incorrect design features which fail to show the correct information in an appropriate format.

Databases

Databases can be used for a variety of purposes as we have already mentioned. A typical database will offer at least the following facilities:

- a personally definable recording format
- a personally definable input format
- file searching facilities
- file sorting facilities
- spreadsheet style calculations
- integration with word processing packages to enable a variety of report formats to be outputted

Graphics packages

Graphics packages are a great aid to graphic designers. Rather than use pens or brushes the artist may use a light pen to produce professional graphics material in a short period of time. A graphics package will contain many of the following features:

- the ability to draw geometric shapes
- a comprehensive range of colours
- the ability to fill areas with colours
- the ability to fill areas with patterns
- the ability to move designs around the screen
- the ability to copy designs
- the ability to delete or save designs
- a wide variety of character fonts

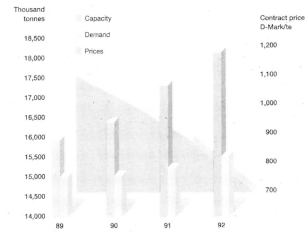

FIG 2.3.3 *A detail from BP's Annual Report and Accounts Report 1992 showing their use of computer software in the presentation of statistics.*

- access to a 'library' of pre-drawn graphics known as clip-art
- the ability to print the finished graphic design

Graphics packages are commonly used in business not only for their artistic capabilities, but also to produce charts, graphs and diagrams.

Desktop publishing

Desktop publishing packages combine the abilities of graphics and word processing packages. They enable the user to produce professional documents, books, posters and articles.

Desktop publishing packages will have a number of facilities available, such as:

- the ability to import text from a word processing package

- the ability to produce text in many fonts and sizes
- the ability to organise text in column form
- the ability to import graphics from other packages
- the ability to 'scan in' (digitally read) pictures and illustrations and convert them to an appropriate size and shape
- the production of various geometric patterns
- the merging of text, graphics and illustrations

Accounts packages

Accounts packages offer the user a variety of different facilities. These include:

- payroll systems which produce payslips and maintain employee records
- sales accounts which maintain records of debits and credits. These packages also give details of orders

GROUP PROFIT AND LOSS ACCOUNT

52 weeks ended 27th February 1993 (1992 – 53 weeks)	Note	1993 £m	1992 £m
Sales at net selling prices		8,128.5	7,595.6
Value added tax		547.0	498.2
Turnover excluding value added tax		7,581.5	7,097.4
Cost of sales	1	6,849.0	6,435.9
Gross profit		732.5	661.5
Administration expenses		155.3	158.2
Operating profit	1	577.2	503.3
Net (loss)/surplus on sale of properties	1	(2.3)	0.5
Interest receivable less payable	3	31.5	65.5
Profit after interest		606.4	569.3
Employee profit sharing	4	25.5	23.8
Profit on ordinary activities before taxation		580.9	545.5
Tax on profit on ordinary activities	5	163.3	149.9
Profit for the financial year		417.6	395.6
Dividends	6	138.7	122.3
Retained profit for the financial year	20	278.9	273.3
		pence	pence
Earnings per share	7	21.45	20.43
Adjustment for loss/(surplus) on sale of properties		0.12	(0.02)
Adjusted earnings per share excluding (loss)/surplus on sale of properties	7	21.57	20.41
Fully diluted earnings per share	7	20.86	19.97
Adjustment for loss/(surplus) on sale of properties		0.11	(0.02)
Adjusted fully diluted earnings per share excluding (loss)/surplus on sale of properties	7	20.97	19.95
Dividends per share	6	7.10	6.30

All group operations for the financial year are continuing.

FIG 2.3.4 *Tesco PLC Profit and Loss Account for the period ending 27 February 1993.*

made and received. In addition, they provide a credit control system

- purchasing accounts which provides a similar service in relation to organisations' buying needs
- general ledgers which maintain and update financial summaries and will automatically produce the following:

  - trial balances
  - trade and profit and loss accounts
  - balance sheets

Stock control packages

A balanced stock control system is imperative to most organisations and these packages should alert the organisation to the following:

- quantities of products stored
- prices of products
- minimum stock levels
- reorder levels

A good stock control system will also provide a warning to management as to when there are excessively high stock levels of a particular product in the warehouse.

Sales

A sales order processing system should provide the following facilities to the organisation:

- order validation
- order checking
- cross-check with customer's credit status
- production of a picking list for the warehouse
- back order monitoring so that orders which were not fulfilled in the past may be fulfilled when the item comes into stock

Invoicing

This may often be part of a larger computer package. In some cases a separate invoicing software package may be employed. The main function of this package is to:

- store customer details
- produce invoices from orders
- assign codes to each product ordered
- provide integration facilities with sales and accounts packages

Computer aided design and manufacture

Computer aided design is a very flexible and quick

system which enables the user to design complex items such as:

- cars
- ships
- buildings
- clothes
- machinery

Computer aided design is essentially a highly sophisticated graphics package which understands the requirements and specifications relating to the item being designed.

Computer aided design requires complex calculations to be made and may only be satisfactorily used on powerful computers.

Computer aided manufacture (CAM), as the title suggests, is involved in the actual manufacturing process. It can control the following:

- automated production lines
- robots
- manufacturing systems
- process control

Organisations often use an integrated CAD/CAM system which allows the CAD produced design to be relayed straight to the production line where the process is monitored by the CAM system.

Management information systems

Management information systems offer a number of features to the organisation:

- they can produce information of a sophisticated nature
- they can provide information at a crucial period of decision making
- they can aid the decision making process
- they can process information stored in databases

Essentially, an MIS system should assist managers in making decisions by allowing them access to hitherto unobtainable forms of data.

student activity

What would you expect to find in a management information system and how would you make the best use of its abilities and functions?

EVALUATION OF INFORMATION PROCESSING SYSTEMS

Just how effective an information processing system is in relation to an organisation's business activities can be measured in terms of the following:

- **Security** – whether the system is secure both as far as the business is concerned, and in terms of its compliance with the requirements of the Data Protection Act.
- Whether the system is **efficient** in terms of its collection, processing and storage of information.
- Whether the system is **cost-effective** in the sense of suitability for its purpose and whether all the features of the package have been fully implemented.

We shall look at these three key considerations in some detail.

SECURITY

A good information processing system should provide a range of controls in order to enable it to carry out its functions efficiently and in a secure manner. These are:

- prevent loss of information through software error
- prevent loss of information through procedural errors such as incorrect key strokes
- prevent loss of information as a result of accidental hazards such as loss of power
- protection of all information from being disclosed to unauthorised individuals
- protection of all information from accidental modification
- protection of all information from deliberate corruption
- restriction of access to this information

In certain circumstances, which are often beyond the control of the organisation itself, files may suffer permanent or temporary damage. These hazards are:

- fire
- flood
- mechanical malfunction
- programming errors
- human error
- malicious damage

Most organisations will ensure that they have back-up files housed in secure locations which can be loaded back into the system should the master files be damaged.

We shall deal in the next section with the provisions of the Data Protection Act 1984 as they relate to information processing systems.

EFFICIENCY AND COST-EFFECTIVENESS

Just how efficient an information processing system is may be dependent upon the way in which the system was originally designed. This can be a slightly more complex consideration, and includes the following:

- how the components of the information processing system were selected
- whether they fit the purpose of the information processing system itself
- how the information processing system interrelates with the administrative procedures required to operate the system
- whether the information processing system is backed up by a sufficiently powerful computer to run it. If the computer is not sufficiently powerful, users may experience reduced response times as the computer desperately tries to handle the complex system
- whether the system fits the purpose for which it was purchased. If the system was designed to handle a lower level of business activity than the organisation is now experiencing, then it may find difficulties in handling all the information it is required to process
- the implementation of the system itself may be acceptable on a mechanical level, but, the users of the system may not be trained sufficiently and would be thus unable to operate it efficiently

In terms of cost-effectiveness, the basic equation is that the cost of the system should be less than the value of the information it produces. When one considers the costs of adopting an information processing system, one must include the following:

- hardware costs
- software costs
- maintenance costs
- specialist staff costs
- training costs
- insurance costs
- security systems instalment costs
- the costs of providing the necessary legal working environments for such equipment

student activity

In pairs, consider the circumstances in which an organisation may find that manual systems of communication and information storage are more preferable to electronic methods.

DATA PROTECTION ACT

Most organisations keep detailed records which may include the following:

- customers' names and addresses
- customer transactions
- customer credit information
- specific information regarding customers, such as their political affiliations (in recent years certain high street banks have admitted that they keep details of customers' political allegiances)
- staff records
- personal information regarding employees' domestic situations
- disciplinary action taken against employees

Organisations obviously store a great deal more information than this, but the Data Protection Act relates specifically to the way in which this information is used. The Act attempts to prevent this information being used to harm an individual. The Act requires all organisations or individuals who hold personal details regarding other individuals on computer to register with the Data Protection Registrar. If an organisation or individual fails to do this, then they may be fined up to £2,000.

The Registrar needs to know the following:

- what sort of information is held
- what use is made of the information
- who else has access to this information
- what methods were used to collect the information

The Registrar must ensure that the data conforms with the Act. Specifically this means that the Registrar must ensure that the information complies with the codes given below:

- that the information has been collected in an open and fair manner
- that the information is only held for lawful purposes
- that the uses to which the information is put are disclosed to the Registrar
- that the information held is relevant to the purpose for which it is held
- that the information is accurate

- that the information is up to date
- that any irrelevant or inaccurate information is destroyed
- that individuals can be told about the existence of the information
- that individuals can challenge inaccurate information
- that the information is kept confidential
- that the organisation takes steps to ensure that unauthorised access is avoided

student activity

Consider, from a personal point of view, the Data Protection Act and try to assess the range and amount of information which may be stored by organisations concerning you.

INDIVIDUAL RIGHTS AND ACCESS TO INFORMATION

As you will have seen from the list above, an individual about whom an organisation has information stored, does have specific rights. These include:

- access to that information
- the right to challenge inaccurate information

If an organisation fails to comply with the Data Protection Act in this respect, then the individual affected has a right to be compensated.

There are some exceptions to this. These are:

- where the individual has supplied the information him/herself
- where the organisation has taken all 'reasonable care' to acquire the information
- where the information relates to payroll matters
- where the information relates to pension details
- where the information is used only for statistical purposes and, in addition, it does not specifically identify individuals

SECURITY

As with any data storage facility, the organisation will take steps to ensure that unauthorised access is avoided. The Data Protection Act, however, makes this a legal requirement and therefore, unauthorised access can mean fines for the organisation which has suffered the breach of security. The sensitivity of some of the material stored is such that it could be used for criminal or other unlawful purposes by an unauthorised entrant. The sensitivity of the information is further heightened by the fact that the individual whose information is stored in the system may be unaware that it is actually there. If unauthorised entry is gained and this information is used by others, then the individual may suffer as a result.

USERSHIP

The Data Protection Act attempts to ensure that stored information is only put to specific lawful purposes. While it is difficult to maintain this degree of certainty about the usership of the information, most organisations tend to use stored information for its specifically stated purpose only. Problems will inevitably arise when there is an interchange of this information between different organisations. The organisation which initially collected the data may have had a specific purpose in mind. However, the organisation which has acquired the information may have different motives altogether. The transmission of sensitive information from one organisation to another can pose considerable problems both to the individual and to the Data Protection Registrar. In particular, information stored regarding an individual's creditworthiness may include a number of inaccuracies which have not been identified. If the individual subsequently discovers that inaccuracies have been made then it is a difficult task to trace the transmission and use of the original inaccurate information in order to ensure that all information stored at whatever location is, indeed, accurate.

EFFECTS OF TECHNOLOGY

The overall costs and benefits of adopting an information processing system can effectively be measured in both strict **financial terms** and additional considerations such as **working conditions** and **job satisfaction**. We will look at the main costs and benefits relating to the installation of information processing systems below.

SPEED AND ACCURACY

Speed in this respect refers to the organisation's ability to respond in an efficient and appropriate manner in a short period of time. It does not necessarily follow that the installation of information processing systems should in itself achieve this. **Accuracy** refers to error-free processing of information but, as we have seen already, the system is only as good as its original designer and the operators using it.

COSTS

Costs take many forms, both those which are immediately tangible, e.g. purchasing costs, and those which are far more difficult to quantify. Here is a list of the main costs that may be incurred both – financial and otherwise:

- hardware purchases
- software purchases
- hardware and software installation costs
- additional insurance to cover potential damage to equipment and information
- a maintenance contract, which is essential to ensure that both the hardware and software are regularly inspected
- an allowance for depreciation of the equipment and its eventual replacement
- the cost of necessary changes to lighting

- the installation of window blinds
- the provision of air conditioning in the room which houses the mainframe computer
- the possible need to acquire alternative premises to house some or all of the computer systems
- the payment of any additional specialist staff who are needed
- consumables such as tapes or disks

Benefits

Although improved efficiency may be seen as a primary goal in using information processing systems, it is not necessarily an automatic **benefit**. The system is only as good as its operators.

The installation of information processing systems should ensure that resources are better controlled and financial controls more stringent, but again these benefits are not automatic.

Productivity should improve as a result of the installation of information processing systems, by allowing the organisation to expand without necessarily taking on more staff.

student activity

Carry out an audit of the institution in which you are undertaking this course and assess their implementation of measures to ensure that electronic technology is being used to its best effect.

HEALTH

By referring to Unit 5, you will see a number of pieces of legislation which refer directly to the installation and use of computer systems. Below are some general points concerning health and safety:

- health and safety regulations must be adhered to
- regular breaks will need to be given to operators
- additional planning may be necessary to ensure that there are sufficient operators available to run machines during the working day
- an office environment which relies on the use of computer information processing systems should find itself to be a more clean and efficient working environment
- equally, on the factory floor, a production line which relies on a CAD/CAM system should be less dangerous and potentially hazardous to employees

SKILLS

Obviously, the need to offer skills training is essential to ensure the efficient use of information processing systems. In addition, there are a number of problems arising out of new skills demands; these are:

- training will need to be given in the use of new hardware, software and systems
- it may be necessary to redeploy certain members of staff
- it may be necessary to make certain members of staff redundant
- employees who presently lack appropriate computer skills may feel at risk
- certain job tasks will suffer from de-skilling
- while some jobs may suffer from de-skilling, there is a general trend after the implementation of information processing systems for most individuals to feel more satisfied with their jobs. They have been freed from the tedium of many tasks

ACCESS TO INFORMATION

Access to information – while beneficial in many situations – can also present a number of problems. Here are some of the advantages and disadvantages of enhanced access to information:

- there is a greater opportunity for fraud to be perpetrated as it is easy to hide such fraud within the processing systems
- in order to ensure that the main frame is protected from unauthorised access, a secure room must be provided
- security systems will need to be put in place to make sure that the hardware and software are safe from unauthorised tampering
- to comply with the Data Protection Act, the organisation must ensure that measures are taken to keep the information confidential and secure
- with clear operational procedures which are aimed at restricting access to information, a computer information processing system should be more secure than its traditional counterpart
- there is an opportunity for individuals within the organisation to readily share information
- as a result of the above point, decision making at all levels should be enhanced

UNIT 2

a s s i g n m e n t

'ADMINISTRATION, COMMUNICATION AND INFORMATION'

In order to fulfil the criteria and provide evidence for this Unit, you will be required to look at the three main uses of electronic technology.

In the role of an Administration Manager of a Limited Company, you have been given a total budget of £30,000 in order to purchase the necessary computer equipment and software to provide a range of support services to the organisation.

You must research the available equipment and software on the market in order to provide the following:

- information processing
- data storage
- internal communications
- financial recording, monitoring and control
- document production
- general administration back-up systems.

You should justify your choices in terms of their:

- accuracy
- efficiency
- speed
- costs
- cost-effectiveness
- security
- health implications
- skills required
- access

You should present your findings in a word processed report for the attention of the Board of Directors.

UNIT 2

t e s t   q u e s t i o n s

1   An agenda shows:

(a)   Items for discussion
(b)   Company policy
(c)   Directors' reports
(d)   A record of discussions undertaken.

2   Minutes of a meeting show:

(a)   Items for discussion
(b)   Company policy
(c)   Directors' reports
(d)   A record of discussions undertaken.

3   Which of the following is not used for internal communication?

(a)   Telephone
(b)   Letter
(c)   Memo
(d)   Report.

4   Which of the following forms of communication have revolutionised business communication in recent years?

(a)   In-house magazines
(b)   Memos
(c)   Facsimile machines
(d)   Letters.

5   In an electronic office, which of the following would not normally appear?

(a)   A word processor
(b)   A photocopier
(c)   Electronic mail systems
(d)   Pocket calculators.

6   Which of the following computer software packages is designed to manipulate figures or numerical data?

(a)   Word processing
(b)   Spreadsheets
(c)   Databases
(d)   Desktop publishing.

7 The best description of a database is:

(a) An ideal method of sending messages
(b) The best system to calculate the organisation's turnover
(c) An information storage system
(d) A software package which can deal with numerical calculations.

8 A LAN is:

(a) A network computer system
(b) A form of information processing package
(c) An enhanced telephone system
(d) An aspect of the Companies Act.

9 NVCs are:

(a) Non-viable competitors
(b) A network computer system
(c) Non-verbal communications
(d) Non-vocational courses.

10 VAT is not applicable to one of the below; which is it?

(a) Cars
(b) Petrol
(c) Televisions
(d) Books.

ELEMENT 3.1

Analyse market research

1 SOURCES OF INFORMATION
experts, general public, primary and secondary data

2 RESEARCH METHODS
postal questionnaires, interviews, telecommunications

3 CRITERIA FOR SELECTION OF RESEARCH METHODS
time, cost, speed, accuracy, ease of use

4 RESEARCH INSTRUMENTS
closed questions, open questions, interview schedules, monitoring

5 ANALYSIS
statistical techniques, trend analysis, qualitative techniques

SOURCES OF INFORMATION

Millions of pounds are spent on marketing research in the UK alone each year. Nearly 10 per cent of what you spend in the shops ends up being spent on marketing research in one guise or another. Let's try to define it:

> Market research is the systematic collection and analysis of data which looks specifically at the customer's attitudes, needs, opinions, and motivations within the context of political, economic and social influences.

Simply put, marketing research is using **scientific** methods to collect **information** that is **relevant** to the product or service in question. Scientific? What information? Relevant?

In order to reduce risk a company needs to know about the intended market for the product it is going to launch. Market research refers to the research into markets specifically, but strictly speaking, marketing research refers to any aspect of the marketing process that requires investigation.

Marketing research covers the obvious markets, but also what we noted in our first definition. Broadly speaking there are three main sources of information that the marketing researcher is interested in:

1 Information within the company which already exists but which may not be in a particularly usable form.

2 Information external to the company which again already exists and is much more expensive to track down.

3 Information which may or may not be within the company, and is usually external to the company, but which does not exist in a usable form at all. Commonly this information is customer opinion, attitude or buying traits.

We can further identify these types of information and categorise them in a more simple way:

1 Information within the company, such as sales figures, is known as **internal information**.
2 Information external to the company, such as government reports or published marketing reports, is known as **secondary information**.
3 The third information source, often characterised by market research opinion polls, is known as **primary information**

Marketing research makes a positive contribution to a business by helping in the decision-making process. There are many different types of marketing research. Here are the main ones:

1 Market and sales research:

- estimating market size of new markets
- estimating potential growth of an existing market
- identifying market characteristics and segments
- identifying market trends
- sales forecasting
- collecting data on existing customers
- collecting data on potential customers
- collecting data on competitors

2 Product research:

- customers' attitude to new products
- comparing competition with own products
- finding alternative uses for existing products
- market testing proposed products
- investigating customer complaints
- packaging research
- generating new ideas for new products

3 Research on promotion and advertising:

- choosing the right advertising medium
- analysing effectiveness of advertising
- establishing sales areas
- evaluating present sales techniques
- analysing sales force effectiveness
- establishing sales quotas

4 Distribution research:

- location of distribution centres
- handling products (efficiency)
- transport costs and comparisons
- storage efficiency and needs
- retail outlet location

5 Pricing policy:

- demand
- perceived price
- costs
- margins

The scope of marketing and market research is very broad. In fact almost every aspect of the production, promotion, sales and after sales life of a product is scrutinised at some point for one particular purpose or another.

PRIMARY DATA

Information systems, if set up correctly, should channel useful information to the marketing department of the company. A marketing information system worth anything should only pass on the useful information and should sift out the irrelevant. There are four facets of information that are useful and should make up the elements of a marketing information system:

1 **Internal accounting** – which reports orders, sales, stock, incoming cash and outgoing cash.
2 **Marketing intelligence** – a firm set of procedures that ensures that information on new developments that may affect the business is collected and collated.
3 **Marketing research** – systematic collection and analysis of information useful to the decision makers of the company.
4 **Analytical marketing** – a system that analyses relevant marketing data in a scientific manner.

SECONDARY DATA – EXPERT AND GENERAL PUBLIC

Before an organisation goes to the expense of paying for primary research it is prudent to look at what information is already available. Surprisingly, whatever the subject, there will be something. Secondary data, which are either already in existence under your noses but not in the right format, or readily available from somewhere else are a great deal cheaper than starting from scratch.

Published data which are available in most good commercial reference libraries, and often in the main libraries in larger towns, include some of the more obvious (and weighty) tomes as well as some seemingly rather boring and starchy items. In the book line there are titles like *Regional Trends* or the *General Household Survey*, *Datastream* is a computer database facility and *Prestel* can be accessed via a TV with an adaptor. Other sources are local chambers of commerce, which have good libraries and links and leads to other sources of information.

RESEARCH METHODS

When secondary data cannot provide you with the information that you need, you are left with no choice but to get the information for yourself. This is also known as 'field' research as the information that you want is actually out there somewhere in the market waiting for you to get at it. There are four main methods of research;

1 the personal interview
2 the telephone interview
3 the postal survey
4 the panel.

The choice depends on many different variables, which include the following considerations:

1 Your budget.
2 Time available; some of the above will obviously take longer to complete than others.
3 Accuracy needed, crudely the more accurate the more expensive. You pays your money, you takes your choice!
4 Who do you want to survey? Consider basic problems like literacy or reluctance in putting 'private' thoughts on paper.
5 Where are the people you want to survey? They could be scattered across the country (like a magazine's readership) or concentrated (like the users of a local amenity).

Let's now look at the four main types and try to identify the advantages and disadvantages of them:

The personal interview

This is a very common method of gathering research information. The interviewer can select the 'victim' and question him or her face to face. The most frequently used method is to ask questions from a formally struc-tured questionnaire – often with a predetermined range of answers.

Here are the advantages:

- high response rate due to choosing the respondent each time
- a fairly low rate of refusal to answer
- if structured well the questionnaire is easy to analyse
- misunderstood questions can be explained
- deliberate 'wrong' answers can be eliminated easily
- additional information can be noted without asking the respondent (e.g. age or sex)
- answers are not considered, they are immediate and probably more truthful
- you can ask reasonably personal questions
- because the respondent does not have to read the questionnaire it can be longer and more involved

There are several disadvantages though:

- the cost is high as you will have to pay for the inter-viewer's time
- there may be interviewer bias in noting down the answers; after all some answers may have to be inter-preted by the interviewer
- there may be some inaccuracies if the respondent is in a hurry to leave and will just say anything to get it over with
- interviewers will need to be selected and trained before they can begin the task
- speed of collection is related directly to length of the questionnaire and the availability of appropriate respondents

The telephone interview

This method is very popular in the United States, but very prone to a low response rate due to people's reluc-tance to be canvassed for information on the telephone.

It is, after all, an invasion of privacy, although the person can always hang up! Otherwise the technique is almost identical to face-to-face interviewing where the interviewer goes through a set questionnaire and notes down the answers.

These are the advantages:

- it is a very quick way of getting through a good many interviews
- the interviewers need only be in one place, and can be supervised easily
- costs are lower than for personal interviews
- the sample can be spread across the country without incurring high travel costs
- you can access those who are hard to track down by other means

The disadvantages are:

- you cannot get to people who do not have a telephone
- without asking you cannot tell age or social class
- you will inevitably annoy people by phoning at the wrong time of the day
- it is harder to get the attention of the respondent
- how can you prove who you are and what you really want?
- ex-directory subscribers are not accessible

The postal survey

Accompanied by a letter, these surveys are sent to a sample of the population in the hope that they may return them answered. Often a second letter is sent after a period of time to remind the chosen sample to fill in the questionnaire. These questionnaires are often found in magazines and are tied to a particular company which will offer discounts or a small free gift as an incentive for filling in the questionnaire. Above all the questionnaire must be straightforward and easy to fill in otherwise the respondent will not bother to do it.

The advantages of this system are:

- you can reach a wide sample of the population
- much cheaper than the personal interview
- no field expenses
- no training of interviewers
- no bias from the interviewer
- easier to reach harder groups, e.g. readers of specialist magazines etc.
- the sample is not rushed to fill in the questionnaire and may choose to consider answers more

There are, however, quite a number of disadvantages:

- it is unlikely that the sample will be representative. You will only get responses back from those who have bothered to fill them in.
- the refusal rate is high. Response will definitely depend on how easy the questionnaire is to fill in

- there is a strong possibility that questions may be misunderstood
- questions need to be highly structured, giving less scope for additional information
- mailing lists are expensive to keep up to date, they are very labour intensive
- plenty of time should be put aside for a slow trickle of replies over the weeks
- personal questions should be avoided as these may stop respondents from filling in the questionnaire
- the answers may not come from the person that the questionnaire was intended for. The respondent may be a different person or he or she may have asked the opinion of someone else

The panel

This information-gathering technique relies on asking the same people a range of questions over a period of time. This method is often used to check on changing attitudes for example. There are three main types of panel, the first of which is the **consumer purchasing** panel, where data are collected by a number of methods and which looks at customers' purchases and attitudes to particular products or types of product, such as washing powder or toothpaste. The second type is the **test** panel, where a group of people are asked to 'field test' new products as they come out; this is particularly useful in the household product line or specialist equipment such as hospital products. Finally, and this is where audience figures for TV and radio come from, is the **audience** panel. Here viewing patterns are looked at, both individually and as members of families.

Geographically, the respondents can be anywhere and you can ask very detailed questions and expect intelligent and useful responses.

These are the advantages:

- good trend indicator
- you can analyse changes and adjust them according to external factors that have influenced them
- you can collect very detailed information about the habits and attitudes of individuals which is very valuable background information

There are some disadvantages, of course:

- the panel can be easily upset by deaths or by panellists moving away from an area
- you are likely to attract the more intelligent as panellists and miss out on the less intelligent and this may affect your sample
- the panellists may adopt uncharacteristic behaviour as they know you are 'watching' them
- it is expensive to recruit panellists in the beginning
- you will continually have to replace lost panellists
- you will have to reward the panellists in some way, however small

student activity

Which of the above techniques would you use for the following research problem, and why? Note down the advantages and disadvantages of the choice that you have made and compare these with the advantages and disadvantages of the other techniques.

Research young women's attitudes to the types of advertising that are directed towards them.

CRITERIA FOR SELECTION OF RESEARCH METHODS

Having decided that you desperately need some marketing research done you now have a choice. You could get your own people to do it for you, or you might decide that it would be better to get in a professional organisation to do it for you. Before we look at the pros and cons of hiring an outside marketing research agency against the 'do it yourself' option we should say something about how you know whether an agency is bona fide or not

The Market Research Society (the MRS) was founded in the late 1940s and is the professional body for market researchers in Britain. Its name flies in the face of what we have already said in that market research is just a part of marketing research, but the society was established simply for market researchers and has, over the years, opened its doors to a wider membership.

The Industrial Marketing Research Association, better known as IMRA, in association with the Market Research Society has published a code of conduct which attempts to lay down the ground rules of market research. It specifically attempts to protect the interviewee from unscrupulous researchers who are trying to use the camouflage of market research as a sales technique. It further warns that researchers should not try to get the response they want by influencing the interviewee, neither should the person interviewed be bombarded by junk mail as a result of being put on someone's mailing list. Market research should not be used to get people to divulge private information about an individual or to let out industrial secrets.

Having laid down these rules the two organisations can only hope that their members do follow them. Indeed the vast majority do, though some companies, but not the better-known ones, give market research a bad name. Have you ever been stopped in the street and asked your opinion only to discover that the questioner wants to sell you insurance? Ever been called to the front door and asked about energy saving and to your horror, after twenty minutes of pleasant banter, found that the person sitting in your front room with a cup of your tea is a double glazing salesperson! The big companies, of course, do not resort to these underhand methods of getting your attention, but they can get tarred by the same brush. It gives them a bad name, let's be honest, wouldn't you slam the door in the face of a poor double glazing salesperson? Or a stone-cladder? Perhaps our reaction to them is a deeper and more complicated fear or loathing?

In order to protect legitimate researchers, the MRS supplies them with identification cards, but would you know one if you saw one? Fake researchers can easily claim that the letter they are showing you establishes their credentials and that the information you give them will not be used for any other purpose except market research. It is a difficult and potentially damaging problem and there does not seem to be a readily workable solution.

student activity

What are the pros and cons of carrying out research yourself?

TIME, COST, SPEED, ACCURACY AND EASE OF USE

What then of the argument about using insiders or outsiders? There are six main areas of consideration, not all of them necessarily relevant to each case but several will be important each time. The first area of consideration is that of **cost**. An obvious thought really, as it is clearly more expensive to 'buy in' help from outside than to use your own staff. But what about the cost of using people from within your organisation? If they carry out the research they can't do their normal work. Is there a cost to the organisation if they fail to do this work?

Secondly there is the question of **expertise**. Do your own people have the skills needed? Some research techniques are fairly basic and do not require a great deal of skill or experience, but some are quite sophisticated. Similarly, the analysis of the data needs to be carried out by the right person. Perhaps the analysis is beyond your immediately available skills.

On the other hand, **knowledge** of the product or service is much more likely to be the domain of your insiders. You would have to teach the outside organisation about you, your company and your products or services. This is both time-consuming and expensive.

It follows from what we have said above about 'in house' people and their knowledge of the company and what it is about, that they may be too close. The question of **objectivity** is important. Conclusions drawn from the research may be unconsciously biased and tainted by their own preconceived ideas and prejudices.

The question of equipment, more commonly called **resources**, is another key factor. Specialist computer programs or particular testing equipment may be needed as may the ability to sample people in different parts of the country. It may not prove possible or economically viable to train your own people to use specialist equipment or indeed to buy what you need just for this one exercise.

Finally, and by no means less importantly, there is the question of **confidentiality**. No matter who you use, once information about a new product or process leaves the confines of your own company and direct control there will be a nagging feeling about its safety. In most cases the fear is irrational and unfounded and the information is probably more safe than when it was with you! But people do worry, and not without reason, since millions can be made through industrial espionage. Many companies, for a variety of reasons, **never** use outside marketing agencies. These include such household names as Marks & Spencer and Sainsbury's. In their highly competitive market secrecy is vital and disclosure disastrous.

It would be fairly obvious to most people that you do marketing research for a reason. That reason should invariably be that you will gain more in the long term from what you have learnt than it cost you in the short term to find out. Easier said than done! Calculating the costs of research is fairly easy: you will know how many people are involved, what equipment you will need, any specialists to pay and what it will cost to process the information to get it into a presentable and usable form. The problem is, how do you work out just what the value of the information is? How can you compare the straightforward costs of collecting and processing data with the benefits derived from your knowledge of it?

Two key thoughts are relevant here. The first is: what is the relative profitability of the alternative decisions open to you before you undertake the marketing research? After all, you might be trying to choose one or another, and the benefit of each should be measurable. The other point is, how will the information directly affect your decision making? Will it make a positive contribution or will it just be another factor to worry about?

Perhaps, if you are still concerned (for financial reasons or otherwise) about whether you need marketing research or not, when you see the phases that the research process needs to go through you will find that simply considering the process directs the mind. In some cases that may be enough for you to get what you want out of the exercise before you have gone through all the stages of the research process.

The first step in the research process has to be to **define the problem**. It is here that you, as the client or director of the research, specify exactly what you hope to achieve from the research. What are the major objectives? If these cannot be achieved then the research is worse than useless.

Next you need to decide what **methods** are to be employed in the collection of the data. As we have already discussed there are effectively three main sources of information. The primary sources of information are usually the ones that cost you money to collect because they are often specific to your needs and involve the more common forms of data collection such as surveys, interviews and observations. The secondary sources tend to be cheaper as they are often already collected but are usually less useful and only helpful as background information.

The third stage is to decide on the **scale** of the information gathering. This is known as sampling. Basically you need to ask just how many people you are going to include in your research. You could probably interview all Conservative Members of Parliament or the residents of one small area of the country, but you couldn't possibly interview everyone who owns a Ford car or all of Britain's smokers. Sampling decisions are crucial because you will need to make up your mind about how many people would be a representative sample balanced against the cost of sampling a larger number.

The fourth stage is making your mind up about how the data that have been collected are to be analysed. Which **statistical procedures** are going to be employed to look at the information? You should consider this question in relation to what you wanted in the first place. What are you looking for? The analysis should give you the answers to the questions you have posed.

The fifth consideration relates to **time** and **resources**. You may well have considered these already before you undertook to start the research but it could be here that you decide not to pursue the research any further. This is where you will have to put a price on the research so that it is also here that you can finally decide whether the research is worth whatever it is going to cost you.

Also you may not have considered just how long it is going to take to collect the data to answer the questions that you want answered. Will the process take too long? Can you afford to wait?

The sixth stage is the point of no return. Having outlined the parameters of the research and looked at how much information you are going to collect and how to analyse it to get the answers that you want, and of course put a monetary figure on the whole exercise, it is here that you get the go-ahead or not. **Agreement** here on the five preceding stages is vital otherwise the research process terminates straightaway.

student activity

How would you decide on the cost effectiveness of research? Work out a simple research process and try to cost it. The results may surprise you!

The final three stages, seven, eight and nine, are the putting into practice of what you have already agreed in the first five stages. Namely they are: collecting the data, analysing it and then reporting back on the findings to the person or persons that the research is for.

RESEARCH INSTRUMENTS

The key point to remember is that a well constructed questionnaire will give far better results than an ill-considered one. If things are unclear you run the risk of annoying the respondent and losing their co-operation. Questionnaires have different types of questions, they fall into four main categories, we shall look at these in a little more detail.

CLOSED QUESTIONS

The respondent is asked to answer the questions from a range of set answers. Usually the answers are simply yes or no, but in other cases may include 'don't know'. The questions could offer a wider range of answers but the more answers the more likely that the respondent will get confused.

OPEN QUESTIONS

The respondent is given the opportunity to answer the question however he or she sees fit. There is no multi-ple choice of preferred answers and the questionnaire has to be structured in such a way as to allow plenty of space for the response.

DIRECT QUESTIONS

These are very similar in some respects to a closed question style. They require an exact or specific answer, sometimes a simple yes or no and at other times a more detailed but specific answer. An example would be: 'What do you think of the Sega Mega Drive?'

INDIRECT QUESTIONS

These are very general and attempt to discover attitudes that the respondent has about certain issues. A series of questions will be asked that will build up a detailed picture of attitudes or behaviour. As the interviewer has to interpret much of what is being said and will note down what he or she see as the more important parts of the response you do need to have well-trained interviewers.

Additionally, the time spent with each respondent is longer than any other method, hence it is expensive. What this type of questioning does reveal can be very interesting and it is unlikely that the other forms of questions can get so much in-depth material.

Having looked at the different types of question we can breakdown the actual types of questionnaire into two basic categories, the structured questionnaire which relies mainly on the closed question with the occasional open question and the unstructured which mainly makes use of the direct and indirect questions.

Structured questionnaires are simple to fill in by just ticking the appropriate box, whereas the unstructured questionnaire must rely on the skills of the interviewer as the questions themselves are merely a guide to the direction in which the interviewer should go.

As a guide for the interviewer in unstructured questionnaires there are two main ways of measuring and recording the respondent's attitudes. The techniques are known as the Likert Scale or the Semantic Differential Scale.

Table 3.1.1 shows a Likert Scale question.

The Semantic Differential Scale asks respondents to mark their opinion on a sliding scale of seven(which is the usual). There is an example in Table 3.1.2.

In both cases the researcher would compile the results and reach an 'aggregate' total for each of the questions. In other words the researcher would look at both the range of answers to the questions as well as discovering which answer was the most common.

INTERVIEW SCHEDULES

During the process of questionnaire design, the scheduling of the interviews will prove to be an important factor. As we will see later, with regard to the size and nature of the sample of interviewees, the time element in particular may be uppermost in the organisation's considerations. Accuracy and depth of detail may be the more important requirements of the research. The interviews may be longer and have more 'cross-checking' features to ensure that the interviewee is consistent with responses and that the interviewer has fully

TABLE 3.1.1 *A Likert Scale Question*

What do you think are the advantage and disadvantages of fresh vegetables against frozen ones? Tick the appropriate box.

	Strongly Agree	Tend to Agree	Don't agree or disagree	Tend to disagree	Strongly disagree
Fresh vegetables are more healthy					
Fresh vegetables are less convenient					
Frozen vegetables are better quality					
Frozen vegetables are more expensive					

TABLE 3.1.2 *The Semantic Differential Scale*

Please rate your day out at the Theme Park, please circle the number you have chosen:

very good value for money	7	6	5	4	3	2	1	poor value for money
very good range of rides	7	6	5	4	3	2	1	poor range of rides
food stalls very good	7	6	5	4	3	2	1	bad food, poor service
staff helpful & courteous	7	6	5	4	3	2	1	bad mannered
great family day out	7	6	5	4	3	2	1	not good for families
strongly recommended	7	6	5	4	3	2	1	will not recommend

understood the responses.

In order to identify the requirements of the questionnaire, and to ensure that it conforms and provides the information required, it is essential that the organisation carries out a pilot survey first. This is achieved by designing the questionnaire and getting a relatively small number of people to fill it in. It is not the information gathered that is important at this stage. It is the speed and accuracy of the data collected and understanding of the questionnaire in general. If some of the questions are ambiguous, then they will have to be reworded.

The interview schedule may now be decided. The organisations must decide exactly how, when and where the questionnaires will be filled in by the respondents (or interviewers on their behalf). The key scheduling criteria are:

- *Random or non-random?* Will the respondents be chosen at random, or chosen to reflect characteristics of the population that the organisation has already identified? A good example of this would be to ask predominantly female respondents regarding the purchase of baby milk or perfume.
- *Single or multi-stage?* Will the sample be collected at the same time (on the same day or same week), or will the sample be collected over a number of days or weeks?
- *Single unit or cluster?* Will the sample be collected from one geographical location or several?
- *Stratified or unstratified?* Will the respondents be chosen according to socio-economic criteria or other 'class based' considerations such as their type of home?

- *Proportionate or disproportionate?* Will the sample reflect the percentage breakdown of the population in relation to various criteria? For example, will the sample include more female respondents to reflect the fact that females outnumber males in the population?

ELECTRONIC MONITORING

Modern technology has allowed researchers to gain access to very valuable data which, in the past, was all but impossible to obtain. Family television viewing patterns can be monitored using a 'black box' attached to the TV set. Each individual in the family has a code number and simply keys in their code when viewing a TV programme. This is attached via a slightly more sophisticated version of a remote control. The viewing data is collected by a mainframe computer via the telephone line using a modem. Additional data is collected by the researchers when the family shops in the supermarket. The family uses a special 'credit card' identification card at the check-out. In this way, the researchers can assess the effectiveness of advertising in relation to changes in the buying patterns of the family.

Storage and analysis of data is rarely carried out manually these days. Research organisations will use a variety of specialist software such as:

- Electronic Data Processing
- Bar Codes
- Minitab
- Statistical Package for Social Sciences (SPSS)

Using these packages has enabled researchers to deal with large samples in an efficient and rapid manner.

ACCESSIBILITY OF SAMPLE

The **accessibility** of the sample, or the ease in which you will be able to find the right kind of respondents for your market research will pretty much dictate the method of collection. As we have seen earlier in this Unit, the various collection methods can handle the problems of accessibility. For instance, you may wish to collect data from respondents who are geographically remote. In this case, you will not want to have to arrange personal face-to-face interviews. The solution would be to carry out the research using the telephone or by simply sending the questionnaire to them.

ANALYSIS

Whenever people are involved you cannot guarantee 'bug-free' results. By this we don't mean that the researchers can get it wrong (they can though, sometimes!) but if you are asking people's opinions or looking at their behaviour you begin to realise that people are pretty unpredictable creatures!

Here are some of the more common types of error:

1 *Sampling errors.* This one is the researcher's fault. He or she has incorrectly chosen the target sample and it does not represent a true cross-section at all.

2 *Non-response errors.* This is another researcher's error. This time he or she has not received responses from all of the intended target sample. This may be partly related to the first error.

3 *Data collection errors.* Most commonly these occur when the respondent, either in a questionnaire or in an interview, gives answers that he or she thinks the researcher wants to hear. Alternatively, the respondent may not really understand the question and may give a wrong answer entirely. In other cases, when the question is read out by the interviewer he or she may intentionally or unintentionally introduce a bias in the tone of his or her voice. Less commonly, some respondents will deliberately give the wrong answer – who can resist it sometimes! Equally an interviewer may be dishonest and put down completely spurious answers for some reason or another.

4 *Analysis errors.* A researcher may have wrongly interpreted the findings of his or her research or may have incorrectly tabulated the information in some way by overlooking something. In some cases analysis errors are the direct result of having collected the wrong information or not having asked the one vital question that should have been asked.

5 *Report errors.* Having collected the data and even having analysed it correctly a researcher can still come to the wrong conclusion! The old saying that there are lies, damned lies and statistics holds true. You can interpret almost anything from a set of statistics. Ask the Labour Party or the Conservative Party to give you the same interpretation of unemployment figures and then sit back and watch them swear blind that they are right and the other party is wrong. Misinterpretation is either a common error or a positive skill depending on your point of view!

6 *Accidental errors.* These are nobody's fault really. What happens if you plan to run your research period over a year and something happens to ruin your research? A competitor may launch a new product or the weather may suddenly change, or the interest rates might fall. Anything can happen, all beyond your control.

student activity

Discuss the following statement:
  Market research is completely unreliable and inevitably prone to misinterpretation anyway, so it is not really worth doing.

STATISTICAL TECHNIQUES

Sampling is absolutely necessary, unless of course you have the time, money and resources to carry out a census of the entire population! Often, though, the size of the sample may depend on other considerations. Firstly, the smaller the sample the less likely you are to change the attitude of the market you are investigating. The second thought is that the size of the sample will affect the accuracy of your findings. If the sample is too small or unrepresentative of the market then your results will be very inaccurate.

So how do you get it right? You have to ask yourself three basic questions, firstly what is the **target population**? Secondly, which of the **sampling methods** (of which there are five) will you choose? Finally, with reference to such things as time and resources, you will need to determine what your **sampling size** will be.

What is the **target population**? Basically this is the part of the total population that the study is directed at. Your prospective respondents should be part of the total population whom you have chosen from directories or maps or perhaps selected after a more general questionnaire to a much larger population.

Selecting the **sampling method** is crucial and you will need to pick the one that most closely matches your pocket and time.

1 *Random or non-random sampling.* Random samples are simply that, each and every member of the total population has an equal chance of being part of the sample. This method has two main advantages, firstly a statistical relationship exists between the sample and the population, and secondly the composition of the sample is not influenced by interviewer bias. Non-random samples, when respondents are chosen to reflect the characteristic elements of the population that the researcher is trying to look at, can be as effective and useful as a totally random choice of respondents. You need far fewer people in a non-random sample, but true reliability rests on the following; your statistics of the structure of the population need to be as up to date as possible, the

GREAT YARMOUTH COLLEGE

JARROLDS OF GREAT YARMOUTH SHOPPING SURVEY
Conducted by Great Yarmouth College - June 1992

AGE:
☐ <20 ☐ 21-30 ☐ 31-40 ☐ 41-50 ☐ 51-64 ☐ 65+>

SEX: ☐ Male ☐ Female

EMPLOYMENT:
☐ Full-time ☐ Part-time ☐ Unemployed ☐ Self-employed
☐ Housewife ☐ Retired

HOME LOCATION:
☐ Gt Yarmouth ☐ Gorleston ☐ Caister ☐ Norwich ☐ Acle
☐ Lowestoft ☐ Bradwell & Belton

Other (please state):..

TRANSPORT: ☐ Car ☐ Bus ☐ Train ☐ Walk

HOW OFTEN DO YOU SHOP AT JARROLDS?
☐ Once a week ☐ Once a month ☐ Occasionally ☐ Never ☐ More than once a week

WHAT DO YOU SHOP FOR?
☐ Books ☐ Maps ☐ Gifts ☐ Cards ☐ Knitting yarns
☐ Pens ☐ Stationery ☐ Office equipment ☐ Art/students materials

Other (please state):..

WHAT DO YOU THINK ABOUT THE RANGE?
☐ Very good ☐ Extensive ☐ Reasonable ☐ Poor

WHAT IMAGE DO YOU HAVE OF JARROLDS?
☐ Upmarket ☐ Middle market ☐ Down market

WHAT ABOUT THE PRICES?
☐ Fair ☐ Competitive ☐ Expensive ☐ Very expensive
☐ Much the same as other shops

WHAT DO YOU THINK OF THE STAFF AND SERVICE?
☐ Helpful ☐ Friendly ☐ Efficient ☐ Knowledgable ☐ Unhelpful
☐ Don't care ☐ Slow ☐ Unfriendly

WHERE WOULD YOU SHOP IN PREFERENCE TO JARROLDS?
☐ W H Smith ☐ Palmers ☐ Boots ☐ Clintons ☐ Occasions
☐ Argos ☐ Index ☐ Woolworths

Others (please state):..

WHAT DO YOU LIKE BEST ABOUT JARROLDS?:..

WHAT DO YOU LIKE LEAST ABOUT JARROLDS?..

WHAT WOULD YOU LIKE JARROLDS TO STOCK?:..

ANY OTHER COMMENTS:..

....

TIME OF INTERVIEW: ☐ am ☐ pm **LOCATION:**..

DAY OF WEEK:
☐ MONDAY ☐ TUESDAY ☐ WEDNESDAY ☐ THURSDAY ☐ FRIDAY ☐ SATURDAY

FIG.3.1.1 *This shopping survey was commissioned by Jarrolds, an office supply and stationery company and bookseller. The sample consisted of some 1,200 respondents. Research was carried out over two weeks with clearly defined limits to age, gender and socio-economic group.*

questions need to be carefully designed and you have to control the interviewers' choice of respondents.

2 *Single stage or multi-stage sampling.* The larger the sample the more likely it is that you do not sample your entire sample at the same time. A well-organised multi-stage sample will systematically look at various areas or classifications of respondents.

3 *Single unit or cluster sampling.* Single unit sampling selects each respondent individually regardless of his/her geographical position. Cluster sampling concentrates on one area and draws all of its respondents from quite a small geographical area.

4 *Unstratified or stratified sampling.* Stratified sampling attempts to segment the population into groups which have the same basic characteristics and then treats each of these groups as a separate entity when sampling them. It has its advantages which include: making sure that the sample is representative and the chances of choosing the wrong people to sample are reduced. It is used most frequently in industrial marketing research where the samples are stratified to make sure that similarly sized companies are sampled. The ACORN system (meaning A Classification of Residential Neighbourhoods) provides a useful framework for consumer marketing research if you want to carry out stratified sampling.

5 *Proportionate or disproportionate sampling.* Following on from stratified sampling, there is the technique of proportionate sampling, which ensures that you use an equal percentage of respondents from each group. Disproportionate sampling is cheaper as you can sample more from one group and then simply reduce it to the correct percentage after you have analysed all the results.

We have already mentioned the size of sample, which is usually governed by the amount of money that is available but is also affected by the degree of precision that you are demanding from the research. The larger the sample, crudely, determines just how accurate the results are likely to be.

The other major factor of precision is to make sure that you have correctly interpreted the responses. Some may have been rather confusing and you will have to make your mind up about how you are going to deal with these. You could ask the respondent to clarify a confused answer but this is a rather expensive solution. You could, alternatively, decide to sample more than you need and simply discard the useless responses.

Now that you have a pile of completed questionnaires how do you analyse them? The simplest way, and the most common, is to tabulate the results. This basically means calculating the number and percentage of respondents who choose each of the answers. You will probably have come across such averaging methods as means, medians and modes; these are also useful in working out what your findings mean.

Most marketing research analysis is limited to working out averages or percentages, but careful coding can cut down analysis and may be imputted to computers. Computers can be put to good use when working out the relationship between different variables. The report itself is usually set out like this:

> Title page
> Table of contents
> Summary
> Introduction/Objectives
> Research Methods
> Findings
> Conclusions
> Recommendations
> Appendices

The technical details of the sampling are usually consigned to the appendices as the reader is often not very interested in such information in detail. Sampling design and questionnaire design will often be found here for the same reason.

It is important to consider these last two things before pen is put to paper; don't use jargon or language that the reader will not understand. Equally try to write for your reader and make the report easy to follow. Whenever possible try to use diagrams or graphs. A good graph will say something that a thousand words cannot.

Companies must be able to predict their sales, and they also need to have some clear idea about potential profits and their cash flow. Miscalculations can be disastrous, an inefficient use of resources can mean that they will lose out against their competitors. Forecasting sales is an essential part of the process of being efficient and aware of what may happen in the future. Traditionally it is a company's Accounts Department or Accountant that is left with the task of sales forecasting. They are conservative creatures in the main and have a tendency to underestimate. It is the accountant's responsibility to prevent the organisation from overspending and he or she will therefore try to curb spending by underestimating sales forecasts, thus turnover and of course profit. The other common set of circumstances is that underestimating will make the actual sales figures or production levels look all the better by being higher than was expected. There is a danger, though, that if the organisation gears itself up for the lower figures then it will be unprepared for the higher demand or the need for production increases.

Arguably then, a company's Marketing Department should be responsible for the sales forecasting. However marketing directors have not, traditionally, had to be very numerate and it is perhaps this factor – amongst more historical ones – that prevents the Marketing

Department from wanting to take control of this vital area and causes it to be left to the Finance or Accounts Department instead.

Marketing Departments are automatically involved if a new product or service is being launched and it is interesting to note that companies that find themselves in competition with new competitors will tend to over-state the level of competition in the market and devalue, in market size terms, the potential sales overall.

There are, effectively, three different types of fore-cast, very imaginatively known as short, medium and long-term. Broadly speaking they fall into two main types of forecasting:

- forecasting for the whole market or industry and then working out what share of the market your particular organisation might be able to grab. This method is known as the **'top down'** approach as the forecast is obtained from data outside the organisation
- forecasting sales by analysing previous sales data. This method is known as the **'bottom up'** approach as the data are collected from the organisation itself

Let's now have a look at the three types of forecasting that we mentioned earlier:

1 *Short-term forecasting.* This looks at about three or so months ahead and is made for immediate tactical reasons. It often looks specifically at seasonal trends and tries to smooth the cash flow and production.
2 *Medium-term forecasting.* This looks at up to one year ahead and is linked closely to budgeting. Usually this forecast forms the basis of the organisation's planning. It looks at probable sales as well as equipment and manpower needs.
3 *Long-term forecasting.* This can look quite a way into the future, perhaps as long as 20 years, more commonly, though, five or 10 and is strongly related to the major strategic decisions that the organisation will have to make. It depends very much on the nature of the business as to how long long-term is; for example in the car industry it would be no more than 10 years, but in the raw materials field, arguably, as long as 20.

The forecast determines the organisation's budget and it is the sales budget that will generate sales. A **budget** is what is **planned** to happen and the **forecast** is just a **prediction** of what might happen. The budget, then, is much more controllable, whereas the forecast might be affected by countless outside factors. Equally it is vital that all three, from forecast, through budget to sales budget, are linked and 'aware' of each other; after all many companies have suffered from 'over successful' sales forces that have been let down by serious short-falls in production.

We do not propose to go too deeply into the techniques of forecasting as we feel it is not strictly necessary to explain this fully.

QUANTITATIVE AND QUALITATIVE TECHNIQUES

Sales forecasting techniques are divided into two main categories, **qualitative** and **quantitative** techniques. Qualitative techniques rely very heavily on subjective opinion. Quantitative techniques rely far more heavily on mathematical computations and have two subdivisions known as time series analysis and casual.

Let's look at the techniques a little more closely:

Qualitative technique – consumer survey method

This technique asks the consumer or user for his or her opinion of the product or service. This is a basic market research technique. It is most valuable when there are a relatively small number of consumers and their opinions are more likely to give a better and more accurate forecast.

Qualitative technique – the panel or jury method

In this method a group of experts are asked for their views on the market, and on the basis of their opinions a forecast is worked out. Sitting in committee, the experts will thrash out the various considerations and arrive at a joint decision (which may be an average in the case of disagreements). This is an expensive technique since it tends to be manpower heavy and is arguably less accurate than some of the more mathematical approaches.

Qualitative technique – salesforce composite method

In this technique each manager is asked to make a fore-cast for his/her particular area of responsibility. This is then linked to things such as sales targets and quotas. The salesperson's figures are compared to the area manager's estimation of the true state of affairs and if the figures differ wildly then manager and salesperson will meet and resolve the differences. Salespeople, a pessimistic breed, have a tendency to underestimate, and this should be compensated for by the inclusion of the area manager's estimates.

Qualitative technique – delphi method

This is rather like the panel or jury method, but the members of the group (usually around 20 or so) do not meet and only correspond or speak to one another on the telephone. The system is designed to get each member of the panel to give his or her true feelings without being exposed to group pressure and the feeling that he or she should agree with the majority. A truer result should come out of this method. This system is not really used for product or customer considerations as the nature of the technique tends to make its use far more general, for example the panel could be asked what they think will be the impact of a new process or technique of production on the market.

Qualitative technique – Bayesian decision method

This is quite complicated to explain, but in a nutshell, a diagram is drawn, like a network of points linked together which includes all the possibilities that the person drawing it thinks should be considered. The group looks at all the possible future outcomes and then tries to evaluate them in terms of their expected profitability or advantage to the organisation. The one that is identified as the best alternative in the future is chosen and aimed for. This is both a subjective (in the sense that it is your opinion of the most likely future) and objective method (since once you have agreed the range of possibilities you then have to agree the most likely one and the best chances you have with it).

Qualitative technique – testing methods

These are usually employed when there are no sales figures to help anticipate demand. Product testing involves a small number of respondents and summarises their opinions and attitudes to a new product or service. This technique is only really of any use for new products where the product is launched in a small geographical area. One of the other main problems is that, as with most new products, the cheaper it is the more likely people are to try it out and not buy it again after the novelty has worn off. It is a brave organisation that bases its future on this technique alone.

Quantitative technique – moving averages

This is a simple example of the time series analysis mould. Taking a period of sales, say over 10 years, you simply add all the sales figures and then divide them by the number of years. In this way you have, crudely, an average. Sales forecasts are then calculated by extending the trend line and following the average into the future.

Quantitative technique – exponential smoothing

This technique helps to overcome the inaccuracies that often plague the previous technique. Taking into consideration the different weighting over the period of sales figures (for example, inflation may have distorted the turnover by making it appear, in relative terms, disproportionately high). This technique smooths out the 'blips' and aims to give a much more accurate trend and hence a more accurate forecast.

Quantitative technique – time series analysis

Sales figures inevitably fluctuate. What any forecaster is looking for is the underlying trend. Fluctuations may be simple to identify, such as seasonal changes, but some require deeper investigation. Time series analysis analyses any deviation from the average trend, and then adds them back into the forecast once the trend line has been worked out. Not surprisingly this particular method requires a considerable grasp of mathematics and as this is a text on business we are gladly willing to say no more.

Quantitative technique – Z-charts

Z-charts provide a year's worth of data. In order to make full use of these the forecaster must prepare several, from previous years, to be able to compare them visually, and see if there are any common general trends. In this way a prediction may be made. This is of course rather subjective and the technique is rarely accepted as a serious forecasting tool. A Z-chart has months along its horizontal axis and number of units sold on its vertical axis. The bottom line of the Z is the monthly sales, the diagonal line is the cumulative sales, and the top line is the moving annual average.

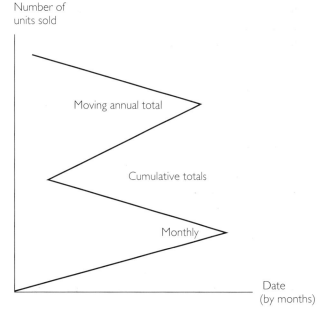

FIG 3.1.2 *This graph shows the form of a Z-chart.*

Quantitative technique – leading indicator

This technique uses linear regression to establish a relationship between something measurable (such as sales figures for units sold) and what has to be forecast. On a diagram one set of criteria is measured on one axis and another on the other. The aim is to see if there is a correlation (or relationship) between the two. If the measurements come close together in a more or less straight line, the correlation is said to be linear, and there then is a close relationship between the two sets of data. The technique is increasingly dependent on a computer and some very useful software packages have taken the headache of working this technique out.

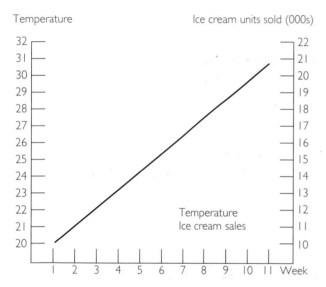

FIG 3.1.3 *This graph shows how temperature predictions could be used as a predictor or lead indicator for ice cream sales.*

Quantitative technique – simulation

As with the previous example this technique also relies on the use of a computer. Simulation uses trial and error, systematically going through each and every possibility in trying to work out the forecast. The more complicated the situation the more complex the simulation and hence the more variable and more numerous the probabilities.

Quantitative technique – diffusion models

This is complicated; diffusion theory makes the assumption that new products have four basic criteria:

- the idea that has created the product
- how this new idea is to be communicated to others
- the social system in which the product is to be sold
- any time considerations

The technique then breaks down the idea or innovation into three further sub-categories which try to identify the product's life cycle. Forecasting is made from relatively small amounts of data over short periods of time during the launch of the new product. Assumptions are made that those who purchase the product after the initial launch period will imitate the early buyers. In other words, buying habits will be similar throughout the life of the product.

Sales forecasts must be incorporated very early in the decision-making process. As competition becomes keener then planning must become more scientific. Having researched and forecast the organisation can maximise its efforts in targeting the segment of the market that most closely resembles its potential customers.

Use consumer trends to forecast sales

1 CONSUMER CHARACTERISTICS
demographic, age, gender, taste, lifestyle, conscience spending (i.e. green etc.)

2 CONSUMPTION PATTERNS
increasing/decreasing

3 ECONOMIC INFORMATION
social trends (income/spending), GNP, employment statistics, growth indices

CONSUMER CHARACTERISTICS

The need to identify and attempt to satisfy the needs of specific target markets is central to the concept of marketing. To do it efficiently is important, to do it more efficiently than your competitors can be vital. Relating the product or services to the needs of the market-place means that your approach is 'market oriented'. In order to do this successfully you must undertake market research and try to forecast your sales. Alternatively, your approach could be 'product oriented', in other words, you look at the market as being made up of identical, but potential purchasers of your product.

The single most important factor to have had an effect on marketing, certainly in recent times, is the realisation that markets are made up of very different sub-groups or sub-markets. As identifying these sub-markets has become more refined, the elements of strategy and marketing have been honed to them specifically. Most products are designed for a particular market and not the general public as a whole. Not surprisingly businesses are interested in the most commercially attractive parts of a market. This is known as **target marketing**. It relies strongly on good research

and is, in itself, the logical conclusion of research work.

A market is a very difficult thing to define. Broadly speaking there are three ways of describing a market. Firstly, it can be the **physical** (geographical) **place** where goods or services are sold, for example Malaysia is a market. Secondly, a market is also the actual **demand** for a specific product or service. Thirdly, it can be the set of **conditions** that determine the price of a product or service. For example you could say that the market for personal stereos is £x million per year.

The most commonly accepted definition of a market identifies **a group of people with needs, what their purchasing power is and what their buying behaviour is**. A further refinement is that this market is not just **existing** customers but should include those who are **potential** ones.

There are three stages which have to be carried out systematically in order to target the marketing successfully. We will have to look at these in some detail, but here are the three stages in brief:

▌ market segmentation

2 selection and evaluation of a market segment
3 product positioning.

As specialised market segments have developed and been identified, there has been a growth in the number of companies which offer goods and services that are much more closely related to the customer.

It is true to say that certain types of goods and services have always been purchased by certain parts of the population and not by others. Initially segmentation was very crude, and was limited to categories such as rich or poor, fashionable or utilitarian etc. Common sense was the key rather than scientific segmentation. As competition became more fierce in almost every market, businesses paid more attention to the market. All markets have certain features that are similar, but not identical. As a result it is highly unlikely that one product would be ideal for everyone.

Take a look at any supermarket shelf and examine the products. Just choose one, say the soap. Each product has its own distinctive qualities, from simple things such as price to subtle aromas and the creaminess of the lather. More recently other considerations and approaches have been made: liquid soap (convenient and non-messy), perfume-free (for sensitive skins) and environmentally friendly (fully bio-degradable). There is a wealth of different products for different tastes, but take a look at the labels on the packets and you will see

that certainly less than a dozen manufacturers are offering this multitude of soap products. They have identified their market, broken it down and refined their segmentation and now cater for sub-groups within the market successfully.

DEMOGRAPHIC, AGE, GENDER AND LIFESTYLE CHARACTERISTICS

In order to identify your target market segment you must look at a number of variables. The first six variables are known as demographic factors and are the basis of segmenting the market:

- age
- sex
- family size and life cycle
- social class
- neighbourhood
- education

Then there are more specialist variables which relate to other criteria:

- benefit segmentation
- usage segmentation
- loyalty
- geographical and cultural segmentation

Each of these variables needs further explanation.

Age

Age strongly affects the purchasing behaviour of individuals. In the younger age groups (18–24, for example) fashion, records, take-aways, magazines and newspapers tend to be the big areas of purchasing. This is known as the youth market and is a specific target for certain products. Age is one of the most important considerations even if it is the easiest to research.

Sex

Sex is again a straightforward variable to measure, but is, in many cases, crucial. Certain products and services are specifically female (such as women's clothes – mostly, and cosmetics). Some products do not cater for one sex or the other in particular whereas for others the slant of the advertising is quite clearly towards one sex or the other. Some brands of cars are definitely aimed at males (Land Rover) and others at women (Vauxhall Nova). Some cars are labelled 'women's cars' and their advertising reflects this.

Family size and life cycle

Family size is a straight categorisation of 1–2 members, 3–4 members and 5+ members. The size of the family simply and most decisively determines the size

FIG.3.2.I *Tesco PLC through consistent market research has managed to focus closely on satisfying the needs of customers. The company has developed stores, introduced new products, new pricing policies, customer service standards and technical innovations, all driven by the aim to satisfy customers.*

of the pack bought and the frequency of purchase. The family **life cycle** defines the stage which the typical family has reached and directly reflects their demand for products and their consumption rate. The stages are:

- young
- young, single with no children
- young couple, youngest child under 6
- young couple, youngest child 6 or over
- older couple with children 18+ at home
- older couple with no children at home
- older and single

There are some rather crude assumptions here as well as the basic assumption that the family unit is still the best social unit to measure. This categorisation may need refinement and eventual replacement.

Social class

Social class is in fact a mixture of both social class and income and again is a rather crude classification based on the 'head' of the household and does not therefore take any account of a second wage earner (in other words married women are ignored in the main). This socio-economic classification was established by the National Readership Survey:

A – Higher managerial, administrative or professional
B – Intermediate managerial, administrative or professional
C1 – Supervisory, clerical, junior administrative or professional
C2 – Skilled manual workers
D – Semi-skilled and unskilled manual workers
E – State pensioner, widows, casual and lowest grade earners

Good examples of the occupations which fall into the categories are:

A – directors, senior doctors, cabinet ministers
B – headmasters/mistresses, solicitors, bank managers
C1 – teachers, nurses, clerks
C2 – foremen, blacksmiths, electricians, plumbers
D – lorry drivers, porters, cleaners
E – pensioners, part-timers/casual workers

Although this categorisation has been criticised it is still extremely useful, despite the fact that some of the boundaries between the categories are a little blurred these days.

student activity

What is the purpose of dividing markets into segments? How useful do you think social class is in helping to segment the market?

Neighbourhood

Neighbourhood classification is a relatively new measure of segmentation. The ACORN system (meaning A Classification of Residential Neighbourhoods) identifies some 38 different types of residential neighbourhood according to their demographic, housing and socio-economic characteristics. The classification is based on the Census of Population in Great Britain:

A1 – Agricultural villages
A2 – Areas of farms and smallholdings
B3 – Cheap modern private housing
B4 – Recent private housing, young families
B5 – Modern private housing, older families
B6 – New detached houses, young families
B7 – Military bases
C8 – Mixed owner-occupied and council estates
C9 – Small town centres and flats above shops
C10 – Villages with non-farm employment
C11 – Older private housing, skilled workers
D12 – Unimproved terraces with old people
D13 – Pre-1914 terraces, low-income families
D14 – Tenement flats lacking amenities
E15 – Council estates with well-off older workers
E16 – Recent council estates
E17 – Council estates, well-off young workers
E18 – Small council houses, often in Scotland
F19 – Low-rise estates in industrial towns
F20 – Inter-war council estates
F21 – Council housing for the elderly
G22 – New council estates in industrial towns
G23 – Overspill estates, high unemployment
G24 – Council estates with overcrowding
G25 – Council estates with worst poverty
H26 – Multi-occupied terraces
H27 – Owner-occupied terraces, Asians
H28 – Multi-let housing with Afro-Caribbeans
H29 – Better-off multi-ethnic areas
I30 – High status areas, few children
I31 – Multi-let big old houses and flats
I32 – Furnished flats, mostly single people
I33 – Inter-war semis, white collar workers
I34 – Spacious inter-war semis, big gardens
I35 – Villages with wealthy older commuters
I36 – Detached houses, exclusive suburbs
I37 – Private houses, well-off elderly
I38 – Private flats with single pensioners
I39 – Unclassified

The classification breaks the country down into units of 150 dwellings, with the predominant type being the classification that is adopted for that unit. There are certainly some properties and occupants that do not fit into any of the above categories.

The largest users of this system are the direct mail companies, financial institutions, gas and electricity companies, TV rental companies, credit card companies, travel companies, companies holding guarantees for goods, manufacturers requiring addresses for promotions, charities and political parties.

The ACORN system has further proved to be of use in the siting of stores and determining locations for posters. In general terms it is useful when you are trying to target without wasting a vast percentage of your mail shot as it enables you to eliminate areas that are unlikely to be interested in your product or service.

student activity

Can you identify your home in one of the above classifications? Is your home representative of the immediate area? What kind of assumptions would an organisation make about your local area?

Education

Education is a rather less useful form of classification than it has been in the past. In effect it notes the purchasers' level of formal education, making the assumption that those with a higher level of formal education are more likely than those with a lower level to consume wine, classical music records or gourmet food, for example. Largely, this is far too crude a measurement. A useful element is the link with newspaper readership, TV viewing and job types. As a rule (although still a generalisation), better-educated people are more likely to read higher-brow newspapers such as *The Times*, the *Guardian* or the *Telegraph*, they are more likely to watch the more 'arty', 'informative' or 'worthy' commercial TV programmes, such as the 'South Bank Show'. Also with better education come better jobs, another reason for this measurement to be useful to the company wishing to reach a specific target.

The Terminal Education Age (TEA) classification system is all but redundant. It works on the basis of noting the age at which a person left full-time education. With the changes in education over the past few years and increasing emphasis on part-time study and the opportunities these offer, the question of when you left full-time education is quite irrelevant.

TASTE, CONSCIENCE ('GREEN SPENDING') AND OTHER FACTORS

Taste simply refers to the particular likes and dislikes of consumers. These are often taken to reflect their life-styles and individual cultures. A forward-thinking Marketing Department will even be able to shape tastes

Avon's Environmental Mission is to:

- **Conserve usage of energy and raw materials.**
- **Reduce waste to a minimum.**
- **Recycle materials as much as is possible.**
- **Avoid pollution of air, land and water.**
- **Improve the working environment.**
- **Meet – and exceed where possible – environmental regulatory standards.**
- **Support local community environmental initiatives.**
- **Train employees in good, environmental practices.**

FIG.3.2.2 *Many organisations have recognised the consumer's interest in environmental issues. Avon UK state that both their management and employees are highly committed – in every aspect of their business – to finding ways to demonstrate this. They have taken special steps to care for the environment.*

by the creation of particular forms of fashion, music and life-styles.

Conscience spending, more commonly known as 'green spending' is an increasingly important aspect which must be considered by Marketing Departments. With the general increase in the amount of information available, coupled with consumers' ability to comprehend it, many individuals have become aware of and concerned about environmental impacts caused by business activity. Specifically, organisations realise that consumers are interested in many of the following:

- CFCs
- E numbers
- additives
- animal testing
- health conscious eating
- resource wastage
- disposal of waste

Other key, but non-demographic features are detailed below.

Benefit segmentation

Benefit segmentation simply groups together consumers on the basis of why they have bought a particular product. Different people buy the same product for a whole list of different reasons. Some people have had satellite dishes bolted on to their homes because of special offers inducing them to try them, or because they want to watch more sport, or films or twenty-four hour news, or for their children's entertainment, or as a status symbol, or to be the first on the street or out of boredom with existing television stations. All are valid reasons for purchasing the product. The key to this segmentation method is for the company to have already identified what the major benefits will be to the potential consumer, then to profile those people, measure its product or service against its competitors and capitalise on an, as yet, unsatisfied market segment.

Usage Segmentation

Segmentation by usage recognises that consumption rates of products or services are not evenly distributed. If a company can identify the heaviest users of a product or service it can target its marketing strategy to capture more of them. The fact that beer drinkers tend to watch sport on television leads to the profusion of alcohol advertising during sports coverage.

Loyalty

The **loyalty status** divides consumers into four groups according to their loyalty to a product (known as brand loyalty):

- *hard-core loyal* – these consumers have total commitment to a particular product and have been long-term purchasers
- *soft-core loyal* – these consumers have a divided loyalty, but only between two or three products. They tend not to have a pattern of purchasing, they simply buy one brand or another at whim
- *shifting* – these consumers seem to have a pattern and switch their loyalty totally to another product for a period and then switch back after a while for no apparent reason
- *switching* – these consumers have no loyalty to a brand whatsoever. They may be heavily influenced by special offers and promotional gimmicks

The key to this segmentation identification is to find out very quickly why consumers are switching from your product to another, the reason for your inability to keep consumers long term, and to take steps in your marketing strategy to stop this trend.

Geographical and cultural segmentation

Geographical and cultural segmentation recognises that certain parts of the UK are substantially different from other areas. The regional differences are marked, particularly in food consumption. The differences may be traditional, for example the eating of black pudding, or economic. In other words in a poor area people's eating habits are likely to be different from those in more prosperous areas. Purchasing behaviour is strongly linked, of course, to what funds are available to the individual. Areas which have high levels of immigrants or those with different ethnic backgrounds tend to have alternative tastes and therefore need to be treated as a separate market segment.

Product positioning

Product positioning is designing the company's product and marketing mix to fit into a particular place in the consumer's mind. With market research a company can ascertain the position of a competitor's products and then decide whether to compete by offering a very similar product or attempt to fill a gap in the market. Multi-dimensional scaling or MDS is an increasingly popular way of positioning a product in your own mind's eye. If you can imagine a sliding scale working both horizontally and vertically, with the extremes noted at the end of each line, acting as a scale, you can then place a product or service at any point along that scale.

Once a company has established its product positioning it is ready to finalise the details of its marketing mix.

Companies find it difficult to cater for the mass market. They have increasingly considered target marketing which has enabled them to focus their efforts. By being able to identify specific target areas they can develop marketing strategy, advertising, pricing and distribution. The research stage is vital, as haphazard or confused results here mean that the entire target marketing exercise is thrown into doubt.

Successful target marketing has benefits for both parties. The **company** can become more competitive and can achieve greater sales and better profitability, while the **consumer** is hopefully more satisfied since the product or service more closely accords with his or her specific needs.

CONSUMPTION PATTERNS – INCREASING/DECREASING

The cost of developing new ideas gets greater as the development continues from initial idea to the launch of the finished product. Having established that the objective is to eliminate any potential losers as early as possible, how can a company fully satisfy itself that it is making the right decision to proceed? Comprehensive analysis and forecasting are the obvious things to do. Once an idea has reached the development stage we are talking about big money investment.

What do the stages look like?

- new ideas
- the screening process
- marketing analysis
- product development
- testing the product
- launch of the product

The 'fall-out' rate during this process gets less as the product gets closer to launch; this is the reverse of costs, which get higher and higher as the product reaches launch. In order to make sure that the product goes no further than its usefulness should allow, the marketing staff of the company must carry out research and compile as much information as possible on the potential of the product. Estimates must be made as to costs and the product's price needs to be set.

The sales potential also needs to be established. This may be obtained either from looking at competing products or by consulting the sales force as to their impressions of potential sales.

By the time the product is reaching the end of its development the marketing department should have made as many projections as is possible. These should include the necessary budgets and potential profitability.

There are several key ways of working out the sales potential of a new product or service. This form of forecasting is somewhat different from normal forecasting based on 'known' products, and takes the following into account:

1 The **overall value** of the product, in terms of what it generates, is one way of predicting the sales potential. Some companies rely on this value approach and miss the main point. Value just looks at the total revenue generated and does not take into account many of the more obvious features such as sales, reductions in price or inflation, for example. It is far more useful to look at the number of units they think will be sold and thus consider volume rather than value. You can then convert the volume figures into value ones at a later date if you need to.

2 Forecasting, to some extent, relies on the ability to **predict**, make guesstimates or assumptions. Price is a prediction, since you do not know what the 'going rate' will be when the product is available. You have to make assumptions on everything from the economic situation to the impact of a change in government. The reasonings behind these assumptions are as important as the assumptions themselves as these reasonings need to be looked at and appraised. The reasonings tie the assumption to the predicting person's view of the future, his or her version of the reality of the forecast. In order to make sure that the forecast is not wildly out, three forecasts are usually made:

- the **pessimistic** forecast, in which all the worst possibilities are considered to have occurred
- the **optimistic** forecast, in which all the best possibilities are assumed to have happened
- the **'most likely'** forecast, in which the best and worst possibilities are put together and an average situation is predicted. This is the version that is used for most planning exercises.

The forecasting techniques used are identical to those already discussed in an earlier chapter, but specifically, here are the most typical ones that relate to new products, with a brief description of each:

1 *The survey method.* Through market research a sample of potential customers is questioned about their likely purchases. They are asked to assume that the new product is available for sale and to decide whether they think that they would buy it and in what kind of volume. The questions asked would not necessarily be direct and would include questions that would attempt to look 'behind' the potential customers' buying habits.

2 *The delphi method.* This is a method that attempts to get a general view of the product's possible sales from many different groups of people. The discussion panel, or forum, may include managers, retailers, wholesalers and sales personnel. In other variants a group of experts are asked to discuss the sales potential with the objective of arriving at a consensus. This can be an expensive and time-consuming business but does offer a great opportunity to cover all the aspects, chances and possibilities.

3 *Sales staff predictions method.* This involves discussion of a particular product with the sales staff and getting them to assess its sales potential. This is not often used with a completely new product since the sales force's knowledge of a totally new product is limited and not very objective.

4 *The trial method.* A particular shop or a small chain in one area is chosen as the ideal average shop. The product is offered for sale here either to anyone who cares to buy, or and more usefully, to a select panel of buyers who again have the choice of whether to buy or not. This is a cheaper form of test marketing and is slightly more controllable.

5 *The moving average method.* A large number of 'new' products are simply modifications of ones that already exist. If this is the case then the moving average method is easy to employ. A series of sales figures are looked at and the underlying trend is worked out, in other words, the average sales figures. If the sales figures were 10, 12, 6, 8, and 4, the underlying trend would be 8. Uneven daily, monthly or yearly sales can be 'smoothed out' by this method and the true trend can be worked out.

6 *The exponential smoothing method.* This is similar in nature to the moving average smoothing of the figures, but this requires a little more consideration and skill. Later figures are compared to earlier ones and the researcher then weights the different figures in accordance with what he or she sees as their relative importance. If sales were high in a shop during the tourist season and then fell to a lower level after the season had finished then the researcher would probably decide that the weighting should be placed on the non-seasonal sales figures. The biggest problem with this technique is that it is only as good as the person who is determining the weightings.

7 *The time series analysis method.* The previous two methods are examples of time series analysis. The main characteristic is to smooth out the troughs and peaks and come up with an average figure that ignores short-lived increases and decreases.

8 *The lead indicator method.* When new products come on to the market it is often hard to predict sales. In this technique a similar product is chosen as the indicator of potential sales. The researcher analyses the sales figures of the existing product to help predict the sales of the new one.

9 *The diffusion model method.* This is perhaps the most useful for predicting sales of products that have no track record. Products tend to have a life cycle and this method attempts to predict what the life cycle will be like. As the first sales figures come in any initial prediction of the life cycle may be modified or radically rethought.

10 *The general analysis method.* Every company should take a regular look at itself to try to analyse the basic assumptions it makes about its operation, sales and profits. Forecasting is an integral part of this and will be based on the following:

- sales
- direct costs
- gross margins
- development costs
- marketing costs
- overheads
- cash flow

New products are slotted into this framework and their contributions, negative or positive, are factored into the calculations. New products are not always expected to pay for themselves immediately, but some products' lives will be cut very short if the projected profitability is not good enough, or if the company has to wait too long before the product will turn in a profit.

student activity

Which of the above methods would you use to assess the potential of the following products:

a new snack bar
a new radio station aimed at the under-21s
a new environmentally friendly washing powder

ECONOMIC INFORMATION

Organisations use statistical forecasting techniques to attempt to predict various national trends. Broadly, these fall into the following categories:

- social trends (including income and spending)
- gross national product (GNP)
- employment statistics
- growth indices

We shall look at each of these in more detail.

SOCIAL TRENDS

Social trends, in addition to showing data on average incomes and average spending, also show many of the following:

- population size
- breakdown of population by gender
- breakdown of population by age
- various regional variations
- birth rates
- death rates
- health
- migration

Income and expenditure statistics also show trends relating to household types and socio-economic groups.

student activity

Identify the sources of information for the above social trends and assess their accessibility.

GROSS NATIONAL PRODUCT

The gross national product shows the overall level of business activity within the UK. It is, in some respects, a more valuable indicator of the nation's wealth and potential than gross domestic product, since it includes both exports and invisible earnings. Statistical information gathered on general ouput from UK industry and inflation levels is also related to the gross national product.

EMPLOYMENT STATISTICS

An important economic indicator is the level of employment in the UK. The statistics should be able to identify key areas of growth or decline as well as identifying

potential shortfalls or gluts in skills nationally. Again, there may be regional variations in these figures, depending upon the reliance on particular forms of business activity.

student activity

Where would you find the gross national product of the UK? Compare the GNP of the UK with those of the following countries:

USA
Germany
Japan
Jamaica

student activity

How are employment statistics calculated?

GROWTH INDICES

The purpose of an index is to reduce a mass of data to a common level so that valuable comparisons may be made. This is particularly useful in the comparison of figures over a period of time. The main indices used are:

- price index numbers which measure changes in price
- quantity index numbers which measure changes in quantity
- value index numbers which measure the value of products and services

A common feature of all these indices is that they are all based on 100. This gives an easy base from which to work out the index number. The base number which equals 100 is the first year of data collection and all increases or decreases in subsequent years can be readily compared to the figure 100. The formula is quite simple:

$$\text{Quantity index number} = \frac{\text{Quantity in year}}{\text{Quantity in base year}} \times 100$$

Indices can be particularly valuable when one is looking at trends over a period of years, although it is important to realise that the index numbers may, in fact, be hiding much of the true detail. National income statistics, for example, which are prepared by the Central

Statistical Office, are published on a monthly basis in the Monthly Digest of Statistics.

student activity

As a manufacturer of processed foods, what information from the Central Statistical Office would you be interested in looking at before launching a range of new pre-packaged meals?

Investigate marketing activities

1 OBJECTIVES OF MARKETING
increase sales, increase market share, enhance product image, enhance corporate image, quality assurance

2 MARKETING ACTIVITIES
research, developing products, pricing, packaging, advertising, promoting, distributing, selling, after-sales service

3 MARKETING MIX
product range development, price, packaging, sales, promotions, distribution, consumer service

4 ETHICS
integrity, honesty

5 AUTHORITIES
Trading Standards Authority, Advertising Standards Authority

OBJECTIVES OF MARKETING

The success of a company is generally assessed in terms of the growth of its sales and profits. If the company sets out its objectives it can try to deploy its resources to best bring about progress. If progress is not forthcoming then it should be able to redeploy its resources to better effect. Diversification may well be the key to achieving growth. We will look at this in some detail shortly.

There are three main methods of expanding the company's activities:

- **Specialisation** is the adaptation of the company's existing range of products. The idea is to cater for additional markets. Growth is expected by getting into new markets with what you already offer rather than trying to launch new products.
- The company may diversify by **acquiring other companies**. The buying company will not just buy in new products or lines but the accompanying staff and expertise of the bought company.
- **New products** can be acquired by either developing them yourself, buying them in from other companies or by licensing the product from another company.

The basic purpose of all forms of marketing is to be able to communicate with the potential customer. The idea, of course, is to get them to buy the product or service that is on offer. However, to assume that selling is all that marketing communications are about is a gross oversimplification.

What then are communications and what are the questions we should ask?

- What is the **objective** and **purpose** of the sender of the message? Who is the **sender** of the information? This is known as the **control analysis**.
- What is the **substance** of the message? This is known as the **content analysis**.
- Who are the **intended audience** for the message? Who is it directed at? This is, amazingly, known as **audience analysis**. Segmentation and targeting play their part here.
- Through which **media** is the message sent? How is the message sent to the target segment? This is known as the **media analysis**.
- Finally, what happens once the message has reached the **listener**? This is known as **effect analysis** and looks at the response to the message.

From the communicator of the message, the message must try to reach the audience, and one of the major problems here is that the channels that are used can often be inadequate for successful communication. For example an advertisement may be reproduced very badly in a magazine or newspaper, or perhaps the double glazing salesperson may be interrupted by the phone ringing.

There are some ways around these possible interruptions:

- the use of attention seeking methods – this involves the use of a gimmick or something that attracts and keeps the attention of the listener. A good example of this would be the use of a jingle in an advertisement. In visual terms perhaps the best example is that used by Silk Cut cigarettes.
- repetition of the most important part of the message – this involves repeated use of a caption, headline or slogan to reinforce the message.

student activity

Can you think of an example of how repetition can work to help you remember the message which is being put across to you?

Communicating relies on the listener understanding what is being said. In all cases words or phrases that are likely to be misunderstood by the listener should not be used. Jargon must be avoided or explained. Misinterpretation means that the message will not get through to the listener in the way that the communicator of the

message wishes it to. Advertisers are often accused of being out of touch with the audience, not knowing what their attitudes and opinions are. By the same token, those who have the technical expertise and knowledge of a product may be incapable of communicating with the audience as they cannot communicate in non-jargon or non-technical terms.

student activity

Can you think of an advertisement which attempted to be too clever or used jargon terms and as a result, failed to get its message across?

The key to this problem is for the communicator and the audience to have some shared idea of the product. Having identified any problem that the audience may have in understanding the message, the communicator should be able to adapt the communication of the message to suit the audience.

Everyone has a slightly different set of beliefs and attitudes, some may be peculiar to him/herself, others may be shared with friends, relatives or the like. If a message goes completely against the individual's set of beliefs and attitudes then it is likely that his or her understanding may be distorted in some way. Some believe that a greater effect may be achieved by confronting these beliefs and attitudes, the reasoning being that the audience is more likely to remember such a message simply because it was so odd.

We've talked about having marketing communications objectives, but what are they? Here are some of the more common ones in the consumer field:

- to tell customers about a new product
- to put the record straight about a product (in other words to straighten out misconceptions)
- to get customers to use a product more often
- to remind customers that the product exists
- to tell customers about special offers and promotions
- to educate customers about a product, perhaps telling them how to use it
- to build a company image
- to build a product image
- to try to obtain a degree of customer loyalty to the product

The objectives may differ slightly if the marketing communication is aimed at other companies:

- to provide information about your company
- to provide information about your product(s)
- to pre-warn about forthcoming promotions
- to offer trade incentives or offers
- to educate the trade on the uses of your product(s)

There are of course limitations to how effective your communications will be. No matter what you do, not all of your communications will get through to the right person, consumer or trade.

Now that the objectives are set, the company has to decide which are the best ways in getting the communication to the intended audience. Before we can look at the different ways in which to communicate we will need to consider a number of things. Firstly, the basic ground rules:

- how can we satisfy, once we have identified them, the audience's interest in the information we have on offer?
- how can we maximise our expenditure? We have to try to make the costs as cost-effective as possible
- how much of the information can be communicated to the audience in ways that will not cost us anything? We may be able to secure editorial coverage in newspapers and magazines, we may be able to offer promotions that other agencies will willingly handle for us or we may be able to offer support to charities or the like for little capital outlay

INCREASING SALES

It is without doubt that organisations cannot exist without ensuring that sales income exceeds the costs incurred. Profits are essential, whether the business is a sole trader or a multinational.

> **Today, an increasing number of businesses are recognising the commercial advantages to be gained from the high quality of service, state of-the-art technology, competitive pricing, and comprehensive management reporting provided by Mercury Communications.**
>
> **In addition, Mercury users benefit from an innovative product line and the highest standards of customer care.**

FIG 3.3.1 *Mercury Communications are a prime example of an organisation which markets many of its services to businesses. This illustration is an extract from its brochure on the Mercury 2200 service which is specifically designed for business users.*

Organisations will endeavour to increase profitability by an overall increase in sales. It should be noted that not all organisations have this profit motive in mind at all times. There is always the danger of trying to expand too quickly. This is known as over-trading and occurs when the management finds it impossible to obtain sufficient working capital to run its operations.

Marketing provides a useful series of tools with which to increase sales. We have mentioned many of them already. Whether marketing's responsibility is simply to inform potential customers or concentrate on enhancing product image, the sales increase motive will usually remain paramount.

SURVIVING AND PROTECTING MARKET SHARE

As we have already mentioned, there are legal mechanisms in existence to ensure that an organisation does not control too much of a particular market. However, it is always the goal of most organisations to increase their market share within acceptable levels. Operating in a highly competitive market, most organisations find themselves not really able to increase their market share but concentrate instead on maintaining their market share. They do this by trying to retain customer loyalty through a series of marketing activities, in addition to normal promotional events. Organisations can suffer from sudden downturns in their market share when other organisations drastically reduce their prices. The inevitable response is to reduce prices in line with the new levels. Alternatively, an organisation may choose to enhance its products and services by offering non-price competitive options to the customer. A good example of this is the recent range of 'money back offers' made by car manufacturers. The car manufacturers have not used pricing in a competitive sense, but have chosen to offer an additional range of enhancements to ensure customer loyalty and the gradual expansion of their market share.

> *student activity*
>
> Can you identify an organisation which seems to control a large percentage of a particular market?

ENHANCING PRODUCT IMAGE

The enhancement of product image encompasses many of the activities an organisation will employ to protect their market share. Promotions or sponsorships have become particularly popular in recent years. There are

FIG 3.3.2 *Allied Lyon's Tetley Tea sponsors the British TV series 'The Darling Buds of May'. With an audience of 13 million viewers in the USA the organisation considers this an ideal way of enhancing its product image.*

a number of organisations which have sponsored television programmes. The image of the television programme helps to enhance the customer's perceptions of the product. However , National Power were unfortunate in their sponsorship of the coverage of the 1990 World Cup. The unexpected defeat of the English team not only curtailed television coverage, but also certainly damaged National Power's credibility. Martell Cognac, which sponsored the disastrous 1993 Grand National, similarly suffered a loss of face as a result of the fiasco.

ENHANCING CORPORATE IMAGE

Marketing plays an important role in enhancing corporate image. An effective and well-managed company should be market sensitive and should aim to create greater customer satisfaction. PR cannot possibly succeed in its goals if the company is unable to show itself

GUIDELINES FOR USE AND REPRODUCTION OF THE LOGOTYPE

The logotype shown below is the copyright of Anglia Television Limited, and may not be reproduced or transmitted in any form or by any means without the prior permission of Anglia Television Limited. The logotype consists of both the symbol and the words 'Anglia Television Limited' and must be used in its entirety.
Applications of the logotype must conform to one of the standard designs shown on the artwork supplied. No other arrangement of the symbol and wording, or typestyle, or colour is permissible; nor may the logotype be linked to any other typography or graphic device.
For any circumstances where the specifications given are not suitable, please contact the Public Relations Manager for further instructions.

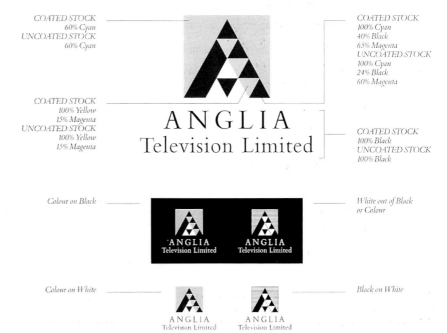

FIG 3.3.3 *Anglia Television is another prime example of an organisation which has produced clear guidelines for its logo to enhance its corporate image. You will notice the Anglia logo on many programmes such as 'The Chief', 'Survival' and 'Nightmare'.*

capable of performing well and demonstrating reasonable efficiency. Good trading performance coupled with strong customer loyalty goes a long way in maintaining a sound and positive corporate image. Marketing can help PR in the following ways:

- *product publicity* – getting your products (particularly new ones) on to the TV or featured in newspapers and magazines
- *informing* – continually feeding information to the public and other interested groups
- *media relations* – co-ordinating advertising, sales promotions, press releases etc. with the PR effort. It is in the company's interest to release as much information as it feels able to in order to counteract any chance that lack of information may mean that the public misunderstands or has a negative vision of the company
- *creating awareness* – by fostering a strong and positive attitude to the company this will help add to the reputation of the company's products and services. In circumstances where the company's reputation is not very good, PR and marketing can make sure that the company's name is kept away from the brand name of a product and that the product does not suffer as a result of the poor reputation
- *developing a corporate image* – marketing can be involved throughout the whole process, starting with market research that attempts to find out what expectations towards the company are. Secondly, it can analyse customer behaviour, target policy, advertising and selling and try to readjust perceptions of the company. Thirdly, it can optimise marketing opportunities and then broadcast the company's successes and at the same time be honest about mistakes. Finally, by using promotional skills, it can pass on information about successes and failures and develop the company's powers of information dissemination.

QUALITY ASSURANCE

Although some may not necessarily relate quality assurance directly to sales, it is an essential part of marketing activity. In this respect, a Marketing Department will endeavour to manipulate consumer perceptions so that they believe a product is of a higher quality than it is. Perceived quality is very important and is related to the position a product has in the market place.

BS 5750 offers organisations the opportunity to obtain government validation that their product or service has reached a sufficiently high standard. While the criteria for the awarding of this standard are somewhat confused in many instances and may not necessarily be applicable to non-manufacturing processes, many organisations are moving towards gaining this standard.

FIG 3.3.4 *Marks & Spencer take quality assurance very seriously. In this illustration we see Operations Supervisor Roger Hodson checking the read-out of a chilled food cabinet to ensure the perfect freshness and absolute safety of Marks & Spencer's foods.*

MARKETING ACTIVITIES

The Marketing Department of an organisation will involve itself in nearly every aspect of the organisation's activities. We have mentioned many of the activities already. This section of the book looks at the specific marketing responsibilities.

RESEARCH

Research, as you now know, is a very important issue for all business organisations, and it takes many forms. Research falls into two distinct categories, consumer and industrial research. They each have peculiarities of their own and need to be examined separately.

Consumer market research

A **purchase** means that someone has bought something. This may appear obvious, but we have to look at this simple fact in rather more detail. A good start is to look at different types of product purchases and how they satisfy particular demands.

The most common sort of purchase is the 'non-durable' type. This category includes food and all the other goods that can be used quickly. 'Durable' goods include all the other sorts of product that take some time to be used: furniture or electrical goods are examples of these. The third main category is services, which includes haircuts, education and all sorts of professional advice like that of a solicitor.

Goods themselves need more detailing and categorising. They fall into three main areas:

- **convenience goods** are those that are bought on a regular basis. They include most types of food, but also include anything that is a spur of the moment purchase. These are products which are bought with little planning or forethought
- **considered purchases** are those that people take a little longer to decide on before parting with their money. Examples of these would be clothes, holidays or luxury food items.
- **special purchases** are those that people really take some time to buy. They have in-depth knowledge of the product and can readily compare the competing products and will tend to buy the best they can afford rather than search for value for money. These sorts of goods include things like cameras.

student activity

Think about the sorts of things you buy. Then try to categorise them into the three main areas outlined above. Where do you think the bulk of your purchases are, what sort of percentage would you assign to each of the three?

What then of the **competition**? There are precious few areas of business activity that have no competition. Some of the competition an organisation must face is direct, while other forms are indirect. Almost every product or service a consumer could possibly need is available from a multitude of different suppliers.

Indirect competition refers to the various ways in which a particular demand may be satisfied. Consider a person looking for something to cook food with. He or she may purchase a gas oven, an electric oven, a microwave or a solid fuel cooker or even a barbecue! These are all direct competitors. An example of an **indirect** competitor would be restaurants or take-aways which would satisfy the purchaser's needs to some extent.

student activity

Identify some other examples of indirect competition. How can you best compete against indirect competition?

The last form of competitor is even harder to fight against. We have already discovered that purchasing power is limited and that businesses must compete for what funds are left available after the necessities of life have been paid for. What happens when someone is looking for a new car and decides to buy a new three piece suite with the money instead, or perhaps spends it on a holiday abroad? This is known as **competing needs** and we must therefore extend our definition of competition to cover anything that might induce the prospective buyer to spend money on something other than the product you are trying to sell him or her.

If marketing is all about meeting the needs of buyers, then we need to know a lot more about customers, whether they be individuals or organisations. The two markets have different characteristics and we shall have to look at them separately.

Let's ask some questions and then try to answer them:

- **Who** buys the product or service? This question is answered once we have segmented the market and identified exactly who our 'ideal' sort of customer is. By obtaining this knowledge we can then tell precisely where to find these people and match the product or service far more closely to their needs.
- **What sort** of products or services do they buy at present? This question follows on from the first very closely. Having discovered who buys we need to know what their buying habits are. What other products or services do they consume and is this knowledge useful in persuading them to buy our product or service?
- **Where** do they buy the product or service? Simply speaking, this is the place, geographically, where the product is purchased. Is it in a supermarket, the corner shop, at a specialist stockist, petrol station, through a mail order catalogue or by phone?
- **When** do they buy the product or service? Is there a pattern in their purchases? Is the product bought daily, like a newspaper, or is it monthly, like the monthly supermarket shop? Some products and services are only bought very infrequently, like Xmas trees or fireworks.
- **How often** do they buy the product or service? This is a question of frequency. Does the buyer only buy infrequently. An example of which is a car, or quite frequently, an example being a monthly magazine? If the business knows this it can gear its production to fulfilling the demands much more closely.
- How **loyal** are they in their purchasing? This looks at how reliable people are in staying with one product, and is also known as **brand loyalty**. Certain products rely on loyalty and indeed have strong levels of loyalty. Competitors will attempt to undermine this loyalty by offering incentives to switch brands.

Even though we have looked at these basic questions there are still some other fundamental questions we must examine. What makes someone buy something? It is a difficult question, so let's start by stating the obvious: they think that they **need** it. Fine, but what **prompts** that feeling of need?

The feeling of need can be aroused by a number of different factors. Some are straightforward: we need to buy food because we get hungry and need to consume food to satisfy that need. Other feelings of need are slightly more complex and the key to being a successful business is to stimulate that very essential feeling of need in people. Make them want what you have got! A successful business further needs to know exactly how to pander to these needs and satisfy the customer so that the next time they get that feeling of need they come to you.

Once you have identified that you need something **what do you do** about it? Hunger is easy to satisfy (in most countries) you just eat. But what about more complex needs? The first thing that comes into play is the memory. You try to remember what you did the last time that you felt that need. If you can't remember you might ask a friend, you might look in the Yellow Pages or you might consult a magazine that contains relevant information.

Now that you have discovered the various ways of satisfying your need you have to weigh up the **alternatives**. Your cultural values might come into play here, or perhaps your prejudices. Some people will never buy foreign cars, others will not buy South African produce. In most cases it is an objective decision that determines ultimate choice. Weighing up the pros and cons can be a difficult and complex task, but in most cases the choice is straightforward and almost automatic. Businesses need to be aware of the decision-making process and help the customer arrive at the right decision as far as that particular business is concerned and buy their product.

Even when you have decided what to buy it may still take you some time finally to buy it. Luxuries such as new cars or stereo systems are most likely to be affected in this way. The business must attempt to shorten this period of wavering to as short a time as possible and make sure that the prospective purchaser hands over the cash for his prospective purchase as quickly as possible. This often means that incentives are offered to speed up the decision making and win that sale.

Satisfied buyers pay huge dividends. If a buyer is pleased with a business's product he or she is more likely to buy the same product again, more likely to recommend it to others and more likely to be a fertile source of ideas for improvements and changes in the future. Knowledge of a brand name and, most importantly, knowledge that the particular product or service is worthwhile and reliable signals loud and clear to other potential customers.

FIG 3.3.5 *Customers who present this exclusive members' card will have a dividend automatically recorded on their share account. This incentive scheme comes from Ipswich and Norwich co-operative Society Limited.*

Industrial market research

Now that we have looked at the various aspects of individuals' buying considerations let's turn our attention to how organisations buy and what their habits are. We will start by answering the same questions that we posed for individuals:

- **Who** buys the product or service? This is as complicated as knowing about individuals. The seller of the product or service needs to know as much about his buyers as he possibly can. What size is their organisation? What are they? Distributors? Retailers? Segmentation is as vital in industrial marketing as in consumer markets. Who makes the decisions? Is it an individual or a group of people? Is there one buyer? What about the input of various managers and decisionmakers, where do they come in?

- We can identify various **types** of people who are involved in the buying process within an organisation, from the person who first brought up the idea that the purchase was necessary through to the decisionmaker who approves the purchase. We should not forget all the other people who, to a greater or lesser extent, will be involved. There are often technical considerations to be thought about, such as, is the prospective purchase compatible? From whom and where will the product be bought? The list is endless and the provider of the product or service must be able to answer questions from any of these quarters.

- **What products or services** do they buy? Broadly speaking the types of purchases fall into three main categories. Firstly there are the basic raw materials and parts, secondly what is known as capital equipment. This includes machinery and other accessories. Thirdly there are regular supplies and services; some of these are obvious, such as paper or office supplies, but this category may include the services of auditors or solicitors.

- **How** do they buy these products or services? This process is rather like that of consumer buying habits. Starting with the recognition that something is needed, it moves on to determining what exactly is required of the product or service (a specialist may be needed to determine what specifications should be considered). The next stage is the inevitable search for suppliers of the product or service, followed by an evaluation of them and what they are offering. The next phase may differ greatly from that of consumer purchasing, as the buying organisation now negotiates with the selling organisation as to the exact nature of the conditions of sale. This may include obvious things such as price and payment terms plus such matters as technical guarantees that the product or service will perform in a particular way. The

final part is again of vital importance and concerns the buying organisation's attitude to the seller organisation and how they perform in after-sales service and the like. This is likely to trigger further purchases as surely as price.

student activity

How important is after-sales service? How do companies stress the support they offer their buyers? Ask this question both of consumer products and of organisational ones.

The industrial marketing manager is usually further removed from the end-user market than the marketing manager in a consumer orientated company. In this sense the industrial marketing manager will find him or herself much more in need of good market research.

So what is industrial market research? It tries to provide information that helps the company understand the markets in which it operates now and may operate in the future. This type of market research is perhaps better described as market intelligence. The information should be collected on a rolling basis and look forward to what the market may be like in the future.

The field research is different from that in consumer research. Sampling has to be modified as it is not so easy to obtain a clear picture of market as it is of the consumer market through the eyes of the consumer.

Sampling can be on a much smaller scale because of the size of the markets involved in industrial marketing. Interviewing skills need to be better as the respondents tend to be specialists and far more sophisticated than their consumer counterparts.

Smaller businesses tend to lag behind in realising that market research is important. Their research budgets are invariably small as they seem to think that they can get all the information they want from their sales force.

Despite the size of the budgets the costs of industrial marketing are much smaller than those of consumer marketing. We have seen that it is difficult for the sales force to recognise the truth as they cannot very easily be objective. Nevertheless, few companies are willing to spend anything at all on research.

Outside consultants, if employed, will open up many new possibilities in the thinking of a company in the industrial field. Senior management in many medium and small companies are blissfully unaware of the possibilities of research. Marketing research can highlight the shortcomings of the company's marketing effort and show how the problems can be rectified with surprisingly little effort.

DEVELOPING PRODUCTS

Like any living thing the majority of products have a limited life. A product's life cycle starts with its birth, or introduction on to the market, then its growth in the market, its maturity stage when it is a fully established product and its declining phase when it is fading out of existence. Let's look at these stages in a little more detail.

The introduction of the product

The most important consideration here is to establish the product on the market. Awareness of the product's existence must be built up in the minds of retailers, wholesalers and, of course, the customer. Advertising is the usual method. Once a product is established in the minds of the potential buyers it must overcome any resistance to the acceptance of something new on the market. As orders begin to roll in the important point is to ensure that sufficient supplies of the product are available as nothing can kill a product off at birth more quickly than its non-availability.

The growth stage of the product

Having successfully launched the product and generated that initial interest and orders, companies often find it necessary to continue to promote the product so as to maintain its place in the market. This period of a product's life is usually its most profitable since demand may not yet have reached a peak and most of the initial costs have been recouped in the introductory period. It is at this time that the company will look for other potential markets to move into with the product and will also attempt to dislodge competitors from the market.

The maturity stage of the product

A company will look to extend this period of a product's life for as long as possible. In this stage the product delivers much needed profit and turnover for the company. Competition must be beaten off by the strong establishment of a brand image and a firmly rooted share of the market. Customers are still important. They must be able to obtain the product readily, and must still be encouraged to be loyal to it as this should guarantee a steady level of purchases.

Older products may be on the verge of decline but it is possible, by careful thought, to provide them with a new lease of life either by reintroducing them into the market or by introducing them into new markets. We will look at product modification in more detail later.

The decline stage of the product

Sooner or later something will happen that will forever kill off potential sales. It may be any of the following:

- the product becomes technically obsolete
- customer attitude to the product changes
- a better product has appeared on the market
- sales have peaked and are falling off
- it is no longer profitable to produce it

Once any of the above has occurred the company is faced with having to do something about it. Among their options are:

- stop spending anything on the product in excess of the cost of producing it
- raise the price and milk the last possible sales out of it and let it die a natural death
- divert spending on to other products
- decide that once demand reaches a particular level production will cease and wait until that happens before acting
- maintain production at a minimum level to supply demands arising from brand loyalty
- maintain the product at present levels and hope that additional marketing activities can rejuvenate the product
- put the decline down to changes in trends and fashions and wait for the product to become fashionable again

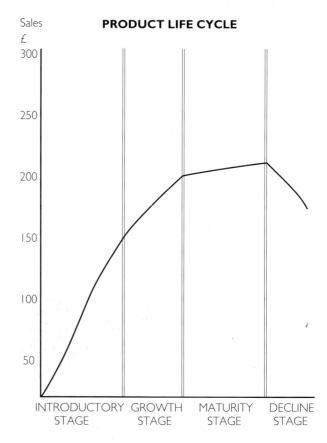

FIG 3.3.6 *This graph shows the common form of product life cycles.*

Launching the product is the most expensive stage so far. So you'd better have got it right! TV advertising costs are enormous, promotional costs across the board from sales promotions through poster campaigns to incentives to stockists often cost more than half of the total revenue that the product generates in the first year. Manufacturers are looking for a successful product, that's all that counts really. If the product turns in a profit after taking into consideration all costs after the third year, then they think they have succeeded. Lessons are learnt very hard, and only around 10 per cent

Don't settle for an ordinary credit card

What would you expect a credit card to give you? Convenience? An extra financial resource for unexpected expenses? Flexibility?

Of course, these things are very important, and you'll get them all with a Barclaycard.

But today, you really should be looking for much more. And with Barclaycard you'll find it. Because by possessing a Barclaycard you'll have access to a whole range of complimentary benefits and services:

International Rescue – helps solve problems when you're abroad.
Purchase Cover – insurance for most Barclaycard purchases.
Travel Accident Insurance – for travel paid for with your card.
Barclaycard MasterCard – a second, totally separate account.
Free Additional cards – for your partner.

You don't have to bank with Barclays to apply for a Barclaycard. So if you're looking for your first credit card, or to improve on your existing card, look no further. Barclaycard gives you so much more.

FIG 3.3.7 *Even the well-established Barclaycard is continually re-packaged and re-launched as can be seen from this recent leaflet, 'Barclaycard – so much more than a convenient way to pay', August 1993.*

of products that reach the launch stage can be considered successful. In success terms this means that they still exist after the first year.

To avoid massive spending and possible massive losses, a company may wish to mirror its test market launch. Gradual launches are very popular since the costs can be limited and the returns more accurately assessed. Advertising and PR can be mobilised to fill in the gaps in the public knowledge of the product.

A successful business should always try to have a range of products within its product mix at various stages of their life cycles. Companies which rely on one product and one product alone are in constant danger of getting into a position that might mean that they have lost their 'golden egg' and do not have a newly hatched one to replace it. Businesses need a steady flow of profitable products so that the more mature products help pay for the new ones, which in turn will pay for the next generation of profit makers.

In the field of product development there are two major strategies: one concentrates on being the first into a new field and is called **proactive** product development and the other is somewhat safer as the company responds to changes by copying other companies' leads; this is known as **reactive** product development.

The dangers with having a proactive policy are that you are forever breaking new ground and taking the risks. There is a high risk of failure, but with that risk comes the possibility of great rewards. The first company to create a product for a waiting market should be well placed to make very good profits. A reactive policy is much safer, as you can learn from any mistakes made by the proactive company and avoid them. The proactive company has, after all, taken all the risks and if you are ready to react you can profit from the market that it has just opened up. You can often make as much, if not more, by being a very fast reactor as by being the proactor but you are spared all the inherent risks.

How can you tell whether a product or service is likely to take off? The company must look at the advantages its product might have over the competition and weigh up whether they are promising enough to take the risk. These are some of the key considerations:

- does the product accurately meet the requirements of the target market?
- does it have advantages in design, style, reliability or quality?
- how does it perform and stand up to the demands that will be made on it by the customer?
- does it make the customer's life easier (in the case of a labour-saving device)?
- does it add to the customer's ego or self-image (in the case of a designer product)?
- does it offer the customer the chance of respect from others (in the case of a status symbol)?
- is it likely to be seen as a superior product when compared to other competing brands?
- are its presentation and image right?
- does it cost less to produce than the competition?

FIG 3.3.8 *Tesco's own label products coupled with their highly successful multi-saver price promotions offered discounts or free products on 400 items in their largest stores. It was promoted on television, in the press and in the stores themselves with the quotation, 'Tesco has never given away so much free!'*

- can you expect a reasonable profit margin?
- can you offer a consistent and reliable product or service?

A brand is a name that is given to a particular product or range of products. In many cases this brand name is simply the company's name, such as Ford or Heinz. In other cases it may be a completely different name such as Nescafé, or it may be the overall name for the entire range of goods such as Marks & Spencer.

student activity

Make a list of the brand names that you can think of, writing down as many as you can in five minutes. See how many of them are actually company names and how many are really product names.

Branding basically exists to differentiate a particular product from its competitors; it is all to do with helping the customer identify the product easily. The choice of a brand name is often absolutely vital, and many brand names are household names, indeed some have become part of the language such as Hoover. We all say that we are going to hoover the living room, and rarely say that we are going to vacuum it. Such is the power and penetration of the brand name into our lives.

With the dominance in the supermarkets of 'own label' products the brand name has a new meaning to the customer. If you have the choice of buying Nescafé or Sainsbury's own label coffee what is there to help you make up your mind? The price is different, the Sainsbury's own label brand is cheaper, you may get more 'bulk' for your money, but what do we really think of the choice? Nine times out of ten you will probably reach for the Nescafé, but why? Probably because you think that the Nescafé is 'better', but better in what respect – better quality? Perhaps. Now change the situation around and compare Nescafé with Maxwell House: why do you buy one rather than the other? Customers go into a shop with a mental list of their preferred brands. What all the marketing, sales promotions and advertising are geared up to do is to put their particular brand name into your memory so that, when you are faced with a choice of branded or own label products, your decision-making process is speeded up and you reach for the brand they want you to reach for.

This branding goes further and tries to encourage you to see a company's entire range as having the same reputation (a good one, of course). This multi-product branding really does pay dividends, especially when a company is launching a new product that has the same brand name as existing products. In such a situation the new product will find sales and will be accepted more quickly. The company must be careful, however, since this is a two-edged sword. A poor product can bring a bad reputation to an otherwise good and reliable brand name.

Other companies prefer to trade under a range of brand names. Their various brand names in the same market, appear to be competing, but often they are complementary products. A good example of this is United Biscuits which trades under several household-known brand names including Maxwell House and McVities. Two products, in all but brand name, can then be aimed at different market segments with different images, prices and marketing strategies.

student activity

Visit your local supermarket and have a look at the competing brands of washing powder, liquid and fabric conditioners. You will be amazed to see just how many of them are produced by the same company. Each brand has its own identity and advertising campaign, but is this just a clever way of selling the same thing to different people?

FIG 3.3.9 *Just as tangible products can be promoted, services regularly appear on British television. The Alliance and Leicester spearheaded its 1992 campaign with a series of popular television commercials featuring Stephen Fry and Hugh Laurie. This attracted much new business and a Silver Award from the Institute of Practitioners in Advertising.*

As we have noticed some manufacturers have their own brand name, others sell under the brand name of a retailer. The manufacturers who produce particular Marks & Spencer products will also produce their own brand products. This method of production is very useful to the manufacturers since it enables them to increase their own production runs and simply change the labels. It also means that they can sell a large proportion of their production runs without having to promote and market them themselves. In other cases producing own label products for retail chains is the only way to get them to stock your goods.

What this relationship does mean is that retailers like Sainsbury's, Marks & Spencer and Tesco are in a very powerful position. They control the pricing, the distribution and the marketing. The manufacturer is very much in their hands. The retail chain will be able to demand that pricing is in their favour, the specifications of the product meets with their approval, that stock levels are maintained at a particular level and that they receive priority treatment even above the manufacturer's own label products.

The use of a name coupled with the brand name also helps to identify a particular product. Ford is the company name and also the brand name, but in addition, all of Ford's makes or models of cars have a name of their own. The Fiesta, Sierra, Escort and Orion are all examples of Ford's product names. The use of these names helps the customer decide by enabling him or her to recognise and select a product in a potentially confusing situation. Ford could just call all of their cars

Ford cars and give them a number or describe them as the £13,000 Ford car. Each product name establishes a specific image by which the customer can identify the product. The choice of name for a product has to be carefully thought out. An inappropriate name is death to a product.

A product name helps to position a product in the market. The name should convey something to the prospective buyer that he or she can relate to. A boring or inappropriate name will need to have much more spent on it in marketing and promotion than a name that inspires the customer and is remembered.

student activity

There are hundreds of product names that tell you actually nothing about the product. The name portrays nothing and without advertising and promotion you would not have a clue what it was. Why do you think producers decide to call a product by such a name?

Once you have decided on a name you need to protect that name. Unless trade names are registered as trademarks there would be nothing to stop anyone giving their product the same name as yours. Successful products can be imitated but they cannot be copied and the same thing goes for names. You cannot even attempt to partly copy a name; for example you could not name your car the Furd Curtina, or you would find yourself very quickly in court! Registered names and trademarks are very valuable commodities, as the name represents all the effort and expense you have put into making that product what it is.

Finally there is the question of how you present your product, physically. Its packaging and overall look are very important since you want people to notice it and recognise it after you have spent all that money promoting it. The first consideration is a very practical one: what does the packaging need to achieve in terms of the actual protection of the product? In the case of food the packaging needs to seal out the world and prevent the product from deteriorating. The packaging needs to be robust enough to survive the handling from factory to warehouse, to shop, to customer's home. It has to be the 'right' size: it needs to be able to fit easily on to the retailer's shelves perhaps, or maybe it is just a question it looking right in their store. Is the packaging safe and convenient for the customer? Can it be opened easily?

PRICING

Pricing is placing a value on a product or service. A product or service has to have a price so that the prospective buyer knows what he or she will have to pay for it. Prices can be fixed, as they are in most cases, where the seller has determined a particular price and the buyer must pay that price if he or she wants the product or service. The other type of price is the negotiable price. Here the buyer haggles with the seller until they have agreed a price and then the transaction is made.

Prices occur at various levels of the distribution chain. The supplier of the product may sell to a wholesaler, who then sells to a retailer, who then sells to the customer (the final buyer in the chain). At each sale a price is set based on the price that the was paid for the item, plus a mark-up to cover costs and to include a profit.

Most business organisations are in the market to make a profit and the financial performance of a company is often measured in the following major ways, all of which involve pricing.

The first way is to look at the company's **turnover**, or the revenue received from sales. More important is the percentage margin of gross profit that makes up a part of this turnover. This relates to what the company charges for the products or services it sells. The other major way is to look at the **rate of return on capital assets** (like machinery) and at how cost-effective these items are. This relates to what the company paid for the capital assets in the first place.

The generation of sales revenue is determined by what the buyer (perhaps a wholesaler or retailer or even the retail customer) is willing to pay for the products or services the company is offering. Conversely, the cost to the company in relation to capital expenditure is based on what the suppliers of those capital assets charge for their products or services. A value has thus been set at both levels of buying and selling.

A company may be able to distribute well, or create effective advertising or be generally efficient, but if it does not get its pricing right it will inevitably fail. The price may be too high, in which case no one will be prepared to buy the product, or it may be too low, in which case the company will not make a sufficient profit on the sale. Also the company's pricing may be confusing in which case sales may suffer or be delayed. It is, above all, imperative to get the pricing right, as the very survival of the company depends upon it.

Many different factors determine price. Pricing policies may differ greatly from company to company. Pricing decisions have to be made by suppliers wishing to sell their goods to retail chains and they in turn must set a price at which they will sell the goods on to the customer. In the case of finished goods (like cars, TVs and stereos), the price the retailer charges the customer has to be agreed to some extent with the supplier of those goods. After all, the customer generally expects to pay roughly the same price for a product no matter where he or she goes to buy it. The profit margin that the retailer wants is dependent upon that business's needs and the competition it faces and the supplier must allow a standard profit margin for most retailers and a greater one for those who buy the product in greater bulk.

student activity

Is there much deviation in prices? Just how controlled do you think prices really are?

PACKAGING

Packaging has really come into its own over the past few years for a number of reasons, the most important of which are the growth of self service as a retail tool and the need to ensure that the product gains as much shelf space as possible through easy and efficient distribution by virtue of its packaging.

The demand for different and more flexible packaging has led to the widespread use of plastics, foil and treated paper and card. New printing technology has allowed hitherto unusable materials to carry product information, photographs and logos. Packaging has assisted the massive change to supermarket shopping where nearly 90 per cent of the weekly shopping is now done, all self service.

student activity

How has convenient packaging affected the way we shop? Why are there so few retail outlets that offer 'unpackaged goods?

Packaging design itself needs to fulfil a number of functions, which include the following:

- *protection* – the product needs to be protected against the environment, rough handling or time itself
- *convenience* – easy handling, easy to store and easy to open. How many of you have had milk cartons spray you with their contents even if you follow the directions on the packaging?
- *easy storage* – the package should be a regular size, easy to stack and store
- *easy to use* – functional packaging that is easy to use, perhaps incorporating safety features
- *convenient to transport* – costs may be cut by packaging the product in light-weight materials that are strong enough to survive the journey

FIG 3.3.10 *Geest import bananas from the Windward Islands and since these are comparatively fragile fruit, they require careful handling and packaging at all stages of their distribution.*

- *reusable packaging* – a product's packaging can be designed to be reusable by the use of refills. Other products, such as coffee jars, can be reused as a storage jar for other products. In this case the shape should be important so that the container is recognisable even after the label has been removed

- *assist product image* – the shape, as we have mentioned already, should be recognisable and help to enhance the product's image
- *corporate identity* – similar to product image, but here a range of products may have similarities to each other to help foster an image of overall identity which assists in maintaining brand loyalty
- *display advantages* – a package that is easy to arrange, stack and display has great advantages in the supermarket. A regular sized package is likely to be easier to stack in bulk, but at the same time should be attractive to the customer
- *differentiation* – a different shape, or strikingly different artwork, can be used to give the impression that the product is different. The widespread use of seasonal packaging in particular is a good example of this

student activity

Do you think that packaging is important? What makes some packaging work and some not?

Packaging's main function is to protect the product inside. There are several key features to be considered:

- damage during handling is perhaps the most common form of hazard to the package. Most damage is done before the product reaches the customer. Damaged goods must be replaced and are inconvenient both to the retailer and to the customer
- theft cannot be easily avoided, but certainly a good packaging system will inhibit this. The main problem is the number of handlers there are from manufacturer to customer
- food, clothing and sensitive machinery are particularly prone to contamination by dust or other small particles. An air-tight package is therefore essential
- seepage of liquids in particular is a problem and they should be protected from leaks, or evaporation. This holds true for powders too
- flavour loss or changes in flavour may be the result of non-air-tight packaging or packaging that lets in the light
- moisture changes can damage products; frozen foods need a constant moisture level as do seemingly tough products like paints
- insects may attack poorly protected products and do untold damage to them
- mould may attack a badly packaged product and can irretrievably affect the quality of the product

student activity

Try to put the packaging considerations into order of priority for the following products:

- a range of milkshakes
- a range of hi-fi and audio equipment
- a range of self-assembly furniture

How do these priorities differ?

ADVERTISING

All branches of the media maintain audience figures and profiles, and by examining each branch's profile of its audience, the planner can attempt to match the company's product and message with the appropriate medium. It is unlikely that any one branch of the media will get the message to all of the proposed target audience, in which case several different media will have to be used. Given below are approximate figures showing the number of adults that might see advertisements in particular media. These figures represent what is known as 'opportunity to see' or OTS, which is the basic measure of the potential coverage of each major medium.

Outdoor advertisements (posters, buses etc.)	nearly all of the adult population
Television advertisements	over 90 per cent
Sunday newspapers	approx. 75 per cent
Daily newspapers	nearly 70 per cent
Radio	nearly 40 per cent
Weekly magazines	approx. 40 per cent
Monthly magazines	30–40 per cent
Cinema	under 3 percent.

student activity

What is unfair about the percentage shown for cinema audiences? What is there about cinema audiences that makes the cinema so expensive?

Unfortunately the choice of medium is not quite as simple as this. If the planner could choose his or her medium by only considering the effectiveness then life would be easy. The question of cost effectiveness must be looked at. It costs more, amazingly, to advertise in certain media than in others. Not surprising you might say. Your £1.00 goes further in some media than others and these costs are compared below. The cost is per thousand of the adult population.

Outdoor advertisements	around 30p
Television	about £3.25 (varies according to region)
Newspapers	nearly £3.00
Magazines and colour supplements	approx. £1.40 (but differs greatly according to magazine's popularity
Cinema	£18.00 plus
Radio	around 80p

student activity

Why bother to advertise in any other media than TV and outdoor posters? After all, aren't you likely to reach the bulk of the target audience?

This price comparison is not entirely fair as we have not considered the size or length of the advertisement or the use of colour's. As a rule there are some average sizes and typical methods of use, and these are what the prices above are based on; here are some examples:

Newspapers	full page black and white advertisement
Colour supplements	full page colour advertisement
Television	30-second slot
Outdoor advertisement	figure is very rough average as the costs of various advertising positions differ enormously.

As we have already mentioned, you can advertise on TV, or elsewhere for that matter, and still not make an impact. You can look at the cost-effectiveness of different media, choose the best for your budget and still not have an impact. The key is the **frequency** with which you advertise. Marketing writers have called this the 'threshold', by which they mean that you have to advertise beyond a certain minimum in order to have any effect at all. This threshold is worked out on the OTSs basis, so if you wanted the target audience to have ten OTS then you would have to show the advertisement far more often than ten times.

student activity

How would you work out the OTS and make sure that your audience does see the advertisement the required number of times?

It isn't enough just to work out the CPT (Cost Per Thousand). As we have already seen, we are not comparing the different media fairly. We can only make assumptions and make very rough comparisons between the different media. Certain media have advantages over others for certain products. When working out a media plan and schedule the planner must consider the following:

- the budget
- using the right media to reach the right target audience
- the need to cover the whole audience (in other words make sure all of them are reached in some way)
- the need to make sure that the target audience has the opportunity to see the message
- achieving this in a cost-effective way
- the need to make sure that the media helps in increasing the impact of the message

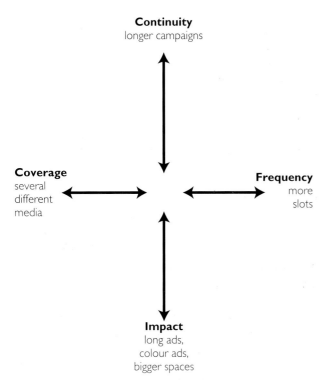

FIG 3.3.11 *A diagram which illustrates the media-planner's dilemma.*

Taking account of all of these considerations means that the media planner has to compromise. The key considerations are the continuity of the campaign, the overall coverage (in different media etc.), the impact and the frequency. It is a rare media planner indeed that is capable of satisfying all these considerations.

In order to take account of the relative merits of each of the media it is appropriate to look at their advantages and disadvantages.

Television

Up until quite recently viewing was almost equally divided between the BBC and the IBA. The IBA of course includes the fourteen regional independent stations plus Channel 4 and TV AM. Naturally, ITV's viewing figures, regionally, reflect fairly closely the demographic spread of the population. The station's share of the audience ranges from some 22 per cent in London and the Thames area to less than 1 per cent in the Channel Islands

1 *Advantages*

(a) TV is extremely useful in getting simple and uncomplicated messages to the vast majority of the population. Most homes have a TV set and therefore on a purely statistical basis everyone has the opportunity to see an advertisement.

(b) Generally speaking the impact should be good. Creativity is high and is assisted by the use of colour and sound.

(c) It is widely agreed that people are more receptive to advertisements in a relaxed atmosphere (homes are usually relaxed, but not necessarily so).

(d) The sophisticated collection and analysis of viewing data helps the media planner target the audience more accurately.

(e) In a highly competitive market such as this, attractive discounts are offered to new or for that matter, regular advertisers.

(f) The regional nature of independent television further helps the planner to segment the country into manageable advertising areas.

2 *Disadvantages*

(a) Production costs, apart from the most basic of advertisements, are high.

(b) Air time can be extremely expensive at peak times. For example, in the Thames region a 30-second peak-time slot would cost in excess of £40,000, dropping to as little as £2,000 in the Border region which only caters for 1 per cent of the population.

(c) High-income and well-educated groups tend not to view as often as the rest of the population. Therefore, television may not be the right medium for them.

(d) Tests have proven that viewers' attention wanders during advertising breaks.

(e) The population's wide use of the video recorder may mean that advertisements are not viewed at all when a programme is played back.

The available advertising time is at present strictly limited, only seven minutes per hour being allowed for advertising purposes. Charge rates are calculated according to particular times of the day, assumed audience size and demand from other advertisers. To buy a 30-second slot on all regional TV stations in peak time would cost well in excess of £100,000.

The Anglia Region

County Boundaries
Airports
Cargo Ports
Ferry Ports
(MS) Main Studios
(NC) News Centres

FIG 3.3.12 *This map illustrates not only the organisation of Anglia Television, but also the infrastructure of the area*

Magazines

With well over a thousand magazines available in the UK alone, the advertiser has the choice of specialist or general interest magazines that are released with frequencies ranging from weekly to quarterly. The range of magazines is really quite bewildering and is constantly changing, but many have done a lot of work that helps the advertiser by specifically catering for a particular audience by offering the right sort of editorial material.

I *Advantages*

(a) Segmentation and targeting can be precise as the magazine may well have done this for its own purposes and, by providing a full reader breakdown, can save the advertiser from having to undertake this him/herself.

(b) Special interest magazines have a considerably longer life than most other magazines. The editorial content is well read and the advertisements are given much more attention than those in general interest magazines.

(c) Magazines tend to have a longer life than newspapers and have a much higher 'pass-on' rate (more than one person reads the magazine).

(d) Advertisements that appear in well-known and respected magazines may well have increased impact and credibility by being in these particular magazines.

(e) The better quality paper and more sophisticated printing techniques used in magazines allow the advertising of up-market products with colour advertisements.

2 *Disadvantages*

(a) There is quite keen competition for the attention of the reader with many high quality advertisements and interesting editorial material.

(b) The readership breakdown is far less complete for magazines than for newspapers; indeed for smaller circulation magazines there may be no independent audits of their true circulation figures available.

(c) An advertiser should not expect an instant response from an advertisement as the 'shelf-life' of the magazine is comparatively long, as is the 'digesting' period after the buyer has purchased the magazine.

(d) Magazine publication schedules have long lead and cancellation times for advertisements and these make 'spur of the moment' advertising very difficult.

(e) High quality advertisements inevitably mean high production costs to create the original for the advertisement.

In many respects the world of magazine advertising is much like that of newspaper advertising. Magazines tend to vie for advertising far more aggressively than newspapers and will often offer special deals for new advertisers and regulars far more readily than newspapers. As one of the disadvantages points out, magazines have relatively early copy dates and require advertising copy as much as two to three months prior to the publication date. Costs vary enormously, women's weekly magazines can be as much as £20,000 per full colour page. The range and scope of advertising in magazines is huge and ultimately will suit anyone's pocket.

student activity

Compare the relative costs of TV and magazine advertising. What are their advantages and disadvantages over one another?

Newspapers

There is a considerable choice in national newspapers available to the potential advertiser. Sales figures (or circulation figures) differ widely. Far and away the most successful newspapers are the *Sun*, and the *Mirror*, both boasting sales between three and four million per day. Several other major papers have sales in excess of a million with the 'heavy' newspapers barely mustering half a million each. A distinction should be made between the daily papers and the Sunday papers as some three million additional sales are made on Sundays. Nearly 15 million newspapers are sold daily whereas over 17½ million are sold on Sunday.

1 *Advantages*

(a) Over 85 per cent of the population can be reached by the combined sales of national and local newspapers. However, a great many individual advertisements would have to be placed in different papers to reach them all.

(b) Each newspaper has a distinctly different readership which allows for accurate segmentation.

(c) The flexibility of short or long notice is a key feature of daily newspapers.

(d) Many people tend to believe the printed word more than any other form of advertising.

(e) Many national newspapers offer the facility of split runs; in other words a company may advertise in the Mirror just in the North of England should it wish.

(f) The message that a company is trying to get across may be long and complex, such as financial advertising and this form of advertisement is best suited to a newspaper.

(g) Many newspapers have now begun to offer special advertising features on certain days, e.g. Monday may be jobs, Tuesday may be property.

(h) An increasing number of newspapers are offering colour supplements. Despite the fact that many papers have gone over to colour reproduction, at least for part of the paper, there are grave misgivings about the quality of colour reproduction on newsprint. The availability of colour supplements helps to alleviate this problem.

2 *Disadvantages*

(a) Most people view newspaper advertisements as boring. They lack impact, although colour has helped improve this.

(b) The bulk of newspapers are only read on the day they come out, therefore the advertisements have a very short life.

(c) The growth of the free newspaper market has diluted available income. Further, it has meant that many newspapers are simply composed of advertisements with very little editorial material. Advertisements simply 'get lost' in the mass.

Reader loyalty can compensate for a number of the criticisms. Equally, certain prestige titles attract a disproportionate amount of advertising compared to their readership. Editorial support for new products is very much a feature of certain titles and greatly enhances the impact of the advertisement itself.

student activity

Is there any point in advertising in local weekly free sheets? Are they just papers full of advertisements pretending to be newspapers? How would you objectively assess their value?

Radio

The 1990s has signalled an explosion in radio. Independent radio as run by the IBA tends to be very middle-of-the-road in its appeal. Networking (rather like the TV version), where the same programme is simultaneously broadcast across the entire independent local radio (ILR) network, is becoming more common and offers very exciting possibilities for the advertiser.

I *Advantages*

(a) This medium is ideal for urgent and immediate advertising announcements.

(b) With widespread stereo use, sound-effects and gimmicks are far more effective than on TV.

(c) A company can advertise precisely to a set area (independent local radio has clearly defined broadcast areas).

(d) Production costs for radio advertisements are comparatively cheap.

(e) Good discounts are available for both new and regular advertisers.

(f) Short notice may be given to the stations for bookings and cancellations, so flexibility is high.

2 *Disadvantages*

(a) National campaigns are difficult to plan and co-ordinate due to the local nature of the ILR network.

(b) Radio has the reputation of being a 'low-impact' medium, used as background 'sound' and not concentrated on as much as the TV.

(c) As with TV, national advertising can be expensive if one adds up the air time across the whole network.

There are two main routes through which radio air time sales are made, firstly there are 'brokers' who handle the sales for each of the stations through their contacts with the London advertising agencies. Secondly the stations sell air time locally through their own offices and sales force. Capital Radio in London heads the price league with a cost approaching £1,500 for a 30-second peak slot, dropping down to under £10 for an off-peak slot on one of the smaller and more remote stations. Discounts can be very attractive as it is rare to buy a single spot. The most common advertising package offered is known as the Total Audience Package (TAP) which aims to reach a cross-section of the listeners at various times of the day over a period of time.

student activity

Radio advertising is a relatively young medium. Do you think that you can accurately target the segment to which you wish to pass on your message? How well do radio stations detail their audience figures?

Outdoor advertising

Outdoor advertising does not just mean static poster sites. It also includes advertising carried on buses, taxis and at train stations. Other 'sites' include sports stadiums (such as football pitches), balloons (the really big ones!), milk bottles and even parking meters!

The most obvious form of outdoor advertising is the poster and you will find these literally everywhere. They do lack the impact of TV, magazine or newspaper advertising, but do serve to remind people about the advertising message.

I *Advantages*

(a) Very high OTS.

(b) Very low CPT.

(c) Wide range of colour available.

(d) Wide choice of sites.

(e) Good opportunities to be the only advertisement in view at any one time, little direct competition.

(f) Sites tend to be sold on a quarterly basis. The gradual effect of the poster may make people sub-consciously notice the advertisement and take note of it over a period of time.

(g) Great opportunities to have very innovative advertising such as the three-dimensional advertisement with models, cars or similar 'stuck' on to the poster.

2 *Disadvantages*

(a) Printing costs are high for the short runs needed for posters.

(b) There is a long booking and cancellation period.

(c) Very debatable research into site 'audiences'.

(d) Can be missed easily and not even looked at by the 'audience'.

(e) Only short snappy messages tend to work.

(f) Graffiti can be a problem.

(g) Prime sites are often monopolised by 'big' advertisers.

(h) Sites are usually not available individually and a package of sites is sold to the advertiser who has no control over where the advertisement is shown.

Most outdoor space is sold by a handful of contractors. They sell a package of mixed sites which are meant to get the advertisers' message across to the intended target audience. Popular sites are often tied up literally for years with the TC (Till Countermanded) system, and this can be frustrating.

Costs vary immensely; some 400 sites sell for around £70,000 per month. Bus rears cost around £50 each per month and are usually available in multiples of 50.

student activity

Do you notice poster or bus advertisements? How would you assess their effectiveness?

Cinema advertising

There are now under a thousand cinemas in the UK, but the medium is gradually fighting its way back as a form of entertainment after a period of decline. Attendance figures show that it is a medium that tends to attract the younger age groups.

1 *Advantages*

(a) Local advertising is possible, and cheap.
(b) Ideal for targeting the younger age group.
(c) Great impact, the audience's attention is held by the 'big screen'.
(d) Reproduction, both of sound and picture, is very good.

2 *Disadvantages*

(a) Low audience figures.
(b) Production costs are high, as expensive as TV advertisements. In addition to this prints of the advertisement are needed for each cinema and these cost several hundred pounds each.
(c) Buying 'space' can be difficult as the medium is not as developed as others.

There are two main sellers of cinema advertising space, but data on audiences are still sparse. Packaging of advertising 'slots' is popular and advertisers can buy slots either in similar towns or areas (such as seaside towns) or in all the cinemas in a particular city. If an advertiser wanted to buy a thirty-second slot on all of the available screens in the UK it would cost in excess of £40,000.

student activity

Do production and duplication costs outweigh the advantages in cinema advertising? Do you think it would be feasible just to concentrate on TV advertising?

SALES PROMOTION

Sales promotion, known as 'below the line expenditure' in sales and marketing, is hard to explain in theoretical terms, but easier to describe by means of examples. If you buy something that says '10p OFF!' or save wrappers from a snack bar for that very valuable Mr Blobby Mega-Mix tape, or 'BUY 2 GET ONE FREE', they are all examples of sales promotions.

Sales promotions account for up to half of all marketing expenditure. This half includes many sales promotions that most people never get to hear about. Trade sales promotions are very common, such as bulk order discounts or rebates based on the amount spent in a year with a supplier. In the latter example, a target is set by the supplier and if the buyer reaches a certain level of purchasing over the year he or she will obtain a higher (retrospective) discount level. In strict terms these types of sales promotions should not really be counted.

Sales promotion has one main aim, to increase sales. This may seem fairly obvious, but the tactic is deeper than what advertising aims to achieve. Sales promotions try to encourage larger, and more frequent purchasing from the buyer.

Most sales promotions are short-term campaigns. Some types of goods are very dominant and regular users of sales promotions. Breakfast cereal producers offer sales promotions, for example, though not to increase sales by this means, since they keep up one promotion or another for virtually the entire year. So why do they do it? By offering plastic Turtle figures, one brand of cereal temporarily has an edge over the cereal that doesn't. For cereal producers, and indeed for petrol companies, sales promotion replaces the need to cut their prices to attract more sales. Price wars do nothing for any of the companies involved except reduce their profits, and no one wants that.

student activity

Why bother with sales promotions? Surely resorting to these means that your advertising campaign is not working?

Sales promotions have become increasingly popular in past years. There are three main reasons for this:

- costs to reach consumers through other more conventional forms of advertising have rocketed over the last few years
- sales promotions can directly appeal to the consumer, or for that matter to the trade, very easily
- sales promotions can be used as an adjunct to other forms of marketing and advertising and are often used in conjunction with advertising campaigns

The major types of sales promotion fall into two main categories, firstly those which seek to put pressure on the consumer to buy (or for that matter the distributors) to buy more, and secondly the type of sales promotion that aims to increase goodwill.

Money off

This can be a very simple form of sales promotion. The pack can be reprinted to include a 'special price' on it. If the budget does not run to that then stickers can be printed to be slapped on to the pack, avoiding the costs of changing the original artwork. The key to this technique is to let the distributors know in good time about the sales promotion and back up the 'special pack' or sticker price with point-of-sales material and displays.

Money-off promotions are a very effective way of inducing customers to try a new product, or perhaps persuading them to change brands. Indirectly this form of promotion can help to persuade existing stockists to take larger orders as a result of expected increased demand.

student activity

Do you think that money-off promotions actually work? Have you ever been convinced to buy something because the price has been 'reduced'?

Self-liquidating premiums

This form of promotion offers the customer the product at a greatly reduced price provided that he or she has several proofs of purchase (usually part of the packet) of the product. The manufacturer is able to offset the cost of this form of promotion by buying in bulk. The offer must be attractive in order to ensure that the target market segment responds well. This form of promotion can be used in two main ways:

- it can act as a counter to a price cut by a competitor
- it can aggressively increase the level of purchase among existing customers

Eye-catching displays and point-of-sale material greatly increase the customer's awareness of the brand and will also work as an inducement for the retailer to devote more shelf space to the product. Self-liquidating premiums are less common now, though in the past they were the major form of promotional activity, second only to money -off promotions.

student activity

Devise a self-liquidating premium for a product of your own choice.

Free premium offers

The objective of this sort of promotion is to encourage a customer to sample a new or existing product. Its most common form is for a sample of the product to be attached to another product. In this way the customer cannot avoid the free sample. This form of promotion is often used when a product is being launched for the first time.

student activity

Visit a local store and see how many free premium offers you can find. How do the free samples relate to the product to which they are attached?

Free samples

In this sort of promotion teams of door-to-door distributors are employed to push the free sample through the customer's letter box. An important point to note is that the sample pack is smaller than those available in retail outlets, and this ensures that the retailer is not deprived of potential business. Retailers may take grave exception to the distribution of free samples in their area if they feel that this will diminish their own sales, and it is vital that their permission is gained before delivery is made. This particular form of sales promotion is most common when geographical availability of a product is patchy and the produce is seeking to stimulate demand in new areas.

User competitions

This form of promotion has a two-fold objective. Firstly, it seeks to maintain brand loyalty. Secondly, it hopes to increase the frequency of use and purchase from existing customers. It is unlikely that new customers are attracted by this sort of promotion. The competition must be attractive and it is directly related to the desirability of the prize or prizes. Each and every entrant must have (or at least feel that they have) a fair chance of winning. Competitions are subject to tight controls in law and must conform to such legislation which requires an element of skill to be involved. Competitions are useful in encouraging retailers to give shelf space to displays related to the competition.

student activity

Devise a realistic competition. How does the competition relate to the product you have chosen?

Personality promotions

Several companies have created fictitious characters which are associated with their products. Point-of-sales displays and other advertising material feature the character and seek to enhance customers' awareness of the product range by association.

student activity

Make a list of fictitious characters related to products. Did you remember the product first and then the character, or the other way around?

Quantity discounts

This form of sales promotion is aimed specifically at the retailer or distributor. Higher discounts are offered on orders made in bulk. This sort of offer is meant to encourage higher stock levels, thus increasing sales and freeing the manufacturer's warehousing for other products.

Trade premium offers

This can be seen as a form of quantity discount, but actually the manufacturer gives away additional stock if the buyer purchases a specified amount. This can be an attractive offer as the retailer will not have 'paid' for the free bonus products and can achieve a better profit margin on the whole order overall. An additional benefit is that stock levels in retail outlets are increased.

Trade competitions

This is a form of competition which is aimed at the retailer as opposed to the consumer. The retailer may be required to devote additional space, perhaps a window display, to promote the product. The prizes must be attractive to ensure retailer interest or may, perhaps, offer the chance of additional discounts. The objectives are three-fold – firstly, to increase the retailer's efforts to sell the product, secondly to gain larger display areas in the outlet, and thirdly, to educate the retailer.

Exhibitions and fairs

There are two main types of fair. A **Trade Fair** seeks to increase retailers' goodwill and attract new stockists and distributors. A **Consumer Fair**, such as the Ideal Home Exhibition, endeavours to persuade customers to sample the product and perhaps to see it in operation – in the case of a household appliance.

student activity

How can the effectiveness of consumer fairs be assessed?

DISTRIBUTION

It may sound obvious that a company needs to ensure that its products are available. After all, if they are not, how can the customer buy them? Two words accurately define distribution – **availability** and **accessibility**. Even the most elementary analysis of a company's operation should identify that these are principal concerns, yet it is a failing of a great many companies that they have not ensured that availability is good. Customers are notoriously lazy, and if a particular product is not available and easily accessible, they will not seek it out, they will buy elsewhere. As often as not, the customer will seek the easy way out and buy what is available, and not necessarily what is best or ideal.

Distribution can be a complex problem and directly relates to the network that a company has set up to ensure that the product is on the shelves when the customer shops. Middlemen are used extensively, but there is a cost to be paid for middlemen handling any stage of distribution. In order for them to distribute a company's products they need to be given a cut of the company's profits. It would seem logical, if possible, for manufacturers to do their own distribution and keep all the profit, but most manufacturers find themselves in a position where they must use middlemen, or even, where it is better to use middlemen.

The main role of the middleman is to make the product more available and more accessible. They do this by performing the following:

- they buy in bulk from the manufacturer and sell in smaller quantities to the customer
- they help relieve the manufacturer's storage problems by storing the product themselves
- they assist in reducing delivery times to customers by holding a buffer-stock for the manufacturer
- they are able to deliver smaller quantities of products in a more flexible way than manufacturers could ever do
- they can promote the manufacturer's products on a local basis with great efficiency

- they can offer credit to their customers which does not affect the manufacturer's cash flow
- they may be able to have some flexibility in setting the price according to local market demands
- they can offer useful after-sales services on a local basis
- they can offer a personal-touch in direct sales which a manufacturer, given its broader base, cannot hope to achieve

student activity

Do the advantages of using a middleman outweigh the loss the manufacturer suffers in terms of profit margin?

Good distribution leads to the customer having a good impression of a company. Efficient distribution can be costly, but it is the job of the Distribution Manager to ensure that the right goods are delivered to the right place at the right time undamaged. Here are some considerations to take into account in order to maintain an effective distribution:

- being **reliable** – long delays are extremely irritating. It is a good tactic to offer slightly longer delivery times but be able to guarantee them, rather than promise short delivery times and never be able to achieve them
- there is no point in getting the goods to the customer on time if they are not in a fit state. Strict controls over packaging, handling and transportation are key features in making sure that the product is delivered **undamaged**
- should the product be defective, prompt **replacement** is vital.
- the customer is equally concerned that the product **continues to function** as required. If it fails in some way then the customer quite rightly demands that the product be repaired or replaced
- distribution managers must consider balancing **minimum order size** with the possibility of losing custom and goodwill if they have set too high a minimum order level.

student activity

Minimum order levels often prevent smaller retailers from stocking product lines. Is the setting of a minimum order level good policy?

A manufacturer must consider how many middle men are required between the company and the customer. Just what kind of distribution network is suitable largely depends on the product. The number of levels or tiers can vary from none, in which case the manufacturer

supplies direct, to as many as three or more. The most common is one tier where large retail chains buy direct from the manufacturer and then sell on to the customer. Two-tier channels are still common where small retailers lack the buying power to buy direct from the manufacturer and are forced to purchase via a wholesaler. Most manufacturers do not religiously stick to one type of channel, they may well use a combination of several types of channel. The type of network a manufacturer chooses depends on three main considerations:

1 *Intensive distribution* – this strategy aims to get the manufacturer's product into as many outlets as possible in order to maximise availability and accessibility. For example, convenience or impulse-buy products require great availability and accessibility as, after all, you the customer buy a can of Coca-Cola almost anywhere.

2 *Exclusive distribution* – this is the opposite of intensive distribution. Accessibility and availability are deliberately restricted in order to make the product appear exclusive. Outlets are chosen carefully as their image and ability to handle the product are key considerations in whether they are allowed to stock the manufacturer's products. It would, for example, be unusual to find a solid gold Dunhill cigarette lighter in a corner shop tobacconist!

3 *Selective distribution* – as with most things, there is always a compromise. The manufacturer may wish to have intensive distribution but by the nature of the products made, this may not be possible. There is little point in convincing a pet shop to stock the latest Nicam stereo television. The manufacturer may wish to have intensive distribution in all relevant outlets, but would consider it futile to extend distribution beyond this.

student activity

Which is the most appropriate distribution network for the following and why?

- milk
- baked beans
- exotic fruit and vegetables

Manufacturers should try to avoid any conflicts which may affect their channels of distribution. Each member of the network is interested in a smooth distribution which maximises profits and lessens expenses. Competing distributors are likely to come into conflict. Healthy competition between outlets should be encouraged, but if price cutting becomes a tool of competition this will have a detrimental effect on a manufacturer's brand image, and this should be avoided.

Manufacturers should try to manage their distributors with a strong policy on pricing, the level of discounts available (and how this may be passed on to the customer) and, at the same time, offer enough freedom to give the outlet sufficient motivation to stock the brand. Manufacturers must offer good margins, display and sales promotional material and joint advertising.

In the UK in particular, retailers are very strong. In some respects, they even control the manufacturers. Big retail chains demand much more say in the type of products available, delivery times, quantity levels, packaging and price. Manufacturers would be foolish to ignore them. Own brand labels can be seen as a retailer's reaction to poor performance by manufacturers, and these have cut deeply into manufacturers' profits. Some manufacturers which produce own label products are virtually sub-contractors, and only the larger manufacturers have been able to combat this trend.

student activity

Do you think that retailers who enjoy a strong position should dictate their requirements to the manufacturer?

SELLING

The process of selling inevitably involves high levels of contact with the customers of the organisation. To be truly effective, in terms of influencing customers' perceptions of the organisation. A Sales Department should take the following points into consideration. They will be guided, to some extent, by the Marketing Department. In many cases, as we have mentioned, the Sales Department will be an integral part of the marketing operations of the organisation.

To create sales for the product or service

The aims of this technique are as follows:

1 To attempt to tell customers **where** they can obtain the product or service.
2 To attempt to tell customers **how** they can obtain the product or service.
3 To try, obtain and maintain the customer's **loyalty** to the product, service or organisation.
4 To state that the product or service offered is much **better** than any of the competition.
5 To try to get across the fact that the organisation offers a **range** of products and services and that all of these products and services offer the same standard of excellence.

student activity

In pairs, think of some phrases or slogans that organisations have used to try to create sales. Are they interesting and convincing enough to work?

Having made this list, now try to create some of your own. Are they any better? If so, why? If not, what makes the professionals' slogans better?

To influence customer perceptions regarding a product or service

The aims of this technique are as follows:

1 To try and heighten **customer awareness** of the organisation in general.
2 To try and create a **positive image** of the organisation and its range of products and services.
3 To inform the customer about the **range** of possibilities offered by the organisation, in terms of products and services as well as advice and guidance.
4 To link any popular public **trends** (such as environmental issues) with the organisation's range of products and services.
5 To link the range of products and services with any recent changes in **legislation**.

student activity

Individually, over the next few days monitor your local independent television station. Pay particular attention to the advertisements. How much do they really tell you about the organisation that produces the products or services they are promoting? Do you actually remember anything about the advertisement apart from the product or service itself? What kind of image is the organisation trying to create with the style of advertisement it is using?

After your period of investigation, tell your ideas to the rest of the group.

These techniques can be best remembered by using a word which is made up from the first letter of the following words. The key word to remember all of this is AIDA:

- **Attention** – get the customers' attention by showing them something that they will remember
- **Interest** – try using some trick or design that will make the customers read or watch your advertisement. These may include special offers, a competition or the use of a celebrity

- **Desire** – make the customers really want your product or service. Tell them that they will really benefit from buying it
- **Action** – this is the real key to it all. Make it as easy as possible for the customers to obtain your product or service

AFTER-SALES SERVICE

Many organisations consider themselves to be fully well aware of the needs and wants of their customers. Indeed, all of their activities revolve around the satisfaction of customers. Organisations consider customers to be of vital importance since this is the key to business success. If an organisation manages to keep the customer in mind at all times, then inevitably it will increase its market share, provide better services than its competitors, maintain its current customers and attract new ones.

FIG 3.3.13 *Fisons Instruments is one of the world's leading scientific instrument makers. They have a strong commitment to customers support and service. To optimise their after-sales service they use a computerised customer support system to log the service record of each instrument to improve its longevity and quality of performance.*

The exact nature of customer service may differ slightly depending upon the sector in which the organisation operates. In this respect, we are concerned with two major sectors. We will look at these shortly.

What exactly are customer services? Let us try to identify them:

- giving the customer information and help
- processing refunds and dealing with replacements
- handling customer complaints

- giving advice on after-sales service
- taking steps to prove that the organisation is interested in the needs and wants of the customer
- answering the telephone promptly
- replying to all forms of communication from customers
- trying to avoid releasing any confusing or misleading information
- always being polite and courteous
- offering a quality service throughout all aspects of the business activity
- trying to remember the names of all regular customers

student activity

In pairs, in the role of owners of a fish and chip shop, decide which of the above you think would be important customer service considerations for your establishment?

Let us now consider the two principal sectors.

1 *The private sector.* Private sector organisations are primarily interested in profits. It is a simple equation – the more customers, the more sales, the more profit. An organisation that has this equation in mind will try to find out exactly what a customer wants. It will take all steps necessary to ensure that it can provide everything the customer might need. It will even take account of possible changes in trends and fashions to try to predict what customers might need in the future. As we have already seen, an organisation that takes all of the above into consideration can be known as a market-orientated organisation.

2 *The public sector.* Public sector organisations did not have to consider customer service to any great extent until recently. They did not have to worry about profits since they were financed by central or local government. The situation has changed to some extent, but we have seen great changes in the attitudes of public sector organisations as they have become aware of the demands of customers and how these relate to the possibility of the organisation's survival. Hospitals, for example, now face the prospect of competition from the private sector. Even tax offices have implemented a customer service programme which aims to deal with customers courteously and efficiently. To ensure that some of the larger public corporations deal with customers in a fair manner, the Government has set up a 'watchdog' or 'ombudsman' to monitor their behaviour. Privatisation may be just round the corner for many of the public sector organisations, so they need to prepare themselves and adopt customer service techniques that are in common practice in the private sector.

Even if an organisation has established a range of customer service provisions, it must still try to improve this service. It will do this by constantly monitoring a variety of areas in which customer service plays a part. These areas of concern include the following:

Monitoring the sales performance

Sales will increase if an organisation manages to attract more customers, or if it convinces its existing customers to purchase more products or services. A well-organised company will keep a close check on the number of enquiries made by customers and how many of these have been turned into actual sales. In order to facilitate this monitoring system, the company may enter all of the names and addresses of customers who have made enquiries on to a database. It will then be an easy matter to cross-check actual orders and see what percentage 'conversion rate' has been achieved. Another way of monitoring sales performance is to see how often existing customers re-order products or services. Repeat purchases are the life-blood of an organisation. Organisations must take strenuous steps to ensure that customers who regularly re-order are treated well; they may be offered extended credit facilities to ensure that they stay loyal to the organisation.

Requesting feedback

An organisation takes customer service seriously will be interested in the attitudes and opinions of the customer. The customer may have very valuable things to say about products or service and may offer useful solutions to difficult problems. There are several ways of obtaining customer feedback. These include the following:

- employees asking the customer directly what they think about a product or service
- 'unknown' employees posing as customers who will visit a branch of the organisation to assess the behaviour of the staff there
- the setting up of a consumer panel which aims to obtain feedback in an informal situation. Normally, this will take the form of a group of customers talking about products and services with a selected group of employees. Very valuable information may be gained from this, including new ideas for products or services

---

student activity

In pairs, in the role of employees of an organisation that is involved in the manufacture, wholesaling and retailing of cast iron park benches. Draw up a list of discussion areas for a Consumer Panel. At present, the organisation can only offer four different versions in three different colours.

Discuss your list with those of the remainder of the group.

Monitoring complaints

The easiest way to monitor complaints is to see how many returned goods the organisation receives. In all cases, these should be accompanied by appropriate paperwork detailing the exact nature of the problem. A customer who returns to the organisation dissatisfied may well now be satisfied after he or she has received a replacement of faulty or damaged goods. The organisation will cross-reference the number, type and source of the faulty or damaged goods and see if there are any common features, such as a large number of faulty goods from a single supplier.

Carrying out market research

Market research is useful in discovering what both existing and potential customers think about the organisation and its range of products or services. Although the information is based upon opinion, organisations place a great emphasis on the reliability of these data and will often act upon them directly. A market research questionnaire itself must be clear and easy to fill in. In some cases, organisations will offer an incentive or reward for customers to complete the questionnaire.

Monitoring after-sales service

Having established an after-sales service, an organisation will be keen to ensure that it is functioning correctly. A series of procedures will need to be in place to make sure that the after-sales service matches the promises made when the product or service was initially sold to the customer. Although a large proportion of customers may not need after-sales service, the organisation will want to ensure that it is available on demand.

THE MARKETING MIX

The **marketing mix** is the combination of strategies and tactics, company policies, techniques and activities, to which resources can be allocated in such a way that the company's marketing objectives can be achieved. The marketing mix itself is concerned with the practicalities of achieving the marketing objectives, in other words, how can the company's marketing objectives be translated into workable marketing plans and sales activities? The marketing mix should comprise of the following:

1 *Strategic considerations*, i.e. what products or services should the company produce, and how is it to satisfy the target market's needs? These choices will be limited by the level of the company's resources, thus the company should limit its activities to what it deems to be potentially fruitful for markets and products.
2 *Tactical considerations*, i.e. what sales tactics or promotional tools will the company employ in its attempt to achieve its sales objectives?
3 *Planning considerations*, i.e. what is the company's long-term commitment to a product or the development of a new product?
4 *Resource considerations*, i.e. how much of its resources can be channelled towards advertising and sales promotions, and when can the company expect a return on research and development?
5 *Operational considerations*, i.e. to what extent does the company expect its Marketing Department to generate marketing and advertising copy and material?

The marketing mix aims to ensure that:

● the **right product** is available
● the **price** is right
● the product is **available** in the necessary outlets
● the product is available **when** the customer needs it

In conjunction with these four basic points the marketing mix should also be responsible for making sure that the appropriate promotional tool is employed to help persuade the customers that they should consider the company's product and make the purchase.

The marketing mix can be more clearly defined as relating to the following, which are known as the four 'P's:

● product
● price
● place
● promotion

student activity

How does an organisation determine which is the appropriate promotional tool?

The four parts of the marketing mix are extremely interdependent and cannot be considered separately. Here are some examples of the interdependence:

● the brand image of a product should be reinforced by the pricing policy, in other words, a customer will be prepared to spend more on what is considered a reputable brand. The price charged is relative to the customer's perception of the product and not necessarily its quality.
● the level of advertising and sales promotion can strongly influence the customer's perception of the product
● if a company intends to distribute a product intensively there will be a large sales force promoting the product in every market, and making sure that it is available where and when demand requires it

If the company makes alterations to one aspect of the marketing mix, this will mean that there will be a knock-on affect to other parts of the marketing mix. If the price is reduced significantly, then this may affect the customer's image of the brand, and may affect the product's standing in the market. This is not to say that a slight adjustment to one of the aspects of the marketing mix will not pay dividends. Slight alterations may be seen in a positive light by the customer, and it is therefore the skill of the marketing manager and his understanding of how the four main elements interrelate that determine the success or failure of the company's marketing objectives.

student activity

How would the marketing mix in a retail outlet and a wholesale organisation differ?

Managers, in particular Marketing Managers, are responsible for planning, organising, directing and controlling within their area of influence. All these controlling tasks are fundamental in assisting the manager to make decisions. The formulation of marketing plans, and any strategy allied to them, is strongly linked to the manager's ability to control the resources at his or her disposal. Like most tasks in business, success depends on getting things done by individuals within the company. The management of human assets needs careful handling as motivation, training and selection are the key features of leadership.

We all have ideas of what a manager does, and indeed, there are many theories of management. Most managers learn how to manage the hard way through a process of trial and error. This is not a satisfactory set of circumstances, as companies need a manager to be effective immediately. Out of this need has arisen some concept of a scientific approach to managerial skills. This professionalisation, in theory at least, requires a manager to use his or her experience as a base, and from this, to establish basic principles of management, and then try to transfer these fundamental skills to aid both him/herself and others in making decisions. There is a wide variety of basic principles, some appropriate to all management decisions, and others specifically created to cope with special problems. The basic elements which we have noted already, are planning, organising, directing and controlling, and these are relevant to the formulation of a marketing plan and indeed to marketing management as a whole.

Planning is an essential feature of a manager's responsibilities. Marketing planning requires the manager to set a series of objectives from which he or she formulates a strategy. Within this strategy some notion of a time scale which considers the implementation and achievements of these plans has also to be set. Just how these objectives are set very much depends on the nature of the business. However, there are a number of basic steps;

- analysis of performance, both current and past, of all products
- a review of marketing opportunities and possible threats
- relating these plans to the overall corporate objectives

Once the marketing objectives have been decided, the manager must determine which route to take to achieve these objectives. Many of the key phrases and tactics are taken straight from military terminology, such as flanking, or encirclement. Broadly speaking, a marketing strategy is the way in which the company proposes to achieve its marketing objectives. It should always include consideration of the following:

- the selection of marketing targets
- market positioning
- an appropriate marketing mix

The choice of the marketing strategy should always take into consideration the company's strengths and weaknesses. It also requires a good knowledge of the market's needs. Marketing strategies represent the overall route to achieving the marketing objectives, and any market-ing tactics that are employed are the fine tuning which adapts the strategy to help ensure that the route is as smooth as possible. In many cases a good strategy has failed because of a company's lack of attention, or the use of an inappropriate tactic. By the same token, a poor strategy can be saved by clever tactics. The real difference between strategy and tactics is unclear. Tactics can be seen as a part of strategy, but strategies are nothing without a good tactical sense. If a Sales Manager's strategy is to increase his customer base, then he needs an appropriate tactic to achieve this. At the same time, if the company's strategy is to increase business, then the Sales Manager's strategy becomes the company's tactic. Here are some broad distinctions between strategy and tactics:

- tactics tend to be more detailed than strategies
- tactics relate to a shorter time period than strategies
- tactics tend to be more flexible than strategies
- the range of tactics is wider, usually, than the range of strategies

Time scales for achieving marketing objectives may vary greatly. As we have noted elsewhere, these marketing objectives are expressed as being short, medium or long term in their nature and may range from one month to ten years or more. Setting the objectives and then placing a time scale to them depends on the company's decision as to how much of its resources is to be committed to achieving the objective.

The marketing plan. Most companies tend to set an annual marketing plan which begins with their analysis of their current situation, then looks at their products and the markets in which they are attempting to sell them. In developing this annual marketing plan, information should be gathered on the following factors:

1 company sales
2 profits and profit trends
3 a detailed analysis of each product
4 a detailed analysis of each customer by type
5 market sizes
6 market volume
7 analysis of competitors' share of markets
8 company's sales and profit projections

Sales forecasts are a central feature of setting objectives and strategy and tactics should then flow from this. Sales forecasts and budgets are very much interrelated with the annual marketing objectives and any strategy and tactics which are applied to them.

PRODUCT RANGE DEVELOPMENT

As we know a product is something that **satisfies a customer's needs**. We should broaden this definition somewhat and include services as well as products. Of course, even though a need exists, it may be that at present neither a product nor a service exists to satisfy it, or what exists cannot satisfy the level of need at present.

The **product mix** is the range of a particular company's products. Each of these products is linked to a particular need within a particular market. Product mix should not be confused with product line which usually refers to the range of products that is aimed at one particular market.

A collection of product lines make up the product mix and the extent of this product mix is known as the **product mix width**. Everything that has a width has a depth! In this instance the **product mix depth** refers to the number of products that make up any one of the product lines. The final definition to try to remember is the **product mix consistency**. This relates to how the individual product lines fit into the product mix. Are they complementary? Are they different, requiring different approaches in sales and marketing techniques? Perhaps they demand very different sorts of technology or industrial process?

We have seen that marketing strategy basically comprises of three main areas:

- the setting of the means by which the company intends to achieve its objectives
- the period of time over which these objectives are proposed to be met
- the resources that are available and those that will be used to achieve the objectives

The fundamental goal is **profitability** and gradual **growth**, in line with the growing profitable nature of the company. This, of course, can be achieved by a number of different methods. They include the following:

- the research and development of new ideas which can become profitable products and services
- the purchase of other companies in allied areas that may complement the company in some way
- a merger with another organisation that relates in some way to the market interests of the company
- subcontracting or licensing the production of other products from other companies to increase the product range with the minimum of investment and delay

Profits are the key to continued, or for that matter any, growth. The company needs to take a serious look at its resources which will, in turn, generate the profits it desires. These resources, of course, include the following:

- finance
- plant
- manpower

- organisational ability
- recognition of the company's marketing possibilities

A satisfactory marketing mix is dependent upon the recognition of the market's needs, the recognition of the company's objectives and the planning of a strategic marketing philosophy which incorporates the various methods of obtaining these objectives. Consideration of the needs of the market must look at how to best serve all the different segments of the market. Any decision that arises out of this should ensure co-ordination in the application of the company's efforts to reach each of the market segments. The development of the marketing plan should involve a clear definition of the problems and will include the following:

- the collection of the facts
- the analysis of the data
- the selection of the appropriate marketing mix
- choosing the appropriate solutions

The elements that make up the marketing mix are very diverse and may include both external and internal considerations. Among the external factors that may affect the marketing plan are the following. Socio-economic influences can effect the markets of the users of the company's products. Government regulations, including restrictions on business, can also have an impact on the long-term plans of the company. Considerations that we have looked at elsewhere include seasonal changes, changes in market demand, technology, product obsolescence and competition. Here are some of the major internal elements that make up the marketing mix:

- market research
- product quality, pricing, development and range
- sales force, aids and promotion
- after-sales service
- advertising
- stock levels
- credit
- public relations
- packaging
- sampling

Having a good idea is often the basis of a new product. Some ideas come quickly and others are years in the development. Some products are very innovative, while others are simply copies or adaptations of existing products. Other products have very little in the way of innovation or 'new product' appeal and are absolute and shameless copies made just to cash in on the success of the original product.

Good idea or bad, all products started off with an original idea. Having established this, any organisation wishing to develop new products should address itself to the problem of creating the right sort of environment and atmosphere to encourage new ideas and hence new products to flourish. Here are some of the ways in which the development of new ideas and products may be encouraged:

1 **Brainstorming** can be a very useful and thought provoking way of getting people to come up with innovative ideas. Eight to twelve people are housed in comfortable surroundings under the direction of a person who is given the role of suggesting useful key words or phrases to help stimulate the creation process. The members of the brainstorming group then shout out the first word that comes into their heads no matter how stupid the word might seem. The other members of the group respond to that word and come up with another word. It works on the same principle as word association and eventually something useful might come out of it. The brainstorming sessions are usually taped or perhaps recorded with a video camera and the results are played back and analysed.

2 A **suggestion box** fixed to the wall of the most used part of the factory or office may result in something useful being generated internally from one of the members of the workforce. This has proved especially effective for some businesses and they now offer financial incentives for good ideas and to help encourage more members of staff to contribute. Payments to staff are usually based on how much money the company will save from adopting their suggestion. Indeed the bulk of suggestion box ideas have more to do with cost cutting and efficiency than with new product ideas, but a fair percentage of ideas may well be for new products.

3 The concept of **forced relationships** is an interesting one. With this technique two or more seemingly unrelated items are considered together. Take a kettle, a clock and a radio – put them together and what have you got? A pair of scissors? No, a Teasmade!

4 **Marketing research** should help develop many new ideas, though many, of course, will be utterly impractical or unprofitable. In the consumer field, however, the number of 'free' ideas obtained from the public is amazing. General market research cannot be expected to generate much in the way of specific ideas, it needs to be taken a step further and people need to be asked specifically about their unsatisfied needs and have the answers coaxed out of them.

5 **Research and development** is an area of high cost and employment in certain companies. Some companies need to spend vast sums of money on R&D just to keep up with their competitors. The highest costing areas are electronics, drugs and computers, amongst others.

6 The **sales force** themselves often feel that they are the least consulted and the most full of ideas. It is an unwise company that ignores what is, effectively, its 'eyes and ears' in the market place. The sales force are out in the real world day after day, they above all know what the market needs and can pass on the thoughts and needs of the company's customers as well as their own.

7 Looking at what the **competition** is selling can be very useful, but is also fraught with dangers. Most companies keep an up-to-date collection of their competitors' brochures and sales literature, and some may even buy and investigate thoroughly their competitors' products. This makes good sense, but really, if the product they are looking at has not been properly market tested in the first place the copiers will just be buying themselves a headache. Who wants another version of something nobody wants? Even if the product is OK then the copiers will probably be too late to make much impression on the market by the time they get the copy ready for sale.

student activity

Try word association yourself, in groups of no more than about six. What do you think the chances are of coming up with something truly original using this technique?

Having thought up all these new ideas we must now concentrate on reducing the number of ideas to the most viable ones. Most companies use a **screening process** to assess the suitability of ideas for the market. A company should also be aware of how the idea will fit into the company's overall strategy and should ensure that it is an enhancement and not a diversion. Here are some of the more common screening methods;

1 How compatible is the idea with the **existing strategies** of the company? There are a great many good ideas that can be eliminated fairly quickly as they do not fit in with the company's strengths and available resources. The company must have staff capable of developing the product, and a sufficient financial buffer to cope with the inevitable costs of development. We must not forget, of course, that the company should also have the necessary marketing skills to launch the product. If any ideas are allowed to go further than they really should, in other words if the idea cannot be exploited successfully, then this mistake will inevitably weaken the company and add to its financial burdens.

2 How does the idea compare with the company's **existing products**? If a new product fits well into an

existing product line it will create fewer difficulties and demands on the company's resources. Compatibility means being able to use the same distribution channels, sales teams and sales techniques etc. A totally different product that is incompatible will cost disproportionately more. A compatible product has several advantages over and above costs; it may fill a hole in the product line, its availability doing much to improve the image of the range, and it may generate additional sales as a knock-on effect to the rest of the range.

3 **Will it pay?** Even if the product is compatible there are no guarantees that it will be feasible to produce it. The concept of value engineering looks at all the direct and indirect costs and assesses a product's likelihood to turn in a profit.

4 **Is the concept sound?** There really is no point in making something that no one is likely to buy. The trouble with a new product or idea, is that no one has any idea about it and the more revolutionary it is, the greater the problem. How can you react to something that does not exist? Customers will not have a understanding of the new product and will, naturally, be biased in favour of a brand or competitor that they already use as they cannot see yours. Since few companies are prepared to go to the expense of making the product until they have obtained customers reactions, a compromise solution is to test the concept as it is. The company will make the product as 'real' as possible by using drawings and possibly fake packaging. The new product can then be discussed with the potential customers and a more accurate idea can be obtained.

5 **How many can we sell then?** If all the above hurdles have been jumped then the final step in the screening process should be to assess the likely demand. The aim of this is to identify any product that will sell, but not in sufficient numbers to warrant production. Perhaps sales will not even cover the costs of development?

student activity

How many brilliant ideas do you think have been lost by businesses because they have not been prepared to take the chance? What affect do you think this has had on the development of new technology, for example?

As a general guide the screening process should be undertaken as quickly as possible. Time and resources pumped into ideas and products that really have no chance of success are just a waste of money. It is very easy to make mistakes and throw out good ideas and take on useless ones, but it is better in the long run to be

ruthless since the costs of development can be cripplingly high.

Now that the product has survived the analysis stage of its life, it changes from idea to being a real thing. The product has to be developed, made, packaged and given an identity of its own. There are three main stages to consider:

1 Making the product itself will involve a number of different people such as research and development staff, designers and other technical staff. A **prototype** is made which is similar to what end product is likely to be, in terms of appearance and performance. This is tested and on the basis of the results of these tests mass production will be approved or not. It is important to note that not only does the product have to work, but it has to do what the marketing department wants it to do.

2 **Packaging** can be vital; indeed in some instances the packaging is an important as the contents! The product may have to fit into the standard image of the company, following its colours or logo, for example. The package must also be functional and protect the product, or keep it fresh.

3 Giving a product an **identity** is of course very important. The brand name should either help to describe the product or be a short and memorable one. In some cases it is important to match the brand image with the market segment very carefully so that potential customers see it as a positive image that enhances desirability.

student activity

How soon in the development of an idea should it be given a name? Does this really matter?

Test marketing is the last chance the company has to rectify any mistakes or misconceptions about the product or iron out any problems with the product. The costs of launching a product nationally can be astronomical and any problems that might occur which could affect the long-term chances of the product need to be eliminated.

The first major way of testing the product is in a **test market**. Effectively this is a small area of the country, usually one with low TV advertising costs (such as those of Border TV). The advertising is run in that area alone and the product or service is available within that area only. Some products or services are not advertised on TV at all, but only in the press or radio. However, the principle remains the same: if the test market is successful then a national launch may be attempted, but if it is not then the company must figure out why not.

Perhaps the product itself is no good or perhaps some other fault, in advertising or elsewhere, is the culprit. The availability may be patchy or the product may be too pricey. Whatever the cause, it has to be found.

In some cases it may prove difficult to test market the product, particularly if it is a seasonal one, like plastic Xmas trees. Not much point in test marketing them in July, is there! Or maybe the product needs to be kept under wraps. In the case of technically advanced equipment, it may prove impossible to risk letting the opposition have any chance of hearing about the new product.

To get over this secrecy problem and also to help market test a product that needs to be in use to prove its worth in 'real' work conditions, potential customers may be asked to test the product 'in situ', under special arrangements with the manufacturer. If the product proves to be capable of coping with the rigours of real use then it is ready to be fully launched.

PRICE

There are several basic considerations to take into account when determining price. The main ones are listed below:

1 All prices are dependent on the **level of demand**. The phrase often used is 'we'll charge what we think the market will bear'. This means that if a business can still sell at a higher price than it needs to in order to make a profit then it will. The basic economic rule of supply and demand operates here. Luxury goods that are in short supply will command a higher price than perhaps they are really worth simply because more people want them than can be supplied. On the other side of the coin there are many products that are very cheap because they are in sufficient supply and people will not pay exorbitant prices for them.

2 **Competition**, as we have already noted, plays an important role in the pricing policy of a company. The more suppliers there are, the more likely the price is to be low. Perfect competition, a condition that is quite rare, means that the price has stabilised because there is just enough supply to meet the demands and the competing companies need not cut prices as they cannot supply more even if they wanted to. Where there is imperfect competition in a market it means that companies are vying for more business by cutting prices in an attempt to control more of that market. The opposite of both of these occurs when a company has a monopoly in a market. Again this situation is rare, but where it does exist, it effectively means that the company can charge exactly what it likes for the product. An example of this is the drugs market where a new drug which cannot be copied by other companies (due to patenting) may be the only available cure for a disease or complaint. Companies are always having to try to double-think their competitors and work out what they think the opposition is planning price-wise and be ready to react quickly to it. They will also have to be prepared for customers' reaction to price changes and try to predict any consequent changes in demand as a result of the change. Too low a price, even if the company can afford it, can cause customers to lose confidence in the worth of a product, or in its quality. Decisions in this area are key ones and the consequences may be very serious if they are not considered properly.

3 The **market segment** that the product or service is aimed at will often determine price. Some products aimed at a market that requires cheap and plentiful supply, like most foodstuffs, will demand a low price. On the other hand some markets rate price very low in their scale of importance and will demand high reliability and good design.

4 Consumer attitudes and behaviour to price are known as **price sensitivity**. Some look for value for money, and in their case *price* changes can radically change their buying habits. Other customers may consider price to be directly related to the performance and reliability of the product, so that changes in *performance* and *reliability* are their measure of value.

5 As we have already realised, each time a product changes hands from the time when it is raw material until it reaches the 'end user', a price change occurs. The product's price is different at each stage in the channel of **distribution**. At each stage discounts from the 'asking price' of the product are demanded. Sometimes these discounts are passed on – which is why it is often cheaper to buy a radio from Argos than from the local electrical store. It is not the case that the local store is marking up the price more than Argos, rather it is almost certainly the case that Argos is passing on part of the benefits of its bulk purchase discount.

6 In certain cases products cost a great deal to **design and develop**. The company must recoup these costs. The most obvious way is to include a portion of these costs in their pricing. High prices can be maintained until the company has sufficient competition to drive the price down to a lower level.

7 An obvious consideration is that of **costs**. Above all, the cost that a company incurs in buying, making or growing the product must be integrated into the price. Simply speaking, the cost plus the desired profit determines the price.

8 Considerably beyond the control of the business are general **economic trends**. These include changes in the following:

- the price of raw materials needed by the company
- the productivity of the labour force
- labour costs
- the rate of inflation
- the interest rate

student activity

Can you think of products and services that have had to change their prices constantly due to circumstances beyond their control?

Pricing is, as we have discovered, closely linked with the value or perceived value of a product or service. This can often equate to what people see as the quality of the product or service. The higher the quality, broadly speaking, the higher the price.

In some cases this quality is linked to the brand name and much stock is set on the customer's awareness and loyalty to that brand. It is an accepted fact of life that established brands command a higher price than brands that are new and unknown. In order to command a higher price the company must seek to establish the name of the brand and at the same time stress its quality and its superiority to other competing brands. If a brand is seen as the 'market leader' or the brand that every other brand is trying to copy, then it can command a higher price regardless of the pricing policy of the competition.

student activity

Think of some examples of where prices are high because businesses have the edge in terms of customer awareness and high brand status.

Most companies sell a range of products that are related to one another. In cases such as this they tend to have a pricing policy that encompasses their whole range. Let's look at this philosophy and at how their pricing policy differs from the single product approach:

- Some of their products may be very **competitively priced**. In other words, each sale generates only a small profit. The reasoning behind this is that these products have **high volume sales** and generate useful turnover. As long as the fixed costs are covered and a profit is achieved then the company is content.
- The concept of the **'loss leader'** is well known in certain markets. The idea is that the product is sold very cheaply, perhaps barely covering the costs and is available only to stimulate sales of the rest of the product line. Often supermarkets will advertise very cheap basic products with the intention that customers are enticed into the store and will buy other more expensive (and profitable) items.
- The idea of **offering products cheaply at the bottom end of their range** is again a common tactic, particularly in the car market. A cheap basic vehicle is offered, which it is hoped will satisfy the customer's initial needs. The customer, if satisfied, will come back to trade in the vehicle for a more expensive model. Good trade-ins are a key to this tactic.
- The company may decide that one of the products in the product line is the **one against which all the other products may be compared**. A price is set, usually for the most popular product in the range, and the others have their prices set in relation to that product, either more or less expensive.

student activity

Make a list of the types of products or companies that offer after-sales service. Compare their prices with those who do not offer this service. How much of the price do you think is related to the provision of after-sales service?

Another major consideration is that of **after-sales service**. In certain markets this is vital and may well be the deciding factor as to whether the customer buys one product or another. The availability, quality and cost of this service must be factors in a company's pricing policy.

The stage in its life cycle that a product has reached can often determine its price.

- When a product is **first launched** its price is set to achieve as many sales as possible and to grab as much of the market as quickly as possible. Alternatively, the price may be pegged higher than would normally be expected, in order to recoup the research and development costs or simply to gain additional profit from the novelty value of the product.
- As a product becomes **established** in the market, the sales policy will change. Perhaps the price has to include paying for a heavy advertising campaign or maybe the product's price rests at an 'acceptable level' and stays there.
- When a product reaches the **end of its useful life**, for example competitors have produced a 'better' or more modern version (or indeed the company itself may have done), the price has a tendency to fall as the company either attempts to get rid of the last of the stock or finds another market for cheaper and slightly obsolete products (perhaps abroad).

student activity

Is there any value in continuing to produce a product which has reached the end of its useful life? Do you think that if the organisation which produces it offers it at a sufficiently low price, then demand will be stimulated?

After the company has identified the segment of the market that will be its main target it may well find that pricing may play an important role. Some market segments are more sensitive to price than others. Pricing should mirror the needs of the segment that is the target. Unless it considers this factor the company may never discover that the product, although desired by that segment, is not priced correctly. Market research should help to identify the importance of price.

Luxury goods are developed specifically for a target market segment. The company's pricing policy will tend to depend on factors such as the exclusive nature of the product and image the price. In such a market neither price nor competition is as important as in the mass market.

student activity

Do you think that some companies charge too much in the name of exclusivity?

Linked to the patterns of demand for a particular product or service are seasonal variations in price. In other words, the price may be different at different times of the year. It is more expensive to go on holiday to Greece in July and August than in April or November. This is because the demand in July and August is much greater, hence, going back to supply and demand, the holiday companies can charge more. Conversely, by offering April and November at, relatively, quite cheap prices the tour companies are also hoping to attract sales in these off-peak months.

One of the golden rules in selling is **not to confuse the customer**. One thing that confuses and annoys the customer most is regular price changes. A **stable** price structure is vital, as is a **consistent** price structure that does not charge you three times as much for twice as much in volume!

Added to this is the role of **psychological pricing**. When we see an advertisement proclaiming 'UNDER £20!' we think, 'great, what a bargain'. The trouble is, the price is only 1p under £20, £19.99! The point is that we see the £19... and not £20... and the sale is more certain! We all fall for the most simple trick time and time again.

The use of **discounts** and the quoting of prices excluding VAT are other versions of the same pricing trick and the concept of the 'trade-in' is similar in its effect. The true price is hidden and only the wary or alert will spot the real hidden price behind all the 'offers'.

Competitors in a market always try to set their pricing structure in relation to one another. There is nothing to be gained and a lot to be lost by setting your price in such a way that it bears little relation to the opposition's price. Having compared like products a company will always try to undercut the competitors' price, even though this may mean having to accept lower profit margins.

A way around this problem is to establish a brand identity that does not allow a direct comparison with competitors. The use of 'own brand' labels in supermarkets is a good example of this.

As often as not a particular product or product line is dominant in the market. It is this product that 'sets' the price and all other companies wishing to compete must fall in with the dominant company's pricing policy. The key to survival in such cases is to be willing to accept lower margins and have a very controlled set of costs. In some cases the larger or more dominant company has cut the prices of its product line in order to make it impossible for other companies to even obtain a foot hold in the market or to force out smaller of weaker companies that do not have the ability to survive on lower margins of profit.

PACKAGING

Many people consider **packaging** to be the fifth 'P' in the marketing mix. As we pointed out in the previous section on marketing activities, packaging plays no small role in selling a product. It not only fulfils a range of functional duties, such as protecting the product, it also allows the organisation to clearly identify the product's brand image. This is often done by novel packaging designs, colours and shapes.

SALES

Arguably, some marketing experts consider the sales **people** to be the sixth 'P' in the marketing mix. As we have already seen, sales fulfil a series of vital activities which are aimed at convincing the customer to purchase the product. The solid integration of the sales and marketing functions of an organisation is imperative if the company is to ensure that full use is made of the complementary nature of these operations.

PROMOTIONS

Promotions can be easy to mount, or alternatively, may be very complex and intricate operations. Whatever the level of complexity and time allocated to their running, it is still very difficult to measure the effects they have on sales. So many other variables affect customer demand that it is almost impossible to quantify their effectiveness. One way of overcoming this is to clearly define objectives and judge changes in relation to all the other trends. There may be clearly laid out objectives such as increasing brand loyalty, or simply increasing sales. Whatever the objective is, a careful monitoring and evaluation process must be put in place to determine the level of success.

DISTRIBUTION

As we have already seen, distribution itself plays no small role in the overall success of an organisation. As we will see later, the range of activities for which the distribution arm of an organisation has responsibility is wide and diverse. Again, the integration of the distribution function of an organisation with the marketing and sales divisions will allow full exploitation of the availability of specialist skills.

CONSUMER SERVICE

Increasingly, consumer services, often known as after-sales services, are coming to play a key role in the maintenance of customer loyalty and awareness. Customer service itself should be 'a cradle to grave' approach which aims to:

- constantly update customer knowledge of the organisation and its product range
- offer periodic special offers and events to existing and potential customers
- using customer databases, periodically mailshot customers
- offer extensive information and advice before, during and after the product has been sold
- offer a prompt and efficient response to all customer queries and complaints
- always ensure that staff are well informed as to company policy
- always ensure that staff have received sufficient training in customer relations and are at all times courteous and polite

INTEGRITY, HONESTY AND AUTHORITIES

Social marketing has so far defied any attempt at a universally acceptable definition. This is mainly due to the fact that the boundaries of social marketing have yet to be agreed. Marketing should act in conjunction with the public interest by attempting to serve the needs and demands of society, as well as, of course, making a profit for the company involved. We will try to be brave now and attempt to define social marketing anyway.

Social marketing takes account of the consumer's needs for wider satisfaction beyond product satisfaction alone.

In other words, consumers place a value on their quality of life as well as on the quality of their possessions. In its wider context social marketing refers to the study of markets and marketing in general within the social system as a whole. There are two good examples of the former definition, both of which are related to our case study at the end of this Unit. Firstly, there is the question of people's need for cosmetic products. Alongside this is the consumer's horror at the use and abuse of animals in their development. This has provided an excellent niche for companies supplying 'cruelty-free products', such as The Body Shop. Secondly, there is the thornier issue of cigarette smoking, and the growing demand for total abolition as against the availability of 'less dangerous' brands. In this case too, animals, particularly dogs, have suffered terribly in the cause of allaying smokers' fears and enabling the development of the lower tar cigarette. It is clear then that people place a high importance on social and humanitarian values and this directly relates to their choice and subsequent purchase of products.

Let us now turn our attention to the wider issues, of which the above social concerns can be considered micro-elements. Marketing's major successes in what is known as the post-industrial age have been in providing for our material needs. A direct consequence of this has been ecological disasters, widespread pollution, congestion in our cities and mountains of waste. We cannot blame marketing alone for these phenomena, but it must shoulder some of the responsibilities and seek to find new products and indeed, production methods, which help to minimise, or preferably, eliminate, harmful effects.

If the principal task of marketing is to satisfy the needs of customers in an efficient and profitable way, then it must attempt to do this in a socially responsible manner. What exactly is **social responsibility**? Is it enough to produce 'safe' products? Is honest advertising sufficient? Or does a commitment to reduce pollution suffice? All these questions are elements of social responsibility. Many commentators now see marketing as having a social responsibility to influence customers' values. This goes far further than simple economic considerations. In markets where there is a clear link between the product and its inevitable social effects, e.g. a car, pollution and congestion, companies must be prepared to satisfy the customer while at the same time making sure that satisfaction does not get in the way of social cost. If a company is able to get this balance right, then its image is greatly enhanced.

student activity

Do you think that organisations would be prepared to reduce their profits in exchange for the consumer viewing them as more 'socially responsible'?

Many companies involve themselves in **welfare issues** such as poverty and education. They can be powerful movers in social attitudes and change. The cynical view of these companies' motives is to reduce their efforts to mere image building. Despite this, companies have begun to mobilise their expertise to develop social roles.

We must return to the question of **boundaries**, and if we must make such a decision, it should lie in the consideration of a company's willingness and ability to influence social attitudes. By successfully incorporating a social angle in its marketing policy, a company can be seen to relate to social issues as well as any elected representative could.

Having noted all of this, and appreciated certain companies' efforts in this field, we must not walk away with the idea that they are not interested in simple profit. What it does mean is that profit is no longer the only objective. Profit is the key to any company's continued success, and even the most enlightened and aware company cannot conceive of being involved in social issues without the funds that profit provides.

Less than 30 years ago, there was little or no protection for consumers under the law. In fact, the phrase that was most often used was 'Let the buyer beware'. In other words, consumers had to rely on their own common sense and feelings as to whether a product was suitable or fit for use. Nowadays, however, there are certain standards laid down by law, as well as voluntary agreements and codes of practice adopted by industries or particular businesses that provide a considerable degree of protection for consumers.

The consumer can quite rightly expect to receive goods and services which not only match the description, but are not faulty, dangerous or unfit for use. Over the years the law has developed to provide guidelines for transactions and to offer a means of dealing with disputes between the supplier and the consumer. The law further tries to address the imbalance between the power of a large organisation, which will have the backing of specialists and lawyers, and the vulnerability of the individual consumer.

Acts of Parliament relating to consumer protection fall within both the civil and criminal areas of the law.

CIVIL LAW

Civil law covers disputes between individuals and suppliers. When a transaction is made, this is, in effect, a contract. If one side suffers a loss in any way from the contract, then the injured party may sue.

CRIMINAL LAW

Criminal law tends to deal with more widespread abuses related to sales transactions. If an organisation sells a product that is harmful or dangerous to the community in general, then it will be the Government (through the Law Courts) that will take action against the organisation. Under criminal law, an organisation or individual found guilty is liable to fines, imprisonment, or both.

CONTRACT OF SALE

As we have already said, when goods or services are provided, the consumer should expect that they are fit for the purpose for which they were intended. If a product does not meet the consumer's requirements, then he or she may expect a replacement. If the product is wholly unfit then the consumer may expect his/her money back. These basic rights form part of the **Sale of Goods Act**. The companion law is the **Trade Descriptions Act**. This makes it a criminal offence to wrongly describe a product. In other words, any description of the product must be accurate.

The **Weights and Measures Act** attempts to ensure that the quantity stated on the box, container or bag matches the weight of the contents inside. It is an offence under this Act to claim a particular weight and supply a lighter one.

The **Food and Drugs Act** deals with food and medicines specifically. Under this Act an organisation cannot supply a harmful product and must always make sure that any instructions as to the use or preparation of the product are clear. For example, uncooked red kidney beans contain a toxic substance which is eliminated by cooking them for the correct period. Suppliers of this product must ensure that any packaging states very clearly the potential hazards. Also under this Act, rules apply to certain prepared foodstuffs such as sausages.

Sausages must contain a defined amount of meat to be called a sausage. If they do not, then they must be alternatively labelled.

THE CITIZENS' CHARTER

The **Citizens' Charter** sets out consumer rights which indicate that, particularly as far as public services are concerned, the consumer should expect a certain level of service. It states that if the service does not meet this standard, the consumer should expect compensation. This system is regulated by a number of separate organisations (some of which we will look at later). It is further suggested that once an organisation's services reach a particular standard, then it will be able to claim a 'Chartermark'. This Chartermark is intended to give consumers a clear indication that they will receive a high quality service.

The first phase of the Citizens' Charter is for organisations to release a list of 'promises', which clearly state exactly what consumers should expect from that organisation. From this set of promises consumers should now know what their rights are as regards services are.

The main reason for the development of the Citizens' Charter is to control publicly run organisations, such as local authorities and to maintain some level of control over 'opted-out' organisations, such as hospitals or schools and colleges.

student activity

In groups of three, in the role of manager of a local authority's refuse collection service, produce a Citizens' Charter covering your promises of service.

Compare your charter with those of the remainder of the group.

GUARANTEES AND OTHER LEGAL PROTECTION

A guarantee or a warranty is basically an undertaking by the manufacturer to replace or repair a product, or parts of a product, should they prove to be defective, and to do this free of charge, and as quickly as possible. A typical guarantee would include the following:

- the product will be repaired free of charge if faulty because of **defective materials** used in its manufacture
- the product will be repaired free of charge if faulty because of **defective workmanship**

- the product will be repaired free of charge if found faulty within the **first 12 months**
- the manufacturer will require a **proof of purchase** such as a receipt or credit card voucher
- the product must be repaired or replaced only at the **manufacturer's service centre** or approved service centre.
- If it is discovered that the fault is not the result of defective parts or workmanship, but due to **negligence** by the consumer or retailer, then the manufacturer is not obliged to repair or replace free of charge.
- optionally, the consumer may choose to **extend** the guarantee or warranty period by paying an additional charge. In this case, the manufacturer extends its offer of replacement or repair for the period purchased.

We will be looking at the Sale of Goods Act and the Trades Descriptions Act later on in this Unit, but there are some other laws which similarly protect consumer rights:

student activity

In pairs, discuss the warranties you would expect to find when purchasing a pocket calculator.

THE CONSUMER PROTECTION ACT

This Act is primarily concerned with price and the pricing policy of organisations. No doubt many of us have been caught out when purchasing a product, to find that the price quoted is not the price in reality. This may be because the sale period has ended, the price quoted did not include VAT, or the claimed price reduction is untrue. This Act states that the organisation must clearly state the 'real' price of a product, not make unfair or untrue comparisons between products and price, and not make false statements about price reductions.

You will often see, particularly in a sale, one of two statements on a price ticket:

- that the product was available for a period of time at a previously higher price. It may not necessarily have been available in that store, but in an alternative location owned by that organisation, and this fact will be stated on the ticket
- that the product has been specifically bought in and offered at a low price for the sale period only

The Consumer Protection Act further covers the consumer who is offered unsafe goods whatever the circumstances.

THE SUPPLY OF GOODS AND SERVICES ACT

This Act was created to cover loopholes in the Sale of Goods Act. The older Act did not include services, hired goods or part exchanges. All goods or services 'purchased' under these conditions are now covered. In respect of services this Act protects the consumer against poor workmanship, long delays and hidden costs.

OMBUDSMEN

An ombudsman's job is to ensure that any complaints between an organisation and the consumer are fairly dealt with. The Ombudsmen Scheme has been extended from its original form which dealt only with government departments, to a variety of different business activities. These include the following:

- *the health service* – an ombudsman deals with complaints from both staff and patients
- *local government* – an ombudsman investigates complaints concerning local government and services which they provide
- *legal services* – an ombudsman operates to consider complaints against solicitors and barristers
- *insurance industry* – an ombudsman investigates unfair small print on insurance policies, inefficiencies and insurance companies' responses and communications with consumers
- *estate agents* – an ombudsman protects the consumer against false descriptions of properties and 'gazumping' (which is allowing another buyer to offer a higher price after a lower price has already been accepted).
- *banking* – an ombudsman attempts to control bank charges, unfair interest rates and generally poor service
- *building societies* – an ombudsman looks at complaints regarding surveys on homes carried out by a building society's valuer.
- *investment* – an ombudsman considers complaints regarding poor or misleading investment advice.
- *pension schemes* – an ombudsman investigates complaints regarding personal, company or state pensions.

CONSUMER ASSOCIATIONS

Although any truly reputable organisation will go to great lengths to ensure that its products or services meet all the necessary standards and demands, there is a need for independent evaluators. The Consumers' Association itself looks at various products and services within a particular area and releases its findings in the magazine *Which*.

In addition to this organisation there is the National Federation of Consumer Groups, which co-ordinates local consumer groups. These local consumer groups investigate products and services available in their regions and like the Consumers' Association, publish their findings. They also are very active in campaigning for changes and further protection for the consumer.

MEDIA

Newspapers, television and radio are often at the forefront of campaigns in support of the consumer. They will often bring to the public's notice abuses and dangers in products or services. In some cases, they will be responding to a public outcry concerning a product or a service. At other times, they will be responsible for investigating a product or a service and discovering some aspect which they believe the public should be made aware of.

There are many consumer-orientated programmes and features that have had a very positive impact in changing organisations' attitudes, service and products to the benefit of the public.

WATCHDOG BODIES

Some of the watchdog bodies have been set up by the Government in order to monitor organisations' activities, particularly in their dealings with the public. Others have been set up by a particular industry to keep a check on their member organisations. This has been done to ensure that standards are maintained and that any adverse publicity resulting from a disreputable trader does not damage the industry as a whole. Some examples of these watchdog organisations are:

- *The Office of Fair Trading* – this is a government body whose brief is to take care of consumer interests as well as those of traders. It releases a range of codes of practice in an effort to improve standards of service. In addition, the Office of Fair Trading will ensure that organisations compete fairly and that no single organisation controls the sole supply of goods or services. An organisation which does so is known as a monopoly.
- *Citizens' Advice Bureau* – the principal duty of this chain of offices is to act as a mediator in disputes between organisations and consumers. They are also responsible for a variety of other advisory matters, not necessarily relating to consumer rights.
- *Trading Standards Department* – this organisation

investigates various complaints relating to short weights, false or misleading offers and matters relating to credit.

- *National Consumer Council* – this council is responsible for representing the consumer in disputes and problems with government departments, nationalised industries, local authorities and other businesses.
- *Environmental Health Department* – this organisation operates a series of local offices which investigate matters relating to food and hygiene. They have the power to enforce legislation relating to food hygiene and may even close businesses which break the regulations.
- *British Standards Institution* – this organisation which operates on funds received from the government and voluntary donations, is concerned with setting minimum standards in all aspects of business and industry. It is best known for the BSI Kitemark which denotes that a product has been manufactured and reached the standards laid down by the British Standards Institute.
- *Consumer and Consultative Councils* – these organisations have been set up to monitor the operations of nationalised industries, and to ensure that they do not abuse their monopoly in terms of charging too high a price or providing a poor level of service.
- *Trade Associations* – there is a large number of these organisations, which deal with specific industries or services and offer assistance, information and advice to their members. In addition, they also devise a voluntary code of practice to which all members are expected to adhere and offer guidelines on how con-

sumers should be treated, particularly with regard to complaints. An example of these organisations is ABTA (Association of British Travel Agents).

- *Advertising Standards Authority* – this independent organisation is involved in ensuring that all advertisements are 'legal, decent, honest and truthful'.
- The *Chartered Institute of Marketing* – this is another independent organisation that attempts to ensure that its members have high professional standards, particularly in terms of honesty and integrity. Their British Code of Advertising Practice gives the advertising industry a clear set of rules to follow.
- *Independent Broadcasting Authority* – this organisation monitors the activities of television and radio stations and ensures that particular standards are maintained. Recently, it has been concerned about a new marketing technique known as 'placement' which involves popular programmes featuring and recommending particular brand names or products. Although placement is well established in America, the IBA has ruled that it is unacceptable in Great Britain.

student activity

In groups of four, contact and obtain leaflets or brochures from at least six of the above organisations. Having done this, summarise the main areas of activity of each of the organisations and compile your findings in the form of fact sheets which could be made available via the Citizens Advice Bureaux and local libraries.

UNIT 3

a s s i g n m e n t

'MARKET RESEARCH FORECASTING AND LAUNCHING OF PRODUCT'

In order to fulfil the criteria in this Unit, you will need to carry out some market research, make some short-term predictions on consumer demand and estimate the effectiveness of any marketing activities proposed.

In consultation with your tutor, you may choose a product or service which would meet the following criteria:

- it is **appropriate** for the supposed demand of the local area
- it is **feasible** in the sense that it does not require a great deal of start-up capital
- it would be the kind of operation that a **small business** could handle
- there would be sufficient **information sources** available for research purposes

Specifically, the process you will have to follow is, firstly:

(a) identify a **market need**
(b) choose appropriate **research methods**
(c) use the correct research methods to **collect the data**

(d) analyse and draw conclusions from the data
(e) write a word processed **report** on your findings

You may then move into Phase 2. The specific activities involved here are:

(a) identify the characteristics of your proposed **customers**
(b) assess any likely **economic impact** on your proposed product or service
(c) use general trends such as economic and social trends to assist you in **forecasting sales**
(d) make a short term (one to five year) prediction of potential **consumer demand**

The final phase includes the following activities:

(a) identify appropriate **marketing activities**
(b) compare your choice of marketing activities with that of the **competition**
(c) formulate a proposed **product life cycle**
(d) consider your **marketing mix**
(e) take into account any **ethical considerations**

You should present your findings in a final word-processed report and be prepared to orally present the highlights of your information gathering exercises.

UNIT 3

test questions

I What is the ASA?

(a) Automated Segmentation Audit
(b) Advanced Standards Association
(c) Advertising Standards Authority
(d) Association for Selected Analysis

2 The best way of describing marketing is:

(a) Market research
(b) Distribution channels
(c) Advertising and promotion
(d) All of the above

3 Which of the following are considered as internal data?

(a) The company sales figures
(b) Analysis of government expenditure
(c) Analysis of the competition's company reports
(d) None of the above

4 Test marketing is often used by organisations to fulfil which of the following roles?

(a) Identify a clear market for a product
(b) Gauge reaction to a product
(c) Collect data on family expenditure
(d) Act as a method of collecting consumer opinion

5 Which of the following is an example of 'own labelling'?

(a) Heinz
(b) Crosse and Blackwell
(c) Buitoni
(d) Tesco

6 Which of the following is best described by saying that a product is sold for little or no profit to attract extra custom?

(a) Loss leader
(b) Premium
(c) Money off
(d) Special prices

7 When a product has reached its maturity stage, which of the following is true?

(a) Its sales have fallen
(b) Its sales have stopped rising
(c) Sales are decreasing
(d) Sales have ceased

8 A supplier of electrical components would be most likely to advertise in which of the following?

(a) TV
(b) National newspapers
(c) Trade newspapers
(d) Radio

9 Direct mail can be described by some as being

(a) Mail shots
(b) Trade mail-outs
(c) Direct offers
(d) Junk mail

10 How would an organisation best assess the effect of its advertising campaign?

(a) The organisation was able to relocate
(b) More products were bought
(c) More enquiries were made by potential customers
(d) The number of complaints received reduced

Investigate human resourcing

1 HUMAN RESOURCING

recruitment, retention, performance, termination, health and safety, employee representation and consultation, training and professional development

2 EMPLOYEE RELATIONS

representation, consultation, trades unions, staff organisations, multi-skilling, team work

3 TRAINING AND DEVELOPMENT

vocational/professional qualifications

4 LEGAL REQUIREMENTS

conditions of employment, individual rights, equal opportunities, equal pay, health and safety at work

5 TYPES OF REDRESS

industrial tribunal, civil legal actions

6 BUSINESS PERFORMANCE

productivity, level of absenteeism, quality of service, profit

HUMAN RESOURCING

It may be already clear to you that **human resources** are perhaps the most important resource used by an organisation. The management of human resources needs to tread a very careful line between the needs of the organisation and the needs of the employee. Most managerial functions concerning employees will be dealt with by the Personnel Department. We will be looking at the responsibilities of this department later in this Unit. Specifically, the management of human resources involves the following:

- recruitment of employees
- retention (the keeping) of employees
- measuring the performance of employees
- terminating employment of employees
- health and safety matters relating to employees
- employee representation and consultation
- the training and professional development of employees

We shall look at these aspects of the personnel function initially here, but in more detail later in the Unit.

RECRUITMENT

Element 4.3 covers all of the main aspects of the recruitment process. However, the main steps in this process are:

- the need for a new post is identified
- a personnel specification is designed
- a job description is written
- an advertisement is placed in the media
- appropriate information and application forms are duplicated in anticipation of candidates responding to the advertisement
- initial contact is made by candidates, either in writing or by telephone
- information packs and application forms are despatched to candidates
- completed application forms are received
- organisation sifts through application forms and propose candidates for short-listing
- short-listed candidates are sent letters of invitation to attend an interview

- acceptance letters are received from candidates in response to invitation
- references are taken up prior to interview
- interview panel is formed and given an interview schedule
- interviews take place
- written confirmation of job offer is sent to successful candidate
- in most cases, unsuccessful candidates are sent a courtesy rejection letter
- successful candidate responds to written confirmation by accepting the job in writing
- successful candidate, if applicable, sends letter of resignation to current employer
- contract of employment is sent to successful candidate
- full job description and staff manual, etc. are sent to successful candidate
- candidate joins new organisation
- candidate completes necessary documentation (such as tax forms, etc.)
- candidate goes through organisation's induction programme
- new employee begins job according to job description provided

These steps will be looked at in more detail later in the Unit, but you should also refer to the section in Unit 5 concerning employment legislation.

RETENTION

Once an organisation has obtained competent staff, and has probably spent considerable sums of money in terms of training and development, it will, of course, be very keen to make sure that they **stay** with the organisation. Particularly in times of high employment, organisations will install a number of facilities and processes designed to ensure that employees are content with their present job role. In times of high unemployment, some of these facilities and processes are discarded as employees are easier to replace. Organisations which take this view are perhaps being rather short-sighted, since the recruitment and training of new personnel is as expensive in times of economic recession as it is in times of boom.

Remuneration

Remuneration is the level of **payment** for a particular job. Normally, the level of payment is arrived at to ensure the following:

- that it attracts suitable staff
- that it keeps staff in the organisation's employ for a considerable period of time

FIG 4.1.1 *This illustration shows the front cover of Tesco Retail Staff Handbook which includes details on the benefits of employment, company policy, terms and conditions of employment and termination details.*

- that it motivates the staff by offering a reasonable payment package, or the opportunity to earn extra related to individual or organisational performance
- that it helps towards the general objectives of the organisation, in terms of competitive rates of pay and linking pay increases and bonuses to overall organisational performance

Welfare

A good employer will offer a range of social facilities to his/her employees. In some cases, this does not go beyond a Christmas party. The ideal employer would provide many of the following:

- sports and social club
- company outings
- season ticket loans
- subsidised crèche or nursery facilities
- regular health checks for employees
- interest in the welfare of the employee's family
- understanding regarding compassionate leave (perhaps in the event of a death in the family)
- understanding regarding paternal leave (for the father of a new-born child)
- subsidised canteen facilities and meals
- staff discounts

PERFORMANCE

A further, more recent, addition to the list of welfare facilities is **staff appraisals**. While these are considered by some with suspicion, a good employer will use staff appraisals in a positive manner. On the one hand, they do look at staff skills and assess how good the employee is at doing a job, on the other hand, they try to look at the ambitions of the employee.

Regular staff appraisals will consider the following:

- the employee's ambitions within the organisation
- the employee's concerns about the job he/she is doing
- the interests the employee may have, and the direction he/she wishes to go in
- the promotion prospects of the employee
- how the job he/she is doing may be improved to give further satisfaction to the employee

TERMINATION

Termination of a contract of employment between the employer and the employee can only take place if one or other or the parties to the contract breaks it. The employee may not be dismissed without good reason. Let's look at the reasons for dismissal of an employee breaking the contract:

Dismissal

This word basically means that the employer is terminating the contract of the employee for having broken the contract; the reason often relates to disciplinary matters, behaviour or conduct. The employer has to give the employee notice that he/she intends to dismiss him/her. In some cases, the dismissal may be instant, but this is usually restricted to very serious matters.

If the employer puts the employee in such a position as to make it impossible for him/her to stay with the organisation, this is known as **constructive dismissal**. Courts have found in favour of employees who have been put in this position by the unfair attitudes and actions of the employer. Examples of such actions would include:

- changes in **wages** without informing the employee
- changes in the **location** of the job without consultation
- changes in **duties** required without negotiation
- changes in **job description** without negotiation

In all of these examples, the employer has decided, on his/her own, to change certain conditions of work. In some cases, this action will break the original contract of employment. In some cases, an employee may resign as a result of a series of events. In these cases, an industrial tribunal would look carefully at the stages of events and decide whether this is constructive dismissal. Some of the breaches of the contract of employment may relate to sexual harassment or discrimination on the grounds of race or colour. (For further details please see the relevant Acts later on in the book.)

student activity

In pairs, try to identify at least three different situations that an employee may find him/herself in which could be construed as constructive dismissal.

All contracts are a matter of interpretation, and we will look at this aspect shortly.

Unfair dismissal

The employee's right not to be **unfairly dismissed** from a job is a very important one. The laws relating to this stop employers feeling that they have the right to hire and fire as they see fit. It is, however, a very complex issue. Whether an individual employee is entitled to a claim of unfair dismissal is a much argued subject.

Generally speaking, to qualify for a claim for unfair dismissal, the employee must:

- have worked for the employer, as a full-time member of staff, for at least two years

- if a part-time worker, working eight hours a week or more, he/she must have been in employment for five years
- the individual must not be of pensionable age (currently 60 for women and 65 for men)
- Police officers cannot claim unfair dismissal even though they may qualify in terms of service
- individuals who are paid only a share of the profits are exempt
- employees who work for the organisation outside the UK are exempt
- employees on fixed period contracts are exempt (and this will be expressly stated in their Contract of Employment)
- members of the Armed Forces are also exempt on service grounds

In cases of dispute between the employer and the employee, an organisation called ACAS (the Arbitration and Conciliation Service) will assist and attempt to resolve the conflict. An official, working for ACAS, will try to get the two parties to agree rather than having to resort to the courts for a settlement.

Causes of dismissal

An employer will nearly always have a **reason** for dismissing an employee, whether the reason is right or wrong. There are, essentially, five main reasons:

- *Capability and qualifications.* These two reasons relate to the employee's fitness or competence to do the job. In this sense capability means skill, health, physical or mental ability. Qualifications, on the other

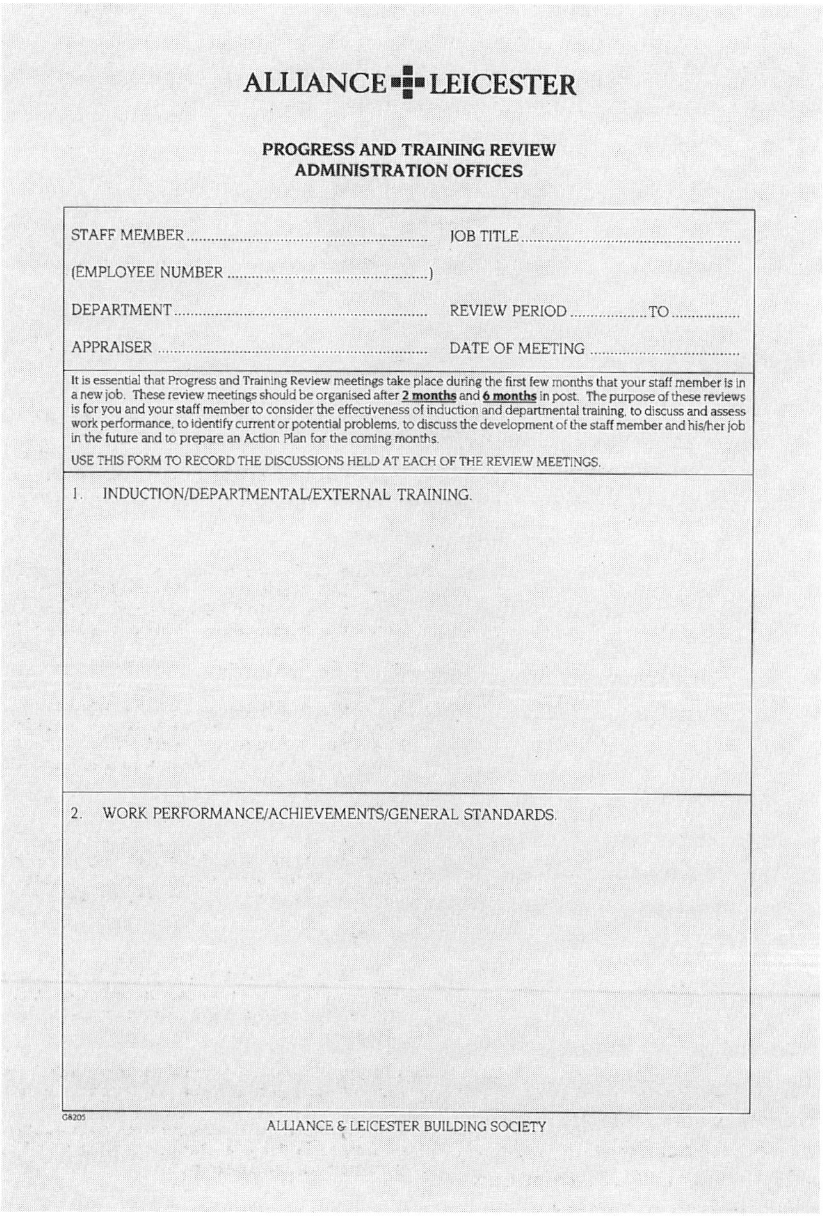

ALLIANCE ✠ LEICESTER

PROGRESS AND TRAINING REVIEW
ADMINISTRATION OFFICES

STAFF MEMBER .... JOB TITLE ....

(EMPLOYEE NUMBER ....)

DEPARTMENT .... REVIEW PERIOD .... TO ....

APPRAISER .... DATE OF MEETING ....

It is essential that Progress and Training Review meetings take place during the first few months that your staff member is in a new job. These review meetings should be organised after **2 months** and **6 months** in post. The purpose of these reviews is for you and your staff member to consider the effectiveness of induction and departmental training, to discuss and assess work performance, to identify current or potential problems, to discuss the development of the staff member and his/her job in the future and to prepare an Action Plan for the coming months.

USE THIS FORM TO RECORD THE DISCUSSIONS HELD AT EACH OF THE REVIEW MEETINGS.

1. INDUCTION/DEPARTMENTAL/EXTERNAL TRAINING.

2. WORK PERFORMANCE/ACHIEVEMENTS/GENERAL STANDARDS.

ALLIANCE & LEICESTER BUILDING SOCIETY

FIG 4.1.2 *Staff appraisal can begin at the induction period of an individual's employment with an organisation, as can be seen by this progress and training review document used by the Alliance and Leicester Building Society.*

hand, refers to the academic, technical or professional qualifications relevant to the job. Capability is an easier reason to define and explain. Basically, if the employee is shown to be incompetent or shows serious errors of judgement, then the employer has grounds for dismissal. Qualifications can be more complicated. If the employee is taken on by the employer on the basis that he/she must achieve a certain level of qualification, and then fails to do so, the employer may dismiss the employee.

student activity

Identify the necessary capabilities and qualifications of an individual employed in the following occupations:
- accounts clerk
- bus driver
- hairdresser

- *redundancy.* If the employer closes down the business, or part of the business, he/she may no longer need the services of some or all of the employees. In such cases, the employer must consult the employees, have fairly selected those to be made redundant and offered them alternative employment, if available. There are always ways around this problem of redundancy; for example, the employer could freeze recruitment and redeploy the existing employees, or reduce the number of hours that all of the employees work.
- *misconduct.* Misconduct is a very wide area and includes the following:
  - absenteeism – where an employee is away from work too often
  - lateness – where an employee constantly turns up late for work
  - insubordination – where an employee refuses to carry out instructions from a superior

In order to comply with the Employment Act 1989 all staff must receive a written statement detailing the Society's Grievance and Disciplinary Procedures.

STATEMENT ON THE GRIEVANCE PROCEDURE

STAGE 1

In the first instance, any member of staff wishing to raise a grievance should refer the matter to their immediate Supervisor who will discuss this informally. The member of staff must make the application in writing, and make it clear to their Supervisor that the issue is being raised in accordance with the Grievance Procedure.

STAGE 2

If the grievance is not resolved, or if the employee considers that they have not been treated fairly, they may apply to the Regional Controller, Administration Office Controller, Assistant General Manager or General Manager within 5 working days.

STAGE 3

If the grievance is still not resolved, or if the employee still considers they have not been fairly treated, they may appeal to the Managing Director (Designate), Mr Kevin Southwood. This would be the final stage for those who are not members of the Staff Association.

STAGE 4

Any issues still not resolved may be considered by the Joint Consultative and Negotiating Committee. This can only be considered with the agreement of both parties and the member of staff must be a paid up member of the Staff Association.

STAGE 5

This is the final stage of the Grievance Procedure, at which time any unsolved items may be submitted to a mutually acceptable arbitrator, whose decision shall be binding on both the Society and the Association.

If any issue remains unresolved 5 working days after commencement of any stage, it may be referred to the next stage of the Procedure.

At any stage in the above procedure an employee has the right to be accompanied by a Representative of the Staff Association or a nominated colleague.

FIG.4.1.3 *As can be seen from this extract, again from the Alliance and Leicester Building Society, the organisation complies with all requirements of the Employment Act 1989.*

- incompetence – where the employee shows on several occasions the inability to do the job
- immorality – where the employee behaves in a way that is unacceptable, perhaps sexually or morally
- breaking safety rules – where an employee endangers his/her life or the lives of others by not taking heed of the safety rules, perhaps deliberately
- theft – where the employee has stolen the property of the employer

In reality then, the employer can identify a number of reasons for dismissal due to misconduct. This may mean that a employee having an affair at work, an employee wearing offensive badges or T-shirts, or indeed, an employee involved in questionable activities outside the work place, could be dismissed under misconduct guidelines.

- *Statutory contraventions.* This reason for dismissal relates directly to an employee doing something which breaks a legal requirement. Good examples of this would be a lorry driver who is banned from driving due to drink-driving, or an employee who works for a butcher and grows a beard! (This would be against hygiene and food legislation).
- *Other reasons.* This broad area covers all other reasons not covered above, and is therefore a difficult category to summarise. Examples of reasons included here would be gradual deterioration in the output or performance of an employee, or in certain cases, the sexuality of the employee.

Fairness and dismissal

The employer really needs a **valid reason** for dismissing an employee. The employer's conduct must be fair towards the employee. The employer must not single out an individual because of his/her gender. Women have the right, of course, to be pregnant. If the employer chooses to dismiss an employee on the grounds of his/her gender, then there would have to be very strong reasons to link gender with the requirements and nature of the job.

If an employer dismisses an employee for any form of misconduct, he/she must be able to prove the employee's guilt In one particular case, all of the employees of a shop were dismissed after stock had been disappearing over a number of months. A tribunal held that the employer could not dismiss all of them as he/she did not have sufficient grounds to dismiss when perhaps only one of them was the culprit. The employer had not 'proved' the guilt of all employees.

Within the category of fairness, it would be safe to assume that the following are 'fair' reasons for dismissal:

- sexual harassment of other employees or customers
- racial harassment of other employees or customers

- wilful destruction of the organisation's property
- negligence
- long-term bad timekeeping
- sleeping at work
- gross insubordination
- inability to do the job the employee was appointed to do
- fraud, including the falsification of records
- inability to do the job as a result of being under the influence of alcohol
- inability to do the job as a result of being under the influence of illegal drugs
- fighting – when the employee has assaulted another person on the premises of the organisation
- unauthorised entry to confidential computer records

On the other hand, dismissal would be unfair if the reasons for it related to the following:

- *race* – an employer cannot dismiss an employee on the grounds of his/her race
- *religion* – an employee cannot be dismissed on the grounds of his/her religious beliefs
- *sexual discrimination* – an employer cannot dismiss an employee because he/she is a homosexual or a lesbian, unless it affects the standard of the work, or the individual is sexually harassing other members of the workforce
- *pregnancy* – as we have already said, a woman cannot be dismissed because she is pregnant. However, if the pregnancy affects her ability to do the job in total (e.g. the woman may be a labourer or have to carry heavy weights) then there are reasonable grounds
- *criminal record* – if the employer finds out that an employee has a criminal record, but it does not relate to the job, then he/she cannot be dismissed. However, some criminal records may relate to the job, such as fraud and accountancy! In such cases, the employer is within his/her rights to dismiss the employee
- *trade union membership* – an employee cannot be dismissed for being a member of a union.

student activity

Why do you think it is necessary for the above forms of discrimination to be classed as illegal?

Disciplinary procedures

The approved **disciplinary procedure**, as recommended by ACAS, should be both fair and impartial. It includes the following features:

- that all stages of the procedure should be **written**

down as a record of events
- that copies of the procedures should be **available** to all employees
- that the employer should clearly state **who operates** the procedure within the organisation
- that the employer should clearly state **who is involved**
- that thc employer clearly states what kind of **disciplinary action** will be taken against particular types of disciplinary matters
- that the employee has the right to have a friend, colleague or Trade Union **representative present** during all disciplinary interviews
- that in most cases, apart from really serious matters, an employee is **not dismissed for a first 'offence'**
- that the employee has the right to **appeal** against a decision made by the employer
- that all proceedings should be administered in a **fair** way
- that the employee should not be **unfairly discriminated against** throughout the whole process

Normally, the actual disciplinary procedure would work along the following lines:

1 *Verbal warning.* If the employee's conduct, behaviour or performance does not reach suitable and acceptable standards, then he/she will be given a formal verbal warning. This is the first official stage of the proceedings, and will not last for ever, provided the employee reaches acceptable standards. If the employee does, then he/she will not move on to the next stage, and the matter will be dropped.
2 *Written warning.* If the employee persists with the same behaviour that resulted in his/her receiving a verbal warning, or if the 'offence' is serious enough, then a written warning will be issued. This is usually written by the employee's immediate supervisor.
The written warning details the complaint against the employee, and clearly states exactly what the employee must do to remedy the situation. The warning will also state how long the employee has to 'mend' his/her ways. If the employee persists then inevitably the next stage of the procedures will occur. Again, if the employee complies with the requirements of the written warning then the matter will be dropped. The employee may also appeal against this written warning through the usual channels.
3 *The final written warning or suspension.* If the employee continues to fail to improve his/her conduct, behaviour or performance, then normally a final written warning will be given. If the conduct has been sufficiently serious the employee may automatically be given a final written warning, rather than go through the first few procedures. Just as the first written warning gives details of the complaint and a stern warning

that dismissal is imminent should there be no improvement, so too does the final written warning. As an alternative, the employer may wish to suspend the individual for a maximum of five days without pay. This is known as *disciplinary suspension.*
4 *Dismissal.* The final stage in the disciplinary procedure is dismissal itself. To reach this point, the employee must have failed all the requirements as laid down in the written warnings. The employee's most senior, but related, line manager will make the decision to dismiss the employee. The employee will be given a written statement which includes the reasons for his/her dismissal and the date of termination of cmployment. Further, it will say how the employee may appeal.

student activity

Write your own version of a formal written warning. What general tone should be taken? What needs to be said?

HEALTH AND SAFETY

As we will see in Unit 5, the area of health and safety has come under the scrutiny of both the UK Government and the EC in recent years. There has always been an obligation, as far as the employer is concerned, to provide some level of protection for employees. Many employers, in the past, have openly ignored guidelines and put their employees at risk in various ways. Since the introduction of the legislation, particularly in the last 40–50 years, employers now face considerable penalties for any breaches in health and safety policy.

Safe working conditions

An employee can quite rightly expect to work in conditions that are not hazardous to life or health. The central piece of legislation which protects the employee, and gives the employer strict guidelines to adhere to, is the Health and Safety at Work Act 1974. (This is covered later on in the book in much greater detail.)

It essentially sets out that the employee must work in an environment that is healthy, and safe and considers the welfare of the individual. The employer is ultimately responsible for any hazards or accidents which may be caused by his/her not taking note of the legislation. Very heavy fines may be incurred if the basic features of the legislation are broken.

Safe working conditions include many of the more obvious dangers to the employee, such as:

- fitting protective guards on dangerous machines;
- taking care that any hazardous or toxic chemicals are

housed in safe and leakproof containers

- ensuring that the quality of the air is good enough
- not requiring employees to carry out duties which could result in their injury, such as falling from a gantry above the factory floor

The laws cover many matters, from whether the employer is taking care to think about the health and safety aspects of the workplace, to whether the training needs of employees are regularly monitored. The Health and Safety Executive sends out inspectors to make sure that nothing is amiss. Also an employee is appointed as each organisation's Safety Officer.

student activity

In the role of an employee of a manufacturing organisation, what would be your key health and safety concerns?

EMPLOYEE REPRESENTATION AND CONSULTATION

Many organisations, while recognising that employees are a valuable resource in terms of their work output,

2. COMPANY POLICY

Health and Safety

We are committed to looking after the health and safety of all employees and customers. If you see anything you think is unsafe please tell your manager straight away. This may prevent an accident happening.

+ The Company's Health and Safety Policy is on your Staff Notice Board. Please familiarise yourself with it.

Accidents

By law we have to keep records of all accidents involving staff or customers. You must tell your manager straight away about even minor accidents.

If you are nearby when an accident happens please act quickly and sympathetically.

Always observe safety regulations and make sure that neither you, your colleagues, nor members of the public are exposed to danger.

Fire and Emergencies

For your own safety you must know the procedures for evacuating the building. Get to know the fire exits and fire alarm call points. Never block fire exits or the routes leading to them for any reason.

+ The Company's general fire and emergency procedures are on the Staff Notice Board and at the fire alarm call points in staff areas. Your manager will tell you what the procedures are in your area.

Tesco Retail Staff Handbook

FIG.4.1.4 *This is a sample from Tesco Retail's Staff Handbook, which outlines the company policy on health and safety.*

have largely ignored their ability to offer specialist knowledge which could aid the operations of the organisation. To this end, as we will see later in the Unit, some employers have installed schemes aimed at tapping this hitherto unused resource. Sceptics will often claim that many of these schemes are simply paper or PR exercises aimed at trying to appear to be more enlightened. Many progressive organisations have installed very effective forms of employee representation and consultation. As regards representation, the traditional forms obviously included trade union organisations. In recent years many of these trade unions have decreased in terms of size and power, while, at the same time, staff associations have become more common. We shall look at these two different forms of employee representation later in this Unit.

TRAINING AND PROFESSIONAL DEVELOPMENT

With employees being a resource, organisations will be keen to develop them, as with any resource. In the case of employees, development takes the form of constantly updating their knowledge, abilities and skills. An employee who is fully conversant with all new techniques of working practice will obviously be a far more valuable employee. As we will see, again later in this Unit, training itself falls into two main categories – vocational and non-vocational. Professional development takes a variety of forms and may include both vocational and non-vocational aspects.

EMPLOYEE RELATIONS

Employee relations become increasingly important as job tasks become more complex. Individuals who have a responsibility for key organisational activities need to feel that the organisation offers them rather more than monetary rewards. To this end, a complex infrastructure has gradually evolved in many organisations to support, in particular, their key employees. We will find that although this is largely related to the retention of these employees, there is, in some organisations, a feeling that employees (particularly those with long service) deserve some level of ownership.

EMPLOYEE REPRESENTATION AND CONSULTATION

There are various forms of **employee representation and consultation**. Many organisations have formed a Joint Consultative Committee in which employees are given the opportunity to involve themselves in the organisation's decision making.

These committees hold regular meetings at which decisions made by the management are relayed to the workforce and a forum for discussion is provided. Such committees also meet to discuss and negotiate on matters relating to industrial relations, such as working conditions, disciplinary procedures and pay.

These committees will take the form of:

- an advisory body
- a consultative body
- a negotiating body

If the committee is of the last type, then usually its decisions are binding on the organisation.

Another form of employee consultation is known as **employee participation**. This has come about because employers have recognised that the workforce has considerable skills and good ideas which could be used for the mutual benefit of employer and employees. There are various versions of employee participation, and they include the following:

- *quality circles* – where employees meet on a voluntary basis to discuss their work and how systems and procedures may be improved
- *employee briefing sessions* – where the employees are given useful and relevant information regarding the objectives of the organisation
- *transferring of responsibility* – when employees take on some of the management-related decision making
- *Worker councils* – which are largely consultative ; they generally concentrate on welfare issues and can often be an alternative to unions
- *Worker directors* – where employees attend meetings of the Board of Directors. In Europe, this idea has proved to be very successful in improving the quality of decision making at Board level. It also gives the Board the opportunity to hear the workforce's views at first hand rather than relying on the various layers of management to relay the employees' wishes and ideas. Further, this system tends to mean that the employees are more committed to decisions made by the Board. Finally, it helps reduce employer/ employee conflict, as the employees have a greater idea of the overall problems faced by the organisation

student activity

Assess the impact of the above forms of employee consultation in the light of reduced labour disputes in the UK.

TRADES UNIONS

Although trades unions have been the subject of a range of legislation to restrict their activities, the primary need for their existence still remains.

In effect, there are four different types of trade union, but the distinction between them is becoming increasingly less obvious.

1 *Craft Unions.* These are the earliest type of trade union, which were formed to cater for craftsmen who had received an apprenticeship. The membership of a Craft union consists of individuals who work with the same basic range of skills. These unions are still relatively powerful, since they control the number of skilled craftsmen entering the workforce. Craft unions restrict their membership by having very strict entrance qualifications and charging high membership rates.

There are still some fields in which it is still the case that you cannot work in that field unless you are a member of a specific union.
2 *Industrial unions.* Traditionally, these unions were formed to cater for all employees (regardless of grade and job) within a particular industry. Good examples of this type of union are the National Union of Mineworkers and the National Union of Railwaymen.
3 *Occupational unions.* Unlike the industrial unions, the occupational unions recruit from a wide range of different industries, but always from the same occupational group. A good example of this type of union would be the National Union of Public Employees, which recruits manual workers from hospitals, councils, schools and colleges.
4 *General unions.* Initially, these unions catered for those individuals not covered in the three categories above. The first general unions concentrated on unskilled workers, offering a wide range of benefits for a relatively low subscription rate. General unions have thrived in recent times as new industries have emerged and older, more traditional ones have declined. Often, these general unions are the result of several smaller, more specialist unions merging with one another.

Whatever type of union exists in the workplace, the basic functions of unions remain the same. A union exists to **protect and promote the interests of its members**. It essentially does the following:

- acts as a pressure group, which promotes the **interests** of its members
- acts as a pressure group, which protects the **position** of its members
- acts as the main instrument of **bargaining** with the employer.

All unions are formed and financed by the members. They are run by full-time officials, voted or appointed into place by the members. Unions are independent of the employers, they do not rely on them for funding. The union must also organise its own facilities and not rely on the employer to offer space within the organisation's own premises.

Trades unions carry out a multitude of different tasks in the pursuit of looking after their members' interests. Some of the major functions include:

- protecting the wages of members, particularly in times of recession
- negotiating the working hours required by the employer
- negotiating the working conditions of the employees
- monitoring health and safety
- providing a range of benefits, including pensions, sick pay, unemployment pay and injury benefits
- representing the interests of the members in times of dispute with the employer

In addition to these tasks, unions undertake a number of political duties relating to employment. They will actively negotiate with the government and opposition parties to further the cause of their members.

With a few notable exceptions, all employees are entitled to join a trade union and take advantage of the benefits offered, both protection and facilities.

student activity

To what extent do you think that trades unions, despite their relative lack of power, can have a positive impact upon employers' decision making?

STAFF ORGANISATIONS

Staff organisations have, in many organisations, either replaced trades unions or been the only option, as far as employees are concerned. Staff organisations tend to have the following features:

- they have been designed by the employer
- they are run by the employer on behalf of the employees

- they are subsidised or fully funded by the employer
- they do not have the same roles or objectives as trades unions
- they are generally 'no strike' organisations
- they are the main route by which organisations consult their workforce
- they tend to offer a similar range of welfare facilities to trades unions
- they are invariably separate organisations and not linked nationally
- membership is usually compulsory
- they are viewed with suspicion by trade unionists since they lack the power associated with independent employees' organisations

Trade Union Membership

We recognise the Union of Shop, Distributive and Allied Workers (USDAW) as the sole representative and negotiating union for all grades excluding senior store management.

Senior store management are represented by the Supervisory, Administrative and Technical Association (SATA) which is a separate division of USDAW.

Our relationship with USDAW has developed over many years and we encourage you to join.

FIG.4.1.5 *Tesco Retail's staff handbook makes it clear that company policy is to recognise the Shopworkers's union USDAW.*

MULTI-SKILLING

Since the introduction of trade union legislation aimed at reducing the power of employees in relation to employers, the subject of demarcation has all but disappeared. In the past, demarcation was a common reason for industrial disputes. Demarcation is essentially to do with the clear definition of job descriptions, tasks and roles. Trades unions fought against the blurring of these definitions. Multi-skilling requires individuals to perform a broader range of activities within the workplace. It is now commonplace for a machine operative to undertake most basic forms of machine maintenance. Previously, demarcation demanded that any maintenance work should be carried out by an individual employed specifically for that task. While multi-skilling offers greater job satisfaction in terms of giving greater job variety, it has meant the loss of many jobs. A fringe benefit of multi-skilling has been, in some cases, higher rates of pay. Multi-skilling has also given organisations the following benefits:

- since machine operatives carry out most maintenance, there will be less 'down time'
- machinery, as a result of this, will be more productive
- following on from these two points, the organisation should be more competitive
- a natural result of all of the above is that the organisation should be able to offer better pay and conditions to its workforce

TEAM WORK

Employees rarely work in an organisation alone. Often teams are created, either formally or informally to carry out specific tasks. A team consists of a group of individuals working together towards a single, common objective. When working as a member of a team, people need to know which members of that team have power and authority, and who is directing the joint efforts of the team. A successful team member needs to be able to communicate with others easily in order to allow interaction between the members of the team. Many organisations spend considerable time and effort in the following areas in order to develop successful teams:

- training and re-training their staff in interpersonal skills
- paying for residential training programmes aimed at enhancing team building
- funding in-house seminars and workshops

TRAINING AND DEVELOPMENT

Training basically falls into four separate categories, these are:

1 *On-the-job training* – which refers to training carried out while at work. It may be delivered by in-house training personnel or by 'bought-in' specialists.

2 *Off-the-job training* – which refers to training carried out at a location other than the workplace. It may require access to specialists or specialist equipment, not necessarily available in the workplace.

3 *Part-time training* – which refers to the 'mode' of training itself. This category includes day-release, evening classes and short courses. This type of training is usually paid for, at least in part, by the employer and relates directly to required job skills.

4 *Full-time training* – which refers to short or long-term training courses which take the employee out of the work situation for an extended period. Such training may be necessary because the employee needs to be trained in a complex area which could not be taught on a part-time basis.

Many organisations run special courses, either at the workplace or in an alternative location. The nature of the training may involve specialist management skills, health and safety or supervisory skills. It is usually key personnel who are chosen to attend these courses and they are then expected to pass on the knowledge they have acquired to the rest of the members of their work teams.

The types of skill required for business can range from knowledge of new software packages to more general managerial skills. The area of work which the individual is involved with, will dictate the type of training he or she needs. Personal skills development has become a very popular area of training in recent years and will attempt to offer guidance in the following areas:

- time management
- stress management
- supervisory skills
- management skills

TRAINING DEPARTMENT INDUCTION COURSE

The programme will include:-

– the functions of building societies

– Alliance & Leicester's main products

– business objectives and your role in helping to meet them

– Alliance & Leicester customer service

– communication and teamwork

– telephone techniques

– education and training opportunities

FIG 4.1.6 *The Alliance and Leicester Building Society is one of many major organisations to consider the importance of training from the very beginning of an individual's working life with the organisation.*

Attendance confirmed by: _____

(Training Officer)

Date: _____

- assertiveness
- communication skills
- counselling skills
- negotiating skills
- coping with meetings
- leadership skills

VOCATIONAL/PROFESSIONAL QUALIFICATIONS

Most people will start their careers with few or no qualifications. Most individuals will have at least some basic understanding of English, or Mathematics, but it is only when they begin to consider what their career goal may be, that they should start to gain qualifications which will help them achieve their goal. Depending on the time and effort put in, individuals can slowly progress in their collection of qualifications. At the same time, particularly if the individual is in work, he/she will be gaining additional responsibilities as a result of the qualifications he or she has achieved.

Whether we are considering training or qualifications, we must make two more important distinctions which relate to the nature of the course of study, and concern whether it is **vocational** or **non-vocational**.

Vocational

Vocational training or qualifications are those which relate directly to a job or job area. It does not necessarily matter whether the individual is in work or not, since the programme is designed to offer the learner the opportunity to practise the type of skills required for a particular job. This has become a very popular area, much supported by employers, who see this as the only useful and relevant way of preparing individuals for work within industry or technology.

Non-vocational

In some respects, you would think that a non-vocational course is the opposite to a vocational course. This may not necessarily be the case. Typically, a course which falls into this category will not have a direct relevance to a particular job and may be more general in nature. Alternatively, non-vocational courses may be academic and provide a wide range of knowledge which is not necessarily applied. Individuals who have followed such courses would need to undertake further training to learn how to put into practice the extensive knowledge they have gained.

LEGAL REQUIREMENTS

CONDITIONS OF EMPLOYMENT

Contracts of employment

As we have seen so far, the employer has a number of duties towards the employee. This can be seen very clearly in the **contract of employment**. This really formalises the relationship and is seen as a legally binding document on both the employer and the employee.

A contract of employment should lay down all of the following points:

- **job role**; what is the precise nature of the job
- **job title**
- **pay details**; how it is paid, frequency of payment
- **additional payment details**, such as which salary/wage scale the individual will be placed on, when overtime can be undertaken, how bonuses and commission may be earned
- start **times** and finishing times of work
- total **number of hours** worked per week, before overtime
- number of paid days off for **holidays** etc. and any restrictions on when these may be taken

- **sick leave** and **maternity leave** details, duration and entitlement to such leave
- **pension schemes**, with details of contributions made by employer and employee
- **grievance procedures** details, who is the Grievance Officer and the processes of the grievance procedure itself
- period of **notice** to be worked/given
- number of weeks or months notice required (by either side) in the event of **resignation** or **termination** of employment

In addition to these legally required details, the employer may wish to inform the employee of the following:

- **rules and regulations** to be followed by employees
- **codes of behaviour** expected of the employees
- the nature and availability of sports, and social activities and welfare facilities offered
- a full **organisational chart** so that the employee identifies where he/she fits into the overall scheme of things

Compliance with contract – employee

Just as the employer will be expected to fulfil his/her obligations as set out in the contract of employment, so too will the employee.

The employee will be expected to comply with all aspects of the contract of employment, and furthermore will be required to accept responsibility for his/her actions at work.

Confidentiality is important; the employee should also take care not to release any information of a sensitive or secret nature to the media or competitors.

---

student activity

To what extent do you consider contracts of employment to be a very one-sided affair in favour of the employer?

INDIVIDUAL RIGHTS

Working to the terms of the contract

The employee has a responsibility to the employer to work in a loyal, conscientious and honest manner. He/she is also expected to accept any reasonable and legal directions from his/her superiors. In essence, this means adhering to the terms of the contract of employment. As we have seen, the contract of employment can be a very detailed document and is considered to be a legally binding contract once both parties have signed. By law, all employees must have received a contract of employment within 13 weeks of beginning employment. The employer is required to exercise a duty of care towards his/her employees, provide sufficient work to do, pay the employee at due times and maintain a number of records on behalf of the employee. These will include details of:

- PAYE deductions
- National Insurance contributions
- Pension scheme contributions

The employer must take care when advertising a job, as the advertisement is considered to be the beginning of the formation of the contract of employment. Once a candidate for a particular job accepts employment on the basis of the advertisement details, then much of the contract of employment has already been decided. Before an employer finally accepts a candidate as an employee, he/she will usually take up references. If a prospective employer receives unfavourable references about the candidate, then he/she is quite within his or her rights to withdraw the job offer. In reality, just how an employer interprets the content of a reference is open to question.

A contract of employment is really like any other contract. It gives both parties rights as well as obligations. The contract, as we mentioned earlier, identifies formally what was really agreed during the interview or selection process. Normally, a contract of employment will contain the following commitments, either directly, or by inference:

- the employer will pay wages
- the employer will provide work
- the employer will pay any reasonable losses or expenses incurred by the employee in the course of his/her work
- the employer will provide a reference if required by the employee
- the employer will provide safe working conditions and working practices
- the employer will not act in such a way as to breach the trust and confidence given by the employee
- the employer will provide necessary information relating to the employee's work, pay, conditions and opportunities
- the employer will always act in good faith towards the employee

In addition to the obvious obligations the employee may have, he/she will also be expected to:

- act in good faith towards the employer
- account for any cash received from other sources (this is to make sure that the employee does not accept bribes or fees from external organisations in the pursuit of his/her normal activities)
- keep trade secrets confidential
- obey any reasonable orders and give faithful service to the employer

---

student activity

What do you understand by the phrase 'act in good faith'?

EQUAL OPPORTUNITIES AND EQUAL PAY

Equal opportunities

Even in these modern times, there are many individuals who are discriminated against on various grounds. Within employment, employees are protected to some extent by a series of laws and regulations, which we look at in some detail later. The main groups who suffer from discrimination are:

1 women

2 ethnic minorities
3 the disabled
4 those with an alternative sexual orientation
5 the young
6 the old
7 certain religious groups

Many organisations have adopted equal opportunities policies, although they are not yet required to do this by law. The **Equal Opportunities Commission** has designed a standard policy which employers can use. This covers a variety of different situations, and includes the following:

- that to have an equal opportunities policy is a desirable thing
- that it should be strictly adhered to
- that all forms of direct and indirect discrimination are clearly defined
- that the organisation states its commitment to equal opportunities and further states that it is in the best interests of the organisation and its employees
- that all employees are made aware of the policy
- that staff are trained to maintain the policy
- that any preconceived ideas which employees may have regarding those who are subject to discrimination are addressed
- that both recruitment and promotion are equal for all
- that training is offered on an equal basis to all
- that the employment contract does not inadvertently discriminate against anyone
- that the organisation's facilities are open to all
- that an individual is nominated to monitor the policy
- that the policy is regularly reviewed and updated according to need
- that any grievances relating to discrimination are dealt with in a prompt and fair manner
- that no individual suffers victimisation in the course of his/her duties within the organisation

Equal pay

The concept of equal pay for an equal day's work is the foundation of several pieces of government legislation. We shall be looking at these in some detail later.

HEALTH AND SAFETY AT WORK

Compliance with health and safety at work legislation – employers

We will be looking at health and safety in much greater detail later, but essentially, employers and employees have an obligation to ensure a safe working environment. If the legal requirements are broken by either party, in effect one side or other has been negligent, then the aggrieved party may begin legal proceedings. In effect, the health and safety requirements with which any employer must comply are:

- to provide a safe working environment
- to provide adequate welfare facilities
- to ensure entrances and exits are safe
- to ensure equipment and systems used are safe and regularly serviced
- to make sure that items needed for use in handling or storage are safe
- to make sure that dangerous or toxic materials are housed in safe containers
- to provide instruction, training or supervision regarding working practices and materials used
- to ensure that all accidents are rigorously investigated and the causes promptly dealt with

Compliance with health and safety – employees

Just as the employer must take heed of the requirements of the legislation, so must the employee. Employees may, however, suffer harm or injuries which are not necessarily the fault of the employer.

If an employee is negligent and causes injury to him/herself or another person, then the employer can find him/herself in a difficult position. The employee may claim that it was not really his or her fault. As long as the employer provides safe working conditions, then apart from accidents caused by negligence, there should be no real concerns here. We will look at the employer's role in preventing accidents later.

Another possible area of concern is when an employee deliberately puts someone else's life in danger. Depending on the circumstances, he/she could not only be dismissed, but be the subject of criminal and civil proceedings.

TYPES OF REDRESS

In certain cases, when an employee feels aggrieved at treatment by an employer, particularly in disciplinary matters, he or she may have to resort to some form of redress. The most common types are given below:

- If an employee chooses to **appeal** at any stage in the disciplinary procedure, he/she must inform his/her superior within two working days. The manager will consider the appeal, but, his/her decision is final. The manager may choose to uphold the decision to discipline the employee, but may not increase the severity of the action taken against the employee.
- It is recommended that all disciplinary matters should be **considered at length** and that employees have the right to state their side of the argument. As we have said, all disciplinary meetings or interviews should take place in the presence of a trade union official or colleague.
- Normally, an employee is given two **verbal warnings**, followed by a final written warning before being dismissed. It should be remembered that the disciplinary code of the employer must be reasonable and fair. If an employee thinks he or she has not had sufficient opportunity to state his/her case, then he or she may choose to refer the matter to an industrial tribunal.
- Employers are not legally obliged to follow the above disciplinary process, but many nevertheless do so. After all, employers are unlikely and unwilling to face the disruption and expense of an industrial tribunal.

student activity

At what stage in the disciplinary procedure would an individual be advised to consult a legal expert?

INDUSTRIAL TRIBUNAL

Industrial tribunals were set up by the Government as a kind of court. They are there to try to obtain an agreement between the employer and the employee and have the power to demand reinstatement of the employee or to award financial compensation if reinstatement is not practicable.

CIVIL LEGAL ACTIONS

Employees may resort to civil law in order to gain redress if they have not received satisfaction via an industrial tribunal. Civil action may be taken in the following ways:

- in the Magistrates Court, where the employee may obtain only a limited financial compensation from the employer
- by attempting to construct a case in relation to the Law Reform (Contributory Negligence) Act 1945
- by attempting to construct a case in relation to the Employers' Liability (Defective Equipment) Act 1969
- by applying to the Court of Appeal
- by claiming breaches of the Employment Protection (Consolidation) Act 1978
- by applying for compensation in line with the Unfair Dismissal (Increase of Compensation Limit) Order 1991
- after the process has taken some time, the employee may apply to the Court of Appeal using the Industrial Tribunals (Interest Order) 1990

The usual method of redress, particularly for unfair dismissal, will be a cash compensation award. This compensation is usually the same as a redundancy payment. The calculation of the basic award follows the following guidelines:

- $1\frac{1}{2}$ week's pay for each year of employment provided the employee was not younger than 41
- 1 week's pay for each year of employment provided the employee was not younger than 22
- $\frac{1}{2}$ week's pay for each year of employment if the employee is younger than 22

student activity

Following the guidelines above, calculate the payments due to the following individuals:

- a 23-year-old who has been working for the company for five years and receives £250 per week
- an individual who is 42 years old and has been working for the company for 16 years and receives £380 per week

An employee who is close to the age of retirement can suffer from considerable disadvantages as a result of his/her age. For employees over the age of 64, lose 1/12th of the award for each month worked after they have reached their 64th birthday.

Compensation is presently limited to £10,000 under the Unfair Dismissal (Increase of Compensation

Limits) Order 1991. Where a tribunal or court orders an employer to reinstate the employee, then subsequently he or she fails or refuses to do so, an additional award may be made. This will be between 13 and 26 weeks' of pay up to a maximum of just over £200 per week. Special awards may be made, particularly in cases when employees have been dismissed in relation to trade union membership or non-membership. They are entitled to a single week's pay multiplied by 104, or £13,180, whichever is the greater. The maximum payment under this special award is just over £26,000.

If the employee has had to wait a considerable length of time for the dispute to be settled, then he/she may be entitled to interim relief.

BUSINESS PERFORMANCE

One of the important aspects of business performance, that organisations need to monitor and measure is the number of employees compared with the level of profitability of the organisation. It is somewhat difficult to relate these two aspects in a crude sense. Therefore, the organisation needs to have a series of specific measuring devices available. These relate to:

- productivity of labour
- the absentee rate
- overall quality of service

We shall now look at these three in more detail:

PRODUCTIVITY

Productivity is essentially the amount of output derived from a series of inputs. The simple equation is:

$$\text{Productivity} = \frac{\text{Output}}{\text{Input}}$$

This formula may be used to show the efficiency of either an organisation or the economy in general. Productivity may increase in the following circumstances:

1 increase output while keeping inputs static
2 increase output more quickly than increases in input
3 keep output static while input decreases
4 decrease output while input is reduced at a lower rate

The productivity of labour obviously depends on the nature of the organisation. It is usually measured by taking the number of products produced as the output and the number of employees as the input.

In order to determine the true productivity of an organisation, however, we must look at more than just labour levels. We must use what is known as a **multifactor productivity ratio.** The formula to calculate productivity using this is rather more complex:

$$\text{Productivity} = \frac{\text{Output}}{(\text{Labour costs} + \text{material costs} + \text{fixed costs})}$$

From this formula we are able to determine whether the organisation's activities are capital intensive or labour intensive. These terms refer to the following features of an organisation's activities:

1 *Capital intensive.* This means than an organisation is more reliant upon equipment and machinery than labour and thus spends much more of its available resources on capital items. This is particularly true of organisations which employ high levels of information technology, automation and other technological equipment.
2 *Labour intensive.* This means that an organisation is much more reliant on the individual skills of employees than upon machines to perform the bulk of the job tasks. It is common to find this sort of organisation in traditional manufacturing areas, agriculture and the traditional craft areas.

In order to monitor productivity over a period of time, the government and business organisations employ a productivity ratio. In a manner similar to the system of calculating indices which we have looked at already, this ratio enables a comparison to be made between organisations operating in the same sector, as well as more general country to country contrasts. The productivity index formula looks like this:

$$\text{Productivity index} = \frac{\text{Productivity ratio in given time period}}{\text{Productivity ratio in base year}} \times 100$$

The government uses a type of productivity formula in order to calculate the productivity of the nation in general. This formula looks like this:

$$\text{National productivity} = \frac{\text{Total national output}}{(\text{Land} + \text{labour} + \text{capital employed})}$$

Organisations can measure productivity more precisely by considering specific productivity totals. Generally, labour, capital and materials productivity are useful calculations to make. These formulae are:

$$\text{Labour productivity} = \frac{\text{Sales income}}{\text{Wage costs}}$$

$$\text{Capital productivity} = \frac{\text{Sales income}}{\text{Current value of capital items}}$$

$$\text{Materials productivity} = \frac{\text{Sales income}}{\text{Value of materials employed}}$$

LEVEL OF ABSENTEEISM

It has been calculated that absence from work for the typical employee – including authorised holidays and unauthorised absences – amounts to around 20 per cent of the average 250-day working year. Some 200 million working days are lost through sickness alone. This costs the country some £9 billion per year. The absentee rate is far higher in the public sector, where it approaches 5 per cent on average, than in the private sector where the figure is around 3 per cent Interestingly, organisations which offer good quality canteen facilities and smoking bans throughout the organisation have absentee rates of less than 3 per cent

The main reasons for absenteeism (which does not include absence through sickness) are:

- stress
- low morale
- child-care commitments
- comparative ill-health after sickness
- domestic problems
- transport complications
- simply not wanting to go into work

Another factor which is related to absenteeism is the staff turnover percentage. The usual calculation used to reach this figure is:

$$\text{Percentage turnover of labour} =$$
$$\frac{\text{Number of employees terminating employment}}{\text{Number of employees}} \times 100$$

In order to reduce staff turnover, organisations employ various retention policies, which we have already looked at. In some organisations, however, although staff turnover is not necessarily a problem. This is particularly true of organisations where the general requirements in terms of job skills and experience are limited. Good examples of such jobs would be routine food processing, basic warehousing duties and unskilled manual workers.

Labour turnover can be categorised in terms of whose decision causes it::

1 *Voluntary.* This is when an individual chooses to leave an organisation of his/her own accord, for whatever reason.

2 *Involuntary.* This is when an individual leaves an organisation as a result of one of the following reasons, which are largely beyond his or her control:

- retirement
- Ill health
- death
- moving house to a new area
- pregnancy

3 *Management Decisions.* This is when the management of the organisation decide to terminate the employment of particular individuals for the following reasons:

- dismissal
- redundancy

QUALITY OF SERVICE

As we have already seen, **quality assurance** – in terms of both customer service and after-sales service – is often part of a marketing function. In recent years, many business analysts have levelled the charge of poor quality of service against UK businesses. As we will be looking at the ways in which business activity is monitored in Unit 6, we will only cover the main aspects of quality at this point. Essentially, we need to try to compare the new views on quality with traditional quality concerns. We shall look at the traditional view first:

- quality should be considered secondary to making a profit.
- by improving quality the organisation will incur higher levels of cost
- it should be a goal of the organisation to minimise quality defects
- quality control is the principal concern of quality controllers
- most quality problems are derived from poor workmanship
- once quality problems have been identified they should be remedied

The newer philosophy on quality control looks at things in a radically different manner. We have listed the aspects in the same order so that you can compare the opposing views:

- quality is the most effective way of maximising profits
- higher levels of quality will lead to lower costs (since there will be fewer complaints and fewer defective products)

- to achieve total quality the organisation should have no defective products leaving the factory
- it is the responsibility of every employee, regardless of his/her status in the organisation, to ensure that quality is maintained in every area of the organisation's activities
- management should shoulder the blame for quality problems
- all quality control problems should be eliminated at the earliest possible opportunity

In relation to the quality of service, organisations will employ most, if not all, of the above criteria. They will expect employees to take as much care in the servicing of customers as they do in the production of the product in the first place.

student activity

List the criteria that could be used to ensure quality in a retail operation.

PROFIT

Increasingly, pay and employee performance is linked to the profit made by the organisation. This linkage is made either, in a direct or formal manner (in the case of profit sharing or performance bonuses), or in an implied or informal manner (in the case of annual salary or wage increases).

Profit can be measured in either gross or net terms. The former refers to the profit level attained by the organisation before the deduction of selling, distribution and administration costs. The latter is the difference between the organisation's sales revenue and all costs.

Profit sharing relies on a profit being made. If the organisation does not make a profit, then there is no profit share to be distributed. The profit share is given either in cash or shares, the most popular (in terms of the recipient) is cash, which accounts for some 80% of the payments.

The distribution of profit sharing attracts income tax relief, providing the scheme has been registered by the organisation. Profit sharing has a number of advantages and disadvantages.

1 Advantages

(a) Employees realise that their contribution to the organisation is important.
(b) Employees are cost conscious.
(c) Management are monitored by the employees in terms of their performance.
(d) Profit sharing leads to the feeling of joint ownership.
(e) Profit sharing leads to greater employee loyalty.

2 Disadvantages

(a) It is hard to directly link job tasks with the profit figures.
(b) Lazy or inefficient employees receive the same as hard-working and well motivated ones.
(c) Profit calculations are complex and may lead to mistrust by the employees.
(d) If the profit levels drop, but not as a result of poor performance by the employees, then this may cause ill-feeling.
(e) Poor or inefficient management has a larger impact on the profit levels than individual employees' efforts.

Investigate job roles in organisational structures

1 TYPES OF BUSINESS ORGANISATION
sole trader, partnership, co-operative, franchise, private limited company (Ltd), public limited company (plc), public corporation

2 STRUCTURES
hierarchical, flat, devolved, static, dynamic

3 JOB ROLES
director, manager, team member

4 JOB DESCRIPTION
job title, position in the structure, responsibilities, competences

5 PERSONAL SPECIFICATION
personal attributes and development, qualifications, experience

6 PURPOSES
to match applicants with vacancies, to match business objectives to jobs, to train and develop employees

TYPES OF BUSINESS ORGANISATION

There are many ways in which a business can be organised, from a small one-man business to a multinational. You will find that the majority of the earlier business organisations in this section are representative of the private sector, but we have covered the public sector in some detail in our considerations of public corporations, for example.

THE SOLE TRADER

The **sole trader** is perhaps the most common type of business organisation although in recent years the num-bers of such businesses have been declining, for a number of reasons, which we will look at later on.

The sole trader is responsible for all actions that the operation undertakes. This individual will be responsi-ble for borrowing all the money required and actually running the business day-to-day. Perhaps the most com-mon sorts of sole traders are craftsmen and women – plumbers, decorators, electricians, mobile hairdressers, window cleaners and chiropodists.

Sole-trade businesses cover a very wide range of activities, but they all have some features in common, including the way they got started, and the fact that the businesses can always normally be run by one person, although that person has to be very flexible and needs to be willing to work very long hours.

There are quite a number of advantages to setting up as a sole trader:

1 there are no real legal formalities to complete before commencing to trade
2 there are no real legal requirements governing the layout of their accounts
3 the annual accounts do not have to be audited
4 decisions can be made quickly since only one individual is involved
5 all the profits and indeed losses belong to the owner
6 the owner has the freedom to run the business his or her own way

There are also a number of disadvantages:

1 capital is limited to the owner's savings or profits or any other money he or she can borrow
2 the owner has sole responsibility for debts – if the owner does fall into financial difficulties he/she may have to sell their own personal possessions to meet the business debts
3 responsibility for a range of activities falls upon the shoulders of the one person which runs the business. So, in other words the owner is responsible for running the business – dealing with paperwork, customers, filling in tax returns and dealing with day-to-day contact with any employees or subcontractors he or she might use
4 the success of the business is always dependent on how hard that sole trader wishes to work
5 any unforeseen accident or illness could seriously affect the business since all responsibilities rest on the shoulders of that one person

student activity

Consult your Yellow Pages directory, and try to identify at least 10 local sole traders.

PARTNERSHIPS

A **partnership** may be formed as a way to overcome the problems a sole trader may have in raising capital. A partnership consists of between 2 and 20 people who set up in business together and share the responsibilities for that business. Each partner is required to contribute some capital and they share out the profits and the losses between all of the partners. The control of the business is the responsibility of all of the partners and decisions made by one partner are always binding on the others.

In partnerships, all partners have what is known as unlimited liability. This means that any debts incurred by the partnership have to be met by all the partners.

Individuals may enter into a partnership with one another without any real formal written agreement, but in practice they usually draw up a partnership agreement. Essentially this is a set of rules which will hopefully help avoid disagreements between the partners.

The agreement usually includes the following:

1 the amount of capital to be contributed by each partner
2 the ratio in which the profits and losses are to be shared. Usually this is worked out in relation to the amount of capital each of the partners has put in. So, in other words, the more capital each partner has put in, the more profits he or she will be entitled to
3 the salaries, if there are any, that are going to be paid to specific partners
4 the rules for admitting and expelling partners
5 the voting rights of partners – they may have an equal or an unequal share of the decision making
6 the rules for ending the partnership

On the question of limited liability, there is an option which allows a partnership to have limited liability for some members of the partnership – this is known as a **limited partnership**. In such partnerships, certain partners are known as **sleeping partners**. They take no part whatsoever in the decision-making process of the business, and should the business fail they stand to lose no more than their original investment in the business. Therefore, they have a limited liability. In contrast, the other partners, known as the **general partners** still face unlimited liability. In law, there must always be at least one partner with unlimited liability.

The most common form of partnership, though, is the ordinary partnership where all partners play an active role in the running of the business. In the event of losses being incurred, each partner has unlimited liability.

It is very important for people setting up a partnership with unlimited liability that all the partners you are trustworthy, hardworking and honest. Otherwise, the mistakes of one partner can affect all the others financially.

Partnerships are commonly found in the accounting and legal professions, where specialists will join together in a partnership to make the business more attractive to prospective clients.

There are a number of advantages and disadvantages in setting up a partnership. The advantages are:

1 as we have said earlier, it is easier for partners than sole traders to raise capital because all of the partners can pool their resources and have access to more capital

2 partners can share their expertise and their efforts

3 partners can arrange to cover one another at times of illness or holidays, or even lunch breaks

4 a partnership, like a sole trader, has the advantage of not having to publish its accounts or have them audited.

5 additional capital can be raised by introducing more partners to the partnership

There are a number of disadvantages too:

I a partner is personally liable for all of the firm's debts

2 disagreements can arise between partners about the amount of effort that each of them puts in

3 partnerships can only raise limited amounts of capital as compared with businesses like limited companies (which we will talk about later on)

4 decision making can be slow since all partners have to be consulted

5 the death or retirement of a member can bring a partnership to an end if such a rule is written into the deed of partnership

6 all profits must be shared

student activity

Investigate at least five local accountancy firms and try to discover the number of partners in each of these businesses.

CO-OPERATIVES

Co-operatives are an increasingly popular type of business organisation. In the past co-operatives were found only in agriculture or retailing. More recently there has been a growth in the number of co-operatives in services and in small scale manufacturing.

FIG 4.2.1 *The Ipswich and Norwich Co-operative Society Limited is one of many co-operative business in the UK.*

In a co-operative all the people who form part of that organisation join together to make decisions, share the work and also share the profits.

The first successful co-operative was a retail co-operative. It was set up at the end of the last century in Rochdale when weavers joined together to start their own shop selling basic grocery items. Their profits were shared as was the amount of money that they spent, and everyone had an equal say in how the shop was run.

The basic idea behind the Rochdale Co-op still stands and Co-ops may be seen in the High Streets throughout the country. Nowadays, the co-ops are registered as limited liability companies.

Another major area in which co-operatives are found is in production, both in manufacturing and food production. In this type of organisation all the members share the responsibility for the success or the failure of the business and work together, making decisions together and taking a share of the profits.

These co-operatives suffer from a number of problems:

- they often find it difficult to raise capital from banks and other bodies because the co-operatives are not in business just to make a profit
- the larger co-operatives have discovered that they must set up a solid management structure in order that decisions can be made
- in food production, several farmers will set up what is known as a Marketing Co-operative where each farmer takes responsibility for a particular part of the production of a food, whether it is packaging, distribution, or advertising.

student activity

Again consulting your local Yellow Pages, try to identify any co-operative organisations in your local area. In which business sectors are they operating?

THE FRANCHISE

The **franchise** is a form of organisation which has been imported into the UK and the rest of the world from America, where over a third of all retail businesses are operating on what is known as a franchise basis. Again, this is becoming a very popular form of business organisation in the UK. The main features of franchising are as follows:

I Franchising really amounts to hiring out or licensing the use of product lines to other companies. A franchise agreement allows another company to trade under a particular name in a particular area. The firm which sells the franchise is known as the **franchisor**.

2 The person who takes out the franchise needs a sum of money for capital and is issued with a certificate from the franchising company. This person is known as the **franchisee**. The franchisee usually has the sole right of operating in a particular area. Some examples of franchises can be seen in many of our High Streets – Pizza Hut, Prontaprint, Body Shop and Spud U Like.

3 Another important feature of the franchise agreement is that the franchisee agrees to buy all of its supplies from the franchisor and the latter makes a profit on these supplies.

4 The franchisor also takes a share of the profits made by the franchisee's business, without having to risk any capital or be involved in the day-to-day management of the business.

5 The franchisee on the other hand benefits from trading under a well-known name and enjoys a **local monopoly**. In other words each franchisee is the only business to operate under that name in a particular area.

6 The franchise agreement allows people to become their own boss without the normal kind of risks of setting up a business from scratch.

student activity

In the role of a potential franchisee, investigate the franchise opportunities open to you. Which information sources would you use in order to find this information?

PRIVATE LIMITED AND PUBLIC LIMITED COMPANIES

The **limited company** is fast becoming one of the most common forms of business organisation.

A limited company is a separate organisation in law from its shareholders and directors.

As with a partnership, individuals put capital into the business – these are known as **shareholders** – and they own part of the business and will share any profits that are earned. They elect a number of **directors** who will actually run the business on their behalf.

The law requires a **meeting** of shareholders once a year, and minuting of matters that may be discussed is required. Shareholders really have little part in the day-to-day running of the business, although they may also be directors.

A number of companies acts have been passed over the years which protect the interests of shareholders, as well as those of creditors who are owed money by limited companies.

It is relatively simple and reasonably cheap to set up a company. In order to set up a limited company, two documents must be drawn up.

1 The first is known as a **Memorandum of Association**. This is really the company's rule book. The kinds of thing that you would find in a memorandum of association are:

- the **name** of the company
- the **address** of the registered office
- the company's **activities**
- the type and amount of **capital** which has been invested to set the company up

2 The second is what is known as the **Articles of Association**. This deals with the inside working of the company. It details the following:

- the procedures that have to be followed at an **Annual General Meeting**, known as an AGM
- the duties of the **directors** of the company
- the **voting rights** of the shareholders
- how profits and losses are **distributed** among shareholders
- details of how **accounts** will be kept and recorded
- details of how company **officers** will be appointed
- the rules and procedures of issuing **shares** and transferring shares to other people.

Once these two documents have been drawn up, the next step is to send them to Companies House. If everything is in order, the Registrar of Companies will issue a Certificate of Operation, which in effect is like a Birth Certificate.

There are essentially two different types of limited company. Both of them have a minimum of two shareholders.

The first is known as a **Private Limited Company**. You can always tell that a company is a private limited company when the word **Limited** or **Ltd** is written after the company name. The shares in a private limited

FIG 4.2.2 *Eric Parker is the Chairman of Cunard Steamship Company Limited and Deputy Chairman and Chief Executive of Trafalgar House PLC.*

company are not freely available to the general public and the transfer of shares is agreed only by the Directors. Private limited companies are usually family concerns, or were originally family concerns. This is the form of organisation often chosen when a sole trader [want] to expand, or wish to maintain control of the company.

The second type of limited company is a **Public Limited Company**. These tend to be larger concerns. They are allowed to raise capital through selling their shares on the **stock exchange**. This gives them greater flexibility in raising capital. They still only need two people to form a Public Company, and there is no stated maximum number of shareholders.

The process of creating a Public Company is very similar to that of creating a Private Company. Once a Public Company has received its Certificate of Operation it will prepare a **prospectus**, which is basically an invitation to the public to buy shares. The people forming the company must decide how those shares are to be sold, and how many shares will be allocated to each prospective buyer.

The **Registrar of Companies** will then issue a **Trading Certificate**. This means that the business is now up and running.

One feature common to both types of Limited Companies is that they must file a set of **audited accounts** with the Registrar of Companies. This set of accounts must include:

- a Directors' Report
- an Auditor's Report
- a Balance Sheet
- the source of application of funds
- an explanation of the accounts.

We will deal with all these items later on in the book.

It is also necessary for public limited companies to file an **Annual Return**. This gives the details of the Directors, Shareholders and any other information that is actually required by law. All this information is kept on file at Companies House, and is always open to inspection by members of the public for a small fee.

There are a number of advantages in setting up a limited company as compared with being a sole trade or partner:

1 shareholders have limited liability
2 it is easier to raise capital through shares
3 it is often easier to raise finance from banks
4 it becomes possible to operate on a larger scale since, when additional capital is required, additional shares are offered to the public
5 it is possible to employ specialists
6 suppliers tend to feel a bit more comfortable in trading with legally established organisations

7 directors are not liable, provided they follow the rules
8 it is easy to pass shares in a company down from one generation to another and in this way control may be kept by the same families
9 the company name is protected by law
10 there are tax advantages attached to giving shares to employees
11 a company pension scheme can give better benefits than those that are available for the self-employed
12 the ill-health of shareholders does not affect the running of the business.

There are a number of disadvantages associated with becoming a limited company:

1 the formation and running costs of a limited company can be expensive
2 decisions tend to be slow since there are a number of people involved
3 employees and the shareholders are actually distanced from one another
4 all the affairs of the company are public, with the audited accounts and annual returns that the company makes being produced
5 legal restrictions under the various Companies Acts, are fairly tight and there are very heavy penalties for companies which break the rules
6 large companies are often accused of being impersonal to work for and to deal with
7 rates of tax on profits are often higher than those that sole traders and partnerships have to pay

student activity

Study a local private company. Who actually **owns** it and who **controls** it? Is this the same person or group of people?

THE PUBLIC SECTOR

There is a vast range of public sector organisations with an equally vast range of objectives.

We are going to look at three main areas:

- the government itself
- the people who operate and work in the public sector
- how they relate to the public.

Government

It depends on your point of view whether you approve or not, but the fact remains that the government is involved very deeply in the business life of this country, as indeed are governments throughout the world.

The prosperity of a country, which is measured by the success of the businesses in that country, can be either helped or hindered by the kind of policies which its governments adopt. The influence of the government is far-reaching. Increases in government expenditure or the creation of controls over businesses, or indeed support for business in a particular area, can have a marked effect.

The government has the means to create wide-scale changes in business activity. Here are some examples:

1 If the government were to **increase interest rates** this would reduce the general level of spending in the economy, and at the same time it would make it difficult for businesses which have borrowed money to finance projects.
2 When the government gives a **contract** to one firm rather than another firm it can make the future of the business very secure, or indeed destroy its possibility of surviving.
3 If the government reduces the **personal taxes** that people pay then this may, in fact, prove to be beneficial. The more money a person takes home, the more inclined that person is to work harder. This is known as increasing productivity.
4 If the government were to **reduce taxes** on a particular product, for example, lead-free petrol, then this could affect the demand for that product. This in turn can lead to changes in how the product is supplied since the supply would need to be increased to match the increased demand.

The government plays a massive role in the economy in general. Here are some examples:

1 Some goods and services are actually **provided** by the government because it is felt that every single person is entitled to that product or that service. good examples of this are health or education.
2 Some goods or services, from which everyone benefits, can only be provided by the government if they are actually going to be provided properly. A good example of this is the police force.
3 The government is very interested in trying to reduce **inequality**. This could mean that people who are relatively well off pay a higher tax. This in turn generates money to give to those who are less well off. Some people, however, think that inequality is a good thing because it gives people an incentive to **help themselves**. Any increases in taxation, of course, will mean that those who are earning higher salaries are taxed more, and in turn they could be less motivated.
4 The government needs to make sure that the **economic system** as a whole is running well. It passes laws to protect consumers or to prevent companies from controlling particular goods or services. It will take measures against polluters or those involved in anti-social behaviour. In other words the Government really sets the rules by which all businesses must comply.

Over time, as the situation changes, the government finds itself required to make amendments to the rules. How do they change? Who loses and who benefits when they change? We will look at these questions later on.

PUBLIC ENTERPRISES

When we think about governments we automatically tend to think about Downing Street, the Houses of Parliament and Whitehall. Although these are important and they are places where the Government can be seen in action, the government has many other parts, including organisations which are controlled by the government in some way. These are known as **public enterprises**, or **public corporations**. Here are some good examples of these:

- British Rail
- British Coal
- the Bank of England
- the Post Office

FIG 4.2.3 *BP, now a successful multi-national, was once publicly owned.*

Since 1979, however, many public corporations have been returned to private hands. Examples of these are:

- British Telecom
- British Gas
- electricity generation

But why did the government get itself involved in running these organisations in the first place? Here are some of the reasons:

1 One of the main reasons is to **avoid waste and duplication**. In the past many services were offered by different companies. Essentially they were offering the same thing. For example, in the past private railways ran similar services from the same towns, often having lines running parallel to one another.

2 Many of these organisations offer services which **could not be run profitably**. The big debate here is whether a private company would invest in supplying gas or electricity or water to a remote village when even in the long term it would not be able to make a profit.

3 The **larger the organisation the more benefits** there are in terms of production. Organisations which produce lots of output are able to buy their raw materials more cheaply, their labour can be more concentrated and consequently their prices can be lower.

4 The government is always interested in the **level of employment**. In setting up a public corporation the government might be taking this into consideration. Good examples of this thinking are Tax Offices and Social Security Offices, where vast headquarters have been set up in relatively remote areas of the country that are suffering high unemployment.

5 One of the biggest arguments in favour of public corporations is that the government itself needs to **control vital basic goods** and **services** which everybody needs. These are known as the infra-structure. This includes the transport network, water and energy. It is argued that the government has a responsibility to make sure that this is supervised and maintained well.

The process of **privatisation** which turns public corporations into companies owned by shareholders is proceeding rapidly and is sure to step up in the 1990s.

One of the ways of safeguarding the running of a public corporation is to set up an independent body which keeps an eye on it. This organisation copes with complaints that are made against the enterprise and tackles the enterprise should it wish to put up prices or cut services.

Although these public corporations operate independently, they are controlled to some extent by government at all times. It is the government's responsibility to make decisions about closing down parts of the business or investing large sums of money to improve it. On a day-to-day basis the chairperson of the enterprise and the other managers will make decisions about

wages, prices, industrial relations, but the government does still interfere when these decisions affect the public.

We have seen that a limited company needs to make an annual report to its shareholders. So too does a public corporation, but it presents its annual report to the government minister who is responsible for taking care of it. This government minister makes a report in Parliament to the Members who will then make criticisms or support the corporation and how it is being run. At the same time a committee made up of Members of Parliament meets on a regular basis to keep an eye on the day-to-day running of the corporation and reports back to Parliament on how it is being operated. This is known as a **Select Committee**.

In addition to public corporations, there are two other areas where the government gets involved in the business world.

- The first is when an activity is actually run by a **government department**. A typical example of this is Customs and Excise. They deal with the supervision and collection of taxes due on products entering and leaving the country
- The second is when the government has a **shareholding** in a public company

Perhaps the most common form of government organisation is one which touches our lives the most, and this is **local government**. In the UK certain services are run by locally elected councillors. These **councils** usually run business organisations such swimming pools, sports centre, bus services, car parks, shopping centres and public conveniences.

Just like public corporations, local council activities have been affected by privatisation. The particular process used by councils is that of **tendering**.

The local council details the service it wishes to offer for tender. Companies which are interested in running the service put sealed bids in to the council explaining what it would cost to run the service and what they would be providing. The company that offers the lowest tender is given the job. It is then the council's responsibility to monitor how effective the company is in providing the service. If a company fails to reach certain standards then the contract is taken away from it. Local government pays for these services by receiving a grant direct from central government and by collecting local taxes. These are variously known as **rates, community charge** and **council tax**.

Local councils also subsidise loss-making activities such as parks which obviously provide benefits to the community.

student activity

Why do local councils offer subsidised loss-making activities to the community?

CHARITIES

These organisations are often called non-profit making organisations in the sense that their sole purpose is not providing a profit for the shareholders or owners. Many charities do indeed make a profit, but this is channelled to whichever deserving cause they represent.

> The British Union for the Abolition of Vivisection (BUAV) was established in 1898. Today, as the country's largest anti-vivisection society, the BUAV is leading the campaign to end animal experiments.
>
> The BUAV has a strict policy of condemning violence, and campaigns entirely within the law. Our activities involve educational, political and investigative campaigning at a national, regional and local level.
>
> In recent years the BUAV has led a successful and high profile campaign, *Choose Cruelty-Free*, against testing cosmetics on animals. Now the society has teamed up with European groups to campaign on this issue within the EEC, forging important international links. In addition the BUAV's powerful *Health With Humanity* campaign tackles the controversial issue of using animals in medical research. The BUAV has also undertaken a major enquiry into the trade in ex-racing greyhounds to laboratories and an undercover investigation into the UK's largest contract testing laboratory.

FIG 4.2.4 *The British Union for the Abolition of Vivisection is a registered charity which campaigns to end animal experiments.*

An organisation with a 'charitable status' is exempt from many of the legal obligations of a normal organisation. This is not to say that they must not comply with such things as health and safety, or contracts of employment, but that any profits they make are not taxable.

In recent times, in addition to the standard charities like Dr Barnardo's, Oxfam, Help the Aged, many schools have adopted this form of organisation.

We have now looked at the main types of business organisation but there are a number of others which are worth mentioning.

1. *Multi-national.* Most people will have heard of this term, which refers to businesses like MacDonalds and Woolworths. These are private sector companies which have divisions or subsidiary companies in various countries. They may well be PLCs.
2. *Multiple.* These are usually found within retailing, where a chain of businesses has branches in numerous High Streets and stores across the country.
3. *Nationalised..* Nationalised industries are state-owned, like the Coal Corporation and British Rail. Many other businesses were nationalised industries in the past and have now been privatised by the Conservative Government and have become public limited companies. Another type of nationalised industry is known as a public corporation. These are large operations like the **energy** industries which are now in the process of being privatised.

FIG 4.2.5 *Geest PLC is a major multi-national with interests throughout the world.*

Perhaps the strangest form of business organisation is known as a **Quango**. This stands for 'Quasi Autonomous Non-Governmental Organisation'. These are organisations that have been set up by the government to carry out a specific task. In other words, they have been set up to take responsibility for a certain area of the government's business. A good example of this is the Equal Opportunities Commission.

student activity

Identify five other QUANGOs other than the Equal Opportunities Commission.

STRUCTURES

Many factors influence the organisational structure of a business or enterprise. In order to appreciate the important demands that an organisation must meet, we must look at private and public-sector organisations separately.

PRIVATE-SECTOR ORGANISATIONS

The structure depends on many factors. These include:

1 the **number of employees**, in effect the actual size of the organisation
2 **Type of premises used**. A multi- or split-site organisation with a number of different branches would need to be organised in a radically different manner from an organisation which is based in a single building.
    An organisation which is regional, national or international will base its organisational structure around logical groups of employees.
3 **Type of business**. If the organisation is in the **primary sector**, it is likely to be organised in such a way as to allow as efficient processing of the raw materials as possible, and may be based around a single mine, forest or quarry.
    A **manufacturing** organisation may either carry out all of its processing procedures on a single site, or need to transport partly finished goods to other specialist sites. Organisation in this case may be based on the single factory unit, or a cluster of factories which contribute towards the finishing of a product.
    Distribution organisations tend to be organised in a regional, national or international framework. Depending on the bulk of goods being distributed, the organisational structure will be complex in certain geographical areas and simpler in others. In other words, if the organisation is busy in one area, the size and complexity will reflect this. As with many organisations, good communications between the regions are vital and a separate part of the organisational structure may concentrate on dealing with communications.
    In the **retailing** sector the obvious organisational structure is that of the **branch**. However, many functions of the business are carried out centrally. These services tend to be of a managerial, financial or buying nature, and this allows the individual branches to concentrate on the selling process.
    Professional services tend to operate on the basis of a number of specialist individuals who are assisted by a variety of support staff. Often these support staff are drawn from a 'pool' of clerical and secretarial employees.

4 The number, type and size of the **clients** may have a bearing on the organisational structure. If the organisation deals with only a handful of clients, then the structure need not be overly complex. On the other hand, if it is dealing with literally millions of retail customers, then the demands on the structure may be much greater.
5 The **past structure** of the organisation and its history may be a good or bad influence on how it is structured. An old-fashioned organisation which has successfully managed to survive for many years may not see the need to change its structure. It may not appreciate the benefits of reorganisation and may be structured in such a way as to prevent the possibility of growth or adaptation to new demands.
6 The **current structure** of an organisation can again be a positive or negative influence on the day-to-day running of the business. If the organisation has recently undergone changes, it will be unlikely to adapt to further changes without encountering considerable problems.
7 The **future needs** of an organisation should directly influence its structure. The needs to constantly react to changing demands, diversify into new areas and respond to changes in legislation, are all strong reasons to consider how the organisation is structured.

As we have seen, the structure of an organisation will vary depending on the nature of a number of factors:

1 the size and nature of the market in which it operates
2 the type of business it is involved in
3 the maintenance of good communications
4 the size of the organisation
5 the number of branches/outlets/sites
6 the type and number of clients
7 how much it is affected by government legislation
8 impact of new technologies
9 nature and extent of responsibilities and obligations
10 past and current structure
11 future plans
12 complexity of business activity

HIERARCHICAL STRUCTURES

The best way to understand what a **hierarchical structure** looks like is to imagine a pyramid. At the top of the pyramid are the owners or major decision-makers of the organisation. As we look further down the pyramid the shape of the organisation broadens as more employees are involved at that level. At the base of the pyramid are the majority of the employees and below them are the customers.

Responsibility, power and authority are all much greater at the top of the pyramid than at the bottom. Decisions flow down the pyramid affecting a succession of layers of employees.

This form of structure can be also referred to as a **'pecking order'** as the higher up the pyramid you are as an employee, the more power and authority you have. Equally, we can see that the lower down the pyramid you are, the less influence you have on the organisation as a whole.

The reason for this hierarchical structure is that important decisions need to be made by those who have expertise and experience along with enough authority to make sure that a decision is implemented. Those at the top of the pyramid take all the credit for success, but also bear the consequences of failure.

Typically, we would see a structure that would begin with directors at the top of the pyramid making decisions for heads of department below to pass on to middle managers who would then tell the junior members of staff to implement them. The higher an individual is in the pyramid, the less likely he/she is to understand precisely how decisions are implemented at the lower levels. These individuals may just have an idea of overall strategy and base their decisions on information received via the various layers below them. Each time information passes from layer to layer, the relative importance of what has been said may change. It is therefore likely that those at the top of the pyramid will have a distorted view of the organisation and how it really works.

For those at the bottom of the pyramid, the directors will seem remote, unable to understand the organisation's needs and unwilling to change decisions which may adversely affect the day-to-day running of the business.

The main advantage of this structure is that each layer sees the organisation in its own peculiar way. Each layer will have different opinions, priorities and interpretation of overall organisational policy.

The main version of the hierarchical structure is the **Steep Pyramid**. In this version of the hierarchical structure, there are many layers of management. The reason for the number of layers may be that the organisation operates in several different locations and needs to duplicate the administration in order to function efficiently. Alternatively, the nature of the business may be very complex, requiring the processing of many orders, messages, pieces of information or complaints.

Because the structure is multi-layered and complicated, those further down the pyramid find it difficult to understand how and why decisions are made and the organisation may find it impossible to make sure that the employees follow through 'corporate decisions' (general statements of policy and procedures). The organisation may also suffer from being 'bureaucratic'. This means that decisions must pass through so many layers that they take a very long time to put into operation, and the systems designed to help implement them become more complicated than they need to be.

FLAT STRUCTURE

This is essentially a version of the hierarchical structure, but it has a number of different features. It should be remembered, however, that this is still a pyramid-style structure, but one with few layers.

The theory behind having fewer layers in the pyramid is that decisions can be made quickly and efficiently. Each layer is able to communicate easily with other layers and the organisation avoids the danger of becoming **'bureaucratic'**. This simpler structure is generally found in organisations operating from a single site where directors and other decision-makers are readily available for consultation and guidance. Employees find it easier to understand the reasoning behind the directors' decisions and therefore feel more a part of the organisation and less isolated.

CENTRALISED STRUCTURES

There are two different ways of looking at centralised structures, both of which contain features of many of the other types of organisational structures. Indeed, they may be actually organised in another form, but will have centralised features.

Centralised Services – this version of a centralised structure involves the re-organisation of key services to provide for the organisation as a whole. In this respect, it would be common to find the reprographics (printing functions) centralised and controlled in such a manner as to provide cross-organisational services. Central control means that the service should be more efficient in terms of work through-put and output, as well as attempting to keep costs down (by the non-duplication of staff roles etc.).

Centralised Decision-making – in larger organisations that do not favour a decentralised approach to decision-making, it may be a preference to concentrate command and decision functions to a few individuals. They will be supported by a variety of employees and will be responsible for cross-organisational decision-making. It is often the case that these organisations are more traditional ones, or rely on the expert knowledge of a handful of individuals that have specialisms.

CONE STRUCTURES

In recent years, some major organisations have recognised that relying on a pyramid structure has prevented quick and necessary decisions and change from taking place. This new form of structure is known commonly as **'decentralisation'**. This is the exact opposite to having centralised services which assist individual branches or sites. Each part of the organisation that carries out a distinctly different function in the organisation is given a level of autonomy. This means that they are allowed, up to a point, to make decisions for themselves without the permission or consent of the directors or the central office. This allows each sub-organisation to be more flexible and responsive to its own needs and customers without having to wait for a central office to consider any points of concern that have been passed on to them. Most typically the structure consists of a central **'holding'** company (these are the owners of several companies who, while they are interested in the profits and decisions made by their companies, do not meddle in the day-to-day business) which has **devolved** (passed down power and authority) **responsibility** to each company forming part of the group.

Line management structure

As we have seen, a typical hierarchy in an organisation consists of a number of **layers**, through which power, responsibility and authority are delegated. This process is known as line management. In other words, each person knows to whom he or she is responsible and from whom he or she should take instructions. A typical example of this would be the Sales Director who is responsible for supervising the Sales Manager, who, in turn, directs the operations of the Regional Sales Managers. They have authority over their own Sales personnel.

Staff management structure

This type of structure refers to **individuals** who carry out a **specialised** function within the organisation. In a typical retail outlet there will be a line management structure which can trace the line of authority from the directors at central office right down to the sales assistants. However, certain members of staff are not directly part of this line. The Personnel Department, for example, does not have day-to-day authority over the branches, but does get involved in matters relating to personnel when needed. Equally, the Marketing Department, which again may be based centrally, will be carrying out functions which do not require reference to the branches. Generally speaking 'staff relationship' describes the liaison between those employees in the organisation who are not part of the direct line of authority.

Line and staff management structure

Most organisations, in reality, have a mixture of both line and staff structures. This can also be described as a **matrix structure**. This particularly suits larger organisations with a number of different sites and complex production/sales operations. The departments which make up the staff side of the organisation tend to service the various lines of authority. In other words, they have responsibilities and authorities which span across a number of lines of authority and provide a specialist service. Good examples of this are the Warehouse, the Buying Department and the Personnel Department.

DEVOLVED STRUCTURE

A **devolved structure** is one where most of the main functions of the organisation, particularly in terms of day-to-day decision making, are made at operational level. In other words, managers in the 'front line' have the power and authority to make decisions (obviously within some guidelines) as they see fit.

STATIC STRUCTURE

Static organisational structures are those which use a form of job enlargement to cope with any additional duties or tasks that may arise. These structures are somewhat prone to over-load in certain areas as perhaps they have not taken into consideration new areas of business activity, which might require additional staff or even a new department to handle new activities.

DYNAMIC STRUCTURE

A **dynamic business structure** is one that will be perfectly prepared to redesign itself as events present themselves. If the previous structure does not suit the current requirements of the organisation, then old structures are discarded. An alternative view of such a structure is that it has been created in such a 'free-form' manner, in other words, there is no real fixed nature to its structure, that it can readily adapt as and when required.

STRUCTURE AND SIZE

The simplest organisational structure is that of the person who works on his or her own. This person would obviously be responsible for everything that the organisation does. Someone, for example, who set up a Mail Order business would be responsible for buying in products, designing the catalogue, getting it printed, carrying out market research to find the kind of person that would buy the products, researching a mailing list, sending out catalogues, taking orders, despatching them, dealing with any correspondence, paying bills, banking cheques, doing the accounts and a hundred other things.

In this situation the individual who is running the business is at the **centre** of everything.

The larger the organisation, the more need there is for people who **specialise** in a particular area. Good examples of these are Bank Managers, Solicitors, Accountants. All of these people have specialist skills and can take some of the responsibility off an individual business person's shoulders.

As a business expands it needs to employ people, some part time, some full time. As the business expands, the person who set the company up needs to think about what has to be done. The business needs to be organised in the best possible way to meet the objectives that have been set for it. The owner of the business needs to define exactly what individuals do. Precisely what departments are responsible for. Who will supervise the employees? Who should tell them what to do? Where does everyone fit into the organisation? And who is ultimately responsible?

This is known as the division of labour and specialisation.

The **division of labour** involves breaking down the process of producing things or providing services into clearly defined specialist tasks. The fact is that if the process is broken down into these separate tasks then production can actually be increased. Instead of one person trying to do everything, everybody who works as part of the production of goods or services specialises. **Specialisation** means being more efficient.

What kind of advantages are there in specialisation?

1 **resources** can actually be **concentrated** where they are needed the most
2 if the worker becomes more efficient at doing a particular job he becomes **more skilled**
3 specialisation allows **greater output**. This means that each item produced is made more cheaply because the labour involved in producing it is less for each unit
4 if people specialise then they can pass on their skills and experience to others and help them become **more efficient**
5 if people specialise then hopefully they can get a better standard of living. By specialising people can develop their own talents and are able to trade what they can do with other people
6 by specialising in one job a person can do that job well rather than doing lots of jobs badly

There are some disadvantages of specialisation:

1 specialisation can often lead to jobs becoming very boring. Simple repetition of the same task day in day out demoralises people and they can become less efficient
2 specialisation is always dependent on how good or efficient the specialists in the previous task were. If they are not as efficient or as fast at every stage of the production this can cause **bottlenecks**
3 there is a tendency in specialisation for workers to become little more than machines. This in turn could lead to **loss of skill**
4 specialising actually reduces a worker's ability to **adapt to change**.
5 those who specialise have only a narrow view of the product or service which they are actually producing. Someone who makes an article from start to finish has a better overview and can help to make things more efficient in the long run.

THE DESIGN OF ORGANISATIONAL STRUCTURES

Many organisations are constructed in a **formal** way. The organisation needs to reflect the kind of activities for which each worker is going to be responsible. Workers can then see exactly what they are responsible for.

Departmental structures

Departmentalisation is the process by which an organisation has certain functions which it carries out grouped logically under a particular manager. There are usually five ways of grouping employees or the things an organisation does. These are:

1 by what they **produce** known as the product
2 by their **function**, in other words what they do for the organisation
3 by **process**, which means how they do it
4 by **geographical area**, which may be various regional offices or separate companies
5 by type of **customer**, for example they may deal with other business organisations, or they may deal with retail

This leads us to look at another form of organisational structure and that is the division by **function**. As we saw above, one of the most common ways of organising the structure of the business is to look at exactly what employees do.

JOB ROLES – DIRECTORS, MANAGERS AND TEAM MEMBERS

Having identified the different types of structure of organisations, employer and employee responsibilities and the legislation relating to employment, we will now look at the specific **job roles** of individuals within an organisation. We will begin by looking at the senior members of an organisation. Some things to bear in mind throughout all of the following explanations of job roles, are these:

- the employer has clearly identified exactly what the employee should do
- at the same time, the employee is well aware of what the employer expects of him/her
- both the employer and the employee are content that the employee is capable of doing the job. If not, then whatever steps need to be taken, must be taken to ensure that the employee can perform to the best of his or her ability.

There are a number of key phrases that we will use continually in describing exactly what the individual job roles are. These are:

- **authority** – can the individual command others to carry out tasks? In other words, does the individual have any real power?
- **accountability** – who is the individual responsible to? How many superiors have responsibility for the individual?
- **responsibility** – what exactly are the tasks or duties related to the job?
- **rights** – what should the individual reasonably expect from the employer? What should the employer reasonably expect from the employee? These questions have already been looked at in much greater detail earlier in the book.

THE MANAGING DIRECTOR

This director is the most senior member of the board of directors. In some cases, the **managing director** is also the chairman of the organisation. It is the responsibility of the chairman to preside over board meetings.

The main roles of a managing director are:

- to exercise all the powers and duties of a director
- to exercise power and responsibility in the name of the rest of the Board on a day-to-day basis. The Board itself will have agreed certain guidelines of conduct and policy which they will expect the Managing Director to adhere to

The Managing Director is chosen by the other members of the Board, who will be looking for an individual with a number of important qualities. Among these may be the following:

- wide business **experience**
- a proven track record of **success**
- the ability to make the right decisions under **pressure**
- being prepared to **answer for any decisions** made and stand by those decisions.
- being prepared to be **accountable** to the Board and ultimately to the shareholders (the Board itself is answerable to the shareholders)
- having a clear idea of the **policies** and **objectives** of the organisation and working towards the fulfilment of these objectives
- excellent **communication skills** and the ability to be a **good ambassador** for the organisation in a variety of situations

It is the managing director who actually is responsible for the implementation of policy formulated by the board, and who represents the board itself at all times. To some extent, the managing director has to interpret the wishes of the board, and develop a clear programme of organisational objectives. Further, he/she must be aware of which key members of staff can be relied upon to follow through his/her policy decisions to successful completion. At all times, the managing director must keep the board informed of any problems, decisions, or crises that may occur which they should be aware of.

FIG 4.2.6 *Deputy Chairman and Managing Director Clinton Silver (left) has special responsibility for merchandise. Managing Director Keith Oates is responsible for finance. These are two key Marks & Spencer PLC executives.*

THE DIRECTORS

Depending on the type of organisation, there must be at least one **director**. In the case of private companies, there need only be one, but a public company requires a minimum of two. A directorship has a dual function, that of direction itself, and, of course, management. The main difference between these two functions is that direction tends to relate to longer-term aims, while management concerns day-to-day decision making.

Direction is essentially the implementation of the board's policies. If a director is an **executive director**, this means that he or she works full time for the organisation and has responsibility for a particular part of the organisation. On the other hand, a **non-executive director** may be part time and may concentrate on a particular aspect of policy with which he or she is experienced.

Management, carried out by executive directors, is, as we have seen, related to day-to-day decision making. Many executive directors find it very difficult to separate the direction and management roles which they are faced with. They may have a good idea of the nature of the organisation's policies, and have a clear impression as to how this policy may be achieved. Unfortunately, day-to-day decision making may mean that the executive director has to make decisions that are at odds with organisational policy. One way around this problem is to organise the board of directors into two separate units. Board members will serve on one or other of the units (with the exception of the managing director who will serve on both). One unit of directors will deal with overall policy, and the other unit will concentrate on day-to-day implementation of policy. In this way, any conflict between policy and management of decision making is avoided.

The main responsibilities of directors are:

- to exercise their power and authority in good faith and for the benefit of the organisation
- to put aside their personal interests and always consider the organisation first
- to endeavour not to be casual or off-hand when managing the affairs of the organisation

A director should therefore display care and skill at all times. Obviously, non-executive directors, who have been included on the Board for their experience and expertise in a certain area, are expected to be even more professional in their conduct on behalf of the organisation. At the same time, these non-executive directors may not have skill or expertise as a Board member. In such cases, they are often assisted by an employee who can guide them as to the processes and procedures required of them.

THE COMPANY SECRETARY

Both public and private limited companies are required by law to have a **company secretary**. Essentially, this is an administrative post. Depending on the size of the organisation, a company secretary may have a variety of different duties. The most common duties are:

- keep all records, as required by law, which include a register of members of the organisation, plus minutes of board and other directors' meetings
- keep all of the organisation's legal documents and the 'seal' secure. The 'seal' bears the organisation's name and registration number
- arrange organisation's and directors' meetings
- ensure that information, as required by law, is sent to the Registrar of Companies
- enter into legally binding contracts on behalf of the organisation

student activity

In pairs, make a list of legal documents which you think a company secretary would be responsible for.

THE AUDITORS

There is a legal requirement to look into the financial affairs of the organisation annually. This examination, known as **auditing** is undertaken to ensure that any facts or figures relating to finance given by the organisation are true and accurate. This auditing is done mainly for the benefit of the shareholders.

It is usual for the auditors to be a professional organisation, not related in any way to the organisation being audited. Only registered auditors can carry out auditing work and there are a number of limitations regarding who may act as an auditor for an organisation. These are:

1 The auditor must not be an officer or servant of the organisation being audited
2 An Auditor may not be the partner of, or employed by, an officer or servant of the organisation.
3 This exclusion of officers and servants extends to any subsidiaries of the organisation and their employees and partners
4 Any individual who has any relationship with the organisation being audited is also excluded.

The auditor, looks at two main areas. Firstly, the organisation's accounts, and secondly what the organisation has said in relation to these accounts to the members of the company.

AUDITORS' REPORT

Kwik-Fit Holdings plc and its Subsidiary Companies

ARTHUR
ANDERSEN

ARTHUR ANDERSEN & CO. SC

18 Charlotte Square
Edinburgh EH2 4DF

To the Members of KWIK-FIT HOLDINGS PLC

We have audited the accounts on pages 16 to 32 in accordance with Auditing Standards.

In our opinion the accounts give a true and fair view of the state of affairs of the Company and of the Group at 28 February 1993 and of the Group profit, total recognised gains and losses and cash flows for the year then ended and have been properly prepared in accordance with the Companies Act 1985.

Arthur Andersen.

Chartered Accountants and Registered Auditor
18 March 1993

FIG 4.2.7 *Statement by Kwikfit Holdings PLC auditors, Aurthur Anderson, that the accounts have been audited in accordance with auditing standards.*

FIFTEEN

---

student activity

In the role of an auditor, which documents would you expect to be given access to by an organisation before completing the audit?

MANAGERS

Below the level of director, there are a number of layers of **managers**. It is the duty of a manager to undertake tasks and duties as delegated to them by a director. In effect, it is the manager who takes responsibility for the day-to-day decision making and implementation of organisational policy. A manager will be accountable to a director, and ultimately to the Board and shareholders via any other managers senior to him/her.

A manager would usually have a far better working knowledge of the organisation than a director. Directors therefore tend not to interfere with basic decision making and are happy to delegate their authority to the various levels of management.

The exact duties of a Manager depend upon the level of responsibility, the department for which he or she is responsible, and the exact nature of the organisation to which he or she belongs. We shall look at specific managerial job roles at a later stage.

FIG 4.2.8 *Managers at various levels play key roles in the decision-making process of the organisation.*

TEAM MEMBERS

It is rare to find employees working in an organisation alone. It is much more often the case that **teams** are created, either formally or informally, to carry out specific tasks. A team is basically a group of individuals working together towards a single, common objective. When working as a member of a team people need to know which members of that team have power and authority, in other words, who is actually directing the joint efforts of the team. To be a successful team member a person needs to be able to communicate with others easily, as the whole point of a work team is the interaction

between its members. Many organisations spend considerable time and effort in training and re-training their staff in interpersonal skills.

Employers have also recognised the advantages of team building and may well be prepared to pay for residential training programmes aimed at enhancing team building.

JOB FUNCTIONS

The jobs people actually do within an organisation are clearly dependent upon three major criteria:

- the **size** of the organisation
- the **type** of the organisation
- the **function** of the organisation

Perhaps a good starting point in trying to assess exactly what a job entails is to try to discover what an organisation needs. Once this has been done, jobs can then be designed to fulfil the various functions required by the organisation. However, things are not always this simple. The majority of organisations have evolved over a number of years and the jobs undertaken by individuals working for them have changed as well. In fact many jobs have expanded to incorporate duties different from those they were originally intended to perform.

FIG 4.2.9 *Teamwork at all levels and in all work situations is a vital component of work activity as can be seen from these Costarican pineapple growers, picking fruit for Geest PLC.*

The result of this change is that some employees find themselves extremely overworked, while others cope well with the tasks required of them, yet others still are underworked (perhaps because technology has replaced the bulk of their original duties). An organisation which allows such an imbalance of work to persist will find that it may well adversely affect the smooth running of the organisation.

The solution appears to be simple, but is not often taken advantage of. Each time an individual leaves an organisation, there is an opportunity to evaluate exactly what his/her job entailed and assess whether certain duties can be merged or reallocated. The more progressive-thinking organisations regularly conduct a process of job review and evaluation. This process aims to look in detail at each job role and see if any features of the job need to be changed to take account of developments in working practices, new or different demands and technological break-throughs.

The smaller the organisation, the more complex each individual employee's job may be. Employees may have to be capable of carrying out a wide variety of duties, unrelated to each other. Not only will the owner of a small business be a managing director, but he may have to cope with recruiting, training and promotion of employees, supervise all aspects of the organisation's operations, work out wages and deal with other financial matters. This individual will rely on his/her small number of employees to carry out their duties largely unaided, but will be able to turn to a number of professionals to deal with certain more complex situations. Good examples of these professionals are an Accountant, a Bank Manager or a Solicitor.

In larger organisations, different functions tend to be split into distinct areas. These include many of the departmental divisions looked at earlier in the book. It would be useful to look again at the various layers of management and authority before considering these divisions in detail;

1 Directly below the level of director are the **senior managers**. In consultation with the directors they will set any necessary policies or procedures to achieve the organisation's objectives. These senior managers, as we have mentioned previously, may well be Executive Directors.
2 The task of implementing organisational policies and procedures is left to the **middle managers**. On a day-to-day basis they will liaise with both the senior managers, in order to clarify organisational objectives, and supervisory managers, who are directly responsible to them.
3 The Managers who deal directly with the work force are known as **supervisory managers**. They are responsible for ensuring that tasks, as directed by the middle managers, are carried out promptly and efficiently.
4 The individuals who make up the bulk of the organisation are the **workers**. Alternatively, these may be referred to as subordinates. It is their role to actually deal with the job at hand. They are often called simply **'staff'** to make a distinction between all types of Managers and all other employees.

It is commonly held that there are effectively only five different types of job, if one considers the skills required to carry them out. These are:

1 *Professional.* This category includes solicitors, accountants, dentists, doctors and architects, all of whom display a certain degree of specialist knowledge of a given area. In recent years, although many professionals would strenuously disagree, new professionals have joined this group. They are in the main related to new areas of work, outside the more traditional professional fields. Examples of these would be computer analysts, personnel managers, marketing executives and a wide variety of business consultants.
2 *Managerial.* This category is a very wide one but essentially features managerial and supervisory posts. Some occupations which we have already mentioned as being professional can also be referred to as managerial, such as personnel directors and marketing managers.
3 *Technical.* This relatively recent occupational category type (although this occupational group has existed ever since there have been machines) essentially refers to those individuals who are responsible for the setting up and maintenance of machinery and technological equipment. Within this category we will find computer programmers, television cameramen and sound recordists and production line technicians.
4 *Administrative.* This category is also a fairly wide one, and includes any job that could be considered clerical or administrative. Typical examples are typists, secretaries, receptionists, word processor operators and switchboard operators.
5 *Manual.* Essentially, this category covers all manual workers who operate various types of equipment and machinery. It is further broken down into three subsections, which are:
   (a) *Skilled* – in this sub-section, we would find tradesmen such as carpenters, plumbers, bricklayers and roofers or tilers. Members of this sub-section usually belong to a Guild or Association for their specific trade.
   (b) *Semi-skilled* – in this sub-section we would find workers who have not been fully trained in a particular trade, but who have been trained to use the equipment or machinery they use regularly for their job. Typically skilled manual workers' assistants or 'mates' would be found in this category.
   (c) *Unskilled* – in this sub-section we would find workers who are not trained for a specific job and fulfil the role of labourer, factory operative, warehouse packer or cleaner.

student activity

List and categorise all the occupations undertaken by your immediate family. Which of the categories listed above covers the majority of these occupations?

Every organisation has its own way of structuring the functions that it carries out. Here are some of the more common ones. Not all the positions described below exist in every organisation. Factors such as the nature of the operations of the organisation and its size and complexity affect the need for functions such as these and for separate departments and staff to carry them out.

The Administration Department

Most organisations have a central administration. The main function of an **administration department** is to control paperwork and to support all the other departments by servicing their needs for secretarial work – filing, mailing, handling data etc.

As offices have become more accustomed to using computers, administration departments have shrunk in size because many of the tasks carried out by such departments can now be carried out simply at the desk-top with a networked computer. We will look at this aspect in more detail later.

One of the functions most commonly still carried out by an administration department is that of **organising office services**. The manager in charge of office services is responsible for training, advising departments about how their space should be organised, supplying equipment, stationery and setting up an effective communication system within the organisation, which obviously includes the telephones and the mailing.

The administration department will also provide a **centralised purchasing service** for office supplies and storage. It also operates as a 'pool' of business stationery and corporate materials, e.g. memorandum and letterhead paper, and will co-ordinate the mass printing of the stationery. Allied to this it will control the large central photocopying facilities, providing a fast and efficient reprographic facility, which may include photocopying, collating and binding of documents.

Traditionally, administration departments have been responsible for arranging insurance for the organisation and the monitoring of leasing agreements (cars, equipment and premises).

The main staff of any administration department are:

1 *Chief administration officer/office services manager.* Will oversee all major functions of the department, allocate work received from other departments (and routine administrative duties) and carry the respon-

sibility for the smooth running of the department.

2 *Secretariat supervisor.* Allocate and monitor all work carried out by the secretaries, audio typists, shorthand typists, word processor operators and typists.

3 *Word processor operator.* Under the guidance of the secretariat supervisor, the word processor operator will undertake work from a variety of different sources and will be responsible for the presentation, safe storage (on disk or hard copy) and ensuring that any deadlines related to the work are met.

4 *Secretary.* This individual usually works directly for one or more managers. It is the secretary's responsibility to ensure that any information in the form of messages, memos, letters, reports etc. is brought to the attention of the manager. In addition, a secretary will also be responsible for routine letter and note-taking, on behalf of the manager, as well as keeping track of all his/her diary commitments (sometimes his personal diary too!) The secretary may also arrange meetings for which his/her manager may be responsible. At all times the secretary will ensure that only relevant information and individuals which really need the time of the manager are brought to his/her attention. A secretary's skills may include the capacity to work with audio tape, word processors and shorthand.

5 *Audio typist.* Responsible for working for several people in the organisation, possibly based in a 'pool'. His/her duties will include typing from audio tapes which have been prepared by various individuals and he/she will need to ensure that this work is completed to the given deadline, in a neat and accurate way.

6 *Shorthand Typist.* Will also work for several individuals within the organisation. He/she will take dictated notes from the Manager and will have the responsibility of transcribing them and typing up the document in a neat and accurate way. A shorthand typist is usually present to note the decisions taken at any company meetings.

7 *Typist.* Involves the typing of routine documents within the organisation. To a great extent this role is gradually being taken over by word processor operators, as increasingly, organisations are tending to buy word processors rather than typewriters.

8 *Messenger.* Involves the distribution of both internal and external documents. The role is particularly useful in organisations which have a number of closely situated sites, or in situations when the organisation's customers are located in the immediate vicinity. Messengers are still used in the City of London, however, many functions of the messenger have been replaced with the availability of facsimile machines, modems and electronic mail.

9 *Records supervisor.* Responsible for ensuring that all

necessary documents are safely, securely and accessibly stored. Despite the fact that technology has substantially reduced the need to store vast amounts of paper documents, there are many reasons why organisations still prefer to have hard copies of documents available for inspection. Upon receiving a request for information, the records supervisor will instruct a records clerk to retrieve and deliver the required documentation.

10 *Records clerk.* Allocated work by the records supervisor. Responsible for retrieving the required information and ensuring its safe delivery by internal mail, personal delivery, or by a messenger. The records clerk will also take note of who has requested the information, the date of the request and the date of return. This 'Out Card' is completed in order to keep track of the documents and ensure their safe return.

11 *Librarian.* Responsible for acquiring and maintaining resources relevant to the organisation's activities. These may take the form of books, reports, periodicals and newspaper cuttings. This resource is then available to all members of the organisation who may need to research into a specific area related to their work. It is the librarian's task to ensure that the information is as up-to-date as possible and that all staff are aware of its availability.

12 *Mail room supervisor.* Responsible for the handling of all internal and external mail. The office is commonly be known as the Post Room. This location acts as a central collection point of letters, packages and parcels. Some may be bound for literally any part of the world and others may be internal mail or bulletins. The various pieces of mail will either be collected by a mail room assistant, or delivered by various individuals within the organisation. It is the mail room supervisor's responsibility to make sure that all outgoing mail is weighed, franked and made ready for collection by the Post Office. The mail room supervisor will also note (for internal cost allocation) the postage totals for each department within the organisation.

13 *Mail room assistants.* Working under the instruction of the mail room supervisor, the mail room assistant may carry out a variety of different tasks:
- collect mail from the various departments
- deliver mail received each morning to the relevant person(s). Before this can be done, the mail needs to be sorted and perhaps re-routed to another site
- weigh, frank and put outgoing mail into the correct Post Office bag ready for collection or delivery to the Post Office
- note postage costs of each department and ensure that the mail room supervisor has up-to-date figures for these

- ensure that the Post Office leaflets kept in the Mail Room are current

14 *Telephone/switchboard supervisor.* Since many organisations rely heavily on the external and internal telephone systems, this key post is vital to the smooth running of most operations. This supervisor ensures that all telecommunication needs are met and that the switchboard system is capable of fulfilling all the demands of the organisation. In addition, the supervisor will make sure that the switchboard is constantly staffed and at times when the organisation is closed for business, that an answerphone can record incoming calls, or can give useful information to callers.

15 *Switchboard Operator.* In many cases, a customer's first contact with an organisation is via the telephone. It is therefore most important that the switchboard operator answers the calls swiftly and is helpful and responsive to the caller. A good switchboard operator will instantly know exactly who the caller needs to speak to (despite the fact that the caller may not ask for a named individual) and will know from memory the extension number of most members of staff.

16 *Cleaning supervisor.* All organisations, whether or not they have a constant flow of visitors, need to ensure that the premises are kept as clean and tidy as possible. Organisations which have sensitive technological equipment may even need to ensure that the work areas are as dust-free as possible. The cleaning supervisor will allocate his/her cleaning staff according to the demands of each particular work area. Periodically, floors and windows may need to be given special attention and may require specialist equipment/subcontractors to carry out the necessary work.

17 *Cleaners.* A cleaner is usually given a particular area of the premises for which he/she is responsible. The main cleaning duties will include emptying of bins, clearing away of empty boxes and packing materials, hoovering and dusting and routine general cleaning duties. Specialist cleaners may be employed to sanitise telephones, clean word processors with anti-static sprays and clean carpets or polish floors.

student activity

Draw up an organisation chart which shows the operations of an administration department. You should include all of the above posts.

Indicate with arrows the lines of responsibility and decision making.

The Accounts/Finance Department

The **accounts department** supervises all matters involving finance. Again computers and calculators are used extensively. An accounts department is split up into two further sections.

- the day-to-day accounting procedures are handled by the **financial accounting section**. Essentially they keep track of all incoming and outgoing cash or credits
- the **management accounting section** concentrates on analysing the figures and trying to predict possible income and outgoings into the future.

The accounts/finance department will record and monitor the following: sales, purchasing, manufacturing costs, running costs (lighting, heating, etc.), dividends to shareholders, payment of salaries and wages and departmental and organisational budgets.

At all times, the accounts/finance department must know whether the organisation is operating at a profit. This is achieved by checking that revenue from sales is greater than costs. The directors, shareholders and senior managers will need to have access to this information instantly. This is presented in various forms, such as balance sheets and profit and loss accounts. We will look at these in much more detail later in the book.

The department is also responsible for maintaining records of financial transactions required by law, e.g. the payment of tax and national insurance and pension fund arrangements.

The officers of this department are:

1 *Company accountant.* It is the **company accountant's** responsibility to maintain an up-to-date record and analysis of income and expenditure. The company accountant will have a number of accounts specialists who will be monitoring, on his behalf, various financial aspects of the organisation. At any time, the company accountant may be asked for detailed information regarding the financial status of the organisation, and must be able to respond immediately. There are a number of legal and statutory requirements which organisations must fulfil and it is the responsibility of the company accountant to ensure that all of these obligations are met. The company accountant is directly accountable to the board of directors for his/her actions and decisions.

2 *Accountants.* There are a variety of **accounts specialists** who are employed to carry out specific monitoring and analysis of financial data. These accountants will oversee the flow of data received regarding sales, purchases, running costs and other expenses. In addition, they will provide essential accounting information such as gross profit, net profit, turnover and relative profitability of different areas of the organisation. In larger organisations they may keep track of the performance of investments in other organisations and regularly monitor the financial strengths and weaknesses of subsidiary companies.

3 *Credit controller.* This individual will monitor the orders placed and the payment history of customers in order to establish their reliability as payers. Each customer will have a set **credit limit** (rather like an agreed overdraft) and the credit controller will endeavour to make sure that customers do not exceed this limit. In cases of late or non-payment of invoices, it is the credit controller who will contact the customer in question in an attempt to secure payment. The credit controller will take into account how long the customer has been purchasing from the organisation and may well look back into the past to see if there have been any previous problems with regard to payment.

4 *Accounts clerk.* An **accounts clerk** carries out the routine day-to-day accounting duties, as directed by either the chief accountant or senior accountants. This may involve either manual figure work, or the use of the increasingly popular range of accounting software. It is usually the accounts clerk's role to prepare figures for analysis by the more senior accountants. In some organisations, one duty of an accounts clerk is to maintain and issue petty cash to those who request it by the presentation of a validly signed voucher (e.g. for the purchase of sundry office items).

5 *Payroll clerks.* Working closely with the personnel department, the payroll clerk is responsible for ensuring that the correct wages or salaries are paid to every member of staff. The payroll clerk must be familiar with income tax and national insurance and pension scheme contributions. Depending on the size of the organisation, the payroll clerk may have to undertake these tasks manually, or in a larger organisation, he/she may be assisted by a software package. In some organisations where the wages structure is complex, or is related to performance and output, this job may not be as straightforward as one may imagine.

student activity

In the role of an accounts clerk, what action would you need to take should the following arise:

1 You are processing a cheque which has not been signed.
2 You receive petty cash vouchers which do not correspond with the attached receipts.

The sales department

The **sales department's** main responsibility is to create orders for goods and services. Many organisations employ a large sales force which operates either, in the case of retail stores, on a local level, or, in the case of organisations which supply to other organisations, on a regional basis.

The greater the emphasis on selling to individual customers, the larger the sales force, and those organisations which rely on heavy advertising to stimulate interest in their goods or services can have a relatively small sales team.

In terms of organising the efforts of the sales employees, the sales department will draw up a detailed **sales plan** which will include targets to be met by each area or region of the sales force. Also included in this will be the level of profit which can be expected from each and every product.

Working closely with the marketing department, the sales department will regularly supply sales information regarding sales levels, activities of competitors and requests from customers for new or improved products. The sales force compile the **raw data** about their sales figures on a weekly basis for interpretation by the sales manager, who will then pass it on for analysis by the marketing department.

In order to stimulate sales, the sales department will develop a range of 'point of sale' material (including posters, leaflets and boxes with the company logo) and other promotional materials.

The officers of this department are:

1 *Sales manager.* This job entails the co-ordination of the organisation's sales efforts. The **sales manager** is usually located at the head office with an administration staff who monitor the performance of the various national, regional and area sales managers and teams. In positions such as this, a considerable amount of the salary is related to sales performance. Periodically, the sales manager will visit his or her sales team in the field to assess their effectiveness and to keep in touch with current customer demands.

2 *Assistant sales manager.* Deputising for the sales manager, this individual will take on a range of sales-related responsibilities and may often be the first point of contact for the various members of the sales force. It will be the assistant sales manager's role to help the sales manager formulate the sales policy of the organisation.

3 *National sales manager.* In larger organisations, there is a need to co-ordinate the sales effort on a country-by-country basis. National sales managers are usually given considerable freedom to formulate a sales policy which is the most effective for the country in which they operate. Normally, a national sales manager will have a wide knowledge of the country in which he or she works and may even be a national of that country. Other organisations may not have national sales managers, as they may have entered into an agreement with a foreign company which will represent the interests of the organisation in the field.

4 *Regional sales manager.* Just as different countries have their own peculiarities, regions within a country also have theirs. Different sorts of industry and commerce tend to cluster around particular towns or cities. The regional sales manager will have an intimate knowledge of the needs of these businesses, which may be different from the national needs. The regional sales manager will be located within the region for which he/she has responsibility and will be required to regularly analyse any changes in the local economy which may affect sales.

5 *Area sales manager.* Working under the direction of the regional sales manager, an area sales manager will be responsible for a part of the region. In some cases, this may mean a single city or county. Again, a good working knowledge of the needs of the area is essential in co-ordinating the sales effort. The area sales manager will regularly accompany sales representatives when they visit customers and be able to offer on-the-spot advice and guidance.

6 *Sales representatives.* These individuals form the backbone of the sales team. Constantly on the road, visiting both existing and potential customers, they will be in direct contact with their area sales manager via mobile or car phones. Since the bulk of their salary is directly related to the sales they generate, they are always under pressure to meet their targets in order to achieve their bonuses. The image of the sales rep. in his company car, is easy to visualise. In reality, they may be very well trained sales people, with an expert knowledge of their field and extremely useful to their customers. They are, after all, the first point of contact and may well become a useful 'partner' in building up a business.

7 *Tele-sales assistants.* Working from central, national, regional or area offices, these individuals will not only take **direct orders** for goods and services from the customer, but will also receive regular orders from the sales representatives. Operating with up-to-date lists of customer contacts from the sales representatives, they will attempt to gain new sales or arrange for one of the sales representatives to visit the business. They will be particularly well trained in telephone skills and have any useful information to hand via a desktop computer.

8 *Invoice clerk.* The role of this individual is to process all orders generated by either the sales representatives or the tele-sales team. Essentially, the documents produced will form both a list of required products

for the warehouse to despatch and a record for the accounts department of products sold. The invoice clerk will be in regular contact with the warehouse to ensure that the sales team is aware of the stock levels of each product.

student activity

In the role of the sales director prepare a memo which answers a note from the personnel department. The note states that at the end of the month you will lose the services of your invoice clerk. Your memo should state your reasons for wanting to keep this individual.

The marketing department

The main function of the **marketing department** is to try to identify customer requirements. There is also an element of trying to predict customer needs into the future. The marketing department works very closely with the sales department, and it is important that the two communicate well.

The starting point for most marketing functions is to carry out extensive research on a particular market to try to discover exactly what consumers want, where they want it, how much they want to pay for it, and the most effective way of getting the message across. This is known as **the marketing mix**. We will look at this again in more detail later.

The marketing department will need to work closely with the R & D department and the production department in developing attractive and sellable products. This work will also include the constant updating of existing products to cater for changes in taste and demand.

One of the more obvious responsibilities of the marketing department is the design and development of advertising ideas and marketing campaigns. This design and development process will take account of the needs of the sales department and any other interested area of the organisation.

As a part of its regular market research procedures, the marketing department will monitor changes in trends and fashions that affect their customers. Some information is readily available as statistical tables published by the government, but much information must be researched as required by the organisation itself.

The staff of this department are:

1 *Marketing manager.* Marketing managers are responsible for planning, organising, directing and controlling the marketing efforts of the organisation. Increasingly, they are professional individuals who are well versed in formulating a marketing plan which is workable within the limitations of the organisation.

In effect, they are responsible for establishing the organisation's marketing objectives (known as the **strategy**) and deciding how the overall objectives may be achieved (known as the **tactics**). All organisations have a **'Corporate Image'**, which means that everything the organisation produces, from letterheads to finished products, has the same overall look. The marketing manager will decide exactly how the corporate image relates to each and every aspect of the company.

2 *Assistant marketing manager.* Deputising for the marketing manager, and co-ordinating the efforts of each of the product/brand managers are the main responsibilities of the assistant marketing manager. It will be this individual's role to implement the marketing strategy across all aspects of the organisation and to ensure that the corporate image is consistent.

3 *Product/Brand manager.* A **product manager** is responsible for co-ordinating the marketing plan relating to a single product. A **brand manager**, on the other hand, may be responsible for a range of products which have the same brand name. In both cases, the individuals will have to organise all activities relating to their product(s), including advertising, sales promotions, launches, re-launches and packaging.

4 *Marketing research analyst.* Millions of pounds are spent each year on marketing research. Nearly 10 per cent of the retail price of every item is spent on marketing research alone. Marketing research is the systematic collection and analysis of data which look specifically at the customer's attitudes, needs, opinions and motivation and anything which influences these. In order to minimise the risks involved in launching a new product, the organisation needs to know as much as possible about the potential customer, competition and any other factor which may affect sales. This specialist will use existing statistical data, as well as commissioning new market research as may be required.

5 *Advertising manager.* An advertising manager will be responsible for co-ordinating the advertising budget of the organisation. Working in close co-operation with various other members of the organisation, the advertising manager should be able to identify the best media for the advertising of the product. Additionally, the advertising manager will negotiate with magazines, newspapers, radio and television companies to achieve the best possible price. In many organisations, the advertising manager's function is taken over by an outside advertising agency which places and co-ordinates all advertisements.

6 *Promotions manager.* There is a narrow line between the responsibilities of a **promotions manager** and an advertising manager. Essentially, the promotions

manager will co-ordinate all other marketing strategies apart from advertisements. These will include special offers, competitions, trial offers, money-off vouchers, point of sale material and exhibitions.

The information technology/computer services department

The **information technology/computer services department's** responsibility includes computing (hardware and software), maintenance of databases, telecommunications, and other technological office developments.

As most organisations are now incorporating computers into almost everything they do, the number of truly separate information technology/computer services departments is diminishing.

The information technology/computer services manager must not only be aware of new developments in technology, but must also know how to use them. They will also supply all support and guidance to help others accomplish this too.

The staff of this department are:

1 *Departmental manager*. It is the responsibility of this departmental manager to provide a round-the-clock and comprehensive service back-up for the organisation's computing and data processing requirements. Within his/her area of influence, the manager will co-ordinate the design of computer programs to manipulate data for the various departments.

2 *Assistant departmental manager*. Under the direction of the departmental manager, this assistant manager will be responsible for acquiring and maintaining all computer software and hardware. In order to carry out this task, he/she will delegate various aspects to specialist managers. In co-ordination with the departmental manager, they will ensure that sufficient support is given to all computer-based communication systems within the organisation.

3 *Data processing manager*. This individual will maintain a detailed record of the organisation's stored information, which will be constantly updated and always accessible. The manager will also ensure that sensitive information is protected from access by any unauthorised person. On a regular basis, the data processing manager will also make sure that back-up copies of all data stored have been made and kept in secure and fireproof locations.

4 *Computer services manager*. The **computer services manager** will keep a constant overview of new developments in order to inform the departmental manager of more efficient ways of storing and manipulating data. It will also be this individual's responsibility to install and maintain new or updated versions of software as they become available. Further, his/her team of servicing engineers will regularly check all of the organisation's computer equipment. In some organisations, this service function has been bought-in from computing service specialists.

5 *Computer programmers*. These specialist individuals will create computer software needed by the various departments, so that information may be processed and analysed according to changing needs.

6 *Computer operators*. These individuals will be responsible for the inputting of data and the manipulation of existing information at the request of various departments within the organisation. Routinely, they will update information from a variety of sources, deleting or modifying as required. Increasingly, organisations have become more reliant on computer-based information and will need constant access to reliable and contemporary data.

The research and development department

By working closely with the marketing department, who keep a constant check on competitors' products and services, the **R & D department** may be informed of the need for a new product. Equally, the R & D staff may be developing new products or ranges of products in their own right.

The main function of the R & D department is not only to design new products, but to work out the most efficient and logical method of producing them. The R & D staff will, after a number of exhaustive tests, pass on their designs and proposed methods of production to the production department, which will then be responsible for putting the product into production.

Routinely, the R & D department will test random samples of products being manufactured to ensure that they comply with the quality standards set by the organisation, as well as by government legislation. In some organisations this function is separated from the R & D department and is supervised by a Quality Assurance/Control department.

The R & D department will also test competitors' products to see how they have been manufactured and whether the organisation's products compare favourably to them. Additionally, they will keep a close eye on the technological advances made within their area to see if the design and production processes used can be improved.

The R & D staff are:

1 *Research and development co-ordination manager.* It is the responsibility of this manager to co-ordinate the development of products and services to prototype level. All products and services must be rigorously tested before they are put into production and offered to the customer. The individual who will fill this post is likely to be a technical expert within a specific field. He/she will be aware of the technological requirements and any production problems related to these. Normally, this manager will be given clear instructions as to the organisation's requirements for a new product or service, but will have to work very closely with the production manager in order to develop a product which the organisation is capable of producing.

2 *Researchers.* Once the departmental manager has been given a brief to develop and test a new product or service, **researchers** will investigate all aspects of this product or service. They will refer to any scientific reports which relate to the area of interest, as well as investigating competitors' products. In effect, they will produce a report which offers a series of alternatives from which the developers can work. This report will also be circulated to any other interested party in the organisation.

3 *Product/Service developers.* These individuals are specialists in their own field. They will have been chosen for their knowledge and ability to apply their skills. It is their responsibility to work from the information given to them by the researchers and to develop a working version or versions of the product. This product will then be subjected to exhaustive testing to ensure that it meets the requirements of the organisation, safety tests and the needs of the customer. At all stages of the development, the production department will advise the developers of any production considerations.

student activity

What kind of R & D would be carried out by a manufacturer of frozen foods?

The production department

The **production department** is involved in all functions which revolve around producing goods or services for the customer.

This department monitors levels of wastage to ensure the most efficient use of resources and checks the costs of raw materials and parts purchased to make sure that profit margins are maintained.

As new products are developed, and technology changes, the production department will be responsible for purchasing all the necessary plant and equipment required, as well as organising the production process.

In consultation with the sales department, the production department must make sure that it can manufacture or supply customers with the quantity of goods required at the time they have been requested. The tight monitoring of production levels means that the production department should know how long it would take to produce sufficient products to fill a particular order. Advance planning and close liaison with the sales department are vital to ensure that deadlines can be met.

Regardless of how many units of products are being produced, the production department is also responsible for the maintenance of quality. Each product must meet a number of strict quality standards and must to all intents and purposes be exactly the same every time. Periodically, products will be randomly selected from the production line and tested by either the R & D department or the quality assurance/control department.

A good production department will monitor methods of production used by all major competitors and allied industries and will take steps to implement any useful methods of production used elsewhere.

Increasingly, as production becomes steadily more automated, the production department will also have to design computer programs which can handle the new processes.

The staff of this department are:

1 *Production manager.* The **production manager's** responsibility is to manufacture products to the correct specification, quality, price and safety levels. Production managers tend to be quite technical individuals, who understand the production process intimately. He/she will work closely with the R & D manager, as well as the sales manager. It is the production manager's role to turn new product ideas into finished products and supply the regular needs of the sales department.

2 *Assistant production managers.* These individuals will be given the responsibility by the production manager to oversee the smooth running of the various production lines. They will work in close co-operation with the production line managers to ensure that

production levels and product quality are maintained in relation to demand. The assistant production managers will be technically competent and may have a good working knowledge of the machinery.

3   The buyer. **The buyer** is required to ensure that he/she has purchased sufficient stocks of raw materials and components to enable the production lines to run efficiently. The buyer must be able to predict demands for all raw materials, components and machinery by close examination of sales figures, past, present and projected. An essential duty of the buyer is to obtain all items at the best possible price. The buyer may be able to negotiate favourable extended credit terms from regular suppliers. He/she will also be responsible for making sure that all items ordered are received in good time.

4   *Production line manager.* This individual is responsible for the smooth running of a part of the production department which produces a single product or product range. The production line manager will be given quotas to achieve by the production manager or assistant production manager and will have to organise his/her staff to meet the deadlines.

5   *Production line supervisor.* It is this individual's responsibility to deploy the members of his/her work team to the maximum possible effect. The supervisor will monitor the performance of both the work team and the machinery and regularly report to the production line manager regarding any potential problems. This supervisor is the main point of contact between the employees and the management structure of the organisation. In the event of potential problems with the machinery, he/she will liaise with the service engineers.

6   *Service engineers.* It is the service engineer's role to ensure that any defects or breakdowns in machinery within the production department are swiftly and efficiently dealt with. They will inform the production manager and the relevant production line manager regarding any need to close down a production line for the purposes of maintenance, servicing and cleaning. The service engineers need to keep a stock of basic components in order to repair machinery on the spot.

7   *Production line operatives.* Depending on the type of production employed by the organisation, the production line operatives are responsible for either a repetitive task or a series of related tasks. Many production lines have been developed so that only routine duties need to be carried out by humans. In these cases, production line operatives tend merely to feed the machines with raw materials and components and do not actually take part in the production process itself. In situations when the production is less automated, production line operatives are involved in the

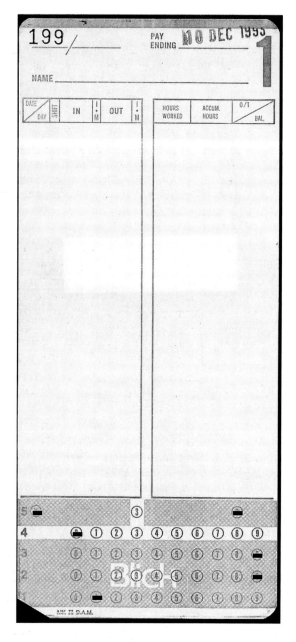

FIG 4.2.10 *This is a clocking-in card used by employees at Sharp Electronics (UK) Ltd.*

production of goods to completion. Many organisations run their production lines continuously and therefore require their production line operatives to work shifts.

student activity

In the role of a production manager, design a time sheet for completion by employees, to replace a system similar to that used by Sharp.

The stores/warehouse

This department has the responsibility for safely housing a variety of the organisation's property. This may take the form of products ready to be sold, various packaging materials, part-finished goods or raw materials, presently unused equipment and machinery and bulk amounts of stationery and corporate materials.

This service department must keep a careful check on the stock levels of all items for which it has overall responsibility, and should inform the relevant department should stocks begin to approach their minimum stock level.

The staff are:

1 *The warehouse manager.* The **warehouse manager** is responsible for the smooth running of the warehousing facilities of the organisation. He/she co-ordinates all warehouse staff in an effort to ensure that goods both inwards and outwards are dealt with in a quick and efficient manner. The warehouse manager designs the storage facilities in such a way as to enable easy access to the most used items. He/she must also keep a close eye on the stock levels of all stored equipment, products, components and raw materials.

2 *Operatives.* The warehouse operatives take their instructions from the warehouse manager. They are responsible for reporting any problems to their immediate manager, and to ensure that they carry out their tasks in a quick and efficient manner. Upon receiving an order via the sales department, warehouse operatives 'pick' the order and pack it ready for distribution. Others may be concerned with the goods inwards part of the warehouse operation, and check goods received against orders made by the organisation. Should there be any discrepancy, the warehouse manager should be informed and he/she will contact the relevant person. Some warehouse operatives operate machinery such as fork-lift trucks.

student activity

There are many rules and regulations which control the working conditions of a driver. Research the laws and restrictions which relate to this occupation.

The distribution/transport department

The main function of this department is to co-ordinate the organisation's transport needs. This will include the purchasing or leasing of vehicles (company cars, etc.) and servicing and maintaining delivery vehicles. As an integral part of this transport service, the department has to maintain records such as insurance, vehicle registration, road tax, service records and leasing and purchasing agreements.

Some organisations provide a delivery service to the customer, and in such situations it is essential that the most efficient and cost-effective delivery routes are used. These are increasingly worked out with the aid of computer packages, specifically designed for this purpose.

As with most departments, when training or re-training needs are identified, the distribution/transport department will liaise with personnel department to organise training programmes.

The staff of this department are:

1 *The distribution manager.* This manager's duty is to design, run and maintain a cost-effective way of ensuring that products reach their correct destination, in a suitable state, at the right time. The distribution manager works in close co-operation with the sales department who inform him/her of orders placed by customers, as well as expected delivery dates. The distribution manager tends to control the operations of the warehouse and all storage facilities. He/she informs the production department when stock levels reach the re-order level. This information is received from the warehouse manager.

2 *The transport manager* The transport manager's responsibility is to maintain and run the fleet of delivery vehicles which service the distribution requirements of the organisation. He/she will liaise closely with the distribution manager, the warehouse manager and the sales department. The transport manager is also responsible for keeping service records and vehicle registrations, as well as any related insurance for the fleet. He/she also negotiates any leasing or purchasing agreements relating to vehicles. He/she directly co-ordinates the efforts of the drivers, vehicle service engineers and the administration staff within his/her department.

3 *Drivers.* The drivers are directly answerable to the transport manager, who issues them with delivery rounds. In certain cases, particularly in larger organisations, there may well be a need to have regional distribution points which will have small warehousing facilities and attached drivers/delivery men or women.

The personnel department

The main function of the **personnel department** is the recruitment and organisation of individuals required for the various functions required to run the organisation.

This primary responsibility is achieved through a close monitoring process which begins with the selection of potential employees, through promotion and training of existing members of staff, to the termination of employment (through retirement, redundancy, those who leave to go elsewhere and those who are asked to leave).

Close liaison is maintained with all other departments to identify the various training needs of staff. This may include the induction of new employees, additional training (perhaps to cope with new technology) and retraining (e.g. when a job has been replaced by a new process and the employees have been redeployed to a new area).

The personnel department maintains all records relating to employees, including holiday entitlements, sickness records, qualifications and experience, salary, pension contributions and entitlements and confidential reports from line managers. Some of this information is very useful in identifying training needs, as well as matching existing staff to new vacancies within the organisation. Much of this information is of a confidential nature, and is restricted by the Data Protection Act, which we will look at later in the book. A further useful function of this information is to provide background for confidential counselling of employees. This will take account of any welfare or social difficulties employees may be experiencing.

The personnel department is the main negotiator for the organisation in matters relating to trades unions and associations and general problems regarding pay and conditions of employees.

In many medium to large organisations a wide range of social activities and facilities are provided. These may include such things as subsidised catering, sports and social clubs, non-trade union employee associations and season ticket loans The personnel department is responsible for running these..

Any organisation which truly values its key personnel will take all the steps necessary to ensure that they are happy and contented in their work. If these key employees feel that they could achieve a higher salary, better working conditions or a wider range of fringe benefits (e.g. company cars, a better pension scheme or reduced rate mortgages), then they will be seriously considering leaving the organisation. The personnel department is responsible for monitoring and expanding the total package offered to employees and ensuring that it is better than that offered by competitors.

The staff of this department are:

I *The personnel manager.* The **personnel manager** is ultimately responsible for the recruitment, retention and welfare of all staff. In this role the personnel manager will be involved in the designing of job descriptions and job specifications, the interview process, any training required by employees, staff problems and handling any necessary documentation relating to termination of employment for whatever reason. The personnel manager will also be involved in the co-ordination of staff facilities such as catering, sport, leisure and social activities. He/she will monitor and fulfil any staff development requirements. The personnel manager is the main point of contact with the management structure in trade union negotiations.

2 *The assistant personnel manager.* This individual deputises for the personnel manager in a variety of situations, and has regular duties delegated to him/her. The **assistant personnel manager** is usually the first point of contact for employee problems and individuals enquiring about possible vacancies within the organisation. The personnel manager and the assistant personnel manager between them offer a confidential counselling service to all employees. The assistant personnel manager is also responsible for the maintenance of comprehensive staff records.

3 *Clerical assistants.* Routine personnel duties, such as the maintenance of staff records and work logs are carried out by **clerical assistants** in the personnel department. Various duties are delegated to them by either the personnel manager or the assistant personnel manager and it is essential that these are carried out with confidentiality always in mind.

---

student activity

In the role of personnel manager, draft an advertisement for the following position

JOB TITLE	CLEANER
HOURS	07.00–09.30 DAILY
PAYMENT	£2.73 PER HOUR
PREVIOUS EXPERIENCE PREFERRED	

The customer/public relations department

Increasingly, organisations have recognised the value not only of responding to customer needs by adapting or expanding product ranges, but also of providing particular employees whose sole responsibility it is to liaise with the public and the media.

The **customer relations department** is the main point of contact for customers who have complaints about products or services supplied by an organisation. A smooth, efficient and courteous response to customer complaints is a key feature in making sure that the organisation's reputation is maintained. Many products now have on their labels a short sentence stating that if a customer has any problem with the product, he/she should simply return it to the manufacturer for a refund or replacement. This is an offer in addition to the legal requirement that a product must be fit for the use for which it was intended and has gone a long way to enhance organisations' reputations for being fair.

A **public relations department** traditionally was the main way in which organisations passed on news and information about their activities and products to the media and other interested parties. In recent years, organisations have recognised the need to project a strong, positive image to the public. This role has expanded to include close contact with the public. Requests for information about an organisation and its operations are dealt with by the public relations department, which may well have developed a range of booklets and other materials for this purpose. Many larger organisations, whose products or activities are of interest in the field of education have also developed teaching packs and other educational literature for supply on request.

It is the public relations department which writes press releases and product news to be distributed to extensive mailing lists of newspapers, magazines, journals and specialist organisations. The public relations department also advises members of the management of the organisation as to how they should respond to questions from the media, and provide specialist support for conferences and seminars.

The staff of a public relations department are:

1 *The Public Relations Officer.* The **public relations officer** is responsible for fostering a good relationship with the media, in the hope that they will consider giving the organisation both editorial space and favourable news reporting. He/she maintains a comprehensive data base of media contacts, from which extensive mail shots will be made. The public relations officer is also responsible for the writing of press releases. He/she also produces a range of booklets and leaflets concerning the operations of the organisation.

2 *The Customer Relations Officer.* While the public relations officer is concerned with media and news coverage, the **customer relations officer** concentrates on existing and potential customers. He/she responds to customer enquiries, providing a range of information packs on request. In addition, the customer relations officer also co-ordinates activities with the **community projects department**. In cases when a customer has a serious complaint about the products or services of the organisation, the customer relations officer will be available to assist in the solving of any problems.

The community projects department

In many of the larger organisations throughout the UK a **community projects department** has been set up with a responsibility to make sure that the local community is made aware of exactly what the organisation is doing. In some organisations this work is carried out by a public relations officer. Other areas in which they are involved are liaison with other local businesses, close contact with the local education service and maintaining an effective environmental policy.

FIG 4.2.11 *BP believe that the best way of contributing to the community is to create wealth by carrying on their business in an ethical, safe and profitable manner. BP's world-wide expenditure on community support is over £20 million per year.*

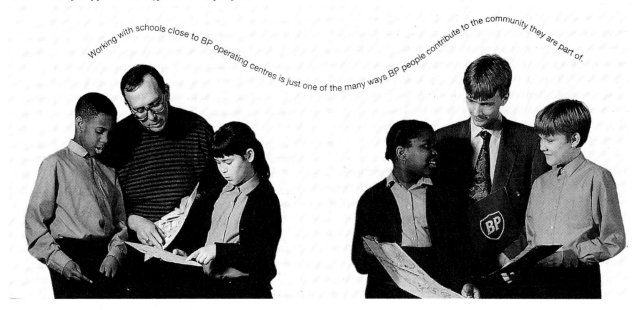

Working with schools close to BP operating centres is just one of the many ways BP people contribute to the community they are part of.

Such departments are not usually large, and may consist only of:

| *The Community Projects Officer.* Many organisations, having recognised the need to form a closer relationship with the local community, have appointed a **community projects officer**. In several respects, the duties of this individual are somewhat similar to those of the customer relations officer. However, the community projects officer tends to concentrate on the immediate locality. He/she will organise, with the assistance of other local organisations, a range of activities in order to heighten the public's awareness and appreciation of the organisation. This may take the form of sponsoring local events, financing community projects, or offering the organisation's facilities to local groups.

JOB DESCRIPTION

When an individual joins an organisation, he/she will be given a job description which has been drawn up by the appropriate line manager or the personnel department. The job description will state the key purposes of the job and list the responsibilities, usually in descending order of priority. It will also make it clear to the employee who he/she is responsible to and what he/she is responsible for. In addition, the job description may also include the following:

- details of any equipment to be used
- details of any records to be maintained
- details of any parts of the organisation's premises which the employee may be responsible for
- the date of issue of the job description

A job description can be revised and reissued to the employee should it become necessary to do so.

If the organisation carries out staff appraisal for its personnel, then the job description is a useful reference for such interviews.

Obviously, a job description cannot contain every single detail of the tasks to be carried out by an individual. This is particularly the case when the individual is at the higher level of management – items like the ability to make 'off the cuff' decisions and deal with open-ended transactions could not be put on to paper in a realistic way.

The job description will include the following:

JOB TITLE

The job title assigned to a particular collection of tasks, duties and responsibilities should attempt to be as appropriate as possible. If the job involves some form of supervisory or managerial responsibility, then it is normal for the job title to be suffixed by the word 'supervisor' or 'manager'.

POSITION IN THE STRUCTURE

The job description, as we have said, should clearly state at what level this job will be in the overall structure of the organisation. It is normal for the job holder to know precisely to whom he/she is accountable and for whom he/she is responsible. In addition the position in the organisational structure will determine the post-holder's inclusion on circulation lists and attendance at meetings.

RESPONSIBILITIES

The job description must also clearly state the responsibilities of the postholder. These may simply relate to specific job tasks and duties, but in the case of supervisory or managerial positions, they may also relate to these supervisory or managerial functions. The specifics of responsibility should be made very clear to the postholder, although they may be couched in rather general terms. It is only when the individual postholder has acquired some experience of the job itself that he/she will know precisely what is being demanded of him/her.

COMPETENCES

As we will see in the next section, a job specification will clearly state the exact nature of the competences required for the particular post. In general terms, the job description will presuppose certain levels of competence. These may relate to experience, conventional qualifications or general skills.

PERSON SPECIFICATION

A person specification covers the main characteristics which will be required to undertake the job. These will include:

- the **physical make-up** of the individual – how he/she looks and whether he/she can speak clearly
- the current **attainments** of the individual – qualifications, driving licence, if applicable, and previous experience
- the **intelligence** of the individual
- the **aptitudes** of the individual – depending upon the job, this may include social skills, listening and communication skills or legible handwriting
- the **interests** of the individual – any relevant sports or leisure activities, particularly any positions of responsibility held in relation to these
- the **disposition** of the individual – whether, for example, the individual is capable of coping with a variety of problematic situations such as dealing with customers, for which tact and diplomacy may be required.
- the **circumstances** of the individual – these will include domestic situation and personal relationships and, the availability and willingness of the individual to work overtime or at weekends.

This person specification is used in relation to the job specification from which the job description has been written. A typical job specification will include the following:

- physical attributes required
- proficiencies required
- manual skills required
- knowledge skills required
- personality traits preferred
- social skills preferred

The specification itself is usually expressed in the following manner:

- what particular **work** will need to be carried out
- what **knowledge** that person will need in order to carry out the tasks
- what **judgements** will need to be made by that person
- what **factors** the individual will have to take into account in the course of his or her duties

PERSONAL ATTRIBUTES AND DEVELOPMENT

As we have already mentioned, the personal attributes will be clearly defined within the job specification or the person specification. However, not all potential employees will be expected to have all of the skills already. An employer should be able to identify an individual who has the potential to fulfil all of the

requirements of the job. To this end, it may be a condition upon which the individual is taken into employment, that he/she engages in staff development. The personal attributes already present in the individual should form a useful basis upon which to develop the individual as an ideal employee. Development will normally take the form of on-the-job (learn as you work) or off-the-job (studies undertaken outside the work environment) training. We have already dealt with the nature of staff development earlier in this Unit.

QUALIFICATIONS

Qualifications may form an important part in determining whether a particular individual obtains a position. Certain occupations require particular levels of competence related to qualifications as a base. The acquisition of qualifications by the individual may be vital in certain career paths. An applicant for a more junior post may not be expected to have proceeded along a specific qualifications path to its logical conclusion. Most employers will encourage individuals to undertake additional studies either within or outside work time. Some employers will be prepared to at least partially finance such additional studies.

In certain career paths, particularly in the professions, the minimum entry requirements in terms of qualifications may be high. An employer in these fields will expect the individual to have pursued several years of personal study.

Most occupations, to a greater or lesser extent, will offer some kind of opportunity to attain additional qualifications. As we have mentioned, individuals will be encouraged to pursue these at the earliest possible opportunity.

EXPERIENCE

Many people will attest that there is no substitute for real experience. It is obviously very difficult for younger employees to obtain experience. To this end, many courses (like GNVQ) attempt to replicate real work situations. Many people entering the job market in their mid to late teens have already had some minimal level of work experience. Perhaps this may have been carried out while at school or college. Employers are keen to see this as otherwise they have no real indication of whether the individual can cope in a working environment.

Recently employers have begun to recognise the concept of transferable skills. This rather tricky area attempts to identify skills performed in alternative situations which may not necessarily relate to the intended work duties. With this in mind, two systems in particular have been developed to cope with transferable skills and all of the problems relating to them. These are:

1. *APL (Accreditation of Prior Learning)* – this particularly relates to the level of entry on to a vocational course. Previous studies may have been at a comparable level to those being considered and as such may allow the individual to be credited with the knowledge he/she has gained. With this credit the individual may become exempt from certain studies on the programme.

2. *APEL (Accreditation of Prior Experiential Learning)* – this rather broader method of gaining credit can allow an individual to be exempt from certain studies without having previously attended a formal programme of study. Provided evidence can be produced that the individual has experience in the area, then credit will be given. This is particularly useful for individuals returning to study after having spent periods of time in the working environment.

student activity

In the role of an assessor of transferable skills, consider the credits that may be given to an individual in the following circumstances:

- a female candidate who has recently returned to study after having brought up two children
- a male candidate who has spent the last five years as a clerical assistant in an accounts department
- a candidate who has recently left the armed forces. The candidate's previous job was as an aircraft fitter and the chosen course of study is business and finance

PURPOSES OF JOB DESCRIPTIONS AND PERSON SPECIFICATIONS

Obviously, the main purpose of job descriptions and person specifications is to ensure that the individual matches a series of desired criteria. It is clearly necessary, when actually employing someone, to match particular **needs** of the organisation. These fall into three main categories:

- accurately matching potential employees with existing vacancies
- making sure that the job design relates to the overall business objectives of the organisation
- being prepared to provide additional training and development if required

We shall look at these three areas in more detail, although many of these aspects have been considered earlier in this Unit.

MATCHING APPLICANTS WITH VACANCIES

Once it has been established that there is a need to create or fill a vacancy, an organisation, via the personnel department, will try to ensure that the applicants match the vacancy as closely as possible. By careful wording

and framing of the job description and the person specification it may be possible to dissuade unsuitable candidates from applying for the post. This is not always necessarily the case, and many unsuitable candidates are certain to apply. If the personnel department is properly prepared, it should have mechanisms in place to sift out the unsuitable candidates so that it may concentrate on the more suitable ones. In all cases, the organisation will try to identify individuals who not only have the basic skills, experience and qualifications required, but also have the potential to be developed.

In order to understand exactly what the demands of a particular job are, an organisation will attempt to analyse the post. In many cases, this may be the first opportunity the organisation has had to look in detail at the exact nature of the job. As a result, the organisation has a chance to redesign the job in line with recent developments. In other words, the organisation can try to figure out better ways of getting the job done.

MATCHING BUSINESS OBJECTIVES TO JOB

There are two main methods by which to measure whether a particular post corresponds with the overall business objectives of the organisation. These are:

Job appraisal

Organisations have recognised that if they do not take a constant interest in the way in which jobs are carried out, then there may be a tendency for certain individuals to gradually shed parts of their responsibilities. In order to monitor this, organisations have gradually adopted a **job appraisal system**. The appraisal system aims to measure employee performance. The criteria used to measure this performance may include the following:

- completion of a particular project
- reaching a particular sales target
- completing a course of study
- improving general knowledge of work procedures and practices
- improving communication skills
- meeting particular deadlines

It is usual for the organisation and the employee to agree a schedule of performance, whereby the individual will be expected to meet all these criteria by certain dates. The specific criteria will have been decided at an appraisal interview conducted by the individual's immediate superior. Organisations have developed a range of forms and guidance material to assist the appraisal process. In many cases, the individual's prospects within the organisation and, indeed, his or her pay level, may be determined by the appraisal system. There are two varieties of appraisal, known as open and closed:

- **open**, where the appraisal is carried out with the full knowledge and involvement of the individual
- **closed**, where the individual is involved to a lesser extent and much of the appraisal is carried out by his/her immediate superior on a confidential basis

Job evaluation

In order to address business objectives with the job more specifically, organisations may use job evaluation systems. Such a system will attempt to rank jobs on a league-style basis and thus assign importance, pay and benefits accordingly. The criteria used in this process may include the following:

- how many staff does this postholder have responsibility for?
- at what level in the hierarchical structure is this post?
- how much financial responsibility does this post hold?
- how much equipment is directly related to this job post?
- how important are the decisions made by the postholder in organisational terms?
- how far-reaching are the decisions made by the postholder?

TRAINING AND DEVELOPING EMPLOYEES

As you will already know from previous sections in this Unit, employers are interested, to a greater or lesser extent in the training and development of their employees. In some respects, training and development are considered a 'perk' and only available to those whom the company consider to be worthy of the experience. In a general sense, training and development are vitally important at all levels of the organisation. Individuals may need to have their skills and knowledge of the working environment constantly updated. Without competently trained and experienced staff, an organisation cannot hope to be truly competitive. Organisations will appreciate that for every organisation which does not value training and development of the staff, another will put these high on its list of priorities. An organisation which ignores training and development needs faces the prospect of being left behind in the race to gain market share.

FIG 4.2.12 *This is the first page of the staff appraisal form used by the Department of Trade and Industry. Its staff appraisal system is a comprehensive scheme which assess individual's competences.*

Evaluate job applications and interviews

I RECRUITMENT PROCEDURES
application methods, selection methods

2 INTERVIEW TECHNIQUES
preparation, assertiveness, body language, framing questions, listening

3 LEGAL OBLIGATIONS
equal opportunities, contract of employment

4 ETHICAL OBLIGATIONS
honesty, objectivity

RECRUITMENT PROCEDURES

The main purpose of offering a new post to prospective candidates is to meet an identified organisational need. As we have mentioned, it will involve the definition of the following:

- a job description
- a job specification
- a person specification

Before we look at the methods of **external** recruitment, we will first consider the question of **internal** recruitment. It is often possible for an employee currently engaged by the organisation to fill a job vacancy. There are advantages and disadvantages for both the individual and the organisation in considering internal recruitment. The **advantages** are:

- the individual knows a great deal about the organisation
- the organisation can save considerable sums of money on recruitment costs
- the organisation can save considerable sums of money on induction costs
- promotion within the organisation is seen as an incentive to other employees

The disadvantages are:

- since the individual already knows the policies and procedures of the organisation, it may be the case that the individual can offer no new ideas or innovations
- an external candidate usually works very hard in the initial period of employment
- the individual who has filled the vacant job position will have to be replaced
- by choosing one individual the organisation has had to ignore or overlook other individuals within the organisation

In order to seek external candidates, the organisation must begin its recruitment campaign by **advertising** the vacant post. An advertisement should include the following:

1   the job title
2   a brief job description
3   the nature of the organisation's business
4   the market sector in which the business is active
5   the geographical location of the vacancy
6   the salary range
7   the organisation's address
8   a specific person to whom all applications must be made
9   a telephone number for candidates to contact
10 qualifications required
11 experience required
12 any limitations the organisation may wish to place upon the post (age or additional skills required)

Another method is to use a **commercial employment agency** which will attempt to recruit on the organisation's behalf for a commission or a fee. As a variation of this, the organisation may decide to employ a temporary person. In this case, the organisation pays the employment agency and the employment agency then pays the individual after having taken its commission.

The final alternative is to use a **government-run employment agency** which will fulfil a very similar role to that of a commercial employment agency. The major difference is that such agencies do not, at present, require commission or a fee to fill a post. Local job centres, career services or employment services are the main agencies involved.

APPLICATION METHODS

Potential applicants will use a variety of sources in their attempt to discover a job which suits their skills, experience and aspirations. Essentially, they may use the following:

- the national daily press
- Sunday newspapers
- professional journals
- trade journals
- television
- radio
- local daily newspapers
- local weekly newspapers
- Free newspapers
- career centres
- job centres
- private employment agencies
- word of mouth
- self-advertisement

In responding to an advertisement, an applicant needs to consider the following questions:

- am I in a position to apply for this post? (This may include the preparation of a **curriculum vitae** and a cross-checking of present skills with skills required)
- what do I already know or what can I find out about the organisation offering the post?
- does the organisation have a good reputation?
- how does it treat its staff?
- are there any possibilities for personal development?
- are there good promotion prospects?
- is it clear to whom I will have to apply?
- do I need to send a letter of application to obtain additional information about the post?
- is the job really for me?
- will I discover that the job is really unsuitable?
- how will they react if I turn down the job after having gone through all the processes of recruitment?

These considerations may involve the following:

- obtaining, then filling in an application form
- writing a letter of application
- researching the organisation
- preparing a curriculum vitae

The advertising organisation may require applicants to write a letter of application. The basic rules about writing a letter of application are:

1 clearly state in the first paragraph that you are applying for a **particular post**
2 state in this first paragraph **where** you saw the advertisement for the vacancy
3 indicate any **enclosures** such as an application form or cv
4 use the letter of application to **summarise** your major strengths as detailed in your application form
5 stress your **suitability** for the post
6 be **enthusiastic**
7 keep the letter of application **short**, no more than one side of A4
8 many recruitment advisers recommend that this letter of applications is **hand-written**
9 use the correct **tone**
10 use the correct **layout** for a business letter
11 make sure that the letter is **formal** and uses the correct salutations and complimentary close
12 state that you are **available** for interview
13 state that you are able to **start** the job
14 make sure that you take a **photocopy**
15 make sure that any examination **certificates** required have been photocopied and do not risk sending the originals

Alternatives to sending a letter of application are the filling in of a standard application form or sending your curriculum vitae. We shall consider these two items separately.

An **application form** may appear to be somewhat daunting in the first instance, but, having reached this stage in your application for the post, it is worthwhile attempting to fill in the details. There are a number of guidelines to consider when filling in an application form, these are:

1 photocopy the original and always fill in a **rough copy** first
2 spend some time considering the more **tricky questions**
3 make sure that you have spelt everything **correctly** and used the right grammar
4 when filling in the personal details, although this is relatively straightforward, make sure that your answers are **legible**. It is, after all, this first part of the application form that will give a valuable first impression to the reader
5 if asked whether you have any **specific skills**, emphasise the ones which you think are particularly useful for the post
6 in mentioning your **achievements**, try to identify something you have done which can show personal

development or initiative on your part
7 make sure that you know the examining board and date of all **examinations** and qualifications undertaken or in the process of being undertaken
8 carefully consider the inevitable **open-ended questions**, such as 'Why have you applied for this post?' In order to answer these questions you will need to have carefully read the details about the post including any skills or competences required.
9 choose your **referees** with care and make sure that they are well-respected members of the community
10 before entering anything on to the original application form, make sure that you have **answered** all of the following questions:

- have I answered everything?
- are there any time periods in my life unaccounted for?
- have I actually answered the questions, or have I simply stated something?
- is my approach positive?
- do I think that the reader will gain favourable impression of me?
- do I need to attach any proof of qualifications or perhaps a photograph?
- have I been honest and can I substantiate anything I have claimed?

Turning to the **curriculum vitae**, this is normally sent when the organisation asks you to 'send full details'. The purpose of a cv, which means 'course of life' is to summarise all of your personal details and past experience. The way in which cvs are produced is very much down to the individual. Indeed, cvs should be designed to match the specifications of the job applied for.

The style of the cv should be **concise** and **clear**. It should include only the **relevant** facts and figures and should be in note format.

The content of the cv will obviously depend upon the post you are applying for. You should ensure that it fulfils the following criteria:

- it should be no longer than two sides of A4
- it is a summary
- it is well presented
- the tone is positive and optimistic throughout

Additionally, your cv must be **typed** and you should keep a copy of it and read it before the interview.
With regard to **covering letters** which often accompany application forms or cvs, you should use the following guidelines;

1 produce a **rough draft**
2 state the **post** for which you are applying
3 quote any **reference numbers**
4 say where you saw the **advertisement**

5 identify any **points** made in the cv or application form which relate directly to the post

6 give **reasons** for applying for the post

7 state convenient **interview dates**

student activity

Write a standard covering letter to accompany the cv you prepared in the previous activity.

SELECTION METHODS

An organisation will receive an enormous number of applications for every post advertised. Trying to match applications to the job and producing a short list of potential interviewees provide the organisation with a number of problems. It is likely that the organisation will reduce the number of applicants to a manageable figure (usually under 10 interviewees). The organisation will have to put into progress a series of elimination procedures which may take the form of pre-selection interviews or tests.

Once the short list of candidates has been agreed, the organisation will have to arrange the interviewing panel and agree dates with the interviewees. At this time it will also seek references on each of the interviewees.

During the interview itself, the organisation will endeavour to follow the following guidelines in order to give an accurate assessment of each candidate:

1 the interviewer should be familiar with the **job description**

2 the interviewer should be familiar with the **job specification**

3 the interviewer should have read the **application forms**

4 the interviewer should have read the **references**

5 an interview **strategy** should have been agreed

6 a decision should have been made with regard to the **formal nature** of the interview

7 a decision should have been made as to how interviewees are **graded** and selected

8 A list of potential **questions** should have been prepared. These should be framed so that they can identify:
- facts about the interviewee's qualifications and experience
- the interviewee's attitudes and opinions

At the interview the following procedures should be adhered to:

1 candidates should be **welcomed** formally to the organisation

2 candidates should have the **interview procedure** explained to them

3 members of the interview panel should **identify** themselves

4 any **questions** asked should be clear and unambiguous

5 interviewees should be given **time** to answer questions and given an opportunity to have questions rephrased if they find difficulty in answering

6 the answers interviewees give should be carefully **listened to**

7 the panel should be prepared to ask **follow-up questions** arising from an interviewee's answers

8 interviewees should be offered the opportunity of **asking questions** at the end of the interview

9 interviewees should be **thanked** at the end of the interview

10 interviewees should be told about the **next stage** of the selection process

Once the interviews have taken place the organisation will then have to follow the following procedures:

1 contact the successful and unsuccessful candidates

2 invite back the successful candidate so that he/she can be given any additional information including potential start dates

3 organise any other procedural activities such as a medical

4 contact personnel department and inform them of the details of the successful candidate

5 prepare a contract of employment and arrange payroll details

student activity

In the role of personnel manager, write a letter informing firstly a successful candidate and secondly a candidate who, on this occasion, has been unsuccessful.

Selection decisions may rest upon a number of key considerations. Essentially, they will relate to the job description, job specification and person specification. Specifically, these are:

- the **educational** attainments of the candidate
- the **physical** attributes of the candidate
- the **background** of the candidate
- the special **skills and knowledge** of the candidate
- the **disposition** of the candidate
- the **motivation** of the candidate

INTERVIEW TECHNIQUES

Having reached the interview stage in the recruitment process, the candidate will have received a letter which tells him/her the date and time of the interview. It is now time for the candidate to begin preparations for the interview phase itself. This section will consider the nature of these preparations and aspects of interview technique, including:

- assertiveness
- body language
- framing questions
- listening skills

PREPARATION

The potential interviewee will reply to the organisation with a letter or telephone call accepting the interview date. As we advised earlier in this unit, the candidate will have kept photocopies of the application documents. Now is the time for him/her to re-read all of this documentation and begin to draft a list of possible questions which might be asked. As we mentioned earlier, it would be wise for him/her to find out as much as possible about the organisation. Specifically, this information should include:

- the **nature** of the organisation
- the **products and services** of the organisation
- the **markets** in which the organisation is involved
- the typical **customer** of the organisation
- the obvious **competitors** of the organisation

This information may be obtained from company reports, articles in the press, libraries or, if the candidate is particularly keen, by trying to obtain a tour of the organisation.

The final phases of preparation for the interview should include the following:

- knowing the most reliable and direct route to the organisation
- testing this route, beforehand if possible
- listening to the radio on the day of the interview to find out if there are any traffic hold-ups
- choosing suitable clothes to wear at the interview
- ensuring one is well groomed
- males should have shaved or ensured that their beard is neatly trimmed
- females should not wear too much make-up
- ensuring sufficient travelling time to allow for any possible delays
- in the event of arriving early, the candidate should not enter the premises more than 10–15 minutes before the expected arrival time

ASSERTIVENESS

The question of assertiveness needs to be carefully considered. The interviewee must attempt to get his or her point of view across at all costs, but should not be too aggressive. With regard to speech itself, he/she should take heed of the following points:

- while replying to a question, he/she must look at the person asking the question
- be positive and optimistic in his/her responses
- he/she must not lie
- he/she must always answer the question that has been asked
- if he/she does not understand, he/she should ask for the question to be repeated

BODY LANGUAGE

The effective use of non-verbal communication is essential in making full use of one's communication skills. In essence, the interviewee should attempt to:

- not fidget
- take care not to use distracting mannerisms
- use facial expressions appropriately to express oneself
- use the hands for appropriate gestures

Typically, non-verbal communication can relate to the following parts of the body:

- head
- hands
- fingers
- legs
- feet

Interviewers will be looking at how the interviewee sits and whether he/she are displays signs of nervousness and discomfort.

FRAMING QUESTIONS

We have already mentioned the nature of questions which may be asked by the interview panel. The nature of any questions asked by the interviewee should take the following into account:

- he/she should ensure that his/her questions are clear and understood
- he/she should ensure that his/her questions are not covering ground already passed over

- the questions should not be of the sort that could be considered to be sarcastic or cynical
- the interviewee should not try to be funny
- questions should be asked at the appropriate time
- the interviewee should never butt-in or interrupt one of the interviewing panel

General speaking skills include:

- careful control of accent
- clear pronunciation
- good articulation, with particular attention to fully rounded endings to words
- emphasis on the key part of answer or question
- projection of the voice so that all of the panel can hear

LISTENING

Just as it is important for the interviewee to develop speaking skills in the interview situation, it is also most important to make full use of all listening skills. For a good communicator, listening is as essential as speaking. Particular listening skills include the following:

- concentration on what is being said
- avoiding distractions
- preventing the mind from wandering
- repeating key words or phrases to oneself
- paying particular attention to the gestures and posture of the speaker
- looking at the speaker's non-verbal communication
- being alert for pauses in the speaker's speech
- being ready to respond when required
- giving the speaker feedback, perhaps by nodding
- being alert for opportunities to give personal responses

student activity

Can you think of six questions that you would wish to ask at an interview? Why would they be necessary?

LEGAL OBLIGATIONS

Laws relating to the recruitment of staff have already been considered elsewhere in Unit 4 and Unit 5. However, there are a number of specific **legal obligations** with regard to the interviewing of prospective employees.

If an organisation fails to comply with the legal requirements then an individual may have recourse to law via a court or industrial tribunal. In order to avoid possible legal action an organisation should ensure that the recruitment criteria are clear and that any terms of employment are made obvious to the candidate. We will need to consider both **equal opportunities** and obligations regarding the **contract of employment** in this section.

EQUAL OPPORTUNITIES

We would not be incorrect in stating that it is an organisation's right to choose an individual for a particular post. However, there are a number of pieces of **legislation** which limit this freedom of choice.

Under the Disabled Persons (Employment) Act 1958, an employer is required to have a minimum of 3 per cent of the workforce as registered disabled persons. The only exception to this is if the organisation has an exemption certificate.

Similarly, the Rehabilitation of Offenders Act 1974 protects ex-offenders from discrimination on the grounds of their past life. The Act states that an individual who has a past conviction need not mention 'spent' convictions on his/her job application forms or at interview. He/she must, however, mention any convictions that are not 'spent'. (The length of time that must pass before a conviction is 'spent' depends on the gravity of the offence.)

Under the Employment Protection (Consolidation) Act 1978 an individual cannot be discriminated against on the basis of union membership.

In certain cases, prospective employees are discriminated against on the grounds of:

- racial origin
- gender
- sexual orientation
- religion
- age
- disabilities

Legislation now exists to protect prospective employees in all of these circumstances. The legislation covering most of the above reasons for discrimination is contained in the Race Relations Act 1976 and the Sex Discrimination Act 1975.

CONTRACT OF EMPLOYMENT

The tricky problem regarding employment contracts concerns when the contract of employment actually **begins**. A job advertisement is not an offer of a contract. However, if a candidate is offered the job, then the contract of employment has, in effect, begun. An additional problem here is that an employer may choose to place conditions upon the acceptance of the individual for the post. Particularly, these may relate to the following:

- the taking up of satisfactory references
- the perusal of an educational qualifications certificate
- a medical examination

If the prospective employee fails to fulfil any of the above, then the offer of the post is invalid.

We will cover contracts of employment in considerable detail in Unit 5.

ETHICAL OBLIGATIONS

It is in the best interests of both the interviewee and the organisation to ensure that **honesty** and **objectivity** prevail throughout the recruitment process. We shall look at these two fundamental basics of ethical obligation in more detail:

HONESTY AND OBJECTIVITY

It is prudent for the organisation to act in an **honest** and **upright** fashion throughout the recruitment process since it does not necessarily wish to mislead prospective employees. Great resentment will occur if an employee subsequently discovers that claims and promises made by an organisation during the recruitment process are not capable of being fulfilled. The organisation does not wish to gain a reputation for untruthfulness as this may deter prospective applicants for other posts from applying.

Objectivity is a key element at every stage of the recruitment process. All those involved in the recruitment process should ensure that they consider only the facts in assessing applicants. An application form often asks whether the applicant knows any individual working for the organisation. If he/she does know someone else, then it is in the best interests of both the individual and the organisation to ensure that this person does not have any input into the recruitment process.

Objectivity should ensure that the organisation chooses the **best** candidate for the available post and that no other criteria such as prejudices or preferences have had an influence upon the selection.

Although the issues of honesty and objectivity are not necessarily covered in employment law, an organisation wishing to abide by the spirit of these pieces of legislation, as well as prevailing acceptable behaviour, should attempt to take note of both of these considerations.

UNIT 4

a s s i g n m e n t

'HUMAN RESOURCES, JOB ROLES, ORGANISATIONAL STRUCTURE AND JOB APPLICATIONS'

To fulfil the criteria of this Unit, you will need to consider human resource considerations, job roles within organisational structure and the process of applying for a job.

In consultation with your tutor, investigate a local business organisation. Your goals are to see how human resource management is improving the performance of the business.

Having done this, select two individuals within the organisation and prepare job descriptions and person specifications for each job role.

Now select a partner and compare how the roles differ in the different organisational structures.

Using your partner's job descriptions and person specifications, compile letters of application to simulate the application process. You should also include a curriculum vitae.

Present these letters of application and cvs to your partner, who will then devise an interview technique and process to simulate a real interview.

After this process, discuss the interview and both interviewer's and interviewee's performance.

You should present your summary of the whole process in the form of a written appraisal for presentation to your tutor.

UNIT 4

t e s t q u e s t i o n s

I Under government legislation, which of the following is responsible for health and safety issues?

(a) The owner of the organisation
(b) The managers of the organisation
(c) The employees
(d) All of the above

2 If you had to describe manpower planning which of the following would you choose?

(a) The carrying out of a staff audit
(b) Forecasting and planning staff needs
(c) Forecasting the immediate demands for labour
(d) Organising to ensure that sufficient labour is available

3 Which of the following is the main purpose of staff appraisal?

(a) Motivation
(b) Job satisfaction
(c) Identifying training needs
(d) An initial stage of the disciplinary procedure

4 To ensure that delegation works efficiently the delegator should make sure that the person has sufficient:

(a) Power and authority
(b) Intelligence
(c) Communication skills
(d) The general ability to fit in at all levels

5 A democratic leader has which of the following characteristics?:

(a) Believes that rules and regulations are paramount
(b) Seeks to include subordinates in all decisions
(c) Requires instructions to be carried out to the letter
(d) Thanks employees for working hard

6 Which of the following created hierarchy of needs?

(a) Taylor
(b) Maslow
(c) Herzburg
(d) Major

7 Approximately what percentage of the working population are currently trade union members?

(a) 80 per cent
(b) 70 per cent
(c) 50 per cent
(d) 40 per cent

8 What do you understand by the term division of labour?

(a) Knowing what your job tasks are
(b) Carrying out a set pattern of tasks daily
(c) Each employee working to a set series of tasks
(d) The organisation offering different incentives to workers

9 If an individual is paid for individual units of production completed what is this known as?

(a) Profit sharing
(b) Piece rate
(c) Overtime
(d) Commission

10 What do you understand by the term collective bargaining?

(a) Trade unions acting as negotiators for the employees
(b) Making decisions in group meetings
(c) Organisations in the same industrial sector agreeing policy
(d) The decision-making process within co-operative organisations

Investigate employment in business sectors

I INFORMATION SOURCES
data sets, UK employment law, EC

2 EMPLOYMENT FEATURES
*full-time, part-time, permanent, temporary, pay and benefits,
provision of training and professional development*

3 EMPLOYMENT TRENDS
*changing contractual arrangements (e.g. full-time, part-time,
temporary and permanent), balance of employment between manufacturing and services,
balance of employment between skilled and unskilled*

4 ECONOMIC RELATIONSHIPS
*technological and social change and aggregate labour supply,
general and specific skills, patterns of wage differentials
(e.g. males and females – different wage rates), skill shortages and unemployment*

We will investigate the nature and conditions of employment in a market economy in this Unit. Specifically, we will attempt to identify the economic relationships between employment and various other key influences on the economy in general.

INFORMATION SOURCES

To begin with, we shall focus on the sources of information regarding employment and the legislation which relates to employment itself.

DATA SETS

In order to accurately assess the status and trends of employment within the UK, it is necessary to refer to a number of sets of data prepared by the Government and other agencies. Primarily these sets of data are prepared for a specific purpose and may not necessarily match the exact requirements of the reader. Potential sources of these sets of data are:

The Department of Employment

The **Department of Employment** release fairly general figures derived from their censuses (these include regional and national employment figures). They also supply a great deal of data which contribute towards *Social Trends*, *Historical Abstracts* and other labour statistics. Via their network of Job Centres, they are also able to supply data on local employment trends.

Local authorities

These authorities keep data on local employment trends and provide information to prospective employers on the availability of specialist skilled labour.

The EC

The EC is concerned with Europe-wide employment trends and tries to monitor the comparative trends from country to country. They will also be concerned with trends in particular industries throughout the EC.

student activity

Using your research methods, assess the relative usefulness of these three main areas of information

UK AND EC EMPLOYMENT LAW

Employment legislation is considered by many people to be a minefield of legal requirements and restrictions. Many of the laws have been designed to protect the individual employee in situations where he/she may be unfairly treated by a powerful employer. Some may say that the laws have only served to reduce the number of full-time employees, as employers move towards part-time and short-contract labour, which is not so comprehensively protected by law. All of the following laws are currently in force in the UK, although another whole batch of laws and regulations are contained within the EC's proposed Social Charter (which at the time of writing the UK Government has opted not to accept).

Disabled Persons (Employment) Act 1958

An employer with 20 or more employees must employ a minimum of 3 registered disabled persons. Certain organisations can obtain an exemption certificate due to the hazardous nature of their work. On the other hand, certain organisations are required to give disabled persons priority in selection and recruitment to particular positions, e.g. electronic switchboard operators, etc.

The Factories Act 1961

This Act covers a wide range of different organisations, focusing on the use of machinery. The key features of this piece of legislation are:

- the employer must provide toilet and washing facilities
- premises should be adequately heated and ventilated
- the employer must make sure that floors, stairs and passageways are not obstructed in any way
- all floors should have a non-slippery surface
- potentially dangerous machinery should be fenced off to protect employees
- the employer must ensure there are adequate fire escapes, well signposted and regularly maintained
- fire doors themselves should never be locked or obstructed

The Offices, Shops and Railways Premises Act 1963

This Act concentrates on conditions within shops and offices and provides a number of clear guidelines to the employer, including:

- in work areas, the temperature must never drop below 16oC
- the employer must ensure that there is an adequate supply of fresh air
- following on from the Factories Act 1961, this legislation states that the employer must provide enough toilet and washing facilities in relation to the number of staff. He must also make sure that there is hot and cold running water as well as soap and clean towels
- again, following on from the Factories Act 1961, this legislation states that an employer has to provide suitable lighting wherever employees are expected to work or move around
- the employer must ensure that there is at least 12 square metres of working space per employee

Equal Pay Act 1970

This important Act stated that women, performing a similar job to men, should be treated in every way equally. This includes not only pay and conditions, but opportunity for promotion and recognition.

Race Relations Act 1970

This very complicated piece of legislation aims to protect individuals against discrimination on the grounds of race, colour, nationality, national origin or ethnicity.

The Rehabilitation of Offenders Act 1974

Individuals who have criminal convictions need not necessarily mention these on their job application forms or during interviews. Some convictions, after a certain period of time, are considered to be 'spent' (no longer applicable). If an employer subsequently discovers that an employee has 'spent' convictions and decides to dismiss him/her because of them, then this is illegal.

Health and Safety at Work Act 1974 and EC Directives on Health and Safety

Before this Act, employees were protected against hazardous working conditions under a number of different pieces of legislation. HASAW aimed to bring all of these together and extend the protection of employees under a single Act. The main points of this Act are:

- it stated general duties of an employer across all types of industry and commerce
- it created a system by which HASAW could be enforced (by the Health and Safety Executive and Local Authorities)
- it created the Health and Safety Commission which aimed to help employers understand the regulations and develop codes of practice
- it was backed up by the imposition of a series of legal obligations on the employer who risked facing criminal proceedings for failure to follow them
- it imposed of minimum safety regulations and introduced improvements to the working environment

The work of HASAW has been followed up by a number of EC Directives covering such areas as safety signs at work, employees handling hazardous materials and guidance regarding avoidance of major hazards.

New regulations and codes of practice are being designed continually and now cover nearly all work activities, both in the private and the public sector. Steps are now being taken to cover any gaps in the legislation, or to make it easier to understand and implement.

Sex Discrimination Acts 1975 and 1986

The original Act covers discrimination on the grounds of gender. It is equally applicable to both males and females. The Act also covers discrimination relating to marital status.

The amended Act of 1986 extended protection against discrimination to employers employing five or fewer people. It also included for the first time employees working in a domestic capacity for private employers and employees working for professional associations.

Employment Protection (Consolidation) Act 1975 and 1978

The original Act, substantially amended in 1978, covers the main features of a **contract of employment**. In addition, it requires employers to provide a Contract of Employment within 13 weeks of commencement of employment. We will be looking at contracts of employment in much more detail later in the book.

Employment Act 1980–1990

Since 1979 successive governments have taken steps to limit trade union power. The main points of each of the laws are as follows:

1980

Picketing (attempting to prevent other employees, customers, deliveries etc. from entering or leaving the premises during industrial action) was restricted to the premises involved in the dispute and was not permitted at any of the organisation's other premises. The Act also restricted 'blacking' (employees refusing to handle goods from an organisation whose employees are in dispute). It also became illegal to sack an employee who refused to join a trade union, whereas before this certain occupations required compulsory membership of a trade union (known as a 'closed shop'). These 'closed shops' were further restricted by the law requiring 80 per cent of employees to agree that there should be one in existence.

1982

This law restricted the reasons for calling an industrial dispute in the first place. The reasons had to be related directly to employment matters and could in no way be political. A more damaging part of the Act, as far as trades unions were concerned, was that they could now be sued by employers for any loss of business to other organisations as a result of industrial action. A trade union's funds could now be seized by the Courts to pay for damages.

Following on from the restrictions made on 'closed shops' in 1980, the law stated that trade union members must vote on whether 'closed shops' should continue.

1988

For the first time, individual members of trades unions were given the right to take their union to Court to prevent industrial action. This right only applied when the union itself declared there should be industrial action, and a ballot had not been taken. Union members were also protected under this law against disciplinary procedures for not having taken part in industrial action. Employees could now work for organisations which had 'closed shops', and not join the union, in the knowledge that they would keep their jobs.

1989

This amended Act required employers to provide some form of document which stated the terms and conditions under which an individual is employed. This is **not** a contract of employment, and does not have all the detail of one.

1990

This Act outlawed the dismissal of an individual who refused to join a union. Secondary action (union members taking industrial action in support of other union members) was made illegal. Unions became responsible, legally and financially, for any unofficial industrial action taken by members. All industrial action had to be approved by a majority of members in a secret ballot. Any union members involved in unofficial industrial action could be singled out by the employer and dismissed.

Trade Union Act 1988

This Act clearly stated that all industrial action must be agreed in advance by a majority of union members in a secret ballot.

EC Directive 'An Employer's Obligation to Inform Employees of the Conditions of Employment Relationships' 1991

The most important feature of this EC Directive is a change to the nature of the **contract of employment**. Employers are now required to provide the following information, within two months and not the original 13 weeks:

- the location of the work
- the job title
- the type of job (by categories)
- a job description
- paid leave entitlements
- hours of work
- collective agreements made organisationally/nationally

This is the first stage of a comprehensive range of legislation designed to ensure that employees throughout the EC have an employment contract, and know exactly what is required of them. The intention is also to treat employees working on a part-time basis as equals to full-time employees in most respects.

Trade Union Reform and Employment Rights Act 1992

This law was designed to assist the rapid creation of jobs by clearly stating exactly what an employer has to provide for the benefit of the employee. This includes a written statement which covers the main conditions of employment (pay, holiday entitlement and hours worked).

Female employees are entitled to take 14 weeks maternity leave in the knowledge that their job is secure for them to return to should they desire to do so after the pregnancy.

Employees who have responsibility for ensuring that Health and Safety Regulations are adhered to and whose employers have broken those regulations, are protected under this law from having the employer take action against them.

Management of Health and Safety at Work Regulations 1992

This major piece of legislation aims to provide a systematic and well-organised set of guidelines in relation to health and safety. They include the following:

- employers are required to assess any potential risks employees may have to face and take preventive measures to cope with them
- this risk assessment must be continually monitored by a group of employers working closely with at least five employees
- employers are required to employ specialists whose sole responsibility it is to implement the preventive measures, as well as to provide information for all other employees within the organisation
- employers are further required to carry out regular screenings of their employees to make sure that they have not suffered any ill-effects as a result of carrying out their duties. If appropriate, any health hazards which have been identified should be addressed immediately
- employees who have been given the duties of Safety Representatives should be regularly consulted, provided with time and space to carry out their investigations and given the authority to act on them

Health and Safety (Display Screen Equipment) Regulations 1992

This Act is designed to protect employees who spend considerable amounts of their working hours in front of a computer screen. The main points of the legislation are:

- employees must receive sufficient breaks from the screen
- work should not be repetitive and the employee should be given a variety of tasks
- basic safety requirements must be satisfied as regards the screen itself, the design of the keyboard, as well as the shape and height of the desk and chair being used
- regular eye tests must be provided by the employer and if the employee needs special spectacles in order to carry out his/her tasks, they should be provided by the employer
- efficient lighting should be provided in the room where the employee is using the computer, as should proper ventilation

Provision and Use of Work Equipment Regulations 1992

This Act covers all equipment from major production line machinery to hand-held tools. The legislation requires employers to:

- take into consideration how and where equipment will be used, and choose the least hazardous methods of production
- purchase only equipment that conforms with any applicable EC Safety Directive
- ensure that employees are given sufficient information to enable them to use any equipment safely. Where appropriate, training and retraining should be offered
- ensure that all equipment is regularly serviced
- ensure that potentially dangerous machinery has appropriate guards to prevent injury
- provide protection for those using hazardous materials
- ensure that work is carried out in an environment which has sufficient light
- display any relevant warnings regarding potential dangers

Manual Handling Operations Regulations 1992

These regulations were implemented to assist in the avoidance of unnecessary injury at work. This directive covers lifting, pushing, pulling, carrying and moving objects at work, and offers advice as to the correct manner by which these should be carried out.

Personal Protective Equipment at Work Regulations 1992

The term 'personal protective equipment' includes life-jackets, harnesses, head, hand and foot protection, glasses and goggles and clothing designed to be visible at all times and in all conditions. The Directive states that the protective equipment must be fit for the purpose for which it is intended, as well as actually fitting the employee. The equipment must conform with EC regulations and it must be suitably stored, cleaned regularly and replaced if defective. In addition, employees must be trained in the correct use of the equipment.

student activity

Assess these pieces of legislation in terms of the relative protection they offer employees and employers. On balance, who do you think is the better protected?

EMPLOYMENT FEATURES

The nature of employment in the UK has changed significantly over the past few years. We shall be looking at particular reasons behind these changes later on in this Unit. Here we will be considering the types of employment available. Essentially, they fall into the following categories, although you should be aware that some of the categories are not necessarily as clear as one may first imagine:

- full-time employment
- part-time employment
- permanent employment
- temporary (including seasonal) employment

Some of the categories of employment may need to be joined together to get a full picture of the nature of a particular type of employment. In other words, an individual may be in full-time employment, but on a temporary basis. Conversely, an individual may have a permanent position, but be part-time.

student activity

In your own estimation, what do you think the percentage is of each of these types of employment? Compare your estimation with official statistics.

TYPES OF EMPLOYMENT

Nearly everyone, at some stage, considers starting their own business. However, this is not always practical. Equally, organisations do not necessarily employ people on a full-time basis; they may find it more useful to offer them employment on various terms.

The range of **types of employment** is very broad and includes the following:

1 *Self-employed.* A self-employed person is usually an individual, or perhaps a group of individuals, responsible for finding and completing all their own work. Typical examples of self-employed people are plumbers, electricians, decorators, gardeners and bricklayers. Many professionals are also self-employed, such as accountants or solicitors. As a self-employed person's business grows, it may employ other people directly.
2 *Employed.* This is perhaps the most common form of employment but it is not as straightforward as it may first appear. An individual may be employed on a full-time or part-time basis. The former refers to an individual employed for a full working week and a part-time employee would work for fewer hours a week than a full-timer, and the hours worked would

be set around busy times or perhaps weekend or evening work.

3 *Permanent.* Whether the employee works on a full-time or part-time basis, permanent refers to the fact that he/she has a commitment from the employer to continued employment. This gives the individual a certain level of job security and knowledge that he/she has a long-term future with the employer.

4 *Temporary.* This form of employment is on the basis of a short-term or perhaps seasonal contract with the employer. The contract usually states the duration of the employment period and may cover such things as maternity leave, exceptionally busy periods of the year, holiday periods, long-term sickness leave or any unusual work load. The employer may often use Job Centres, private employment agencies or direct recruitment to obtain staff.

student activity

In the role of a temporary worker, what comparative job security do you think you have as opposed to a permanent employee?

5 *Flexible working arrangements.* Such arrangements, commonly known as flexi-time, allow some 2.5 million people to take advantage of the opportunity to arrange their hours to suit themselves within certain limits. All employees will be expected to be at work during the core time (usually 10 a.m. – 4 p.m.) but they can then choose to make up the rest of their hours at some point between 8 a.m. and 6 p.m. In addition, employees may choose to work extra hours and build up days off.

6 *The compressed working week.* Certain organisations choose to close early on Fridays, or perhaps close on Fridays altogether. This means that employees must work longer hours between Monday and Thursday. This can prove to be a suitable arrangement since the organisation can concentrate its business activities on the four full working days and the employees can enjoy an extended weekend.

7 *Compressed annual hours.* Certain employees will find that their contracts simply stipulate the number of hours they will be expected to work throughout the

FIG 5.1.1 *This is a timesheet as used by employees of the dti. Note that it includes a full breakdown of all work and activities and tasks undertaken.*

TIMESHEET

RE	STAFF NAME	GRADE	STAFF No.	STAFF DIARY
DIVISION	COST CENTRE CODE		WEEK ENDING	TOTAL TIME / OVER-TIME

DESCRIPTION OF WORK	ACTIVITY/TASK CODE PROJECT	JOB	SUB-JOB	TOTAL TIME	OVER-TIME	MON	TUES	WED	THUR	FRI	SAT	SUN
				.	.							
				.	.							
				.	.							
				.	.							
				.	.							
				.	.							
				.	.							
				.	.							
				.	.							
				.	.							
				.	.							
ANNUAL LEAVE			* 01	.								
BANK HOLIDAY AND PRIVILEGE LEAVE			* 02	.								
SICK LEAVE			* 03	.								
If continuation sheets are used enter totals on last sheet, strike through the TOTALS boxes on this and intermediate sheets and enter the number of continuation sheets attached in the box below.			TOTALS	.	.							

COMPLETED BY ________ GRADE ________ DATE ________

AUTHORISED BY ________ GRADE ________ DATE ________

year. With such arrangements, they may be able to work extremely long hours for short periods of time and then be able to benefit from long breaks at the end of these work periods.

8 *Job sharing.* Job sharing has become increasingly popular in recent years. Employers have discovered that job-share arrangements are very beneficial to the organisation, since the job sharers approach the job in a fresh and positive manner, only having had to work for a part of the week. They also benefit from the fact that there are two people with different ideas to solve particular problems. Individuals involved in job sharing will be able to choose the hours they work, in consultation with one another and the employer. Ideally, this type of arrangement suits individuals with other commitments outside the workplace, such as child care.

student activity

Identify at least three occupations in which job shares would be appropriate.

9 *Home working.* It is now possible for individuals to undertake their job tasks at home via a computer linked to their employers' premises. (This is also known as tele-working.) An individual, within certain limitations, may in this way be able to engage in full or part-time employment as well as fitting in other commitments. It was supposed that this form of work would be very common by now. However, many organisations have discovered that it is unsuitable since it may result in the individual becoming isolated through lack of social contacts throughout the day and thus becoming unmotivated.

student activity

Identify three occupations in which home working would be appropriate.

WORKING CONDITIONS

The number of different types of job is as varied as the number of different organisations, perhaps more so. Working conditions within an organisation can differ depending upon an employee's department, site or rank. Factors which may differ include the technology used, the physical surroundings or the number of people one works with. Furthermore, individuals' qualifications differ, as do the ways in which these are used in the context of a specific job. Obviously, the way in which

individuals are paid, and how much will differ, but the legal requirements governing pay are similar for all. Individuals' training requirements and needs may be different, as may be the opportunities people have to gain additional qualifications and training. We need to consider all of these points in turn:

The basic **working conditions** are governed by health and safety rules (we will look at these in more detail later). It has long been realised that employees work much better if the employer takes note of the following:

- that the workplace is well lit
- that the workplace is kept at a constant temperature, regardless of the weather
- that the workplace is pleasant and well-decorated
- that the workforce is kept fit and well, so as to reduce sickness
- that the hours worked are relatively flexible to take account of the employees' external commitments
- that the workforce receives regular training and the opportunity to gain additional qualifications
- that skills are rewarded, financially, in relation to their value to the organisation
- that, with age, additional payments are made so as to encourage experienced workers to stay with the organisation
- that trades unions are accepted, and that there is a regular dialogue with them
- that pay and conditions, overall, should be attractive and competitive

Having said all of this, there is a vast difference in how these points are adopted by individual employers. The physical working conditions of a person in an administrative job are very different from those of a person working in industry. The former will enjoy relatively luxurious conditions, with carpets, curtains or blinds, comfortable seating, and above all, a clean environment. In a factory, you may find a completely different set of conditions. The environment may be dirty and noisy, the employee may be on his/her feet all day, the job may be physically demanding and the hours longer.

If you examine the nature of jobs in the different sectors of industry, you will find a wide variety of conditions. When we consider industrial working conditions we may have to look also at the following:

- where is the work? Is it outside or inside? Is the work in a hot or cold environment?
- does the employee work on his/her own? Is there much opportunity for contact with others during the working day?
- do the hours differ? Is there a requirement to start work early, finish late, or do regular shift work?
- is the work carried out in a clean environment? Does

the employee need to have regular health checks as a result of the environmental features of the workplace?

- how safe is the job? Putting health and safety aside, is the job itself dangerous? Is it physically demanding in the sense that it may result in injury?
- does the employee have to wear protective clothing? Is the job sufficiently physical, dangerous, or unsafe to mean that the employee has to wear some kind of equipment or protection?

student activity

Assess the working conditions in the following occupations:

- a butcher
- a sales representative
- a sales assistant in a retail outlet
- a nurse

It is in the **manufacturing** sector that we will probably find the widest range of working conditions. Even organisations, producing the same goods, only a few hundred yards apart, may be radically different. The conditions may depend upon how much has been spent on updating old machinery and improving the overall environmental conditions.

The **production process** in a factory obviously depends upon what is being made. An organisation that produces fairly small numbers of products or components will be comparatively small in terms of both numbers of employees and space provided. In contrast, an organisation which makes cars on a production line will need enormous amounts of space, considerably more staff and larger premises. The size of the production process does not really have a bearing on how noisy and unsafe the conditions are, but this is inevitably related to investment in new techniques and machinery.

Administration jobs, despite the fact that they may be a part of the same organisation as the production process, often have completely different working conditions. They may be housed on a separate site, or away from the noise and demands of the 'shop floor'. Depending upon the nature of the administrative work carried out, and the demands placed upon it, we may find another variety of working conditions:

- the administration section may be cramped, with severe lack of space and amenities. This may be due to the fact that the administrative unit is only seen as servicing the main operation of the organisation, namely – making things
- the offices may be reasonably spacious, but functional, since no one outside the organisation such as customers, will ever see them

- the office space may be plush and well-appointed. This will be due to the uses to which the offices are put. In other words, customers may regularly visit and it may be considered important that they be impressed by the furnishings and the image of the premises
- the offices may be relatively small and highly automated. In this case, the organisation may have invested heavily in computers and technological equipment, partly to ease the work load and partly to reduce the numbers of administrative staff
- usually, the physical conditions of the administrative section will be a mixture of several of the above. It is the case, quite often, that administrative departments have grown and are not particularly well planned. Having the right people to hand is not always possible, since the administrative department may well be split up in a series of rooms, or even different sites
- The concept of a purpose-built administrative block has proved popular over the years, but often it is the production process that takes first place when considering investment

The **service sector** offers yet another broad range of working conditions. Since this sector includes many occupations from postmen to teachers and policemen to retail assistants, we can see a massive difference in conditions at work. The conditions will usually revolve around the nature of the job itself. If we take two contrasting examples, we can see the problems:

- a **teacher** will have a room to use as an office. A **retail worker** may only have a small rest room, as no real administrative work needs to be undertaken
- the **retail worker** will carry out the bulk of the job on the shop floor, the **teacher** may use a variety of different classrooms in the course of a day
- the **teacher** will deliver a predetermined course of study, and in some respects the day is mapped out ahead. The **retail worker**, on the other hand, will not know the demands to be faced until they happen
- The **retail worker** will have to cope with a variety of different customer problems. The **teacher**, meanwhile, will deal with the same customers (students), but may not be able to predict what they will demand

Contracts of employment

Most of the conditions of work are laid down in the contract of employment (which we have dealt with in an earlier section) The following information must be included in the contract:

- the names of the employer and the employee
- the date on which the employee began working for the organisation

- the employee's pay (either the amount or the scale)
- when, in terms of frequency, the employee is paid
- the employee's hours of work
- the employee's holiday entitlements (if applicable)
- the employee's holiday pay entitlements
- the employee's right to sick pay due to injury
- the employee's right to sick pay due to illness
- the length of notice (from both sides) required to terminate employment
- the employee's pension rights
- the employee's job title

A good contract of employment would also cover, in brief note form, such things as the disciplinary rules and grievance procedures.

Over and above the main contract, the employer is required to take note of a variety of different legislation, which we will deal with later. Essentially, the legislation provides the following protective rights for employees:

- to receive a contract of employment
- to receive a pay statement which details pay and deductions
- to have a period of notice when terminating employment
- to join a trade union is desired
- to have maternity leave
- to return to work after maternity leave
- not to be unfairly dismissed from employment
- to receive a redundancy payment
- to receive equal pay for equal work
- not to be discriminated against

student activity

What action could you take if your employer failed to supply you with a contract of employment within the first 13 weeks of your employment?

Not all of the above rights come into force immediately. An employee may have to wait before he/she is eligible. Equal pay, trade union membership and maternity leave are immediate. The employer must give the employee a contract of employment within 13 weeks. The others, including maternity pay, the right to return after pregnancy and redundancy payments come into force after two years.

PAY AND BENEFITS

Most people, who are in work, get paid in one way or the other. The exception to this, are those who are involved in some kind of voluntary work. Although most people are paid, they receive their reward in a variety of different ways:

- those paid strictly according to the hours worked
- those paid for working a certain number of hours in a week
- those paid for working a certain number of hours in a month

These are the basic ways in which pay is worked out, but there are others (less common) which we will look at shortly.

It goes without saying that some people are paid more than others. The reasons for these differences may include:

- the employee's period of service with the organisation
- the age of the employee
- the qualifications of the employee
- the training undertaken by the employee
- if the employee performs exceptionally (see later)

Other employees receive a range of perks or benefits, such as company cars, health care, subsidised canteens or season ticket loans. These perks may be offered to keep valuable staff and to ensure that the organisation is more competitive with other organisations. In some cases, the perk is more valuable to the employee than actually receiving the cash alternative.

Despite the pay differences, two things remain the same. Everyone has to pay Income Tax and National Insurance. We will look at these in a little more detail later.

One more distinction exists between the ways in which people are paid. This is the difference between salaries and wages. Let's contrast the two:

1 **salaries** tend to be paid to clerical and managerial staff who are paid on a monthly basis, whereas **wages** tend to be paid to manual workers who are paid on a weekly basis
2 the **salary** is paid either every four weeks (i.e. 13 times per year), or at the end of each calendar month. The **wage** is paid, usually on a Friday, or at the end of the working week
3 **salaries** tend to be paid either as 1/12th or 1/13th of the total quoted salary for the whole year. **Wages**, on the other hand, tend to be paid according to the quoted weekly pay rate, or the hourly rate times the number of hours worked
4 **salaries** are usually paid by bank credit transfer into the bank account of the employee. The **wage** is paid either in cash, or by cheque (which can often be cashed in a local bank by arrangement with the organisation)

5 **salary-paid employees** are not usually paid for any overtime that they may have to do. The overtime is considered to be a duty of the employee – this is particularly true of managerial staff. The **wage earner** is paid overtime according to the number of extra hours worked

6 the **salary-paid employee** will always receive the same payment every month, since it is a proportion of the total yearly pay. **Wage earners** will earn money according to how many hours have been worked, and consequently they may earn different amounts each week

7 both **salary** and **wage** earners are often paid in arrears. This means that the employee has actually worked a period of time or hours before being paid. The salary worker will have probably worked for a whole month before being paid, the wage earner will have only worked a week before receiving a pay packet

These distinctions have become a little less obvious in recent years. Organisations have taken on many more part-time workers, both manual and clerical. Some of these individuals will be paid on a weekly basis or on a monthly basis.

student activity

On balance, which do you think has the most benefits, wages or salaries?

Earlier, we mentioned that there are some less common ways of being paid. Some of these payment methods may be in addition to a basic salary. It is more likely to find these additional payments in the case of sales people, or other employees which make a positive and visible contribution to the profits of the organisation.

1 **Commission** is often paid to sales people based on the income they generate for the organisation. They will often be on a relatively low basic salary, or none at all, and rely on the commission they earn for their income. In this way, the organisation positively encourages employees to work hard and make profits for them, but the obvious problem is that in cases when the sales people have had a bad week or a bad month they will earn very little. This can mean that employees paid on this basis tend to leave the organisation if things are not going well.

2 **Bonus payments** are made, in addition to a basic salary, when specified sales targets are made. Employees may also receive bonus payments when the organisation is particularly busy, in holiday periods for example. It is usual for an organisation to pay a bonus at Christmas time, or after the annual accounts have been calculated and have shown exactly what

profit has been made. In most cases, the bonus payment is then linked to the productivity of the employees over a given time period

3 **Profit sharing** is another alternative source of extra income for the employee. This particular form of payment involves the organisation calculating its overall profit, then identifying a portion of it for distribution to the employees. Normally, the organisation will pay employees a certain amount for every year worked. This means that the longer an employee has been working for the organisation, the bigger the share of the profit payout he or she will receive

4 **Expenses** form the final type of additional payment to the employee. Expenses are not really an additional payment at all, they are simply the repayment of monies already spent, or which will be spent by the employee. These payments will include meals, petrol, hotel bills, travel and in some cases a clothing allowance. In many cases, the employee will not have to 'claim' these expenses and will be issued with a company credit card instead.

Tax, national insurance and other deductions

We have, so far, been considering the pay of the individual employee. However, employees do not actually receive this full amount at all. All salaries and wages are subject to a number of **deductions** from this **gross pay** (this means the total amount earned by the employee before deductions). What is left after the deductions is commonly known as **net pay**.

From the gross pay, as we have said, are deducted various forms of 'charges' against the employee. Some are required by law, such as Tax, and others are voluntary, such as pension contributions.

Tax is deducted by the employer on behalf of the Inland Revenue. Employers are required to make these deductions, and promptly pass on the monies to the government department. The deduction process is complicated, but includes the following procedures:

1 The Inland Revenue calculates the employee's eligibility for various personal allowances, in other words, how much an individual can earn before he or she must pay tax. These personal allowances are based on the marital status of the individual and other criteria.

2 Once these personal allowances have been calculated, an individual will pay tax out of every pay packet or monthly pay cheque. This system is known as PAYE (Pay As You Earn) and is the most common way to pay tax.

3 A self-employed person pays tax in a very different way. After having completed the end of year accounts, the self-employed person sends in the 'return' to the Inland Revenue and then they calculate how much

**Inland Revenue
PAYE**

Instructions to Employer

- **Employee with no P45**

  If a **new** employee does not produce Parts 2 and 3 of form P45
  - ask him to read the Note to Employee below and complete Certificate A or B if appropriate
  - complete the back of this form yourself and follow the instructions on form P8. If this tells you to send form P46 to your Tax Office you should do so straightaway.

- **Employee previously paid below the limit**

  If an **existing** employee's pay rises above the taxable limits
  - complete the back of this form and follow the instructions on form P8.

Note to Employee

As you have not been able to produce Parts 2 and 3 of form P45, you should consider Certificates A and B below.

If this is your first regular job since leaving full-time education and you have **not** claimed unemployment benefit* since then, you should sign Certificate **A** below. This may enable your employer to operate a correct PAYE code for you straight away.

If this is your only job or your main job, you should sign the Certificate **B** below. Your employer will use the emergency code.

If you are unable, or do not want to sign either Certificate, your employer will deduct tax at the basic rate.

- **Certificate A**

  I declare that this is my first regular job since leaving full-time education and that I have not claimed unemployment benefit* since then.

  Signature _____ Date _____ 198 __

- **Certificate B**

  I declare that this is my only or my main job.

  Signature _____ Date _____ 198 __

P46   *including supplementary benefit paid because of unemployment

FIG 5.1.2 *Form P46 issued by the Inland Revenue gives instruction to the employer regarding the calculation of tax for employees.*

tax should be paid. They will usually allow the tax to be paid in two instalments over the following year.

The process as far as the wages department is concerned, follows the following procedure:

1 The deductions of each employee will be calculated on a form known as a **P11**. This will take account of any personal allowances that the individual is entitled to.
2 The wages department will then generate a **pay slip** for each employee which details the exact nature of the deductions made.
3 Once a year they will generate another form known as a **P60**. This will detail all pay received, tax deducted, National Insurance contributions made and any statutory sick or maternity pay for the whole year.
4 If an employee changes his/her job in the course of the year, the wages department will issue a **P45** which details the employee's tax code, total pay to date, any tax due and all tax paid to date. This must then be given to the employee's new employer to ensure that his/her tax is calculated correctly.

National insurance is paid by all employees, and a contribution is made by the employer too. Self-employed individuals pay their NI on a quarterly basis direct to the Department of Social Security. The national insurance contributions are collected to provide a range of benefits and services which include the following:

- unemployment benefit
- state pensions
- statutory sick pay
- statutory maternity pay
- child benefit
- industrial disablement benefit
- widow's benefit
- death grants

The DSS is a large and complex government organisation that has both central administration in London and a spread of regional offices throughout the country.

We have now looked at the two statutory (compulsory) forms of deduction from the employee's pay packet. These are not the only deductions made from the pay packet, however, There are a number of possible voluntary deductions.

The first, and possibly the most common, is the pension. Essentially, there are four forms of pension. They are:

1 **SERPS** (State Earnings Related Pension Scheme) which is a government-run pension scheme
2 **company pension schemes** which are run and administered by the organisation on behalf of its employees
3 **personal pension schemes** which have been set up by a pension or assurance company to meet the individual demands of the employee
4 **occupational pension schemes** (also known as superannuation) which are run and administered nationally for all members of an occupational group (such as teachers)

Other types of deduction include the following:

- trade union subscriptions, which are paid by an individual who belongs to a trade union
- social/leisure club subscriptions, which are paid by the individual who uses the facilities offered by the organisation
- charitable donations, which can be paid directly to the charity, before Tax and National Insurance is deducted

TRAINING AND PROFESSIONAL DEVELOPMENT

There is an extremely wide variety of **training** and **qualifications** available to the employee. The exact nature of the training or the qualifications is dependent upon the nature of the job. For some jobs individuals will require constant training or updating of qualifications, whereas for others will they not need anything beyond basic training to be able to carry them out. Despite the availability of so many courses, upwards of one-third of the population still does not have any formal qualifications.

You will find further details about training and professional development in Unit 4.

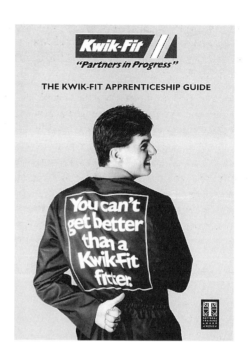

FIG 5.1.3 *Kwik-Fit are one of the few remaining major organisations to offer an attractive apprenticeship package.*

EMPLOYMENT TRENDS

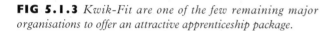

As we mentioned earlier in this Unit, the nature and type of work in the UK has changed greatly over the last few years. There are clearly identifiable **trends** which relate to the balance between full- and part-time workers, the relative importance of industrial sectors and the requirements for skilled labour. We shall be looking at these specific trends in more detail.

CHANGING CONTRACTUAL ARRANGEMENTS

One of the major changes in the UK economy since the end of the Second World War has been a reduction in employment in the manufacturing industries. While this has been coupled with the growth of the service sector, organisations have tended to employ fewer people. As a result of this decline and the introduction of technological innovations, individuals have had an increase in their leisure time and there has been a general rise in the overall standard of living.

Consequently, there have been considerable changes in employees' contractual arrangements with their employers. In essence, this has meant there has been a move away from permanent full-time posts to alternative types of employment. It is now common for organisations to employ their workers on a permanent part-time basis, or alternatively, on a full-time temporary basis. This gives the organisation flexibility to respond to periodic changes in demand. Costs, too, remain low as the organisation does not have to employ individuals at times when demand is low. With a large pool of suitable labour available, the organisation can also pick and choose from those seeking work.

BALANCE OF EMPLOYMENT BETWEEN MANUFACTURING AND SERVICES

The manufacturing sector has certainly become more efficient in recent years, but at the same time it has become smaller. Measuring this relative size we must consider the number of individuals employed in the manufacturing sector and the proportion of the gross national product which manufacturing contributes. It was the United States that began the trend towards having a larger service sector which contributed more than the manufacturing sector. All developed nations have followed this example. There are, essentially, three main reasons for this trend:

1 there is a tendency for the more developed, and therefore the richer nations, to spend a higher proportion of their income on **services** than on manufactured goods
2 it is easier to gain more **productivity** in the manufacturing sector by the application of automation than can be expected in the service sector

3 as nations become more developed and richer they are able to use their profits to **purchase** considerably cheaper manufactured products from less developed countries

The service sector has been hit considerably during the recession as the trends have been reversed and the developed nations have become poorer. The automatic reaction in such a situation is to reduce the consumption of services. The base demand for manufactured goods remains fairly constant, although there have been some notable exceptions. These exceptions are in areas where less developed countries have used the recession as an opportunity to 'catch up' with the developed nations.

The service sector tends to be divided into the following groups:

- financial services
- distribution
- retailing
- health
- education

Each area has also been transformed by the application of technology. This has led to a rationalisation of the levels of employment in each of these areas within the service sector.

BALANCE OF EMPLOYMENT BETWEEN SKILLED AND UNSKILLED

Another aspect of the application of technology has been to reduce, in relative terms the importance of skilled labour. Many traditional crafts have been replaced by machines. Technology has enabled semi-skilled workers to be substituted for skilled labour. This has naturally led to a reduction in wage costs. Although workers can be retrained, they may find it difficult to obtain work which provides not only a similar standard of living, but the same level of job satisfaction that a skilled job would give them.

Alongside this comparative reduction in the number of skilled workers there has been a gradual decline in the size and power of the trade union movement. As traditional skilled work has been replaced by technology, the number of craft unions has declined. In the semi-skilled or unskilled sectors, trade union membership is still reasonably buoyant, but many unions have recognised the need to merge in order to sustain their membership and power.

ECONOMIC RELATIONSHIPS

As you may have realised, we cannot consider employment in isolation. We must look at the economic relationships which exist across the whole of the economy. Technological and social changes have affected the labour supply. In this regard a number of other factors need to be taken into consideration, including:

- the availability of particular skills
- wage differentials
- skills shortages
- unemployment

TECHNOLOGICAL AND SOCIAL CHANGE AND AGGREGATE LABOUR SUPPLY

Coupled with the technological changes that we have already mentioned, there have been a number of key social changes which have affected the aggregate labour supply.

The first of these is the change in the **age structure** of the workforce. The high birth rates in the 1950s and 1960s have created a 'bulge' in the population in the 1990s. This 30–40 year-old age group now makes up the majority of the working population. However, with the birth rate falling in the 1970s and 1980s the number of 16-year olds entering the market in the early 1990s has drastically fallen.

The ageing nature of the population is reflected in the ageing workforce. By the end of this century over one-third of the working population will be over 45. As there is a tendency for people to retire earlier, the pressures on the remaining population have meant that there are enormous strains on the pension and benefits systems. The government has encouraged many individuals to take up their own pension schemes and there are rumours that the government is considering the reduction or termination of state pensions in the future.

The other major trend in employment has been the growth of the self-employed sector. Upwards of 3.5 million people are self-employed and over 50 per cent of these operate in the service sector. Unfortunately this sector, which has been generating considerable wealth for the nation, has been hard hit by the recession.

As we will see later in this section, women suffer from

discrimination at nearly all levels of employment. By the end of this century women will have taken up nearly 50 per cent of the available jobs and many will be adult women returning to work after bringing up their children. During this period the number of men available in the labour market has remained relatively stable. Men who find themselves jobless before retirement age, have found it increasingly difficult to find another job. Employers have discovered that women tend to be more flexible in terms of the type and method of employment they can undertake.

The main reasons behind the increase in the availability of women in the labour market are:

- the growth of **single parent families**, which means that women who find themselves needing to support their children, must seek work in order to provide for their families
- there has been a change in **social attitudes** which has allowed the relative importance of a woman's salary to be considered an important and vital element of a family's income
- there is a trend for women to have **children at a later stage in their lives**. This point has led to the increased availability of younger women in the labour market
- with the passing of various pieces of legislation, **gender discrimination** has become unlawful
- women who are in professional or managerial work are much more likely to **return to work** after having had children
- there is a widespread availability of **child-care facilities**
- it is more **socially acceptable** for women to return to work after having had children
- with the decline of heavy industry and the **growth of the service sector**, women have greater opportunities in the job market
- many women tend to favour **part-time work** which may be undertaken alongside their other commitments
- the creation of maternity leave and child benefit has further re-inforced the **flexibility** of women in the job market

GENERAL AND SPECIFIC SKILLS

As we have mentioned, with the decline of traditional industries, there has been a gradual increase in the growth of the service sector and light manufacturing industries. Individuals engaged in these areas of business activity do not require the level of expertise and are thus more flexible in terms of their skills and competences.

If an employee has basic skills, then it is possible for him/her to seek employment in a wide variety of different business activities. As regards specific skills, there has been a general reduction in the level of skill requirement, primarily caused by the introduction of technology.

This relative devaluing of skills is known as de-skilling. This process, although gradual, allows employers to replace expensive employees who are highly trained with comparatively cheaper employees who are only partially trained.

PATTERNS OF WAGE DIFFERENTIALS

We should begin by considering this point from two different perspectives. The first is the relative differences in the wage rates earned by **men** and **women**. It is often the case that women who hold a similar post to a man will receive a lower rate of pay. Many will see this as a traditional approach to setting pay levels. However, strictly speaking, this is illegal. Many employers will get around this problem by assigning different job titles to men's and women's roles. A man, for example, will be defined as a manager, a woman as a supervisor. By this method, the employer is able to 'legally' offer different rates of pay. Coupled with this is the relative difficulty women find in obtaining promotion or personal development within the work situation. If their ability to compete with men is impeded by their lack of access to training and development, then this may be the subject of legal action.

Obviously, **regional** differences in pay exist. An employee in the South of England will earn up to 50 per cent more than an employee in Northern Ireland. Comparisons between the North (and Scotland) and the South of England show that a worker in the South may earn up to 25 per cent more. While these relative pay differentials may seem unfair, it is generally accepted that in areas where employees receive lower rates of pay, the actual cost of living is considerably lower. Factors which will also affect the pay differentials include the **'weighting system'**. This gives the employee an additional payment, such as a London weighting, in an attempt to offset the relatively high cost of living in that area.

student activity

Identify two specific areas which suffer from adverse wage differentials.

SKILLS SHORTAGES AND UNEMPLOYMENT

The economy and particular industries will suffer from periodic skill shortages. There may be many reasons for the lack of availability of suitably skilled employees. There is always a mismatch between the number of individuals seeking employment within a particular industrial sector and the demand for that labour. In certain areas there will be an oversupply of labour available. In others, there may be short- or long-term shortages. These shortages can be alleviated by employees' willingness to move and find suitable employment. In many cases, however, the employer may have to take on unskilled or partially skilled labour and install a training and development programme to bring them up to full skilled levels. As various traditional forms of employment have declined there has been a tendency for those who have lost their jobs to seek retraining. With good management and a knowledge of the needs of the market, retraining programmes can be designed which will then provide suitably retrained staff to match industrial needs. Training institutions, which should have close contacts with the industry where their trainees are destined to seek employment, should endeavour to be aware of the current status of that job market.

With regard to unemployment, we are really considering a situation where there is total mismatch between the skills and experience available and the requirements of the labour market. It is certainly the case that some unemployed do not have any readily transferable skills to offer. However, there are training programmes available through which an individual can develop his/her own range of skills. We have already considered the nature and reasons for unemployment, but we should note that there are two distinct types of unemployed, these are:

1. **Voluntarily unemployed** – who are those not prepared to work for the wage rates offered. They may be perfectly capable of working and would probably be prepared to take a job if the pay was acceptable. Also in this category are those who decide that they would rather work in an unpaid capacity (such as doing voluntary work) than take a salaried position.
2. **Involuntarily unemployed** – specifically, as we have mentioned already, these will include:

- the frictionally unemployed
- the seasonally unemployed
- the structurally unemployed
- the cyclically unemployed

Many theorists would state that unemployment is inevitable, as there is insufficient demand in the economy. If the individuals who make up society do not have sufficient funds to enable them to buy goods and services, then there is not enough money available to keep everyone in work. A possible reaction to this, in government terms, would be to spend more money. This would create that additional demand. The workers employed as a result of this government funding would then demand additional products and services which could then, in turn, mean the employment of others to supply them. Classical theorists suggest that if many individuals are unemployed, then wages will fall. This will reduce the cost of producing goods and services. As a result, demand will increase because the price of the products and services will be lower, therefore, more workers will need to be employed to supply the higher demand.

student activity

Assess the unemployment situation in your local area and assign percentages to the various forms of unemployment.

Analyse external influences relating to employment

1 EXTERNAL INFLUENCES
media, trades unions, legislation, government, technology, competition

2 ACTIONS
wages policy, responses to changes in demand, wage differentials

3 ECONOMIC RELATIONSHIPS
demand for labour and demand for the product, the supply of labour

EXTERNAL INFLUENCES

Any study of the external influences on employment will include many of the following aspects of personnel policy:

- changes in the level of employment as a result of changes in demand
- adjustments to the size of the workforce in response to a decline in market
- changes in the proportion of part-time and full-time employment
- changes in working hours
- changes in the wage or salary structure
- changes in training and personal development requirements
- changes in recruitment policy in line with legislation
- changes in the provision of staff welfare facilities
- trade union influences
- technological impacts on the workforce
- the impact of a competitor's business activity

We shall consider some of the specific external influences relating to employment in the first part of this element and then consider an organisation's possible actions and then the overall economic relationships relating to labour.

student activity

Consider the above list closely. In your estimation, which are the most important considerations? Try to put them in some form of ranking order. Why have you chosen this order?

MEDIA

The availability of information has led to a gradual improvement in the overall knowledge of most individuals in society. The **media** have, perhaps, a disproportionate impact upon the formulation of policy. Sensationalist headlines may adversely affect a business. It does not necessarily follow that a media concern is necessarily a consumer concern. Despite this apparent disparity of importance, the media do wield a tremendous influence on the employment market.

The media have been charged with adversely affecting the fortunes of various organisations. Sometimes, upon the most flimsy evidence, an organisation will be damned for its use of a particular production process or the safety of its products or services. 'Bad press' may, of course, be countered by considered and well-organised public relations operations. However, this is merely a reaction to damage already done. The media will, inevitably, highlight the most extreme of situations and cases and will thereby affect consumers' perceptions of the organisation. Should an organisation suffer at the hands of the media there are a number of unfortunate outcomes.

One worrying result of bad press is that a number of key groups who interact with the organisation will form the wrong opinions about that organisation. Investors, for example, may withdraw their funds and seek alternative investment possibilities. Suppliers may lose confidence in the organisation and reduce their credit facilities. Buyers and consumers may also lose confidence and look for alternative sources of products or services. In extreme cases, the government may step in and demand that the organisation make immediate changes to the situation as well as financial amends for any losses incurred by other parties. Many of you will remember the recent disastrous promotional campaign run by Hoover. They offered almost unconditional free flights to any consumer who bought their products. In the event, the sales promotion was seriously oversubscribed. Hoover had simply miscalculated the level of demand. They did not have sufficient mechanisms in place to handle the volume of enquiries and applications. As a result, thousands of disgruntled consumers formed a very negative opinion of the organisation. It is without doubt that many of these consumers will never consider purchasing Hoover products in the future. What began as an attractive sales promotion campaign rapidly became a disaster. The media took great pains to highlight personal 'tragedies' suffered by consumers at the hands of Hoover's mismanagement of the promotion.

On the other hand, the media do provide a useful service to the consumer by means of their interest in potentially hazardous products and services. An organisation which is identified as producing unsafe products and services will suffer a loss of market share, and consequent loss of profitability as a result. The inevitable outcome is that they will have to shed workers. The media will also highlight bad practice in certain areas of business activity. If organisations undertake dubious trading practices, particularly in the direct sales field, then they may suffer total ruin at the hands of the media.

student activity

Do the media have a disproportionate influence on the economy and business activity? After all, they are unappointed 'guardians' of society. Should we pay such close attention to their opinions?

TRADES UNIONS

Many individuals consider that **trades unions** are an unwanted relic from the past. If unions did not exist then employers would be free to make any claims upon their employees that they saw fit. Employers will always seek to obtain labour at the lowest possible cost. Employees, on the other hand, will always try to obtain the highest possible wage. In a society without trades unions, employees would have to compete with one another, gradually reducing their pay claims in order to remain employed. Equally, without trades unions employers would be able to group together in an attempt to secure the best possible wage rates for themselves.

Trades unions came into existence as a result of employees realising that if they grouped together then they could secure for themselves better pay and working conditions. This collective bargaining aspect at the heart of trade union activity has enabled imbalances to be addressed.

The main objectives of trades unions are:

- to obtain the best possible rates of pay for their members
- to obtain and retain the best possible working conditions for their members
- to constantly improve the conditions of employment for their members
- to protect their members against unfair action taken by employers
- to attempt to ensure full employment for all of their members
- to attempt to obtain job security for all of their members
- to attempt to have a greater say in the policies formulated by employers
- to try to influence government policy
- to represent their members in cases of dispute

Trade union membership, and consequently their influence, has declined throughout the 1980s and 1990s. In 1979, prior to the avalanche of anti-union legislation, there were 13 million trade union members. This meant that almost half of the working population were members of a trade union. Presently, this total has been reduced to nine million (40 per cent of the workforce). The main reasons for this decline in membership are:

- the general increase in unemployment
- the changes in the structure of employment and industry (there are more 'white collar jobs' which are less likely to be unionised)
- the increase in the number of women in the workforce and the fact that, as the majority of these jobs are either part-time or temporary, they tend not to be union members
- political action against trades unions

Trades unions interact with employers and the government in the following ways:

- *nationally* – the National Advisory Council has representatives from the TUC. This organisation's role is to create guidelines for collective bargaining. In addition, trades unions interact with employers concerning rates of pay and conditions of service. These functions are carried out by full-time union officials.
- *locally* in the case of local disputes and grievances, trade union representatives seek to negotiate on behalf of the individual trade union members concerned. Often trade union officials who work at local level are unpaid.

student activity

How much are the professed objectives of trades unions at variance with the objectives of employers?

LEGISLATION AND THE GOVERNMENT

The **government** has three main roles in relation to employment. Sometimes the government has difficulty in balancing these three, often conflicting, functions. The three main functions are:

1 legislative
2 mediation
3 as employer

Successive governments have introduced a range of **employment law** (for further details of which see the first element in this Unit). The government also operates as a **mediator** between employers and employees via QUANGOs such as ACAS. The government is also a major **employer** in the UK, although, in recent years, there has been a move to reduce the extent of direct employment by setting privatisation plans in motion.

The government, at all times, will be interested in how UK industry is performing and will consult various business organisations in the course of their deliberations in the formulation of government policy.

student activity

Many people believe that the present government fails in its task of mediation. It is said that it inevitably comes down on the side of the employer. Do you think this is true, and if so, why does it do so?

TECHNOLOGY

The development of **technology** has, as we have seen, had wide implications for the labour market. In the final analysis, however, it is an employer's choice whether to make use of technology and replace traditional working practices. Since organisations tend to have the profit motive as their major concern, it is inevitable that they will seek to replace inefficient working procedures with new technology at the earliest possible opportunity. In this respect, technology is not strictly speaking an external influence on employment. It is very much for the organisation, in its role as employer, to decide whether to make use of it.

Technological advances have been bitterly resisted by certain trade unions and groups of employees. Technological unemployment is inevitable in a market economy, but it is very different to bring about changes in attitudes towards this technology.

student activity

Could an organisation seriously hope to survive in this day and age without the application of technology?

COMPETITION

The overwhelming majority of organisations face some form of **competition**. We must take a broad view of the nature of competition, however, since strictly speaking, all organisations compete with one another. After all, there are only limited amounts of funds available to finance the purchase of products and services. Clearly, an organisation's ability to compete is related to matters such as the development of products, their pricing strategies and their promotional policies. An organisation will always attempt to monitor and maintain its customers' loyalty. The actions of a competitor may be hard to predict and as a result, sudden, if temporary, negative effects are bound to occur. An organisation faced with such a situation will seek to reduce its costs and, since one of the highest costs a business faces is its wage bill, members of the workforce may be discarded. In order to be in a position to react positively to sudden increases in competition, an organisation will attempt to keep its workforce at the absolute minimum at all times. As a result, there is an increasing tendency for organisations to adopt alternative methods of production which do not rely on high levels of manpower.

ACTIONS

Just how an organisation responds to these external influences may depend on the nature of its business activity. Specifically, we will be considering the following areas:

- wages policy
- responses to change in demand
- wage differentials

In certain cases, however, it is not the organisation that takes steps to react to these external influences, but the government.

WAGES POLICY

The individual **wages policy** within an organisation will attempt to address the following considerations:

- how much will we have to pay in order to **attract** the right kind of staff?
- how much will we have to pay in order to **retain** our staff?
- should we pay our staff **basic pay** only?
- should we pay them by **performance**?
- should we pay them by **piece-rate**?
- what proportion of our total costs are **wages**?
- how should we decide on the **differentials** between different grades of job?
- how should we decide on the level of **pay rises**?
- should we offer any **other monetary rewards**?
- what kind of **fringe benefits** should we offer?
- should we offer employer **contributions to pension schemes**?
- what mechanisms need to be in place to ensure that our pay policy is **consistent** throughout the organisation?

As we have said, the government may attempt to insist upon certain restrictions when an organisation considers its new pay policy. In order to control inflation, the government may consider the restriction of pay settlements as a key objective. Indeed, the government tends to set the basic levels of pay settlements by beginning with its own employees. A low pay settlement in the public sector should signal similarly low pay settlements in the private sector. In recent years, in order to control inflation, the government has favoured extremely low pay increases or no pay increases at all. Unfortunately for the government, it has not chosen to extend this pay settlement restriction to Members of Parliament. This, has caused considerable ill-feeling throughout the country.

A government's wages policy is an integral part of its overall economic strategy. With the increasing closeness of European countries, there have been moves to try to agree pay increases throughout Europe. These moves face a number of basic problems, however, since the differences in pay throughout Europe are enormous. Governments will find it difficult to justify similar pay levels in countries which enjoy different costs of living.

student activity

Why should the pay settlements of public sector employees have any bearing on those of the private sector?

RESPONSES TO CHANGES IN DEMAND

The relationship between the labour market and **demand** is a very close one. Demand will, in effect, dictate the number of individuals in work. Obviously, higher levels of demand will mean that there can be higher levels of employment. As demand drops, however, employment will drop proportionately. Organisations have discovered that demand does not necessarily drop proportionately throughout all industrial sectors. Unemployment levels may therefore differ from sector to sector and cause many problems in relation to **regional unemployment**. This is because the congregation of particular industries in a given geographical location tends to mean that some regions have been hit harder by drops in demand.

An organisation must be able to reduce its costs very quickly if demand decreases. This has led, as we have seen, to changes in the nature of employment: organisations will offer employees limited work opportunities and fixed-term contracts. In this way, organisations can respond quickly to fluctuations in demand for their products or services and adjust the level of their work force accordingly. Although this may be an ideal situation for organisations, it does lead to many problems which require solution on a nation-wide basis. The government has tried to alleviate situations such as this by creating **development areas** to encourage organisations to recruit and retain higher levels of labour. This has worked, to some extent, but only temporarily. Once the area loses its development area or assisted area status, the full force of the market will impact upon the organisation and its workforce.

WAGE DIFFERENTIALS

Obviously, the ability of an organisation to pay high levels of wages depends upon the productivity of its workforce and its ability to sell its products in the market place. There is an enormous disparity between the wage levels paid in different sectors of the economy.

The *New Earnings Survey* (Department of Employment 1991) identified some 10 levels of pay throughout the economy. These are:

- Top tenth – doctors, solicitors and bank managers
- Ninth tenth – accountants, production managers and police officers
- Eighth tenth – scientists, electricians, teachers
- Seventh tenth – sales representatives, librarians
- Sixth tenth – car workers and laboratory technicians
- Fifth tenth – factory workers and debt collectors
- Fourth tenth – secretarial workers, clerks and caretakers
- Third tenth – receptionists and warehouse staff
- Second tenth – cleaners and waiters
- Bottom tenth – kitchen porters, hairdressers and beauticians

This is not a comprehensive list of different classifications of employment. We should also consider the other major method of identifying types of employment. This is the distinction between **manual** and **non-manual** employment. As we have already mentioned in Unit 4, there are further divisions to be considered in relation to socio-economic groups. You will also find additional information about socio-economic groups in the Market Segmentation section of Unit 3. Broadly speaking, a socio-economic classification divides the working population into some six major categories.

Outside all of these classifications, there is a group known as the under-class, which has suffered considerably in the recession. This group includes the following:

- those with no qualifications
- pensioners
- ethnic minorities
- single-parent families

Members of this under-class lack power and the financial independence enjoyed by the majority of individuals in society. According to some agencies, the young who have no formal qualifications may number at least 100,000 individuals. Obviously, wage differentials are totally irrelevant to this under-class, as their income is wholly reliant upon benefits.

ECONOMIC RELATIONSHIPS

When considering the economic relationships which have an effect upon employment, we must return to the notion that the workforce is perhaps the most important factor in production. It is essential for organisations to have a ready supply of potential employees with the correct skills and experience to ensure efficiency of production.

We will be considering the specific economic relationships between **labour** and **demand**. In addition, we will also look at the **supply of labour** itself.

DEMAND FOR LABOUR AND DEMAND FOR THE PRODUCT

Certain employees will only be required when there is a demand for their specific skills and talents. Individuals who have specialist skills and are not flexible in terms of being able to offer alternative skills may find themselves at risk in times when demand decreases. Equally, individuals who have a skill which is in the process of being replaced by technological advance will also find themselves in a difficult position. If there is a decline in the aggregate demand (this is the combined demand for all products and services by consumers) there will be a comparative reduction in the demand for labour. If there is a rise in this aggregate demand, then it follows that unemployment will fall.

The government has the power to control or at least influence the aggregate demand for products or services. In other words, by selecting the correct policy it may actually be able to reduce unemployment. This technique is known as **aggregate demand management**. However, in the light of the present government's wish to reduce the overall amount it spends, use of this policy may not be a viable option. Since recent governments have experienced a deficit between income and expenditure and have had to rely on making high demands on public sector borrowing, there may not be sufficient funds to consider aggregate demand management.

The **individual output** of some employees may be fairly easy to calculate, especially those on production lines. The measurement of performance of an administrator, however, proves to be a much more difficult task. The question of efficiency is important here. Indeed, the organisation may have to make some fairly subjective assessments of the output of each individual. In trying to assess the relative efficiency of each employee, the organisation will attempt to identify key members of staff. This core of employees should largely be untouched by changing levels of employment.

Employment within an organisation is unlikely to remain static. A number of factors may influence the number of workers that an organisation can afford to employ. Increases in wage rates may have to signal the discarding of inefficient members of the workforce. Increasingly, wage rates have been linked to productivity and a simple equation is often used to determine pay increases. If the organisation increases its productivity and its profits by a certain percentage, then the workforce can likewise expect a similar percentage increase in wage.

student activity

If an organisation chose to use an increase in wage rates as a method of discarding inefficient members of the workforce, try to identify the criteria they would use in selecting workers for dismissal or retention.

THE SUPPLY OF LABOUR

The **availability of labour** is, in some respects, restricted by government legislation. If we use the basic premises that it is illegal for those under 16 to work and it is generally accepted that those over 65 will retire, then this leaves the remaining individuals as the real workforce. Those who do not work can be considered to be economically inactive. In other words, they do not contribute to the economy in any way.

The supply of labour is further restricted by the government attempts to increase the school leaving age through encouraging individuals to move into further and higher education. The individual's working life is further shortened by successive governments' attempts to encourage early retirement. Interestingly, these fly in the face of recent government policy to increase women's retirement age to 65 instead of 60. This change will inevitably mean that more women in their early 60s will be actively seeking work in the labour market.

student activity

Assess the impact upon women who have recently discovered that they will have to work an extra five years.

On a personal level, an individual can obviously choose to work or not to work. He or she can also decide exactly how hard he/she wishes to work. Some individuals may consider that maximising their leisure period is desirable, while others will work as many hours as possible. These choices will obviously relate to an individual's personal lifestyle, expenditure and commitments.

As pay increases, more individuals will be enticed into the job market or will show a greater willingness to work longer hours. In other words, as wage rates increase, so too, does the labour supply.

Reductions in income tax may also increase the number of individuals seeking work. Certainly, in some areas, this is true, but other individuals may consider that the reduction in tax merely means that they can work shorter hours. Not all employees, of course, have the option to reduce their working hours as they may be employed on a contract which fixes their hours.

The supply of labour available to specific industries may be affected by the following:

- wage levels offered
- relative wage levels compared to similar industries
- the skills required
- the expertise required
- the general availability of these skills within the labour market
- the length and expense of training for qualifications required

The wage level is usually linked to the employer's perceived value of the skills offered. Specialists or experts can obviously demand higher wages. However, there are many individuals who undertake extremely onerous and vital job roles but are paid extremely low wages. Perhaps job satisfaction remains the sole motivator in these cases. Unfortunately, employers recognise this and will be keen to take advantage of it.

Certain **regional** considerations affect the supply of labour. In other words, the location of the industry affects the availability of appropriate employees. When we consider the geographical mobility of labour, we can see that certain individuals will be more or less willing to relocate or travel considerable distances in order to fill a post. The financial incentives related to relocation must be good enough to recompense the individual for the upheaval. An unemployed individual, who has identified a suitable post in a remote geographical location may find it extremely difficult to make the move.

A final factor to consider in terms of the supply of labour is the industrial immobility of labour. This means that an individual's ability to move from employment in one industrial sector to another is restricted by his or her specialist skills.

student activity

In the role of a job seeker, assess your relative mobility. Try to identify any major reasons which would prevent you from considering relocating in order to take up employment.

Evaluate the workforce performance of business sectors

1 FEATURES OF WORKFORCE PERFORMANCE
wages, benefits, conditions of work, health and safety record, training policy, equal opportunities policy, productivity, specialisation, motivation, redundancy

2 DATA SOURCES
business media, employer and labour organisations, individuals, policies on: training, remuneration, benefits, equal opportunities, health and safety

3 ECONOMIC RELATIONSHIPS
investment in human resources, effects of trades unions and governments on wages, health and safety, training and equal opportunities, effects of foreign investment

FEATURES OF WORKFORCE PERFORMANCE

Assessing the work performance of individuals within an organisation is the role of the personnel department. We have considered the functions of this department in detail in Unit 4. However, a key issue in recent years has been their involvement in **performance appraisal**. There are a number of different ways in which organisations appraise performance. These include:

- performance evaluation
- performance review
- personnel rating
- merit rating
- staff assessment
- staff appraisal

We shall focus on the measurement of individuals' performance in terms of their **personal attributes** and **motivation**. Let us begin by considering personal attributes.

In the recruitment process, an organisation will have taken care to ensure that any individuals chosen as potential employees match a certain standard in terms of **qualities or abilities**. Perhaps they were tested formally. However, it is only when an individual is actually in work that the organisation can monitor and assess these qualities and abilities. Another factor relating to personal attributes is an individual's **preferences** regarding involvement in certain forms of work. Individuals approach different tasks in a variety of different ways, depending upon their interest in undertaking them. Equally, we may use the term preference in relation to an individual's willingness to undertake different types of job roles and working hours. A good organisation will not impose new working conditions on an individual without prior consultation. Within the range of personal attributes we must also consider **attitude**. An employee should always have a positive attitude towards the organisation and the work that he/she does. Unfortunately many jobs do not always live up to the expectations of the employee. In other cases, an individual's attitude to work may be related to perceived job security. The final consideration when we are looking at personal attributes is the question of an individual's **motivation**. This will affect his or her efficiency and willingness to undertake a variety of tasks. The **morale** of the staff is of paramount importance and should be closely monitored by managers. Morale can be measured quite easily by comparing the output of various workers, or, in certain cases, asking the staff to complete anonymous questionnaires.

There are two distinct types of **appraisal system**, which we can call formal and informal systems. Let us look at these in more detail.

Formal systems of appraisal

This form of appraisal has a number of key considerations. These are:

- they tend to be expensive
- administration costs are high
- managers may feel embarrassed
- there is a sense of confrontation
- employees look upon these systems with distrust
- there is a sense that the system may not be objective
- the system is out in the open
- employees are normally told how they will be judged
- employees are usually given the opportunity to rectify any negative assessments

ASSESSMENT SHEET

✔ box appropriate for each assessment area

	CENTRE	DIVISION

VISIT DATE	Above Standard	Acceptable	Below Standard	Unacceptable	REPORT FOR THE MONTH OF (✔)
TIME-	Always on time ☐	Seldom late ☐	Frequently late ☐	Persistently late ☐	JAN ☐
APPEARANCE	Always clean, tidy and well presented ☐	Generally well turned out ☐	Often untidy ☐	Persistently unkempt ☐	FEB ☐ / MAR ☐
ATTITUDE AT WORK	Exceptional attitude and co-operative at all times ☐	Good attitude usually co-operative and helpful ☐	Poor attitude can be unco-operative and unhelpful ☐	Bad attitude Hostile and Aggressive ☐	APR ☐ / MAY ☐
INITIATIVE	Takes correct action without supervision ☐	Usually acts on own ☐	Requires frequent supervision ☐	Requires constant detailed direction ☐	JUN ☐ / JUL ☐
KEENNESS	Very interested and very keen to learn ☐	Reasonably interested and keen ☐	Slight interest not very keen ☐	No interest in learning new skills ☐	AUG ☐ / SEPT ☐
QUALITY OF WORK	Consistently high quality ☐	Good ☐	Fair, room for improvement ☐	Continually makes errors ☐	OCT ☐ / NOV ☐
PROGRESS	Has made exceptional progress ☐	Has made progress ☐	Has made poor progress ☐	Little or no progress ☐	DEC ☐

Apprentice _____

Manager _____

Partner _____

R.M. _____

COMMENTS ON ANY ACTION TAKEN:

Signed _ _ _ _ _ _ _ _ _ _ _ _ (Apprentice)

Signed _ _ _ _ _ _ _ _ _ _ _ _ (Manager)

Date _ _ _ _ _ _ _ _ _ _ _ _

SEND TO THE PERSONNEL MANAGER BY THE END OF EACH MONTH

Kwik-Fit

20

CEN 78A

FIG 5.3.1 *This assessment sheet, used by Kwik-Fit aims to consider the personal characteristics and attitude of the individual. Our example comes from their apprenticeship training programme.*

PERFORMANCE APPRAISAL

GUIDELINES AND PREPARATION DOCUMENT FOR EMPLOYEES

INTRODUCTION

These guidelines have been developed to help you prepare for the Performance Appraisal process and should be used in conjunction with the Appraisal and Training/Development Planning record sheet.

In this document the appraisal process is explained under three main headings:

1. PREPARATION AND TIMING
2. COMPLETION OF RECORD SHEET
3. POST APPRAISAL ACTION.

These issues are discussed more fully below.

1. PREPARATION AND TIMING

Successful performance appraisal preparation is best achieved by:

- reading the guidelines and completing the forms well in advance of the appraisal meeting – the appraisal documentation should be issued to you 7 to 10 days prior to your meeting
- agreeing a date/time with your Manager/Supervisor for the appraisal interview
- contributing to the meeting which should be viewed as a two way exchange of information and ideas.

All appraisals should be completed by the end of January.

2. COMPLETION OF THE APPRAISAL TRAINING/DEVELOPMENT PLANNING RECORD SHEET

The format of this preparation document is very similar to that of the record sheet which covers four major sections:

- achievement of objectives/targets for previous year
- methods of working
- dealing with people
- objectives/targets for next year.

Each of these is explained in more detail overleaf.

FIG 5.3.2 *This Peugeot Talbot performance appraisal form 'Guidelines and Preparation Document for Employees' shows the criteria upon which employees are being appraised.*

Informal appraisal systems

Informal systems of appraisal may have the following features:

- they may be a rather haphazard affair
- there may be no formal feedback procedures
- managers may find it difficult to make constructive criticisms
- criticisms may be misunderstood by the employee
- there is an opportunity to exchange views
- as there is no formal feedback procedure, this means that the manager carrying out the appraisal cannot easily report back to his/her superior

The main purposes of appraisal are:

1 to identify employee weaknesses
2 to identify employee strengths
3 to determine salary increases
4 to determine who deserves promotion
5 to aid the internal communication process within the organisation
6 to determine staff development needs

As we have mentioned, there are a variety of different staff appraisal systems. However, the organisation needs to ensure the following:

- that the management is fully committed to the appraisal system
- that time to carry out the appraisal process is identified and made available
- that the system is not overly complex
- that there is an agreed timetable for the overall implementation of the appraisal system

- that managers receive training in order to carry out their appraisal role
- that employees, as appraisees receive guidance and information to assist them

In designing the appraisal system, the organisation has a number of alternative techniques to choose from. These are:

1 *Merit rating*. In this system, each employee's characteristics are graded on a scale which ranges from outstanding to unacceptable. Each particular characteristic has been identified and may also include some rather subjective characteristics such as attitude and aptitude.

2 *Comparison with objectives*. Having set a series of objectives for the employee, the manager will then compare performance with these identified targets. Obviously, some objectives are fairly easy to measure, but many are open to interpretation.

3 *Behaviourally anchored rating scales*. This technique is basically a complex version of the merit rating system. The manager carrying out the appraisal, in consultation with the personnel department, will consider the job description of each employee, they will then create a list of duties and tasks and agree levels of performance required.

4 *Narrative reports*. This system requires the appraising manager to summarise features of the employee's work. In many respects, this is rather like a school report. It is open to bias and does not take into account the fact that the manager may not necessarily remember all the incidents that occurred over the appraisal period.

5 *Critical incident report*. This is an ongoing system in which the appraising manager is expected to record examples of good or bad work performed by the employee. He/she will then pass on the information to the employee in the course of an appraisal meeting. This should be held as soon after the incident as possible. The system does take considerable amounts of time and may unnecessarily interrupt the smooth running of the department.

It should be noted that the information gathered in the course of an appraisal comes under the Data Inspection Act 1984. The individual being appraised has the right to inspect any information gathered.

Following the appraisal the employee and the appraiser will draw up an action plan which will include all aspects covered in the appraisal interview. This will form the basis of the next appraisal meeting. There will be an opportunity at this meeting for the employee to respond and offer evidence that matters identified in the previous appraisal interview as being unsatisfactory have been rectified.

WAGES

Wages can be used as both a motivator and an indication of workforce performance. Financial incentives should create higher output. As we have mentioned earlier in this Unit, individuals may receive performance-based pay, calculated in various ways in relation to their efforts within the organisation.

The short-term result of using financial incentive schemes to affect employee output is that individuals do work harder. However, incentive schemes may not in the long run create greater productivity. There are, of course, the higher administration costs to be considered in running such a scheme, but many other factors may affect the productivity of the organisation. Where circumstances beyond employees' control have led to reduced productivity, employees may feel aggrieved at their loss of performance-related pay.

Perhaps **individual** bonus schemes and financial incentives are an answer to this problem. If an organisation can identify a method of measuring an individual's performance, then it is more assured of getting the best out of its employees. Organisations will favour such systems as piece work or bonus schemes linked to target achievement.

Performance-related pay was designed to reward short-term achievements and individuals who consistently reached their targets. Individuals who were considered to be only satisfactory in terms of their performance would receive only a basic pay increase. The higher-performing managers would receive much higher levels of pay increase. In order to run this system in a fair and consistent manner the organisation must ensure that a review system is in place. This must monitor such factors as favouritism and other subjective criteria.

student activity

If financial incentives are proven to increase productivity, then why is it that many employers frown upon this kind of scheme? What other methods of increasing productivity could be used instead of financial incentives?

BENEFITS AND CONDITIONS OF WORK

Perhaps the best way for an organisation to ensure that employees derive the most tangible **benefits** and enhanced **conditions of work** is for it to consider the various methods of managing the **work process** itself. There have been a number of different attempts to design systems which allow an individual within the work situation to enjoy better conditions of employment. We shall have a look at these in some detail:

Job rotation

Many individuals suffer from boredom as a result of having to do repetitive and simple tasks. Under this system, individuals are trained to obtain the skills required in order to carry out many **different tasks**. This will give them a vital variety of different work experiences. Two points of caution should be noted here: firstly, an organisation must take care not to rotate staff too often as inefficiency will be a net result; secondly, an individual who moves from one comparatively boring job to another will, in no way, be more motivated.

student activity

Referring back to the job roles covered in the previous Unit, design a job rotation system for the administration department.

Job Enlargement

Particularly on a production line, an employee will be expected to undertake a series of **highly repetitive tasks**. Not only will they be repetitive, but individually they will take only a short period of time each. An assembly line worker who is simply riveting a front door panel on a car every four minutes will not be receiving a great deal of job satisfaction. Job enlargement means that this individual will be given a greater variety of tasks to perform in the production process. In our example, the riveter would be able to rivet the rear door panels too! Other organisations have taken the job enlargement system to its logical conclusion. They have replaced individual employees carrying out repetitive tasks on the production line altogether by robots. The employees now maintain the robots and carry out a wide variety of other duties.

student activity

How would you 'enlarge' the job of an invoice clerk?

Group work

Extending the job enlargement programme even further, organisations have created **groups of workers** who complete a whole task. The group will be responsible for all aspects of the production process and will, in effect, turn raw materials into finished goods.

A further variation on this technique is to allow groups of workers to operate autonomously. They agree between themselves how, when and by whom certain tasks within the production process are to be carried out. There is a supervisor involved, but this person is really considered to be a problem solver and a communicator with the rest of the organisation.

student activity

How would group work help in the running of an administration department?

Job enrichment

Following the theories of Herzberg, a **job enrichment** programme aims to provide for the employee's full psychological development. There is a notion here of 'stretching' the employee and making him/her develop skills in a variety of different areas. This challenge is intended to increase the motivation of the individual.

HEALTH AND SAFETY RECORD

As we have seen earlier in this Unit, organisations are required to undertake many procedures in order to ensure that their employees' working conditions are both **healthy and safe**. Careful monitoring of the health and safety record by the organisation will give some indications as to the effectiveness of its procedures. An organisation with a poor health and safety record is likely to have some inconsistencies in its health and safety training programmes. Measuring health and safety records against work performance can show some levels of efficiency or relative inefficiency. One could state that a poor health and safety record indicates a poor workforce performance. Conversely, a good health and safety record may be an indicator of efficient working practices.

student activity

How would an engineering company measure its health and safety record? By the number of lost fingers? Would the health and safety record really be a clear indicator of the performance of the company?

TRAINING POLICY

Workforce performance should not be considered to be solely the responsibility of the employee. The employer may have a positive impact upon workforce performance in other ways than simply by offering financial incentives. By implementing a comprehensive and well-structured **training programme**, the employer will be able to identify and rectify shortcomings in the skills and qualifications of the workforce. Although this may be an expensive method of increasing workforce performance, an organisation which takes a longer view will be able to count on increased productivity and greater staff loyalty and motivation in the future.

student activity

Should training really be used as an incentive to workers? How might the training programme reflect the corporate policy?

EQUAL OPPORTUNITIES POLICY

The **equal opportunities policy** of an organisation will be created to ensure that regardless of the gender, age, sexual orientation, race, colour or religion of an employee he/she is not precluded from advancement within the organisation. While a great many equal opportunities aspects are covered under various pieces of government legislation, there are still many instances of discrimination on one ground or another. In terms of workforce performance, and assuming that there are no discriminatory practices prevalent in the organisation, all individuals should be in a position to progress as far as their natural abilities will take them. Equally, the policy should also include clear statements as to the make-up of the workforce in general and allow for the inclusion of all minorities at every level of the organisation. Many organisations ensure that all their communications with the public, including advertisements of posts within the organisation, include a short line which states that the organisation is an equal opportunities employer.

PRODUCTIVITY

For most organisations, faced with a bewildering selection of workforce performance measurement techniques, the bottom line is impact upon **productivity**. While wishing to satisfy its employees' needs, an organisation must be aware of its own organisational objectives. If the working conditions of employees are changed, then these alterations must also be beneficial to the organisation. Organisations will accept short-term productivity losses but will expect considerable improvements once the new working systems have become established.

SPECIALISATION

An alternative method of ensuring that workforce performance increases is to encourage the **specialisation** of the workforce. This will entail the detailed training and development of individuals who perform specific tasks. It is hoped that, through specialisation, the organisation will enjoy greater levels of productivity while, at the same time, employees will be much more motivated. Specialist knowledge in a particular area provides the individual with a larger degree of independence and should make him/her far more efficient.

MOTIVATION

Just as the way in which an organisation may choose to manipulate the working conditions and practices of individuals within the organisation may improve employees' **motivation**, an individual may derive inherent job satisfaction from the successful completion of tasks. We can consider this to be something of a cycle. The employer reorganises the working conditions and practices of the individual, who, in turn, is more motivated. This motivation is transformed into higher work performance, for which, in turn, the employer rewards the individual. The reward serves as a further motivator which increases productivity yet more. Obviously this cycle can be easily broken by either the employer or the employee not responding to a stimulus from the other. Some individuals may be motivated purely by being able to perform better. They may gain satisfaction in this way from the job itself.

REDUNDANCY

If all attempts to motivate workers and increase workforce performance fails, an organisation has one final recourse. It may have no alternative but to make individuals **redundant**. Organisations should take care to ensure that the selection of individuals for redundancy does not breach any current legislation. Alternatively, an individual may choose redundancy rather than accept changes in working conditions, or what he or she sees as unwarranted work performance demands from the employer.

By opting for redundancy an employee may receive, in addition to a standard redundancy payment, 'enhancement', in the form of extra payments. The organisation may be perfectly prepared to pay these enhancements as it may have had no alternative but to remove the individual.

DATA SOURCES

Businesses are able to obtain a variety of information regarding workforce performance from a number of organisations. As we mentioned in Unit 1, the forms of information sources will vary according to the type of information required. In addition, the nature of the information they require will be dependent upon the particular aspect of the workforce performance that they are analysing. In order to obtain relevant information organisations may seek assistance from the following sources.

BUSINESS MEDIA

Several organisations provide a wide range of quantitative information regarding the comparative output of various organisations. This information is extremely useful in assessing the comparative performance between similar organisations in the same industrial sector. A full list of useful business media may be found in Unit 1.

EMPLOYER AND LABOUR ORGANISATIONS

Similarly, the CBI, industrial employers' organisations and trades unions compile information regarding productivity and workforce performance in all areas across industrial sectors. This information, although UK wide in its coverage, provides a good indicator as to the relative success or failure of businesses. This is particularly useful when an organisation wishes to consider comparative productivity or performance against foreign competition.

student activity

Obviously, the CBI and the TUC have radically different views on productivity and performance. Try to identify their relative stances on these two issues.

INDIVIDUALS

Management consultants or specialists may offer either quantitative or qualitative assessments of industrial sectors based on their knowledge and experience. Organisations tend to regard these consultants as being privy to useful insights which may enable them to obtain a competitive edge in the market place.

POLICIES ON TRAINING, REMUNERATION, BENEFITS, EQUAL OPPORTUNITIES AND HEALTH AND SAFETY

Organisations will formulate their policies on many different issues in line with government policies and in later years, the EC's Directives. In essence these will form part of the organisation's corporate plan and some may be key objectives within that plan. As we have mentioned, organisations will attempt to adhere to legislation as closely as possible and perhaps offer additional ranges of benefits and schemes to their employees. These will obviously be linked to work performance and productivity and in times of recession they are often the first casualties. An organisation which is suffering in poor market conditions will be tempted to cut corners and take considerable risks. In addition to the shedding of jobs the organisation may wish to make cost-cutting exercises which impact upon its declared policies.

ECONOMIC RELATIONSHIPS

As you will by now be aware, it is impossible to consider any element in the economy in isolation. The government will involve itself at almost every stage of the economic activity of the nation. It will be particularly concerned with the manipulation of employment related issues and the availability and appropriateness of human resources. Since we have already established that human resources are indeed the most important factor in the production process, then this resource needs further support from both government and business organisations.

INVESTMENT IN HUMAN RESOURCES

Through education and training the government strives to ensure that all industrial sectors are provided with the necessary raw human resources to carry out all necessary business activities. By creating a comprehensive educational system with all necessary back-up provisions, the government attempts to match employers' needs. In many cases, decisions are made with reference to employers' organisations. It is for this reason that in recent years the further education market has expanded to provide both vocational and non-vocational programmes of study to match changes in the employment market.

Organisations will also expend considerable sums of money in the provision of training and development facilities for their employees. We have considered these aspects in further detail in Unit 4.

Both government and organisations see a direct relationship between investment in human resources and improved productivity and performance. It is for this reason that both are keen to encourage training and development. The government has sought in recent years to manipulate the availability of courses which do not match the immediate requirements of the industrial sectors. Some people have found it impossible to obtain places on courses which are not currently favoured by the government in terms of their 'pay back' potential. Courses which have suffered in the main have been the Arts and Social Sciences. The government recognises the need to encourage individuals to train and develop within the areas of Science, Languages and Engineering in particular.

student activity

Why has the government identified these study areas as being particularly important?

EFFECTS OF TRADES UNIONS AND GOVERNMENTS ON WAGES, HEALTH AND SAFETY, TRAINING AND EQUAL OPPORTUNITIES

The government has a far more obvious and direct impact upon a number of issues relating to employment and workforce performance. It is keen to encourage organisations to link many of these related issues directly to performance and productivity Trades unions, however, despite the reduction in their power, have sought to maintain a balance. Trades unions consider that individuals should receive a fair day's pay for a fair day's work. Organisations, on the other hand, may not use the same criteria. The assessment of a fair day's work is very subjective. Some of the methods used to evaluate workforce performance already mentioned in this element try to put some kind of quantifiable measure on these issues. Trades unions are not wholly convinced.

EFFECTS OF FOREIGN INVESTMENT

When considering the effects of foreign investment and workforce performance we must to begin with refer to the concept of 'Japanisation'. Japan has enjoyed, until relatively recently, a consistent economic success. Its annual rate of economic growth has far exceeded those of the rest of the western world. It has succeeded in holding down prices while increasing productivity. Japan's GDP is three times greater than that of the UK with a population only twice the size of the UK.

Many different individuals, governments and agencies have investigated the cause of this amazing level of success. They have identified a number of key points. These are:

- the Japanese respect for authority
- the relative unimportance of the individual compared to the group
- Japan's cultural cohesiveness
- the Japanese feelings of duty
- the Japanese education system
- Japanese loyalty to companies
- national pride
- desire to maintain their reputation
- employees' willingness to compromise

If the Japanese are so successful in their home market, then why have they decided to establish a number of production units in Europe and particularly the UK? The Japanese chose Britain in particular of the following reasons:

- the use of the English language
- the availability of a high quality workforce
- stable government
- relatively stable economy
- comparatively low wage costs
- a well developed infrastructure
- government incentives
- comparatively good labour relations

The Japanisation of UK industry has been effective as Japanese organisations tend to adopt the following criteria:

- their organisations are innovative
- they are growth orientated
- they are prepared to introduce new products at early stages of their development
- they are receptive to change
- they favour group decision making
- they have excellent communication systems
- they are essentially community organisations

Employees who have joined Japanese organisations enjoy the concept of **lifetime employment**. They receive a number of **benefits** which include comprehensive training and personal development prospects.

From the government's point of view, Japanese investment in particular has been greatly welcomed. It came at a time when UK industry was unable to invest any significant sums of money in developing new industrial processes. The benefits which have accrued from these Japanese organisations establishing themselves in the UK have been massive cash injections into the economy, the building up of the infrastructure and the providing of employment in unemployment black spots throughout the UK.

student activity

Try to identify an organisation in your area that has been 'Japanised'. What are the features of this organisation that make it different?

UNIT 5

assignment

'BUSINESS SECTORS, EMPLOYMENT AND PERFORMANCE'

In order to fulfil the criteria of this Unit, you will have to investigate the various business sectors, how external factors affect employment and the measurement of work performance. The focus is, however, on employment, and to this end, you will be able to follow your study of two business sectors throughout the whole Unit Assignment.

Your first task, in consultation with your tutor, is to select two different business sectors. You should choose these carefully as you will be expected to collect data from both the UK and the EC.

Having chosen your two business sectors, you should concentrate on researching the following areas:

1 present employment levels

2 external influences relating to employment in these sectors
3 how economic factors influence decision making within these business sectors
4 methods of assessing workforce performance

You should use as wide a variety of different research methods and sources as possible in your efforts to obtain as much data as possible on your two chosen business sectors.

You should present your findings in the following forms:

1 a full word processed report
2 a series of posters which identify key features of your research
3 an oral presentation supported by appropriate illustrative material

UNIT 5

test questions

I Which of the following is deducted from a worker's pay at source?

(a) VAT
(b) Corporation tax
(c) NI
(d) Supplementary benefit

2 Which of the following cannot be considered to be a fringe benefit?

(a) Overtime payments
(b) Company discount
(c) Company car
(d) Staff uniforms

3 What do regional assistance grants aim to do?

(a) Offer incentives to the unemployed to relocate
(b) Provide finance for the region to advertise on television for companies to relocate
(c) Give financial assistance to organisations wishing to set up in the area
(d) Increase the level of unemployment benefit in that region

4 Which of the following is least likely to mean an increase in wages for employees working in the manufacture of fridges?

(a) Increased productivity
(b) Increased demand
(c) Minimum wage legislation
(d) Greater training opportunities

5 If an individual only works during the summer period and is unemployed for the rest of the year what is this known as?

(a) Structural unemployment
(b) Unfortunate unemployment
(c) Regional unemployment
(d) Seasonal unemployment

6 What is off-the-job training?

(a) Undertaking training while unemployed
(b) Attending training courses during your lunch hour
(c) Attending training at your work placement
(d) Attending training related to work but not on the premises

7 What is a subsidy?

(a) A payment made by government to support an industrial sector
(b) A wages policy
(c) A form of industrial relations
(d) A contractual obligation

8 Which of the following is not a feature of work performance?

(a) Health and safety record
(b) Wage differentials
(c) Motivation
(d) Redundancy

9 What is remuneration?

(a) Demand for a product or service
(b) An equal opportunities consideration
(c) Pay and wages
(d) Technological development

10 What are wage differentials?

(a) Earning different amounts each month
(b) Being able to receive wages in cash or by credit transfer
(c) The changes in pay over the past few years
(d) Differences in earnings for doing the same work

ELEMENT 6.1

Explain financial transactions and supporting documents

1 PURPOSES
monitoring performance, recording purchases and sales, generating accounts, meeting legal requirements

2 PURCHASES DOCUMENTS
orders placed, goods received note, purchase invoice

3 SALES DOCUMENTS
orders received, delivery note, sales invoice, statement of account

4 PAYMENTS DOCUMENTS
pay slip, cheque, petty cash voucher

5 RECEIPTS DOCUMENTS
receipt, cheque, paying-in slip, bank statement

6 SECURITY
authorisation of orders, invoice against orders and goods received notes, authorised cheque signatories

ABOUT THIS UNIT

Element 6.1 and Element 6.2 have been combined in the following section. As you can see from each element's 'range' headings, listed above and in the tinted box on page 246, both elements do have a number of themes in common.

Taking the range of Element 6.1 as its specific heading this first part of Unit 6 ensures that all the performance criteria and the full range of both Elements

6.1 and 6.2 are covered. The information and documentation provided will enable students to produce the necessary evidence for both units:

- clear explanation of the purposes and use of financial transaction documents regularly used in business
- the production of a set of clearly and accurately completed financial documents
- understanding of the need for clarity and accuracy in documentation

ELEMENT 6.2

Complete documents for financial transactions

1 PURCHASES DOCUMENTS
orders placed, goods received note, purchase invoice

2 SALES DOCUMENTS
orders received, delivery note, sales invoice, statement of account

3 PAYMENT DOCUMENTS
pay slip, cheque, petty cash voucher

4 RECEIPTS DOCUMENTS
receipt, cheque, paying-in slip

5 REASONS FOR CORRECT COMPLETION
accuracy, reliability of data, consequences of error

6 CONSEQUENCES OF INCORRECT COMPLETION
incorrect purchases, incorrect sales, incorrect payments, incorrect receipts, incorrect accounts, wrong information about business performance

PURPOSES

MONITORING BUSINESS PERFORMANCE

Financial information is essential to all organisations in order that they can review their own performance. It is necessary to keep information up to date and accessible for the following reasons:

1 for the **planning** and **control** of the organisation's activities
2 in order to keep **shareholders** informed of the organisation's performance
3 to ensure that **creditors** are aware of the perform-
ance of the organisation
4 so that the government legislation is adhered to
5 for prospective investors who may wish to become involved with the organisation.

The only way that an organisation can monitor its business performance is to obtain information and feedback. This information can be placed into two categories:

- *Quantitative* – this is a precise measurement of what has been achieved. It may be a percentage – for example, the organisation has achieved 45 per cent of the market share in a certain area.

- *Qualitative* – this is not so precise. It takes the form of opinions stated when an organisation receives feedback from customers or clients when carrying out market research.

We have mentioned organisations' **'goals'** and **'objectives'** earlier in the book. Organisations would use this quantitative and qualitative information to indicate whether they have achieved these aims, or whether they have to change their plan of action in order to achieve them.

student activity

Using the information given above, write a list of the reasons an organisation would need to monitor financial performance.

Obviously, the information an organisation requires would not be restricted to one particular area. The information would be needed from as many areas as possible. It would also be vital that this information is accurate – false or misleading information could lead to a series of wrong decisions, which, in turn, would lead to the organisation achieving poor performance.

Different managers within the organisation would deal with different information in order to monitor the business performance of their particular area of work. For example, we may consider the areas of **strategy** and **tactics**, which we have mentioned before.

- managers dealing with **'strategy'** would make policy decisions regarding the future of the organisation. They would need precise information from all areas of the organisation. They would also need information from competitors and customers of the organisation in order to compare their performance with those of others.
- managers dealing with **'tactics'** would need information from the 'strategy' managers. They would deal mainly with information from inside the organisation and would try to ensure that deadlines are adhered to and met
- other managers would need information from both 'strategy' and 'tactics' managers. This would enable them to ensure that the day-to-day running of the organisation is smooth and trouble-free. Any problems they deal with would be short-term operational ones.

So, in order to monitor business performance effectively, an organisation needs to produce reliable, accurate and informative material which can be used by a series of personnel. How, then, do they achieve this? Firstly, they need to record all purchases and sales generated by the organisation.

RECORDING PURCHASES AND SALES

We look in more detail at the actual documents used for these transactions later in this unit. But what is the purpose of such documents?

All organisations will have a budget. Whether the organisation is large or small, it will have an objective which it must try to meet. It would be impossible for managers to monitor the performance of an organisation if documents relating to the amount of money spent and the amount of money coming into the organisation were not readily available and accurate.

Obviously, the larger the organisation, the more documentation it will generate. In addition to this, a larger organisation is more likely to purchase goods on a credit basis. This means that it will order and receive goods when the need arises, and pay for them on a monthly basis. Such an organisation is likely to generate its documents by computer software packages, although it is not unusual for an organisation to still be handling transactions manually.

In the same way, an organisation sells its products to customers or clients on a credit basis, and receives payment for them on a monthly basis.

Because so many transactions are dealt with in this way, mistakes such as the following could easily occur unless the organisation records all transactions:

- goods being sent to the wrong customer
- incorrect goods being despatched to a customer
- delay in payments for goods
- complaints being received from customers
- loss of business because of confusion with customers

The activities of different organisations vary, although all organisations use the business documents they generate to plan and control the way the organisation performs. The documentation may relate to the day-to-day work of a small number of workers, or it may relate to a specific job of the production line.

Whatever the activity, the accounts department would need to be fully aware of the financial transactions taking place within the organisation. Because so much credit business is conducted nowadays, the accounting team need copies of each document received or sent out of the organisation in order that they can generate the accounts of the business.

GENERATING ACCOUNTS

Staff of the accounts department meticulously record in **Ledgers** all the financial transactions of the organisation. This process of using Ledgers to record is known as **Double Entry Bookkeeping**. The following would be used by most organisations:

1 *The sales ledger*. All goods or services sold by the organisation will be listed in the **sales ledger**. These customers are **debtors** of the organisation until they pay for the goods or services received.

2 *The purchases ledger*. All goods or services bought by the organisation will be listed in the **purchases ledger**. The organisation will remain a **creditor** of these businesses until it pays for the goods or services received

3 *The cash book*. receipts and payments of both cash and cheques are recorded in the **cash book**.

4 *The general ledger*. Items such as expenses, assets and liabilities are recorded in the **general ledger.**

In addition to the purchases and sales, the Accounts Department would also need to record information regarding the following:

- bank transactions
- timesheets and clock cards
- wages and salaries
- tax and insurance details of staff
- petty cash transactions

Much more information about these ledgers and other accounting procedures is given later in this unit.

The accounts department records this information not only in order to provide details of the transactions for the benefit of monitoring business performance, but also to meet legal requirements laid down by government legislation.

MEETING LEGAL REQUIREMENTS

An enormous amount of government legislation has been passed to determine the way organisations operate. This can vary from the way food is handled in a food production organisation, to laws governing the health and safety of office workers.

In order to ensure that they comply with these legal requirements, larger organisations employ specialists to keep up to date on such laws. These specialists make sure that they familiarise themselves with all existing legislation and pass this information on to all members of the organisation.

Whatever the size or type of organisation, laws can influence the way it operates. Laws governing business organisations in this country fall into two main areas:

- **common law** – these laws tend to be historic. They could have been in place for many years, although it may not be clear where they originated. Common law can determine, for example, that land or pathways belong to the public, and therefore they cannot be taken over or built on by anyone

- **statutory law** – these laws can be very complicated, and come about as a result of Acts of Parliament. An example of a statutory law is the Health and Safety at Work Act of 1974. These laws are passed to ensure that organisations and employees adhere to certain restrictions. They can be updated should they become out of date, but a new law needs to be passed in order to do this.

In recent years, the existence of EC law has meant that organisations within the UK have with comply to additional legislation.

Details of UK and EC legislation governing the way an organisation operates are given in other units of this book.

PURCHASES DOCUMENTS

All organisations need to buy raw materials and services in order to produce or provide their own goods and services. These materials and services may take several forms – raw materials needed on their production line, the services of specialists, e.g. cleaners or consultants. In order to obtain these materials or services, the organisation will have to complete a series of purchase documents requesting them. It may help you here to refresh your memory concerning the types of goods or services an organisation may require:

1 *Materials*. These can take several forms. They may be raw materials, which the organisation will need to produce its products. They may, however, be things like headed paper needed to produce letters from the organisation, or cleaning products to assist in the sanitation of the production lines. These types of product are known as consumables, and they are all ordered on an **Order Form**.

2 *Components*. Examples are furniture, new computer equipment, new buildings etc. These are dealt with in a different way from materials, and a special purchasing system will be in effect within an organisation to deal with these purchases.

3 *Services*. In order to purchase a service from an individual or another organisation, it would be necessary to complete a **contract**. The organisation raising the

contract would state clearly the terms of the contract, and this would be signed by a representative of the organisation, plus the person providing the service. This contract would be legally binding on both sides.

The **purchasing department** would be responsible for buying materials or services for the organisation. This involves the completion of a series of documents. Before we look at these documents in detail, there are a number of terms you may find it helpful to revise:

1 *Trade discount.* This discount is given to an organisation because it is placing a large order. It may also be given if the organisation buys goods on a regular basis from the same company, or if that company is in the same field as the organisation itself.
2 *Prompt payment discount.* This discount is given to an organisation if it pays its bill on time. The term – 5 per cent one month – means that the organisation can deduct 5 per cent from its bill if it pays within one month of receiving the goods ordered.
3 *Cash discount.* This discount is given if the organisation pays its bill immediately. The term – $2^{1}/_{2}$ per cent cash discount – means that the organisation can deduct $2^{1}/_{2}$ per cent from its bill if it pays by cash or by cheque immediately the goods are received.

The following are the common forms of document that an organisation uses before purchasing goods or services:

1 *Letter of Enquiry.* This will be sent to several companies which sell the goods or services required by the organisation. It will help the purchaser find out information before placing an order. This information will include the following:

- price details
- details about the goods
- delivery dates and times
- discounts available

student activity

Using the format given in Figure 6.1.1, write a letter of enquiry to a supplier requesting five typists' chairs.

2 *Quotation.* This will state the price of the goods required, the expected date of delivery and any discounts the company may offer. The organisation will then choose the company with the best price, terms and delivery times.

student activity

Looking at the example of a quotation given in Figure 6.1.2, why do you think all the different sections are necessary? What does each one mean?

3 *Estimate* As with a quotation, the organisation may ask several companies to offer **estimates** to carry out a piece of work. This is not as accurate as a quotation, but again the organisation would choose the company offering the best deal.
4 *Tender.* An organisation may put a piece of work, or a service, out to **tender**. This means that any company interested in doing the work will 'offer' to do the job for a price. There will be a closing date for tenders to arrive with the organisation, and on that date all tenders will be opened. Again, the organisation will choose the company offering the best deal.

Many companies issue **catalogues** of the goods, products or services they provide. Purchasing Departments would keep stocks of these catalogues, and would need to update them when new price lists are issued.

Once the purchasing department has decided which company they intend to order their goods from, they will issue an order form to that company:

student activity

Look at the three completed quotation forms in Figures 6.1.3, .6.1.4 and 6.1.5. If you had sent letters of enquiry and received these three quotations, which one would you choose and why?

ORDERS PLACED

Order form

These are always numbered and dated. This ensures that they can be traced easily should discrepancies occur during the buying process. The distribution of an **order form** is as follows:

- the top copy will go to the supplier of the goods
- one copy will be kept by the purchasing department for its records
- one will be needed to check the goods when received to ensure the order is complete and accurate
- one will be sent to the accounts department so that it can pay for the goods when received

Our Ref JT/DEC/JS

25 January 199-

Office Equipment Centre
114 Middle Road
Tottenham
LONDON
NR31 6AW

Dear Sirs

We are interested in purchasing two office desks in pine finish.
We would prefer a three-drawer model, with the drawers on the
left of the desk. In addition, we are interested in an office
chair in black with arm rests.

Would you kindly let us have your quotation for supplying these
goods and include details of your terms and delivery dates.

Yours faithfully

J Sutherland
Chief Buyer

FIG 6.1.1 *An example of a letter of enquiry.*

QUOTATION

REFERENCE NUMBER   DATE

TO

In reply to your enquiry dated _____

We have pleasure in quoting you for the following:

Prices include delivery by:

Delivery:

Trade Discount:

Cash Discount:

VAT: Value Added Tax at   % must be added to the price
       quoted.

FIG 6.1.2 *An example of a blank quotation form.*

QUOTATION

REFERENCE NUMBER   1124   DATE   30 Jan 19..

TO

    Smith and Sons
    47 Rosamoss Lane
    Wisbech
    Cambs.

In reply to your enquiry dated __25 JANUARY 199.__

We have pleasure in quoting you for the following:

    2 PINE   DESKS @ £171.00 EACH   TOTAL £342.00

    1 CHAIR
    @ £170.00 EACH   TOTAL £170.00

Prices include delivery by: COMPANY VAN

Delivery: 3 weeks

Trade Discount: 1.5%

Cash Discount: 2.5%

VAT: Value Added Tax at 17.5% must be added to the price
      quoted.

FIG 6.1.3 *Completed quotation form (1).*

QUOTATION

REFERENCE NUMBER 411   DATE   27 Jan 19..

TO

    Smith and Sons
    47 Rosamoss Lane
    Wisbech
    Cambs.

In reply to your enquiry dated   25 JANUARY 199.

We have pleasure in quoting you for the following:

2 PINE 3-DRAWER LEFT HAND DESKS
@ £175.00 EACH   TOTAL £350.00

1 OFFICE CHAIR WITH ARM-RESTS
@ £173.50 EACH   TOTAL £173.50

Prices include delivery by: COMPANY VAN

Delivery: IMMEDIATE

Trade Discount: 2.5%

Cash Discount: 2.5%

VAT: Value Added Tax at 17.5% must be added to the price
     quoted.

FIG 6.1.4 *Completed quotation form (2).*

QUOTATION

REFERENCE NUMBER 5731   DATE   2 Feb. 19..

TO

Smith and Sons
47 Rosamoss Lane
Wisbech
Cambs.

In reply to your enquiry dated   25 JANUARY 199.

We have pleasure in quoting you for the following:

2 PINE 3-DRAWER LEFT HAND DESKS
@ £173.00 EACH   TOTAL £346.00

1 OFFICE CHAIR WITH ARM-RESTS
@ £170.00 EACH   TOTAL £170.00

Prices include delivery by: COMPANY VAN

Delivery: 6 weeks

Trade Discount: 1.5%

Cash Discount: 1.5%

VAT: Value Added Tax at 17.5% must be added to the price
      quoted.

FIG 6.1.5 *Completed quotation form(3).*

ORDER FORM

| TO | ORDER NUMBER |
| | DATE |

| DELIVERY ADDRESS | SPECIAL INSTRUCTIONS |

REF NO	QUANTITY	DESCRIPTION	UNIT PRICE	AMOUNT

ORDER AUTHORISED BY: ....

FIG 6.1.6 *An example of a blank order form.*

Advice note

This is sent by the seller to the purchaser before the goods are to be despatched. It informs the purchaser that the goods are on their way and ensures that any delay is noticed immediately.

Delivery note

This is sent with the goods and lists the items that have been despatched. The purchaser will check this to ensure all goods have arrived.

GOODS RECEIVED NOTE

This document is used internally within an organisation to inform the department requesting the goods of their arrival. The distribution for a **goods received note** is as follows:

- one copy to the department ordering the goods
- one copy to the accounts department

During the purchasing process, it could be that any of the following may occur:

- *missing goods* – when the goods received do not tally with the original order for some reason
- *additional goods* – when goods extra to those ordered are received
- *incorrect goods* – when goods different to those ordered are received
- *damaged or faulty goods* – which makes it essential that goods received are checked before signing for them

PURCHASE INVOICE

Once the goods have been delivered to the purchaser, the seller will send a copy of the **purchase invoice**. This invoice will list the quantity and description of the goods sent, as well as the total price owing. The invoice will also state a time by which the payment should be made, and will list any discounts made available to the buyer. The organisation buying the goods will check the **invoice** against the **order form** and the **goods received note** to ensure that they all tally. It will check for the following:

1 the order number is correct
2 the goods listed match those delivered
3 the quantity listed matches that delivered
4 the price listed matches that quoted
5 the calculations are correct
6 the discounts are as agreed
7 the 'carriage' – this will show how the transport of the goods should be paid for. 'Carriage paid' means that the seller is covering the cost of transportation. 'Carriage forward' means it is the buyer who should pay
8 the VAT – if the goods are subject to VAT then this will be added to the total cost of the invoice

All invoices contain the letters E & O E at the bottom of them. This stands for 'errors and omissions excepted' and helps to ensure that the supplier can send a further invoice if a mistake is found. Most organisations show their VAT number on the invoices they issue.

Supplementary invoice

If items have been delivered, but have been omitted from the invoice, the supplier will send a **supplementary invoice** to cover the difference. A supplementary invoice will also be sent if the customer has been undercharged for some reason.

Credit note

The supplier must issue the purchaser with a **credit note** if he/she has listed items on the invoice by mistake (i.e. goods not sent), meaning that the invoice total is too high, or when any faulty goods have been returned. A credit note will **decrease** the price on the invoice.

GOODS RECEIVED NOTE

NO	DATE RECEIVED	ORDER NO	DELIVERED BY
QUANTITY	DESCRIPTION	NUMBER OF PACKAGES	STORES REF

RECEIVED FROM	ENTERED INTO STOCK		RECEIVED BY
	DATE	INITIAL	
SUPPLIER			STOREKEEPER

FIG 6.1.7 *An example of a goods received note.*

INVOICE

TO				NUMBER	
				DATE	
				TERMS	
YOUR ORDER NO				DESPATCH DATE	

QUANTITY	DESCRIPTION	UNIT PRICE	TOTAL PRICE	VAT
	Gross Value			
	LESS Trade Discount			
	Net Value of Goods			
	PLUS VAT @ %			
	INVOICE TOTAL			

E & O E

FIG 6.1.8 *An example of an invoice.*

CREDIT NOTE

TO   NUMBER

                                            DATE

ORDER NUMBER   INVOICE NUMBER

QUANTITY	DESCRIPTION	UNIT PRICE	TOTAL PRICE	VAT
	Gross Value of Goods			
	LESS Trade Discount			
	Net Value of Goods			
	PLUS VAT @ %			
	CREDIT NOTE TOTAL			

FIG 6.1.9 *An example of a credit note.*

STATEMENT

TO

DATE

NUMBER

TERMS

DATE	DETAILS	DEBIT	VAT	CREDIT	VAT	BALANCE

PAYMENTS RECEIVED AFTER THE END OF THE MONTH WILL NOT BE SHOWN ON THIS STATEMENT.

FIG 6.1.10 *An example of a statement of account.*

student activity

Using the example of a blank credit note in Figure 6.1.9, why do you think each of the headings is needed and to what use will they be put?

Debit note

This will **increase** the price on the invoice. It may be issued when there has been a mistake on the original invoice, or when goods have been sent in error (i.e. too many sent).

Statement of account

Each month the purchaser will receive a **Statement of Account** from the seller. It will list all transactions that have taken place during the month and will have two columns – the debit column and the credit column. The debit column shows the purchases that have been made. The credit column shows the payments that have been made.

student activity

Using the example of a blank statement of account in Figure 6.1.10, why do you think each of the headings is necessary and to what use will they be put?

SALES DOCUMENTS

The size of a sales department will depend on the size of the organisation and the type of industry it is involved in. The main objective of any sales department is to generate sales for the organisation and to record the transactions in a reliable and accurate way. As we have mentioned earlier, the sales team may work on a regional or area basis, and the information and documentation generated by them may be used by one central department.

THE SELLING PROCESS

It may be that the organisation has received a **letter of enquiry** from a prospective customer. The sales department would have replied to this by sending either a **quotation** or a **catalogue and price list** to that customer. As a result of this initial enquiry, the organisation might receive a firm **order** from the customer.

ORDERS RECEIVED

The completion of an **order form** by a customer is a legally binding contract that he/she wishes to purchase the goods from the organisation. It is normal for the order to be on credit terms for the customer. In such cases it would be necessary for the sales department to send a copy of the order to the credit control department of their organisation.

It is essential for any organisation to **control the credit** allowed to customers or prospective customers. It would greatly endanger the performance of an organisation if bills were not paid promptly and serious problems regarding the company's **cash flow** could result. When a new customer applies for goods on credit, the organisation may contact a bank for a **reference**. Alternatively, it may apply for a **trade reference'** from an existing supplier of goods to the customer. Once the creditworthiness of the customer is verified, the sales department will generate the following documentation:

ADVICE NOTE

This would be issued to the customer either shortly before the goods are despatched, or as they are being sent. This informs the customer of the expected date and time of delivery, as well as the method by which they are being sent.

DELIVERY NOTE

This is sent with the goods and describes the content of the parcels/packages being delivered. A signature by the customer is usually necessary as acknowledgement that he/she has received the goods.

student activity

Look at the example of a delivery note given in Figure 6.1.11. Why do you think each of the headings is necessary and to what use will they be put?

DELIVERY NOTE

TO

NUMBER

YOUR ORDER NUMBER

DATE

THE FOLLOWING ITEMS HAVE BEEN DESPATCHED TODAY TO _____

_____ BY RAIL/COMPANY VAN/POST*

QUANTITY	DESCRIPTION	NUMBER OF PACKAGES

I certify that the goods received have been checked and are in good condition

Signed: .... On behalf of: ....

Date: ....

I certify that the number of packages delivered is correct according to the number stated above, but that the goods have not been checked

Signed: .... On behalf of: ....

Date: ....

* Please delete as appropriate

FIG 6.1.11 *An example of a delivery note.*

SALES INVOICE

The sales department would issue an **invoice** to the customer once he/she has received the goods. The invoice would contain the following information:

1 a number
2 the original order number
3 the VAT registration number of the supplier (usually)
4 the name and address of the customer
5 the quantity of goods
6 a description of the goods, including any reference or code numbers used by the organisation for stock reference
7 the price of the goods
8 the discounts allowed to the customer, if any
9 the VAT calculation
10 the total amount owed by the customer

If there is any mistake or discrepancy in the invoice, the organisation may issue one of the following documents to the customer:

- *Credit note.* If the customer has been charged too much on an invoice, or if the goods received have been faulty or damaged, then the selling organisation would issue a **credit note**. This will decrease the price on the invoice.

- *Debit note.* If the mistake has resulted in the customer not being charged enough on the invoice, then the selling organisation would issue a debit note.

When the customer pays for the goods received will depend on the credit arrangement made. It is usual, though, for invoices to be paid within one month of receipt. In order to obtain payment it may be the policy of the organisation to issue a 'Statement of Account' to each of its customers, once a month.

STATEMENT OF ACCOUNT

Rather than pay each invoice individually, a customer may prefer to settle his/her account on a monthly basis. A **statement of account** summarises the transactions between the supplier and the customer and would contain the following information:

1 the VAT registration number of the supplier
2 the name and address of the customer
3 the date and description of all goods sent
4 the price of all goods sent
5 the date of any payments made
6 details of any credit or debit notes issued
7 the balance owing by the customer

PAYMENTS DOCUMENTS

All organisations have commitments to make payments to other organisations or individuals on a regular basis. These payments will take a variety of forms, and the method used will depend on the **commitment** involved. Nowadays it would be highly unlikely for a large organisation to use cash to make payments. It is more likely to use cheques or other banking facilities.

One of the highest commitments in terms of financial outlay for an organisation is usually the payment of wages and salaries to its employees.

Some employees are still paid in cash on a weekly basis. Others receive a cheque on a weekly or monthly basis. More commonly though, employees will receive their salary by means of a **bank transfer**. Whichever method of payment, each employee should receive a **pay slip** or **pay advice note** at the time of each payment. This document is produced by the organisation from details kept on an individual pay record.

An individual pay record will be kept by the accounts or wages section of an organisation. It contains the details of income tax codes and contributions, national insurance contributions and pension contributions of each employee within the organisation.

PAY SLIP

The **pay slip** or **pay advice note** will be produced from the individual pay record of the employee, and will be issued at the time of payment of wage or salary. The pay slip or pay advice note will contain the following information:

1 *gross pay* – the amount earned before any deductions are made
2 *statutory deductions* – income tax and national insurance contributions
3 *superannuation* – contribution to the organisation's pension scheme
4 *voluntary deductions* – this might include trade union subscriptions or social club membership
5 *net pay* – the amount received once the deductions have been taken from the gross pay

CHEQUES

When a cheque is issued, it is an instruction to the bank to pay the sum of money to the person named. Because of the increased popularity of using cheques as a method of payment (more than eight million each day), it has become a very expensive system for banks. They have used new technology to try to reduce the cost and to increase the efficiency of cheque payments.

Certain conditions limit the use of cheque payments:

- unconditional – means that payment cannot be dependent upon any conditions being met
- the cheque must be written in ink or printed on a computer
- cheques will not be accepted for payment if they are not signed by the drawer (the person paying the money)

- the amount of the cheque must be written in words as well as figures
- the person receiving the money must be named (the payee)
- the life of a cheque is six months – after that it becomes out of date
- any amendments to the cheque must be initialled by the drawer

student activity

From the example of the cheque given in Figure 6.1.16, identify the following:

- payee
- drawer
- account number
- sort code

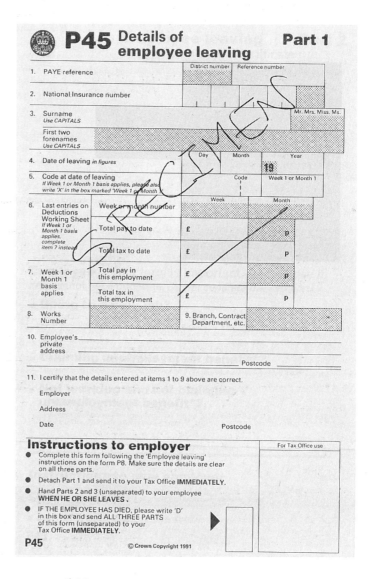

FIG 6.1.12 *The P45, one of the forms issued by the Tax Office for completion by employers regarding the tax situation of their employees.*

Because banks have found cheque payments so expensive and time-consuming, several other banking facilities have been introduced to allow money to be paid or transferred:

1 *Direct debit system.* Regular payments can be made from one account to another using this system. The customer informs the bank of the date and amount of payment, and the bank transfers the funds accordingly. With a **direct debit**, the organisation receiving the funds can vary the amount, although it is required to inform the customer prior to taking this action.

2 *Standing order system.* Regular payments can be made using this system. A customer can instruct his or her bank to pay by **standing order** on a certain date for a fixed amount. The recipient cannot change the amount unless the customer informs the bank of the change in advance.

3 *Bankers automated clearing service* (BACS). This system is used for both direct debit and standing order payments, as well as salary transfer. It reduces the amount of paperwork involved in each transaction.

The necessary information is supplied to the bank on magnetic tape or disk and is processed via the BACS computer centre. Once the information has been processed, the necessary payments are made automatically.

PETTY CASH

As we have said, most organisations use cash very little for payments. It is likely, however, that an organisation will keep a certain amount of cash for payments of a low-value nature. This is known as **petty cash**. The cash would be kept securely and safely by an individual who deals with small purchases on a daily basis. This may be for such items as window cleaning, tea and coffee or small items of travel for employees. The most commonly used system for recording petty cash transactions is known as the **imprest** system: A certain amount of money is kept for petty cash purposes. This is called the **'float'**. The process for obtaining petty cash is:

FIG 6.1.13 *The End of Year Return, another of the forms issued by the Tax Office for completion by employers regarding the tax situation of their employees.*

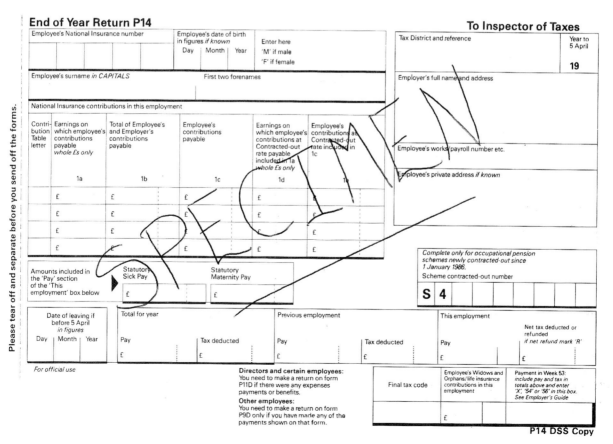

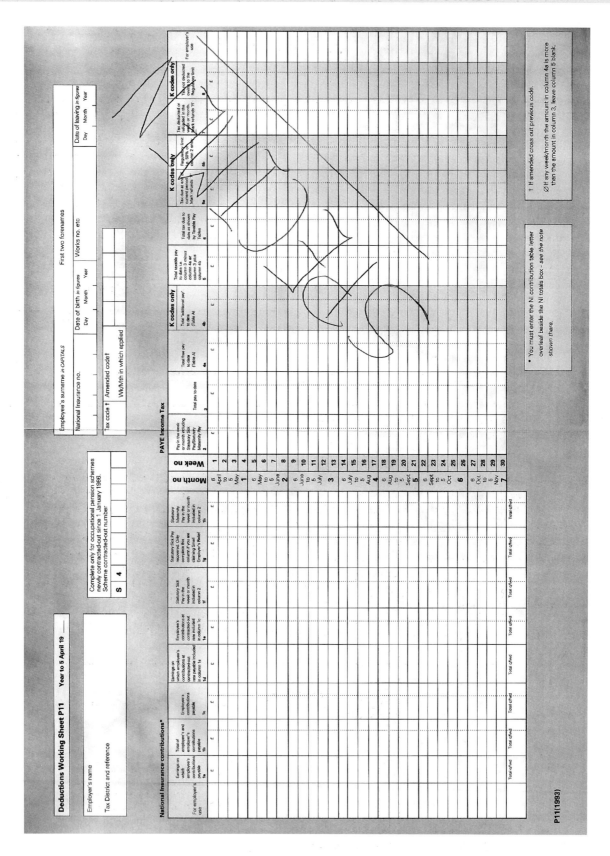

FIG 6.1.14 *The P11 Deductions Working Sheet, another of the forms issued by the Tax Office for completion by employers regarding the tax situation of their employees.*

PAY ADVICE

N.I. Number	Tax Code	Basis	Year	Period	Pay No	Pay Centre

GROSS PAY	STANDARD DEDUCTIONS	VOLUNTARY DEDUCTIONS	NET PAY
Code		Code	
Total Gross Pay		Total Deductions	

Hours worked Normal Overtime	TOTALS TO DATE	VOL DEDUCTIONS
		Code Balance Owed

A LIST OF CODES AND ABBREVIATIONS USED IS SHOWN ON REVERSE

FIG 6.1.15 *An example of a pay slip issued to employees advising them of their salary details.*

1 the person requesting the money completes a petty cash voucher. This contains the number of the voucher, the reason for the payment (i.e. what has been purchased), the amount paid, the VAT charged, the signature of the person claiming the money and the signature of the person authorising the payment

2 the person requesting the money takes the petty cash voucher to the person responsible for dealing with these payments (the **petty cashier**).

3 the petty cashier checks that the voucher has been authorised and makes the payment from the 'float'

4 the petty cashier transfers the amount paid on each voucher to the petty cash book. The petty cash book is sectioned into columns – for example:

- money received into the petty cash
- dates of payments from the petty cash (transferred from each voucher issued)
- details of each payment made (also transferred from each voucher issued)
- the number of each voucher
- the amount of each voucher

_____ 19 _

£ _____

573054

Pitman Bank plc

SPECIMEN

_____ 19 ___   40-51-20

21 East Bridge Street
Linton Bridge Yorkshire

Pay _____ or order

_____ £

GENERAL ENTERPRISES LIMITED

⑅573059⑅ 90⑅ 5I20⑉ 00893912⑅

FIG 6.1.16 *An example of a blank cheque.*

PETTY CASH VOUCHER

Folio ......

Date ...... 19..

For what required	AMOUNT	
	£	P

Signature ....

Authorised by ....

PETTY CASH VOUCHER

Folio ......

Date ...... 19..

For what required	AMOUNT	
	£	P

Signature ....

Authorised by ....

- the VAT charged on each voucher
- a series of columns which enable the analysis of petty cash spent on specific items; headings may be:
  - Postage
  - Travel
  - Stationery
  - Sundries

5 on a regular basis the petty cashier will request money to bring the 'float' back to its original amount

6 usually about once a month the petty cashier will total each of the columns and deduct the total amount issued from petty cash from the original amount of the 'float'. This is known as **'restoring the imprest'.**

student activity

Using the petty cash vouchers given in FIG 6.1.17, complete for the following:
- 2 jars of coffee @ £2.95 each
- 4 boxes of paper clips @ £1.25 each
- Window cleaner, payment for 2 weeks @ £2.50 each week

FIG 6.1.17 *Examples of petty cash vouchers.*

FIG 6.1.18 *Example of a petty cash book.*

PETTY CASH BOOK						Folio								
DR		(Imprest System)					CR							
RECEIPTS AND PAYMENTS						ANALYSIS OF PAYMENTS								
Imprest		Date	Details	Voucher Number	Payment		VAT							
£	p				£	p	£	p	£	p	£	p	£	p	£	p

RECEIPTS DOCUMENTS

Just as we expect a receipt for goods we have purchased from a shop, so an organisation expects a receipt for goods or services it has bought.

In order to provide evidence that the purchase has taken place, a **sales receipt** is issued. This receipt will include the following information:

1 The name and address of the organisation selling the goods
2 the VAT registration number of the organisation selling the goods
3 the date the transaction took place
4 a description of each of the goods purchased
5 the cost of each of the goods purchased
6 the total cost of the goods purchased
7 the payment method

RECEIPTS, CHEQUE AND PAYING-IN SLIP COUNTERFOILS

Receipts must be kept in order to prove that the purchase has taken place. They need to be produced if the goods need to be returned for any reason, perhaps because they are faulty, or because they are unsuitable. Normally goods will not be exchanged nor will a refund for goods be given unless a receipt can be produced.

Other documents that prove that a transaction has taken place are the **paying-in slip** or **bank giro credit** form produced by banks or a **cheque counterfoil** kept by the person paying money in. This would contain the amount of the payment, as well as the date and details of to whom the payment was made (the payee). Paying-in slips show the following information:

- the **date** the transaction took place

- the **branch** of the bank where the transaction took place (plus its code number)
- the **account name**
- the **account number**
- the **amount** of the transaction
- the **name and signature** of the person paying in the money

A paying-in slip is normally used to pay money into one's own account.

A bank giro credit slip can be completed to allow a transaction to take place from one account to another, and can be used for paying bills and for the payment of salaries.

An organisation would use these documents as receipts to be included in the **cash book** produced by the accounts department.

THE CASH BOOK

The organisation would keep a cash book to record receipts and payments made by both cash and cheque. Normally a cash book is two-columned. This means that the page has two columns on the left-hand side of a page for receipts, and two on the right-hand side to record payments.

- the first left-hand column is to record the **receipt of cash**
- the second left-hand column is to record the **receipt of cheques**
- the first right-hand column is to record the **payment of cash**
- the second right-hand column is to record the **payment of cheques**

```
+--------------------------------------------------------------------+
|                                                                    |
|              CASH RECEIPT                                          |
|                                                                    |
|   Number .......   NUMBER ................ DATE ...........        |
|                                                                    |
|   Date .........   RECEIVED FROM ..........................        |
|                                                                    |
|   From .........   ........................................        |
|                                                                    |
|   .............    ........................................        |
|                                                                    |
|   .............    THE SUM OF .............................        |
|                                                                    |
|   .............    ........................................        |
|              £    p                              £    p            |
|                                                                    |
+--------------------------------------------------------------------+
```

FIG 6.1.19 *An example of a receipt.*

The cheque columns are usually headed with the word 'bank' and termed 'money in bank' as opposed to 'cash in hand'.

Usually it is necessary to make transferrals between the columns of the Cash Book, for instance, when putting cash into the bank. This means that cash is no longer regarded as **'cash in hand'** but **'money in the bank'**. This is known as a **'Contra Transaction'** and is shown in the cash book by the letter 'C'.

At the end of each month the accounts department would total the columns in the cash book. The column with the smallest amount would be deducted from the column with the largest amount. This figure would be brought down as the **balance** for the beginning of the next month.

basis, although they can be requested by an organisation or individual on a more frequent basis.

In order to check the figures in the cash book with those appearing on a bank statement, a **bank reconciliation** has to be undertaken. It must be taken into account that the cash book and the bank statement may not tally. This could be due to time differences

- items may have appeared in the cash book but not yet appeared on the bank statement
- cheques which have been recorded in the cash book may not yet have been cleared by the bank
- standing orders and direct debits may appear on the bank statement but may not have been entered in the cash book

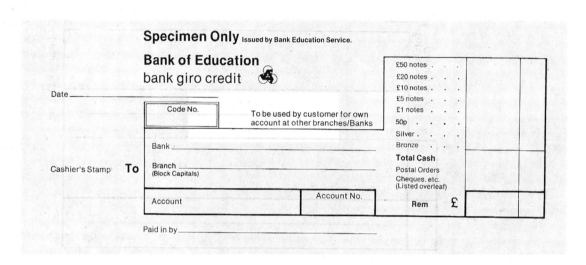

FIG 6.1.20 *An example of a bank paying-in slip.*

It is important that the cash book calculations are checked for accuracy. The amount of **'cash in hand'** should be physically counted to ensure that it tallies with the entry in the cash book. There are several reasons why a discrepancy might be found:

- an error when entering the amounts in the cash book
- an error when totalling the columns in the cash book
- incorrect entry because all receipts were not entered
- theft of some of the money

BANK STATEMENTS

As with the 'cash in hand' amounts, so the **'money in the bank'** columns should be checked. This, however, is not quite so straightforward. In order to check these transactions, a **bank statement** must be obtained. These are normally issued from a bank on a regular

- bank charges may have been incurred – these will appear on the bank statement but may not appear in the cash book
- bank interest may have been paid – this will appear on the bank statement but may not appear in the cash book

In order to carry out a bank reconciliation with the aim of producing a bank reconciliation statement, the following steps should be undertaken:

- identify those items that appear both in the cash book and in the bank statement
- if items appear in the bank statement but do not appear in the cash book, then the bank columns in the cash book should be updated. The updated bank column should then be balanced.

Timing differences can now be identified. A bank reconciliation statement should now be produced.

SECURITY

It is very important that an organisation has security high on its list of priorities. There are different reasons for an organisation to take steps to ensure security measures are complied with.

1 *Security of cash.* Not everyone is honest, and money kept in an insecure way may tempt such people.
2 *Security of documentation.* Throughout the book, we have mentioned several times the importance of keeping and storing documents and various data securely. This is particularly the case with any financial transactions an organisation might make, and is the main reason why the checking of such documents for accuracy and neatness is so important.
3 *Correct procedures.* The security of such documents going out of the organisation is not the only consideration, however. Safeguards have to be taken to ensure that employees follow the set procedures for the completion of documents. This is another form of security.

The three main aspects of security of financial transactions relate to authorisation of orders, reconciliation of invoices against orders and goods received notes, and authorisation of cheques. Let's look at these three main points in more detail:

student activity

In the role of the accountant responsible for security, list the actions you would take to ensure that financial information is safely stored but accessible both within the organisation and from outside.

AUTHORISATION OF ORDERS

It would be very disadvantageous to an organisation if there were not an individual, or a group of individuals, who had the overall say as to what could be ordered. Obviously, this has to be someone with the right amount of authority within the organisation, who knows its financial commitments. This person or persons has to know what goods are needed and the urgency of this need.

It makes sense then, that each department within the organisation should have a person who can authorise requests for goods or services. These people will have a budget to work to and will only be allowed to spend a certain amount of money each month or year. You already know that these budgets will have been set by the organisation – we have discussed this before.

The goods ordered obviously have to be products or services that are required to carry out the work in hand. Again, the authorisation of the order is the responsibility of the Departmental Manager.

INVOICES AGAINST ORDERS AND GOODS RECEIVED NOTES

As we already know, **invoices** will be checked thoroughly before being sent out. Some organisations may be more thorough than others. It may be that each person checking the invoice has to sign a **verification** to that effect before passing it on to the next person.

As we have learnt earlier in this section, reconciliation means the checking of details against details sent. This will be done when an organisation receives an **invoice**. The person responsible for receiving the invoice will check it against the **order sent** and the **goods received note** to ensure that all the details on the invoice are correct.

If the invoice is correct, then it will be sent to the accounts department for payment, either immediately to claim the discount offered, or when the statement of account arrives.

But what if there are discrepancies? If an error on the invoice is discovered when it is compared with the order and the goods received note, then the following steps would need to be taken:

- if it is only a small error and the organisation has a good relationship with the supplier, then a **telephone call** is probably all that is needed. In this case the supplier would most likely send the organisation a replacement invoice.
- however, if the error is a large one, it would be in the interests of the organisation to have this **in writing.**

Obviously, if a series of errors or discrepancies appeared on the invoice of the same supplier, the organisation might well consider changing its supplier for that particular product or service.

student activity

Using the invoice in Figure 6.1.21 and the goods received note in Figure 6.1.22 list the discrepancies you can find.

INVOICE

TO	Smith and Sons 47 Rosamoss Lane Wisbech Cambs.		NUMBER	457663
			DATE	31 January 199.
			TERMS	2.5%
YOUR ORDER NO 156387			DESPATCH DATE	30/1/9.

QUANTITY	DESCRIPTION	UNIT PRICE	TOTAL PRICE	VAT
2	OFFICE DESKS (THREE LEFT HAND SIDE DRAWERS)	£175	£350	£95.00
1	BLACK OFFICE CHAIR WITH ARM-RESTS	£173.50	£173.50	£33.30

Gross Value	£523.50
LESS Trade Discount	12.50
Net Value of Goods	£511.00
PLUS VAT @ 17.5%	£128.30
INVOICE TOTAL	£382.70

E & O E

FIG 6.1.21 *A completed invoice.*

GOODS RECEIVED NOTE

NO 101356	DATE RECEIVED 30 JANUARY 199.	ORDER NO 156387	DELIVERED BY COMPANY VAN
QUANTITY	DESCRIPTION	NUMBER OF PACKAGES	STORES REF
2	OFFICE DESKS	3	BAY 47
2	BROWN OFFICE CHAIRS	1	BAY 48

RECEIVED FROM	ENTERED INTO STOCK		RECEIVED BY
	DATE	INITIAL	
SUPPLIER			STOREKEEPER

FIG 6.1.22 *A completed goods received note.*

AUTHORISED CHEQUE SIGNATORIES

You may already know that when you open a bank account yourself, the bank will ask you to sign a form so that it has an example of your signature. The same thing applies to an organisation.

For reasons of security, it is not possible to allow just anybody to sign a cheque on behalf of the organisation. To make sure that all cheques that leave the company are authorised to do so, it is normal for an organisation to allocate people with authority to be **cheque signatories**. This means that their signatures will be held by the bank, and only cheques signed by them will be authorised for payment.

Under these circumstances, the accounts department would complete all the details on the cheques to be sent. The authorised cheque signatory would sign all the cheques in a batch. Sometimes, on the other hand, the number of cheques leaving an organisation might be very large, in which case the organisation would have a rubber stamp made of the signature to cut down on the time spent signing cheques.

The number of cheque signatories depends on the size of the organisation. In a small organisation it may be that only one person can be authorised as a cheque signatory. On the other hand, in much larger organisations, two, three, four or five people may have this authority. It is a form of security, to have more cheque signatories when cheques for very large amounts of money are regularly signed. The people signing them are then protected from any allegations regarding their 'right to sign', as they have witnesses, and their colleagues have signed as well. Also, if there are several people authorised as signatories, cheques can still be signed if one of the signatories is absent.

By using the above methods of ensuring security of documents leaving the organisation, it is protected to some degree from fraud or theft or misuse of company funds.

Identify and explain data to monitor business performance

I USERS

owner(s), providers of finance, tax authorities

2 REASONS FOR MONITORING

solvency, profitability, taxation, maintaining finance, comparisons with targets, improving performance

3 KEY COMPONENTS OF ACCOUNTING INFORMATION

forecasts including balance sheet, profit and loss account, cash flow; actual information including balance sheet, profit and loss account, cash flow, aged debtors, aged creditors

4 PERFORMANCE OF BUSINESS

solvent, profitable, achieving targets, comparison with targets

BUSINESS PERFORMANCE

As we have already said, it is important for an organisation to monitor the business performance. We have discussed the type of information such monitoring can produce, i.e. quantitative and qualitative, and the necessity of this information to an organisation achieving its goals or objectives. We have also discussed the strategy and tactics managers within an organisation.

We have realised from this discussion that, however large or small an organisation, or to whatever sector that organisation belongs, each has to deal with financial information of one kind or another.

But **who** uses this information, and **how**? We will look at these questions in more detail now.

USERS OF THE ACCOUNTING PROCESS

The accounts department of an organisation will devise a system of obtaining and recording information which can be used to keep a tight rein on the financial activities of that organisation. The decision-making process of the organisation will be assisted and speeded up when this information is summarised to good effect by the accounts department. Decisions about the performance of the organisation cannot be made without the necessary data, and the accountants within the organisation should be readily able to provide this information. They may do this in several ways:

1 *By the reliable recording of financial transactions*. Each time a transaction takes place, it must be recorded. Without this system it would be impossible for an organisation to judge its performance and to forecast future development. The information obtained from transactions should be recorded either manually or through a computerised system. These business activities should be recorded in an orderly and organised way to make information easily and readily accessible.

2 *By breaking down information into different categories*. It would be impossible to analyse information obtained from a variety of sources regarding the organisation as a whole. In order to make the information reliable and easy to use, it is necessary to categorise the data.

3 *By summarising the data produced*. The accounts department would be required to summarise the information obtained from its accounting systems, for example breaking it down either into departments or specific products the organisation sells.

The information produced from such accounting processes would be useless if it were too complicated. The management responsible for decision making and planning for the future of the organisation, would probably need the financial information to be interpreted. Other parties who would be likely to need to have this information interpreted would be:

- shareholders or prospective investors in the organisation
- suppliers of the organisation who might want to check their creditworthiness
- a bank from which the organisation has requested a loan
- the Inland Revenue and Customs and Excise departments, which need accurate information in order to assess the organisation for tax purposes
- the employees of the organisation who would want to know how financially stable their jobs are

- agents representing investors who would want to know if the organisation is a viable institution for their clients to invest in.

Larger organisations may employ accounting personnel with expertise in different areas, whose skills are deployed in different ways to benefit the organisation. These specialist accountants fall into two main areas:

1 *Financial accountants*. These individuals would deal mainly with the way documents and transactions are recorded and the best way to interpret and present the information gained from them.

2 *Management accountants*. These individuals would deal mainly with providing information about the future of the organisation. They would provide forecasts and plans which would help the organisation achieve the goals set for the future.

In order for a person to be called 'qualified' in the accounting profession, he or she would usually have passed a series of examinations set by a professional body. Normally, these are examinations in Chartered Accountancy, Certified Accountancy, Management Accountancy or Public Finance Accountancy.

We mentioned earlier some of the people likely to need information about the business performance of an organisation. Among these people are those who are likely to be investing money in one way or another in that organisation Those people are the providers of finance. Obviously they would need to have a firm statement, from someone who knows what he or she is talking about, concerning the financial position of the organisation.

PROVIDERS OF FINANCE

As already mentioned, specialist accountants plan for the future of the organisation. They would look at the current situation of the organisation and forecast any likely changes they foresee from analysing the data and putting these forecasts to the best advantage of the organisation in terms of meeting aims and goals.

When an organisation is first set up, or when it needs to provide extra finance for future developments, it will be necessary to draw up a **business plan**. When the organisation needs extra finance, the business plan should provide the information required by all involved in the process.

student activity

In the role of a managing director of an organisation, list the items you would want to see on a business plan. Imagine that you need this plan to obtain additional finance for a project the organisation is undertaking.

The identity of the providers of finance depends not only on who is prepared or in a position to offer finance but also on the way the organisation wishes to obtain its money. It might be useful here to look at the various types of organisation separately:

Sole trader

A sole trader often finds it more difficult than any other type of organisation to raise funds, maybe because this type of organisation carries with it a large amount of risk. Very often a sole trader will expand by taking a **partner**. Obviously, nobody would consider entering into a partnership agreement unless he or she had available very detailed information about the financial stability of the business.

student activity

In the role of a sole trader, list the possible providers of finance that you can think of. Now discuss your thoughts with the rest of your group.

Partnerships

When a sole trader business becomes a **partnership**, it benefits from the additional capital that can be ploughed into the organisation, as well as the additional expertise. However, because there are several restrictions which limit the activities of a partnership, particularly as to the number of partners that can be involved, the opportunities for partnerships to raise capital for the organisation are limited. In order to overcome this problem and to raise additional capital for the business, many partnerships offer themselves as a **registered company**. By legally becoming a registered company the business can offer shares in the organisation. Naturally, no one would wish to purchase shares without detailed information on the financial stability and future prospects of the organisation.

student activity

List the factors to be taken into consideration before a sole trader would enter into a partnership. What would be the sources of finance?

Private limited companies

These types of organisation are subject to restrictions on the rights of members to transfer shares, as well as limits on the owning of shares by the public. A private limited company might try to raise additional finance so that it could become a public limited company. It is obvious that before any such development could take place, a full and detailed breakdown of the financial stability of the organisation would be required.

Public limited companies

It is much easier for a **public limited company** to obtain additional finance. Once it has been listed on the Stock Exchange it has the following alternatives available to it:

1 *Issue of a prospectus.* A public limited company can inform potential shareholders of the dealings of the organisation by producing a prospectus. This invites people to buy shares. Naturally, this is expensive to produce and market. An organisation would need to be financially viable before undertaking such a course of action or before this sort of venture could be successful.

2 *Make an offer for sale.* If a public limited company wanted to raise additional finance it would issue shares to an 'issuing house'. (This may be a concern such as a merchant bank.) The shares are then offered at a fixed price by the issuing house to prospective buyers. Once again this is a very expensive venture to undertake.

3 *A rights issue.* The public limited company could offer shares to its existing shareholders at a special price. This is a cheaper way to obtain additional finance, but again the shareholders are not likely to invest any further money unless the organisation can prove its financial viability.

The following are ways organisations may choose to increase their finance:

1 *Profit retention.* An organisation might decide to plough back into the business any profits remaining after the Inland Revenue have taken their corporation tax from the business' profits, and the shareholders have received their dividends.

2 *Borrowing money.* An organisation could approach any High Street bank for a loan, although merchant bankers are available to provide a more specialist service from a business and financial point of view. The Stock Exchange also provides a long-term loan service, as does the government. The Loan Guarantee Scheme set up by the Government and the Rural Development Commission's scheme both enable organisations to increase their finance.

Chairman's statement   Barclays PLC

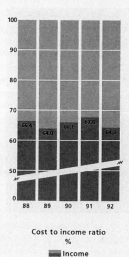

Cost to income ratio
%
■ Income
■ Cost

The 18% improvement in operating profit before provisions arose from higher levels of activity in many of our businesses and from increases both in non-interest income and in efficiency. Our commitment to better cost management is reflected in the improvement in the cost to income ratio. Bad debts are, of course, an expected cost in a banking business, but the levels of 1992 were unacceptable and we know we have made mistakes. As a result, we have reviewed the way in which we manage credit policy and portfolio risk, have strengthened credit risk management and are developing a number of tools to improve risk assessment and control.

The provisions of £2.5 billion have arisen predominantly in the United Kingdom, but we have also seen higher levels in parts of Europe, where the trend is not encouraging. However, there has been a welcome fall in the United States. While we have suffered quite substantially in the property and construction markets, a high percentage of the UK bad debts have arisen in the small and medium-sized businesses, of which thousands went into receivership or liquidation during 1992. Although we have made some poor lending decisions, it would have been difficult for us to escape without substantial provisions when we hold about 25% of the corporate market and our customers have been so badly affected by the downturn in business activity.

It is unfortunate that, in some cases, relations in the UK between banks and their customers became strained as a result of the recession. Because of the important part that banks play in the economy, they are sometimes wrongly perceived as utilities rather than commercial businesses. We have been accused of not passing on interest rate cuts, as well as being unsympathetic to the problems of business. All customers with borrowings linked to base rate, however, had the full benefit of the substantial base rate cuts. On the other hand, there is also no doubt that the risk in our lending has increased. It is an obvious, but sometimes overlooked, fact that the interest margin on a loan should reflect the degree of risk and it is quite clear that over the last few years, lending margins have contracted to a level at which this risk is not properly rewarded.

Banks are sometimes wrongly perceived as utilities rather than commercial businesses

FIG 6.3.1 *Report of the Chairman (Andrew Buxton) to shareholders concerning financial transactions and the situation of Barclays PLC, from their account 1992.*

New lower rates

BARCLAYLOAN REPAYMENT TABLE

All rates and repayment figures in the accompanying Barclayloan booklet (December 1992/January 1993) should be ignored as they have been superseded by those shown in this table. This should be read in conjunction with the accompanying booklet.

The examples in this table are to give you an idea of typical repayments. If the size or period of the loan you have in mind is not shown please ask your branch for a quotation.

The premium for Barclayloan Protection is a once-only payment made when the loan is taken. It is usually added to your loan. However, if you wish you can pay the Barclayloan Protection premium separately in cash.

To apply for a Barclayloan you must be aged 18 or over (20 in Jersey). A written quotation is available on request from your branch or from Barclays Bank PLC, Personal Sector Marketing Department, PO Box 120, Longwood Close, Westwood Business Park, Coventry CV4 8JN.

☐ Loans with Barclayloan Protection

☐ Loans without Barclayloan Protection

	LOANS UNDER £2,500 APR 22.4%			LOANS OF £2,500 TO £4,900 APR 19.9%			LOANS OF £5,000 AND OVER APR 18.9%			
	£100*	£500	£2,000	£2,500	£100*	£500*	£5,000	£10,000	£100*	£500*
12 MONTHS										
Total to repay £	120.24	601.80	2407.56	2974.32	118.92	594.84	5921.28	11842.68	118.32	592.08
Includes premium £	8.05	40.27	161.07	198.99	7.96	39.80	396.14	792.28	7.92	39.61
Monthly repayment £	10.02	50.15	200.63	247.86	9.91	49.57	493.44	986.89	9.86	49.34
Total to repay £	111.36	557.04	2228.16	2755.08	110.16	551.04	5486.64	10973.40	109.68	548.64
Monthly repayment £	9.28	46.42	185.68	229.59	9.18	45.92	457.22	914.45	9.14	45.72
24 MONTHS										
Total to repay £	136.80	684.72	2739.84	3348.24	133.92	669.60	6637.44	13274.64	132.72	663.60
Includes premium £	11.68	58.42	233.72	285.61	11.43	57.12	566.18	1132.33	11.33	56.61
Monthly repayment £	5.70	28.53	114.16	139.51	5.58	27.90	276.56	553.11	5.52	27.65
Total to repay £	122.64	613.20	2453.28	3005.04	120.24	600.96	5962.32	11924.40	119.28	596.16
Monthly repayment £	5.11	25.55	102.22	125.21	5.01	25.04	248.43	496.85	4.96	24.84
36 MONTHS										
Total to repay £	154.80	775.08	3101.04	3749.40	149.76	749.88	7400.88	14802.48	147.96	739.80
Includes premium £	15.22	76.04	304.22	367.81	14.70	73.57	726.06	1452.16	14.52	72.60
Monthly repayment £	4.30	21.53	86.14	104.15	4.16	20.83	205.58	411.18	4.11	20.55
Total to repay £	134.64	672.84	2691.72	3268.44	130.68	653.76	6462.72	12925.80	129.24	646.20
Monthly repayment £	3.74	18.69	74.77	90.79	3.63	18.16	179.52	359.05	3.59	17.95
48 MONTHS										
Total to repay £	174.72	872.16	3489.60	4175.52	166.56	834.72	8208.48	16417.44	163.68	820.80
Includes premium £	18.59	92.83	371.32	444.32	17.74	88.84	873.38	1746.83	17.46	87.35
Monthly repayment £	3.63	18.17	72.70	86.99	3.47	17.39	171.01	342.03	3.41	17.10
Total to repay £	147.36	735.84	2943.36	3545.76	141.60	708.96	6987.84	13976.16	139.68	698.88
Monthly repayment £	3.06	15.33	61.32	73.87	2.95	14.77	145.58	291.17	2.91	14.56
60 MONTHS										
Total to repay £	196.20	983.40	3933.60	4657.20	186.00	931.80	9117.60	18236.40	181.80	911.40
Includes premium £	22.58	113.13	452.40	535.63	21.45	107.17	1048.55	2097.20	20.95	104.83
Monthly repayment £	3.27	16.39	65.56	77.62	3.09	15.53	151.96	303.94	3.03	15.19
Total to repay £	160.20	802.20	3208.20	3835.80	153.60	767.40	7537.20	15075.00	150.60	753.60
Monthly repayment £	2.67	13.37	53.47	63.93	2.55	12.79	125.62	251.25	2.51	12.56

*Shown for calculation purposes only

BARCLAYS

Published by Barclays Bank PLC, Personal Sector Marketing Department. Reg. No. 1026167. Registered in London, England.
Reg. Office: 54 Lombard Street, London EC3P 3AH. BB620028. Item Ref. 9951235. March 1993. Barclays Bank PLC is a member of the Banking Ombudsman Scheme (UK branches only).

FIG 6.3.2 *The repayment table for loans provided by Barclays Bank PLC*

3 *Leasing equipment*. If an organisation wishes to obtain more up-to-date equipment to enhance its production process, then rather than expend money to purchase this, it is possible for it to lease the equipment. Another company owns the equipment and a contract is drawn up between the lessor (the owner of the equipment) and the lessee (who is hiring the equipment). This contract would state the rent and conditions regarding maintenance and breakdown service.

4 *Government assistance*. This scheme was set up to assist, in particular, small organisations which require assistance. The government provides a range of schemes either centrally or at local level.

5 *Overdrafts from the bank*. This method of providing finance is the one most commonly used by organisations. If a short-term cash flow problem has arisen, the organisation can arrange for its business account to have a short-term overdraft facility. Interest is paid while the account is overdrawn, and organisations should always ensure that they are aware of the fact that an overdraft can be made repayable on demand.

6 *Credit buying*. As we have mentioned before, many organisations purchase their goods on credit. This is a useful way of obtaining goods before actually having to pay for them. It should always be remembered, however, that goods eventually have to be paid for, and it would not be in the interests of the organisation to jeopardise its relationships with suppliers by not paying its accounts on time.

Naturally, any provider of finance to an organisation would want guarantees concerning the current financial and potential future of the organisation. Sometimes they will also ask for a **personal guarantee** from the main shareholder of the organisation that any repayments will be met. They will also demand **security** or **collateral** against the amount of the loan. By safeguarding themselves in this way, then these providers of finance would have priority over other lenders or creditors when claiming money should the organisation fail.

student activity

In the role of an organisation wishing to obtain additional finance, list the factors you would need to consider. How many different alternatives do you have?

TAX AUTHORITIES

The business performance of any organisation is also of great interest to the Inland Revenue and Customs and Excise departments. In 1992 the government raised almost £178 billion in taxes. The tax authorities are interested in all organisations, but the reason for their interest in various organisations may differ. The taxes that business have to pay include the following:

- **corporation tax** is tax paid on business profits and all organisations have to pay this on profits over a certain amount.
- **business rates** to their local councils
- employers have to pay a contribution to the government of **national insurance** for each employee
- **value added tax** also has to be paid and **charged**
- customs and excise duty

All companies must comply with certain legal requirements.

1 *Auditing.* All registered companies in the UK are required by law to have their final accounts **audited** by a registered accountant annually. This means the checking of records to testify that the accounts show a 'true and accurate view' of the financial position of the organisation. The auditors will be specialists who are employed by the organisation to carry out this task and they will prepare an audit report when their enquiries have been completed. This Audit Report will state:

That the financial statements have been audited in accordance with Auditing Standards. In my opinion the financial statements give a true and fair view of the profit and the state of affairs of the Company as at 30 April 19...and of the source and application of funds for the year then ended, and have been properly prepared in accordance with the Companies Act 1985.

2 *Registrar of Companies.* In addition to annual auditing, all organisations must issue a set of accounts to the Registrar of Companies, together with the following:

- a copy of their Directors' Report – this will include a summary of the business activities of the organisation
- a copy of the Audit Report
- a copy of the accounts of each company within a group
- a copy of the accounts and details of any subsidiary companies of the organisation

student activity

In the role of an auditor, list the documents that you would expect to have access to during your audit. What information would you gain from these documents and why?

AUDITORS' REPORT

To the members of Fisons plc

We have audited the financial statements on pages 31 to 51 in accordance with Auditing Standards.

In our opinion these financial statements give a true and fair view of the state of affairs of the Company and of the Group at 31 December 1992 and of the profit and cash flow of the Group for the year then ended, and have been properly prepared in accordance with the Companies Act 1985.

Price Waterhouse

Chartered Accountants
and Registered Auditor

Southwark Towers
32 London Bridge Street
London SE1 9SY
30 March 1993

FIG 6.3.3 *A copy of the Auditors' Report sent to the members of Fisons PLC after completion of the audit.*

REASONS FOR MONITORING

We look at the reasons for monitoring business performance in several other Elements within the book. However, the reasons for monitoring are as follows:

1 to ensure the organisation is solvent
2 to measure the amount of profit the organisation is making
3 to ensure the organisation is complying with legislation regarding the payment of taxes
4 to ensure the organisation is making enough profit to maintain payments
5 to compare actual progress with the objectives set in the original business plan
6 to identify areas where the organisation could improve its business performance

If an organisation is to trade successfully, it is important that it is always aware of its current financial situation. In order to monitor its business effectively, an organisation must:

1 *Prepare a budget*. The budget must be realistic and achievable. In addition, it should challenge those involved both in production and in complying with the budget itself.
2 *Monitor*. Once the budget has been set, the organisation will need to regularly monitor performance. Monitoring will possibly take place once a month and will be essential if the business is to perform effectively.

The whole process of monitoring can be time-consuming. It is, however, essential if the management of the organisation are to remain in control of business activities. Certain key areas will be monitored:

1 *Sales*. Variances in the **sales price** of certain products and those of competitors will need to be noted. In addition, any variances in the **volume of sales** of particular products and services will also need to be monitored and noted.
2 *Materials*. Careful monitoring of the cost of any **raw materials** will need to be undertaken. Any variances in the cost of materials should be noted, as should any changes in the usage of and demand for such materials.
3 *Labour*. In order to assess the deployment of **labour** within an organisation, the amount of activity of each area of the workforce must be monitored. Should there be any variances in the amount of work undertaken this should be noted. In addition, any changes in the wages of the workforce must be monitored and noted.

4 *Overheads*. Any rise (or fall) in the money the organisation has to allow for the **overheads** (things like heating and lighting) must be monitored carefully as changes could affect the profit margin of the organisation.
5 *Cash flow*. This is dealt with in more detail earlier in this Unit, but suffice to say here that the careful monitoring of the cash flow situation of the organisation is essential.
6 *Aged debtors*. This is often one of the most useful reports available when monitoring is being undertaken. It lists the debt for each customer. Increasingly, these reports are prepared by the use of computer systems. The **aged debtors report** is prepared from the sales ledger of the organisation and states whether customers are paying promptly. Obviously a large number of aged debtors will adversely affect the cash flow position of the organisation.
7 *Aged creditors*. The reverse of the aged debtors, aged creditors are people to whom the organisation owes money. Payment outside the terms of credit can lead to bad feeling with suppliers, which, in turn, could result in their refusing to supply the organisation. Once again an **aged creditors report** is compiled when monitoring is being undertaken. This lists the accounts payable and states whether they are being paid within a reasonable amount of time.
8 *Stock*. It should be the aim of an organisation to keep its **stock levels** to a minimum, but to allow sufficient raw materials to maintain production. In addition, sufficient finished goods should be held in stock to supply the needs of customers. Too high a stock level would mean that too much working capital was being tied up, so it is important that this level is monitored carefully. It is normal to monitor stock levels on an individual product basis.
9 *The balance sheet*. Another reason for monitoring all of the above aspects of business activity is to enable the organisation to produce a **balance sheet**. Some of the items appearing on a balance sheet may fluctuate from one month to another, while others (e.g. the fixed assets) will remain much the same. Increasingly, organisations are preparing their balance sheets by means of computer software, thus enabling this monitoring process to be carried out monthly. If, the organisation decides that once a month is too frequent, the process may be carried out quarterly. If a balance sheet is produced only once a quarter, another form of report needs to be produced so that careful monitoring of the cash available, total debtors and total creditors can be undertaken.

Cash Flow Statement
For the year ended 31 December 1992

Note		1992 12 months		1991 14 months
	£000	£000	£000	£000
12 **Net Cash inflow/(outflow) from Operating Activities**		22,633		(2,007)
Returns on Investments and Servicing of Finance:				
Investment income and interest received	2,137		1,762	
Interest paid	(14)		(155)	
Dividends received from associated undertakings	410		107	
Dividends paid	(4,098)		(4,087)	
Net Cash outflow from Returns on Investments and Servicing of Finance		(1,565)		(2,373)
Taxation				
Corporation tax paid (including advance corporation tax)	(2,851)		(3,791)	
Tax Paid		(2,851)		(3,791)
Investing Activities				
Purchase of tangible fixed assets	(3,185)		(2,581)	
Purchase of unlisted investments	–		(232)	
Purchase of shares in associated undertakings	(1,549)		(3,124)	
Purchase of shares in subsidiary undertakings	(804)		–	
Purchase of short term investments	(1,200)		–	
Sale of tangible fixed assets	417		335	
Sale of investments	14,794		3,334	
Net Cash inflow/(outflow) from Investing Activities		8,473		(2,268)
Net Cash inflow/(outflow) before Financing		26,690		(10,439)
Financing				
Issue of ordinary share capital		–		373
13 **Increase/(decrease) in Cash and Cash Equivalents**		26,690		(10,066)

FIG 6.3.4 *A cash flow statement as produced by Anglia Television for the year ended 31 December 1992.*

CASH FLOW STATEMENT

Year ended 31 December 1992	Notes	1992 £m		1991 £m	
Net cash inflow from operating activities	18	**165.8**		202.4	
Returns on investments and servicing of finance					
Interest received		**22.3**		26.8	
Interest paid		**(40.1)**		(38.3)	
Dividends paid to Fisons plc shareholders		**(60.2)**		(51.6)	
Dividends paid to minority shareholders		–	**(78.0)**	(1.4)	(64.5)
			87.8		137.9
Taxation					
United Kingdom corporation tax paid		**(22.7)**		(29.9)	
Overseas tax paid		**(20.4)**	**(43.1)**	(12.4)	(42.3)
			44.7		95.6
Investing activities					
Purchase of tangible fixed assets		**(111.7)**		(90.7)	
Purchase of businesses	13	**(28.0)**		(54.4)	
Sale of tangible fixed assets		**9.0**		6.9	
Sale of businesses	19	**(24.5)**	**(155.2)**	(6.3)	(144.5)
Net cash outflow before financing			**(110.5)**		(48.9)
Financing					
Issue of Ordinary share capital	20	**1.7**		9.9	
Increase/(Decrease) in amounts borrowed	20	**8.4**		(20.2)	
Decrease/(Increase) in investments	20	**38.5**	**48.6**	(28.4)	(38.7)
Decrease in cash and cash equivalents	21		**(61.9)**		(87.6)

FIG 6.3.5 *A cash flow statement as produced by Fisons for the year ended 31 December 1992.*

In addition to the reasons given above for monitoring business performance, an organisation would also need to look at the following questions:

- are all its products making a positive contribution?
- are all the fixed costs being covered?
- is production on target?
- is the organisation making a profit?
- is the list of aged debtors becoming too large?
- is the organisation still liquid?
- is the organisation still solvent?

In an efficient organisation, monitoring will take place continually, thus eliminating the need to monitor all the above all the time. It is essential, however, that the information about these criteria be readily available.

Balance Sheet
as at 4th September 1993

	Note	£	1993 £	1992 £
FIXED ASSETS				
Tangible Assets	5		35,715,041	30,372,440
Investments	6		3,680,792	2,999,831
CURRENT ASSETS				
Stocks		12,163,778		9,580,020
Debtors and Prepayments	7	3,836,398		3,111,534
Investments	6	11,741,353		9,441,353
Cash at Bank and in Hand		2,932,184		2,516,044
		30,673,713		24,648,951
CURRENT LIABILITIES				
Amounts falling due within one year:				
Creditors	8	18,947,071		14,370,863
Loans	9	346,384		310,434
		19,293,455		14,681,297
NET CURRENT ASSETS			11,380,258	9,967,654
TOTAL ASSETS LESS CURRENT LIABILITIES			50,776,091	43,339,925
LONG TERM LIABILITIES				
Amount falling due after more than one year:				
Creditors	8		1,579,666	
NET ASSETS			49,196,425	43,339,925
FINANCED BY:				
SHARE CAPITAL	12		6,393,491	5,079,725
REVENUE RESERVES	13		42,802,934	38,260,200
			49,196,425	43,339,925

page thirteen

FIG 6.3.6 *A balance sheet as produced by Ipswich and Norwich Co-operative as at 4 September 1993.*

KEY COMPONENTS OF ACCOUNTING INFORMATION

As we have said in this Unit already, financial transactions must all be recorded accurately in order that this information can be used to implement the objectives of the organisation. We have mentioned also, that this information is produced by the accounts department to ensure that relevant and related figures are available so that the managers of the organisation can make decisions and take steps to ensure that the business is progressing well and moving in the right direction. This information is collated in order to produce the **final accounts** of the organisation and these have to be audited to ensure that they are a true and accurate record of the financial position of the company.

Before we consider the key components of accounting information, it may be useful to revise some of the terms used in financial documents:

1 *Assets*. Assets can be **cash, money in the bank, stock** or **buildings and equipment**. In addition, any **money** the organisation may be **owed** by another organisation is also known as an asset (customers who owe an organisation money are known as debtors). Assets are of two types:

(a) *Fixed assets*. These are items which have been purchased and are expected to be kept for a long time. The fixed assets of an organisation might include premises, machinery and vehicles.

(b) *Current assets*. These items can be changing continually. These are the cash, money in the bank, stock held or debtors of the organisation.

2 *Liabilities*. This is the **money owed** by the organisation in one form or another. Liabilities might be long term or shorter term.

(a) *Long-term liabilities*. These items may not be due for payment for over one year. Long-term liabilities might include **mortgages** or **bank loans**.

(b) *Current liabilities*. These are shorter-term items which are probably due for repayment within one year. They might be **creditors** (suppliers of goods to the organisation for which payment is still outstanding), any short-term **loans** or overdrafts from banks or **taxes** owed by the organisation.

3 *Capital*. **Capital** is provided by the owners of the business at the commencement of trading. Because it is provided in this way it is regarded for accounting processes as being owed to the owner by the business. The capital may increase or decrease during the financial year, depending on the profits or drawings (money taken out of the business for personal use).

4 *Working capital*. The **working capital** of an organisation is an important part of the accounts because it is money that is easily accessible, and can be found quickly, unlike the capital which is 'tied up' in fixed assets. The working capital is calculated by subtracting the current liabilities from the current assets.

The **working capital ratio** (the ratio of current assets to current liabilities) depends on the type of organisation and the need of the company to meet short-term liabilities. A working capital ratio of 2:1 is regarded as ideal for many organisations, although some do survive on lower ratios.

5 *Stock*. This is any item(s) of **finished goods** which are held within the organisation in readiness for sale when demanded by customers. When items are sold on credit, the stock is reduced and the business gains debtors.

6 *Gross profit*. This is the difference between the price of buying the raw materials and the selling price of the finished product.

7 *Net profit*. This is the gross profit, less the expenses incurred in the production of the product (e.g. electricity, wages and salaries for the employees and the cost of heating the premises).

8 *The profit and loss account*. All the financial transactions of the organisation for the year will have been recorded. At the end of the financial year (this will vary from organisation to organisation, but will be the same date each year), the accountant will prepare a **profit and loss account**. This will include a summary of all the transactions, both for **expenditure** (money paid out) and **income** (money coming in). The difference between the income and expenditure is known as either the profit or the loss.

9 *The balance sheet*. The profit or loss the organisation has made during the year is transferred from the **profit and loss account** to the **balance sheet**. The balance sheet will also list all the organisation's **assets** and **liabilities** at the end of the financial year.

In order that we can explain the ways in which different types of organisation deal with the accounting information they produce, we intend to look at each type of organisation separately:

CONSOLIDATED PROFIT AND LOSS ACCOUNT

Year ended 31 December 1992	Notes	1992 £m	1991 £m
Turnover			
Continuing operations		**1,211.0**	1,151.8
Discontinued operations		**73.2**	88.1
	1	**1,284.2**	1,239.9
Trading profit			
Continuing operations	2	**117.3**	193.5
Discontinued operations	2	**0.1**	3.9
		117.4	197.4
Profit/(Loss) on disposal and termination of businesses, after charging goodwill of £66.0m (1991 – £2.6m) written off against reserves in prior years	19	**23.3**	(24.6)
		140.7	172.8
Finance charge	3	**(17.1)**	(10.2)
Profit before taxation		**123.6**	162.6
Taxation	4	**(26.9)**	(41.4)
Minority interest		**(1.0)**	(1.4)
Profit attributable to shareholders	5	**95.7**	119.8
Dividends	6	**(60.2)**	(60.2)
Retained profit	17	**35.5**	59.6
Earnings per 25p Ordinary share	7	**13.9p**	17.4p

32

FISONS

FIG 6.3.7 *A consolidated profit and loss account as produced by Fisons for the year ended 31 December 1992.*

LADBROKE GROUP PLC

CONSOLIDATED PROFIT AND LOSS ACCOUNT
FOR THE YEAR ENDED 31st DECEMBER 1989

	Note	1989 £m	1988 £m
Turnover	1	**3,659.5**	2,848.0
Cost of sales		**3,250.9**	2,518.6
Gross profit		**408.6**	329.4
Administrative expenses		**60.3**	53.4
Share of profits of related companies		**5.2**	0.5
Operating profit	2	**353.5**	276.5
Interest	3	**51.3**	24.2
Profit on ordinary activities before taxation	1 – 3	**302.2**	252.3
Tax on profit on ordinary activities	5	**88.4**	78.7
Profit on ordinary activities after taxation		**213.8**	173.6
Minority interests		**6.7**	4.0
Profit for the financial year attributable to shareholders before extraordinary profit		**207.1**	169.6
Extraordinary profit	6	**4.9**	26.0
Profit attributable to shareholders	7	**212.0**	195.6
Dividends	8	**83.8**	69.6
Retained profit for the year		**128.2**	126.0
Earnings per share			
Actual	9	**24.26p**	19.99p
Fully diluted	9	**23.76p**	19.84p

Movements on reserves are shown on page 50, note 24.

FIG 6.3.8 *A consolidated profit and loss account as produced by Ladbroke Group PLC for the year ended 31 December 1989.*

GROUP BALANCE SHEET

AT 6 MARCH 1993

	NOTES	1993 £m	1992 £m
Fixed assets			
Tangible assets	11	3,500	3,670
Investments and loans	12	107	99
Associated undertakings	13	271	252
Total fixed assets		3,878	4,021
Current assets			
Stocks	15	1,201	1,149
Debtors	16	946	904
Cash at bank and in hand		135	104
Creditors (due within one year)			
Short-term borrowings	19	(336)	(363)
Other creditors	17	(1,296)	(1,190)
Net current assets		650	604
Total assets less current liabilities		4,528	4,625
Creditors (due after one year)			
Loan capital	19	(1,617)	(1,671)
Other creditors	17	(46)	(33)
Provisions for liabilities and charges	18	(114)	(141)
Net assets		2,751	2,780
Capital and reserves			
Called up share capital	20	229	228
Share premium account	20	430	405
Revaluation reserve	21	1,247	1,624
Profit and loss account	22	476	423
Shareholders' equity		2,382	2,680
Minority interests		369	100
Total equity		2,751	2,780

Approved by a duly appointed and authorised committee of the board on 26 May 1993 and signed on its behalf by:

Michael Jackaman
CHAIRMAN

Peter Macfarlane
DIRECTOR

FIG 6.3.9 *A group balance sheet as produced by Alliance and Leicester for the year ended 6 March 1993.*

LADBROKE GROUP PLC

CONSOLIDATED BALANCE SHEET
AT 31st DECEMBER 1989

	Note	1989 £m		1988 £m	
Fixed assets					
Intangible assets	10		792.5		600.1
Tangible assets:					
Operating assets	11	2,155.1		1,563.3	
Investment properties	12	757.7	2,912.8	514.5	2,077.8
Investments	13		55.6		42.1
			3,760.9		2,720.0
Current assets					
Development properties	14	258.8		181.9	
Stocks	15	152.4		110.7	
Debtors	16	322.8		227.1	
Investments	17	64.1		16.4	
Cash at bank and in hand		112.6		84.0	
		910.7		620.1	
Creditors – amounts falling due within one year	18	636.5		480.0	
Net current assets			274.2		140.1
Total assets less current liabilities			4,035.1		2,860.1
Creditors – amounts falling due after more than one year	19		1,541.5		823.9
Provisions for liabilities and charges					
Deferred taxation	21		27.9		18.1
			2,465.7		2,018.1
Capital and reserves					
Called up share capital	22		85.6		42.4
Share premium account	23		312.9		342.2
Other reserves	24		2,035.4		1,607.4
Shareholders' funds			2,433.9		1,992.0
Minority interests			31.8		26.1
			2,465.7		2,018.1

Approved by the board of directors on 25th April 1990

C Stein

JF O'Mahony

Directors

FIG 6.3.10 *A consolidated balance sheet as provided by Ladbroke Group PLC for the year ended 31 December 1989.*

THE SOLE TRADER

A **sole trader** may gather documents throughout the year and place them in a ring-binder. Possibly he/she will deal with them personally, or pay a specialist to help with the accounts. It will be necessary for the sole trader to declare annually the financial profit made by the organisation so that tax deductions can be made from the profit. The tax authorities will want to know that the accounts they receive are accurate and represent the financial position of the company. In order to calculate the profits made, it will be useful to prepare the following sets of accounts: a **trading account**, a **profit and loss account** and a **balance sheet**

A trading account

This type of account decides what **gross profit** the organisation has made. In order to work this out, the following calculations have to be made:

the sales (the items sold by the organisation)
minus –
the cost of sales (the items purchased for re-sale by the organisation, with adjustments made for items still held in stock at the end of the year)
equals =
the gross profit

In calculating the **cost of sales**, it is necessary to take into account the value of stocks. **'Opening stock'** is the amount at the beginning of the financial year. **'Closing stock'** is the amount left at the end of the financial year. Therefore, the calculation for the cost of sales is:

the opening stock
plus +
any purchases made
minus –
the closing stock
equals =
the cost of sales

The profit and loss account

This can be added to the bottom of the trading account It covers the same period of trading. Money may be earned from additional items such as rent from premises or commission earned. This extra income is added to the gross profit from the trading account. Any expenses the organisation may have incurred are deducted, e.g. the rent of premises, gas or electricity bills, depreciation on machinery or debts outstanding. The purpose of the profit and loss account is to calculate the net profit of the organisation, and this is done using the following:

the gross profit
plus +
extra income (i.e. rent, commission, discounts)
minus –
expenses incurred
equals =
the net profit

The balance sheet

This document gives an up-to-the-minute picture of where the organisation is. It is normally prepared at the end of a financial period and states the **assets, liabilities** and **capital** of the organisation at that time. It provides information on a business's exact financial position, even though some of the assets and liabilities are short term, while others are ongoing. Whichever applies, the balance sheet must always BALANCE.

THE LIMITED COMPANY

As we have said earlier in the book, a limited company is owned by its shareholders. These shareholders have limited liability, and the organisation is managed by a board of directors (who may or may not be shareholders). There are two different types of limited company – private and public. A review of a few terms might be useful at this stage:

1 *The Articles of Association* which the company produced at the outset of business state the way in which the accounts of the organisation should be kept and recorded.
2 *Share capital* – this is stated in the Memorandum of Association and can be divided into two:
- *Authorised share capital* – the amount the shareholders have authorised the directors to issue
- *Issued share capital* – the amount that has actually been issued by the directors
3 *Shares.* There are several different types of shares:
  - *ordinary shares* – for which dividends are normally expressed as a percentage of the nominal value of the shares or as a monetary value per share
  - *preference shares* – which carry a preferential right to receive a dividend
  - *debentures* – which are split into units like shares and are loans made to the organisation and secured by assets of the organisation

The trading/profit and loss account

This is similar to the trading account of a sole trader, except for the following:

- because the directors are employed by the organisation, their **salaries or fees** have to be included as an expense

- **debenture payments** (because they are similar to loan payments) are treated as expenses

The appropriation account

This appears on the same page as the profit and loss account and shows the way in which the profits are distributed.

Corporation tax is also shown on the appropriation account. This is charged on profits and is paid to the Inland Revenue.

Any **Reserves** shown on the appropriation account are **monies set aside** for a specific purpose in the future. These reserves are part of the profit made which the directors and shareholders have preferred not to distribute as dividends.

Retained profit shown on the appropriation account is **money left over** at the end of the year which has been added to money left over at the end of the previous year and carried forward.

The balance sheet

The balance sheet of a limited company is prepared in the same way as that of any other organisation, except that it states the following:

- authorised share capital
- issued share capital
- reserves
- retained profits

PARTNERSHIPS

Earlier in the book we looked at the ways in which sole traders may venture into partnerships. When a partnership is formed, the following are included in the partnership agreement:

- **profit-sharing arrangements** and details
- the rate at which interest is to be paid on the **capital invested by each partner**
- the rate at which interest is to be charged on **drawings made by each partner**
- the way in which **profits and losses would be shared** between the partners

The differences in the preparation of accounts for a sole trader and a partnership are minimal:

1 an **appropriation account** section is included in the **profit and loss account**. This shows the way in which the profit is divided between the partners
2 a **capital section** is included in the **balance sheet**. This shows each of the partner's capital and current account balances. The capital account of each partner is fixed and only changes if partners decide to increase or decrease their contributions. On the other hand, the current account balances may change because of the following:

- the share of profit is added
- if it applies, the salary of each partner is added
- any interest earned on capital is added
- any drawings from the account are deducted
- any interest charges because of drawings are deducted

NON-PROFIT-MAKING ORGANISATIONS

We have looked at examples of non-profit-making organisations earlier in the book. You may want to refresh your memory by referring back to those pages. Often the accounts of such organisations are termed **Club Accounts**, and would include the following:

1 *A receipts and payments account.* A very straightforward document which simply lists the money received and the money paid out.
2 *An income and expenditure account.* This would include the items from the **receipts and payments account**, and is very similar to a **profit and loss account**. Included in the **income and expenditure account** would be any of the following:

- any subscriptions which have been paid in advance
- any prepayments
- any fund-raising activities
- any profits made from such things as the bar and sale of beverages and soft drinks

3 *The balance sheet.* This is a very simple document to complete once the **receipts and payments** and **income and expenditure accounts** have been produced.

LOCAL AUTHORITIES

Local authorities or local **councils** provide a range of services to the community. These services include libraries, police, fire services, education, transport and housing, although sometimes the responsibility for these services is shared by central government.

Legislation to which local authorities have to adhere lays down procedures for local authority accounting which is very different from that of the private sector industries. One reason for this difference is the fact that local authorities do not have profit making as their main aim. This means that local authorities tend to have a budget for each of the services they provide, and have to raise the funds to meet these budgets.

As with other organisations, local authority spending usually falls into two types:

1 *Capital expenditure.* This is money spent on major areas of outlay like new hospitals or new road systems

2 *Revenue expenditure.* This is money spent on a day-to-day basis for areas of outlay like salaries, upkeep of buildings and road maintenance.

Sources of finance

Local authorities may obtain their finance by a variety of means:

1 *Council tax.* As you already know, since April 1993 residents pay their local authority **council tax** payments. Properties are banded at different levels, with the most expensive houses paying the most tax.
2 *Central government grants.* Local authorities may obtain a grant from central government. These grants fall into two main areas:

- **specific grants** obviously for something specific, such as a new road system or identified new housing
- **revenue support grants** These grants are specific to each area and are calculated on the amount of expenditure the authority is likely to incur during the course of providing its services.

3 *Borrowing.* A local authority may borrow money to help finance major projects. Local authority stock can be bought and sold on the **Stock Exchange** and also a local authority may sell **bonds** in order to take out a temporary loan.
4 *Charges for services.* Local authorities also raise money from the services they provide. These charges may include money from leisure centres and swimming pools, rent from council houses and income provided by homes for the elderly.

Accounting procedures

Legislation insists that local authorities must produce **annual reports** containing the necessary accounts information. These accounts are prepared from the daily records of the authority and contain the following:

1 *Income and expenditure accounts.* An **income and expenditure account** will be prepared for each fund provided by the local authority. For example, the income and expenditure account for a swimming pool will show the payments incurred for the use of the service as well as the expenditure made in order to provide the service.
2 *Consolidated balance sheet.* This will be similar to any other balance sheet but will show the situation for each of the funds provided by the local authority.

We all know how important it is to control the cash we have available, and to forecast how much we are likely to have to spend in the future. As with individuals and their personal money, so organisations of any type have to carry out forecasting and cash-flow control. The reason for cash planning or budgeting is to ensure there is no shortfall in the future. Let's look at these in more detail:

CASH-FLOW FORECASTING

Any organisation requires cash so that it can buy the goods or services it requires to produce its products, improve its products and make a profit. Obviously, the way an organisation uses its cash is vital. It is important that it uses it to the best advantage. An organisation must ensure it has sufficient cash to carry out long- and short-term objectives as well as making sure that the cash coming in is sufficient to cover that going out. An accurate cash-flow position is vital for the smooth running of an organisation.

In order to prepare a cash-flow forecast, an organisation needs to know, or to estimate, what income and expenditure is likely and when it is likely. This information is likely to be broken down when preparing a **cash-flow forecast**. Possible items that need to be considered are as follows:

- money in the bank
- purchases for raw materials
- receipts from sale of goods
- any credit transactions entered into
- any credit given to customers
- wages that have to be paid on a regular basis
- anticipated purchases of new machinery etc.
- rent and rates to be paid
- overheads (such as electricity and heating) to be paid
- any expected income which will be used for the business

Obviously, any cash-flow forecast will need to be amended as trading continues throughout the year. Any number of problems may arise which affect the cash-flow of an organisation, and the timing of money coming in and going out of a business. Regular monitoring is vital if the organisation is to be profitable.

AGED DEBTORS AND AGED CREDITORS

We have already mentioned aged debtors and aged creditors in Element 6.2, but it may be useful to repeat the information here as these are among the key components of accounting information required by an organisation in order to monitor its performance.

CONSOLIDATED CASH FLOW STATEMENT

For the fifty-two weeks ended 27 March 1993 (Note 1)

(c) Disposal of Subsidiary Undertakings

	£ million
Fixed assets	97.0
Stocks	57.6
Debtors	17.1
Creditors	(35.2)
Other loans (b)	(17.2)
Provisions for liabilities	(0.9)
	118.4
Loss on disposal	(31.4)
Goodwill adjustment	10.0
Provision for Habitat Europe	5.3
Total consideration in cash	**102.3**
Deferred consideration *(Note 13)*	18.8
Cash consideration received net of £17.4 million of cash in businesses sold	83.5
Total consideration in cash	**102.3**

The businesses disposed of during the year had the following effect on the Group's cash flows:

	Continuing Businesses £ million	Discontinued Businesses £ million	Total £ million
Operating cash flows	49.4	(45.6)	3.8
Returns on investment and servicing of finance	(22.1)	(0.5)	(22.6)
Taxation	1.8	(1.1)	0.7
Investing activities	(25.0)	75.5	50.5
Financing	(47.0)	0.5	(46.5)
Net cash outflow	**(42.9)**	**28.8**	**(14.1)**

24   STOREHOUSE

FIG 6.3.11 *A consolidated cash flow statement as produced by Storehouse (the merger of BHS, Mothercare and Blazer) for the year ended 27 March 1993.*

1 *Aged debtors.* This is often one of the most useful reports available when monitoring is being undertaken. It will list the debt for each customer. Increasingly, these reports are prepared by the use of computer systems. The **aged debtors report** will be prepared from the sales ledger of the organisation and will state whether customers are paying promptly. Obviously a large number of aged debtors will adversely affect the cash-flow position of the organisation.

2 *Aged creditors.* The reverse of the aged debtors, aged creditors are people to whom the organisation owes money. Payment outside the terms of credit can lead to bad feeling with suppliers, which, in turn, could result in their refusing to supply the organisation. Once again an aged creditors report will be compiled when monitoring is being undertaken. This will list the accounts payable and state whether they are being paid within a reasonable amount of time.

PERFORMANCE OF BUSINESS

The measuring and monitoring of business performance relies on a constant flow of feedback and information from all parts of an organisation. We can further characterise this information and feedback as being of both a **quantitative** and a **qualitative** nature.

- *Quantitative* this refers to strictly measurable performance in terms of facts and figures. This information can be related directly to the goals and objectives set by the organisation
- *Qualitative* this is often a more immediate indicator of whether businesses are reaching their goals and objectives, but can be fraught with personal opinion and conjecture. A qualitative assessment of business performance is derived from personal views, and is not necessarily borne out by the facts and figures produced by key personnel.

SOLVENT

As we now know, **solvency** is a measure of the business's ability to survive. It means that the organisation is able to meet its short-term financial commitments and essentially to operate in at least a break-even situation. Organisations which are on the edge of solvency may consider the monitoring of financial transactions to be even more critical than those who are comparatively successful.

PROFITABLE

The level of **profitability** of a business is measured in relation to its overall productivity and deployment of resources. The levels at which acceptable profit is made differ from organisation to organisation. The profit may relate directly to each unit traded or to the overall turnover of the organisation. In this respect, it is possible for an organisation to be profitable despite the fact that

certain elements of the organisation are only breaking even, or are, perhaps, trading at a small loss. It is essential that all financial transactions are monitored in order to ascertain whether projected profit levels have been achieved.

ACHIEVING TARGETS AND COMPARISON WITH TARGETS

As a matter of course, organisations make forecasts and set targets. However, what is of particular interest to an organisation are the **projected targets** and the **actual performance**. The consistent monitoring of all financial transactions is essential to ensure that the organisation is 'on line' to achieve specified targets.

It is also important for organisations to make constant comparisons (they will not necessarily wait until the end of the year to do this) with projected targets and actual performance so that they can readjust levels of business activity and production as necessary. These comparisons should also identify key problem areas which may require additional financial or advisory input. Areas with particular problems may need a total overhaul of either staff or process. By monitoring financial transactions in relation to targets proposed, an organisation should be able to identify these problem areas before too much damage has been done to productivity, profit or growth.

Organisations use a number of formulae to ascertain whether they are working at full capacity and obtaining the highest possible level of profitability. We shall look at these here, but we shall be considering these in much more detail in Unit 7 and you will find them of particular use in Unit 8:

Gross profit percentage

Gross profit percentage relates gross profit to sales revenue and will rise or fall under certain circumstances. If the percentage falls, then the organisation is comparatively less profitable. If the percentage rises, then a greater level of profitability has been achieved.

$$\text{gross profit percentage} = \frac{\text{Gross profit}}{\text{sales revenue}} \times 100$$

This gross profit percentage is normally calculated at regular intervals throughout the year.

Net profit percentage

Net profit percentage is usually calculated year-on-year and is used to make comparisons with other organisations operating in the same market. As it considers net profit rather than gross profit, it takes into account all of the business's expenses. As a result, the business can identify any increases in the overheads and make adjustments to suit.

$$\text{net profit percentage} = \frac{\text{Net profit}}{\text{Sales revenue}} \times 100$$

Return on capital employed

This formula is one of the more useful ways of measuring profitability. It shows the relationship between the amount of **capital** used in the operation of the business and **profits** generated. Capital employed is the amount of available finance and is usually generated from profits made in the previous year. The capital employed is all of the net assets before any long-term deductions (such as debts).

percentage return on capital employed (ROCE)

$$= \frac{\text{net profit for year}}{\text{capital employed}} \times 100$$

Liquidity

Working out the liquidity of an organisation (the ability of that organisation to turn assets into cash) is an important consideration, particularly when we look at the organisation's ability to pay short-term debts. The easiest way to work out the liquidity ratio of the organisation is to employ the **'acid test'**. The acid test looks at how much money will be available when the creditors require payment. This is best expressed in two ways:

$$\text{current assets} - \text{stock} = \text{current liabilities}$$

or alternatively,

$$\text{debtors} + \text{cash balances} = \text{current liabilities}$$

This acid test ratio will be quite accurate since it only includes assets capable of being turned into ready cash in the short term.

Debtors' collection period and credit periods available to the organisation

There are two other related formulae which we may consider, the **debtors' collection period** and the **credit periods available to the organisation**. The first formula is used when an organisation is trying to improve its liquidity by cutting down the amount of time it gives debtors to pay outstanding bills. Customers who pay late are, in effect, receiving free credit at the expense of the organisation. The ratio shows the average number of days of credit that customers receive at present. Normally, customers receive somewhere and between 30 and 90 days credit as a matter of course. The formula is:

$$\text{debtors' collection period} = \frac{\text{debtors}}{\text{average daily sales}}$$

The other side of the coin is the credit period available to the organisation. This shows the average credit period suppliers are prepared to offer the organisation. By extending the average credit period, an organisation can increase its liquidity. The formula is:

$$\text{credit period} = \frac{\text{creditors}}{\text{average daily purchases}}$$

Use of assets

In terms of the **use of its assets**, a business will try to see how its performance can be improved by better using these assets. This is usually considered from two viewpoints, that of **actual asset utilisation** and that of **stock turnover**.

The asset utilisation formula shows how fixed assets are being used to generate sales revenue. This is, in effect, a method of showing how efficient the organisation is.

$$\text{asset utilisation} = \frac{\text{sales}}{\text{fixed assets}}$$

This formula can be misleading in some respects since organisations require different levels of fixed assets in order to operate.

The **stock turnover** formula shows the average number of days an item of stock is held before it is used or sold. This will vary from organisation to organisation, depending upon the type of business activity in which it is engaged, e.g. a baker could not hold his stock for the same length of time as a jeweller. The stock turnover formula is calculated by adding together the values of the opening stock and those of the closing stock, and multiplying by two. The stock turnover formula is:

$$\text{stock turnover} = \frac{\text{cost of sales}}{\text{average stock}}$$

Gearing

Finally, we should consider the capital structure of the organisation in terms of its utilisation of share capital, loans and other funds. The **gearing** formula makes a comparison between the capital within the business (provided by shareholders) and any long-term loans or other sources of finance. The gearing formula is:

$$\text{gearing} = \frac{\text{interest bearing capital}}{\text{risk capital}} \times 100$$

A high gearing percentage means that an organisation must spend a higher percentage of its revenue on interest payments. Inevitably, this means that the organisation's fixed costs are higher and consequently the organisation is at a disadvantage in comparison to other competitors. In recessions, highly geared organisations have tended to fail as interest rates have increased.

As we have already mentioned, the use of these formulae and ratios is strictly limited to the context in which the organisation operates. They may not be used for making comparisons between organisations because they do not measure size, structure or type of business activity. These formulae and ratios can only show some of an organisation's aspects, but they are useful in identifying the early stages of potential problems.

UNIT 6

assignment

'TRANSACTIONS, DOCUMENTS AND ACCOUNTS'

To fulfil the criteria of this Unit, you will need to learn the **purpose** of documenting financial transactions, how this is done **in practice** and the **uses** to which the information recorded can be put.

In the course of preparing information to monitor business performance you will already have been required to complete a number of documents, using the blank documents available in the teacher's pack. Now using the information you have gained from completing these documents, you need to conduct the following research:

Take the same two organisations that you chose in the Unit 5 assignment. Here you will be looking at their financial transactions. You need to consider which of the business sectors your organisations came from and, having done this, choose the one most appropriate for this particular assignment. Once again you will need to consult with your tutor and seek assistance from the management of the chosen organisation.

In effect, you will design your own **case study** of your organisation. You may find that you can gain permission to spend some work experience time in the organisation, or to 'shadow' an individual within the accounts department for a week or two. If this is the case, you should be very careful to comply with the organisation's requirements with regard to confidentiality of information.

You will assess the information you research in order to cover the following criteria:

- who uses this accounting information?
- how does the organisation use this information to monitor its business performance?
- what information is relevant and why?

You should present your research as a report which assesses the financial situation of the organisation in terms of:

- solvency
- levels of profit
- the setting and achieving of its targets
- the monitoring of targets set

Your findings should be presented in written form, using terminology which shows you have examined all the aspects of accounting procedures.

UNIT 6

test questions

1 Which of the following can be considered a liability of a business?

(a) Petty cash
(b) Stock
(c) Company cars
(d) Bank loans

2 Which of the following would not be considered when calculating working capital?

(a) Premises
(b) Cash
(c) Creditors
(d) Debtors

3 Which of the following is not an intangible asset?

(a) Patents
(b) Goodwill
(c) Land
(d) Trade marks

4 Which of the following would you not expect to find on a payslip?

(a) Gross salary
(b) Net salary
(c) National insurance deductions
(d) Cheque number

5 Which of the following headings would not appear on an order form?

(a) Quantity
(b) Catalogue number
(c) VAT
(d) Total amount ordered

6 Which of the following does not appear on a cheque?

(a) Account balance
(b) Account number
(c) Cheque number
(d) Branch code

7 Petty cash can be recorded using which of the following systems?

(a) The Impost system
(b) The Impest system
(c) The Imprest system
(d) The Improst system

8 Which of the following does not necessarily need to be checked when an invoice arrives?

(a) Discounts
(b) Prices
(c) VAT
(d) Invoice number

9 The formula for calculating debtors' collection periods is?

(a) Sales/debtors
(b) Debtors' average daily sales
(c) Debtors/purchases
(d) Average daily sales/365

10 A Management Information System would be used to

(a) Present reports
(b) Monitor financial transactions
(c) Assist managers in planning
(d) Produce final accounts

Identify sources of finance for a business plan

I ASSET TYPES
land, buildings, production machinery, office machines

2 ASSET FINANCE METHODS
shareholders' funds, mortgage, lease, loan, hire purchase, grant

3 SOURCES OF ASSET FINANCE
investors, banks, building societies, landlord, finance company, government agencies

4 WORKING CAPITAL
cost of raw materials, work in progress, stocks of finished goods, debtors

5 WORKING CAPITAL FINANCE METHODS
equity, overdraft, creditors

6 SOURCES OF WORKING CAPITAL
investors, banks and sellers

ASSET TYPES

Assets are all items of value owned by the organisation. They may include any money owed to the organisation by debtors on orders fulfilled but not yet paid. Assets are either fixed or current and in the first instance, we will be considering the fixed assets of an organisation. These include:

- land
- buildings
- production machinery
- office machines

We will look at these individually in more detail.

LAND

Land can be a valuable asset to the organisation, because of its comparative worth on the open market and the possible uses to which this land can be put by the organisation. Broadly speaking, land may be held either as leasehold or freehold. Land provides the organisation with perhaps its most valuable collateral against which it may borrow.

BUILDINGS

Depending upon the suitability of the building, the organisation probably considers its **premises** to be as important as any land it owns. The building would normally be designed in such a way as to maximise its usage by the organisation. Organisations may own additional premises that are not necessary for their day-to-day business activities, and these may be sub-let or leased to other organisations. This is particularly common in the case of High Street shops, which may own the freehold to the whole building, but lease or rent rooms or whole floors above the retail outlet to other businesses. The value of the buildings will, of course, relate to current market values and, in certain cases, buildings may be very difficult to dispose of in the short term. However, buildings provide a very substantial asset upon which to base applications for loans and financial assistance.

student activity

Carry out an audit in your local area, looking at the various types of buildings used by organisations. Although you can probably think of some other categories of buildings, here is a brief list of different types:

- light manufacturing unit
- purpose-built industrial unit
- purpose-built office block
- converted office accommodation
- office above retail unit
- purpose-built retail unit
- 'traditional' retail unit

Can you identify the types of organisations which use these premises? How suitable do you think these premises are for their intended use?

PRODUCTION MACHINERY

Production machinery includes all of the necessary equipment required to carry out production processes. In this category we also include all necessary spares and certain consumable machinery items. Production machinery suffers from depreciation (this means that the current value of the asset is lower than the original cost of the asset). Because of depreciation, over a period of years, assets in this category will gradually become less and less valuable in real terms to the organisation. A constant updating and replacement of production machinery is necessary, not only to ensure that the organisation makes full use of new technological break-throughs, but also to maintain the relative value of production machinery assets. Typically, production machinery includes all automated, semi-automated and manual machinery of various sizes and complexities.

FIG 7.1.1 *Ladbroke Property is a division of Ladbroke Group PLC, and is involved in the rented office space sector of business. 'Langham Island', a 1.6-acre development in London's West End consist of some 270,000 square feet of office space and adjoins Farringdon Station.*

OFFICE MACHINES

Within this category, we include, of course, typewriters, computers, switchboards, telephones and photocopying machines, for example. In addition, we should also consider office equipment such as desks, chairs, filing cabinets and so on. Again, These suffer, perhaps even more so than production machinery, from depreciation. The value of these assets is related to the current state of the second-hand market, and this, particularly in times of recession, can be very depressed. Office machines tend to have very low values as they are so quickly made obsolete by technological developments. An organisation which has large numbers of typewriters that it wishes to dispose of and replace with computer terminals will find that they have relatively little realisable value.

ASSET FINANCE METHODS

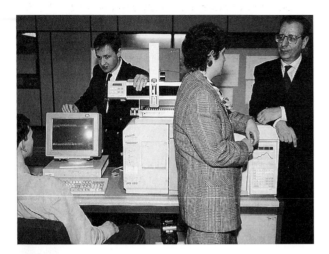

FIG 7.1.2 *The Scientific Equipment Divisions of Fisons develop the MD 800 – a new benchtop system – with a wide range of environmental, clinical and industrial testing potential.*

In order to fund the purchase of the capital assets described in the previous section, the organisation will use a number of methods to raise capital. These include:

- shareholders' funds
- mortgages
- leases
- loans
- hire purchase
- grants

We will now assess the relative importance of and the ease of access to these sources of asset finance. In the next section we will be looking at the actual sources of these asset finances.

SHAREHOLDERS' FUNDS

The shareholders or owners of the business may be a useful source of finance. The issue of shares to raise finance will not only raise this capital but will also spread the ownership of the organisation more widely. Organisations tend to avoid this option since it may mean that they will lose some of their control of the business. There are other methods linked to shareholders which can be considered if the sale of shares is not an acceptable option. Shareholders should receive a proportion of the organisation's profits by means of a dividend. However, the organisation may wish to retain some of these earnings, in which case they are known as **Undistributed Profit.** They may be used for the acquisition of specific assets.

The term capital itself has a number of different meanings, as we will see later in this Unit. In relation to shares, we can consider the following types of capital:

- *authorised capital* – this description of capital refers to the **value of the shares** that an organisation is authorised to issue under its Memorandum of Association
- *issued capital* – this is the value of the organisation's **capital** which has, up to this point, been **issued to the shareholders** in the form of shares
- *paid-up capital* – this is the **amount of capital which has actually been paid** to the organisation on the shares which have been issued. It should be noted that it is possible to issue shares which have not been paid for or have only been partly paid for. This is particularly the case of share issues in the privatisation of public corporations.
- *unpaid capital* – if shares have been issued, but are not at present fully paid, then the outstanding monies are called **unpaid capital.** Shareholders will be expected to pay the unpaid remainder to the organisation either at a specified time or when the organisation calls upon them to do so. The organisation may hold this option in reserve and call upon the shareholders to make the additional payment if it faces difficult financial problems.

FIG 7.1.3 *Storehouse, which includes such well-known High Street names as BHS and Mothercare, produce an Annual Report and Accounts for the perusal of existing and potential investors.*

MORTGAGE

Many individuals have their own mortgage in order to finance the purchase of their homes. A mortgage is a legal agreement signed by the borrower which gives the lender certain legal rights over the property. The principal right given to the lender is the ability to repossess the property and sell it should the borrower be unable to make the required repayments. There are essentially two main types of mortgage.

1 *Repayment mortgage.* This is a mortgage paid monthly. It includes payments to both the capital borrowed and the interest accumulated. At the beginning of the payment schedule, the bulk of the repayments will be interest, but in the latter stages of the payment schedule the larger part of the payment will be towards the capital. It is prudent, and often required, that the borrower take out a mortgage protection insurance policy to ensure that the mortgage is 'paid up' in the event of the death of the borrower.

2 *Endowment mortgages.* The main alternative to repayment mortgage is the endowment mortgage. In this case the borrower pays only interest to the lender. The borrower also makes monthly payments into an endowment life assurance policy which ensures that there is sufficient capital accumulated at the end of the mortgage period to pay off the capital borrowed.

Increasingly, as people have taken out personal pension schemes, they have found it cost-effective to take out mortgages linked to their pensions. In effect, the borrower is able to obtain a mortgage on the basis of the funds which will be available in his/her pension scheme.

Organisations, however primarily use, the first method of obtaining a mortgage since the mortgage will be based upon the organisation itself and not an individual.

Fixed rate		8.55%	
Fixed until		30th June 1998	
Mortgage term		25 years	
Amount of loan £		40,000	80,000
APR	Endowment/pension	**9.0%**	**8.9%**
	Repayment	**9.2%**	**9.1%**
Monthly interest payments (net) £	Endowment/pension	232.63	517.63
300 monthly repayments (net) £	Repayment	279.89	603.27
Total amount payable (Gross) £	Endowment/pension	126,361.00	251,931.00
	Repayment	98,877.00	197,065.00

Notes to the table

1. The net (re)payments assume tax relief at 25% on the first £30,000 of the loan.

2. A non-refundable booking fee of £150 and an arrangement fee of £150 is payable. The arrangement fee can be added to your mortgage and can be waived – see later.

3. The calculations make allowances for typical valuation fees of £90 and legal costs of £150 for a mortgage of £40,000, and typical valuation fees of £130 and legal costs of £180 for a mortgage of £80,000.

4. The figures do not include the premiums for endowment, pension or mortgage protection policies. Mortgage Indemnity may be payable if the loan exceeds 80% of the purchase price or the Bank's valuation whichever is lower.

5. The endowment and pension options are repaid in one lump sum at the end of the term.

FIG 7.1.4 *A detail from Barclays' fixed rate mortgage leaflet which shows repayment schedules and appropriate APRs.*

LEASE

If an organisation chooses to lease equipment, then it is never the legal owner of that equipment. The equipment remains the property of the organisation which leased it. The equipment is leased in return for a regular schedule of payments. The organisation leasing the equipment cannot count the equipment as an asset on its balance sheet and does not benefit from tax allowances related to equipment. The organisation is allowed to count the lease payments as a legitimate business expense and may, in this way, include the equipment on the profit and loss account. There are essentially three forms of leasing agreements. These are:

1 *Short period or closed-ended leases.* These leasing agreements last for up to five years and. A particular benefit to the organisation leasing the equipment is the option to buy the equipment at the end of the lease period at a favourable rate.
2 *Long-term or open-ended leases.* These leasing agreements run for an unspecified time period. They can be ended once the minimum leasing period has been completed.
3 *Reduced payment or balloon leases.* This type of lease offers the advantage of a reduced level of lease repayment during most of the lease period. At the end of this period the organisation leasing the equipment pays a large final payment in order to terminate the lease. This is particularly useful since the leasing company usually allows the organisation leasing the equipment to find another organisation willing to buy the equipment. In this way the organisation can offset some of this final payment by the cash generated from the sale.

student activity

Using the local estate agent(s) as your primary source for research purposes, investigate the relative availability of the following:

● leasehold commercial properties
● freehold commercial properties
● rented commercial properties

Which is the most common and why?

LOAN

Loans are usually negotiated with a finance provider in order to acquire an agreed sum of money which has been earmarked for the purchase of particular equipment or other assets. The loan is usually paid back over a fixed time period with agreed levels of interest and regular payments. The organisation receiving the loan will be required to pay regularly over a number of years and will be expected to meet each payment on schedule. These loans are particularly useful in raising finance to make large purchases. Organisations will be granted loans on the basis of their credit rating. The finance provider will require evidence of income and expenditure so that it can assure itself that the organisation is able to meet all loan payments. Loans can be more easily obtained if the organisation has realisable assets which could be seized should it be unable to maintain the repayment levels.

student activity

Referring back to Figure 7.1.4. write a letter of application to Barclays asking for details and terms and conditions of their available loans. What information do you think you should include in this letter? What information do you think they will subsequently ask you to provide?

HIRE PURCHASE

Hire purchase is not a simple method of purchasing a product. A finance company buys the equipment from the seller and then 'hires' this equipment to the organisation wishing to obtain it. The organisation then has to agree to make regular payments to the finance company until the full value of the goods, plus the interest accumulated over the period, has been fully repaid. In a hire purchase agreement the equipment remains the property of the finance company until all monies have been repaid.

If a hire purchase agreement is broken by the organisation because it cannot continue to make repayments, then certain laws protect the finance company. These laws give the finance company the right to repossess the goods without having to refer to the courts if less than one-third of the repayments have been repaid. If more than one-third has been repaid, then the finance company has to apply to the courts to obtain permission to repossess the equipment. The court will not always grant this permission, but may agree an order by which the organisation can negotiate lower repayments over a longer period of time.

The organisation entering the hire purchase agreement is not the legal owner of the equipment until all the repayments have been made. The organisation cannot, therefore resell the goods while the agreement is still in force. Because the organisation is not the legal owner of the equipment, the asset can be shown on the organisation's balance sheet and it can claim tax allowances from the time it takes possession of the equipment. The amount still outstanding to the finance company will be shown as a liability on the organisation's balance sheet.

The main advantage to an organisation of using the method of hire purchase to obtain equipment is that it is saved the initial outlay of large sums of money. One of the disadvantages, though, is the fact that the repay-

ments include interest in addition to the capital supplied by the finance company and tax relief is only available on the interest the organisation pays.

GRANT

Grants may be available from a variety of government, local authority or QUANGO sources. Increasingly, the EC provides funds for suitable projects, particularly those linked to social and regional development. As we will see, organisations like European Investment Bank will provide financial assistance for projects relating to industrial, infrastructure or energy areas of business activity.

These grants require the organisation to substantiate any claims under the grant framework and the organisation will find itself continually monitored and scrutinised by the grant provider.

student activity

In the role of a sole trader with limited working capital, consider the relative attractiveness of a hire purchase agreement as against outright purchase. What criteria would you use in trying to determine whether a hire purchase agreement is more beneficial to the cash flow of the business?

SOURCES OF ASSET FINANCE

There is a wide variety of **sources of asset finance**. Some sorts of finance, as we shall see, are more expensive and difficult to obtain than others. However, an organisation which is fully conversant with the availability of finance will have investigated all of these at some time. Essentially, they fall into three main categories:

- internal (e.g. investors and shareholders)
- external (e.g. banks and building societies)
- governmental (e.g. loan guarantee schemes, business expansion schemes, EC etc.)

student activity

We have mentioned above the three main sources of asset finance. Before you read any further, can you identify more specific types of asset finance within the three main categories?

INVESTORS

As we mentioned in the previous section, investors can offer considerable levels of finance to an expanding or diversifying organisation. An organisation should be careful to balance the advantages and disadvantages offered to the shareholders and must not always expect the shareholders to provide additional finance at short notice. It requires considerable organisation to inform

and obtain finance from shareholders and, therefore, may not necessarily be the ideal means of acquiring finance.

BANKS AND BUILDING SOCIETIES

Probably the most common way of raising short-term finance is to use a bank overdraft. Many organisations run on a permanent overdraft which allows them flexibility in controlling their cash-flow. The overdraft facility means that an organisation will pay interest on money owed to the bank at a set rate of interest. The basic interest rate of the bank will vary, depending upon the credit standing of the organisation and the security which the organisation can offer against the overdraft. In some cases, when the organisation is considered a poor credit risk, the interest rate may be extremely high.

Banks are not very keen to offer overdraft facilities and may set a number of limitations upon the organisation. These will include:

- the organisation may be required to give precise reasons for requesting an overdraft
- the bank will set a specific time period for which the overdraft is available
- the bank will reserve the right to renegotiate the terms of this overdraft after this period has elapsed
- the bank may decide to withdraw the offer of an overdraft, in which case full payment must be made immediately

- the bank will require a guarantor to ensure that the debt can be recovered
- the bank will not be keen on the organisation using the overdraft to finance the purchase of capital equipment
- the bank should be kept informed of any developments or complications which may relate to the overdraft
- the organisation should not abuse the overdraft facility since this may mean that the bank in the future would give them a poor credit rating

Since the de-regulation of building societies, many have offered very similar facilities to those offered by banks. However, current account holders are not allowed to overdraw on their account. Overdrafts must, in both building society and banks, be prearranged.

student activity

In the role of a business owner, having read the requirements of a bank or building society regarding the provision of do you think that if you accept the offer of a , the bank or building society will impose an overly strict regime on your business? Do you think that, by providing all the information required and remaining within their guidelines, you, will lose control over certain aspects of your business activities?

Merchant banks

Merchant banks offer a wide variety of financial services to businesses. These include:

- loans
- financing mergers
- financing take-overs
- assisting exportation
- assisting importation
- organising the flotation of new organisations on the Stock Exchange
- preparation of a company prospectus

The merchant bank will usually receive a commission on the sales of shares generated by the flotation on the Stock Exchange and will 'under-write' (guarantee that it will buy the shares if nobody else does) the remaining shares.

student activity

Are there any other methods you could employ to organise the flotation of an organisation on the Stock Exchange without having to use a merchant bank?

LANDLORD

Organisations which rent or lease premises from a **landlord** and wish to redevelop or improve the premises may be able to organise at least a partial contribution towards this work. The terms of the contract agreed with the landlord, may oblige him/her to contribute in some way. It may be to the advantage of the landlord to assist since he/she will be able to ask for higher rental payments or, when the next period of lease is negotiated, require a higher leasing payment. Improvements increase the value of the landlord's assets. It should be noted that the landlord must be in agreement with any proposed improvements or developments on the site. If he/she does not agree, this may prove to be an immovable block to any plans. An organisation will, at all times, attempt to ensure that it has a good working relationship with its landlord so that there are no difficulties should the need arise to ask the landlord for a contribution.

student activity

If a landlord refuses to provide sufficient support and financial aid to make premises safe and suitable for a business, what steps could the business legally take?

FINANCE COMPANY

Finance companies also offer a wide range of asset finance options. Typically, they offer the following:

- mortgages
- leases
- loans
- hire purchases

The levels of payment to finance companies again depend upon the status of the borrower in terms of realisable assets and overall credit rating.

Finance companies also provide credit factoring facilities. This, in effect, means that they can purchase or act as an agent in the recovery of bad debts.

Factoring is a useful way of obtaining short-term finance, particularly for an organisation which is suffering a cash flow problem. The organisation sells the right to collect the money owed to it to a factor (often a finance company, finance house or clearing bank). The factor pays the organisation less than the face value of the debt (often up to some 10 per cent less). The factor then attempts to collect the debt in a variety of ways. In this respect, factoring can be considered an asset as the debt has been turned into readily available cash.

student activity

Credit factoring is an increasingly important aspect of ensuring that cash flow remains controllable within a business. Under what circumstances, and at what stage, do you think a business would resort to factoring in order to recover bad debt?

GOVERNMENT AGENCIES

As we mentioned in the previous section, there are a number of sources of finance available via government agencies. These include:

Grant aid schemes

Within this category there are assisted area grants, regional development grants and many other grants specifically targeted towards the re-generation of depressed areas. Organisations can take advantage of these grants if they are willing to relocate or expand within certain areas.

Department of Trade and Industry

The DTI is keen to encourage research and development in new technological areas, such as:

- microprocessing
- fibre optics
- computers

Within the grant system, the DTI will not only provide financial assistance towards the purchase and development of equipment, but also offer specialist advice at all levels.

Local authorities

There is a wide variety of grants available via local authorities. They earmark certain funds for particular development projects relevant to the local job market.

European Community funds

These are funds and grants that have been set aside to provide finance for specified projects. Specifically, as with grant aid schemes, they focus on social and regional development.

Loan guarantee scheme

Organisations which lack the necessary assets as security against loans are able to take advantage of the government's loan guarantee scheme. The Government essentially acts as a guarantor for loans up to £100,000, but with the limitation that it will only stand as guarantor for 70 per cent of this total. This is a particularly expensive way of obtaining finance since the organisation is expected to pay a premium interest rate. It is, however, the only option available to new or small businesses wishing to expand.

student activity

Using the following headings, draw up a list of countries which could be categorised as:

- reasonable credit risks
- fair credit risks
- poor credit risks

What criteria have you used in determining the kind of countries included in each category?

Business expansion scheme

This government scheme allows private investors to obtain large tax concessions by putting their money into new and growing organisations. The tax concession is available on the personal income tax of the investor, up to the value of £40,000. The investment has to be held for at least five years in order to obtain the tax relief. This scheme encourages investors to provide finance for small and medium-sized organisations.

WORKING CAPITAL

As we will see in Unit 8, there are many ways of considering the **liquidity** of an organisation. This liquidity basically equates to the **amount of realisable capital** available to an organisation. Working capital is used to pay immediate debts. If an organisation cannot pay its immediate debts, then it is considered to be **insolvent**. Creditors, such as landlords or suppliers, may be unwilling to allow the organisation to continue its operations if it does not have sufficient realisable assets that can be turned into capital. The main types of working capital are:

- the value of raw materials in stock
- the value of unfinished goods (known as work in progress)
- the value of the stocks of finished goods
- the debts owed to the organisation by other individuals or organisations

COST OF RAW MATERIALS

Organisations, through their stock control system, should endeavour to maintain sufficient stock to ensure that they are capable of producing at an agreed level. They should hold a 'buffer' stock of raw materials which may be necessary should suppliers fail to deliver goods ordered. This buffer stock is also used to ensure that organisations are in a position to increase production at short notice should demand rise. Systems should be in place, in line with available storage facilities, to ensure that organisations can take advantage of reduced cost raw materials if the opportunity arises. Normally, raw materials may be found in three locations:

- *in situ* at an organisation's warehouses
- *en route* to the organisation's warehouse from the supplier
- stock earmarked at the suppliers destined for the organisation

The value of these raw materials is the current market price, although it may be difficult to realise these assets, depending upon their general availability or suitability. Organisations count raw materials as part of their working capital, since it is possible to turn these raw materials into finished goods and thereby offer them to potential customers. In themselves these raw materials have, as we have said, a basic value.

student activity

In a typical manufacturing organisation, which of the above three locations of raw materials is likely to be of the greatest financial value?

WORK IN PROGRESS

The status of partially processed raw materials at the different stages of the production schedule means that the organisation has varying levels of assets throughout the company. Obviously, the closer these part-finished goods are to the end of their production process, the more value will be attached to them. The work in progress may be difficult to identify precisely, since items are scattered throughout the organisation's premises. Typically, work in progress is found in the warehouse and along the production lines. These assets can be somewhat difficult to turn into realisable working capital since they may not have a definite value to a potential buyer.

student activity

In terms of the value of work in progress, how much real value would the following have:

- partially finished garments
- partially assembled household goods
- partially processed food

STOCKS OF FINISHED GOODS

Most organisations try to ensure that they have at least sufficient stocks of finished goods to provide for **potential demand**. Organisations should have identified a particular stock level in relation to **known demand**, but will also have buffer stock available for **unforeseen circumstances**. They may well have overproduced in the past and may have been forced to retain these additional finished goods in the hope that demand might increase in the not too distant future. Organisations which rely substantially upon seasonal trade, such as, those which who sell the bulk of their finished goods around the Christmas period or the summer build up stocks of finished goods in preparation for their major trading periods. Some stock may be held on behalf of customers, although full payment may not have yet been received. Finished goods in this category cannot be classed as potential working capital. Most of the finished goods, however, could be turned into realisable cash should the organisation consider it advisable to do so. Finished goods may make a major contribution to the working capital.

student activity

If an organisation found itself to be in possession of unnecessarily high levels of stock in their finished state, what steps could they take in order to dispose of the excess? Assuming that there is no immediate for their goods at the current price, how would they 'off-load' the excess stock onto the market?

DEBTORS

At any one time organisations will be owed considerable sums of money by a variety of debtors. Some of these may be **bad debts** which may be the focus of **factoring** in the future. The majority of these debts, however, may become **due** after agreed credit periods have lapsed. In this sense, debts can be considered to be **realisable working capital**, as the organisation can substantially rely on the debtors to make the payment when required. Through its credit controller and accounts department, an organisation will ensure that the status of all debts is constantly monitored. It may take steps to encourage debtors to pay on time and it may be necessary for it to offer additional incentives (such as early payment discounts) for this purpose.

WORKING CAPITAL FINANCE METHODS

Organisations use all available methods to ensure that they have sufficient working capital available. Some of the sources of working capital will be considered in the next section. However, the main **methods** of obtaining working capital finance are:

1 equity
2 overdrafts
3 creditors

We shall deal with each of these individually.

EQUITY

The main definitions of equity relates to the initial investments made by the owners of any organisation. The founders of an organisation provide initial sums of money, known as equity, to allow short-term capital to be available. Organisations whose owners cannot raise sufficient funds seek the assistance of financial institutions, which buy shares and thus make up the shortfall in equity. Normally, organisations are reluctant to consider equity finance since, by accepting it they will lose some control over the business. They are keener to use internally generated funds or some form of loan.

OVERDRAFT

The size of an organisation's overdraft depends upon working capital requirements. Generally, the amount is agreed annually with the overdraft provider. As the organisation's customers will always tend to delay their payments as long as possible, it is prudent for the organisation to try to ensure that its working capital is at least equal to the average monthly sales multiplied by the number of months it takes to collect the debts. Overdraft requirements may also be affected by the level of stock, in terms of raw materials, work in progress and finished goods, that the organisation chooses to hold.

Obviously, the more stock is held by the organisation, the less working capital there is available.

CREDITORS

As we mentioned when considering overdrafts, debtors inevitably avoid payment until the last possible moment. Similarly, an organisation which owes money to various suppliers will likewise attempt to avoid payment. In essence, money owed to creditors saves the organisation from having to use up available working capital. Favourable credit periods help to ease pressures upon working capital. By careful consideration of the status of its own debts, an organisation can juggle the various debts owed to ensure that sufficient working capital is available for an unavoidable debt payment.

Recently, the government has been considering legislation which would require organisations to pay their debts on time. What is planned is that legal action would be taken against debtors who consistently refused or avoided payment of aged debts. If the system is fully implemented, then the use of creditors' 'goodwill' as a means to bolster an organisation's working capital would no longer be available.

SOURCES OF WORKING CAPITAL

Just as organisations use a variety of sources for obtaining **asset finance**, they also use a variety of methods to obtain **working capital**. Ensuring that the organisation has sufficient working capital may be a short-term objective and, as such, may have less impact upon the ownership or status of the organisation than the sourcing of asset finance may have. The levels of working capital required by an organisation are constantly changing, because of such requirements as the need to make periodic purchases of materials or to pay debts as they become due. In order to ensure that working capital is always available, organisations have back-up systems to provide the necessary finance.

INVESTORS, BANKS AND SELLERS

We have already mentioned the main **types of finance** available from these sources, but the acquisition of **working capital** can be considered to be a short-term requirement. An organisation attempting to acquire working capital will seek to avoid long-term commitments or drastic and substantial changes to the balance of the ownership of the organisation.

If an organisation decides to retain some profits, to provide working capital, **shareholders** will receive a reduced dividend on their shares. The funds retained may then be allocated to working capital. An organisation can try to balance its requirements in this way without putting pressure on its shareholders. Alternatively, it may ask shareholders for additional sums of money, perhaps in the form of preference shares.

Banks are usually more than willing to provide short-term finance, usually in the form of overdrafts or short-term loans. These have to be clearly defined and to be for specified short periods only. Where the acquisition of working capital is essential to an organisation, it may be forced to consider these relatively more drastic measures.

Short-term financing can be the cheapest finance available. It usually offers the following advantages and disadvantages:

1 *Advantages*

- flexible
- quick to obtain
- usually no minimum amount
- interest rates are comparatively low
- the loan is normally renewable

2 *Disadvantages*

- technically repayable on demand
- vulnerable to sudden changes in the finance provider's policy
- there is a temptation to use it for the wrong reasons
- there may be personal or asset guarantees required

student activity

How would the relative importance of investors and banks as sources of finance to a private limited company and a public limited company differ?

Produce and explain a projected cash flow for a single product business

1 PURPOSES
to support applications for finance, lender's confidence, monitoring of performance

2 CASH IN-FLOW HEADINGS
start-up capital, loan receipts, sales receipts, interest receipts

3 CASH OUT-FLOW HEADINGS
payments for assets, raw materials, wages, running costs, interest payments, loan repayments

4 SIGNIFICANCE OF TIMING
credit periods for purchases and sales, VAT payments, VAT recoveries, wages, salaries

5 CONSEQUENCES OF INCORRECT FORECASTING
incorrect working capital, cash flow problems

PURPOSES

A cash flow forecast or a projected cash flow show the **expected income and expenditure** for a business over a specified period of time. They are vital components in the preparation of a business plan, as well as being useful for more general forecasting purposes. The major benefits of this budgetary control, which is a natural progression from the cash flow analysis, are:

- it requires the organisation to formulate and define all of its **key objectives**
- individuals within the organisation (or perhaps spe-cialists bought-in for the express purpose) will be given responsibilities for aspects of the cash flow projection. An additional benefit is that it is possible to **measure their efficiency in monitoring** their part of the projection
- it also ensures that full note is taken of **cash require-ments** when that finance is actually required
- the various and separate individual budgets of dif-ferent parts of the organisation need to be **co-ordinated** as far as possible

- clear cash flow statements enable all employees and others involved in the organisation to be aware of **cost implications**. In addition, they will hopefully attempt to ensure that the most efficient methods are used to carry out their own functions
- it enables the management to concentrate on issues arising out of business activity which do not automatically fall within the cash flow projections. This particular technique is known as **management by exception**, which means that managers are thus able to concentrate on these exceptions and solve them
- at the same time, the decision makers of the organisation can adopt a **management by objectives** approach, to control the activities of the business

student activity

Try to put these functions of the cash flow forecast in order of importance. Which of the functions above would you consider to be the three most important?

In simple terms, a **cash flow forecast** will enable the organisation to:

- work out the income of the organisation
- work out the expenditure of the organisation
- identify short-term cash flow problems
- identify areas where additional income may be generated
- know, at any point, where money is owed

student activity

Which one of the above would you try to work out first? Do you need to know the figures for this one before you can work out the rest?

Specific **purposes** of the cash flow projection are:

- to support applications for finance
- to obtain lender's confidence in the organisation
- to monitor the performance of all of the business's activities

We shall consider these points in more detail.

TO SUPPORT APPLICATIONS FOR FINANCE

Any potential provider of financial resources will require the organisation to prove that it has a **viable business concern**. A lender will require the organisa-

tion to produce a statement which will include all relevant financial considerations. These considerations will cover all the major income and expenditure of the organisation, together with a reasoned appraisal of the organisation's prospective income and expenditure in the future.

A new business will have to work on reasoned conjecture in order to create a **projected cash flow**. A lender of finance will expect the organisation to have carried out substantial research into its area of business activity and to have considered all potential opportunities and threats at every stage of the business process. In effect, this means that the organisation is expected to be fully conversant with the requirements of providing products or services for a specified market sector and to be aware of the threats that any competitive organisation may present.

A provider of finance will constantly **monitor** the performance of the organisation against the projected cash flow statements and will expect the organisation to do the same. If the organisation's performance is wildly different from the projected performance, then this may give grave cause for concern. The organisation will have to justify any major deviations from the projected cash flow statement and will be expected to set the problems straight at the earliest possible opportunity.

student activity

Apart from the cash flow forecast itself, what other information would you need to present in order to support an application for finance?

LENDER'S CONFIDENCE

During the period in which the organisation is being loaned finance, the lender will be very interested in the **overall performance** of the organisation. Regular meetings will be expected when the lender will demand to see current documentation and proof that the organisation is attempting to remain within the projected cash flow. The lender will be keen to see as much information as possible, but will expect to see specific accepted forms of presentation such as cash flow statements, profit and loss accounts and balance sheets.

It is in the organisation's best interests to ensure that these documents are as accurate as possible since it may need to rely upon the lender for additional finance at a later date. Equally, it will wish to conform with the demands of the lender in order to ensure that a good working relationship is maintained.

MONITORING OF PERFORMANCE

Just as a lender will wish to see relevant documentation completed accurately, the organisation itself will need to be assured that it is on track to attain the projected financial objectives. The process of **monitoring performance** is a vital linking process between actual financial success and the processes of the business's activities. By careful consideration of the figures the organisation will be able to match projections with actual performance. It should be able to adjust and amend its activities according to particular circumstances.

CASH IN-FLOW HEADINGS

We shall now consider cash flow projections in more detail and look at the meaning of the various headings we shall find on a typical statement. To begin with, we shall consider the cash in-flow headings, which are:

- start-up capital
- loan receipts
- sales receipts
- interest receipts

START-UP CAPITAL

In the case of new businesses, start-up capital will include all **cash investments** made by the owners of the business. These investments will be required to pay any initial expenditures and to provide the basis for the organisation's working capital. This start-up capital may be earmarked for necessary initial purchases, including the acquisition of various assets and raw materials. The organisation will take steps to ensure that it has enough initial start-up capital to cover immediate projected expenditure.

LOAN RECEIPTS

Loan receipts, or rather, **the receipt of a loan**, include any monies given to the organisation as a loan. For the

purposes of the cash flow forecast this will be counted as monies received.

TESCO PLC

GROUP CASH FLOW STATEMENT

52 weeks ended 27th February 1993 (1992 – 53 weeks)	Note	1993 £m	1992 £m
Net cash inflow from operating activities	25	639.4	676.4
Returns on investment and servicing of finance:			
Interest received		89.1	123.3
Interest paid		(117.3)	(136.4)
Interest element of finance lease rental payments		(8.0)	(9.1)
Dividends paid		(121.1)	(103.2)
Net cash outflow from returns on investments and servicing of finance		(157.3)	(125.4)
Taxation:			
Corporation tax paid (including advance corporation tax)		(93.6)	(165.4)
Investing activities:			
Payments to acquire tangible fixed assets		(605.1)	(775.7)
Receipts from sale of tangible fixed assets		81.6	54.4
Increase in investment in associated company		(5.5)	–
Net cash outflow from investing activities		(529.0)	(721.3)
Net cash outflow before financing		(140.5)	(335.7)
Financing:			
Ordinary shares issued for cash		21.2	8.9
Issue of 10½% bonds		–	200.0
Issue of ⅛% deep discount bond		–	50.0
E.C.S.C. loan		–	73.8
New finance leases		26.4	33.6
Increase/(decrease) in other loans		1.8	(40.7)
Capital element of finance leases repaid		(30.3)	(24.7)
Decrease/(increase) in short-term deposits		53.2	(93.2)
Expenses paid in connection with share and bond issues		(0.5)	(1.0)
Net cash inflow from financing	26	71.8	206.7
Decrease in cash and cash equivalents	28	(68.7)	(129.0)

FIG 7.2.1 *This is Tesco's Group Cash Flow Statement comparing 1992 with 1993. Note all of the variations of investments and financing considerations. Also note that the figures in brackets are negative amounts.*

SALES RECEIPTS

Although this heading is not strictly relevant before the business has begun trading, the owners of the business must be able to forecast the **probable income from sales**. This sales revenue will probably form the basis of any major decision made by a provider of finance as to the viability of the business. The sales receipts forecast, in other words, must, as accurately as possible, reflect the true expectations of the business's income from sales.

INTEREST RECEIPTS

Similarly, interest receipts are the receipt of **interest from monies invested** by the business. Again, providers of finance will require to know the exact nature of any investments made by the business and the probable income derived in the form of interest.

CASH OUT-FLOW HEADINGS

In this section we will be considering the regular expected expenses of the organisation. These expenses act as a counter-balance to the cash in-flow (or monies received). Once the cash out-flow totals have been deducted from the cash in-flow totals, the organisation is able to ascertain its closing balance for a particular period. The main cash out-flow headings are:

- payments for assets
- raw materials
- wages
- running costs
- interest payments
- loan repayments

PAYMENTS FOR ASSETS

Payments for assets include the costs of all capital assets, such as machinery and office equipment. A new business should be careful to make sure that items such as consumable office materials are not included in this heading. In fact, they belong under the 'running costs'

KINGFISHER PLC ANNUAL REPORT & ACCOUNTS 1992

consolidated cash flow statement

Kingfisher plc and subsidiary companies for the financial year ended 1 February 1992

£ millions	Notes	1992	1991
Net cash flow from operating activities	23	239.8	234.2
Returns on investment and servicing of finance			
Interest received		26.5	14.4
Interest paid		(46.2)	(52.5)
Dividends paid		(57.8)	(52.0)
Net cash flow from returns on investment and servicing of finance		(77.5)	(90.1)
Taxation			
Corporation tax paid		(64.9)	(70.3)
Investing activities			
Purchase of subsidiary		–	(35.3)
Payments to acquire tangible fixed assets		(80.3)	(197.6)
Payments for additions to investments		(6.0)	(40.5)
Net purchase of short-term investments		(3.1)	(20.8)
Receipts from the sale of tangible fixed assets		34.7	194.9
Net cash flow from extraordinary items		–	(4.9)
Net cash outflow from investing activities		(54.7)	(104.2)
Net cash inflow/(outflow) before financing		42.7	(30.4)
Financing			
Issue of ordinary share capital		17.7	3.9
Net purchase of short-term investments		(36.8)	(11.9)
(Decrease)/increase in loans		(6.3)	94.0
Expenses paid in connection with issues		–	(0.2)
Net cash (outflow)/inflow from financing		(25.4)	85.8
Increase in cash and cash equivalents	23	17.3	55.4

FIG 7.2.2 *This is the consolidated Cash Flow Statement for Kingfisher plc. The group includes Woolworths, Comet, B & Q and Superdrug. 'Consolidated' means the total of all income and expenditure for the whole of the group.*

heading. Initially, an organisation may have to earmark considerable amounts of capital to pay for necessary assets. Alternatively, an organisation may be able to arrange for the payments for assets to be made over a number of months, in which case the credit payments will be included under the 'payment for assets' heading each month.

> ### student activity
>
> Looking again at the Kingfisher cash flow statement, note the two headings 'payments to acquire tangible assets' and 'receipts from tangible assets'. Firstly, what do you think the word 'tangible' means in this context? Secondly what is the net cost or income from these payments and receipts?

RAW MATERIALS

Raw materials include all consumable items used during the production process. For organisations which require considerable amounts of raw materials, this may be a significant part of their expenses. In the service sector, however, a business is unlikely to need to put very much down under this heading.

> ### student activity
>
> Try to identify the kind of raw materials necessary to run the following types of business:
>
> - a dress and garment manufacturer
> - a book printer and publisher
> - a baker

WAGES

Under the **wages** heading an organisation totals its entire wage bill. This will include salary payments, weekly wages and any overtime payments. An organisation should be able to predict most of the costs found under this heading quite accurately, with the possible exception of overtime.

RUNNING COSTS

Running costs include the payment of rent and rates, and payments for power and other consumable items such as office stationery. Organisations, particularly in their early stages, will have to ensure that these running costs are kept to the absolute minimum.

> ### student activity
>
> What other running costs can you identify?

INTEREST PAYMENTS

If an organisation has purchased assets by taking out a hire purchase agreement or on credit, it will include these payments under the **interest payment** heading. Again, the amount of cash involved may depend upon the need of the organisation to gain credit at this early stage of its operations.

LOAN REPAYMENTS

If an organisation has had to obtain a loan in order to purchase assets, then it will include these payments under the **loan repayment** heading. Organisations obviously attempt to spread the cost of these repayments over as many months as possible. However, certainly in the case of new businesses, loan repayments may be high as providers of finance will insist upon comparatively high rates of interest.

SIGNIFICANCE OF TIMING

Since a new business operates with very little working capital or reserves of cash, the **significance of timing** both payments and income is vital. Careful control of the budget is essential to ensure that sufficient funds are available when payments must be made. An organisation which does not pay enough attention to the chasing of debts or the recovery of cash from Customs and Excise may suffer serious cash flow problems. The organisation may have to obtain additional unnecessary loans. Such loans can be extremely dangerous for a new business to have to contemplate as, for reasons already stated, borrowing money can be very expensive.

---

student activity

Investigate the available interest rates for new businesses. How will the amount that they wish to borrow affect the interest rate payable?

CREDIT PERIODS FOR PURCHASES AND SALES

Provided an organisation has supplied acceptable business references, it may be given credit by other businesses. The credit period is generally between 30 and 90 days – you will find several references to credit periods elsewhere in other Units. Just as the organisation will expect credit terms from its suppliers, the organisation's customers will expect credit terms from it. This will be particularly true of an organisation that supplies products or services to the trade. Generally speaking, organisations that make direct sales to the consumer are normally able to rely on immediate payment. Although this may take a variety of different forms and may involve other agencies, such as banks or credit card companies, the money received can still be considered to be 'cash in hand'.

The problem of matching the credit terms acquired by the organisation and the credit terms demanded by customers needs careful consideration. Inadequate monitoring, particularly of late payers, may result in unnecessary cash flow problems.

---

student activity

What are the implications for a business that offers 60 days credit to its customers and can only obtain 30 days from its suppliers?

VAT PAYMENTS AND VAT RECOVERIES

Organisations whose turnover reaches the current limit of nearly £40,000 per year will need to be VAT registered. Registration has considerable advantages and disadvantages, depending upon the nature of the business. Let us consider the nature of VAT first, before looking at these advantages and disadvantages.

VAT (value added tax) is essentially a government tax on spending. VAT is added to all items purchased and it is the business's responsibility to collect VAT on behalf of the government. The process of organising this VAT collection includes the following:

- the organisation totals the amount of VAT collected
- the organisation then totals the amount of tax it paid on items bought in
- the balance, if positive (in other words, more VAT was collected than was paid out), is forwarded to Customs and Excise
- if, on the other hand, the balance is negative (in other words the organisation paid out more in VAT than it collected), then the business may claim a refund

Normally organisations are required to present their VAT return quarterly, although in some cases smaller businesses may submit their VAT return annually.

The major advantage of collecting VAT on behalf of the government is that the organisation can make use of this money for the three-month period before it is due. However, organisations should take care to ensure that sufficient funds are available to settle VAT bills, as the Customs and Excise Department takes no prisoners! It will demand payment at all costs. If an organisation's business activity is in an area where the products sold are zero rated, that is, not subject to VAT (such as food, books, magazines and children's clothing), then Customs and Excise will provide a very useful $17\frac{1}{2}$ per cent refund on all purchases made.

---

student activity

Can you identify at least three types of business that will be able to regularly claim VAT from HM Customs and Excise, rather than pay it to them?

WAGES AND SALARIES

Organisations need to ensure that sufficient funds are available to meet any salary or wage bills. When deciding when to pay salaries, organisations will have chosen a particular point in the month when they traditionally have sufficient working capital. With regard to wage earners, an organisation needs to ensure that regular amounts of money are set aside to meet these weekly claims upon the working capital. Organisations tend not to have terribly good relations with their employees if they cannot, for some reason, meet their wages and salaries commitments. You will remember that under employment legislation, particularly that relating to the contract of employment, the employer undertakes to ensure that monies due to employees are made available.

CONSEQUENCES OF INCORRECT FORECASTING

If an organisation incorrectly estimates its levels of expense and income then it may suffer a lack of working capital or more serious cash flow problems. Essentially, an organisation must set aside enough working capital to meet immediate running costs and other expenses. Cash flow problems may be a little more complex, since the problems encountered in one month will have a knock-on effect into the next, and so on, and so on.

INCORRECT WORKING CAPITAL

An organisation that does not have enough working capital has to take drastic measures to ensure that it can obtain additional funding. This may be in the form of a short-term loan to carry it over the temporary lack of working capital. Since working capital is earmarked to pay for essential purchases and running costs, an organisation unable to meet these costs may have to resort to the disposal of assets in order to raise additional capital.

CASH FLOW PROBLEMS

As we mentioned in the previous section, the significance of timing in relation to **cash flow** is all-important. An organisation must try to make sure that sufficient funds are entered in the cash in-flow to compensate for expenditure in the cash out-flow. An organisation that does not pay careful attention to this matter risks running out of money. If this happens, it will obviously have a drastic impact upon all areas of the organisation's activities. It will not be able to purchase raw materials, or any assets, cover its running costs, make interest or loan repayments, or meet the wage bill. There is some degree of flexibility here, in the sense that some cash flow problems may be carried over into the next month. However, this is no real solution, as carrying them over will eat into the available working capital, which has additional complications – as we have already mentioned. Banks and other providers of finance will be quick to recognise cash flow problems and will insist that the organisation takes drastic cost-cutting measures to sort out the problems.

student activity

What short-term solutions can be found for a lack of working capital?

Calculate the cost of goods or services

> **1 DIRECT COSTS**
> *labour, wages, materials, depreciation, power*
>
> **2 INDIRECT COSTS**
> *management, administration, marketing, running expenses*

DIRECT COSTS

An organisation can apportion the costs incurred in the production of products or services in either a **direct** or an **indirect** manner. We shall be looking at the indirect costs in the next section. You may also wish to consult Unit 8 for a fuller description of fixed, variable, semi-variable, average and marginal costs. In addition, we have considered there break-even point analysis and an organisation's long-term costs.

The **direct** costs can be defined as being the amount materials actually cost and any other directly linked costs, such as labour. We shall look at the nature of each of these direct costs in more detail below.

LABOUR AND WAGES

The cost of obtaining, training and retaining **labour** is a significantly high cost which must be allocated to each unit of production. As we have seen in many of the previous Units, there are many legal obligations as well as social and welfare considerations, which add to this high cost total.

In order to work out the exact labour and wages costs to be attributed to each unit of production, an organisation must make a careful study of the production process and allocate the appropriate expenses. If, for example, an individual earns £10 per hour and processes 10 units during that hour, then £1 of direct costs may simply be added to each unit. Unfortunately, things are not that simple. There are many other additional costs which an organisation must bear in the employment of individuals. These may include employer's national insurance contributions, pension payments and insurance policy payments. In most organisations, labour and wage costs account for the majority of direct costs.

---

student activity

Using Figure 7.3.1 make the following calculations:

- the percentage increase or decrease in the figures over the two years
- the comparative levels of employment in the three categories identified (show your information in the form of a pie-chart)
- the average wage of the employees, using the 'equivalent number of employees working full time' figure

7 Employees

£ millions	1992	1991
Staff costs:		
Wages and salaries	403.5	372.5
Social security costs	27.4	25.2
Other pension costs	2.1	1.2
	433.0	398.9
Number		
Average number of persons employed:		
Stores	57,087	56,759
Distribution	1,617	1,493
Administration	3,237	3,245
	61,941	61,497
The equivalent number of employees working full time would have been	37,462	37,578

MATERIALS

The costs of **materials** differ according to the sector in which an organisation operates. An organisation that operates in the primary sector has comparatively low material costs. At the other end of the scale, in the tertiary sector, the costs of finished goods to a retailer, for example, will be extremely high. The principal elements that affect the costs of materials should be included in the organisation's overall budgetary controls. In addition, an organisation must also consider the cost of materials in relation to market demands, as these will inevitably cause periodic fluctuations in material costs.

When considering the cost of a product or service in terms of the materials used to produce that product or service, we will only include those materials that are actually involved. We will not consider other consumable materials used by the organisation, as these are classed as indirect costs and are considered under separate budgets.

FIG 7.3.1 *This shows the total wage bill and average number of employees for Kingfisher plc. It compares the figures in years 1991 and 1992. Note that the 'Stores' category refers to the number of retail outlet employees and not warehousing staff.*

DEPRECIATION

Organisations must always consider the **depreciation** factor when attempting to work out a total for direct costs. Depreciation, as we have already mentioned, refers to the relative reduction in the value of assets held by the organisation. The loss of value on machinery used (perhaps the more it is used the less it is worth), or the simple obsolescence of equipment due to technological advances, must be taken into consideration. Depreciation rates will be classed as direct costs and, as such, included in the calculation of costs for each unit.

student activity

Using Figure 7.3.2 what would be your explanation of the following?

- the drop in the amount (in value) of the finished goods totals from 1991 to 1992
- the nature of the stock under the title 'miscellaneous'
- the importance you would attach to the nearly £3m drop in the value of stock over the two years

student activity

With reference to Figure 7.3.3 what do you understand by the terms?

- acquisitions
- revaluation adjustment
- disposals
- net book amounts

❶ Stocks

	GROUP		COMPANY	
	1992 £000	1991 £000	1992 £000	1991 £000
Produce and raw materials	9,177	11,629	-	-
Work in progress	109	122	-	-
Finished goods	226	1,878	-	-
Miscellaneous	2,224	1,626	97	92
	11,736	15,255	97	92

FIG 7.3.2 *This is a detail from Geest plc's Notes to their 1992 Accounts. You can see that there are four main categories of stock, in their case mainly fresh produce.*

Depreciation

At 1st October 1991	–	71	765	40,862	4,989	46,687
Acquisitions	1,334	–	270	14,513	2,289	18,406
Charge for the period	23	212	123	3,839	971	5,168
Revaluation adjustment	–	–	–	1,463	–	1,463
	1,357	283	1,158	60,677	8,249	71,724
Disposals	–	–	–	(388)	(88)	(476)
At 30th September 1992	1,357	283	1,158	60,289	8,161	71,248

Net book amounts

At 30th September 1992	2,001	10,442	740	9,074	2,938	25,195
At 30th September 1991	–	8,860	429	6,817	1,689	17,795

Plant and equipment includes assets acquired under finance leases in respect of which, at 30th September 1992, the net book amount was £3,341,000 (1991: £180,000) after charging £802,000 (1991: £201,000) depreciation for the year.

Technical plant and equipment has been revalued at 30th September 1992 using price index tables published by the Central Statistical Office. The net book amount calculated on a historical cost basis for these revalued assets would have been £8,429,000 (1991: £6,052,000). All other fixed assets are included on a historical cost basis.

A valuation of the long leasehold property carried out by Sallmans (UK) Limited, and dated 18th April 1991 assessed the depreciated replacement cost of the Television Centre, Leeds and 104 Kirkstall Road, Leeds as £23,073,000. This valuation has not been incorporated into the accounts.

FIG 7.3.3 *This is a detail from Yorkshire-Tyne Tees Television Holdings plc's Accounts. It covers the depreciation and disposal of assets.*

POWER

The power used to produce each unit must be considered as a direct cost. This means that the cost of any electricity, gas, fossil fuel or other means of power must be added to the overall cost of each unit. Obviously, certain production processes require disproportionate amounts of power and are thus more expensive in this respect. In addition, we should consider the cost of power needed to light and ventilate the premises in which the production takes place. A certain percentage of these costs will be apportioned to the indirect cost factors also, as administration and warehousing, for example, will similarly benefit from the light, ventilation and warmth provided.

FIG 7.3.4 *BNFL's Calder Hill Power Station, opened in 1956. It is authorised to remain in operation until at least 1996. It remains a solid contributor to the UK's power needs.*

INDIRECT COSTS

Indirect costs are costs incurred in the running of an organisation that cannot be easily apportioned to the production process. In effect, they cover all of the support and management services of the organisation. These indirect costs may be apportioned in percentage terms to each unit produced. However, the optimum balance between direct and indirect costs can be somewhat difficult to ascertain. If an organisation allows its indirect costs to rise in a disproportionate manner to its direct costs and production levels, then we can consider the organisation to be rather 'top heavy'. It will suffer loss of both profit and working capital.

The main forms of indirect cost are:

- management
- administration
- marketing
- general running expenses

MANAGEMENT

Managers, in particular general managers, need to be 'carried' by the organisation as a whole. These managers, who may have specific administration job roles, may not be involved in the production process at all, but their function is essential to ensure the smooth running of the organisation. In this respect, they are vital members of staff and their positions require funding. The normal procedure is to apportion in percentage terms the costs of these managers to each unit of production – as part of the general calculation of indirect costs.

Organisations try to ensure that the number of 'non-productive' managers is kept to an absolute minimum as the costs of such people will inevitably affect both profitability and working capital available.

Managers, by virtue of their position, are more expensive than normal employees and must provide a positive benefit to the organisation.

The more senior the position a manager has in the hierarchy, the more divorced he or she is from the production process. It is therefore difficult to establish any clear criteria that may be used to apportion managers' costs. This allocation of costs is often the subject of much friction within an organisation, as different departments may wish to see a certain percentage of their managerial costs apportioned elsewhere.

Notes on the Accounts CONTINUED

5 Directors' emoluments and other statutory information

The aggregate emoluments of the Directors of British Nuclear Fuels plc for the year were £1,001,451 (1991 £845,104) including fees of £21,737 (1991 £28,057) and payments of £118,805 (1991 £29,800) on retirement.

The emoluments of the Chairman, the highest paid Director, amounted to £191,675 (1991 £162,208).

The emoluments, excluding pension provision by the Company, of the other Directors in the various ranges are as follows:

Range	1992 Number	1991 Number
Nil to £5,000	—	2
£5,001 to £10,000	3	3
£10,001 to £15,000	2	—
£40,001 to £45,000	—	1
£50,001 to £55,000	—	1
£75,001 to £80,000	—	1
£80,001 to £85,000	—	1
£85,001 to £90,000	1	—
£90,001 to £95,000	—	1
£110,001 to £115,000	1	—
£155,001 to £160,000	—	1
£170,001 to £175,000	1	—
£180,001 to £185,000	1	—

Pensions paid to former Directors amounted to £58,910 (1991 £44,101). Included in debtors are interest free loans of £2,042 repaid in April 1992 (1991 £2,917) and £9,000 to Dr W L Wilkinson and Mr K G Jackson respectively. These loans were made prior to joining the Board in accordance with the Company's policy of providing housing assistance to staff who have been relocated.

FIG 7.3.5 *Part of BNFL's costs are the payments to directors. Sir Christopher Harding, the Chairman, is the highest wage earner with an income of £191,675 in 1992.*

ADMINISTRATION

The administration function, as we have seen in Unit 4, plays an important role in the smooth running of business's activities. Regardless of their position in the overall organisational structure, or, indeed, their responsibilities or competences, administrative staff do not play an active or direct role in the production process. As with managers, a certain percentage of administration costs will be attributed to each unit of production and spread across all products manufactured or all services provided.

Administration units operate as separate costs centres in order to ascertain the full costs of running the administration facilities. These cost centres have to be funded from some other part of the organisation. Organisations attempt to reduce their administration costs while attempting to ensure that their administration is as cost-effective and efficient as possible.

student activity

Considering a manufacturing organisation, try to identify the various cost centres.

MARKETING

The marketing function can be an extremely expensive aspect of an organisation's costs. The marketing function includes the following:

- market research
- advertising
- sales promotions
- corporate image development

Again, all of these expenses have to be absorbed by other aspects of the organisation's activities. Typically, a proportion of the initial set-up costs to launch a new product include most of these marketing functions. Continual marketing support for all products and services is essential, as we have seen, to ensure that the organisation retains and expands its market share.

student activity

With reference to Unit 3, identify, in ranking order, the above marketing activities in terms of their cost to the organisation.

RUNNING EXPENSES

The general running expenses of the organisation include:

- rents
- leases
- loans
- mortgages
- salaries
- maintenance
- payment to utilities
- warehousing
- transport
- distribution
- insurance
- business rate
- water rate
- communications

Obviously, these expenses will depend upon the exact nature of the organisation's business activities.

The most common method for costing products or services is known as **absorption costing**. This means that all direct costs are allocated to the product or service as a matter of course and then all the remaining overheads are apportioned to each product or service on a standard basis.

The fairest way of apportioning costs may be related to the time (in the case of wages) that the individual spends related to the production process. A full appraisal of absorption costing requires considerable knowledge of an organisation's overheads and relies upon the organisation reaching full capacity.

student activity

Investigate the business rate in your local area. How is it set? What criteria are used to calculate it? How important a consideration is the business rate when deciding to locate in an area? Identify at least three areas of the country where business rates are very low as a result of central government funding and assistance.

Produce and explain profit and loss statements and balance sheets

I. PURPOSES
secure finance, maintain finance, monitor performance

2 TRADING PERIOD
quarterly, annually

3 OVERHEADS
administration, wages, rent, telephone, interest, travel expenses

4 PROFIT AND LOSS, CONVENTIONAL FORM
sales, cost of sales, gross profit, overheads, net profit

5 BALANCE SHEET, CONVENTIONAL FORM
assets, current assets, current liabilities, share capital, profit and loss brought forward, profit and loss for a period

PURPOSES

Profit and loss statements or accounts and balance sheets form an integral part of an organisation's final accounts. The **profit and loss account** lists the various overheads, also known as revenue expenditure, of the business. This total of overheads is then deducted from the **gross profit** in order to give the **net profit** for the year. In other words, net profit is calculated as gross profit minus overheads for the year. We shall be considering the exact nature of a profit and loss account later in this Unit.

The balance sheet shows the state of the business at a particular moment in time when the balance sheet was constructed. Essentially it lists all of the assets, liabilities and capital at that particular date. A normal balance sheet will consist of an asset column and a liabilities column, the totals of which are exactly the same. Again, we will be looking at the conventional form of a balance sheet later in this Unit.

student activity

Compare the figures in all years from 1989 to 1993 in Figure 7.4.1. What are the trends? Can you identify any significant features on the record sheet? How would you assess the overall performance of the organisation from the point of view of a potential investor?

FIVE YEAR RECORD

SUMMARY OF TURNOVER AND PROFIT:

	1989 £ million	1990 £ million	1991 £ million	1992 £ million	1993 £ million
Turnover	1,221.2	1,310.3	1,208.6	1,179.8	1,139.3
Profit from retail operations	63.0	37.1	17.3	10.0	43.0
Profit from associated undertakings and other income	13.4	2.0	1.3	4.9	5.1
Exceptional items	12.1	(38.8)	(36.6)	-	(31.4)
Interest and other items	(16.0)	(8.6)	0.5	0.9	(1.5)
Profit before taxation	72.5	(8.3)	(17.5)	15.8	15.2
Taxation	(13.7)	2.7	(2.7)	(5.0)	(14.8)
Profit (loss) for the financial year	58.8	(5.6)	(20.2)	10.8	0.4
Earnings per share	14.4p	(1.4)p	(4.9)p	2.6p	0.1p
Dividend per share	8.8p	5.0p	5.0p	5.0p	5.0p

SUMMARY OF BALANCE SHEETS:

	1989	1990	1991	1992	1993
Fixed assets	576.5	498.3	457.6	448.0	356.1
Net current assets	67.5	127.8	88.9	36.5	92.8
Creditors falling due after one year	(110.8)	(122.3)	(77.6)	(26.3)	(6.1)
Provisions for liabilities and charges	(20.8)	(19.0)	(15.7)	(19.9)	(18.9)
Total net assets	512.4	484.8	453.2	438.3	423.9

OTHER KEY DATA/STATISTICS:

	1989	1990	1991	1992	1993
Net cash (debt)/equity (%)	(13.3)	(5.7)	0.9	(4.1)	5.8
Capital expenditure	97.7	61.4	41.8	45.2	41.7
Depreciation	50.3	51.0	45.7	45.2	40.6
Rents	70.5	78.5	76.9	87.5	82.4
Number of stores	1,022	969	719	736	426
Net selling space (000's sq. ft.)	7,118	7,110	6,567	6,452	4,704
Average number of employees	31,658	30,352	26,945	24,440	21,916
Average number of full-time equivalents	19,372	18,822	15,759	14,550	12,453

Notes:

All years have been adjusted to reflect the impact of UITF Abstract 3 on Treatment of Goodwill on Disposal of a Business and FRS No.3 Reporting Financial Performance.

FIG 7.4.1 *This shows the five-year record of the Storehouse group of companies. Note that it contains summaries from both the profit and loss account and the balance sheet and other useful data.*

student activity

Compare Figures 7.4.1 and 7.4.2. What are the major differences? How would you assess the relative success or failure of the two organisations? In the role of a financial advisor, decide which of the organisations offers the better return on an investment.

SECURE FINANCE AND MAINTAIN FINANCE

In order to secure finance and then maintain it, an organisation must be able to provide sufficient and accurate financial information to providers of that finance. They will require access to the organisation's balance sheet as well as the profit and loss account. They may also wish to see other documentation such as order books and other sources of information detailed in Unit 6. If an organisation is unwilling or unable to provide this information then the providers of finance may insist that an external auditor inspect the documentation on their behalf. In this instance, the auditor's costs will usually be passed on to the organisation which has failed to provide the information.

student activity

In the role of an auditor carrying out an investigation into the financial status of an organisation, in addition to the necessary documentation, which individuals within the organisation would you wish to talk to?

MONITOR PERFORMANCE

As we have mentioned in many of the previous Units, it is essential for an organisation to keep a close eye on productivity and general profit levels at all times. The organisation's provider of finance may require it to make adjustments if its performance is not acceptable. It is therefore in the organisation's interest to monitor performance closely.

As we have seen, there are many techniques that can be employed to monitor performance, many of which will specifically relate to the business activity in which the organisation is involved.

student activity

As we have seen from the various accounts documentation illustrated, organisations compare their performance from year to year. What other time periods should also be compared? What value would comparison of shorter periods of time have to the organisation? Does the period of time between reviews of performance have an impact on the organisation's ability to react to different circumstances?

FIVE YEAR RECORD

	1988 £m	1989 £m	1990 £m	1991 £m	1992 £m
Turnover					
Continuing operations	732.2	900.5	1,090.2	1,151.8	**1,211.0**
Discontinued operations	50.7	88.7	96.4	88.1	**73.2**
	782.9	989.2	1,186.6	1,239.9	**1,284.2**
Profits					
Continuing operations	121.9	160.5	218.4	193.5	**117.3**
Discontinued operations	0.2	0.6	7.4	3.9	**0.1**
Trading profit	122.1	161.1	225.8	197.4	**117.4**
Exceptional items	(22.3)	(15.8)	(34.8)	(24.6)	**23.3**
Finance income/(charge)	8.4	2.0	0.9	(10.2)	**(17.1)**
Profit before taxation	108.2	147.3	191.9	162.6	**123.6**
Taxation	(28.5)	(32.1)	(44.6)	(41.4)	**(26.9)**
Minority interests	–	(0.2)	(0.7)	(1.4)	**(1.0)**
Net profit attributable to shareholders	79.7	115.0	146.6	119.8	**95.7**
Dividends	(29.4)	(40.1)	(51.5)	(60.2)	**(60.2)**
Transfer to reserves	50.3	74.9	95.1	59.6	**35.5**
Assets employed					
Long-term assets	266.6	325.6	344.7	380.2	**433.1**
Net current assets	109.5	183.3	149.4	126.8	**169.0**
	376.1	508.9	494.1	507.0	**602.1**
Financed by					
Ordinary shares	147.7	148.8	171.8	172.6	**172.8**
Reserves	181.0	221.8	242.9	273.3	**349.5**
Shareholders' interests	328.7	370.6	414.7	445.9	**522.3**
Minority interests	0.9	1.6	3.4	3.9	**5.7**
Loans	44.6	131.0	70.0	51.1	**68.0**
Taxation accounts	1.9	5.7	6.0	6.1	**6.1**
	376.1	508.9	494.1	507.0	**602.1**
Statistics					
Ratio of activity profit to average operating assets employed	30.3%	31.8%	36.7%	28.8%	**15.2%**
Earnings per share (FRS 3 basis)	14.8p	19.1p	21.5p	17.4p	**13.9p**
Dividend per share (gross including tax credit)	6.67p	8.27p	10.00p	11.6p	**11.6p**
Dividend earnings (times covered)	2.7	2.9	2.8	2.0	**1.6**
Number of shareholders	33,000	30,500	34,000	44,000	**50,000**

FIG 7.4.2 *This is Fisons' five-year record covering 1988–1992. Fisons have used slightly different headings from those used in the Storehouse five-year record, but the information is still clear and precise.*

Earnings per share figures have been adjusted for the bonus element of the rights issues of 1 for 6 in 1988 and 1 for 8 in 1990.

TRADING PERIOD

Trading periods may be considered annually or quarterly. Requirements differ according to the needs and nature of the business activity in which an organisation is involved.

It is essential for organisations to complete quarterly accounts in order to ascertain their VAT liabilities and to give them a clearer indication of their performance over the period. Some organisations may wish to focus on particular quarterly periods for in-depth analysis as their trading activity may rely upon particularly high levels of demand within these periods.

More commonly, for the production of final accounts, the **annual** method is used. This method gives a more accurate picture of the overall trading successes and failures of the organisation throughout the year. When trading periods are annual, this does not necessarily mean that the final accounts have to be prepared at the end of the financial year (i.e. April). Each organisation has its own year end.

OVERHEADS

Overheads are items of expenditure which cannot be directly attributed to the costs of production. They include all of the following:

- administration
- wages
- rent
- telephone
- interest
- travel expenses

Overheads will be deducted from the **gross profit** of an organisation in order to show the true **net profit** of the business.

student activity

As we have already seen, there is a need to monitor these cost and attribute them to a particular part of the organisation. How would items such as rent or administration be apportioned to the activities of the business?

PROFIT AND LOSS, CONVENTIONAL FORM

When organisations provide a service, they are required to produce a profit and loss account. In the service sector, there is no gross profit, so the profit and loss account records the income from clients or customers. Overheads are listed in a similar way to those in a trading account (see Unit 6).

SALES

Sales and **purchases** are items which have been bought by the business, such as machinery and equipment. When they appear on the balance sheet they are classed as fixed assets.

COST OF SALES

The **cost of sales**, or cost of goods sold, is the cost to the business of the goods which have been sold in the particular financial year. The calculation used to arrive at this figure is:

Opening stock + purchases − closing stock = cost of sales

GROSS PROFIT

Gross profit is calculated as:

Sales − costs = gross profit

Consolidated Profit & Loss Account
For the year ended 31 December 1992

Note		£000	1992 12 months £000	£000	Restated 1991 14 months £000
3	**Turnover**				
	Advertising revenue		112,851		127,347
	Sale of programmes		23,319		22,355
	Other revenue		3,278		3,666
			139,448		153,368
	Expenditure on Programmes				
	Acquired programmes	37,240		40,869	
	Own productions	22,436		21,096	
4	Other operating charges	43,121		51,740	
	Rental payable to the ITC/NTL	4,740		5,516	
	Channel Four subscription	18,938		22,208	
			126,475		141,429
	Operating profit before levy and associated undertakings		12,973		11,939
6	Exchequer levy		2,422		8,320
	Operating profit before associated undertakings		10,551		3,619
	Share of results of associated undertakings		1,860		382
	Operating profit		12,411		4,001
	Profit on disposal of fixed asset investments		–		15,911
7	Investment income and interest		2,137		1,762
	Provision for diminution in value of fixed asset investments		–		(13,296)
8	**Profit on Ordinary Activities Before Taxation**		14,548		8,378
9	Tax on profit on ordinary activities		4,941		1,792
	Profit on Ordinary Activities After Taxation		9,607		6,586
	Minority interests		(53)		57
	Profit For The Financial Period		9,554		6,643
10	Dividends		4,098		4,098
	Retained Profit		5,456		2,545
11	**Earnings Per Share**		21.59p		15.04p

	1992 12 months £000	Restated 1991 14 months £000
Statement of Total Recognised Gains and Losses		
Profit for the financial period	9,554	6,643
Unrealised surplus on revaluation of fixed assets (net of deferred tax)	141	227
Currency translation differences on foreign currency net investments	389	70
Total recognised gains and losses relating to the financial period	10,084	6,940
Note of Historical Cost Profits and Losses		
Reported profit on ordinary activities before taxation	14,548	8,378
Difference between historical depreciation charge and actual depreciation charge for the period calculated on the revalued amount	631	1,131
Historical cost profit on ordinary activities before taxation	15,179	9,509
Historical cost profit for the period retained after taxation, minority interests and dividends	6,087	3,676
Statement of Retained Profit		
Profit and loss account at 1 January 1992	47,923	49,110
Retained profit	5,456	2,545
Exchange differences	389	70
Goodwill written off	(751)	(3,802)
At 31 December 1992	53,017	47,923
Reconciliation of Movements in Shareholders' Funds		
Profit for the financial period	9,554	6,643
Dividends	4,098	4,098
	5,456	2,545
Other recognised gains and losses relating to the period (net)	530	297
New share capital subscribed	–	373
Goodwill written off	(751)	(3,802)
	5,235	(587)
Opening shareholders' funds	67,623	68,210
Closing shareholders' funds	72,858	67,623

FIG 7.4.3 *Anglia Television Group plc's Consolidated Profit and Loss Account for the year ending 31 December 1992 shows the wealth of valuable information covered..*

Remember that if costs of sales are greater than net sales then the business has made a loss.

OVERHEADS

The general overheads included in this classification are such items as:

- administration
- wages
- rent
- telephone
- interest
- travel expenses
- non-production-related power
- insurance
- depreciation

NET PROFIT

The **net profit** is the amount that the organisation has earned during the year. This may not be the amount by which the organisation's bank balance has increased during the year, as some of the transactions will not have had an effect on profit but will have affected the bank balance. Good examples of this would be the purchase of fixed assets and owner's drawings. Net profit is calculated as:

Gross profit + income from other sources − expenses = net profit

BALANCE SHEET, CONVENTIONAL FORM

As we mentioned earlier, the balance sheet shows the assets, liabilities and capital of a business at a particular moment in time. The conventional form in which balance sheets are constructed includes the following headings:

student activity

Having now had the opportunity to look at profit and loss accounts and balance sheets again, which do you think is the more valuable document? Consider this value from the point of view of:

- an existing investor
- a potential investor
- the board of directors of the organisation

ASSETS

These are essentially **fixed assets**, in other words, the long-term items owned by the business. They have not been purchased with the intention of selling them, but they are classed as assets all the same, since they could be turned into cash. In a full balance sheet each of these fixed assets listed in terms of its liquidity, in other words, how easy it is to turn into ready cash.

CURRENT ASSETS

Current assets, conversely, are the short-term assets owned by a business. These are assets which change regularly and include stock, debtors, bank balances and ready cash. In a full balance sheet, each of these current assets is listed in terms of its liquidity, in other words, how easy it is to turn into ready cash.

CURRENT LIABILITIES

Current liabilities are liabilities which are due for repayment within twelve months of the balance sheet being constructed. Typically current liabilities will include creditors, bank overdrafts and loans.

student activity

What other forms of current liabilities might an organisation have to consider?

SHARE CAPITAL

Share capital is included in the balance sheet of a limited company. It is stated in the Memorandum of Association of that organisation and can be divided into two:

1 **authorised share capital** – the amount the shareholders have authorised the directors to issue
2 **issued share capital** – the amount that has actually been issued by the directors

PROFIT AND LOSS

The **net total**, either negative or positive, from the profit and loss account is entered on to the balance as this accurately reflects the current profit or loss situation of the organisation.

FIG 7.4.4 *BNFL's Balance Sheet shows how the income and expenditure of the organisation are bassignmentlest questionsalanced in each column.*

Balance Sheets

		Group		Parent	
As at 31 March		**1992**	1991	**1992**	1991
	Note	**£M**	£M	**£M**	£M
Assets employed					
Fixed assets:					
Tangible assets	9	**4221**	3850	**3972**	3590
Intangible assets	10	**31**	33	**—**	—
Investments	11	**58**	40	**327**	300
		4310	3923	**4299**	3890
Current assets:					
Stocks	12	**165**	179	**152**	154
Debtors	13	**183**	144	**184**	153
Investments (short-term deposits)		**487**	568	**476**	560
Cash at bank and in hand		**4**	2	**1**	1
		839	893	**813**	868
Less creditors: amounts falling due within one year	14	**802**	707	**843**	724
Net current assets/(liabilities)		**37**	186	**(30)**	144
Total assets less current liabilities		**4347**	4109	**4269**	4034
Financed by					
Creditors: amounts falling due after more than one year	15	**2612**	2564	**2597**	2552
Provisions for liabilities and charges	16	**992**	874	**967**	850
Accruals and deferred income	17	**83**	99	**65**	79
Capital and reserves:					
Called up share capital	18	**33**	33	**33**	33
Exchange differences		**2**	2	**—**	—
Profit and loss account	19	**612**	521	**607**	520
Shareholders' interest		**647**	556	**640**	553
Minority interests		**13**	16	**—**	—
		4347	4109	**4269**	4034

Sir Christopher Harding
Peter S Phillips   } Directors
25 June 1992

UNIT 7

a s s i g n m e n t

'FINANCE, CASH FLOWS, COSTS, PROFITS AND LOSSES AND BALANCE SHEETS'

In order to fulfil the criteria of this Unit you will need to develop your understanding of the financial considerations of a business to the point where you are able to understand and complete accounting information.

In Unit 8 you will be expected to prepare a **Business Plan**. In this Unit you have to prepare the financial details to support such a plan. It would therefore be advisable for you to consider the nature of your business proposal at this stage.

The stages through which you must work are:

1 Identify the financial requirements of your business
2 Identify possible sources of finance
3 Identify methods of acquiring finance

Once this initial stage has been completed, you will be able to see the financial constraints under which you will have to develop your business.

Your next task is to prepare a cash flow forecast for the first twelve months of your single product business. You will need to explain the significance of all in-flows and out-flows from the business. These explanations will support any attempts to seek finance.

You should use a spreadsheet package to generate this cash flow.

Having completed your cash flow forecast, you must now consider the costs of products and services, paying particular attention to any direct or indirect costs. Again, you may use a spreadsheet package to aid your calculations.

The final phase of this assignment is two-fold:

1 Create a profit and loss statement
2 Create a balance sheet

Explain the uses of these two documents as you will be using them to support your attempts to seek finance from your chosen providers. Again, these documents may be generated using an accounts package.

It is essential that you have completed all phases of this assignment before attempting to move on to Unit 8. You need a firm foundation, in terms of having organised your financial requirements, to ensure that your Business Plan has the necessary authority and authenticity.

UNIT 1

t e s t   q u e s t i o n s

1 Which of the following is not a fixed cost?

(a) heating bills
(b) rent
(c) business rate
(d) wages

2 What is contribution?

(a) selling price + unit fixed costs
(b) marginal costs − selling price
(c) difference between selling price and variable cost
(d) difference between variable cost and margin

3 Which of the following cannot be considered as a business expense?

(a) electricity bills
(b) insurance
(c) stationery
(d) pensions

4 Which of the following is used to calculate the cost of sales?

(a) Opening stock + sales − closing stock
(b) Closing stock + sales + opening stock
(c) Opening stock + purchases − closing stock
(d) Sales − purchases + opening stock

5 If the monthly repayments over a five-year period are charged at 8% and the original loan was for £5,000 what would be the monthly repayments?

(a) £142.17
(b) £118.75
(c) £119.04
(d) £116.83

6 What is factoring

(a) obtaining a loan from the bank
(b) obtaining money from the government
(c) selling invoices to debt collectors
(d) the writing-off of bad debts

7 If two major organisations merged which of the following would not be an advantage to consumers?

(a) the new comparative monopoly position
(b) the new economies of scale
(c) the diversification of potential
(d) the rationalisation of employees

8 Trade discount is given to only one of the following; which is it?

(a) foreign customers
(b) customers also in the business
(c) customers prepared to pay in cash
(d) employees of the organisation

9 Which of the following is aimed at obtaining payment from a debtor?

(a) an invoice
(b) a debit note
(c) a statement of account
(d) a credit note

10 What are running costs?

(a) sponsorship deals with local athletic organisations
(b) payments for assets
(c) payments for raw materials
(d) day-to-day costs incurred by an organisation

Prepare work and collect data for a business plan

1 OBJECTIVES
to make a profit, to break even, to be subsidised

2 LEGAL AND INSURANCE IMPLICATIONS
employment law, health and safety, environmental protection, trades descriptions, age limits, asset insurance, public liability, product liability

3 RESOURCES
human, physical, financial, time

4 EXTERNAL SUPPORT
own organisation, other organisations, individuals

PREPARE WORK AND COLLECT DATA

FOR A BUSINESS PLAN

When individuals or groups of individuals consider starting to run a business, they have a series of different basic choices before them. Essentially, these relate to the nature of the business and whether to start a **new business** or to buy an **existing** one. We shall look at the basic choices in turn, taking first the question of the **nature of the business**. It is easier to think of the nature of the business in terms of which business sector it falls into:

- *Primary sector* - this covers all industries involved in the **production of raw materials**. Remember that it also includes most forms of agriculture and fishing too
- *Secondary sector* - this sector includes industries involved in the **processing of raw materials** in

some way. In other words, industries in this sector turn raw materials into finished goods
- *Tertiary sector* - this relates mainly to the **service industries**. They do not actually involve themselves directly in the processing of materials. This sector includes tourism, transportation and financial services

The choice of which sector your business falls in will largely depend on two main criteria. These are your own **expertise and knowledge** of the business activity and the **potential demand** for the products or services you wish to offer.

Turning to the question of whether to establish a new business or to buy into an existing one, there are a number of possibilities:

STARTING A NEW BUSINESS

This basically means beginning a business from the start. There are a number of risks and costs involved:

- high financial risks
- market research should be extensive
- as you are unknown in the market, you will need time to establish yourself
- mistakes in the first few months can be disastrous
- you will need to carefully consider exactly where to locate the business
- you will need to make an impact quickly to make sure that your cash flow is not adversely affected.

student activity

In the rest of this Unit, we will be considering the purposes and nature of a business plan. However, when a person is thinking about establishing a new business, there is often very little immediately available information which can be used. In the role of an individual considering starting a new business from scratch, what would be your first move in establishing the viability of the business? Who would you need to consult in order to make these initial decisions?

BUYING AN EXISTING BUSINESS

This means that you are buying a business with an existing track record, good or bad. This course has several risks attached to it:

- although the business is established and there are all the benefits of the infrastructure being in place, such a business is much more expensive
- you will be expected to pay extra for 'goodwill', this means the trading name and trading relations with customers which are already in place
- although the business is up and running this does not mean that you will know what to do with it
- you will have to look carefully at all of the assets and liabilities, as you may be buying someone else's mistakes
- constant monitoring is essential since you cannot really rely on what the previous owner claimed about the strengths and weaknesses of the business

EXPANDING AN EXISTING BUSINESS

This opportunity may arise when a business is diversifying or increasing output. While this may not be an option for a person setting up an entirely new business,

student activity

Imagine yourself in the role of an individual considering purchasing an existing business. What financial and other information would you need to see in order to make a considered decision as to whether to proceed? Also, consider whether you would need to use the services of the following, and what specialist knowledge you could gain from them:

- bank manager
- accountant
- solicitor
- surveyor
- management consultant

At what stage would you bring these specialists in?

this could be a way of gaining the advantages of an existing business along with the independence of setting up a new one. A business person may consider taking another partner on, or a small limited company may take in another shareholder to inject cash and expand. This course of action also has some risks attached to it:

- you may not be as independent as you would like
- you should consider why, if the existing business structure was sound, profits acceptable and management in control of the situation, the organisation needs an 'outsider'
- you should also ask why the business has waited until this point to expand
- although diversification is a good idea, since it spreads risk across different business enterprises, it does stretch available resources too

student activity

In the role of a financial provider who is being asked to consider further investment and support to an existing organisation, what information would you need? Consider your response to the following two situations:

1 The organisation is making a considered and logical expansion to its business activities. The organisation appears to be reasonably financially sound.
2 The organisation largely requires the additional finance to bolster existing business activities and intends to make only minor investments into new markets. The organisation seems to have a variety of problems associated with both its operations and its management.

What would you insist upon before giving additional funding, particularly in the latter case?

BUYING A FRANCHISE

A successful business may offer its name, operational procedures, products or services to interested parties under a franchising arrangement. Inevitably, there are some risks:

- while it is easier to obtain a loan to buy a franchise than to buy some other businesses, the franchisor may require quite high 'set-up' fees
- franchises are considered to be low risk, in general, but they are also fairly low in returns. The franchisor will require a share of all of the profits that you make
- franchises are usually restricted to very tight geographical areas, and you will not be allowed to operate outside your specified territory

student activity

Investigate the availability of franchise business opportunities. What criteria would you use in deciding which franchise to opt for? Bear in mind that you should choose a franchise in a business activity which you have some knowledge of or interest in.

Compare the start-up capital required, support from the franchisor and business expansion potential of the opportunities available.

OBJECTIVES

We can best look at the various objectives of businesses by first realising that not all organisations have the same set of objectives. Indeed they may consider some of the objectives detailed below to be of no importance at all. Others may have identified versions of the main objectives. In any case, organisations will put the following objectives into a different order, and may consider that some are vital, others important and the rest desirable. In the business world, it is often difficult to make sure that you obtain all of the benefits and successes that you intended.

student activity

Referring to Figure 8.1.1, how would you identify these short-, medium- and long-term objectives? Do you think that personal objectives may differ from those of a business? If so, why?

TO MAKE A PROFIT

This is perhaps the most obvious of all of the objectives, and yet, not all organisations will consider this to be the most important consideration. Perhaps, as we shall see from some of the other objectives, the act of survival in a highly competitive world is just as important.

Making a profit has obvious benefits for the owners of a business; the more apparent ones are being successful in their chosen career and obtaining wealth. The employees of the business will benefit too, as they will probably receive better pay and conditions of employment. If the need to make a profit is too powerful and gets out of control, this can have detrimental effects on the business and how it is run. The business may cut corners and risk breaching legislative guidelines, particularly those relating to employees or the environment.

Being profitable, as you will now no doubt be aware, brings additional benefits in terms of the running of the business. These include:

- economies of scale - being able to buy materials more cheaply and producing units at a lower unit cost
- being able to buy environmentally friendly materials
- being able to use environmentally friendly production processes
- being able to obtain the best staff for the job

student activity

How realistic is it to expect a new business to make a profit in the first year? If a new business must manage its finances in a careful and professional manner in the first year, surely survival must be the major goal? Do you agree with this statement?

TO BREAK EVEN

Breaking even, as we know, means covering costs. For most businesses, this is the key factor which will signal their survival or failure. Any organisation which is considering a loan to a business will, at least, insist that in the medium term it must break even. Profits may take a little longer to accrue.

OBJECTIVES

What are your personal objectives in running the business?

Short-term

_____

_____

_____

Medium-term

_____

_____

_____

How do you intend to achieve them?

_____

_____

What objectives do you have for the business itself?

Short-term

_____

_____

_____

Medium-term

_____

_____

_____

How do you intend to achieve them?

_____

_____

What are your long-term objectives (if any)?

1. _____

_____

2. _____

_____

3. _____

4. _____

5. _____

_____

How do you intend to achieve them?

_____

_____

_____

FIG 8.1.1 *Part of Barclays Bank's 'Setting up and running your own business' information pack, which illustrates the need, even before the business has come into existence, of setting out objectives in the short, medium and long term.*

TO BE SUBSIDISED

This objective is the only major exception to the basic requirements of making a profit and breaking even. There are certain circumstances in which an organisation may operate at a loss, but receive funds from another source to ensure its survival. Governments will subsidise organisations operating in designated re-development areas. They will also offer financial assistance to organisations developing new technological equipment. A business which is part of a larger organisation (such as a conglomerate or a multi national), may receive subsidies in the course of the development of its market. The parent company will, in effect, subsidise the running of the business during the expensive start-up period.

KINGFISHER PLC ANNUAL REPORT & ACCOUNTS 1992

Within the markets we target, we've said
we want to build 'market leading quality businesses'.
What do we mean by that?

We want our businesses to be capable of
earning consistently high returns on the capital employed in them.
Kingfisher companies are expected to lead the pack
consistently and in every department.

Consistently is the word to concentrate on.
Customer needs and preferences change all the time.
So our businesses must be geared up to
constant change – up to and including
regenerating their entire retail concept if necessary.

We don't encourage them to base their response to change
on any one element – like design – or on the talent or flair of any one individual.

We ask them to outpace rivals by developing an ethos of continuous innovation.
They are expected to generate a stream of unique advantages –
advantages based on existing strengths, such that competitors can't
even come close to imitating them.

And we're not just talking about developments at the customer interface level.
We aim to stay ahead, for example, in every aspect of management,
cost positioning and infrastructure. In other words,
we want businesses which stay alongside the customer, by
being good enough to drive the markets they're in.

student activity

There are around 300 different types of grants available which are designed to cover the following:

- starting a new project
- acquisition of new machinery
- creating new job opportunities
- expansion of existing business

Try to identify at least one grant which relates to each of the above.

FIG 8.1.2 *This is a statement concerning B & Q, taken from Kingfisher plc's Annual Report and Accounts. It clearly states that they are concerned with consistent customer care, as well as introducing innovative customer services.*

CUSTOMER CARE

Customer care may be a key objective to a business, as the maintenance of goodwill is of prime consideration. Customer care may take various forms, including:

- attractive and efficient premises
- modern equipment

- streamlined processing systems
- extensive staff training programmes
- instant response to customer queries (for example pledging that all telephone calls will be answered within four rings)

student activity

Referring to Figure 8.1.2, what do you understand by the following phrases?

- 'An ethos of continuous innovation'
- 'Customer inter-face level'

SOCIAL RESPONSIBILITY

Social responsibility may take two distinct forms, either towards employees or towards customers. With regard to employees, it may take the form of the provision of various welfare facilities, including crèches and in the case of customers, it may be a regard for the production of socially responsible products and services. While key factors relating to social responsibility are covered

FIG 8.1.3 *This is the opening page from the British Airports Authority's 1993 Environmental Report. Richard Everitt is a member of the company's main board and has specific responsibilities for the implementation of BAA's environmental policies.*

Richard Everitt is a member of the Company's main board, and is responsible for the effective implementation of BAA's environmental policies.

BAA plc owns and operates seven airports in the UK. These account for

73 per cent of the UK's passenger air traffic and 84 per cent of air cargo.

In 1992, over 77 million passengers travelled through our airports –

an increase of 75 per cent over the last decade. The demand for air travel

is likely to double within the next 12 years or so and people's freedom to

travel as they need depends on continued airport development.

Airports have impacts on the environment – that's inevitable. And our

priority is to continue striving to reduce those impacts where practicable.

While BAA has a long history of successful environmental

initiatives, we have never before published an environmental policy.

This report sets out our policy and introduces some of the projects we

have already undertaken and aim to build upon. We will continue setting

new environmental goals and will report each year on our progress.

in various forms of legislation, businesses may take additional steps in order to enhance the working experience of their employees, or to attract additional purchases from customers.

ENVIRONMENTAL CONCERNS

Customers are becoming increasingly aware of environmental issues and, consequently, certain businesses will cite environmental considerations as being key objectives. Specific environmental policies which may be adopted by businesses include:

- the use of environmentally friendly products and processes
- the careful consideration of all waste disposal
- the use of energy efficient heating systems
- the use of bio-degradable packaging materials at all stages in distribution and transportation

student activity

Referring to Figure 8.1.3, you will see that BAA have identified a number of key considerations which relate to their specific business activities. They have funded a number of projects designed to ensure that they minimise the impact of their activities on the local environment. These include the creation of nature reserves and working closely with local authorities on conservation activities.

Try to identify any similar projects which have been undertaken in your local area.

TO ATTAIN POWER AND INFLUENCE

This objective may also have two levels of importance to an organisation. The first relates to the dominance of the market in which the organisation's business activity takes place. The second relates to power and influence at national or international level. On yet another level, power and influence may be related to the comparative importance of an organisation in a particular job market.

LEGAL AND INSURANCE IMPLICATIONS

Businesses, are required to ensure that they have complied with various legal guidelines. For further details of these see Unit 4 – for specific legal requirements with regard to employees and Unit 5 for additional UK employment law and EC directives.

Organisations naturally have to keep accurate accounts of all transactions made. These accounts will be required both by the Inland Revenue and for VAT collection purposes.

Businesses also have to take out a various sorts of insurance in order to protect them from certain unfortunate circumstances and risks. There is a tendency for most businesses to under-insure as the cost of insurance has far outpaced inflation. But a business which is under-insured leaves itself open to potential disaster.

Businesses have to decide which policy best suits them in relation to their business activities. It is now possible to obtain an insurance policy which covers most of the risks faced by businesses. We will be looking at the specific insurance needs of businesses shortly.

student activity

It is wise for organisations to insure various aspects of their business. For an organisation to expose itself to the possibility of theft or fire and their damaging effects is foolhardy.

Barclays, for example, offer the following types of insurance which cover most potential liabilities:

- public liability
- employers' liability
- commercial inclusive policies
- residential building policies
- solo policies (for the self-employed who work at home)
- hotel policies
- nursing and rest home policies
- motor policies
- life assurance policies

Referring to your own intended business, which of the above would you have to consider taking out? Are there any policies available which cover the majority of these risks?

EMPLOYMENT LAW

Particular attention should be paid to providing a contract of employment to all those who work for 16 or more hours per week and adhering to laws relating to discrimination. For a fuller listing of all employment laws see Units 4 and 5.

HEALTH AND SAFETY

Employers' liability insurance covers a business against claims made by employees who have suffered injury in the course of their work. The term employee is a broad one in this respect, and covers all those who are under contract in some way to the organisation.

As we will have seen in Units 2, 4 and 5, **health and safety at work** has become an increasingly complex area for businesses to consider. In effect, a business should ensure that it complies with the Health and Safety at Work Act 1974 in the following respects:

1 Provide safe machinery and equipment
2 Ensure that regular maintenance is undertaken
3 Ensure that all operating procedures for machinery and equipment are carefully monitored
4 Ensure that safe methods of handling all potentially dangerous or hazardous materials are adhered to
5 Ensure that all employees receive sufficient training in safety matters
6 Ensure that employees are well supervised at all times
7 Provide healthy and safe business premises in terms of heating, lighting, ventilation etc.
8 Ensure that access to and exit from premises are both safe and clearly marked
9 Ensure that any visitors to the premises encounter a safe environment

ENVIRONMENTAL PROTECTION

In Unit 1 we looked at the Environmental Act 1990 and its implications for UK businesses. This law and a variety of related EC Directives have been created to ensure that businesses take full account of their social responsibility at all times. These laws, coupled with considerable consumer pressure, have caused businesses to re-evaluate many of their costs of production. There is no doubt that certain products and services have become more expensive as a result of more stringent environmental protection, but, these costs are far outweighed by the positive impacts which both businesses and the country as a whole enjoy.

When considering environmental concerns, a business will attempt to examine the following aspects of its activities:

1 Do any of our **activities** involve any environmental risks?
2 Do any of our **processes** involve any environmental risks?
3 Do we use any **materials** which are particularly environmentally suspect?
4 Do our products (including our packaging and disposal of used products) have any **detrimental impact** on the environment?
5 What types and levels of **waste** are involved at all stages of production?
6 Can we implement any cost-effective ways of **eliminating pollution**?
7 By the implementation of environmental policies, can we be more **efficient**?
8 Is there a real **consumer demand** for environmentally sound products?
9 Is there any **legislation** at planning stage which may adversely affect our business activities?
10 Do we have systems in place to ensure **adherence** to existing and expected legislation?
11 Can we make use of any environmental policies in terms of improving our **corporate image**?
12 What implications will **environmental policies** have on the opinions of our shareholders, investors or providers of finance?

If an organisation decides to install a comprehensive environmental policy, then this should form part of its overall business plan. Commonly, an environmental policy will take the form of a statement which will include the following:

- the business's commitment to make environmental concerns a central part of all planning activities
- an undertaking that a series of processes will be put in place to identify possible environmental threats
- an assurance that the policy is fully endorsed by both senior management and the Board of Directors
- a commitment to communicate policies regarding environmental protection fully to all employees
- a commitment to seek assistance and guidance from external agencies as a matter of priority

One of the problems relating to environmental protection is the constant development of new production processes which are not, covered under the existing environmental protection legislation. Initially, governments and authorities rely on the social responsibility of organisations to carry out their activities in the spirit of environmental protection and existing legislation. It is inevitable that the development of legislation lags behind the development of new industrial processes.

BAA aims to reduce its consumption of resources such as energy and water and to reduce waste where possible. We also promote recycling and the use of recycled materials whenever this is cost effective.

Conserving resources

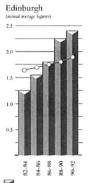

Edinburgh
(annual average figures)

Terminal passengers in millions
O—O Energy consumed in KwH, (10M)

The success of BAA's energy conservation programme can be judged by looking at energy consumption as more and more passengers travel through the Company's airports. For example at Edinburgh, energy consumption went up by only 15 per cent despite a 90 per cent increase in passenger numbers over a 10 year period.

BAA has long recognised the importance of preserving valuable resources, and has introduced various conservation measures as well as commissioning a detailed investigation into the extent to which waste from airports can be recycled. This study will form the basis for a number of new recycling initiatives in the course of this year.

Energy use

In May 1992, BAA signed the Government's "Commitment to Energy Efficiency." The Company's own energy use during 1991/92 was 540 million kWh/year and our airport tenants used a further 660m kWh/year. To ensure that we're using this energy wisely, and thereby helping to reduce air pollution, we've set up energy monitoring throughout our operations. In this way, we can supply managers with the information they need to control energy use more effectively, and set targets for the future. The results can be seen quite clearly at Glasgow, where over the last six years passenger numbers have increased by 50 per cent and terminal facilities have expanded by 60 per cent, but consumption of energy has only increased by 6.2 per cent.

Water consumption

Just as we've done with energy, BAA has also developed ways to save water. A survey of water use at Gatwick led to a £40,000 programme to stop leaks from the mains, saving 140 million litres of water and cutting our water bill by £120,000 a year. Elsewhere, trials with automatic controls on flushing systems in toilets at Gatwick and Heathrow airports have shown that water consumption can be reduced by as much as 90 per cent. At Heathrow alone this could save almost 50 million litres a year.

Waste management

Aircraft arrive at airports with large amounts of waste that has to be disposed of. Each year, Heathrow Airport Ltd has to dispose of around 20,000 tonnes of waste, whilst Gatwick Airport Ltd disposes of around 8,000 tonnes. We have initiated a detailed study of waste management and the type of waste at all our airports to determine possibilities for recycling. BAA also has responsibility for litter control at its airports. With cleaning bills adding up to more than £15 million a year, we are obviously keen to encourage people to dispose of litter in a responsible way. At our airports, we have been actively promoting awareness campaigns such as Tidy Travel Week.

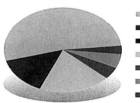

Paper and card 52.7%
Plastic 13.7%
Textiles 0.5%
Miscellaneous 19.9%
Glass 4.8%
Putrescible 5.2%
Metal 3.2%

This chart shows a breakdown of the types of waste handled by contractors for Gatwick Airport. Further research is looking at opportunities for recycling a proportion of this waste.

fourteen

FIG 8.1.4 *This is another page from BAA's Environmental Report 1993, which states its policy of reducing the consumption of resources and, wherever possible, recycling materials.*

student activity

You can see from Figure 8.1.4 that BAA spend £15 million per year on cleaning bills. Can you suggest any ways in which this expenditure could be reduced?

TRADES DESCRIPTIONS

In Unit 3 we looked at the Trades Descriptions Act in some detail. However, there are some key considerations and obligations relating to the providing of products and services that we should look at again. These are:

1 A product must comply with its **description** and any claims made regarding its **performance**
2 **Faulty products** should be replaced or a refund should be made to the customer, without exception
3 Products should meet all existing **safety standards**
4 If a product is found to be unsafe in any way the business may be **prosecuted**

AGE LIMITS

Employees should be 16 years of age in order to be legally in full-time employment. There are some restrictions on the number of working hours for the under 16s in part-time employment. Recently the retirement age has been changed to 65 years for all. Formerly the retirement age was 60 for women and 65 for men. Individuals may, of course, work beyond the normal retirement age, but doing so has implications for their pension rights.

ASSET INSURANCE

Asset insurance attempts to ensure that a business is protected against loss or damage to stock, equipment or processes as a result of various uncontrollable factors. Essentially there are four types of asset insurances:

1 The first type covers **damage** and **loss** to both the premises and the contents of the premises from fire. The term 'fire' used in such insurance in actual fact covers floods, lightning, explosions, earthquakes, storms, riots and vandalism.

2 The second type covers **theft** of all removable assets, including computers, machinery, office equipment, money and stock. An organisation must ensure that its insurance provides cover both for loss on and off the premises. Additionally, a business must be careful to ensure that the insured value is for the replacement value of item(s) and not current value.

3 The third type protects against the **interruption of business activity**. This cover may automatically come into operation if the business has suffered damage as a result of a disaster under the fire cover. This cover insures the organisation against the loss of business while the premises or other vital business equipment are being replaced or repaired. In addition, this insurance covers the loss of production caused by an interruption in the power supply.

4 The fourth form is **'all risks'**. Under this type of insurance a business is covered for damage, loss or destruction of items anywhere within the UK. This insurance will recompense the organisation at full replacement value of item(s).

PUBLIC LIABILITY

A business must ensure that it is covered against injury to a member of the public as a direct or indirect result of any occurrence or event related to the business. This insurance also covers the loss or damage of customers' property.

PRODUCT LIABILITY

In effect as an extension of public liability insurance, a business also needs to insure against claims arising from the use of its products or services. If a customer has suffered injury, loss or damage as a result of faulty products or services, the business may claim against its product liability insurance. This insurance also covers the organisation for legal costs which may be incurred in preparing a defence against any claims that are made under consumer protection legislation.

RESOURCES

Central issues in the business plan of an organisation are the co-ordination and organisation of the resources available or required. We shall be looking at the four main types of resources, which are:

- human
- physical
- financial
- time

HUMAN

Planning the human resources of an organisation basically involves consideration of the following:

- the availability of experienced management
- the exact nature and experience of other staff
- the staff support systems that will be required

In order to maximise the effectiveness of a business in the early stage of its development, the deployment of human resources is essential. We should look at the planning in terms of both short- and long-term considerations.

The short-term considerations include the skills required in the following areas:

- management
- administration
- marketing
- selling
- accounts
- production
- research and development

It does not necessarily follow that all of these specialist skills must be supplied by directly employed staff. An organisation may choose to buy in assistance in some areas. These will include:

- directors who assist in financial terms only
- self-employed individuals contracted to carry out specialist functions
- individuals employed via an employment agency
- employment of younger or inexperienced staff with the intention of training and developing them to fulfil certain roles

FIG 8.1.5 *This is a section from Barclays' Business Plan Form which relates specifically to premises, machinery and vehicles.*

PREMISES/MACHINERY/VEHICLES

Premises:

Where do you intend to locate the business and why?

What sort and size of premises will you need?

What are the details of any lease, licence, rent, rates and when is the next rent review due?

Machinery/Vehicles:

What machinery/vehicles do you require?

Are these to be bought or leased and on what terms?

How long is their lifespan?

PERSONNEL

Estimate the cost of employing any people or buying any services you may need in the first two years

Number of people	Job function	Monthly cost	Annual cost

(Remember to include your own salary and those of any partners you may have in this calculation)

FIG 8.1.6 *A detail from Barclays Business Plan Form, which considers the cost of employing people or employing their specialist skills*

In terms of long-term planning, an organisation will consider the following:

- the maintenance and improvement of output
- the maintenance and expansion of productivity
- maximisation of profit
- ensuring job satisfaction
- maximising the relationship between labour costs and productivity

We looked at the subject of the deployment of human resources in much more detail in Unit 4. The key considerations in relation to the business plan should include the following:

- the precise staff requirements of the organisation
- the availability and implementation of staff training programmes
- the maintenance of good industrial relations with good employees
- the provision of staff welfare facilities
- the consideration of competitive wage levels
- adherence to all health and safety, employment law and other legal requirements relating to employees

student activity

How many of the above considerations will have to be planned for in the initial stages of the formation of the business? How many of them will be developed as and when the situation arises?

PHYSICAL

Planning the physical resources will basically involve consideration of the following requirements:

- premises
- machinery and equipment
- stock
- materials – raw, part-finished and finished

The first major consideration in terms of the physical resources of the organisation is the **premises**. We should begin by looking at some legal implications:

1 *Planning*. It is a legal requirement that a business must obtain planning permission relating to the type of business activity carried out on the premises. All premises have a 'usage designation' which is monitored by the local authority. Particular buildings will be considered unsuitable for certain business activities. An additional consideration here is that a business operating from the home may render the premises liable for the payment of business rates.

2 *Licences*. To trade legally, a business may require a licence. The following types of business will require a trading licence which is monitored by and available from the local authority:

- restaurants, cafes and bars
- food processing and manufacture
- mobile food outlets
- retailers of alcohol
- retailers of tobacco products
- nursing homes and children's nurseries
- scrap metal dealers

3 *Leases, covenants and restrictions*. The lease on premises may restrict the type of business activity allowable. It is also worth considering, before the investment of considerable sums of money on the improvement of a building, the length of the lease, the possibility of renewing it. and whether any renewal is likely to be under agreeable and affordable terms. With regard to covenants and other restrictions, there may be certain by-laws relating to the building. These may not only restrict the type of business activity allowed but also relate to the development of the site.

4 *Environmental*. The location of the premises, and the availability of services to handle various waste and other emissions, may make the premises unsuitable. Environmental legislation does not permit certain sorts of business activity to take place in premises in

residential areas.

Once we have considered the **suitability** of the premises, there are other factors to take into account, such as the basis on which the property may be held:

- Whether **freehold** is available – freehold is a legal term which gives an individual the right to purchase the property outright. A person who owns the freehold of a property may choose to do what he or she wishes with it, provided he or she adheres to any relevant legislation. The freehold option is less likely to be available on business premises as the majority of such premises are available for lease or rent.
- Whether the option is to **lease** – this is when a business or an individual takes out a lease on a property for a specific period of time. The particulars of the lease will include the following:

  – the number of years of the lease

  – the options to renew the lease
  – the rental payable
  – what the leaseholder is required to do in terms of insurance and maintenance of the property
  – whether the payment of a premium is required to secure the property

Other facts to be considered when deciding whether to use a particular property include the following:

- the paying of a chartered surveyor to give a valuation and full survey on the property
- the use of an insurance broker to obtain the most competitive quotation for all necessary insurance
- the contacting of the local authority to ascertain the rateable value of the property
- consultation with an accountant to fully consider all of the financial implications of the premises

The other major consideration with regard to physical

FIG 8.1.7 *Barclays provide a comprehensive pack of information designed to assist individuals in starting and owning their own business.*

resources relates to the fixed assets – which include any machinery, equipment or vehicles used by the organisation. The organisation should consider the following:

- what machinery, equipment and vehicles should be obtained immediately
- whether they should be bought
- whether they should be leased
- which supplier offers the most acceptable terms

Whether the assets are bought or leased will have tax implications. Briefly, these implications are:

1 *Buying*. The gradual loss of value (known as depreciation) of the equipment may be set against tax on the profit and loss account of the business.
2 *Leasing*. The cost of leasing may be entered on to the profit and loss account, thereby reducing profits and thus reducing tax.

An organisation will always try to buy equipment rather than lease it as buying is more tax-efficient in the long run.

FINANCIAL

Planning the financial resources involves consideration of the following factors:

- the capital available from the owners of the business
- the sources of finance needed

We covered the main considerations that must be taken into account in the planning of financial resources in Unit 7. However, later in this Unit we will be looking at some specific aspects of financial resource planning.

In essence, an organisation should try to identify:

- the financial resources required for the purchase and maintenance of fixed assets
- the amount of working capital needed
- how fixed assets will be financed
- how working capital will be obtained
- who will provide finance

Specifically, later in this Unit we will be looking at financial data and forecasting, and in particular, at the following:

- time periods involved
- cash flow forecasts
- start-up balance sheets
- projected profit and loss accounts
- projected balance sheets

TIME

Planning the **time** resources involves undertaking the following tasks:

- accurately charting when all other resources will be required
- co-ordinating all other resources
- constructing a time frame within which all other resources will be needed

Applying a time frame to all of the various resources required to start the business is essential to ensure that the correct resources are available **at the right time**. The level and complexity of planning needed can be very difficult for new business people and they will require the assistance of qualified specialists to enable them to fully plan the time considerations. Typically, an organisation will use two main techniques for its planning – **Critical Path Analysis** and **Gannt Charts**. We shall look at these in some detail:

1 *Critical Path Analysis*. This method relies on the identification of all of the component actions and the minimum time required for each main project. The analysis takes the form of a series of arrows against which are marked the activities and the time required to carry out each activity. Each arrow will come from and go to a node (which is in effect an event). Critical path analysis may be very complex. By tracing actions along a series of arrows and events, a business planner is able to identify the maximum time required to carry out particular projects. In addition, activities which take the longest time to complete are identified as **critical activities**. These will tend to be drawn on the diagram as a thick line. By carefully analysing the completed chart, the planner should be able to identify particular 'bottle necks' and predict potential future problems.

2 *Gannt charts*. An alternative method of illustrating the processes and activities in the planning schedule is to create a **Gannt chart**. This consists of a number

Critical path analysis

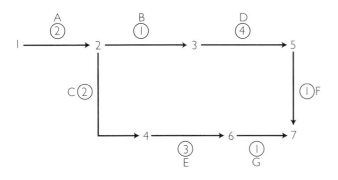

FIG 8.1.8 *This is a simple critical path analysis network. The numbers on their own refer to the stages. The circled numbers refer to the days that the tasks will take to complete. The letters refer to the tasks themselves.*

of activities listed against numbered weeks. The activities are cross-referenced against the week in which the activity is intended to begin and end. The process is continued down the list of activities, with the later activities, which rely on the completion of earlier activities, beginning in the week after the previous activity has been completed. Again, it is necessary to identify critical activities which have major implications on the beginning of other activities.

student activity

Using either a Critical Path Analysis Network or a Gantt Chart, detail the activities and timings which relate to your business in the stages before you actually commence operations.

GANTT CHART FOR PLANNING THE CONSTRUCTION OF A HOUSE

Tasks are broken down into the necessary steps

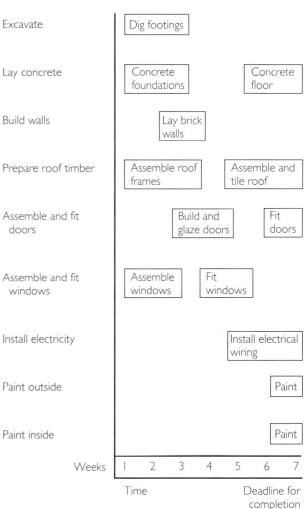

FIG 8.1.9 *An example of a Gannt Chart.*

EXTERNAL SUPPORT

No business, whatever its size, can realistically expect to be able to form a full business plan by itself. It will inevitably require the assistance of specialists to formulate particular aspects of the plan. In some cases, some of the skills needed may be available within the organisation, but may not yet be identified. In other cases, different organisations will be able to offer support and assistance with procedural or legal matters. Alternatively, an organisation may require the assistance of specifically qualified individuals to undertake monitoring and development tasks on its behalf.

OWN ORGANISATION

Certain individuals or departments within the organisation itself will have been identified as being the source of assistance for particular aspects of the business plan. We considered the responsibilities of individuals and departments when we considered their job roles within the organisation structure (see Unit 4). Specifically an organisation would expect the following assistance from each key department:

Association of British Chambers of Commerce, 212a Shaftesbury Avenue, London WC2H 8EW (01-240 5831).

British Franchise Association, Franchise Chambers, 75a Bell Street, Henley-on-Thames, Oxon RG9 2BD (0491 579049).

British Overseas Trade Board, 1 Victoria Street, London SW1 (01-215 7877).

Business in the Community (BIC), 227a City Road, London EC1V 1JU (01-253 3716).
(BIC will be able to provide you with the name and address of your nearest local Enterprise Agency).

In Scotland contact Scottish Business in the Community (SCOTBIC), Romano House, 43 Station Road, Corstophine, Edinburgh EH12 7ES (031-334 9876).

Companies Registration Office, Companies House, 55 City Road, London EC1Y 1BB (01-253 9393).

In Scotland contact the Registrar of Companies for Scotland, 102 George Street, Edinburgh EH2 3JD (031-225 5774).

In Northern Ireland contact the Department of Commerce, Chichester House, 43-47 Chichester Court, Belfast BT1 4PJ (0232 234121).

Co-operative Development Agency, Broadmead House, 21 Panton Street, London SW1Y 4DR (01-839 2988).

Highlands and Islands Development Board, Bridge House, Bank Street, Inverness IV1 1QR (0463 34171).

Institute of Export, Export House, Clifton Street, London EC2 4HI (01-247 9812).

London Enterprise Agency, 4 Snow Hill, London EC1A 2BS (01-236 3000).

Mid Wales Development, Ladywell House, Newtown, Powys SY16 1JB (0686 626965).

Rural Development Commission, 141 Castle Street, Salisbury SP1 3TP (0722 336255). The RDC has regional offices throughout the country.

Small Business Bureau, 32 Smith Square, London SW1P 3HH (01-222 9000).

Small Firms Service, dial 100 and ask for Freefone Enterprise. Alternatively here are the regional addresses:

Birmingham – 6th Floor, Ladywood House, Stephenson Street, Birmingham B2 4DT (021-643 3344).

Bristol – 6th Floor, The Pithay, Bristol BS1 2NB (0272 294546).

Cambridge – 24 Brooklands Avenue, Cambridge CB2 2BU (0223 63312).

Cardiff – 16 St. David's House, Wood Street, Cardiff CF1 1ER (0222 396116).

Glasgow – 57 Bothwell Street, Glasgow G2 6TU (041-248 6014).

Leeds – 1 Park Row, City Square, Leeds LS1 5NR (0532 445151).

Liverpool – 1 Old Street, Liverpool L3 9HJ (051-236 5756).

London – Ebury Bridge House, 2-18 Ebury Bridge Road, London SW1W 8QD (01-730 8451).

Manchester – 3rd Floor, 320-325 Royal Exchange Buildings, St. Ann's Square, Manchester M2 7AH (061-832 5282).

Newcastle – 22 Newgate Shopping Centre, Newcastle upon Tyne NE1 1ZP (0632 325353).

Nottingham – Severns House, 20 Middle Pavement, Nottingham NG1 7DW (0602 506181).

Reading – Abbey Hall, Abbey Square, Reading RG1 3BE (0734 591733).

Stevenage – Business and Technology Centre, Bessemer Drive, Stevenage, Herts SG1 2DX (0438 743377).

Wales – The Welsh Development Agency, Treforest Industrial Estate, Pontypridd, Mid Glamorgan CF37 5UT (0443 852666).

Scotland – The Scottish Development Agency, 102 Telford Road, Edinburgh EN4 2NP (031-343 1911).

Northern Ireland – The Local Enterprise Development Unit, Lamont House, Purdys Lane, Newtownbreda, Belfast BT8 4AR (0232 691031).

Rural Development Commission, 141 Castle Street, Salisbury SP1 3TP (0122 336255). The RDC has regional offices throughout the country.

FIG 8.1.10 *There is a great deal of reliable business information available at low cost, or in some cases, free of charge. Much of this information is produced by organisations which are seeking to sell their services and use this free information as a promotional tool. The available information covers all aspects of business activities including law, finance, taxation, funding and information technology.*

1 *Accounts.* Individuals carrying out accounts functions should be able to identify and construct all necessary profit and loss accounts and balance sheets. They should also be able to give a clear indication of the cost implications of the implementation of particular business plans.

2 *Legal.* The company secretary should be abreast of all current legislation relevant to business activity and should be able to advise the organisation whether new business activities will involve compliance with additional legislation.

3 *Personnel.* The personnel department or personnel manager should be able to identify any additional human resource requirements of any planned new business activities.

4 *Production.* The production manager will be able to advise as to the feasibility of new production requirements. He/she will be able to identify possible suppliers of materials and equipment required to carry out new functions.

5 *Design.* Designers in their research and development role will probably have been consulted at any early stage to assess the viability of new projects. They will be able to identify any cost implications in consultation with the production manager.

6 *Sales and Marketing.* The sales and marketing department or managers will have a clear idea of whether potential new business projects will meet the needs and approval of proposed customers. They will be able to offer advice in the formulation of the marketing plan which we will find to be an integral part of the overall business plan.

7 *Distribution.* There may be distribution considerations, particularly if the organisation is proposing to produce and provide new products or services which have not been associated with the organisation previously. The distribution manager may have to consider alternative distribution and transportation methods in order to ensure prompt and safe delivery of the proposed new products.

8 *Administration.* The administration at various levels of the organisation will be able to provide a key support function to the formulation of the business plan, whether simply in the presentation of the business plan, or whether there are additional considerations that relate directly to the main administration functions.

OTHER ORGANISATIONS AND INDIVIDUALS

Sometimes an organisation formulating a business plan may need to call in other organisations or individuals, either because it is very small or because it is deficient in certain areas. These individuals may fulfil many of the functions considered above, but others may be specialists in particular areas of business development. Examples of other organisations or individuals who may be called in to assist the formulation of a business plan include:

- financial advisers
- insurance specialists
- tax consultants
- solicitors
- architects and surveyors
- design specialists
- management consultants
- marketing consultants

These individuals or organisations will be employed only if it is strictly cost-effective to do so. Their employment will have to show positive benefits for the employing organisation. As we have said, these benefits may relate to the specialist knowledge they possess, or the additional advisory skills they can offer.

It is normal for banks and other providers of financial assistance to be able to advise on the employment of particular organisations or individuals and may well have their own advisers available.

student activity

Figure 8.1.10 listed some sources of information, but, as we mentioned in the last section, there are other specialists and consultants who offer advice and support. Using your local Yellow Pages, try to identify any specialists or consultants who may be able to offer advice and support directly related to your own business. You may also try to find out how much it would cost to use their services.

student activity

How would you identify the expertise available within your organisation? Devise a skills audit sheet for existing members of staff to detail their specialist knowledge.

Produce and present a business plan

1 PURPOSES OF A BUSINESS PLAN
to seek finance, to gain finance, to monitor performance

2 OBJECTIVES
supply of goods or services, achieve sales volume, achieve sales value, achieve market share, make profit, break even

3 MARKETING PLAN
pricing, promoting, distribution, selling, timing

4 PRODUCTION PLAN
premises, machinery, raw materials, labour

5 RESOURCE REQUIREMENTS

HUMAN, PHYSICAL, FINANCIAL

6 FINANCIAL DATA AND FORECASTS
time period, cash flow forecast, start-up balance sheet, projected profit and loss and balance sheet

7 MONITORING AND REVIEW
monthly profit and loss and balance sheet

PURPOSES OF A BUSINESS PLAN

We now need to consider the actual **production** and **presentation** of a business plan. In this business plan, we should include the following:

1 Definition of all of the business **objectives**
2 Measures taken in relation to **financial planning**
3 Measures taken in relation to **resource planning**
4 Measures taken in relation to **production planning**

5 **Market research** undertaken and outcomes
6 **Marketing planning**

The main **objective** of the plan will be to show a potential provider of finance everything they he or she needs know about the business. It must also show that the business is viable and has potential. There is not a standard acceptable format in which to design a business

■ *GO LOCAL. Get advice which is easily accessible and which is based on a sound knowledge of local business conditions.*

■ *Choose your professional advisers well in advance of setting up.*

■ *Don't underestimate the impact that good, and bad, advice can have on your business.*

■ *Don't choose an accountant, solicitor or bank manager just because you have met them at a party.*

■ *Be confident that the firms you appoint can cope with the kinds of transaction you will be requiring them to handle.*

■ *Make sure that the people you are dealing with are properly qualified and that they are members of the relevant professional bodies.*

■ *Have a good idea of how often you will be consulting your advisers, and make sure that you know how much it will cost you.*

■ *Be prepared to grow with your advisers, and make sure that they can grow with you.*

■ *Make sure you UNDERSTAND the advice you receive – YOU are paying for it!*

plan, as the nature and structure of the business will determine the precisely what is included in the business plan. Generally, a business plan will seek to fulfil one of the following criteria:

- to seek or gain finance
- to monitor performance

We shall look at these individually:

TO SEEK OR GAIN FINANCE

To begin with, the business plan will identify the organisation's financial situation. The items to be covered include

- financial resources currently available
- financial resources needed
- prices of production
- prices of products or services
- organisation's ability to repay loans

Having covered these, the organisation should then be able to identify what finances will be required to ensure that it runs in an efficient and productive manner.

In relation to the gaining of additional finance, perhaps to expand or to diversify into a new area of business activity, the organisation will be operating from existing sets of information (particularly forecasts and financial statements) as opposed to the projected profit and loss accounts and balance sheets which would be used in the case of a new business.

FIG 8.2.1 *Barclays provide a useful list of key points to consider when seeking advice and support. These should be borne in mind when engaging in any contact with advisers.*

TO MONITOR PERFORMANCE

Normally, a business plan is **reviewed** at regular intervals so that the decision-makers within the organisation can assess the relative success and progress of the business. It is better to identify a problem at an early stage than to have to react to it once it has developed. Typically, an organisation will use SWOT analysis (strengths, weaknesses, opportunities and threats) to ascertain its current position, both internally and externally. The **strengths** and **weaknesses** identify the organisation's internal situation (the advantages and disadvantages of its structure, processes, size and staff). The **opportunities** and **threats** consider external implications for the organisation, making direct comparisons with competitors and looking at the current status of market in which the business is active.

student activity

It is a good idea to clearly identify your market and consider the most direct competitors and their comparative advantages and disadvantages. Begin this process with reference to your own business.

MARKET

Describe your market _____
_____
_____
_____

Where is your market? _____
_____

Who are your customers? _____
_____

How big is your market? _____
_____

Is your market growing, static or in decline? _____
_____

Itemise the competitive products or services
Competitor's name _____

Competitive product/service A

Name _____ Price _____
Strengths _____ Weaknesses _____
_____ _____
_____ _____

Competitor's name _____

Competitive product/service B

Name _____ Price _____
Strengths _____ Weaknesses _____
_____ _____
_____ _____

Competitor's name _____

Competitive product/service C

Name _____ Price _____
Strengths _____ Weaknesses _____
_____ _____
_____ _____

What is special about your own product or service? _____
_____
_____
_____
_____

Advantages of your product or service over
Competitor A _____
_____

Competitor B _____
_____

Competitor C _____
_____

FIG 8.2.2 *Barclays' Business Plan Form includes a section which asks for a basic analysis of the market and of competitors' strengths and weaknesses.*

OBJECTIVES

A business plan offers an organisation the opportunity to identify a series of **objectives** with the aim of improving the overall performance of the organisation. Although these objectives may differ from business to business, they generally fall into the categories considered below. These objectives also have comparative importance, depending upon the age and development of the organisation and any current problems or opportunities.

SUPPLY OF GOODS OR SERVICES

For an existing business, the **nature of the business activity** undertaken **by the organisation** may already be predetermined. However, for an organisation entering the market as a new business, this objective may be the first of many to be considered. An analysis of present market conditions and the comparative successfulness of existing businesses operating in related areas will be of prime importance. Additionally, to enter a market which provides particular products or services, an organisation will need to ensure that it can source all available resources to maintain production. In relation to the **supply of products or services**, the organisation will also have to look at distribution aspects and see whether it can identify cost-effective methods of bringing products and services to potential customers. A great deal of basic information can be found by referring to statistical information provided by the government or agencies working on behalf of the government, or by the careful analysis of competitors' company reports. Trends in customer spending can provide useful data on which to base the criteria needed to establish objectives relating to the supply of products or services.

ACHIEVE SALES VOLUME

It may be the objective of the organisation to achieve a particular **level of sales** in terms of units sold, in order to obtain full economies of scale. The establishment of the production process may be such that it requires the equipment and machinery to be running at full capacity in order to maintain efficiency. This sales volume will inevitably lead to the saturation of the market with the organisation's products. Perhaps the organisation can achieve this volume of sales by supplying other organisations with part-finished products. Food manufacturing organisations achieve this sales volume by supplying own-label products to wholesalers and retailers. The need to achieve sales volume is particularly common in organisations which produce relatively low value products.

ACHIEVE SALES VALUE

As an alternative to achieving sales volume, the organisation may opt for maximising the **sales value**. This means that the organisation is concerned with the overall revenue accrued from its sales. This objective is equally relevant to both low unit value and high value unit products. Sales value will be particularly important to organisations which have high capital expenditure and require high revenue in order to service existing loans. The maintenance of the high sales value is essential to ensure they maintain their competitive edges as any reduction in the sales value may result in the loss of working capital. In extreme circumstances this may mean that the organisation will lose its liquidity and may have to reduce costs elsewhere, such as by reducing the workforce. Another way of achieving higher sales value is to increase the profit margin per unit. This is a tricky technique, since it may mean that the organisation's products or services may lose their competitive edge in terms of price.

ACHIEVE MARKET SHARE

It will be the express objective of certain organisations to control as much of the market as is possible. Organisations use various policies to **achieve market share**:

- competitive pricing policies (for further details on pricing policy see Element 8.3). Such policies may also have implications for many of the other activities of the business such as advertising and sales promotions
- the provision of adequate after-sales service to ensure that customers are fully satisfied with the products and services provided may increase an organisation's market share
- an organisation begins by identifying a certain percentage of the market that it wishes to obtain. This percentage will be its initial objective, although, as the organisation develops, it will increase this percentage in line with its overall corporate objectives. Careful analysis of the market itself, as well as the relative success or market penetration of the competition, will give the organisation some indication of potential growth in that market. The organisation, at

the same time, may identify other related markets into which it can expand. By doing this, it can, by default, gain more market share, thus achieving both higher sales volume and higher sales value.

MAKE PROFIT

Although **making a profit** may seem to be the most obvious business objective of any organisation, this need not necessarily be so. As we have already mentioned in Element 8.1, certain organisations do not consider the maximisation of profits to be essential in any measurement of success. Indeed, any or all of the previous objectives may take precedence over profit maximisation. The importance of profit motive is very much dependent upon the stage of development that the organisation has reached. In the early stages of an organisation's life, it is unreasonable to assume that profit maximisation is the key consideration. Survival may be the main goal.

BREAK EVEN

Breaking even, or generating enough profit to cover expenditure, may be an objective for an organisation in its early years. By simply breaking even, however, an organisation is not providing additional finance on which to base expansion. It will have to rely on alternative sources of finance if it needs to service any further loan requirements. Breaking even may be a criterion laid down by a parent company or an organisation providing finance. At a particular stage in the development of a new organisation, the parent company may be satisfied with a level of business activity which ensures the continued survival of that operation. This is particularly true of organisations which are suffering in periods of economic downturn. As we have already mentioned in Unit 8.1, other organisations may be able to operate at a loss because they are subsidised either by a parent organisation or by the government.

MARKETING PLAN

We will be looking at many of the specific aspects of the **marketing plan** in the next Element. However, it is important to ensure that the marketing effort is a unified strategy, so, with this aim in mind, there are a number of key aspects of the marketing plan to be considered here. These are: pricing, promoting, distribution, selling and timing.

FIG 8.2.3 *Barclays recommend that you identify the types of marketing and advertising undertaken by your competitors and the most appropriate methods for your business.*

MARKETING

What sort of marketing do your competitors do?

Competitor A
_____

Competitor B
_____

Competitor C
_____

What sort of marketing or advertising do you intend to do?

Method _____   Cost _____

_____   _____

_____   _____

Why do you think that these methods are appropriate for your particular market?

_____

_____

Where did you get your estimates from?

Method _____   Source _____

_____   _____

_____   _____

Construct a form similar to that shown in Figure 8.2.3, and analyse the marketing activities of your most obvious competitors.

Apart from material costs, running costs and the acquisition of assets, what other pricing considerations will affect your pricing policy?

PRICING

The **pricing policy** adopted by an organisation will determine, at least to some extent, its potential success. The organisation will have to consider how its prices relate to those of its competitors and the flexibility available, within its costs and budgets, to offer products and services at reduced or special prices for promotional purposes. The organisation can also consider tactics such as changing the price structure once its products or services are established on the market.

PROMOTING

As we have already seen in Unit 3, organisations undertake a variety of different **advertising** and **promotional activities** to promote their products or services. An organisation will have to consider each type of advertising and promotional activity in terms of its effectiveness against costs. In advertising and promoting its products or services an organisation may have to develop a distinctive form of packaging and provide point of sale material to assist retailers in informing customers about the product or service.

FIG 8.2.4 *This section of Barclays' Business Plan Form, provides a useful summary sheet to consider the contribution of products or services to overall turnover and a breakdown of the costs of materials. These considerations obviously affect an organisation's pricing policy.*

PRODUCT/SERVICE
Description
_____
_____
_____

Contribution of individual products or services to total turnover
Product _____ % Contribution _____
_____ _____
_____ _____
_____ _____

(the figures in this column should add up to 100)

Break down the cost of materials (if any)
Product A
Materials (including packaging, labelling etc.) Cost
_____ _____

*Selling price for Product A: _____
Product B _____

*Selling price for Product B: _____
Product C _____

*Selling price for Product C: _____
(*These are assumptions)
Where did you get your estimates from?
Material Source

CARIBBEAN & AMAZON RIVER

Explore the highlights of the Caribbean - from Trinidad's rich mixture of cultures and traditions to the waterfalls and and lush gardens of unspoilt St Vincent. Sample its most popular destinations - such as St Thomas with its many attractions and fabulous duty-free shopping - as well as locations not featured on the usual tourist itineraries, such as St Barts, Tobago and Tortola. Then cruise into the heart of one of the world's great, mysterious wildernesses, the Amazon, and sail up the river to Manaus, one of the world's most remote duty-free ports.

In St Barts, you'll find a unique mixture of jet set playground and untouched Norman culture, kept alive in villages like Corossol, where elderly women speak an old Norman dialect of their forbears and maintain their formal, centuries-old dress. There's also the scenic beauty of Tobago to discover, the island where history's 'real' Robinson Crusoe lived - where you'll now find secluded beaches and bays. And you can sample the haunting atmosphere of Devils Island, where orchid-draped jungle now encroaches the deserted penal colony where some of France's most notorious prisoners were detained.

Explore one of the world's great wildernesses as Vistafjord sails up the Amazon River. There's colourful Santarem, a gold-prospectors' town settled by Confederate soldiers fleeing the American Civil War. In addition to sights along the river all the way to Manaus, nearly a thousand miles from the sea, where you'll find one of the world's most opulent opera houses, which appears much the same as it did when Jenny Lind and Caruso sang there.

MAR 15 TO APR 1

AMAZON RIVER ADVENTURE

17 NIGHTS FROM £2195

Barbados is delightful combination of British traditions and tropical island charm, where you can snack on Bajan flying fish overlooking a Trafalgar Square older than London's. You can also explore the natural riches of the Amazon River - so wide in some places that only one river bank is visible - home to one-tenth of the world's plant and animal species.

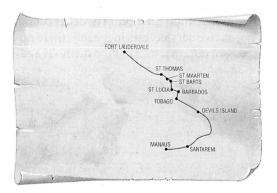

HOLIDAY VFMC		
Tue, Mar 15		
London - Miami		Fly to Miami
Fort Lauderdale		Sail 9.00 pm
Fri, Mar 18		Arrive 8.00 am
St Thomas		Depart midnight
Sat, Mar 19		Arrive 8.00 am
St Maarten		Depart 1.00 pm
St Barts		Arrive 2.00 pm
		Depart 6.00 pm
Sun, Mar 20		Arrive 9.00 am
St Lucia		Depart 6.00 pm
Mon, Mar 21		Arrive 8.00 am
Barbados		Depart 7.00 pm
Tue, Mar 22		Arrive 8.00 am
Tobago		Depart 6.00 pm
Thu, Mar 24		Arrive 1.00 pm
Devils Island		Depart 5.00 pm

Sun, Mar 27		
Santarem,		Arrive 8.00 am
Brazil		Depart 12.30 pm
Alter Do Chao,		Arrive 2.00 pm
Brazil		Depart 6.00 pm
Mon, Mar 28		
Cruising Amazon River		
Tue, Mar 29		
Manaus, Brazil		Arrive 8.00 am
Wed, Mar 30		Disembark 9.00 am
Manaus		Fly to Miami
Thu, Mar 31		Hotel dayroom
Miami		Fly to UK
Fri, Apr 1		Arrive in London

THE AMAZON RIVER

FIG 8.2.5 *This is a detail from Cunard's Cruise Programme 1994. Cunard use their impressive brochures to promote their extensive range of cruises throughout the world. Also note that their pricing policy must accommodate not only the basic costs of the holiday, but the maintenance of high standards of service throughout.*

DISTRIBUTION

As we have already seen, the **distribution policy** is related to many other aspects of marketing activities. The choice of distribution method may depend upon the type of product or service, but, inevitably, there may be a wide variety of different distribution methods available, many of which, at some point, need to be assessed and evaluated in terms of their effectiveness and appropriateness. The organisation will have a clear understanding of what it requires from its distribution network. Its requirements will, of course, relate to speed, efficiency and safety of its products during the distribution phase. Many organisations rely on specialist distribution organisations to ensure that their products and services reach the customers in a fast and reliable manner.

SELLING

An organisation will probably have already identified particular target areas in which to concentrate its **sales operations**. The availability of distribution may have a considerable impact, in terms of cost-effectiveness, on the choice of sales area. Additionally, as we have seen, an organisation may choose to test market its products in a particular geographical area in order to gauge customer reaction before launching them more widely. In relation to the sales effort, the organisation has to ensure that its sales staff are fully conversant with all aspects of the products and services they are selling. This is equally true of suppliers selling to retailers or those selling direct to the consumer.

TIMING

The **timing** of the various phases of the marketing plan is as important as the timing of the overall business plan itself. Certain activities must be undertaken before other key activities may be attempted. For instance, the product must be clearly designed, packaged, labelled and described before the sales force can be fully briefed on it.

One of the key determining factors in the timing process will be the acquisition and analysis of information gained from market research. Sufficient information must be gathered in order to ascertain the nature, size and growth potential of the market, since these factors will determine the direction in which the sales effort will move.

PRODUCTION PLAN

Production plans are written to ensure that the resources deployed in the production process will be adequate to meet the potential orders for products and services. It is essential that the organisation makes sure that it has adequate resources in terms of premises, machinery, raw materials and labour in order to produce the products as and when required. If customers are made to wait they may become dissatisfied with the organisation and look for their orders to be fulfilled elsewhere.

PREMISES

The **location** of the premises is only one of the important questions that need to be considered. In many cases, however, the main prerequisites determining the suitability of premises will be their **cost** and **availability**. In choosing an ideal location for the business, it is prudent to consider its accessibility in terms of:

- markets
- raw materials
- employees
- suppliers
- appropriate support services
- main utilities

Another factor, as we have already mentioned, is the availability – in certain areas in the UK of government development and resettlement grants.

student activity

If you have not already identified potential premises from which to run your business, you should now consider how you will identify the correct type and location of building(s). You will find local estate agents to be a valuable source of information, in identifying the availability of suitable premises. In Element 8.1, we discussed the differences between tenancy and ownership of premises. You will now have to decide, in relation to your available capital, which types of premises are viable for you.

MACHINERY

Depending upon the exact nature of its business, an organisation is more or less reliant upon the guaranteed continuity of production available to it through the use of **machinery** and other equipment. As we have already mentioned, machinery may be a key physical resource and the organisation must ensure that it has a reliable supplier of such machinery, together with such back-up support services as are essential to maintain production. With regard to the most efficient running of the machinery, it may be necessary to consider a continuous production process, by which the machinery is run on a 24-hour, 365 days a year basis. This will have effects upon the acquisition of other essential resources, such as raw materials, and a well-organised labour force (working in shifts). In relation to its premises, the organisation must ensure that the building not only is fit for the operating of essential machinery, but also has the necessary licensing, insurance and usage clearance by the local authority.

student activity

Identify all of the types of machinery you will require to run your business successfully. Again, you should consider the following types of ownership:

- outright purchase
- lease
- rental

In the case of retail operations, the need for machinery may be less important, but, do not forget that you will need to obtain at least a cash register.

RAW MATERIALS

If an organisation requires large supplies of **raw materials**, not only must the location of the premises be right, for they must also be suitable, to ensure that these large quantities can be handled. Locating the business in an isolated part of the UK can mean unnecessary transportation costs which may affect the viability of the business. Although transport and distribution costs have reduced, comparatively speaking, over recent years, it is still a major goal of most organisations to reduce these costs as much as is possible. For this reason organisations operating in the same area of business activity, or in a support function to a number of similar organisations, tend to congregate fairly close to one another. This concentration of organisations is known as the **external economies of scale**. Collectively they achieve these economies of scale by jointly reducing unnecessary costs. In addition, this congregation also ensures that training facilities for staff are available locally. The other major bonus is that smaller support systems, such as servicing contractors and component suppliers, are nearby.

student activity

If raw materials are relevant to your business, you should now have some idea of the sources of these raw materials. Have you been able to assess the reliability of supply? The predictability of price? Try to list at least three potential sources of raw materials. If possible try to find out their credit terms.

LABOUR

Labour costs differ widely from area to area and region to region. Employees in the South East of England earn some 50 per cent more than those in Northern Ireland

and between 15 and 25 per cent more than in the rest of the UK. If an organisation wishes to ensure that it has an adequate supply of skilled labour, then it may be forced to locate in an area where wage levels are comparatively higher. As we saw in Unit 5, the **mobility of labour** has become greater in recent years, but labour is still not as mobile as some employers would wish. Another major reason for locating in a particular area may be to avoid traditional **industrial relations** problems which are associated with an alternative region. In areas where there have been considerable **job losses**, employers can attempt to exploit the situation by calling on the excess labour pool and employing them at comparatively low wage rates. In terms of an organisation's production plan as a whole, the availability of **skilled labour** in sufficient numbers is imperative, to ensure that the production process is fully operational at all times and at all levels.

student activity

Does your business require the specialist skills of any individuals? If so, how will you be able to attract them to your business?

Even if you do not require specialists, how do you intend to advertise the availability of employment? In Units 4 and 5 we looked at the nature and types of employment and identified organisations which could assist in the recruitment of staff. You may wish to refer to these sections in the process of deciding how and where to advertise.

RESOURCE REQUIREMENTS

As we mentioned in the Element 8.1, the resource requirements of a business plan are **human, physical** and **financial**. One of the main functions of the individuals producing a business plan may be the precise identification of the resources needed to ensure that not only production but general business activity is maintained.

HUMAN, PHYSICAL AND FINANCIAL RESOURCE REQUIREMENTS

As we have already mentioned in previous Units, organisations are concerned with ensuring that they gain **economies of scale** at the earliest possible opportunity. For example, the production plan, which makes up part of the overall business plan, will be concerned with the batching of orders so that production runs may be longer, so as to ensure economies of scale. This particular technique can have its own drawbacks, since it may cause delays in the fulfilment of customers' orders. If this does happen customers should be kept informed as to the status of their order at all times.

The **resources** of an organisation can be deployed to ensure that quality is maintained at all levels of production and service. It is not sufficient these days for an organisation to be in a position to supply the products or services required by its customers. They will demand much more. An organisation will begin by considering its human and physical resources in the following way:

1 *Physical resources*. Suppliers will be expected to deliver raw and part-finished materials of the correct quality
2 *Human resources*. The workforce, will be instilled with the notion of quality. Special training in quality and customer service may be required. It may be dangerous for an organisation to ignore these features as it is certain that its competitors will be paying close attention to them.

Although the improvement of quality is a gradual process by which the organisation attempts to make small but constant steps towards perfection, investment is necessary.

The concept of **total quality management** (or TQM) has begun to be generally accepted by most organisations as the basis of appropriate practice. The manufacturing process and all aspects of after-sales service come under the concept of TQM. This approach, Japanese in origin, seeks full quality assurance throughout the organisation. It will hopefully ensure that the organisation:

- is efficient at every stage of its activities
- makes the best use of all available resources
- provides consistency in its production of products and services
- has in place a series of quality assurance measures to feed back information on potential quality problems
- pays particular attention to the concept of customer satisfaction

With regard to the **financial resource** requirements of the organisation, it is essential that frank and honest contact is maintained with providers of finance. All potential problems regarding cash flow or profitability must be discussed at every stage. If there are shareholders, they will require to know the true state of affairs within the organisation, as it may be necessary for them to make additional share capital available to finance short-term cash flow problems or long-term investments. We will be looking at the specific financial data and forecasting methods that relate to business plans in the next section.

FINANCIAL DATA AND FORECASTS

In Units 6 and 7 we looked at cash flow forecasts, balance sheets and profit and loss accounts. These are vital sources of financial data from which to construct meaningful forecasts that relate to the actual level of business activity. We shall consider these and other aspects of the financial data and forecasting in this section.

TIME PERIOD

When a new business is set up, it is necessary to know the financial position of the organisation at the **precise** point when the business is actually set up.

student activity

In order to collect financial data and make meaningful forecasts, you will have to complete cash flow forecasts and profit and loss monthly and quarterly reports. Figure 8.2.6 provides the basis for both forecasting (budget) and actual performance from month to month. Figure 8.2.7 serves as a useful summary of the information in Figure 8.2.6 and allows for reasons to be highlighted and actions taken if budgets do not match actual figures. Figure 8.2.8 is a variation which allows you to work out all income and expenditure as a percentage of turnover.

CASH FLOW FORECAST

A **cash flow forecast** should be constructed for at least the first year of trading, although it is advisable to consider projecting the probable cash flow into at least the first two to three years.

A reasonably constructed cash flow forecast will also be able to show prospective providers of finance when the business may be able to begin to pay back loans.

START-UP BALANCE SHEET

It will be necessary to consider the probable state of the **balance sheet** at the end of the first year's trading. Although the start-up balance sheet may not be able to predict unforeseen expenses it will serve as a base indicator of probable income and expenditure.

PROJECTED PROFIT AND LOSS AND BALANCE SHEET

Taken together, these should indicate whether the business will be in a position to either **break even** or show a small **profit**. From these two information sources, it will be possible to calculate the expected return on capital employed. This is an important ratio and is calculated by dividing the profit by capital employed.

MONITORING AND REVIEW BY USING MONTHLY PROFIT AND LOSS AND BALANCE SHEETS

By constructing a monthly profit and loss account and a monthly balance sheet, an organisation will be able to **monitor** its adherence to its business plan. This control mechanism should be able to identify any causes for concern and allow the organisation to react in time. The normal procedure is for an organisation to create a cash flow forecast which includes the budgeted figures for various items. Then, as the actual figures become available, it can compare these with the budgeted figures. Similarly, it will be possible to compare actual output with production targets and actual sales with projected sales.

BARCLAYS

CASHFLOW FORECAST FOR: _____ MONTH _____ TO _____ MONTH _____

RECEIPTS	MONTH BUDGET	ACTUAL	MONTH BUDGET	ACTUAL	MONTH BUDGET	ACTUAL	MONTH BUDGET	ACTUAL	MONTH BUDGET	ACTUAL	MONTH BUDGET	ACTUAL	TOTALS BUDGET	ACTUAL
Cash Sales														
Cash from Debtors														
Capital Introduced														
TOTAL RECEIPTS (a)														
PAYMENTS														
Payments to Creditors														
Salaries/Wages														
Rent/Rates/Water														
Insurance														
Repairs/Renewals														
Heat/Light/Power														
Postages														
Printing/Stationery														
Transport														
Telephone														
Professional Fees														
Capital Payments														
Interest Charges														
Other														
V.A.T. payable (refund)														
TOTAL PAYMENTS (b)														
NET CASHFLOW (a-b)														
OPENING BANK BALANCE														
CLOSING BANK BALANCE														

N.B. All figures include VAT. Published by Barclays Bank PLC. Corporate Marketing Department. Reg. No. 1026167 Reg. Office: 54 Lombard Street, London EC3P 3AH. Ultimate Holding Company: Barclays PLC. BB16164I October 1988. BE. 997161SC. A Member of IMRO.

FIGURE 8.2.6 _Barclays' Monthly Cash Flow Forecast pro-forma.._

APPENDIX II

CASHFLOW

MONTHLY/QUARTERLY REPORT

Name of Business:

Month/Quarter ended:

	BUDGET £	ACTUAL £	DIFFERENCE £	REASON	ACTION TAKEN
Cash Sales					
Cash from Debtors					
Capital Introduced					
TOTAL RECEIPTS (a)					
PAYMENTS:					
Payments to Creditors					
Salaries/Wages					
Rent/Rates/Water					
Insurance					
Repairs/Renewals					
Heat/Light/Power					
Postages					
Printing/Stationery					
Transport					
Telephone					
Professional Fees					
Capital Payments					
Interest Charges					
Other					
VAT payable (refund)					
TOTAL PAYMENTS (b)					
NET CASHFLOW (a–b)					
OPENING BANK BALANCE					
CLOSING BANK BALANCE					

NB. All figures include VAT

FIGURE 8.2.7 *Barclays' Monthly/Quarterly Cash Flow Report pro-forma.*

APPENDIX I

PROFIT AND LOSS BUDGET

MONTHLY/QUARTERLY REPORT

Name of Business:

Month/Quarter ended:

		BUDGET		ACTUAL		DIFFERENCE	REASON	ACTION TAKEN
		£	100%	£	100%	£		
SALES	(a)							
LESS: DIRECT COSTS:								
Cost of Materials								
Wages								
GROSS PROFIT	(b)							
OVERHEADS (FIXED COSTS):								
Salaries								
Rent/Rates/Water								
Insurance								
Repairs/Renewals								
Heat/Light/Power								
Postages								
Printing/Stationery								
Transport								
Telephone								
Professional Fees								
Interest Charges								
Other								
TRADING PROFIT								
Less: Depreciation								
TOTAL OVERHEADS	(c)							
Net Profit before Tax	(b-c)							
Plus: Previous Mths/Qtrs 1.								
2.								
3.								
TOTAL YEAR TO DATE								

NB. All figures exclude VAT

FIGURE 8.2.8 *Barclays' Monthly/Quarterly Profit and Loss Budget Report proforma.*

Produce a sales and marketing plan

1 PURPOSES
support application for finance, set targets, monitor performance

2 PLANNING ACTIVITIES
naming, pricing, promoting, sales targets, timing, distribution, after market

PURPOSES OF A SALES AND MARKETING PLAN

As we have seen, a business plan, but a sales and marketing plan in particular, will assist management in **controlling business** in a much more efficient manner. Specifically, the sales and marketing plan aims to:

1 focus upon the main factors to remain **competitive**
2 identify and systematically consider the business's opportunities for **expansion**
3 prepare a series of counter-measures to address **potential problems** in the future
4 set identifiable **goals** and results hoped to be achieved from them
5 identify the precise criteria relating to the **achievement** of goals and objectives
6 set out a series of measurement systems to **monitor** the progress of achieving goals and objectives
7 provide necessary information and supporting data to be used when negotiating with **providers of finance**

Drawing up the sales and marketing plan consists of a number of steps which are common regardless of the organisation's business activity or market involvement. These are:

1 an assessment of the organisation's historical performance
2 an assessment of the organisation's potential performance
3 a detailed analysis of the competition's performance
4 a global investigation of the market potential and any possible opportunities or threats
5 a clear indication of the main objectives of the owners of the organisation
6 the development of strategic plans
7 the writing of an action plan which details tactics required to fulfil the strategic aims of the organisation

student activity

In order to assist you in the formulation of a sales and marketing plan, it would be advisable to consider the following questions:

1. do you understand the market?
2. what types of people buy your product or service?
3. do you know when they buy?
4. do you know how often they buy?
5. have you assessed the product or service they are buying at present?
6. what is the size of your market?
7. is the market growing, declining or remaining the same?
8. will you be able to obtain a big enough share of the market in order to be successful?
9. does the market have any geographical boundaries?
10. is it local or national?
11. what is the cost of reaching this market?
12. do you know how much your customers will be prepared to pay for your product or service?
13. can you supply the product or service which the market wants?
14. can you supply the product or service when the market needs it?
15. do you have any existing orders?

In relation to the product itself, or the service you provide, there are other elements to consider:

1. do you understand the product or service you are supplying?
2. do you know who you are competing against?
3. is your product or service at least as good as those of your competitors?
4. are there any legal implications concerning the establishment of your business?
5. are there any environmental implications concerning the establishment of your business?
6. have you ever sold this product or service before?
7. Can you be assured that you can follow up your existing line of product or service with new innovations?

If you are able to answer these questions, then you are some way towards formulating a sales and marketing plan.

SUPPORT APPLICATION FOR FINANCE, SETTING TARGETS AND MONITORING PERFORMANCE

The main purposes of producing a sales and marketing plan are to support applications for finance, set targets and monitor performance. The identification of a specific **purpose** may influence the way in which the plan is structured. However, whichever purpose is being considered, an organisation must make a number of assumptions based upon the information available. These assumptions will include:

- probable labour costs
- probable raw material costs
- government intervention
- social changes which may affect demand
- technological changes which may affect demand
- consumer spending patterns
- activities of competitors

By considering these factors, the organisation will begin to establish its objectives, strategies and overall policies. As a result of this exercise, some specific goals or action plans may be established.

An organisation will usually undertake a marketing **audit**, also known as SWOT analysis, which will attempt to identify any patterns in its trading activity as well as its overall performance in various areas. To begin with, the organisation will try to identify the particular internal strengths of the organisation and will then compare any weaknesses it may have with its competitors' current capabilities. The external environment itself plays no little part in the impact on an organisation and is to a large extent beyond that organisation's control. The organisation will not be able to predict sudden changes in government policy, economic prosperity, population changes, legislation or indeed changes in government.

As we have said, an organisation will begin by defining **key marketing objectives**, which will be statements concerning the preferred achievements of the organisation in the future. These objectives should be clear, be capable of being put into action, be consistent with corporate policy and be measurable in terms of their performance and impact on the organisation as a whole. Additionally, these marketing objectives will be defined as being long or short term in their nature.

When considering the strategy and action plan which will derive from the identified key marketing objectives, the organisation will consider the **marketing mix**, in that it will examine how these objectives will impact upon product, price, promotion and place.

The written sales and marketing plan will be **monitored** and reviewed on a regular basis and should be flexible enough to allow amendments to be made. An annual updating of the plan will allow constant development and adaptation to current circumstances.

Although there are no clear guidelines for writing a sales and marketing plan and no universal format, it is common to find the following features in most such plans:

- key **marketing objectives** identified
- **sales forecasts** calculated
- past, current and future **product policies**
- analysis and description of all **markets** relevant to the organisation's business activities
- a full breakdown of **customers** by use of market segmentation techniques
- an analysis of past, present and proposed **market research**
- statements on **pricing policy**
- statements on **distribution policy**
- statements and analyses of **advertising**, past, present and future
- statements and analyses of **sales promotions**, past, present and future
- **budget** allocations and statements
- **timing** of all activities, usually expressed in terms of an action plan

PLANNING ACTIVITIES

As we have seen in the previous Element, an organisation's marketing plan needs to be fully developed in order to interact efficiently with its overall business plan. Specific considerations are detailed below, but these do not necessarily cover all considerations as different organisations will have different priorities and objectives.

NAMING

As most organisations offer more than one product or service, the identification of each product or service is essential. As we have seen, this will mean the assigning of a product name or brand to each of them. This **naming** process will also aim to identify some of the specific advantages or benefits which may accrue from the use of the product or service. This is often known as the 'unique selling proposition' (USP), which helps the organisation position the product in the market place. Considerable market research will already have been undertaken to ensure that, at least for the most part, the organisation's perception of the product or service match that of the consumer.

FIG 8.3.1 *Kwik-Fit's name aptly describes the whole ethos behind the operation.*

student activity

If you have not already considered this, you should now think about naming your product, service or organisation. Although it is a comparatively easy task to buy an 'off the peg' company, the name of the organisation may not necessarily be appropriate to your line of business. Many organisations will simply name themselves after the founders of the business. Others may choose names which relate to the area of business activity in which they are involved. Whichever is the case, you should carefully consider what you do call your business, since the name will be with you for a considerable length of time.

PRICING

Pricing policy may relate to the level of contribution that the organisation expects from each of its products or services. This contribution, as we have seen, is equal to the price charged less all variable costs. In addition, in its pricing policy, an organisation will take into account the pricing policies of competitors within the market.

All products, to some degree, contribute towards all of the fixed costs of the organisation. Again, as we have already seen, once the fixed costs have been covered, the contribution itself becomes profit. Pricing policy is a key aspect of the overall marketing plan. Products must generate a sufficiently high contribution in order to assist the organisation in terms of its solvency, liquidity and profitability.

The different forms of pricing policy are commonly described as follows:

Penetration pricing

This is an initially low price, set in order to gain market share. In setting a low price, the organisation relies upon profits from other areas of business activity to temporarily subsidise a new product or service in its initial launch period.

Price skimming

If the organisation is in the fortunate position to be first into the market with a new product or service, it may be able to charge a considerably higher price to people who wish to be the first to take advantage of the new item. This pricing policy is often used when the demand for a product is price inelastic.

To recover investment quickly

This policy is designed to achieve a fast profit and return on the investments made. Prices are set without any specific regard to demand for the product or service.

Psychological pricing

Organisations recognise that there are particular price barriers which should not be breached as they will affect customers' willingness to purchase products. Thus an organisation will price a £10.00 product at £9.99 in order to artificially stay within the preconceived boundary.

Customary pricing

organisations may set their prices according to the customers' expectations of how expensive a product should be. If the price is higher than expected, then sales will be affected.

Odd pricing

This is a form of psychological pricing, in which the price appears to be much more acceptable at a level between two clear and even prices, such as 19p instead of 18p or 20p. To some extent, odd pricing has become a feature of many products with the inclusion of VAT.

Prestige pricing

Certain products or services may be given the image of being exclusive by the setting of an artificial price, which is far in excess of the real value of the item. This form of pricing is particularly true of all luxury goods and is, perhaps, one area of pricing where the comparative competitor's pricing levels are irrelevant.

Cost-plus pricing

This is a simple form of calculating the price of a product as it is linked to the total cost incurred in producing,

distributing and promoting the product and a specified profit margin.

Target pricing

Target pricing is used to achieve the break-even point and relies on several assumptions being made regarding demand. The target price may relate to the position the product has reached in its life cycle.

Life-cycle pricing

This form of pricing relates to the comparative demand for the product at various points during its life cycle. When there is a high demand, the price may be increased, and when demand falls, so too will the price.

Discrimination pricing

This pricing policy is one that is used in particular in the service industries when normal demand is low. Certain 'quiet' periods of the day, month or year are identified as times for discrimination price policies to be implemented. In other words, customers find that it is cheaper to make use of the service at these quieter times and this generates additional demand.

Competition pricing

Many organisations consider their competitors' pricing policies when setting their pricing levels. From a careful consideration of their competitors' price levels, they are able to ascertain what is the accepted price and can set their pricing levels in relation to this 'standard' price. This is a good way of product positioning.

Promotion pricing

This form of pricing is used to attempt to maintain market share by the use of particular promotional devices. These devices include short-term price reductions or the offering of more volume or weight of product for the same price.

Trade discounts

Organisations which purchase products or services from a supplier, and are not at the end of the distribution chain, do not have to pay the full recommended retail price for the item. They pay a price known as the **trade price**. This trade price is related to either the total value of the order or the number of products ordered.

Early payment discounts

In order to persuade customers to settle their accounts as early as possible, organisations may offer additional discounts. These assist the cash flow of the supplier. At the same time, these discounts allow the purchasers to make a bigger profit when they sell on the product or service. A variation of the early payment discount is the discount available to those who choose to pay in cash immediately. Such payments save the supplier from the delays associated with payment by cheque, such as waiting for the account to be cleared, or waiting for a cheque to be sent on in due course.

Quantity discounts

This is a common form of discount and enables customers to obtain the products or services at a lower unit price by purchasing in bulk.

Tenders

Tendering has become an increasingly accepted method of pricing. Here it t is the supplier of the product or service who sets (in isolation) the price he/she wishes to be paid for that product or service. An organisation wishing to purchase a product or service calls for tenders to supply it and several organisations will simultaneously put in tenders to provide it. The buyer will then assess these offers and choose the best in terms of price and other criteria.

student activity

Having read the various forms of pricing policy, try to identify the ones which would be most appropriate to your own business. Why have you chosen them? How will you use them? Are there some which you would feel are wholly inappropriate?

PROMOTING

Within the **promotion** area, an organisation should consider all forms of advertising, promotional methods and public relations. Each specific activity will have its own objectives, and will need to be designed in such a manner as to achieve its goals. All activities should be monitored and any variations in the manner in which these activities are undertaken may affect the achievement of the required outcomes. All forms of promotional activity will, of course, have financial implications in terms of costs but, at the same time, they will be expected to contribute in some particular way. A careful assessment of each activity, can show whether they are successful or failures. Since many millions of pounds are spent on promotional activities, campaigns need to show positive benefits to be repeated in the future.

SALES TARGETS

The sales force will be set a variety of **sales targets**, in whatever form the organisation chooses. These will be reached and assessed in relation to the effort expended and any related promotional activity. It is usual for most sales personnel to have quotas expressed in a variety of different ways, and the successful meeting of these quotas will be placed in the overall financial context of the organisation. Particular concerns will be the number of effective man hours sales people use to achieve a particular sales volume. In other words, what returns can the organisation expect from the various inputs made?

TIMING

Again, the **timing** of all aspects of the planning process is essential to the effectiveness of all activities. Co-ordination of activities and co-operation between various parts of the organisation will be included when considering the timing implications. Particular promotional activities must be coupled with increased effort on the sales front. Equally, distribution will have to be geared to provide the necessary back-up for expected increases in demand. The launching of new products, in particular, will involve crucial timing considerations and may involve many employees engaged in a variety of roles within the organisation.

DISTRIBUTION

The way in which a product or service is **distributed** will directly affect the success or failure of an organisation. Distribution channels must be analysed in order to show the following:

- how the **distribution network** is integrated
- **effectiveness** of the distribution network in general
- **costs** at various stages in the distribution process
- other **resource considerations** relating to the distribution network

Organisations constantly attempt to increase the efficiency and effectiveness of their chosen distribution methods and to identify alternative methods more appropriate to their market position.

AFTER MARKET

The term **after market** refers to all activities and processes undertaken by the organisation in relation to product support after sales have been achieved. As we saw in Unit 3, many organisations have developed sophisticated customer service and after-sales service systems. Many organisations have recognised that the provision of these services may have a considerable impact on the willingness of consumers to choose their organisation as opposed to others in the same field.

assignment

'THE BUSINESS PLAN'

In order to complete this Unit and **GNVQ Advanced Business**, you will be required to prepare and produce a **Business Plan.**

You should follow the stages given below and should be, by this stage, in a position to understand all the implications, both internal and external, of a business's' objectives, commitments and strategies.

The stages you should follow are:

1 create a **flow chart** which shows all of the legal, insurance and resource implications of your business
2 draft a **business proposal**, which may have been already agreed in relation to your activities in Unit 7

In this next stage you will be required to create a **five-part business** plan for presentation to a potential provider of finance. Your tutor will either take the role of this provider of finance or have arranged an individual from the local business community to adopt this role.

Specifically, the five-part business plan should consist of:

> the organisation's **objectives**
> a **marketing** plan
> a **production** plan
> a clear indication of **resource requirements**
> the **financial support data** which was completed in Unit 7

You will receive feedback on your achievements and performance in the oral presentation. Any advice or guidance will be particularly useful as you move into the final stage of this assignment.

Your final task is to prepare a full **sales and marketing plan** for a single product. You should ensure that it includes an estimated budget and a comprehensive timing schedule. You should present this sales and marketing plan in word-processed form to your tutor. It should be supported by any other information which you think is particularly relevant in enhancing your plan.

test questions

1 Which of the following cannot be considered to be a key resource?

(a) Human
(b) Financial
(c) Tax liabilities
(d) Time

2 Which of the following would not be included in a business plan?

(a) Marketing plan
(b) Financial forecasts
(c) Sales plan
(d) Owner's annual holiday entitlement

3 What is SWOT?

(a) An accounts package
(b) A method of analysing strengths and weaknesses
(c) A communications technique
(d) A cash flow forecast

4 For which of the following people would you primarily prepare a business plan?

(a) Bank manager
(b) Solicitor
(c) Local trading standards officer
(d) Your employees

5 Which of the following can be considered a good example of long-term finance?

(a) Cash
(b) Factoring
(c) Loan
(d) Overdraft

6 Which are the correct five elements that you would find in a business plan?

(a) Objectives, marketing, production, resource requirements, financial data
(b) Objectives, marketing, production, resource requirements, distribution
(c) Objectives, marketing, production, resource requirements, pricing policy
(d) Objectives, marketing, production, resource requirements, advertising

7 Which of the following is not a reason for producing a business plan?

(a) Gaining finance
(b) Seeking finance
(c) Product development
(d) Monitoring performance

8 How do you calculate total revenue?

(a) Fixed costs + variable costs
(b) Price × quantity sold
(c) Revenue costs
(d) Average revenue × output

9 Primary market research is carried out in which of the following ways?

(a) By interviewing people
(b) By researching existing data
(c) By investigating company records
(d) By designing a business plan

10 Which of the following is not one of the major objectives of a business?

(a) To achieve sales volume
(b) To achieve sales value
(c) To break even
(d) To be in a position to borrow money

Glossary of
business terms

Absorption costing   This is a technique which assigns the costs of materials and labour and other overheads to each unit of production.

Acid test   This is an accounting measure which aims to ascertain a business's ability to pay its short term **current liabilities** with its **current assets.**

After-sales service   These are customer services provided by an organisation to its customers; they include maintenance, repair and advice.

Annual report and accounts   This is a yearly report to the company's shareholders which includes a **balance sheet** a **profit and loss account** and other information that is required by law.

Appraisal   *See* **performance appraisal**.

Arbitration   This is a method of settling an industrial dispute through a third party.

Articles of association   These are the rules concerning the relationship between individuals within an organisation.

Assembly line   This is a method of organising the machinery and labour in an organisation in which the product is assembled in a series of operations along the line.

Asset   This is an item which is owned by a business or an individual to which a monetary value can be attached.

Authorised share capital   Also known as **registered share capital**, this is the maximum amount of **share capital** that an organisation can issue at any time.

Average cost   This is the total cost divided by the number of units produced.

Bad debt   This an accounting term which refers to money owed by customers or borrowers which is unlikely to be paid.

Balance of trade   This is the relative position of a country's imports and exports.

Balance sheet   An accounting term which refers to a statement of a business's **assets** and **liabilities** on the last day of a **trading period**.

Bank rate   This is the level of interest charged by a country's central bank. It forms the basis of the lending rate for all other loans.

Bankruptcy   This refers to the position of a business which is unable to pay its **debts** when they fall due.

Board of directors   This is a group of individuals who are responsible to the **shareholders** for the running of a business.

Brand   This is the name, design, symbol or term which is used to identify an organisation's product or service.

Break-even   This is the point when **output** matches **fixed** and **variable costs**.

Budget   This is an organisation's allocation of money and resources for particular projects.

Budgetary control   This is an accounting system for controlling **costs** and **revenue** by comparing actual results with estimates.

Capital   This can be defined either as the **funds** invested by a business to acquire **assets** or physical **assets** such as machinery or equipment.

Capital employed   This refers to the total funds which have been invested in a business.

Capital expenditure   This is the **expenditure** on the acquisition of **fixed assets**

Capital goods   These are goods bought by a business for use in the production of other products or services.

Cash account   This is an account which records all of the company's **incomings** and **outgoings**.

Cash flow   This is a system by which an organisation monitors **revenue** and **expenditure** on a monthly basis.

Collateral   This is an **asset** which a borrower is required to deposit or pledge against a loan which will be sold by the lender if the loan is not repaid.

Collective bargaining   This is the negotiation process between employers and representatives of the workforce.

Competition These are other organisations with which an organisation must contest in order to gain and maintain **market share**.

Consolidated accounts This is the aggregate or total of all accounts from a group of companies.

Contract of employment This is an agreement between an employer and an employee in which the employer lays down the conditions of service and the rewards for work undertaken.

Contribution This is the difference between **sales revenue** and **variable costs.**

Corporation This is a publicly registered company which has a separate legal identity from its owners.

Corporation tax This is a tax levied by the government on **profits** made by a business.

Cost This is the **expenditure** on **resources** incurred by a business.

Costcentre This is a technique used by some organisations to manage **costs** by attributing them to certain areas of the business's activity.

Cost of living This is the level of prices of products and services usually measured in order to monitor **inflation** via the **retail price index**.

Cost of sales This is **expenditure** incurred in the process of obtaining sales.

Cost price This is the cost of a product which a business incurs in the course of its production.

Creditors These are individuals or organisations to which a business owes money.

Current assets These are **assets** owned by a business. They include **stock**, money owed by **debtors** and cash.

Current liabilities These are all the obligations a business has to pay out money in the near future.

Current ratio *See* **acid test**.

Debentures This is a means of financing a business through fixed-interest loans secured against **assets**.

Debt This is simply the amount of money owed by one person an organisation to another.

Debtors These are the people or organisations which owe money to a business.

Demand This is the amount or quantity of a particular product or service required by organisations and other customers.

Depreciation This term can be used to describe the fall in value of either an **asset** or a currency.

Direct costs This is the total of **materials** and **labour costs** that can be related to the production of a product.

Direct labour This is a recognisable portion of the workforce which is involved in any aspect of producing a product.

Director This is an official of a business who is elected by **shareholders** and given the power and responsibility to run the organisation on their behalf.

Discount This is a deduction from the list price of a product.

Disposable income This is the amount of money which an individual has left after paying compulsory deductions.

Distribution This is the process of storing and transporting products to consumers via various channels.

Diversification This is the process which occurs when a business expands its business activities into new **markets**.

Dividend This is a payment made by a business to its **shareholders** in return for providing **share capital**.

Economies of scale This is a beneficial reduction in the **average costs** of producing a unit which is obtained by an increase in the size of the business.

Elastic demand This refers to the **demand** for a product which changes as a result of a price change.

Elastic supply This refers the **supply** of a product or service which changes in response to price changes.

Equity This is **ordinary shareholders'** funds.

Expenditure These is the **outgoings** or expenses incurred by a business.

Financial management This is advice, usually obtained from an outside source, which allows a business to analyse the flow of money through the organisation.

Financial year Usually taken to mean the period from 1 April to 31 March the following year.

Finished goods These are the **stocks** of completed products being stored by the organisation.

Fiscal policy This is how the government controls the level of spending in the economy by changing the level of its **expenditure** and of taxation on individuals and businesses.

Fixed assets These are **assets** such as machinery and buildings bought by a business for long-term use.

Fixed costs These are **costs** incurred by an organisation which do not vary despite changes in the level of **output**.

Franchise This is a business arrangement by which one organisation grants another the right to trade under its name and supply its products or services.

Goodwill This is the reputation, expertise and contacts of a business, for which a prospective buyer must pay a premium above the **asset** value of the business.

Gross domestic product This is the total value of all products and services produced in the economy in a year.

Gross national product This is the total value of all products and services produced in the economy plus any income from investments abroad.

Gross profit This is the difference between **sales revenue** and **cost of sales** before selling, distribution and administration are taken into account.

Holding company This is a company which controls another company.

Income   This is the money received by an individual or organisation.

Incomings   *See* **revenue**.

Industrial relations   This is the management of the relationship between the employer and the workforce.

Inelastic demand   This refers to the **demand** for a product or service which does not change regardless of price changes.

Inelastic supply   This refers to the **supply** of a product or service which does not change even if the price changes.

Inflation   This is a general increase in prices which is usually measured in terms of its effect on the whole economy.

Input   These are all of the resources used by a business to produce its products and services.

Insolvent   This refers to a business which has suffered **bankruptcy** and cannot pay its **debts**.

Interest   This is a charge made for borrowing money.

Inventory   This is a comprehensive list of all **finished goods, work in progress** and **raw materials.**

Issued share capital   This is the amount of **authorised share capital** which a business can issue to **shareholders** in order to raise **capital**.

Job analysis   This is the identification of the tasks which make up a particular job role.

Job description   This is a statement of the tasks and responsibilities which make up a job.

Job enrichment   This is when workers are given greater freedom in performing their tasks.

Job evaluation   This is a system by which the relative worth of a job is linked to grading and pay.

Joint venture   This is a business owned by two other independent organisations which have pooled their expertise and **resources**.

Labour costs   This is the total of all **expenditure** which can be attributed to the workforce.

Leaseback   This is an arrangement which involves the selling of **assets** to a third party and then **renting** them back at an agreed rental.

Ledger   This is an accounting record which keeps a running total of the business's financial transactions.

Legislation   Rules, regulations and directives imposed by the government or the EC.

Liabilities   This is a form of **debt** or claim on the **resources** of a business in relation to money owed.

Limited liability   This is a type of liability in which a **shareholder** is only liable for the amount of money that he or she actually invested in the business.

Liquidity   This is the relationship between a business's **current assets** and its **current liabilities**, in other words, the organisation's ability to pay its **creditors**.

Loss leader   This is a product sold at a reduced price in order to attract customers to purchase additional products.

Managing Director   This is the **director** of an organisation who is responsible for the day-to-day management.

Margin   This is the difference between the **cost price** and the **selling price** of a product.

Marginal cost   These are extra **costs** incurred by a business when it increases **output**.

Market   This is the situation when the buyer and seller of a product or service come together.

Market leader   This is a product or service which has the largest **market share**.

Market research   This is the collection and analysis of data regarding a particular **market**.

Market segmentation   This is a method of dividing the **market** into segments to target them more accurately.

Market share   This is the percentage of the total value of the market which is held by an individual organisation.

Marketing   This is a process by which an organisation attempts to identify customer needs and satisfy them.

Marketing mix   These are the measures which an organisation employs to attract buyers to purchase its products or services.

Materials   These are the items required in order to produce a product. They may take the form of **raw materials** or components.

Memorandum of Association   This is a legal document which governs the relationship between the business and all external individuals and organisations.

Merger   This is the mutually agreed combining of businesses into a single business.

Mixed economy   This is an economy in which products and services are provided by both private and public enterprises.

Monetary policy   This is how the government controls the level of spending in an economy by regulating the supply of money through the control of interest rates.

Monopoly   Officially this is when an organisation has 25 per cent **market share**.

Motivation   This is the willingness and enthusiasm of a worker to carry out tasks.

Net profit   This is the difference between a business's **sales revenue** and total **costs**.

Opportunity cost   This refers to the next best alternative foregone. In other words, when decisions are made, the opportunity cost is all the benefits that would have been gained by making an alternative decision.

Ordinary shares   Also known as **equity**, these are essentially certificates issued to providers of long-term finance. In exchange for this long-term finance, ordinary **shareholders** are entitled to receive **dividends**.

Outgoings   *See* **expenditure**.

Output   These are the products or services produced by an organisation.

Overheads   These are **costs** which cannot be directly attributed to a product.

Partnership   This is an organisation owned and controlled by two or more individuals.

Performance appraisal   This is the process of evaluating the performance of an employee, the purpose of which is to improve performance.

Planned economy   This is an economy in which the majority of production is owned and controlled by the State.

Privatisation   This is the transferring of public ownership to private ownership.

Product life cycle   This is the sales pattern of a product over its period of existence.

Profit   This accrues when an organisation's **sales revenue** is greater than its total **costs**.

Profit and loss account   This is an accounting statement which shows an organisation's **sales revenue** and **costs** which relate to that revenue during a specific **trading period**.

Profit centre   Just as **cost centres** are used to attribute **costs** to various parts of the organisation, profit centres are those which make money for the organisation.

Profit margin   This is the difference between the selling price of a product and the cost of producing it.

Promotion   This is a method of attracting the attention of consumers.

Public relations   These are the methods employed by an organisation to enhance its public image.

Raw materials   These are basic items, usually produced in the primary sector of the economy, which are destined to be converted into finished products.

Registered share capital   See **authorised share capital**

Renting   This is a method of acquiring an **asset** which is owned by a third party and may be used by the organisation in return for regular payments.

Resources   These are the human, physical, natural and time items which can be identified as being 'owned' by an organisation.

Retail price index   This is a measure used to determine the rate of **inflation**.

Revenue   This is the income of an organisation derived from sales, interest from loans and other investments.

Sales forecast   This is a method of predicting future **demand**.

Sales promotion   These are methods used by businesses, other than advertising, to increase their sales.

Sales revenue   This is a key item of **revenue** derived from the monies paid by purchasers of a business's products or services.

Selling price   This is the price charged by an organisation for its products or services after taking into account the **costs** incurred in producing it and having added a **margin**.

Share capital   This is the money which has been obtained from **shareholders** investing money in the organisation.

Shareholders   These are essentially part-owners of an organisation who have made long-term investments in it.

Sole trader   This is a business owned and controlled by a single individual.

Stock   These are the organisation's **assets** in the form of **raw materials, work in progress** and **finished goods**.

Stock control   This is the process of controlling all **stock** of **raw materials, work in progress** and **finished goods,** in order to make best use of warehousing facilities and stock holding costs.

Supply   This is the amount of products or services that organisations are willing to offer to the **market**.

SWOT   A system by which an organisation can identify its internal strengths and weakness and the external opportunities and threats.

Trading period   This is a specified period of time, a month, a quarter or a year, which is used to monitor business performance.

Turnover   This is the amount of money taken in a business. It can also refer to the number of people entering and leaving employment.

Unit cost   See **average cost**

Unlimited liability   This is a type of liability in which the owners of a business are responsible for all losses.

Value added   This is either the difference between the **cost** of producing a product and the price obtained for it, or an additional benefit offered to a purchaser in order to convince him or her to buy.

Variable costs   **costs** which may change in direct proportion to the organisation's level of business activity.

Wage differential   This is the difference between the wage rates for different groups of workers.

Working capital   This is an accounting term which identifies the organisation's short-term **current assets**.

Work in progress   These are products which are in the process of being turned into **finished goods**.

Index